D1563889

In the Mind's Eye

In the Mind's Eye

JULIAN HOCHBERG

on the Perception of Pictures, Films, and the World

Edited by
Mary A. Peterson
Barbara Gillam
H. A. Sedgwick

OXFORD
UNIVERSITY PRESS

2007

OXFORD
UNIVERSITY PRESS

Oxford University Press, Inc., publishes works that further
Oxford University's objective of excellence
in research, scholarship, and education.

Oxford   New York
Auckland   Cape Town   Dar es Salaam   Hong Kong   Karachi
Kuala Lumpur   Madrid   Melbourne   Mexico City   Nairobi
New Delhi   Shanghai   Taipei   Toronto

With offices in
Argentina   Austria   Brazil   Chile   Czech Republic   France   Greece
Guatemala   Hungary   Italy   Japan   Poland   Portugal   Singapore
South Korea   Switzerland   Thailand   Turkey   Ukraine   Vietnam

Copyright © 2007 by Mary A. Peterson, Barbara Gillam, and H. A. Sedgwick

Published by Oxford University Press, Inc.
198 Madison Avenue, New York, New York 10016

www.oup.com

Oxford is a registered trademark of Oxford University Press.

Library of Congress Cataloging-in-Publication Data
Hochberg, Julian E.
In the mind's eye : Julian Hochberg on the perception of pictures, films, and the world
/ edited by Mary A. Peterson, Barbara Gillam, and H. A. Sedgwick.
p. cm.
Includes bibliographical references.
ISBN-13 978-0-19-517691-9
ISBN 0-19-517691-X
1. Visual perception.   I. Peterson, Mary A., 1950–   II. Gillam, Barbara.
III. Sedgwick, H. A.   IV. Title.
BF241.H55   2006
152.14—dc22
2005019299

9 8 7 6 5 4 3 2 1

Printed in the United States of America
on acid-free paper

Contents

Part II *Commentaries on Julian Hochberg's Work*

Overviews

Schematic Maps and Integration Across Glances

Local Processing, Organization, and Perceptual Rules

Pictures, Film, and Dance

Part III *Julian Hochberg: Biography and Bibliography*

Credits

Chapter 1: Article originally appeared as Hochberg, C. B., & Hochberg, J. (1952). Familiar size and the perception of depth. *Journal of Psychology, 34,* 107–114. Reprinted with permission of the Helen Dwight Reid Educational Foundation. Published by Heldref Publications, 1219 18th Street NW, Washington, DC 20036-1802, http://www.heldref.org. Copyright © 1952.

Chapter 2: Article originally appeared as Hochberg, J., & McAlister, E. (1953). A quantitative approach to figural "goodness." *Journal of Experimental Psychology, 46,* 361–364.

Chapter 3: Article originally appeared as Hochberg, J., & Beck, J. (1954). Apparent spatial arrangement and perceived brightness. *Journal of Experimental Psychology, 47,* 263–266.

Chapter 4: Article originally appeared as Hochberg, J. (1956). Perception: Toward the recovery of a definition. *Psychological Review, 63,* 400–405.

Chapter 5: Article originally appeared as Hochberg, J. (1962). The psychophysics of pictorial perception. *Audio-Visual Communication Review, 10,* 22–54. Reprinted with permission of the National Education Association.

Chapter 6: Article originally appeared as Hochberg, J., & Brooks, V. (1962). Pictorial recognition as an unlearned ability: A study of one child's performance. *American Journal of Psychology, 75,* 624–628. Copyright © 1962 by the Board of Trustees of the University of Illinois. Used with permission of the University of Illinois Press.

Chapter 7: Article originally appeared as Hochberg, J., & Galper, R. E. (1967). Recognition of faces: I. An exploratory study. *Psychonomic Science, 9,* 619–620. Reprinted with permission of the Psychonomic Society.

Chapter 8: Article originally appeared as Hochberg, J. (1968). In the mind's eye. Invited address read at the September 1966 meeting of the American Psychological Association, Division 3. Reprinted in R. N. Haber (Ed.), *Contemporary theory and research in visual perception* (pp. 309–331). New York: Holt, Rinehart and Winston. Reprinted with permission.

Chapter 9: Article originally appeared as Hochberg, J. (1970). Attention, organization, and consciousness. In D. Mostofsky (Ed.), *Attention: Contemporary theory and analysis* (pp. 99–124). New York: Appleton-Century-Crofts.

Chapter 10: Article originally appeared as Hochberg, J. (1970). Components of literacy: Speculations and exploratory research. In H. Levin & J. P. Williams (Eds.), *Basic studies on reading* (pp. 74–89). New York: Basic. Reprinted with permission of the publisher.

Chapter 11: Article originally appeared as Hochberg, J., & Brooks, V. (1970). Reading as an intentional behavior. In H. Singer & R. B. Ruddell (Eds.), *Theoretical models and processes of reading* (pp. 304–314). Newark, DE: International Reading Association. Copyright © 1970 by the International Reading Association. Reprinted with permission of the International Reading Association.

Chapter 12: Article originally appeared as Hochberg, J. (1972). The representation of things and people. In E. H. Gombrich, J. Hochberg, & M. Black (Eds.), *Art, perception, and reality* (pp. 47–94). Baltimore: Johns Hopkins University Press. Copyright © 1972 by the Johns Hopkins University Press. Reprinted with permission of the Johns Hopkins University Press.

Chapter 13: Article originally appeared as Hochberg, J. (1974). Higher-order stimuli and inter-response coupling in the perception of the visual world. In R. MacLeod & H. Pick, Jr. (Eds.), *Perception: Essays in honor of James J. Gibson* (pp. 17–39). Ithaca, NY: Cornell University Press. Copyright © 1974 by Cornell University. Used by permission of the publisher, Cornell University Press.

Chapter 14: Article originally appeared as Hochberg, J., & Brooks, V. (1978). Film cutting and visual momentum. In J. W. Senders, D. F. Fisher, & R. A. Monty (Eds.), *Eye movements and the higher psychological functions* (pp. 293–313). Hillsdale, NJ: Erlbaum. Reprinted with permission of Lawrence Erlbaum Associates, Inc.

Chapter 15: Article originally appeared as Hochberg, J. (1980). Pictorial functions and perceptual structures. In M. Hagen (Ed.), *The perception of pictures* (Vol. 2, pp. 47–93). New York: Academic.

Chapter 16: Article originally appeared as Hochberg, J. (1981). Levels of perceptual organization. In M. Kubovy & J. Pomerantz (Eds.), *Perceptual organization* (pp. 255–278). Hillsdale, NJ: Erlbaum. Reprinted with permission of Lawrence Erlbaum Associates, Inc.

Chapter 17: Article originally appeared as Hochberg, J. (1982). How big is a stimulus? In J. Beck (Ed.), *Organization and representation in perception* (pp. 191–217). Hillsdale, NJ: Erlbaum. Reprinted with permission of Lawrence Erlbaum Associates, Inc.

Chapter 18: Article originally appeared as Hochberg, J. (1983). Form perception: Experience and explanations. In P. C. Dodwell & T. Caelli (Eds.), *Figural synthesis* (pp. 1–30). Hillsdale, NJ: Erlbaum. Reprinted with permission of Lawrence Erlbaum Associates, Inc.

Chapter 19: Article originally appeared as Hochberg, J. (1984). The perception of pictorial representations. *Social Research, 51*, 841–862. Reprinted with permission of the publisher.

Chapter 20: Article originally appeared as Hochberg, J., & Brooks, V. (1996). Movies in the mind's eye. In D. Bordwell (Ed.), *Post-theory* (pp. 368–387). Madison: University of Wisconsin Press. Copyright © 1996. Reprinted by permission of the University of Wisconsin Press.

Contributors

ERIN AUSTEN, Department of Psychology, St. Francis Xavier University, Antigonish, Nova Scotia

JEREMY BEER, Henry M. Jackson Foundation for the Advancement of Military Medicine, U.S. Naval Health Research Center Detachment, Brooks Air Force Base, Texas

PAUL M. CORBALLIS, School of Psychology, Georgia Institute of Technology, Atlanta, Georgia

JAMES E. CUTTING, Department of Psychology, Uris Hall, Cornell University, Ithaca, New York

PATRICIA R. DELUCIA, Department of Psychology, Texas Tech University, Lubbock, Texas

JAMES T. ENNS, Department of Psychology, University of British Columbia, Vancouver, British Columbia

PATRICK GARRIGAN, David Rittenhouse Laboratory, University of Pennsylvania, Philadelphia, Pennsylvania

BARBARA GILLAM, School of Psychology, University of New South Wales, Sydney, New South Wales, Australia

MARY M. HAYHOE, Center for Visual Science, University of Rochester, Rochester, New York

HELENE INTRAUB, Department of Psychology, University of Delaware, Newark, Delaware

PHILIP J. KELLMAN, Department of Psychology, University of California, Los Angeles, California

DALE S. KLOPFER, Department of Psychology, College of Arts and Sciences, Bowling Green State University, Bowling Green, Ohio

DANIEL T. LEVIN, Department of Psychology and Human Development, Vanderbilt University, Nashville, Tennessee

ARIEN MACK, Department of Psychology, Graduate Faculty of Political and Social Science, New School University, New York, New York

MARY A. PETERSON, Department of Psychology, University of Arizona, Tucson, Arizona

ZYGMUNT PIZLO, Department of Psychological Sciences, School of Electrical and Computer Engineering (by courtesy), Purdue University, West Lafayette, Indiana

JAMES R. POMERANTZ, Department of Psychology, Rice University, Houston, Texas

DANIEL REISBERG, Department of Psychology, Reed College, Portland, Oregon

H. A. SEDGWICK, State University of New York College of Optometry, New York, New York

DANIEL J. SIMONS, Psychology Department and Beckman Institute, University of Illinois, Champaign, Illinois

ED TAN, Department of Communication, University of Amsterdam, Amsterdam, The Netherlands

JAMES T. TODD, Psychology Department, Ohio State University, Columbus, Ohio

PETER A. VAN DER HELM, Nijmegen Institute for Cognition and Information, University of Nijmegen, Nijmegen, The Netherlands

Introduction

Barbara Gillam, H. A. Sedgwick, and Mary Peterson

How can we best describe the processes by which we attain the visual perception of an extended and coherent world?

One view, which for many years has been the standard model, is that through a series of eye fixations we trigger the creation of a detailed internal model of the world, which we then consult in order to report our perceptions or to control our actions. Recent research, however—grouped under headings such as "change blindness" and "inattentional blindness," among others—has seriously undermined this view, showing that little visual detail is preserved from one eye fixation to the next and that, in the control of action, eye fixations are continually being deployed to reassess relevant information.

An alternative view, which has also had considerable support for some time, is that all the information needed for the perception of the visual world is continuously present in the structured optic array of light reaching the eye from the environment. Thus no internal model is needed. This view, although it may be correct as far as it goes, does not engage directly with the particularities of human perception and so leaves many questions unaddressed.

Contemporary visual theory has reached a junction at which the development of a coherent and well-thought-out middle position is clearly needed—a theoretical position that acknowledges the wealth of available information while also recognizing the particularity of the perceptual processes that are able to find structure and organization within this information, a theoretical position that negotiates successfully between the limitations on the information that can be retained from a single eye fixation and the phenomenal and behavioral evidence for the perception of an extended and coherent world.

At this junction, many leading theorists and researchers in visual perception are turning with new or renewed interest to the work of Julian Hochberg. For more than 50 years, in his own experimental research, in his detailed consideration of examples drawn from a very wide range of visual experiences and activities, and most of all in his brilliant and sophisticated theoretical analyses, Hochberg has persistently engaged with the myriad problems inherent in working out such a middle position. The complexity of Hochberg's thought and the wide range of the areas into which he has pursued the solution of this central problem have, however, limited both the accessibility of his work and the appreciation of his accomplishment.

This book came about as a convergence of two concepts. Peterson had for some time wanted to bring together a series of commentaries on the work of Julian Hochberg from the many influential people in perception who admired him, were indebted to him, and felt that the field as a whole had been influenced by him in ways that should be recognized. Peterson was Hochberg's student at Columbia and now in the thick of her own career was aware of how many colleagues had enthusiasm for such an enterprise. Meanwhile, Sedgwick and Gillam, who were not Hochberg students but long-standing junior colleagues in the perception world of New York City, had another idea. Their concern was that many of Hochberg's important works would be lost because of the relative inaccessibility of the journals in which they were published or because they were in books now out of print. So Sedgwick and Gillam thought that it would be good to collect some of his most significant writings and make them available to a new generation of perception scholars.

At an early meeting of the Vision Sciences Society, we described our ideas to each other over lunch and decided to combine them into a book that would be both a collection of many of Julian Hochberg's major papers and a series of short articles by individuals on the significance of his work both for themselves and for the field more broadly.

The choice of which of Hochberg's papers to include has not been easy because of the wealth of possibilities from which we had to choose. One decision that we made early on was to include only whole articles or chapters. We were initially tempted to include some excerpts because Hochberg has written many important book chapters that are of considerable length, but to include as many of them as we might have wished would have made the length of this book excessive. What decided us against excerpts, however, is that each of Hochberg's papers, even the longest ones, is carefully organized around the development of a theoretical argument, and we feared that some of the coherence and thrust of these arguments might be lost in excerpts.

A second choice we made was to keep some chronological balance in our selections. Hochberg's ideas and interests have of course developed and changed over the course of his long career, but many of the earlier papers are still of considerable interest, either because they examine topics that he has not since revisited, because his earlier positions help us to understand the development of what has followed, or because some readers may still find valuable insights in ideas from which Hochberg has since distanced himself. Certain topics, such as picture perception, have been taken up by Hochberg again and again over the years, and we believe that a great deal can be learned from tracing the changes and continuities in these papers. The casual reader may have some impression of redundancy in Hochberg's repeated treatments of such central topics, but a more careful reading will generally show that, when he takes up a topic again, it is with revised formulations, additional illustrations, and new insights.

Third, we have included papers that show something of the range of Hochberg's thinking and investigations. Although all of his work arguably springs from a few central concerns, he has pursued these in many different directions, and in doing so has often helped to open up new areas of research.

Finally, as mentioned above, we have placed some emphasis on making available papers that are relatively inaccessible, either because they were published in books now out of print, because they appeared in journals not normally read or searched by researchers interested in visual perception, or because, although they appeared in well-known journals, their early dates put them beyond the horizon of online access. One effect of this emphasis on relative inaccessibility has been to place somewhat less emphasis on more recent papers, although a few are included.

The selection of Hochberg's papers included here is arranged chronologically by date of publication. Although it would have been possible to arrange some of his papers into categories (for example, on picture or face perception), many of Hochberg's essays span a number of areas, so we chose to avoid the arbitrariness that would have been entailed in assigning each of the papers to a single category.

Altogether, we have selected 20 of Hochberg's previously published papers to include in the first part of this volume. Although many of the chapters are so broad in their theoretical concerns as to resist easy categorization, we may roughly say that four of the papers (chapters 1, 3, 4, and 13) are concerned with forms of visual information and their interaction in perception. Here, Hochberg introduces and develops the important concept of nonstimulus interresponse coupling and strives to develop strict criteria for an empirical definition of perception.

Five important theoretical papers (chapters 2, 8, 16, 17, and 18) are clustered around Hochberg's investigation of perceptual organization, beginning with his quest to find a more quantitative account for the Gestalt "laws" and progressing into his extensive development of a neo-Helmholtzian concept of "mental structures." As Hochberg writes (chapter 16): "The class of theory proposed by J. S. Mill and Helmholtz—that we perceive by fitting the most likely or expected (global) object or event to the sampled (local) sensory component—remains the one best suited to the widest range of organizational phenomena (including the Gestalt phenomena)." In another highly important and closely related theoretical paper (chapter 9), Hochberg applies his approach to perceptual organization to the problem of selective attention.

A series of five papers (chapters 5, 6, 12, 15, and 19) chronicles Hochberg's long involvement with picture perception. Recognizing that much of the investigation of visual perception has long made use of pictures as stimuli, Hochberg has faced this situation squarely—trying to understand how it is that marks on paper can evoke perceptions so like those evoked in the perception of the world and drawing some of his most far-reaching conclusions about perceptual processes from his examination of this puzzle. In another two papers (chapters 14 and 20), Hochberg explores the perception of moving pictures. Adding the dimension of motion to the static realm of pictures raises a plethora of new issues, such as how we are able to successfully perceive the sudden shifts from one viewpoint, environment, or time to another that are produced by editing "cuts" in movies.

Two papers (chapters 10 and 11) explore the process of reading, showing the productiveness of applying Hochberg's broader theoretical ideas to this important problem and also showing how the more narrow strictures of the reading task can throw light on broader perceptual issues. Finally, one paper (chapter 7) gives an early example of Hochberg's interest in face perception and recognition—a topic that is also taken up in the context of a number of his longer papers.

This project was planned to honor Julian Hochberg on the occasion of his 80th birthday, July 10, 2003, but that date marks only an important milestone in an ongoing career, as evidenced by the new essay Hochberg wrote for this collection (chapter 21). This chapter contains new and insightful contributions to our understanding of visual perception in Hochberg's discussions of his latest views on successive glances, attention, and the mind's eye.

For the other component of the book (part II: "Commentaries on Hochberg's Work"), we asked a combination of former Hochberg students[1] and other leading figures in the field who had expressed an interest in or indebtedness to Hochberg's work whether they would like to write chapters.

One of our authors, James Cutting, writes, "Julian Hochberg is our greatest synthesizer of theories and experimental results in the field of perception, and he has been so for a half century." It is therefore not surprising that a volume based on Hochberg's work and influence would be strongly theoretical in content, would have a broad scope, and would elicit views that do not always agree with each other. We gave our authors free rein to choose any aspect or aspects of Hochberg's work about which to write, and we can judge fashion to some extent by the topics that have been chosen among the many that might have been. A similar book produced 10 years from now would undoubtedly focus on different topics to some extent.

A relatively large number of people chose to write about Hochberg's concepts of schema and schematic map and his related views on integration across glances, especially in relation to change blindness and inattentional blindness (which Hochberg prefers to call "inattentional disregard"). Simons and Levin (chapter 37) and Enns and Austen (chapter 24) show how

Hochberg anticipated many current research developments, including the flicker method of measuring change blindness. Hayhoe's essay (chapter 25) supports and extends Hochberg's notion of schema as incorporating not only the gist of a scene (as suggested by several of the authors here) but also the consequences of actions with regard to the scene. Whether a visual stimulus is noticed depends very precisely on where it occurs in an action. Reisberg (chapter 27) relates active processing to the issue of imagery, arguing for example that imagery inevitably lacks some of the features of perception since it cannot be interrogated in the same way as perceptual input. Intraub (chapter 26) follows on from Hochberg's work on aperture viewing, drawing on his concept of "the mind's eye" to account for "boundary extension" in people's descriptions of scenes. Enns and Austen extend Hochberg's view "that our perception of objects is not everywhere dense" by showing how schemata may be important even in processing very simple stimuli. DeLucia (chapter 28) extends the notion of local processing to an analysis of how judgments are made concerning when an approaching object will make contact with the viewer, pointing out that explanations based on higher-order variables, such as "tau," are inadequate. Mack (chapter 29) introduces some controversy by arguing that Hochberg's idea that what is not encoded is lost fails to account for priming data, which suggest that even unseen content is processed for meaning. Klopfer (chapter 41) shows how the perception of dance is strongly influenced by schemata.

Another topic of strong current interest in perceptual theory, particularly in the form of Bayesian approaches, is the role of rules in perception. Can perception be predicted on the basis of either the likelihood or simplicity of the possible outcomes? These issues have been a major preoccupation of Hochberg's for many years, and he discusses them in his chapter here. Cutting (chapter 30) discusses Hochberg's position and the general issue of rules in perception. Van der Helm (chapter 33) shows how simplicity can substitute for likelihood. Pizlo (chapter 34) discusses Hochberg's account of the simplicity principle in relation to other versions of this principle and to likelihood. Other authors, such as Peterson (chapter 22) and Gillam (chapter 23), also comment on this issue. Gillam's chapter is an attempt to place Hochberg's ideas within cognitive and perceptual traditions.

A strikingly original feature of Hochberg's work is his discovery that depth processing is local and that inconsistencies are not perceptually rejected if far enough apart. Todd (chapter 31) provides some striking new examples, and Pomerantz (chapter 32) discusses the local nature of processing in relation to grouping data. Peterson (chapter 22), in a broad treatment of Hochberg's theories in relation to recent data, ties together the idea that perception is piecemeal with the role of schematic maps and expectancy in determining the response to a single glance and integration across glances. A number of other authors comment on the significance of the local nature of depth processing.

Film is an area in which Hochberg and his wife, Virginia Brooks, were almost alone in discerning profound perceptual significance, and this topic attracted comment and analysis from several of our writers, such as Tan (chapter 38) and Simons and Levin (chapter 37), and mentions by others. In a similar fashion, Hochberg has always been interested in picture perception both in its own right and for what it implies about normal perception. Sedgwick (chapter 39) analyzes Hochberg's contributions here while Beer (chapter 40) shows among other things how Hochberg's work indicates a greater role for pictorial cues than motion cues in many instances.

Kellman and Garrigan (chapter 36) and Corballis (chapter 35) give accounts of their youthful encounters with Hochberg and go on to describe their own work on topics of interest to him: Kellman and Garrigan on what is a form and Corballis on the hemispheric basis of perceptual intelligence.

Topics that could have been chosen and were not include Hochberg's theory of figure-ground perception, his concept of percept-percept coupling (although Peterson discusses it as a methodological tool), and his work on reading. These are just as interesting and thought provoking as any of the ideas that have been written about. Fortunately, they and many other interesting ideas are present in the Hochberg chapters themselves.

We have ordered chapters in the second part of this volume into the following four categories:

A. Overviews: Peterson (chapter 22) and Gillam (chapter 23)
B. Schematic maps and integration across glances: Enns and Austen (chapter 24), Hayhoe (chapter 25), Intraub (chapter 26), Reisberg (chapter 27), DeLucia (chapter 28), and Mack (chapter 29)
C. Local processing, organization, and perceptual rules: Cutting (chapter 30), Todd (chapter 31), Pomerantz (chapter 32), van der Helm (chapter 33), Pizlo (chapter 34), Corballis (chapter 35), and Kellman and Garrigan (chapter 36)
D. Pictures, film, and dance: Simons and Levin (chapter 37), Tan (chapter 38), Sedgwick (chapter 39), Beer (chapter 40), and Klopfer (chapter 41)

The organization of the second part should be regarded as somewhat loose, however, because many of the authors touched on issues from more than one category.

The last, short part of this volume includes a brief account of Hochberg's career and a complete list of his publications.

We are grateful to all of our authors for their enthusiastic participation in this project. We also thank Catharine Carlin, our editor, for appreciating the importance of making Julian Hochberg's work more accessible to a wider audience and for supporting this project so wholeheartedly. Finally, and most important, we thank Julian Hochberg, who while expressing his discomfort at being made so much of, has nevertheless graciously allowed us to reprint this selection of his papers and has added his own contribution to this volume (chapter 21).

Note

1. Chapters by Hochberg's students are those by Jeremy Beer, Patricia De-Lucia, Dale Klopfer, and Mary Peterson.

Part I
Selected Papers of Julian Hochberg

1

Familiar Size and the Perception of Depth

Carol Barnes Hochberg and Julian E. Hochberg

The Problem

Among the "cues" of depth perception and the techniques for the representation of space on two-dimensional surfaces, *familiar size* (2, 9, 28) is unique, being the only one which by its very definition requires past experience.

Thus, while perspective might be a "learned cue," it may instead be that symmetrical tridimensional objects are perceived, autochthonously, in place of less regular two-dimensional shapes (stimulus conditions permitting; cf. 20, pp. 159–160); interposition may be due to learning or, instead, to "completion" *behind* the overlapping object which prevented "good continuation" in two dimensions (cf. 25, pp. 115–118). Such depth "cues" may, as well as not, be direct stimuli for perceived depth, with no need for past experience. This view is opposed by Berkeley's famous "demonstration" that distance has no direct stimuli ("... being a line directed endwise to the eye, it projects only one point in the fund of the eye, which point remains invariably the same, whether the distance be longer or shorter" [6, p. 13]), an argument which apparently makes the exceedingly dubious assumptions (20, p. 85; 26, p. 33n) that we are aware of our retinal images,[1] that a sensation must somehow share the *quale* of its stimulus, and, since there is nothing "depth-like" in the proximal stimulus, that "depth" must come from some nonsensorial source, i.e., inference based on adventitious association (6, p. 201).

Consider, on the other hand, a hypothetical case of pure *familiar size*, with a nearby boy and a distant man subtending the same visual angle and all other possible distance "cues" absent: if the man should be seen, not as a midget standing beside the boy, but of normal size at his true distance, the crucial factor must be the observer's "knowledge" of the sizes of man and boy. Presumably, the perceived distances of man and boy would arise because of discrepancies between (*a*) unnoticed sensory data (the sizes and identifying characteristics of the retinal images) and (*b*) unnoticed nonsensory data (the recognition of the meaning of the images of man and boy, and the

3

knowledge of their average sizes)[2] by means of (c) unnoticed inferential processes (the "trigonometry" which locates man and boy spatially).[3]

Such appeal to the unconscious prodigies of a multileveled human mind (cf. 21, p. 94) is not unfamiliar. If retinal images are compared with those of past experience to form "depth," then the organism must functionally be able to "recognize" them *before* the percept itself, with its depth relationships, is aroused; this implied pre-perceptual homunculus (14) also appears in the "subception" (22) and pre-threshold recognition phenomena of "perceptual defense" (3, 23), and, above all, in psychoanalysis. It is a concept which, with its drastic import, its difficulties (20), and its "solution" by removal of the problem to another sphere, can neither be left hidden as "common sense," nor accepted lightly.

Most of the support for *familiar size* (11) comes from the many demonstrations (5, 8, 30) that a difference (or change) in retinal image size tends to be perceived as a difference (or change) in the distance of objects of constant size. Thus, if a giant playing card is compared to a physically nearer (but smaller) one, the larger card seems nearer than the smaller (1).

However, such situations do not test pure *familiar size*, and while their results do show that larger objects tend to appear nearer than similar smaller ones, they do not show that past experience is at all responsible: there are two variables to be "untied" here (in Brunswik's terminology [4]), the *relative size* of the stimuli, on the one hand, and their "associated meaning" on the other. It is unjustified (and unparsimonious [cf. 27, pp. 88, 102]) to attribute the results to one without controlling the other; only if we assume, with Berkeley, that we "see" our retinal image and that there can be no direct visual stimuli for depth (since they could not be "depth-like") are *unconscious assumptions* "inescapable" (18, p. 198). Otherwise, we are perfectly free to note a "stimulus-bound" (cf. 27, p. 102) correlation between retinal size and perceived distance, or more elaborately, we can hypothesize an autochthonous tendency toward homogeneity by which similar shapes "seek" similar size through appropriate distribution in perceived space (20, 25).

Portions of recent experiments by Hastorf (11) and by Ittelson (17, 18) seem free of this objection. For example, Hastorf's subjects viewed a variable-sized luminous disc *monocularly*, which the experimenter suggested at one time to be a "ping-pong ball" and, at another time, a "billiard ball"; their reports of the disc's distance (and their size settings) in terms of a well-structured *binocular* field were found to change appropriately with the experimental suggestions. However, one can question first whether the effect was truly perceptual,[4] since two-thirds of the subjects perceived that the disc was not really a ball (11, p. 208), and an unspecified number realized that two different names had been given to the same stimulus (and these subjects might even have contributed to the significance of the results, since they " . . . still altered their settings when the suggestion as to the nature of the stimulus was changed" [11, p. 209]). Second, since Hastorf's subjects were *told* the meaning of the forms, the essential element of "pre-perceptual recognition" was absent, i.e., the subject was not required to recognize the object's meaning prior to organization of the percept. (Ittelson's procedure [17] was free from this second objection: the meaning of his stimulus objects was given by their form [normal and out-size playing cards, etc.], not by his suggestion.) Perhaps the same results could be achieved with no stimuli at all, with subjects indicating how large a billiard or ping-pong ball would have to be to appear at a given distance, etc. Pratt (27, p. 103) asks, "What else could the observers have said?...This shift in judgment...was presumably no more than the kind of verbal displacement involved in saying, for example, that a 25 cent piece is smaller than a half-dollar but at the same time larger than a nickel. The object has not changed, but only the units or words used to describe the object in relation to other objects."

Some of the other situations used by Hastorf and by Ittelson seem to involve immediate perception (11, p. 208; 18), but these, on the other hand, are merely additional cases of change or difference in size of like shapes, which we have seen does not necessarily involve past experience. Since we do not know that such size effects and *familiar size* are the same "cues," we cannot attribute the immediacy of one to the inferences of the other. To be sure, "judgmental" processes may modify, and be important to perception. However, if *familiar size* is to support an empiricistic theory of "primary" space perception, involving unconscious inference and pre-perceptual recognition, it must be demonstrated as operative at or below the level of the immediate perception which it is trying to explain, not as some process which may very well be "secondary" or subsequently interacting (26, p. 341) with a prior percept which is organized in depth.

Let us consider two experiments whose results[5] are pertinent to this proposed distinction between *familiar size*, which logically requires past experience, and *relative size* or *size difference*, which does not.

Experiment I

On two-dimensional "reversible-screen" drawings (see Figure 1.1a) were drawn a man, 4¼ in. high, on one panel, and a boy of the same size and approximate contour, on the other.[6] Subjects pressed one telegraph key when the left panel appeared nearer, another key when the right seemed nearer. With space errors controlled or equated (each of the two positions of man and boy on each of the two forms of the "screen" [Figures 1.1a and 1.1b] being presented to a separate group of subjects, no subject seeing more than one presentation), the problem is whether the panel with the boy appears nearer more of the time than that with the man, as might be expected from *familiar size*.

The "screen" presented a labile perceptual situation which at the same time was "structured" enough to yield definite, albeit reversible, depth; it

Figure 1.1. Reversible "Screens" with Figures Drawn on the Panels.

was hoped that this would minimize judgmental processes. The instructions allowed gross qualitative responses of "right side nearer," "left side nearer," "both near," and "neither near"; it was hoped that such loose responses would tap primary depth perception rather than *inspection* (30). Each member of four groups of 15 college students viewed the figure monocularly through a reduction screen at a 70 cm. distance, was shown its reversibility, and asked to allow the screen to reverse as it would and to let his gaze move freely.[7] Ten cycles of depth reversals were recorded on a polygraph; the total time the left panel seemed nearer was subtracted from that for the right panel, and this measure ("d") was compared for the two arrangements on each form of the "screen." Since the boy is on the left in Groups A and C, and on the right in Groups B and D, we would expect (if *familiar size* affects depth in this situation) "d" to be greater for Group B than for Group A, and for Group D than for Group C.

Results: The differences between the mean "d" scores of Groups A and B, D and C in Table 1.1 indicate that *familiar size* was ineffective in this situation.

Table 1.1.
Effect of Man and Boy on Reversible Figure

Group (N = 15)	Screen	Figure on Right Side	d*
A	Fig. 1.1a	Man	−1.42
B	Fig. 1.1a	Boy	−2.19
		Difference: 0.77, t = 0.2	
C	Fig. 1.1b	Man	2.64
D	Fig. 1.1b	Boy	−0.58
		Difference: 3.22 t = 0.9	

*Mean of the difference: time that the right side seemed nearer minus the time that the left side seemed nearer.

Experiment II

It could readily be argued that perspective reversal is unaffected by super-imposed content, so that the above data mean nothing. Against this, we know that the balance of figure-ground alternation can probably be changed by altering the relative size, complexity, and continuity of the parts and of the figures drawn on them (15, 20); by differential figural satiation (13); etc. However, to test whether the figure used here can be so affected, as well as to test the effectiveness of *relative size* as contrasted with *familiar size*, the procedure of Experiment I was repeated with the screen of Figure 1.1b, the boy being on one panel, with a reduced ($\frac{3}{4}$ in. high) version of the same boy on the other panel. Here the variable of *relative size* or *size difference* was tested, expecting that the panel with the larger boy would appear near more than that with the smaller boy.

Results: Table 1.2 indicates that, as expected, the "d" score is significantly greater for Group E than for Group F; accordingly, the perspective reversals *can* be affected, and the boy's failure to seem nearer than a man of equal height, in Experiment I, suggests the inadequacy of *familiar size*, not the intractability of the reversals.

These results also emphasize the need for a distinction between *familiar size* (or "meaning") and *relative size*, or *size difference* of similar objects. For example, if Experiment II had been presented alone it might very well have been adduced by Lawrence, Ittelson, or Hastorf as evidence for *familiar size*, although, taken with Experiment I, it serves rather as evidence against the operation of this "cue." It is true that *relative size* was indeed effective here, as elsewhere, but relative size is not necessarily *familiar size*, has not been shown either to involve past experience or to "assume the subjective identification of classes or types of similar objects" (18, p. 199), and may instead be a direct stimulus for the organization of perceived depth (cf. 27, p. 102), just as other variations of proximal stimulation with nothing "depth-like" about them may nevertheless serve as stimuli for perceived depth. For example, the authors (using the plastic eyecaps described by Hochberg, Triebel,

Table 1.2.
Effect of Large Boy and Small Boy on Reversible Figure

Group ($N = 15$)	Screen	Figure on Right Side	d*
E	Fig. 1.1b	Large boy	17.90
F	Fig. 1.1b	Small boy	−2.98
		Difference: 20.88	$t = 5.5$

*Mean of the difference: time that the right side seemed nearer minus the time that the left side seemed nearer.

and Seaman [16]) created a *Ganzfeld* of homogeneous visual stimulation which "untied" illumination intensity from "texture," and obtained with intensity changes *alone* (12) the characteristic depth differences noted by Metzger (24); Gibson found that in aperture vision with only texture gradients varied, perceived "slant" changed with texture changes (10). It would not be surprising if *relative size* constituted another such depth stimulus.

It is not contended here that *familiar size* is always powerless, even in immediate perception; certainly, qualifications are necessary as to generalizability to more "life-like" situations, and as to possible optimal differences in *familiar size* of the represented objects, etc. These problems of "ecological sampling" (4) are, however, also faced by proponents of this "cue" (cf. 27, p. 89), and it has yet to be shown that *familiar size* as opposed to *relative size* can be of any influence in "primary," immediate space perception. It is premature, therefore, to employ this portmanteau in an empiricist-nativist controversy with such far-flung implications (7, 19).

Summary

Most of the "cues" for the immediate perception of space do not as yet require explanation in terms of past experience. Only if we assume that a stimulus for depth perception must have something "depth-like" about it are explanations in terms of inferences based on learning necessary; unless we then make the equally dubious assumption that we can see our retinal images, such "inferences" must be unconscious. Only the cue of *familiar size* requires past experience; most of the evidence for this cue actually involves, instead, *relative size* (which does not require pre-perceptual recognition of retinal images, past experience, and unconscious inference). An experimental separation of the two "cues" found the latter effective and the former ineffective.

Notes

Thanks are due to Professors E. C. Tolman, H. D. Carter, and L. J. Postman of the University of California at Berkeley, and to Professor J. S. Bruner of Harvard University, for helpful comments and criticisms.

1. The retinal image is probably *never* present in awareness, although under special attitudes (rotation to an assumed frontal-parallel plane, etc.) percepts having some formal similarity to the image may result; consider the facts of phenomenal constancy, the inability to see the blind spot or the two retinal components presumably responsible for the perception of "yellow," etc. Thus, any theory in which "depth" is based on recognition of retinal content would seem committed to call upon *unconscious* processes, not, as Hastorf says, " . . . that some sort of judgment or interpretation, be it conscious or unconscious, must be made . . . if . . . size is to be used as a cue to distance" (11, p. 198).

2. This assumes (as yet without support) sufficient concomitance of a given object's distance, its retinal image size, and some characteristic nonvisual *proximal stimulus* (since visual distance is not supposed to be directly perceived).

3. An alternative view might be that our minds hold a vast number of associations, pairing each retinal image directly with a perceived distance from the observer. This may sidestep "unconscious inference," but it seems difficult to apply to pictures, views through lenses, etc., where relative rather than absolute depth is involved, and to breakdowns and inversions of size constancy (cf. 21, p. 89), etc.

4. Where observation is difficult, or when one is forced to consider magnitude as separately measurable entities and not as single integrated experience, *inspection* or close scrutiny tends to occur, using some concept of magnitude which is essentially ideational and cannot be directly perceived (30). *Perception* as an immediate and compelling experience of depth is not dependent upon deliberation and analysis.

5. The data reported were presented in a paper read at the 59th Annual Meeting of the American Psychological Association, 1950.

6. The figures of the man and boy were modifications of drawings lent by Professor Jerome S. Bruner of Harvard University.

7. It is probable, however, that eye movements have no effect upon reversible perspective (cf. 29).

References

1. AMES, A. Some demonstrations concerned with the origin and nature of our sensations (what we experience). *A laboratory manual* (preliminary draft). Hanover, N.H., Hanover Institute, 1946 (mimeographed).
2. BORING, E. G., LANGFELD, H. S., & WELD, H. P. *Psychology: A Factual Textbook.* New York: Wiley, 1935.
3. BRUNER, J., & POSTMAN, L. Perception, cognition, and behavior. *J. Personal.*, 1949, *18*, 14–32.
4. BRUNSWIK, E. *Systematic and Representative Design of Psychological Experiments.* California: Univ. California Press, 1947.
5. CALAVREZO, C. Über den Einfluss von Grössenänderungen auf die scheinbare Tiefe. *Psychol. Forsch.*, 1934, *19*, 311–365.
6. CALKINS, M. (*Ed.*). *Bishop Berkeley: Essays, Principles, Dialogues.* New York: Scribner, 1929.
7. CANTRIL, H. *Understanding Man's Social Behavior (Preliminary Notes).* Princeton: Office of Public Opinion Research, 1947.
8. CARR, H. *An Introduction to Space Perception.* New York: Longmans, Green, 1935.
9. DUDLEY, L., & FARICY, A. *The Humanities.* New York: McGraw Hill, 1940.
10. GIBSON, J. J. The perception of visual surfaces. *Amer. J. Psychol.*, 1950, *63*, 367–384.
11. HASTORF, A. H. The influence of suggestion on the relationship between stimulus size and perceived distance. *J. Psychol.*, 1950, *29*, 195–217.
12. HOCHBERG, C. B., & HOCHBERG, J. E. Phenomenal depth and discontinuity of illumination in a modified "Ganzfeld." *Amer. Psychol.*, 1951, *6*, 259–260 (Abstract).
13. HOCHBERG, J. E. Figure-ground reversal as a function of visual satiation. *J. Exp. Psychol.*, 1950, *40*, 682–686.

14. HOCHBERG, J. E., & GLEITMAN, H. Toward a reformulation of the perception-motivation dichotomy. *J. Personal.*, 1949, *18*, 180–191.
15. HOCHBERG, J. E., & HOCHBERG, C. B. Reversal as an objective index of "good Gestalt." (In preparation.)
16. HOCHBERG, J. E., TRIEBEL, W., & SEAMAN, G. Color adaptation under conditions of homogeneous visual stimulation (*Ganzfeld*). *J. Exp. Psychol.*, 1951, *41*, 153–159.
17. ITTELSON, W. H. Size as a cue to distance: Static localization. *Amer. J. Psychol.*, 1951, *64*, 54–67.
18. ———. Size as a cue to distance: Radial motion. *Amer. J. Psychol.*, 1951, *64*, 188–292.
19. ITTELSON, W. H., & KILPATRICK, F. P. Perception. *Sci. Amer.*, 1951, *185*, 50–56.
20. KOFFKA, K. *Principles of Gestalt Psychology.* New York: Harcourt, Brace, 1935.
21. LAWRENCE, M. *Studies in Human Behavior.* Princeton, New Jersey: Princeton Univ. Press, 1949.
22. McCLEARY, R. A., & LAZARUS, R. S. Autonomic discrimination without awareness: An interim report. *J. Personal.*, 1949, *18*, 171–179.
23. McGINNIES, E., & BOWLES, W. Personal values as determinants of perceptual fixation. *J. Personal.*, 1949, *18*, 224–235.
24. METZGER, W. Untersuchungen am Ganzfeld: II. Zur Phänomenologie des homogenen Ganzfelds. *Psychol. Forsch.*, 1930, *13*, 6–29.
25. METZGER, W. *Gesetze des Sehens.* Frankfurt am Main: Kramer, 1936.
26. MURPHY, G., & HOCHBERG, J. Perceptual development: Some tentative hypotheses. *Psychol. Rev.*, 1951, *58*, 332–349.
27. PRATT, C. C. The rôle of past experience in visual perception. *J. Psychol.*, 1950, *30*, 85–107.
28. RICHTER, J. P. *The Literary Works of Leonardo da Vinci.* London: Oxford Univ. Press, 1939.
29. SISSON, E. Eye-movements and the Schröder stair figure. *Amer. J. Psychol.*, 1935, *47*, 319–331.
30. VERNON, M. D. *Visual Perception.* London: Cambridge Univ. Press, 1937.

2

A Quantitative Approach
to Figural "Goodness"

Julian Hochberg and Edward McAlister

Empirical study of the Gestalt principles of perceptual organization is, despite their great heuristic value, frequently made difficult by their subjective and qualitative formulation. We wish to suggest here that it may be possible to achieve *parallels* to these "laws" of organization through analysis of the objective stimulus pattern. This approach differs from similar ones (1, 6) in the orienting hypothesis that, other things being equal, the probabilities of occurrence of alternative perceptual responses to a given stimulus (i.e., their "goodness") are inversely proportional to the amount of information required to define such alternatives differentially; i.e., *the less the amount of information needed to define a given organization as compared to the other alternatives, the more likely that the figure will be so perceived.*[1] However, to make this hypothesis meaningful, it is necessary to determine empirically the stimulus dimensions in which such "information" is to be measured. Therefore, we are concerned here mainly with so-called ambiguous stimuli (which evoke no single response with a probability of 1.0), although we will consider a possible theoretical bridge to the conditions of what Gibson and Waddell (2) call "determining stimuli."

An objective definition of perceptual "goodness" requires some measure of *S*'s responses to stimulus figures. One such index might be the *threshold* (illumination, tachistoscopic, etc.), the "best" pattern having the lowest limen; however, this measure is too laborious for any really extensive survey of stimuli, and restricts the variety of stimuli which can be tested, being highly sensitive to recognition effects. Instead, we propose to use as a measure of "goodness" the response frequency or the relative span of time devoted by *S* to each of the possible perceptual responses which may be elicited by the same stimulus. This seems close to the intuitive meaning of "goodness" (3), and its probabilistic nature may permit rapprochement between perceptual laws, on the one hand, and "information theory" (and, eventually, behavior theory) on the other (5).

That the concept of "information" (here meaning the number of different items we must be given, in order to specify or reproduce a given pattern or "figure," along some one or more dimensions which may be

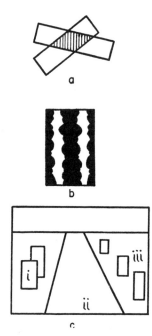

Figure 2.1. Transparency, symmetry, and depth

abstracted from that pattern, such as the number of different angles, number of different line segments of unequal length, etc.) may be useful in approximating figural "goodness" is suggested by almost any random selection of Gestalt demonstrations. The illusion of transparency obtains in Fig. 2.1a when less information is required to specify the pattern as *two* overlapping rectangles (number of different line segments: 8, plus one for notation of locus of intersection; number of angles to be specified: either 8, plus one for notation of angle of intersection or, more simply, one right angle plus the repetition implied in the notation of rectangularity, plus one for notation of angle of intersection; etc.) than, alternatively, as *five* irregular shapes (number of different line segments: 16; number of angles: 16; etc.). In Fig. 2.1b, less information is necessary to specify the symmetrical central black area as figure (number of different angles or points of inflection: 10, plus notation of duplication by bilateral symmetry) than the irregular white areas (number of different angles: 17). Listing the organizational "laws," from "good continuation" and "proximity" to the more general "simplicity" or "homogeneity," one finds translation impressively easy; the eventual utility of such translation depends, however, upon empirical determination of the dimensions of abstraction along which "information" is to be scored (shall we use "number of angles," "number of line segments," a weighted combination of these, or entirely different dimensions?) and upon the demonstration of a quantitative dependence of response frequency on the "information scores."

But can we approach the study of *determinate* (2) perception in this manner? Consider the task of representing spatial depth in two dimensions (Fig. 2.1c). Stimulus part *i* requires less specification as two overlapping rectangles than as L and rectangle; part *ii* requires less specification as a rectangle at a given slant (say $45°$) than as a trapezoid at other slants; finally, in one way part *iii* requires less specification as three identical rectangles at the appropriate distances than as different-sized rectangles at other distances (although here rather involved assumptions are necessary about a size-distance relationship "built in" to the specifying coordinate system, etc.). Now, although each part is ambiguous, if we take all the parts together and if the slant and depth relationships associated with the "best" response to each stimulus part should coincide, the probability of obtaining just these slants and depths will be reinforced. As we add more such "cues," the probability of obtaining alternative depth responses approaches zero, and we may therefore consider *determinate* perception as different from the ambiguous variety, with which we are concerned at present, not in kind, but in degree.

Method

The approach outlined above is of little use unless it is possible to select dimensions for scoring "information" which are in correspondence with empirically obtained response-probabilities. The relative durations of alternate classes of response may be obtained by the usual method of pressing telegraph keys for each phase, but with this procedure *S*s often report that the act of key-pressing altered the percept, which often fluctuated too rapidly to record; moreover, only one *S* can be used at a time. For these reasons, a sampling method was devised in which signal tones were presented by tape recording at "random" intervals and *S*s indicated the phase they had perceived at the time each signal tone sounded. The frequency with which a given response is obtained is assumed to be proportional to the amount of time that response would have been obtained by "ideal" continuous recording.

The problem here was to apply this method to the case of Kopfermann cubes (Fig. 2.2) which may all be seen either as bidimensional patterned hexagons, or as tridimensional cubes (4). Drawings of each cube were presented in balanced order for 100 sec. each to 80 college students, providing

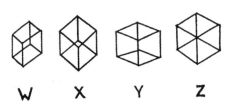

Figure 2.2. The Kopfermann "cubes"

a pool of over 2,600 responses for each stimulus; Ss indicated by pencil code marks which phase they had experienced just prior to each of the 33 signal tones presented at random intervals during the 100 sec.

Results and Discussion

The results obtained correspond roughly to Kopfermann's more subjective findings: that figure which possesses the best phenomenal symmetry as a two-dimensional pattern was obtained least often as a cube (see Table 2.1). In terms of Gestalt theory, we would expect that the likelihood of seeing a figure in two dimensions would not only vary directly with its "goodness" in two dimensions but, in addition, would vary inversely with its "goodness" in three dimensions. However, in this study, we may consider the "goodness" of the bidimensional patterns alone, since the tridimensional phase of each figure is more or less the same cube, the only appreciable difference being the apparent angle with respect to S. That is, we take the relative duration of two-dimensional responses to be proportional to the "goodness" of the two-dimensional patterns, the "goodness" of the tridimensional phases being approximately constant.

The bidimensional patterns may be analyzed for a large number of stimulus properties whose values will yield a relationship similar to that of the four points of bidimensional "goodness" response measures (Table 2.1), and the relationships fit quite well if these properties are differentially weighted. However, data are still needed on many other stimulus figures before a general system of factors and weights can be attempted, so that we are probably safer, at this stage, in merely noting stimulus variables which match the response relationships without employing differential weights. Two such stimulus dimensions fit the responses quite well, namely, the number of angles and the number of line segments (Table 2.1). (Note that

Table 2.1.
Bidimensional Responses to the Kopfermann "Cubes" and Some Two-Dimensional Stimulus Characteristics of the Cubes

"Cubes"	Bidimensional Responses (%)	Stimulus Characteristics		
		Line Segments	Angles	Points of Intersection
W	1.3	16	25	10
X	0.7	16	25	10
Y	49.0	13	19	17
Z	60.0	12	17	7

with the present figures, both dimensions represent the same geometrical fact.) Another dimension is the number of points of intersection required to define each bounded shape in the flat patterns. Any of these scores would be consistent with an inverse relationship between response probability and the amount of "information," as discussed above, required to *specify* a given pattern; it is simple, however, to construct other figures whose relative strengths in alternate response phases may appear, at least intuitively, to be poorly handled by these dimensions, and we will need quantitative data from a wide sample of such figures before general stimulus dimensions can be chosen.

Summary

Probability of alternate perceptual responses is suggested as an approximate quantitative index of "goodness" of figure, and a group technique is presented by which this score can be obtained for ambiguous stimuli. Using the technique to obtain group scores for relative duration of tri- and bidimensional phases of four Kopfermann cube figures, the resulting responses are not inconsistent with the working hypothesis, namely, that the probability of a given perceptual response to a stimulus is an inverse function of the amount of information required to define that pattern.

Notes

A slightly shorter version of this paper was read at the April 1953 meeting of the Eastern Psychological Association.
  1. After preparation of this paper, we have been privileged to see the manuscript of a paper by Dr. F. Attneave, which contains a much more detailed theoretical discussion of the tendency of the organism to perceive in terms of "maximum redundancy"; although this formulation is probably not precisely equivalent to the one proposed here, and the experimental techniques employed are quite different in method and assumptions, we are agreed as to the basic similarity of our general approaches.

References

1. BROWN, J. F., & VOTH, A. C. The path of seen movement as a function of the vector field. *Amer. J. Psychol.*, 1937, *49*, 543–563.
2. GIBSON, J. J., & WADDELL, D. Homogeneous retinal stimulation and visual perception. *Amer. J. Psychol.*, 1952, *65*, 263–270.
3. KOFFKA, K. *Principles of Gestalt psychology.* New York: Harcourt Brace, 1935.

4. KOPFERMANN, H. Psychologische Untersuchungen über die Wirkung zweidi-mensionaler Darstellungen körperlicher Gebilde. *Psychol. Forsch.*, 1930, *13*, 293–364.

5. MILLER, G. A. *Language and communication.* New York: McGraw-Hill, 1951.

6. ORBISON, W. D. Shape as a function of the vector-field. *Amer. J. Psychol.*, 1939, *52*, 31–45.

3

Apparent Spatial Arrangement and Perceived Brightness

Julian E. Hochberg and Jacob Beck

The problems of brightness constancy (e.g., the constancy of perceived object color under different illumination conditions) and of the perceptual constancies in general arise from the fact that changed sensory stimuli frequently elicit unchanged responses (and vice versa) which follow more closely the variations of distal stimuli (objects) than of the sensory-surface stimulus distributions. This raises difficulties for any formulation of a one-to-one correspondence between stimulus and experience (confusingly called the "constancy hypothesis" [5, p. 86]), which at first sight would seem essential to psychological prediction.

Such findings have been used in attempted ("nativistic") refutation of the constancy hypothesis and its associated stimulus-sensation units of analysis (5) and to demonstrate the importance of nonstimulus organizational "forces." Empiricist "inferential" explanations, on the other hand, retain the constancy hypothesis in *sensation*, and ascribe the obtained discrepancies to the effects of past experience in *perception*. Objections to the nativistic position are (*a*) some evidence suggests that the accuracy of the perceptual constancies depends on past experience (1); (*b*) no well-defined analytic units have been presented to supplant the old "sensations," and in their absence precise prediction is difficult despite the considerable heuristic value of the more or less intuitive Gestalt "laws." General objections to the empiricist positions have been (*a*) it is not possible to distinguish between "sensation" and "perception"; (*b*) there is some awkwardness involved in the doctrine of "unconscious inference" and its derivatives, especially when referring to the lower animals in which the constancies appear (7, pp. 605–607); (*c*) any attempt at precise prediction from this viewpoint must await as yet unperformed "ecological surveys" to determine what the past experiences of an organism are likely to have been; (*d*) the constancies also appear to exist without opportunity for past experience (3), and while demonstrated effects of past experience on the constancies do not necessarily refute the Gestalt position, evidence of the reverse seriously injures a thoroughgoing empiricist explanation.

An alternative formulation is appealing: responses may occur in one-to-one correspondence not to what we had previously taken to be the stimuli but to their relationship, without regard to central factors, whether of association or organization. In considering this possibility, we do not have to postulate innate knowledge; we need only seek new dimensions for analyzing the physical stimuli which *are* in correspondence with experience (or response). Gestaltists most frequently sought such invariant relationship not in the stimulus distribution, but in the as yet largely unmeasurable psychophysiologically isomorphic cortical processes; however, one may instead direct attention to the reanalysis of the proximal stimulus pattern as do Gibson (2), Helson (4), and Wallach (6).

Thus, Wallach (6) suggests that we may understand brightness perception by taking as the stimulus not the intensity of illumination falling on a given retinal region, but the relationship of the intensities of illumination falling on adjacent regions. The relationship approximated a *ratio* of intensities in the situations he studied; i.e., the stimuli in the perception of brightness appeared to be the ratios of illumination intensities on adjacent areas, rather than the illumination intensities themselves. Thus, if Ss viewed a variable disk surrounded by a ring of 180 illumination intensity units—degrees of episcotister opening—and were asked to match the variable disk to a disk of 90 units surrounded by a ring of 360 units, they set the variable disk to a mean value of 47 units, only 2 units away from the proportionate 4:1 intensity ratio, which would here be $90 \div 360 \times 180$, or 45 units. If this redefinition of the stimulus will explain all of brightness constancy, we can again effect a one-to-one psychophysical formulation of perceived brightness.

The constancy hypothesis was shaken since the same *absolute* stimulus intensities aroused different brightness responses (and vice versa); can conditions also be found in which the same *distributions* or relationships of stimulus intensity arouse different brightness responses? The object of the present experiments was to determine whether a change in the apparent position of a target surface relative to an illumination source results in a change in the perceived brightness of that surface (cf. 7, pp. 600, 612), even though the actual illumination conditions remain constant.

Experiment I

The apparatus[1] is shown in Fig. 3.1: the main illumination (100 w.) came from above (*a*), this being "indicated" to Ss by the shadow distribution on several cubes (*d*). These "cues" are of considerable importance since, in preliminary experiments, little or no success was achieved without them. The Ss looked monocularly through a reduction screen (*Sc*) at an upright cardboard trapezoid target (*t*) covered with Number 8 Hering gray paper, cut so that its retinal image would be the same as that of a square (*Sq*) lying

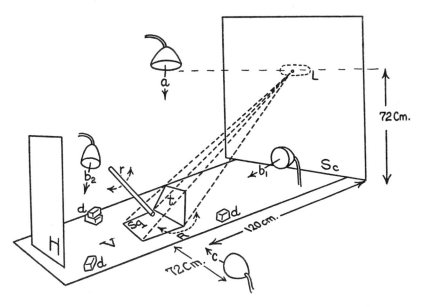

Figure 3.1. Apparatus for presenting the same target at different apparent slants and illumination conditions.

flat on the black cloth surface (V). All Ss ($N = 13$) reported seeing a horizontal square, whose brightness they were then (Judgment I) asked to match quickly and unanalytically to a scale (H) of Hering gray paper patches (Nos. 1, 3, 5, . . . 19). A round rod, r, ½ in. in diameter, 22 in. long, painted white for Group A and black for Group B, was then waved behind the target (trying to avoid any cast shadows visible to S). This was kept up for some seconds, as it was difficult not to "see" the horizontal square (Sq) instead of the upright trapezoid (t); indeed, one S was dropped at this point, unable to see the target as upright. The Ss again compared the target's brightness with the gray scale (Judgment II).

The results (Table 3.1) indicate that the target when apparently upright is reported as brighter than when apparently horizontal. Two questions may, however, be asked: First, while illumination of the rod is not likely to have been responsible for the brightness change since it was black for some Ss and white for others, might not inadvertently cast shadows, or even the motion itself, have been the important factor? Second, if a stimulus is perceived as parallel to the line of regard, it should have a greater apparent area than when perceived as perpendicular to the line of regard (Fig. 3.1); may not the lower reported brightness in the former case be due to the smaller amount of *retinal* illumination per unit of *perceived* surface? The next two experiments were undertaken to test the first question by varying the means whereby the

Table 3.1.
Relative Apparent Brightnesses of the Target with Different
Apparent Positions and Illumination Conditions

Exp.	Group	N	Light Source (Fig. 3.1)	S's Responses	
				Trapezoid Brighter	Square Brighter
I	A	6	a	5	0
	B	6	a	6	0
II	C	15	a	14	0
			b_1	0	14
III	D	5	a	5	0
	E	5	b_1	0	5
	F	5	c	0	0

apparent shift in the target position is brought about, and to test the second by changing the direction of illumination while, of course, holding the apparent size change constant.

Experiment II

The procedure of Exp. I was modified here in three ways: (a) When attempting to make the target appear upright, it was moved through short horizontal arcs (R) instead of having a rod (r) waved behind it. (b) The 15 Ss (Group C) of this experiment ran through the procedure with the illumination coming from above (a), and then repeated the experiment with the illumination coming horizontally from in front of the trapezoid (b_1), with a concealed supplementary source (b_2) to remove the shadow of the target (t) from the cues. (c) The Ss were alternated in each part of the experiment as to the condition to which they were first subjected, the upright target or the horizontal square.

The results (Table 3.1) under illumination from above are the same as those in Exp. I: when seen upright, the target appears brighter than when seen flat. Under illumination from in front (b_1), the results are the reverse: with horizontal illumination, the target appears less bright when seen as upright than when seen flat. Since the change in perceived area consequent upon the change in perceived target position would be the same both when illumination comes from above and from the front, we can reject the amount-of-illumination-per-perceived-surface-area as a determining factor. This suggests that the brightness changes are due either largely or solely to the perceived change in target position with respect to the direction of illumination; this is supported by the results of the next experiment.

Experiment III

Two changes were here made in the procedures of Exp. I: (*a*) The target was changed from flat to upright appearance by shifting from monocular vision to binocular vision (through a larger hole, *L*). (*b*) Illumination was maintained from above (*a*), as in Exp. I, for Group D ($N = 5$); from in front horizontally (b_1), as in the second part of Exp. II, for Group E ($N = 5$); and horizontally from the side (*c*), for Group F ($N = 5$).

The results of Groups D and E show the same changes in brightness as were found in Exp. II. There is no evidence of any perceived brightness changes in Group F, in which there is no change in perceived orientation of the target with respect to the illumination, since the illumination is parallel to the target surface in either of the two perceived positions. These results again suggest that the brightness changes are obtained due to the change in the relationship of the perceived direction of illumination and the perceived position of the surface it falls upon.

Discussion

In general, the results of these experiments suggest that when a surface of a given illumination is perceived as being perpendicular to the direction of illumination, it appears less bright than when the same surface, with the same illumination, seems parallel to the direction of illumination. How does this fit the various approaches to brightness constancy?

A simple one-to-one correspondence of illumination and perceived brightness must as usual be rejected, since the same stimulus arouses different responses. Likewise, any attempt to bring the perception of brightness into one-to-one correspondence with illumination *ratios* is inadequate, since differing responses are here obtained with the same illumination relationships. Either we must view Wallach's ratio formulation (or, for that matter, Helson's "adaptation level" explanation) as incomplete, or hold that there are at least two different kinds of brightness constancy, one bound to the illumination conditions and the other not, an unparsimonious position. The general viewpoint may, however, be retained (as may also a Gestalt organizational one) if the determinants of perceived brightness include not only the peripheral illumination relationships but the "cues" to spatial position and the illumination direction (cf. 7, p. 612). The empiricist or "inferential" position, disconcertingly enough, seems well able to explain the findings, at least by hindsight: thus, to reflect a given amount of light to the eye, a surface parallel to the incident illumination would have to have a higher albedo or brighter object color than would a surface perpendicular to the incident illumination, and would therefore be "inferred" to be brighter.

Summary

In order to determine whether perceived brightnesses can be brought into one-to-one correspondence with stimulus illumination *relationships* any more than with absolute illumination intensities, *S*s made judgments of the brightness of a target which, under constant or controlled conditions of illumination, was made to appear to be either perpendicular or parallel to the apparent direction of illumination. Since substantially the same illumination distributions produced different perceived brightnesses, analyses of brightness constancy in terms of stimulus illuminations cannot at present be considered complete explanations.

Note

1. Modified from one devised by Professor J. J. Gibson to study the relationship between perceived slant and perceived form.

References

1. BRUNSWIK, E. Über Farben-, Grossen- und Gestaltkonstanz in der Jugend. In H. Volkelt (Ed.), *Bericht Über den XI. Kongress exp. Psychol.* Jena: Fischer, 1930. Pp. 52–56.
2. GIBSON, J. J. *The perception of the visual world.* Cambridge: Houghton Mifflin, 1950.
3. GOGEL, W. C., & HESS, E. H. A study of color constancy in the newly hatched chick by means of an innate color preference. *Amer. Psychologist,* 1951, *6,* 282. (Abstract)
4. HELSON, H. Adaptation-level as frame of reference for prediction of psychological data. *Amer. J. Psychol.,* 1947, *60,* 1–29.
5. KOFFKA, K. *Principles of Gestalt psychology.* New York: Harcourt, Brace, 1935.
6. WALLACH, H. Brightness constancy and the nature of achromatic, colors. *J. Exp. Psychol.,* 1948, *38,* 310–324.
7. WOODWORTH, R. S. *Experimental psychology.* New York: Holt, 1938.

4

Perception

Toward the Recovery of a Definition

Julian Hochberg

Perception, a word which once had a fairly limited meaning, has recently acquired a host of new (and frequently mutually contradictory [e.g., 26, 27]) ones. The shattering of the taxonomy of sensation, image, and percept (15, 30) made it difficult to maintain the older definitions (e.g., perception equals sensations plus images). Since then, usage has ranged from a narrowing of "perception" almost to the previous connotations of "sensation" (27), to a widening which includes almost all cognition—e.g., "Symbolization makes possible *perception at a distance* where the immediate percept is only a symbol of a distant event" (26). So loose has the term become that today Murray might call his battery the Thematic Perception Test, and not arouse any great comment. This diffuseness renders the term almost meaningless, and, even if there were no more serious consequences, it tends to promote a feeling of false unity and community of subject matter among diverse disciplines which really use the word in quite different fashions (cf. 29).

When the different definitions of the term are allowed to shift and interact in a single argument, however, serious confusion may result. When pre-, sub-, and unconscious perceptual processes are postulated (1, 17), when the results of presumably "perceptual" demonstrations are the occasion of profound epistemological conclusions (6, 12), and when questions are raised as to whether it is "really" perception (18, 21, 11) that is being investigated—at such points, it is not mere pedantry to ask questions about definitions. "Perception" frequently carries with it the various connotations of "awareness," of a "discrimination" between stimuli, of a conviction of the "real" environmental presence of the perceived object, etc. These concepts are quite complex and as yet ill defined, and their casual intermixture may have methodological as well as theoretical consequences. For example, Bruner, Postman, and Rodrigues (4) attempted to demonstrate that the effect of the previously experienced normal color of an object on its presently perceived color increased as the ambiguity was increased by *increasing the time elapsed* between the presentation of the stimulus and the matching of that stimulus to a color wheel—a procedure more appropriate to the investigation of *memory* than to the traditional usage of *perception*. This is not to say that we must adhere to the old structuralist methods of slicing mental processes, but memorial effects in memory are not quite as critical a phenomenon as would be memorial effects in perception, and the distinction seems worth retaining when the existence of such effects is itself the question at hand. For most purposes such distinctions may actually be as unnecessary as the tendency to ignore them suggests, but this really depends upon the use to which the definition will be put.

It seems to me that there are at present at least two purposes for which a definition of perception is needed: (*a*) to delimit certain characteristics (phenomenal properties) of the *experience* of the subject, and (*b*) to distinguish between the immediate (primary) and less immediate (secondary) functional determinants we assume to be underlying the overt discriminal response. Few attempts have been made recently at explicit definitions for either purpose, and this is what has generated the delightful Freudian paradoxes about "subceptual recognition," the ambiguity about motivational determinants in perception, and the confusion about "ambiguity."

Programs for the Definition of Perception

Perceptual Experience.   One aspect of classical consensual usage is given in a definition by MacLeod: Perception is that process by which things, events, and relationships become phenomenally "here," "now," and "real." Some might object to the "private" and "subjective" nature of the construct; however, aside from such metaphysical objections, the actual problems of applying such definitions experimentally have largely been ignored. Since a "percept" is a construct and not "directly measurable," its definition can be approached with different indices and at various levels.

At the most primitive level, a considerable gain in information could be achieved in many supposedly "perceptual" experiments (cf. 8) simply if subjects were asked whether their reports concerned objects "really seen" as present, rather than inferred or imagined. This is particularly important where the experimental findings are intended to reveal the fundamental dependence of perceptual experience *in general* upon some set of variables other than those immediately involved, e.g., dependence upon learning, upon motivation, etc. Thus, Hastorf (8) attempts to support the empiricist explanation of depth perception by showing that the known size of an object can determine its apparent distance: He instructs subjects that a rectangular stimulus, presented so that its visual distance is indeterminate, is a calling card, an envelope, etc., and obtains different distance matches; the relevance of his findings would be considerably increased, however, by some assurance (in the face of some evidence to the contrary [10]) that his subjects' performance actually entailed perceiving the stimulus as instructed and perceiving the distances as reported. Again, if we have attempted to demonstrate the effects of needs on the perception of length by rewarding longer lines (22), we require some assurance that the subjects are not merely reporting, without *seeing*, greater length (18). Where needed, greater certainty as to the degree to which "immediacy" characterizes the experience and as to the uni- or multidimensionality of the response system could be achieved by the use of psychophysical and scaling procedures. *Whether or not a given response is perceptual in this sense is an empirical matter* (cf. Perky's demonstration of the continuity of image and percept [19]).

Since it seems unlikely that very many modern American experimental psychologists feel quite comfortable when brought face to face, in such bald fashion, with a construct of "conscious perceptual experience," the second purpose for which definition is required is probably more important at the moment (although it cannot be completely untied from this first problem).

The Temporal Primacy of "Perceptual" Processes. A recurring theme (by no means new) is the helpless dependence of perception on internal nonexteroceptive factors of motivation and past experience. Thus, our perceptions of the world—its spatial fabric (16), the objects within it (3), and their dimensions (13) and attributes (4)—are supposedly determined by desire and habit. A percept becomes merely a normal hallucination and, with all knowledge based upon the senses, all our cognitive processes are contaminated and deluded. In extreme cases (6), solipsistic epistemologies—each man being viewed as in an independent, monadic universe produced by the projection of his trigonometric judgments (16) or of his unconscious desires (1) or memories (9)—have been offered as psychological "findings" with great energy and persuasiveness. We are not concerned here, however, with either the philosophical or the factual aspects of this matter, but rather with the definitions of perception involved, implicit or explicit.

By the old structuralist definition of perception, all of this is trivial and at least as old as Bishop Berkeley—by definition, a *percept* is *not* in correspondence with proximal stimulation, but is compounded of sensations and remembered images. *Sensations* alone would be in expected correspondence with the physical world of proximal stimulus energies, while the nature of the world of objects and space would by definition be determined by (in fact, composed of) the associated images of past experience and the judgment-like processes of *unbewusstersschluss*. The Princeton demonstrations of purported experiential determinants in perception should occasion no great amazement to anyone who has the traditional definition in mind, with its temporal primacy of sensation and associated memory trace arousal *before* the arousal of the perceptual process. Similarly, there is little occasion for pleased surprise at the "perceptual defense" claims that unconscious recognition processes intervene between what, in classical terms, would be sensation (itself not always conscious [2]) and conscious perception or overt recognition. Another class of implicit definitions has evidently been under attack here, one which ignores the old sensation-perception dichotomy (14).

However, if we wish to establish anything concerning the effects of, say, judgment as an independent variable upon perception as a dependent variable, we must be sure that the process we have observed as a dependent variable was not, itself, the judgmental one whose *effect* we were presumably investigating (11, 21). Postman (20) seems to tell us that the perceptual response—and, therefore, everything useful we can say about "perception"—follows the "laws of associative learning." However, the main point has been glossed over by Postman, and tends to return us to the earlier problem of conscious experience: *not every behavior measured is an index of the perceptual nature of the response, and not all indices are equally good.* Let us look, therefore, at some examples of perceptual research in which implicit or explicit attempts were made to answer this question.

1. If we reward differently the two alternates of a simple reversible figure-ground pattern, the situation is vastly different from that of rewarding different line lengths. Schafer and Murphy (24) coupled monetary reward with one, monetary loss with the other of two sets of half-faces, which were then combined to form single reversible figure-ground units and presented for tachistoscopic recognition. Here, subjects who report recognition of the previously rewarded half-face cannot be "judging": *If* we assume (23) that only one of the two faces can be figure at one time (there is some doubt about this, however; see 27, 25) and that the tachistoscopic exposure employed does not allow time for a reversal of figure and ground, the subject cannot correctly report a face other than the one he first sees, since he cannot (except by chance) know which it is. *The subject cannot be giving a report which could equally well have been made in the absence of the stimulus.*

2. Wallach, O'Connell, and Neisser (28) found that the shadow of a static wire form, originally reported to be two-dimensional, appeared three-dimensional after viewing the shadow cast by the same wire form in rotation. This would constitute a clear demonstration of the effect of past experience on depth perception if we could be sure that this was not merely recollection by the subjects that "this pattern is one which was cast by a three-dimensional form." The experimenters therefore had the subjects continue to view the same static shadow pattern, and when reversals of perspective were reported with appropriate changes in relative sizes of the parts, concluded that they were dealing with perceived, rather than just judged, depth. The criterion of reversal has been used before (for example, by Hochberg and Hochberg [10] in testing the perceptual effects of "familiar size" on "represented" depth).

Why is perspective reversal considered evidence that the response is perceptual? (*a*) For one thing, spontaneous perspective reversal is known to occur in the presence of certain kinds of stimuli and has not yet been reported to occur in cognitive processes *which take place in the absence of the specific stimulus.* (*b*) More important is the element of "additional information" already noted to be implicit in the Schafer-Murphy criterion: the second (reversed) description of the wire form is only one of an unlimited number of responses which the subject *could* make, but the one which he *does* make is a specific and appropriate function of the distal stimulus. As with figure-ground reversal, but in considerably more complex fashion, the patterns of (proximal) stimulation on the retina must change their function in the delineation of the object (distal stimulus): what were seen as the opposite edges of the same surface become edges of two different ones, etc. The subject must abandon in its entirety his first description of the distal stimulus, yet the second report cannot be made independently of the distal stimulus and depends upon its presence.

Even more striking are the related changes in length accompanying the three-dimensional form reversal. If some wire side *a* was previously seen as equal to and nearer than *b*, it now appears longer and farther away than *b*. This is to be expected in terms of the laws of perspective, but the speed with which this occurs, the ignorance most subjects display with respect to such laws, and their inability to compute such trigonometric relationships (5) make it very doubtful that the response has been a judgmental one.

To summarize, one set of implicit criteria of the perceptual nature of any given response appears to be that the experimenter has some reason to believe that the *presence of the stimulus, and its excitation of neural processes, are necessary (but perhaps not sufficient) for at least certain aspects of that response.* The experimenter should not, in principle, be able to predict the response completely without knowledge of the specific stimulus, else we are dealing neither with sensation nor with perception. To distinguish between the latter requires definition of another concept—that of *ambiguity.*

Perception, Sensation, and Ambiguity

Thus, we have a continuum in place of the older dichotomy between sensation and perception. At one extreme, complete psychophysical correspondence (7) obtains (including most of the area known as *sensation*), and our knowledge of the variance of some aspect of the stimulus object is necessary *and* sufficient to predict completely the response variance of the subject; here, considerations of *needs* and *past experience* are at present gratuitous. At the other extreme, subjects' responses are completely independent of the presented stimulus, knowledge of which is neither necessary nor sufficient for prediction of response, and we are not dealing with perception at all, but with other psychological processes such as judgment, imagery, etc. Between these two extremes lies an important domain (corresponding to some extent to the classical area of *perception*) in which the stimulus accounts for some but not all of the response variance, and here it may be fruitful to inquire as to how much of the residual variance may be sought in factors of motivation and habit.

The criterion underlying this continuum is a concept of *ambiguity,* i.e., the degree of the inter- and intra-individual variability of relationship between stimulus and perceptual response we considered above. (Another definition of ambiguity might be attempted in terms of the extent to which different stimuli are perceived as having more or less of the quality of ambiguousness, but as little is known about this dimension as about the dimension of phenomenal *reality* or *presence* discussed above, to which it seems closely related.) Such ambiguity can never be ascribed to a stimulus alone, but must depend also upon the choice of dimensions along which the subject is requested to make his response. Consider a visual stimulus under any specified constant conditions of seeing—say, a red feather. Is it an ambiguous one? The answer depends in part upon the questions I ask the subject. If I ask psychophysical questions about the form, color, size, etc., I can get very low response variability. If I ask about its warmth, its softness, or its charity, I suspect that response variability will increase, while with respect to flavor or sexual attractiveness, variability will reach really respectable levels. The Rorschach is not an ambiguous stimulus if I am seeking the answer "inkblot," but becomes so only if subjects are asked to respond along dimensions to which the stimulus is partly or wholly irrelevant. In short, whether we are dealing with "sensation," "perception," or "judgment" is not to be determined by either the stimulus or the response dimension alone, but by both as related by the task set.

Summary

The concept of the *percept* or the *perceptual response*, if it is to retain any useful meaning, requires definition at least in those situations where contradictory or controversial statements are made about it. Two sets of defining operations are suggested: (*a*) psychophysical scaling of experimental situations in terms of the immediacy or perceptual quality of the experiences they arouse; (*b*) the requiring of responses which cannot be made, by the naive subject, in the complete absence of the stimulus. The degree to which the presented stimulus fails to determine the response marks the *ambiguity* of the psychophysical relationship under a given task set.

References

1. BLUM, G. S. An experimental reunion of psychoanalytic theory with perceptual defence and vigilance. *J. Abnorm. Soc. Psychol.*, 1954, *49*, 94–98.
2. BORING, E. G. A history of introspection. *Psychol. Bull.*, 1953, *50*, 164–189.
3. BRUNER, J. S., & POSTMAN, L. Perception, cognition and behavior. *J. Pers.*, 1949, *18*, 14–31.
4. BRUNER, J. S., POSTMAN, L., & RODRIGUES, J. Expectation and the perception of color. *Amer. J. Psychol.*, 1951, *64*, 216–227.
5. BRUNSWIK, E. Statistical separation of perception, thinking, and attitudes. *Amer. Psychologist*, 1948, *3*, 342. (Abstract)

6. CANTRIL, H. *Understanding man's social behavior (preliminary notes)*. Princeton, N.J.: Office of Public Opinion Research, 1947.

7. GIBSON, J. J. *The perception of the visual world*. Boston: Houghton Mifflin, 1950.

8. HASTORF, A. H. The influence of suggestion on the relationship between stimulus size and perceived distance. *J. Psychol.*, 1950, *29*, 195–217.

9. HILGARD, E. R. The role of learning in perception. In R. R. Blake & G. V. Ramsey (Eds.), *Perception: an approach to personality*. New York: Ronald, 1951.

10. HOCHBERG, C. B., & HOCHBERG, J. E. Familiar size and the perception of depth. *J. Psychol.*, 1952, *34*, 107–114.

11. HOCHBERG, C. B., & HOCHBERG, J. E. Familiar size and subception in perceived depth. *J. Psychol.*, 1953, *36*, 341–345.

12. ITTELSON, W. H., & KILPATRICK, F. P. Perception. *Sci. Amer.*, 1951, *185*, 50–56.

13. ITTELSON, W. H. Size as a cue to distance: static localization. *Amer. J. Psychol.*, 1951, *64*, 54–67.

14. KOFFKA, K. *Principles of Gestalt psychology*. New York: Harcourt, Brace, 1935.

15. KÜLPE, O. Versuche über Abstraktion. *Ber. ü: d. I. Kongr. f. exp. Psychol.*, 1904, 56–68.

16. LAWRENCE, M. *Studies in human behavior*. Princeton, N.J.: Princeton Univer. Press, 1949.

17. MCCLEARY, R., & LAZARUS, R. S. Autonomic discrimination without awareness: an interim report. *J. Pers.*, 1949, *18*, 170–179.

18. PASTORE, N. Need as a determinant of perception. *J. Psychol.*, 1949, *28*, 457–475.

19. PERKY, C. W. An experimental study of imagination. *Amer. J. Psychol.*, 1910, *21*, 422–452.

20. POSTMAN, L. Experimental analysis of motivational factors in perception. In *Current theory and research in motivation*. Lincoln, Nebr.: Univer. of Nebraska Press, 1952.

21. PRATT, C. C. The role of past experience in visual perception. *J. Psychol.*, 1950, *30*, 85–107.

22. PROSHANSKY, H. M., & MURPHY, G. The effects of reward and punishment on perception. *J. Psychol.*, 1942, *13*, 295–305.

23. RUBIN, E. *Visuellwahrgenommene Figuren*. Copenhagen: Glydendalska Boghandel, 1921.

24. SCHAFER, R., & MURPHY, G. The role of autism in a visual figure-ground relationship. *J. Exp. Psychol.*, 1943, *32*, 335–343.

25. SMITH, D. E. P., & HOCHBERG, J. E. The effect of "punishment" (electric shock) on figure-ground perception. *J. Psychol.*, 1954, *38*, 83–87.

26. SWEET, A. Some problems in the application of cognitive theory to personality functioning. *J. Pers.*, 1953, *23*, 41–51.

27. WALLACH, H. Some considerations concerning the relation between perception and cognition. *J. Pers.*, 1949, *18*, 6–13.

28. WALLACH, H., O'CONNELL, D. N., & NEISSER, U. The memory effect of visual perception of three-dimensional form. *J. Exp. Psychol.*, 1953, *45*, 360–368.

29. WERNER, H. Introductory remarks. *J. Pers.*, 1949, *18*, 2–5.

30. WERTHEIMER, M. Experimentelle Studien über das Sehen von Bewegung. *Z. Psychol.*, 1912, *61*, 161–265.

5

The Psychophysics
of Pictorial Perception

Julian Hochberg

The study of pictures, and psychology as a scientific inquiry, have been intertwined since Leonardo da Vinci's analysis of the techniques for portraying space. As we learn more about perception and learning, we must revise our interpretation of how pictorial communication takes place. Reciprocally, what we have learned about pictorial communication has altered some of our conceptions about the underlying sensory structures and perceptual processes.

This essay presents a brief review of the interaction between systematic psychology and the study of pictorial communication; some hypotheses about the perceptual function of pictures; and some current attempts at psychological treatment of pictorial communication. Since an object or shape must first be perceived before it can function in the processes of communication and education, the conditions which determine pictorial shape and object perception will be our main concern.

Theory of Depth Clues

In the 1580s, Leonardo da Vinci investigated the techniques by which "pictures" could be made: "... place a sheet of glass firmly in front of you, keep the eye fixed in location, and trace the outline of a tree on the glass.... Follow the same procedure in painting ... trees situated at the greater distances. Preserve these paintings on glass as aids and teachers in your work" (11).

A picture is a flat object with a pigmented surface whose reflectance varies from place to place and which in some sense (which we will examine later) acts not as a dappled surface, but as a substitute or surrogate for spatial arrangements of other entirely different objects (19 and 20).

This paper is part of an investigation of pictorial psychophysics supported by the National Science Foundation, NSF-G9601.

Why does Leonardo's method produce a surrogate for the scene being traced on glass? Because such a pane of glass, if perfectly prepared, would provide the eye much the same distribution of light, or *optic array* (21), as would have reached that eye from the scene itself.[1] If a painting had to be perfect in this optical sense to portray an object or scene, this process would hold little interest for the psychologist. However, the optic array produced by a painting must be quite different in a number of ways from that produced by the portrayed object. The picture needs to share only certain aspects of the optic array produced by the real scene, and the question of what these features are and why they are so is what makes pictures important to the psychologist.

The "Laws" of Representational Painting

For many years, pictorial surrogates could be prepared only by some variation of Leonardo's prescription—a large part of the artist's task. (See Figure 5.1.) With the advent of photography, the preparation of such high-fidelity surrogates became a more precise and less laborious task. However, to da Vinci, the glass tracings were not to be pictures in themselves, but "aids and teachers" to the artist. If the artist sets a tracing to some other distance and slant from his eye than that at which he painted it, and views the glass plate as an *object with patterns of pigment* on it, he will discover certain regularities in the tracing, correlated with aspects of the scene he traced: the tracing of the near boy and that of the far one are different sizes; the parallel roadsides converge to a "vanishing point"; the nearer object yields a completed outline while the farther one is "interrupted"; the density of detail of texture becomes progressively greater as the surface being traced recedes in space; the

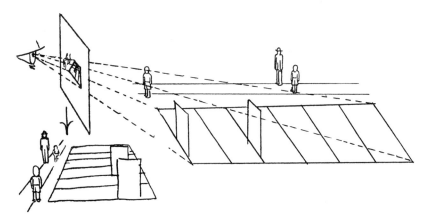

Figure 5.1. Scene, picture plane, and the tracing (or surrogate) which will portray the scene.

shadows which model the objects in the environment appear as areas of different reflectance or albedo. If the artist studies a number of such tracings and compares them with the scenes which they portray, he will discover a set of laws—for example, perspective—or rules by which he can achieve approximately what he would have traced on a glass pane with any real or imaginary scene. Here there are two alternative technical procedures whereby one can prepare pictorial surrogates: we can actually trace the scene with a glass plate or photographic film, or we can employ pictorial rules—perspective, interposition, etc.—in preparing pictures of any given scene.

There is a third method which is most curious: with some training, we can—almost at will—view the *real* world as though it were a *painting* and examine it for its pictorial qualities (aided in this attempt, perhaps, by framing the scene with our hands, sighting with the thumb, squinting, etc.). These properties—mainly the rules of linear perspective—have been extracted as the "visual depth clues," or "cues," and have been used by artist and psychologist alike for almost 400 years. Let us see why they became embedded at the heart of perceptual theorizing.

1. These depth cues seem to compel our observation of space where in fact there is no space. Might not our normal space perceptions depend upon the use of these same cues? Since the retina of the eye is flat, just as is an artist's canvas or a photographer's plate, how else could we possibly perceive space?

2. As noted above, these cues can actually be observed in a peculiar way. That is, if we look at railroad tracks (as shown in Figure 5.1) with the right attitude, we can see the convergence readily enough. Less easily, we can see that the boy at 20 feet looks smaller than the boy at 10 feet.[2] That is, we seem to be able to see the individual pieces of which the optic array is composed. This is what the early psychologists attempted. By careful study of our observations of the world, they sought to break them down into their elementary components or *sensations*—a very serious effort which made a lot of sense. (It still does even though we now know that it can no longer be undertaken with such simple intentions.)

However, let us note one very important point about these depth cues, which have been thought about for centuries and were deeply involved in the most widespread of the psychological analyses of man, starting with what is usually called British empiricism or associationism and culminating with Brunswik and the Princeton School today. Nevertheless, the depth clues were not discovered by *psychologists*, nor even studied much by them; herein lies both a lesson and a *warning* concerning their use.

In 1585, Leonardo systematically investigated them (11). In 1946, Ames constructed demonstrations to separate them (2). Both men were artists, seeking how best to represent the world. For representational purposes, the depth cues are *probably* functioning tools. As cues—as stimulus-variables by means of which we see the world itself—they *have never been shown* to be anything of the sort. Despite a great deal of literature in psychology "explaining" depth perception in terms of these cues, and despite their inclusion and assertion in every textbook on psychology, they have *not*, in general, been shown to be *responsible* for the perception of space *other than in pictures*. Even more to our present point, we don't know too much about their importance in pictures.

Empiristic Theory of Space and Picture Perception

Self-observation of the visual depth cues fit most neatly into what has been the only serious, systematic attempt in common Western thought to set up a scientific study of the mind and its processes. This was the attempt (which we may trace from Locke and Berkeley to Helmholtz and Titchener) to find the "elements" of which mental events are composed. It was an immensely bold and exciting attempt. All present approaches to perceptual problems are marked both by its failures and by the continuing attempt to find an adequate substitute (21 and 31). The task was as follows:

First, it was assumed that *all* thoughts come originally through our senses so that every idea must consist either of sensations—elementary sensory experiences—or of these combined with the memories of previous sensations (called *images*). Thus, it was thought that out of a finite list of sensations one can explain all the infinite variety of things we perceive and know. The task of psychology, like that of chemistry, was to find the elements and the rules governing their combination into the various objects of the world which we can perceive or conceive.

Second, it was assumed that with effort and training we can dissect our own perceptual and conceptual experiences so as to observe the elementary sensations and images of which they are composed. The procedure employed was known as *analytic introspection*. This act of the introspective *psychologist* is almost identical with that of the *artist* when he "sees" the depth cues, which we discussed above. Let us consider a concrete example:

Painters' Observations and Psychologists' Introspections. To casual observation, Figure 5.2 portrays a light-colored cube. Its corners are right angles, its surface is fairly uniformly light. As soon as the point is mentioned, however, one notices that *i* is nothing of the sort; with more careful analysis, one sees that, as at *ii*, the angles are very far from being rectangular and equal, and the local color grades markedly from dark to light. This is a particularly easy kind of introspection to undertake since, after all, angle *d-a-b* really is an acute angle drawn on paper, and the gradation of pigment from one point to the next is quite evident.

The task is much more difficult when you look at a real object such as a box or table. There, to approximate the conditions of Figure 5.2 *ii*, you will need to look at the various parts through a tube or a hole in a piece of cardboard—that is, if you wish to detect the *actual changes in local color* from

Figure 5.2. A light cube (*i*) and its parts (*ii*).

one region to the next as they would be seen if each patch of color had been presented *separately*. It was believed that with suitable training, one could in fact observe the pure sensations by means of analytic introspection. Thus, if one could divorce meaning and past experience from his observations, he would in fact see railroad tracks converge (as in Figure 5.1), the smallness of the boy farther off, the texture-density gradient, and not the spatial qualities at all. (We now know that this accomplishment is simply not possible in the sense attempted.)

Let us now see what this assumption meant with respect to the pictorial cues as such.

Necessary Ambiguity of the Pictorial Depth Cues. One essential property of Leonardo's depth cues is that they must be ambiguous and unreliable indications of spatial arrangements. The very fact that a picture—a pattern of pigment on a flat plane surface—can be prepared which can produce at the eye the same cues as would be produced by a tridimensional object means that these aspects of light are not determinative; that is, they can be produced by at least two spatial arrangements. Indeed, as Figure 5.3 indicates, there is an *infinite number* of different spatial arrangements which will provide the *same* pictorial depth cues.[3] This point concerning the ambiguity of pictorial communication led, via an irrelevant metaphysical issue, down a false but still popular path of psychological theory.

Since the pictorial depth cues cannot suffice to reveal depth to our minds unambiguously, how can we learn about the real world of three dimensions? One response is that there is no such tridimensional real world—the solipsistic vein running strongly through Western thought. Others held that there must be other sources of information from which we

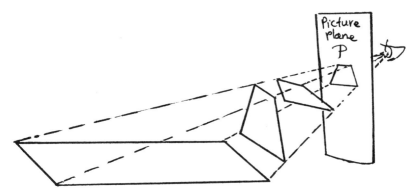

Figure 5.3. The necessary ambiguity of pictorial representation: the trapezoid on the picture plane could be projected by any one of an infinite number of quadrilaterals.

learn about the true state of spatial arrangements. For example, the *convergence* of our eyes, which changes as we look from one distance to another, might serve to convey, by sensations of different degrees of muscular tension, the distance of the object at which we are looking; so might the sensations from the muscles which focus the optic lens (*accommodation*). Similarly, the memory of the greater number of steps which we must take in order to touch the smaller boy in Figure 5.1 would be recalled when we receive the visual sensations of his size.

In short, it was proposed that we do not see space at all and that what we always see is directly *analogous to a picture*, with neither solidity to the parts nor distance separating the near and far objects. Space, it was contended, is a *nonvisual* idea, a tactual-kinesthetic idea (composed of sensations of touch and of muscle action), which past experiences have taught us to associate with the visual depth cues. By such analysis, the world we see becomes an assemblage of patches of color-sensation, differing only in their hue, brightness, and saturation and occupying areas of different extent at different positions in a two-dimensional arrangement.[4] Ideas of tridimensionality derive from the muscular sensations of convergence, accommodation, and locomotion. Even ideas of form—e.g., circle versus square—were thought to consist of the muscular sensations which arise from their "tracing out" by the moving eye of the observer (23 and 51). An object has apparent spatial form because of the cues by which such form is indicated to the observer, and the cues themselves suggest muscular motions in space simply because of the *frequency* with which those cues have been paired or *associated* with the appropriate motions in the past experiences of the observer. A picture, then, is simply the putting together of a set of symbols in a learned and *arbitary* visual language of tactual-kinesthetic spatial suggestions.

This was an attractive idea. We can—at least in some circumstances—"see" the depth cues, rather than the space itself; these depth cues do appear

Figure 5.4.

to suggest space rather than to comprise it. Artists, indeed, have seemed quite willing to accept the depth cues as learned conventions—as arbitrary assemblages of pigment on paper or canvas by which we learn to (or agree to) assign spatial meaning (1 and 2).

Demise of Structuralist Empiricism. This theory of space perception is now untenable. We know now that at least some animals can make spatial discriminations though they have been reared in darkness and prevented from having any associated visual and tactual-kinesthetic experiences since birth (15 and 30).

More important, we simply cannot consider "sensations" of color and position to be the observable and fundamental elements out of which our perceptions of the world are in fact built and, therefore, out of which pictures are composed. One cannot, in fact, observe the elements as though they were presented in isolation. For example, no matter how strongly you try, you cannot see the horizontal lengths in Figure 5.4 as equal—which they are—without covering up the diagonal lines. The number of such examples is immense. Over a very wide spectrum of psychological orientation, no one I know of seriously proposes this analytical task today, although rarely are the consequences of its abandonment followed through.

We shall have to reinquire what a picture is, and how it is that the pictorial cues are at all observable.

What, Then, Are Pictures?

A picture so perfect that it would produce at the eye exactly what the eye would receive if confronted with a real scene (as in Figure 5.1) would have perfect fidelity (19 and 20). However, even with the most perfect photograph or motion picture, there are profound differences between picture and reality. Do these departures from fidelity impair the pictorial communication? Not at all. Photographs have higher fidelity than outline drawings and still more than caricatures, yet the characteristics of a given object may be communicated better as the representational fidelity of the surrogate deteriorates (41). Perfect physical fidelity is impossible and would not be of psychological interest if it were achieved, but perfect *functional* fidelity— "the degree to which the variables to which the eye is sensitive are the same in one array as another" (20, p. 233)—is completely achievable and is of considerable psychological interest. Indeed, findings as to functional fidelity raise a vast area of inquiry. The nature of exaggeration, caricature, distinctive features, etc., in pictorial communication can tell us a lot about the normal perceptual process and its development. We must, however, first ask explicitly what possible essential feature is being retained when an outline drawing is substituted for a high-fidelity photograph.

What Are Outline Drawings?

How can the *lines* of linear perspective represent what we normally confront when we look at a real scene? How can a circle, scribed by a compass on paper, claim functional fidelity to the edge of a dinner plate and the solid form (or margin) of a ball (16, p. 405)?

The first answer which might occur to us is that such pictures are a form of visual language learned much as we learn a foreign language at school. In the typical "paired-associates" procedure, we rehearse "*manger*—to eat, *avoir*—to have" or, instead, we point to the *chaise*, the *fenêtre*, the *porte*. Is this how pictures come to communicate? Are outlines drawn on paper learned symbols for the edges of things in the world? Persistent anecdotes concerning the inability of primitive people to comprehend pictures suggest some support for such doctrine.

1. *That outline pictures are not a learned language* is now clear. It has been established that an individual without any formal training of the paired-associates variety can recognize pictures. A recent study of a 19-month-old child provides confirmation (36). The child had been taught his vocabulary solely by use of solid objects and had received no instruction or training whatever concerning pictorial meaning or content; indeed, he had seen practically no pictures close at hand. Yet he recognized objects portrayed by two-dimensional outline drawings as well as by photographs. The pictures are shown in Figure 5.5 in the order in which they were presented and recognized.

    Thus, if the understanding of outline drawings is learned at all, this must occur not as a separate process but in the normal course of whatever learning may be involved in seeing the edges of objects in the world. In what way can a line on paper be inherently equivalent to the edge of an object?

2. *Lines, ribbons, and edges*—the psychophsics of "flats." What are the characteristics of an edge? At an object's edge, there is an abrupt cessation of surface at *that* distance from the eye and some increase in the distance through empty air (or other medium) which must be traversed before we hit another surface. In Figure 5.6*a*, the cut-out silhouette does not have both a convex nose and a concave expanse of background nesting together at the boundary between the two. Instead, the nose is flesh up to its very edge, which is convex; past that, we have nothing in the same plane, and the material to the left (if there is any) is at a greater distance and extends indeterminately *behind* the convex edge. Note that this is

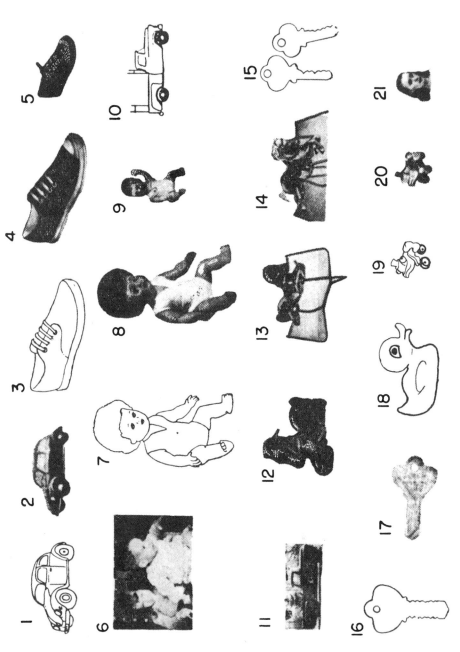

Figure 5.5. Outline drawings are not merely symbols. Drawings and photographs shown here were correctly named by a young child who had no

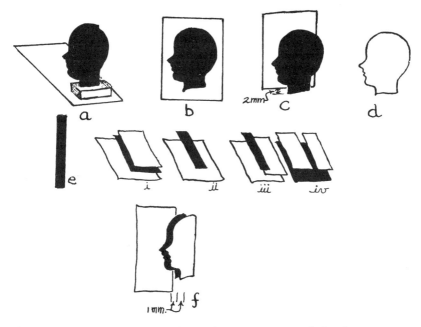

Figure 5.6. What can an outline drawing have in common with the object it represents?

a description of physical properties, of physical objects. We shall see later that this relationship is faithfully reflected in the perceptual qualities of figure-ground contours.

Thus, a printed silhouette on paper, as in Figure 5.6b, provides the eye the same optic array as would an arrangement of two surfaces, one in front of the other, as in Figure 5.6c. There are, of course, some slight differences between the two—in accommodation and binocular disparity, and in relative motion, interposition, etc., for a moving observer—but these differences are negligible. In fact, if we prepare both an actual cutout object, such as Figure 5.6c, and a picture of it as in the inked silhouette of Figure 5.6b, subjects who are asked to compare the picture and the object from a normal viewing distance of about two feet do not spontaneously recognize that one is a spatial array and one is a picture of it (33). In short, a silhouette is a reasonably high-fidelity surrogate for the edge of a planar object.

The same profile appears again in Figure 5.6d, this time in outline. In what ways are this outline and the silhouette of 5.6a the same? Again, let us examine the kinds of physical objects which could provide the same optic array as this picture: In Figure 5.6e, we see that there are six arrangements of surfaces which produce substantially the same optic array as does the ribbon of pigment on the printed page—those shown, plus the mirror images of *i* and *iii*. In three of these—*i*, *ii*, and *iii*—the same surface edge appears as formed the silhouette in 5.6*a*. This is a description of the ways in which a number of different physical surfaces will produce optic arrays similar to that produced by an outline drawing.

We now have to inquire as to what, in fact, people see when confronted by such optic arrays. If we now prepare a multiple-level cut-out object such as Figure 5.6*f*, and ask subjects to compare that object with the outline picture of Figure 5.6*d*, again we find that they do not spontaneously recognize one as a spatial array and the other as a picture.

Let us assume that—either as a result of a great deal of extremely early experience with the world of things and objects,[5] or as the result of being born with appropriately evolved structures of eye and brain—we enter early childhood with the tendency to see an *edge of a surface* each time a sufficiently large luminous discontinuity (or other stimulus for "contour") confronts our eyes. Even the untrained child would see the margins of deposits of pigment on paper as surface-edges.

What kinds of surface-edges are in fact seen when outline drawings are being viewed? Naive subjects asked to describe a line of some specific width using any words *other* than "line," overwhelmingly use a small number of categories—those in Figure 5.6*e*; that is, either the edges of overlapping surfaces or, in rare cases, rods (or wires) and their edges (16, p. 409f.). As the width of the line decreases, the tendency to see a ribbon or wire, with two edges bounding the pigmented region, first increases, then decreases. That is, we pass from a silhouette to a wire or bar, back to some form of silhouette again. And as we increase the angle formed by a line or contour, the preference of one over the other alternative silhouette increases (33).

Subjects' use of words like *edge, surface*, etc., are remarkably subject to suggestion by the questioner. Is all this merely a matter of language, of terms derived from objects, simply because the observer knows no other words which our questions permit him to use?

3. *Edges as elements of shape.* There are several ways in which it appears that for an object's shape to be perceived at all, it must have an edge which can function in only one direction at a time, and which operates only over a limited span or distance. As far as shape is concerned, what isn't edged is not perceived, and what is perceived is edged. Three different measures, in addition to the purely verbal descriptions of Figure 5.6, support this assertion.

a. *Retinal rivalry* between opposing contours. If the views to the two eyes are in marked conflict as in Figure 5.7*a*, the information coming from the left eye, *i*, and from the right eye, *ii*, does not consist of independent points which can fuse to form one single image. Instead, it consists of edges, each of which carries a "halo" of its appropriate field along with it; that is, we see *iii* or *iv* instead of a complete black cross.[6] Edges must originate at some pretty primitive levels in the nervous system.

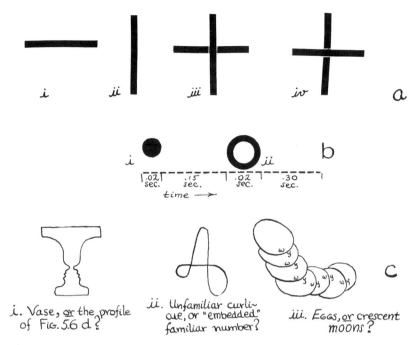

i. Vase, or the profile   ii. Unfamiliar curli-   iii. Eggs, or crescent
of Fig. 5.6 d?   cue, or "embedded"   moons?
                         familiar number?

Figure 5.7. Edge as a prerequisite for *shape*. In group *a*, if the left eye is shown *i*, and the right eye is shown *ii*, we see *iii* or *iv* instead of a solid, complete cross. In group *b*, the sequence of disk, *i*, and annulus, *ii*, will render *i* invisible; in the reverse order, this does not occur. In group *c* are figure-ground alternatives.

b. *Successive contour appropriation* (metacontrast). If stimuli are presented in the same position, but for the durations and order indicated in Figure 5.7*b*, the disk in *b*, *i*, simply is not perceived at all (although there are some secondary effects due to its presentation). The formation of an edge facing in one direction preempts the edge which had just begun to form in the opposite direction, thereby preventing the first shape from being seen (50).

c. *Concealment of forms* in camouflage and "puzzle pictures"; figure-ground phenomena. The previous two sets of phenomena are far removed from normal visual communication. Not so the following: Any and every region of color on a painted or printed surface is, in a very strict sense, shaped in only one direction at a time; if one of the two adjoining regions has a recognizable shape, the shape of the other is lost. Grossly speaking, what is figure has recognizable shape; what is ground is formless and extends behind the picture. See Figure 5.7*c* for some classical examples of figure-ground alternatives.

As a general description, the figure-ground distinction is convenient, but it is not really accurate. A given closed region may be figure in one part, ground in another. For example, in Figure 5.7*c.iii,* each region is figure at *w*, ground at *y*. Similarly, it is incorrect to treat the contour which separates a figure from its surrounding regions as a monolithic phenomenon. Again note Figure 5.7*c.iii.* There, contours are shown to comprise an edge facing in one direction; yet at some distance away, they form an edge facing in another direction.

What is true is that a *perceived* edge, like a physical edge itself, can belong to only *one* surface at a time, but a given surface may extend in front of another surface at one edge, and yet, elsewhere, can itself have another surface extend in front of it. A perceived edge appears to have a limited sphere of influence within which it maintains a direction of surface. Within this critical functional distance range, edges opposite in sign will conflict, forming the famous "reversible figures" which provide research tools to perception psychologists, curiosae for laymen, and interesting exercises for graphic artists (13). Past this critical distance, however, the effects of such conflict disappear, and quite inconsistent and "impossible" physical surfaces can be perceived side by side in apparently peaceful continuity as in Figure 5.8*a.* Very little is known about the perception of pictures of "impossible objects" (40). They are probably very rewarding subjects for study, since the problems of relationship between thing and picture, concept and percept, *unity of structure* and local *psychophysical* determination would all appear to focus here. In an important sense, moreover, all pictures are surrogates of impossible objects. The rigidity and consistency of the objects we see in the world are, then, not predetermined by our prior associations, by our mental categories, nor by overall organizational factors. When we see rigidity and self-consistency between the parts of an

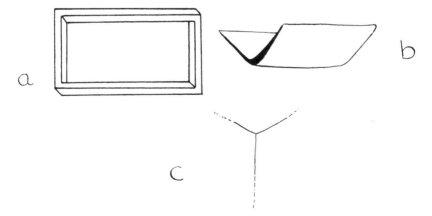

Figure 5.8. *a* is a picture of an impossible object patterned after Penrose (40). *b* shows a bent surface defined by its edge. *c* outlines a corner.

object and between the objects in a scene, these are *imposed* by the relationships between the parts of the stimulus array. If they are missing, an inconsistent and noninvariant world is acceptable to the perceptual system and is communicated to the observer.

In short, outline drawings are surrogates for edges, as are silhouettes.[7] Since any contour can be a surrogate for either of two edges, there is always the possibility that what we want to communicate pictorially will not be seen at all, or will not be seen as we want it to be seen. How can we determine which way an edge will be seen? We shall consider this essential problem in outlining the next school of perceptual psychology, Gestalt theory. First, however, we must complete our consideration of what pictures are.

What Are Pictures of Solid Forms and Volumes?

We have considered outline drawings as surrogates for overlapping plane surfaces like stage "flats." Most pictures, of course, portray much more solid forms (16, p. 405), and spatial features such as slant, curvature, and a dihedral angle can certainly be represented without the use of outlines at all. How can a picture act as a surrogate for such objects and real scenes?

1. *The psychophysics of "models."* What essential features of the optic arrays produced by scenes of solid objects also can be produced by the dappled surface of a shaded or halftone picture? Three classes of such common features have been separately studied so far:

    a. *Textural distributions.* Most common surfaces have inhomogeneities which are more or less uniformly distributed over their substance, and these produce optic arrays whose *texture density gradients*—i.e., the rates of change of the texture distributions—characterize the spatial arrangement of the surfaces, and, therefore, might provide information about spatial arrangements of the surfaces and about the relative sizes of objects resting on them (19, 20, and 21). These gradients can be produced with great fidelity by a pictorial surrogate, particularly a photograph.

    b. *Modeling by shade and shadows.* By virtue of their different orientations to the source of illumination and because of "cast shadows," the optic array produced by objects of uniform surface color will usually contain distributions of shading and shadow. These characteristics of the array are readily produced—within a limited range of illumination ratios—by the pigment density in a painting, photograph, or print.

    c. *Corners and bends.* To the traditional cue of linear perspective (Figure 5.1), and the edge-interposition of stage "flats" (Figure 5.6), we can add at least two other ways in which outline drawings can produce optic arrays equivalent to those produced by curved and angular surfaces. The edge of a bent or curved surface will produce a correspondingly inflected contour in the optic array, and a suitably drawn line (preferably of unequal width) can form a surrogate for these (Figure 5.8*b*). Most important: a corner, which in a sense is an edge facing in two directions simultaneously, can be replaced by lines (Figure 5.8*c*). In these respects a drawing can be a surrogate for a solid form or volume, as well as for silhouettes or "flats."

2. *Pictorial ambiguity.* All these features of the optic array are, of course, ambiguous; the very fact that we can produce them both by real scenes and by flat pictures is proof. The information contained in pictorial surrogates must necessarily be equivocal, and pictures must always be open to alternative interpretations, at least in theory. This inherent ambiguity raises two critical questions about pictorial communication: First, to what extent can pictures actually be optical *surrogates* for what they represent, rather than being merely interpreted as signs or symbols? Second, since pictorial information is ambiguous, what *determines* which of the alternative sets of surfaces and edges will be *perceived*? The answer to this first question will finally tell us what a picture is; the answer to the second will tell us how to make and use pictures, and this finding will return us to Gestalt theory, which first followed structuralism, and to the mainstream of psychological inquiry.

a. "Fooling the eye": mistaking the picture for its object—and vice versa. If we consider a picture to be a surrogate for a scene, we should recognize that it must be an imperfect surrogate. As we have noted before, there are many ways in which the array produced by a picture is different from that produced by the scene being portrayed. The most important of these would seem to be the cues which identify the picture as an object—as a plane surface, itself, at some specific distance and slant with respect to the viewer, and with variable reflectance due to uneven pigment deposits. To the extent that a picture is seen as a dappled surface, it cannot be a surrogate and must be acting merely as a symbol (16, p. 410). Regardless of how realistically a *trompe l'oeil* painter reproduces his scene, no matter how high the fidelity of a photograph, neither the painting nor the photograph can be mistaken for the scene itself if the plane of the picture is effectively *localized* over its entire surface. A number of cues can, in principle, accomplish this destructive localization of the picture's surface.[8] As we remove or reduce the cues, the effectiveness of the picture—the solidity or plasticity of the represented objects—appears to increase remarkably. Thus, everyone knows that the use of a stereoscope to introduce binocular disparity appropriate to the *objects* in the scene rather than to the *surface* of the picture will provide an impression of "relief" or plasticity; that is, one sees the scene, not the picture. However, the appearance of plastic solidity can be obtained with a single picture also, if it is viewed monocularly through a lens or aperture which *hides the edges* of the picture (1, 42, and 48). Indeed, the apparent space in a photographic scene can be made so convincing that observers could throw a ball at a point in it (46). Sonoda reports that such strong "plastic space" was suggested even by extremely simple outline drawings that relative pictorial distances were measured in a comparison with distances in real, freely seen space (47). These experiments provide some reason to believe that the conditions which produce strong plastic effects also mediate more accurate judgments about the characteristics of the represented object—for example, size. Certainly we would expect an increased speed and consistency of spatial comprehension. Equally important is the strong aesthetic value which seems to inhere in pictorial plasticity—a value to which the expensive paraphernalia of both stereoscope and "cineramic" viewing may be largely superfluous. The study of the conditions for, and consequences of, the perception of solidity is still in its infancy despite its obvious importance. We shall survey some closely related problems in the next section. Here, however, let us consider the other side of this point.

After all, pictures are normally viewed binocularly, with clear edges, and with a certain amount of head movement. How important are these cues to the flatness of a picture?

We have seen that it is possible under restricted monocular-viewing conditions to "fool the eye" into taking a flat picture for relief or plastic space. We can also reverse this process and under normal-viewing conditions, we can equally well "fool the eye" into accepting a real scene as a picture. For example, see Figure 5.9.

This tolerance of the optical system for discrepancies between the depth cues may depend upon an ability to attend to some cues and ignore the others. Thus, since we have seen that the effects of an edge (and the unity or rigidity of a surface) extend only over a limited space, perhaps one sees a picture as a tridimensional scene merely by keeping his gaze away from the edges of a picture. This specialized restriction of gaze—and perhaps a decreased attention to the binocular localization through suppression of the contribution of one edge—may well comprise all or most of the "learning" to use pictures of objects or scenes. The traditional primary cues of accommodation and convergence, as well as binocular disparity, would oppose the pictorial depth, of course, but as Smith and Smith point out in discussing their ball-throwing experiment:

> Accommodations and convergence were necessary for the perceptions (i.e., to form clear retinal images), but the latter were otherwise independent of these ocular functions... [which] are probably of no effect as cues for the perceived depths and absolute distances over surfaces which are characteristics of everyday life. (46, p. 231)

Research here awaits a good means of measuring "plasticity."

What is implied concerning the problem of *scale* is another matter. Except in rare cases, the picture is a surrogate not for the original

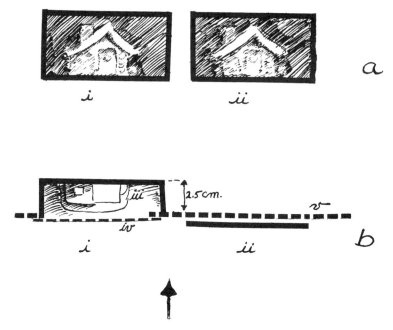

Figure 5.9. Picture and object. From a viewing distance of about 10 feet with unrestricted binocular viewing, observers of the pair, *a*, do not spontaneously notice a difference between *i* and *ii*, despite the cues which must be present to indicate that *i* is a model house—shown from above as *iii* in the top view of the arrangement, *b*. The model was sprayed with paint from an angle which stimulated a direction of illumination at strong variance to that of the room, and was then covered by a sheet of textured cellophane, *iv*. In *b* at *ii*, next to the model house, a picture of the set-up is placed on a common cardboard background, and both are given heavy black borders. The purpose of the textured cellophane is to eliminate the surface-cue differences between *i* and *ii*, but such texture merely makes the surface uneven and does not affect the operation of binocular disparity, accommodation, convergence, or motion parallax. With monocular vision, it becomes extremely difficult to detect which is picture, which is object.

scene but for a reduced and distorted model of that scene; that is, if it is true that savages have difficulty in identifying pictures of their family and friends, it may simply be that they would have evidenced exactly the same difficulty with the miniature simulacra of their friends to which the normally viewed photograph is in fact a surrogate.

b. *Potential pictures.* Because naturally unhomogeneous pigmented surfaces—such as grainy woods, dappled fur, clouded skies—surround us, potential pictures are abundant. These, however, only become surrogates when viewing conditions permit their surfaces to be *divorced* from their own determinate positions in space. Several factors contribute to this "pictorialization" of a surface, some of which we will consider below. The point is that without ever attempting to make a picture as such, we could, by judicious selection from among all of the dappled surfaces which nature produces, select a surrogate for almost any conceivable object or scene which we might desire to portray. This is what is meant by the "suggestion" inherent in the veining of a particular block of marble, the picture which grows by itself, or the cloud pictures and Rorschach ink blots which have been used in the so-called projective techniques.[9] Thus, a picture is defined not by the activity of its creator, but by the intention of the viewer (and partly by the introduction he receives). The artist may construct the picture on bare canvas; on the other hand, he may, as with scratch-board, simply remove what he doesn't want from the pigment on a surface.[10] Similarly, the photographer who seeks out a formation of clouds whose photograph, when suitably presented, can represent a castle or a unicorn, merely puts a frame around the photographically presented surface produced by a light-sensitive film at the rear of a camera.

c. *Multiplicity of scenes portrayed by any picture.* Although a single picture may appear in "plastic" relief, it still lacks the information contained either in a pair of stereoscopic pictures of the same scene, or in the view of a real scene obtained by a moving observer. The scene being portrayed and the dappled picture surface, itself, are only two of many alternative arrangements which will fit the same optic array. An infinite number of slant-shape pairs will fit the "tennis court" of Figure 5.1, and the pair of rectangles might just as well be an L-shaped flat in front of an eight-sided one. The corner in Figure 5.8*c* might be two rhomboid flats butted together at one side. In preparing any picture, *fidelity* alone will not explain nor predict what object or scene will be perceived. Figure 5.10*a* shows three projections of the same object, all equally faithful, yet extremely unequal in their portrayal of the original object.

We do not start with two-dimensional perception and build up, by learned associations, to tridimensionality. The problem is not why we see depth in pictures. Instead, we must ask why we see more or less depth in some pictures, and what conditions improve communication in pictures considered as surrogates for real, tridimensional objects in the world around us.

To offer a good surrogate is simply not enough to *ensure* that the tridimensional object will be adequately communicated. High fidelity may not prevent misperceptions, as every amateur photographer has discovered. For example, an unexpected coincidence of a telephone pole and a prize subject may weld the two into some inexplicable new object. Mechanical measures of representational fidelity are inadequate. The artist and photographer

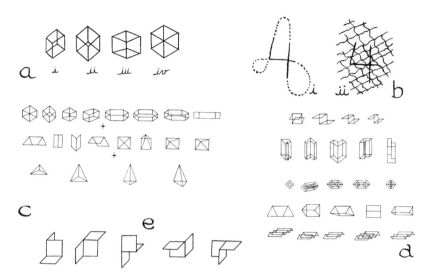

Figure 5.10. Reversible figures: tools for the study of organization.

must still "compose" their pictures if scenes and objects are to be recognizable (and also to lead the eye where it should go—a point we shall consider separately, below). One way they do so is by trying out or visualizing an arrangement, then changing their roles to that of the naive observer in order to discover whether such an observer would see what is intended. Assuming that most people respond in much the same way, and to the extent that they do so respond, it *must* be possible to discover general rules or laws governing perceptual selection. The discovery of these rules comprised the main goal of Gestalt theory. In recent years, as we shall see, some progress has been made toward reaching it.

Psychophysics of Represented Form

The search for new units by which to analyze both the world we perceive and the processes of our nervous system (27)—the "laws of organization"—brought the Gestalt psychologists into the very set of pictorial problems we now have to consider.

The "Laws of Organization"

To know where, in a picture, an edge will be seen and which way it will face is essential in the preparation of pictorial stimuli. Remembering the empiricist tradition, we might as a start hypothesize that we will see what is familiar to us. However, although this assumption may be true in some complex sense, it is certainly not true in any way which we can use, in practice, to make predictions. For example, in Figure 5.7*c.ii* a very familiar shape is in sight yet is difficult to detect. It cannot be the lack of familiarity which conceals it since it is more familiar than the pattern in which it is embedded.

Is it, then, a question of confusion? Is the number invisible because it is presented amid cluttering lines? No, for despite an equal or greater number of lines in Figure 5.10*b.ii*, the number remains clearly in view. It is a matter of *arrangement* of additional lines, not their mere presence. The configuration (Gestalt) decides what will be figure, what will be ground. The point of Gestalt psychology in opposition to structuralism is that there are lawful ways in which the overall configuration determines the action of any part we may consider—for example, which way an edge will face—and that these laws are not to be explained simply in terms of associative learning to assemble the individual local sensations—the patches of color and brightness—as the empiricist structuralists would have it.

This concept providing some means of anticipating and predicting which way edges will face is pretty much what we have been looking for. Unfortunately, the mainstream of Gestalt theory did not go much further than three undertakings: (a) to demonstrate that individual sensations could not in fact be observed when embodied in contexts (i.e., demonstrations that the whole is more than the sum of its parts); (b) to speculate about the underlying kinds of physiological mechanisms which might be responsible for such organization; and (c) to find examples of the laws of organization.

The first two of these undertakings have little purpose today. The last provides an intuitive set of explanations about where contours or edges will form—the "laws of grouping"—and a set of rules which tell us which way they will face—the "laws of figure-ground organization." The Gestalt laws may or may not be convincing to the reader, but they certainly suffer from one major defect: they appeal to intuition to decide what will occur in each case. The reader must decide which alternative has better continuation, which arrangement is more symmetrical, which is simplest. Of the laws listed, that of proximity appears to be most objectively statable, but the least impressive as a predictor. Good "continuation" appears to be subject to measurement and objective statement, as we shall see. "Simplicity," which appears to be the most powerful—at least as an intuitive statement—also appears to be the least easy to state objectively. The next steps, then, are to try to discover the measurable aspects of the physical stimulus-distributions which correspond to these intuitive laws of organization; to subject them to psychophysical research; and to ascertain their relative strengths and efficacies in predicting what will indeed be seen.

Quantitative Statements of Gestalt Laws

A number of attempts have been made to state and measure several Gestalt laws, but since it is difficult to devise pictures in which only one of the laws of organization is operative at any time, these are in general unsuited for the problems normally faced in pictorial representation (cf. 26 and 31). A more inclusive formulation is needed and fortunately is available.

Simplicity and Informational Redundancy as the bases of pictorial depth cues. *Kopfermann* (39) explored a number of reversible-perspective figures like the series in Figure 5.10*a*. These portray either one cube in parallel projection viewed from a number of different vantage points, or a group of different two-dimensional patterns. Figure 5.10*a.iv* appears most readily as a flat pattern; it is only with some effort that we can recognize it as a cube. Figure 5.10*a.i* appears most readily as a cube. What changes from *i* to *iv* to cause a corresponding decrease in tridimensionality?

What the Gestaltists proposed here is a deceptively simple formula: Where more than one organization may be perceived, we will see the *simplest alternative*. This generalization does seem to fit a great many cases. Figure 5.10*a.iv* is simpler as a two-dimensional pattern than as a tridimensional object, and we see it accordingly. Similarly, Figure 5.10*a.i* is simpler as a tridimensional object than as a two-dimensional pattern, and so we see the former. If we review the pictorial depth cues in Figures 5.1 and 5.8, we find that in each case the three-dimensional arrangement is simpler than the two-dimensional alternatives—it is simpler to see one square in front of another than an abutting "L" and square, simpler to see two boys at different distances than a giant and a midget side by side, etc.[11]

The only defect in this "law" is that the measurement of "simplicity" remains to be made explicit. As it stands, an intuitive judgment permits us to explain only after we have constructed a figure and have observed how people react to it. It does not enable us to predict in advance, as any useful law or rule must.

However, "simplicity" need not remain purely intuitive. Several closely related attempts to define it as a physical measure have been made in order to bring the Gestalt hypothesis into usable form (3, 4, 14, 32, and 38). Of these, it suffices to cite two:

> Gestalt psychologists have been vigorously attacked in the past for . . . these concepts, on the grounds that they are subjective, unquantifiable. . . . Such arguments no longer have much weight since organization is demonstrably measurable in informational terms: roughly speaking, organization and redundancy are the same. . . . perception might be conceived as a set of preliminary "data-reduction" operations, whereby sensory information is described . . . in a form more economical than that in which it impinges on the receptors. (4)

Specifically, we might hypothesize "that the probability of a given perceptual response to a stimulus is an inverse function of the amount of information required to define that pattern" (38).

To use such a hypothesis, we must discover the specific physical variables by which to measure "complexity." A first attempt in this direction has proved extremely promising thus far, using only the following three-factor equation:

$$Y_1 = t_1 + t_2 + 2(t_3)$$

where: Y_1 is the predicted relative apparent solidity of each of the different viewpoints from which a particular object can be represented (e.g., i through iv in Figure 5.10a);
t_1 = the number of angles enclosed within each figure;
t_2 = the number of different angles divided by the total number of angles;
t_3 = the number of continuous lines.

This prediction is based on the previous assumptions: The degree to which each of the different drawings of an object appears in its *solid* rather than its flat alternative is proportional to its *complexity* as a *flat pattern*.[12] Study of several "families" of different views (as in Figure 5.10c and d) suggested that the important factors were the three measures given above (32). In each case, these measures refer to flat patterns and are scored on a scale running from 0 for the lowest in each "family" to 10 for the highest. This formula has been tested over a fair range of pictured objects with some success. Correlations between predicted and observed apparent solidities vary between 0.6 to 0.9 for the various categories of pictures which have been sampled by a variety of "random" procedures.[13] There are, however, at least three distinct limitations to the use of this formula at present:

First, it applies only to the different representations of one single object and does not as yet permit direct *comparisons* between the pictures of *different* objects.

Second, it was designed to fit only relatively simple, unshaded drawings consisting of *straight lines.*

Third, there are undoubtedly relevant factors which we have not included and some which we do not as yet even know (35 and 37).

Research here is still very much in progress. We need to test this formula and other quantitative restatements of the Gestalt laws with much wider samples of pictures before we can evaluate their validity and usefulness. Also, the selection of pictures for use in research is itself a problem in need of study since it is all too easy for the artist acting as a psychologist or for the psychologist acting as an artist to select sets of pictures to "prove" his laws. This sampling problem is extremely serious (5), but we can, of course, produce pictures in arbitrary ways, not subject to the experimenter's own choice.

Procedures for generating flat "nonsense shapes" (5) have been used to study the stimulus bases for the apparent *complexity* and connotative meaning of silhouette forms. By means of three-dimensional gridworks and tables of random numbers, arbitrary shapes like those of Figure 5.10e can be obtained. Samples taken "randomly" from the objects surrounding us can be made just as arbitrary, yet are not so unrelated to stimuli we are likely to encounter in the normal run of events (29).

It is evident that the range of arbitrarily produced pictures providing the experimental bases for any rules or theories which can be enunciated today is still dangerously restricted. As long as the perception psychologist finds it necessary to employ only constrained and simplified pictures in his research, it would be very unwise to employ his generalizations with more confidence than these constraints display.

Even with the restricted selection of pictures so far investigated, one major omission has appeared. Observers do not look at an entire picture, but at selected portions (especially those with larger and more complex patterns). This factor of selective attention may set the most important limits of the entire enterprise of attempting to deal with pictorial communication on a scientific basis.

Prediction of Attention

Early psychology was particularly concerned with the origin of spatial ideas of form or tridimensionality. Gestalt thought and inquiry were similarly invested. However, with such complex stimuli as normal pictures, other variables became more interesting. Research on the pictorial communication of metric spatial information—that is, judgments about relative distances, sizes, etc.—is still exploratory, but appears promising (6, 44, 45, 47, and 49). The experiences in which we may be interested may not even be spatial or "physical" at all. They may fit more naturally with the interests of the advertiser, the cartoonist, the pin-up artist, or the aesthetician than with the communication needs of the engineer or draftsman.

Communicating "Nonphysical" Qualities

Just as some believed that the optic array—and, by the same token, any pictorial display—can contain no information about tridimensional space, Berkeley argued:

As we see distance . . . in the same way . . . we see shame or anger in the looks of a man. . . . Without . . . experience we should no more have taken blushing for a sign of shame than of gladness. (7, p. 202f.)

We have seen, however, that we can find bases—whether it is a learned process or not—in pictures for our perceptions of portrayed size and distance. Can we similarly hope to find bases for the communication of shame and anger?

A number of such phenomena as facially expressed emotions (43) seem to be *reliable* in that subjects agree with others in their responses to pictures. Consequently, we know that observers must be responding to some physical aspects of the stimulus, and psychophysical study is at least possible in principle. Scattered attempts have been made to measure stimulus bases for such experiences as "cuteness" (38).

It does, indeed, appear that we can discover psychophysical formulas with which to predict observers' *nonphysical* experiences with some consistency (and we would expect—from the successes of typecasting, the cosmetic industry, pin-up sales—even greater consistency outside the laboratory). It is not difficulty of measurement which slows our progress in this area of inquiry, but rather *the absence of systematic theories,* counterparts of the structuralist and Gestalt theories which motivated inquiry into *spatial form.* At present, we can expect such research to be directed by specific needs, as these appear in other areas of theoretical or practical interest. Of particular interest here is the quality of *visual attractiveness* because, as we have seen, it may influence profoundly our attempts to predict what people will see in pictures, by determining where they will look.

The Psychophysics of "Attensity"

No matter how successful we might otherwise be in our attempts to determine a particular experience on the part of the observer, unless we have some way of knowing (either statistically or individually) where and when an observer will look, we have no way of knowing what his response will be. Upon the success of this last point depends the entire attempt at a psychophysics of pictorial perception. Artists, lay-out men, and advertisers believe that linear composition and other aspects of the stimulus decide where the gaze of the average observer will be directed. Although a great deal of research has been done over the years on the study of eye movements, very little scientific study has been made of the "laws of composition."

Intuitive prescriptions may turn out to be correct. At least grossly, observers do seem to know where they are in fact being "forced" to look. Figure 5.11*a* shows paintings and photographs for which Buswell recorded observers' eye movements photographically (10). The pictures are each divided into 16 sections to show the relative duration of fixation spent within each section. They were not so divided, of course, when they were presented to the subjects.

When other observers are requested to indicate the most prominent regions in Figure 5.11*a*—those which attract their eyes the most strongly or the most frequently—we find general agreement from one set of observers to the next (34). That is, observers are consistent in their judgment of where they are looking, and we can predict what one observer will say from what others have said. In fact, the distributions of judged attention—what we here call *attensity*—are in fair agreement with the photographic records. It is not premature to make two conclusions about the control of fixation and attention:

  a. Even the *untrained* observer has some idea as to what attracts his eye. It therefore seems a good bet that the student of composition can do

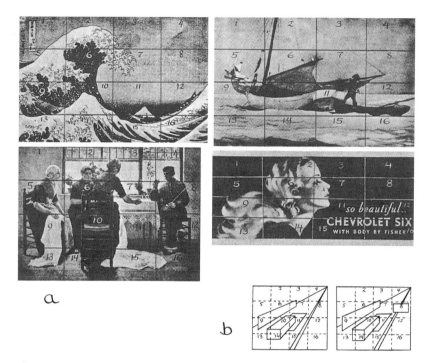

Figure 5.11. Prediction of attention: Group *a* shows pictures used to compare photographic records of where people look (10) with other observers' judgments of *prominence* (34). Group *b* shows examples of the class of pictures for which the psychological prediction of attention is being attempted.

better than chance in guessing where people will look in a given arrangement. Such judgments are probably not merely empty expertise.

b. The fact that observers' judgments are consistent and agree both with each other and with eye-movement records indicates that a psychophysics of attensity must be possible in principle. Is it possible in practice? Preliminary attempts have been made to predict points of greater and lesser attensity in simple pictures (34) such as those in Figure 5.11*b*. In these attempts, several different tentative formulas have succeeded better than chance. The preliminary formulas were obtained with restricted samples of stimuli and with a relatively restricted sample of motivating conditions. The effects of different motives on a freely moving observer beset by varied visual displays—all competing for his active and passive attention—may offer an entirely different set of problems from those being studied.

Further studies, however, should be relevant to tasks in which the observer is set to look at some particular communicative display. Most reading, TV viewing, and instrument searching would be included in this category—one that is not too narrow a field in which to achieve a measure of psychophysical control of visual attention. That measure of control will, in turn, permit the application of whatever other psychophysical knowledge we have obtained.

Summary

Pictorial communication of shape and form is not simply a learned visual language. Whatever processes of learning, if any, underlie our ability to perceive represented surfaces' edges—without which the communication of shape is impossible—in response to outline drawings probably occurs very early in life in consequence of our normal commerce with spatial objects. Although this probability makes the problems of "learning to see pictures" relatively inaccessible, it simplifies the study of the rules which govern edge and surface perception in pictures. The applicability of such rules depends, eventually, on knowing where people will look in a pictorial display. The study of such selective attention and of its stimulus control and educability— although it appears promising—has barely been started.

Notes

1. This is true only if the painting is presented to the eye of the observer from the same distance and in the same orientation as that at which it was painted by the artist.

2. Some training is necessary to observe this difference, and some aid—either the use of mathematical perspective or special viewing devices—is always necessary to see that the farther boy is only "half the size."

3. This is not the only point at which ambiguity is a useful property. It is a valuable research tool for the investigation of psychological laws. Furthermore, the entire psychological testing area of projective techniques—Rorschach ink blots, etc.—rests upon the ambiguity of the pictures employed. Of course, the very existence of nonrepresentational as well as representational art depends upon such ambiguity.

4. In a purely physical sense, this analysis is bound to work. If we make our patches small enough, we know that we can duplicate any scene by an appropriate set of colored dots—cf. TV, halftones, stippling, and pointillism.

5. Repeated exposures in early life might build up neural structures in the brain—that is, "cell assemblies" (23)—which would respond in a unitary fashion.

6. Moreover, the descriptive observations given in Figure 5.6 appear to be duplicated, at least in gross outline, in the fusion-products of retinal rivalry.

7. Why this should be so is as yet unknown. It may be a physiological accident (e.g., byproduct of some edge-responding or contour-enhancing properties of the optical nervous system). It may serve some evolutionary function in its own right. Or it may be an adventitious product of the general learning process. In any case, we can vary the physical and geometrical nature of the stimulus pattern to which

subjects are exposed and determine experimentally the correlated changes in appearance which result (26). This is desirable not only because this technical information is applicable in pictorial communication, but because it tells us something about the machinery of perception as a psychological and physiological process—and we must know what the machinery does and how it acts before it is meaningful or reasonable to investigate what the machinery is like.

8. The traditional cues which would specify the locale of the picture's surface are, of course, those which do the same for any surface: binocular disparity, motion parallax, interposition, accommodation, convergence, etc. However, the effective use of these cues for this purpose has not been studied. We do not know the actual efficacy of such localization.

9. We should note a firm difference in kind between the various projective techniques. The Rorschach technique is not ambiguous in the same sense as is the TAT(25). The Rorschach ink blot does, indeed, contain a number of surrogates for different, alternative objects (18 and 28). These surrogates are not consistent with each other nor necessarily good surrogates. They are, however, just as reasonably interpretable as objects as are the markings on any other picture. Against this, such tests as the TAT ask questions about situation, social intent, life history—sets of responses for which some stimulus determinants may or may not be present.

10. Against this, cf. Gibson (16, p. 404).

11. Only one traditional cue—that of familiar size—cannot be expressed in terms of "simplicity." It was thought that the known size of an object could affect the distance at which it appears to be located. This cue depends for its very definition on past experiences, not upon anything one can say about the stimulus itself. It now appears, however, to be largely or wholly ineffectual (12, 22, and 24.)

12. There are branches of physical science—notably thermodynamics—which also have to deal with problems of configuration. The measures which have been most frequently borrowed for this purpose are closely related to entropy; e.g., the measures of "information theory." As the quotations above suggest, a number of attempts are currently being made to devise and use informational substitutes for the intuitive Gestalt terms.

13. Thus, a correlation coefficient of 1.0 would represent perfect prediction of what observers say they see, while one of 0.0 would represent a complete failure to predict; that is, no relationship was found between the prediction and the reported appearance. Some amendments of the formula are needed for special kinds of pictures. For example, in generating randomly assembled $45°$ oblique projections of the sort shown in Figure 5.10e, right angles are produced which remain unchanged regardless of whether the flat or solid alternative is perceived; they should not be counted in either t_1 or in the numerator t_2. To make this change improves prediction from $r = 0.3$ to $r = 0.8$ for the tested sample of this class of pictures.

References

1. AMES, A. "The Illusions of Depth from Single Pictures." *Journal of the Optical Society of America 10*: 137–148; 1925.
2. ———. *Nature and Origin of Perception.* Hanover: Institute of Associated Research; 1946–47.

3. ATTNEAVE, F. "Some Informational Aspects of Visual Perception." *Psychological Review 61*: 183–98; 1954.

4. ———. *Applications of Information Theory to Psychology.* New York: Henry Holt and Co., Inc., 1959.

5. ATTNEAVE, F., and ARNOULT, M. "The Quantitative Study of Shape and Pattern Recognition." *Psychological Bulletin 53*: 452–71; 1956.

6. BARTLEY, S., and ADAIR, H. "Comparisons of Phenomenal Distance of Photographs of Various Sizes." *Journal of Psychology 47*: 289–95; 1957.

7. BERKELEY, G. "Essay towards a New Theory of Vision, 1709." *Selections from Berkeley*, edited by A. Fraser; 6th edition. Oxford: Clarendon Press, 1910.

8. BERLINER, A. *Lectures on Visual Psychology.* Chicago: Professional Press, 1948.

9. BROOKS, V., and HOCHBERG, J. "A Psychophysical Study of 'Cuteness'." *Perceptual and Motor Skills 11*: 205; 1960.

10. BUSWELL, G. T. *How People Look at Pictures.* Chicago: University of Chicago Press, 1935.

11. DA VINCI, LEONARDO. *Trattato della Pittura*, 1585. (Excerpt quoted from *Experimental Psychology*, by R. S. Woodworth and H. Schlosberg. New York: Henry Holt and Co., 1955. p. 464.)

12. EPSTEIN, W., PARK, J., and CASEY, A. "The Current Status of the Size-distance Hypotheses." *Psychological Bulletin 58*: 491–514; 1961.

13. ESCHER, M. *The Graphic Work of M. C. Escher.* New York: Duell, Sloan and Pearce, 1961.

14. FITTS, P., WEINSTEIN, M., RAPPAPORT, M., ANDERSON, N., and LEONARD, J. A., Jr. "Stimulus Correlates of Visual Pattern Recognition: A Probability Approach." *Journal of Experimental Psychology 51*: 1–11; 1956.

15. GIBSON, E., and WALK, R. "The Visual Cliff." *Scientific American 202*: 64–71; 1960.

16. GIBSON, J. "What Is Form?" *Psychological Review 58*: 403–12; 1951.

17. ———. "The Visual Field and the Visual World: A Reply to Professor Boring." *Psychological Review 59*: 149–51; 1952.

18. ———. "Social Perception and the Psychology of Perceptual Learning." *Group Relations at the Crossroads*, edited by M. Sherif and M. Wilson. New York: Harper & Brothers, 1953.

19. ———. "A Theory of Pictorial Perception." *AV Communications Review 1*: 3–23; 1954.

20. ———. "Pictures, Perspective and Perception." *Daedalus 89*: 216–27; Winter 1960.

21. ———. "Ecological Optics." *Vision Research 1*: 253–62; 1961.

22. GOGEL, W. C., HARTMAN, B., and HARKER, G. "The Retinal Size of a Familiar Object as a Determiner of Apparent Distance." *Psychological* Monographs 71, Issue 13 (Whole No. 442); 1957.

23. HEBB, D. *Organization of Behavior.* New York: Wiley, 1949.

24. HOCHBERG, C., and HOCHBERG, J. "Familiar Size and the Perception of Depth." *Journal of Psychology 34*: 107–14; 1952.

25. HOCHBERG, J. "Perception: Toward the Recovery of a Definition." *Psychological Review 63*: 400–05; 1956.

26. ———. "Spatial Representation." Theme 10. *Proceedings of the International Congress of Psychology.* Brussels, 1957.

27. ———. "Effects of the Gestalt Revolution: The Cornell Symposium on Perception." *Psychological Review 64*: 73–84; 1957.

28. ———. "Psychophysics and Stereotype in Social Perception." *Emerging Problems in Social Psychology*, edited by M. Sherif and M. Wilson. Norman, Okla.: University of Oklahoma, 1957. pp. 117–41.

29. ———. "Toward a Distal Psychophysics of Space-perception: Displays, Pictures and Other Surrogates." (Mimeo.) Paper contributed to Working Group 16, NAS-NRC, 1961.

30. ———. "Nativism and Empiricism in Perception." *Psychology in the Making*, edited by L. Postman. New York: Knopf, 1962.

31. ———. *Perception*. Englewood Cliffs, NJ: Prentice-Hall, 1964.

32. HOCHBERG, J., and BROOKS, V. "The Psychophysics of Form: Reversible-pespective Drawings of Spatial Objects." *American Journal of Psychology 73*: 337–54; 1960.

33. ———. " 'Edges' as Fundamental Components of the Visual Field." Third Annual Scientific Meeting, *Psychonomic Society 8* (abstract), 1962.

34. ———. "The Prediction of Visual Attention." *American Psychologist 18*: 437; 1963 (Abstract).

35. ———. "Graphic Symbols: Things or Holes?" *American Journal of Psychology 76*: 22–54; 1963.

36. ———. "Pictorial Recognition as an Unlearned Ability: A Study of One Child's Performance." *American Journal of Psychology 75*: 624–628, 1962.

37. ———. "Compression of Pictorial Space through Perspective Reversal." *Perceptual and Motor Skills 16*: 262; 1962.

38. HOCHBERG, J., and MCALISTER, E. "A Quantitative Approach to Figural 'Goodness.' " *Journal of Experimental Psychology 46*: 361–64; 1953.

39. KOPFERMANN, H. "Psychologische Untersuchungen über die Wirkung zweidimensionaler Darstellungen köperiicher Gebilde." *Psychologische Forschung 13*: 293–364; 1930.

40. PENROSE, L. S., and PENROSE, R. "Impossible Objects: A Special Type of Visual Illusion." *British Journal of Psychology 49*: 31–33; 1958.

41. RYAN, T., and SCHWARTZ, C. "Speed of Perception as a Function of Mode of Representation." *American Journal of Psychology 69*: 60–69; 1956.

42. SCHLOSBERG, H. "Stereoscopic Depth from Single Pictures." *American Journal of Psychology 54*: 601–05; 1941.

43. ———. "The Description of Facial Expressions in Terms of Two Dimensions." *Journal of Experimental Psychology 44*: 229–37; 1952.

44. SMITH, O. "Judgments of Size and Distance in Photographs." *American Journal of Psychology 71*: 529–38; 1958.

45. SMITH, O., and GRUBER, H. "Perception of Depth in Photographs." *Perceptual and Motor Skills 8*: 307–13; 1958.

46. SMITH, O., and SMITH, P. "Ball-throwing Responses to Photographically Portrayed Targets." *Journal of Experimental Psychology 62*: 223–33; 1961.

47. SONODA, G. "Perceptual Constancies Observed in Plane Pictures." *Experimental Researches on the Structure of Perceptual Space*, edited by Y. Akishige. Fukuoka, Japan: *Bulletin of the Faculty of Literature.* Kyushu University, 1961.

48. WEBER, C., and BICKNALL, N. "The Size-constancy Phenomenon in Stereoscopic Space." *American Journal of Psychology 47*: 436–48; 1935.

49. WEINSTEIN, S. "The Perception of Depth in the Absence of Texture-gradient." *American Journal of Psychology 70*: 611–15; 1957.

50. WERNER, J. "Studies on Contour." *American Journal of Psychology 47*: 40–64; 1935.

51. WUNDT, W. *Outlines of Psychology* (4th German edition); translated by C. H. Judd. Leipzig: Engelmann, 1902.

6

Pictorial Recognition as an Unlearned Ability

A Study of One Child's Performance

Julian Hochberg and Virginia Brooks

Anecdotes about primitive people who are unable to identify pictured objects suggest the hypothesis that pictorial recognition is a learned ability.[1] In a weaker form of this hypothesis, learning might be held essential for the recognition of line drawings (compare Gibson's "ghost shapes"),[2] while the naïve recognition of photographs, with their higher "fidelity," would be admitted. The present investigation was designed to determine whether a child who had been taught his vocabulary *solely* by the use of objects, and who had received no instruction or training whatsoever concerning pictorial meaning or content, could recognize objects portrayed by two-dimensional line drawings and by photographs.

Answers to these questions were desired for two reasons. First, the psychophysical exploration of outline representations has begun to provide some promising, lawful relationship.[3] Although the predictive equations would remain just as interesting regardless of whether they are based on "learned" or "innate" processes,[4] somewhat different sets of further hypotheses might suggest themselves if the entire realm of responses to outline representations of spatial objects turned out to be the product of arbitrary associations between symbols and things—a sort of assigned visual language. Second, if pictorial perception did indeed turn out to be a learned ability in this arbitrary sense (which it did not), we should have a starting point for the investigation of the possible lines of its development and of individual differences therein.

It should be stressed that this investigation does not directly bear upon the general question of nativism vs. empiricism in space perception, which is too broad to be submitted to so specific a test. If space perception were itself an "unlearned" ability, the representation by flat pictures might not be feasible without specific learning. If recognition of solid objects in two-dimensional representation were at least in part unlearned, it might still

This study, assisted by Dr. P. C. Smith and Mrs. Janice Goldstein, was supported by an NIH research grant, B-1586(C2).

develop without formal training as a by-product of a more general process of learning to perceive space.

Training. Since birth, the subject (*S*), a boy, had been exposed to and taught the names of a wide variety of toys and other solid objects. With two exceptions discussed below, the color of each of these objects was either uniform, or it was divided into functional areas (e.g., face coloration, hair shade, and dress color on dolls). That is, no objects were depicted as surface decoration. Even so, *S* never was told (or allowed to overhear) the name or meaning of any picture or depicted object. In fact, pictures were, in general, kept from his immediate vicinity.

This is *not* to say that *S* never had been exposed to pictures. There was a Japanese print on one wall of a room through which he frequently passed; a myriad of billboards fronted the highways on which he traveled frequently; a few times (six in all) he accidentally encountered a picture book (which was gently withdrawn) or caught a glimpse of the label of a jar of baby food (these were normally removed or kept covered). (All these encounters were unaccompanied by instruction or naming-play.) Furthermore, one toy (a top) had pictures of elves on it and, accordingly, it was available for play only under strict supervision to prevent any naming in his presence; and a high chair had a decal of babies on it, which could be glimpsed (without parental comment) only when *S* was being placed in the seat.

The constant vigilance and improvisation required of the parents proved to be a considerable chore from the start—further research of this kind should not be undertaken lightly. By 19 months of age, the child began actively to seek pictures, and continuation of the constraints became both pediatrically and methodologically undesirable. Two incidents terminated this stage of the investigation: (a) *S* became aware of events on the TV set in the next room, managed to obtain a glimpse of the screen on which a horse was being depicted, and excitedly cried "dog"; (b) he squirmed around in his high chair about the same time and, pointing to the decal, said "baby." It was evident that some form of parental response to such identifications would soon become unavoidable. The testing procedure was begun at this point.

Testing: Part 1. The set of 21 pictures listed in the first part of Table 6.1, and shown in Fig. 6.1, was prepared on 3 × 5 in. cards. In all cases but one (No. 12), the series was so arranged that the outline drawing of any object preceded any photograph of the same object; recognition could not, therefore, be made first from the photograph and then transferred to the drawing. The drawings were handed one at a time to *S*, a somewhat unsuccessful attempt being made to convert the test to an interesting game. Responses were obtained by tape recording.

Part 2. Immediately after Part 1, *S* was given a large store of picture books. For a period of one month, he had free (but monitored) access to still pictures, but motion pictures, TV, and picture-naming play still were completely avoided. (It was feared that motion pictures would provide a basis for

Table 6.1.

Stimulus-Presentations and Judges' Interpretations of S's Responses

Part 1				Part 2			
Stimulus Picture	Parents	Interpretation of Responses Judge A	Judge B	Stimulus Picture	Parents	Interpretation of Responses Judge A	Judge B
(1) car	+	car	car	(1a) car	+	car	car
(2) car	+	car	car	(2a) car	+	car	car
(3) shoe	+	shoe	shoe	(3a) car	−	Jody§	Jody§
(4) shoe	+	shoe	shoe	(4a) shoe	+	shoe	shoe
(5) shoe	+	——	——	(5a) shoe	−	——	——
(6) Jody (sister)	+	Jody	——	(6a) Jody	+	Jody	Jody
(7) dolly	+	——	dolly	(7a) dolly	+	dolly	dolly
(8) dolly	−	shoe‡	shoe‡	(8a) dolly	+	dolly	dolly
(9) dolly	−	shoe‡	——	(9a) car	+	car	car
(10) car	+	car	car	(10a) car	+	car	car
(11) car	+	car	car	(11a) rocky	+	rocky	rocky
(12) rocky	+	rocky	rocky	(12a) rocky	+	rocky	rocky
(13) rocky	+	rocky	rocky	(13a) rocky	+	——	——
(14) rocky	+	——	——	(14a) key	+	key	key
(15) keys	+	key	keys	(15a) dog	+	dog	——
(16) key	+	key	key	(16a) spoon	−	——	key
(17) key	+	key	key	(17a) Mommy	−†	——	——
(18) wawaw	−*	wawaw	wawaw	(1c) box	+	box	——
(19) fcahr	+	car	car	(2c) box	+	——	car
(20) fcahr	+	car	car				
(21) Mommy	−	——	shoe‡				

*Since no response could be elicited during Part 3 to the solid object, and since the parents do not agree as to the certainty of the name in previous handling, all identifications of this stimulus are doubtful.
†Much amusement.
‡"Shoe" may be the judges' misinterpretation of S's "thank 0you" in response to being given the pictures.
§Misidentification due to sister's entry into the room.

attaching names or three-dimensional "meanings" to the still pictures which do, after all, appear even in cinema sequences.) A great variety of naming reactions appeared during this period, but special pains were taken not to respond to any of these. Vocabulary building by means of object-naming games continued during this month, but at special times and with no pictures present. At the end of the month, the testing procedure of Part 1 was repeated with the new set of stimuli listed in the second part of Table 6.1 and shown in Fig. 6.2.[5]

Figure 6.1. Pictures Shown *S* in Part 1

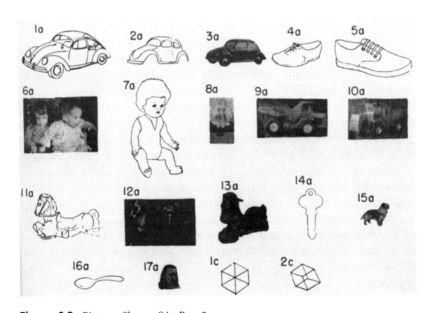

Figure 6.2. Pictures Shown *S* in Part 2

Scoring. A set of objects, consisting of most of those whose pictures appeared in the two testing series, then was presented to *S*, and *his* naming responses were tape recorded. These provided two judges (*A* and *B* in Table 6.1), who had not been present during the two testing sessions, with experience of the child's pronunciation. The judges then were told that those words would be used, in any order and with any number of repetitions, in the recordings of the two testing sessions, and their task was to determine the order of presentation of the objects, using only the child's responses as recorded during those sessions.[6] (This scoring procedure was undertaken separately by the two judges.)

Results. Those pictures which were considered to be correctly identified by the parents (who did know the stimulus series) are shown in Table 6.1; the interpretations of each of the judges also are shown. If we consider only the line drawings which both judges correctly identified in Part 1 (given eight possible names which, they were told, could appear in any order with any number of repetitions), the probability of a chance relationship is well under 0.01. The judges thus correctly identified objects from the *S*'s responses to the line drawings.

It seems clear from the results that at least one human child is capable of recognizing pictorial representations of solid objects (including bare outline drawings) without specific training or instruction. This ability necessarily includes a certain amount of what we normally expect to occur in the way of figure-ground segregation and contour formation. At the very least, we must infer that there is an unlearned propensity to respond to certain formal features of lines-on-paper in the same ways as one has learned to respond to the same features when displayed by the edges of surfaces. "Ghost shapes," as Gibson has called them,[7] may be anemic, but they are by no means deceased. There may, however, be considerable ontogenetic difference in structuring or emphasis; the clear recognition of Stimulus 1*c* as a "box," and the uncertainty of response to Stimulus 2*c*, are certainly not what one would have expected from adult performance.[8] Although order-effects may have been responsible for the poor response to Stimulus 2*c*, the immediate identification of 1*c* was unexpected.

It may be maintained that this ability would not have been displayed by a child who had never been exposed to any pictures at all, and who had not had such extensive experience with patterned surfaces as had the present *S*. This may be true (although consideration of the inhomogeneities of the normal *apictorial* environment make it seem quite improbable to us), but, even if it is, the complete absence of instruction in the present case (the absence of "association" between picture and represented object) points to *some* irreducible minimum of native ability for pictorial recognition. If it is true also that there are cultures in which this ability is absent, such deficiency will require special explanation; we cannot assert that it is simply a matter of having not yet learned the "language of pictures."

Notes

1. The only study in point is that of W. Hudson, Pictorial depth perception in subcultural groups in Africa, *J. Soc. Psychol.*, 52, 1960, 183–208, which is concerned with differences in spatial localization rather than in recognition of objects.

2. J. J. Gibson, What is a form? *Psychol. Rev.*, 58, 1951, 403–412.

3. Julian Hochberg and Virginia Brooks, The psychophysics of form: Reversible-perspective drawings of spatial objects, *American Journal of Psychology*, 73, 1960, 337–354.

4. Hochberg, Spatial representation: Theme 10, *Proc. Int. Congr. Psychol.*, 1957.

5. The object represented in 1*c* and 2*c* was a box constructed of rigid wire, approximately $\frac{1}{8}$ in. in diameter, and 8 in. on a side. Introduced as a toy, it was involved in naming games only during the month which elapsed between Part 1 and Part 2.

6. The judges were permitted as many repetitions as desired. The first two presentations in Part 1 had been edited to remove extraneous chatter. Since the third presentation proved to have elicited "extraneous" responses which might be interpretable by judges as part of the series, editing of the remaining presentations was restricted to the elimination of overly long interruptions; the residual chatter and gabble made judgment a difficult task.

7. Gibson *op. cit.*, 412.

8. Hochberg and Brooks, *op. cit.*, 347.

7

Recognition of Faces

I. An Exploratory Study

Julian Hochberg and Ruth Ellen Galper

Shepard's recognition procedure was applied to photographs to test its usefulness for exploring perception of, and memory for, faces. Recognition was measured as a function of number of faces viewed and of vertical orientation. Recognition accuracy was significantly greater for upright than for inverted photographs, suggesting that faces are not here perceived and stored simply as patterns. Inspection series length did not significantly affect recognition accuracy. Comparison of upright-viewing-and-upright-recognition with inverted-viewing-and-upright-recognition yielded no significant differences in accuracy, suggesting that unlike information stored during upright viewing, information stored during inverted viewing is not strongly tied to orientation.

Shepard (1967) recently reported data suggesting that Ss can retain enough information from single brief exposures of each of approximately 600 pictures of objects to be able subsequently to recognize them all. The present experiments determined that a short version of Shepard's procedure is suitable for exploring how people perceive and remember faces, since recognition scores are high, yet responsive to transformation (i.e., inversion) which reduces the recognizability of faces without changing the stimulus configurations.

Experiment 1

Thirty-two Ss were shown a set of photographs, presented individually, serially, and self-paced. Of these pictures, 15 were presented to S a second time, this time paired with another photograph not previously seen, and S was asked to indicate which one he had seen before.

Subjects. A different group of eight Ss (four male and four female) were used for each of four experimental conditions. Ss were graduate and undergraduate students and a few faculty members.

Materials. Seventy-five pictures of females were selected randomly from a college yearbook after those with glasses or distinctive clothing or

Table 7.1.
Experimental Conditions, Means and Standard Deviations of Errors, Median
Errors, Median Percentage Correct Recognition (Rights Minus Wrongs),
and Range of Mean Viewing Times per Photograph (in sec).

							Range (in sec)
Condition	Inspection Series	Test Series	Mean Errors	SD	Median Errors	Median % Correct	of Mean Times/Photo

Experiment 1

Condition	Inspection Series	Test Series	Mean Errors	SD	Median Errors	Median % Correct	Range of Mean Times/Photo
1	35 Upright	Upright	0.375	0.74	0.0	100 %	7.77–16.20
2	60 Upright	Upright	1.750	1.58	1.5	90	3.60–9.87
3	35 Inverted	Inverted	2.625	1.60	3.0	80	5.69–12.60
4	60 Inverted	Inverted	3.500	2.20	4.5	70	7.30–11.82

Experiment 2

| 5 | 35 Inverted | Upright | 3.500 | 2.27 | 2.5 | 83 | 7.86–18.40 |

backdrop had been eliminated. These were rephotographed and reduced to
3/4 × 1 in. in size.

Procedure. The four experimental conditions are shown in Table 7.1.
Prior to each administration, 15 photographs were randomly chosen
and set aside for use in the Test series. Fifteen photographs to be later paired
with them were also chosen randomly and were then spaced throughout the
Inspection series. Spacing was symmetrical around the middle of the series,
and such that the first and last two photographs in each Inspection series did
not appear in the Test series. Each S was thus shown a different subset of
photographs in the Inspection series, and of pairs of photographs in the Test
series. Inspection series order was random; Test series order followed the
sequence of the "old" photographs in the Inspection series.

Inspection Series. In each condition, Ss viewed the photographs serially, with the aim of being able later to recognize them as having appeared in
the series. No specific information was given them at this time about the
nature of the recognition task. Ss were told that "most people spend about
5 to 15 sec on each picture," but that they could proceed at their own pace.
The only viewing restrictions were that (a) pictures could not be turned or
tilted (this was made explicit only when necessary); (b) once a photograph
had been viewed and placed face down, it could not be viewed again; and (c)
only one photograph could be viewed at a time.

Test Series. Immediately after the Inspection series, Ss were presented
serially with the Test series of 15 side-by-side pairs and told that one member
of each pair would be an old photograph, while the other would be a new
one, and that they were to indicate which (right or left) they had seen before.
Ss were instructed to guess, if uncertain, but to indicate their uncertainty.

The position of the "old" picture was assigned semirandomly, such that the correct answer was "right" for seven or eight of the pairs, and "left" for the others; the correct answer was never the same for more than three sequential pairs.

Experiment 2

When the direction of results in Experiment 1 was apparent, an additional group of eight Ss was run, in which pictures were inverted in the Inspection series and upright in the Test series. Otherwise, procedures were identical to those of Condition 3 (see Table 7.1).

Results

Mean and median errors, SDs, and range of viewing times across Ss are given in Table 7.1 for each experimental condition. Analysis of variance of the errors, after square root transformation, yields a highly significant difference among conditions ($F = 5.14$, $df = 3/28$, $p < .01$), a highly significant difference between upright and inverted conditions ($F = 10.92$, $df = 1/28$, $p < .005$), and no significant difference as a function of Inspection series length ($p > .08$) or the interaction between length and orientation ($F < 1$).

Median Test series recognition scores, corrected for guessing (rights minus wrongs) appear as percentages in column 7 of Table 7.1. An estimate of the numbers of stored Inspection series faces can be obtained by multiplying Inspection series length by these corrected percentages.

Discussion

The significant difference in recognition accuracy between upright and inverted faces in this procedure supports the intuitive notion that something other than pattern storage and pattern recognition is operating in the recognition of faces, since inversion leaves pattern unchanged. Since recognition accuracy in Condition 5 is not significantly different from that of Condition 3 ($t = 0.9$), it may be inferred that the information stored during inverted viewing is not strongly tied to orientation.

Although the effects of such procedural variables as Test series length have not been investigated, the technique in its present form seems usable without further modification, and we are currently applying it to study the effects of such stimulus variables as left-right and negative-positive reversal; ratio of Negro to Caucasian faces in the Inspection series; and expression change between Inspection and Test series.

Note

1. This research was supported in part by Grant GB-5270 from the National Science Foundation.

Reference

Shepard, R. N. Recognition memory for words, sentences, and pictures. *J. Verbal Learn. Verbal Behav.*, 1967, *6*, 156–163.

8

In the Mind's Eye

Julian Hochberg

Introduction

I'm going to talk today about some current attempts to analyze the structure of visually perceived form, and to identify those components of perceptual processing that mediate the known effects of set, of knowledge, and of learning. Most of the work is unpublished, and some is only starting, so what I will say is tentative and groping, and the implications are much less well-thought through than I would wish.

First, a question that would not have been necessary forty years ago, and would not have been possible twenty years ago: When should we talk about *form perception*, let alone analyze it? I am raising this question because we'll need an answer to it that we can use, not merely as a definitional exercise.

The question was unnecessary forty years ago because a formal definition in terms of introspective observation was available and acceptable. In structuralist terms, "perception" could be analyzed into fundamental mental units, and there was good reason to do so, since what one perceived was itself used to predict other mental events.

The question would have been impossible, or at least in bad taste, twenty years ago, because by then two points were well established. They were the following:

(1) The Gestaltists' point: the basic introspective units—the *sensations* and *images* into which it was once thought *percepts* could be reduced, and in terms of which they were to be defined—turned out to be useless for that purpose, even in principle.

This paper is a slightly revised version of an Invited Address read at the September 1966 meeting of the American Psychological Association, Division 3. The unpublished research referred to herein was variously supported by Off. Educ., S—407; by A.F. contr. 19 (628) 5830, with Sperry Rand Res. Center; and by NSF GB 5270. I am indebted to Fred Attneave, Lloyd Kaufman, and Harry Blum for discussion of many of the questions to which this paper is addressed.

(2) The behaviorists' point: no causal status could be attributed to a mental event; and in any case, introspective reports about what one perceives are only verbal responses, not mental events. They are dependent variables, not independent variables.

Now we cannot ignore all that history. Structuralist introspection *won't* work, the old definitions are *not* consistent with the rest of present-day psychology, and the behaviorist arguments, philosophically motivated though they may have been, remain methodologically sound as far as they go. Yet some psychologists continue to talk about "perception," even though they no longer have the original introspective definition, nor do they have the original purposes within which to use it as an independent variable. New definitions in terms of converging operations can and have been devised—Postman (1952); Garner, Hake, and Eriksen (1956); Hochberg (1956). But if it's only an "effect," never a "cause," why pick these particular responses for special definition and for present study?

The answer is that there is clearly a large and important set of problems, important both in and out of psychology, in which this particular dependent variable—"perception"—does in fact seem to have some kind of causal status. Thus, when perception psychologists wish to check whether or not a subject *really* sees some object or event, they usually ask him a question that they do not expect him to be able otherwise to answer. And this means using "perception" as a *construct*, based conjointly on the subject's reports and on the physical stimulus, with which we can more simply predict the subject's behavior than we can by measures taken on the stimulus alone— a use for the construct "perception," which surely should be taken into account in our attempts at definition (Hochberg, 1956). Thus, the general answer to the question of when we should talk about form perception is this: *when we can predict and explain the subject's responses to the world that confronts him more simply and elegantly with the aid of such a construct than without it.*

What criteria are thereby implied for perceptual responses? Before explicating this point in the area of form perception, in which the relevant stimulus measures are still largely unknown, let us first look at an analogous example in the field of color perception, where we are fairly certain of the relevant physical variables.

A primary fact of color perception is this: a single perceived hue may be produced by a great many different sets of wavelengths. However, where *metamerism* holds, it doesn't matter what stimuli we have used to elicit a given color. A yellow may be produced by light of 580 mμ or by a mixture of 530 and 650 mμ, but no matter how it is produced, all lights of that yellow hue will mix with a given perceived blue to produce the same perceived gray, and will mix with a perceived red to produce the same perceived orange. And, where metamerism holds, *laws of color mixture can be stated and used without knowing what wavelengths are employed.* When the painter or photographer uses the "color circle," he is using *perceived color,* which is a dependent variable, a response—as a *cause,* as an independent variable.

Similar response-response relationships have been proposed in the study of perceived distance, of perceived size, and of perceived shape. From Berkeley, through Helmholtz to Woodworth, perceived size has been explained in terms of perceived distance (that is, as though it were causally dependent on perceived distance); perceived shape has been explained in terms of perceived slant, and so on. To illustrate: if you really see the cube's lower face as nearer, as in Figure 8.1B, you will probably see line x as shorter than line y; if you see the upper face nearer, line y will probably look shorter than line x. Your responses are not independent of the stimulus, or of each other.

It seems to me that the following are minimum requirements for calling any set of responses "perceptual" (Hochberg, 1956): If the responses were completely independent of the stimuli, we would be dealing with imagination, with memory, with hallucination; if the responses were dependent only on the stimuli (that is, if there were no interresponse constraints, no perceptual *organization* or *structure*), then talking about a "percept" would be gratuitous, since a simple psychophysical (S-R) correlation would then suffice. But we may in fact gain something by talking about the perceived cube in Figure 8.1A, as we just saw in the line-length example, and there are in fact a great many similar questions that one could ask the subject about what he sees in that figure, to which his answers could be predicted

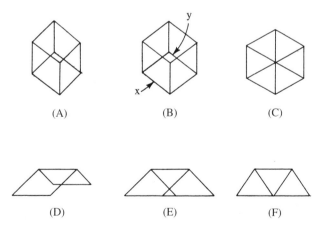

Figure 8.1. Reversible-perspective figures:

	A	B	C	D	E	F
Apparent tridimensionality:	1	2	3	1	2	3
Gestalt complexity, 2D (Kopfermann, 1930):	1	2	3	1	2	3
Measured pattern complexity:	1	2	3	1	2	3

better once we know which alternative arrangement of the cube—which organization—he perceives. This is true because there are many attributes of the specific perceptual structure "cube-with-lower-face-forward," that are different from those of "cube-with-upper-face-forward," and it is the coupling between such attributes that defines the perceptual structure.

In order for such a construct—a "perceived structure"—to be useful, we need to know in advance which attributes are coupled to each other, and how. What determines the inter-attribute coupling in any perceived structure?

Imagine that you are playing a game somewhat similar to Twenty Questions, and that you have to decide whether someone *really* is looking at some object in front of him. You ask him questions about the object—questions which he can answer only while looking at the object. Some of your questions require answers depending simply on the *physical* structure (for example that the diagonal of a square is 1.4 times the length of a side), but other questions depend on the observer's visual system. Some, *but not all,* of the consistencies and couplings of the real physical world are more or less reflected in the perceived structure (that is, in the interresponse constraints) of objects and scenes; some attributes are quite different (as in the geometrical illusions); and some couplings and consistencies of objects in the physical world are, as we shall see, missing from their perceived form. Whether or not it's worthwhile to talk about the subject's "perception," in any specific case, seems to me to be a local, empirical question—a matter of how much it simplifies our description, not a general philosophical issue.

Let me now apply these abstract considerations to the study of form perception. Various problems have been pursued under this name for various reasons. First, of course, the structuralist attempt—by Helmholtz, by Wundt and Titchener—to analyze form into two kinds of content: (1) local *sensations* of color—innate, visual, and meaningless; and (2) associated to each familiar pattern or subpattern by the results of past experience, the *images* (memory) of previous movement-produced tactual and kinesthetic sensations which, because they are the results of commerce with the real world and its physical consistencies, provide structure to the percepts in which they participate. I will not review the reasons for abandoning this attempt, except to note that a major factor was the Gestaltist argument that a form comprises a unit which cannot be analyzed into more elementary parts or elements—an argument which I will seriously dispute.

A second and more neutral set of problems consists of pattern-discrimination and pattern-recognition. I can't see the point of this enterprise *unless we expect some consequences to follow from the fact that the subject identifies one pattern rather than another.* And, of course, although students of pattern-recognition rarely seem concerned with such matters, there are many phenomena that *do* seem to depend on the configuration of the pattern and/or on its perceived form. These are the phenomena of the geometrical illusions, and the Gestalt phenomena of apparent motion, figure-ground reversal, and ambiguous depth.

This is, to me, the most significant set of problems in the field of form perception. Which form a subject reports seeing apparently makes a difference. In fact, in this area, perceived form is important in three ways:

(1) Because we don't have a single physical dimension of stimulation by which to define the stimulus configuration to which a subject is responding, or by which we can decide what it is that two different patterns, which both produce the same form percept, have in common. In fact, we don't even have a limited set of dimensions that we know are relevant to perceived form, nothing analogous to the physical dimensions of luminance and wavelength with which S-R treatments of color perception can be attempted. So, in most nontrivial cases, we have to use human observers to define the stimulus configuration. We can say, of course, that we're merely doing this for convenience and not from permanent necessity, and that we'll surely be able to define the relevant physical stimulus characteristics objectively when we really want to—but *even* if that were true (and I'm no longer all that certain that it is true), the fact at present is that *we need someone's form perceptions (whether experimenter's or subject's) to define our independent variable.*

(2) Because the subject can perceive very different forms in response to the same physical stimulus, and which form he perceives critically determines the other answers he gives to questions about shape, motion, size, depth, and so on.

(3) Because of a third, and more subtle, involuted way in which form perception has causal status in this research area.

These form-dependent phenomena have been studied primarily by Gestalt psychologists, motivated by the belief that effects of a given stimulus pattern all depend upon, and therefore reveal, the underlying physiological processes set up by the physical stimulus acting on the sensory system—underlying physiological processes that are different in configuration from the physical stimulus pattern, and which mediate between the physical stimulus and the final perception. The determinants of the form-dependent phenomena were presumably the "laws of organization" of the underlying physiological process. Since the underlying physiological process is not known, and since the perceived forms' phenomenal attributes were presumed to be *isomorphic* with that underlying process, the alternative percepts that could be obtained with a given physical stimulus pattern were used in effect as measures of the alternative physiological processes that a given physical stimulus could arouse and, thereby, a means of predicting *which* such process and which percept *would* occur.

This point is obscure but important. Consider Kopfermann (1930): Using ambiguous drawings (Figure 8.1), which can readily be perceived in either of two very different ways—that is, as flat two-dimensional shapes or as tridimensional reversible-perspective objects, she demonstrated that *one obtains the flat percept when that is "simpler" in some sense than the tridimensional percept, and vice versa.* Note that prediction (and explanation) of which alternative percept will be obtained was given in terms of the attributes of the alternative percepts themselves (or of their mythical underlying physiological distributions), not in terms of any stimulus measure. The *independent variable* was essentially this: the degree of difference between the simplicities of the two alternative percepts that could be obtained with each stimulus; the *dependent variable* was the relative strengths of the two alternative percepts.

In principle, of course, it must be possible, in any specific case, to replace such a mentalistic explanation with one couched in physical terms. Brooks and I did this in 1960 by finding, empirically, a function of objective measures of pattern complexity (for example, number of angles, number of continuous line segments, and so on) that predicts the judged tridimensionalities of Kopfermann's ambiguous forms. This function sidesteps the subjective variables of "perceived complexity" or "perceived simplicity" as predictors of the subjects' tridimensionality rating and form-naming responses. This start at constructing a *psychophysics of form perception*, in S-R terms, seemed at the time to be moderately successful. We could predict a subject's reports about relative tridimensionality, and about which alternative form he sees, from measurable features of the physical stimulus configuration. We seemed, therefore, on our way to breaking out of the mentalistic circle. But these hopes were premature for two reasons:

(1) It turns out that we cannot yet really define the physical stimulus configurations whose measured attributes we are using as predictive variables.
(2) The function found is wrong, not in detail but in principle.

Let us see first why I say that we can't at present define what the effective stimuli are for form perception; then let us see why the specific psychophysical attempt is basically wrong.

Exotic Stimuli for Presenting Forms to the Mind's Eye

Most form perception research uses luminance-difference contours as stimuli. We cannot, with such displays, decide which form-dependent phenomena occur at the same level in the nervous system, are tied to each other, and therefore have to be explained together. What we did, therefore, was to produce each form in whose relative apparent tridimensionality we were interested by three very different classes of physical stimulus display, some of which bypassed any possible retinal contributions to perceived structure.

Binocular Entry

Forms can be presented postretinally by using stereograms in neither field of which is the form visible (cf. Julesz, 1960): Two identical random matrices of dots were viewed stereoscopically, one by each eye. In one eye's view, a region of dots, corresponding to one of the reversible-perspective figures, was cut out of the matrix and displaced slightly (20 min. of arc); since this produces a binocular disparity for those dots, the figure thereby delineated seems to float in front of the remaining dots. This is schematized in Figure 8.3A, with the displaced region opposite in color from its surround; in actual use, of course, the figure is set off only via stereopsis, not by color.

Momentary Displacement

Take a single regular matrix of dots, and *briefly* displace a subset which delineates a reversible-perspective pattern, as in Figure 8.3D. If a 50-msec displacement of that pattern relative to the rest of the matrix is repeated regularly, with an interdisplacement interval of about 500 msec, a form is "sensed" which displays most of the form-dependent phenomena. Charles Eriksen (1966) is using a very similar technique to study form storage, a field of inquiry to which we shall return shortly.

Successive Aperture Viewing

This last method places the entire problem at a different level and may wipe out at one stroke most of the Gestalt physiological models and the various diffusion models of form perception that have been offered at different times by Köhler; by Hochberg, Gleitman, MacBride; by Sickles; and most recently, by Harry Blum.

In 1965, Parks reported an immensely interesting phenomenon: if a pattern is moved behind a stationary slit so that its parts appear successively in the same place, the entire pattern can be recognized. To Parks, this demonstrates the existence of postretinal visual storage. One might dismiss this phenomenon as the result of eye movements that spread the entire pattern out on adjacent regions of the retina, making Parks' effect a case of parallel stimulation within sensory integration time, that is, not different in principle from any brief exposure. Even were this argument completely true, however, which seems very unlikely to me, it misses an exceedingly important point raised by the Parks effect: that the visual perceptual system

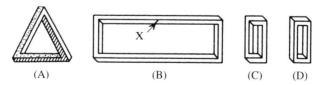

(A)   (B)   (C)   (D)

Figure 8.2. "Impossible" and consistent pictures. A: Adapted from Penrose and Penrose, 1958. B, C, D: Hochberg and Brooks, 1962.

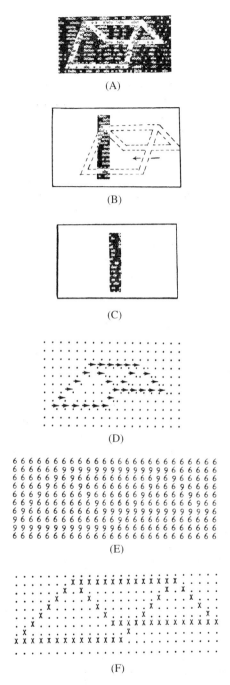

(A)

(B)

(C)

(D)

(E)

(F)

Figure 8.3. Exotic form displays. A: Representation of a binocularly entered (Julesz-pattern) reversible-perspective figure. B: How the stereogram of (A) is moved behind a (binocular) aperture. C: What a monocular view of (B) looks like. D: Figure produced by momentary displacement of subset in dot matrix. E: The same figure outlined in *9*s. F: The same figure outlined in *X*s.

can, under the proper conditions, assemble a set of partial views that fall on the same retinal area over a period of time into a single simultaneous form or scene; and that such scenes synthesized in space out of time must comprise a large part of the normal visual experience on which our attempts at perceptual laws are based. We shall discuss research explicitly directed to this point later on.

Our variation of Parks' procedure was this: Instead of outline drawings pulled behind a slit, the Julesz-pattern dot-matrix stereograms, described under binocular entry above, were moved (via motion picture) back and forth behind a pair of binocular slits (Figures 8.3B, C). Overall figure width was 18° to 23°, slit width was 3°, and time for the entire figure to traverse the slit was 1.5 seconds. Reversible-perspective figures, Muller-Lyer patterns, and so on were clearly recognizable to each of 5 Ss when so presented. Coordinated tracking and "binocular retinal painting" is a barely conceivable explanation for the apprehension of such displays, but (considering the long elapsed times and large excursions, which would place the figure's trailing edge some 20° off the fovea if the latter were tracking the leading edge after it passed behind the slit) to me, a very strained one.

I have tested two families of reversible-perspective figures with each of the above three procedures and, with all of them, subjects rank the apparent tridimensionalities of the figures in the same way that they do with conventional displays. However, these procedures are remarkably abstract ways of getting a form into the CNS. Let me describe what our dot-matrix aperture views look like to me: in the aperture itself, a clearly *sensory* vertical ribbon of dots, with some parts clearly nearer in stereospace; the ribbon of dots—still quite clearly—is part of an entire (largely *unseen*) surface of dots that is moving back and forth *behind* the aperture; and the raised regions are the exposed parts of a shape that is raised from, or floating in front of, the background. Now, unlike what Parks reports for his arrangement, there is no real sensory quality to either the shape or its background, where these are occluded by the mask. I'm completely certain that I only *see* those portions of the shape that are behind the aperture at any moment, but I'm equally certain of the extension of the shape behind the mask. Is this "perception," "apprehension," "imagination"? Perhaps we're not dealing with perception at all, in these situations. Maybe merely *knowing* what the pattern is, is sufficient to elicit the different tridimensionality ratings, regardless of how that knowledge is gained.

How, in short, can we decide whether the observer really perceives these forms as tridimensional, using these exotic display conditions?

This is why I spent so much time before on the matter of defining form perception. We will say that the subject has perceived a tridimensional form if the structure implied in such a statement lets us make predictions that we otherwise cannot. In the present case, characteristic and appropriate *spontaneous reversals* and *apparent motions* are obtained. In all three methods of display, any form which was reported to appear tridimensional, rather than flat, was also reported to undergo spontaneous depth reversal, which is what we have come to expect from such percepts. And this does not happen, as far as I can tell, with knowledge alone. Consider, for example, the reversible-perspective figure outlined in 9s against a background of 6s in Figure 8.3E, and in Xs against a background of dots in Figure 8.3F. In 8.3F, the pattern is clearly perceptible as a figure, and its relative tridimensionality, when compared to other patterns presented in this manner, is what it should be. Spontaneous depth reversal occurs with prolonged inspection. In 8.3E, however, while the subject can name or identify the reversible-perspective pattern by tracing out the 9s with his gaze, the pattern is not perceived as a figure, it does not appear tridimensional, and, of course, patterns presented in this way do not display the expected rank-order of relative tridimensionality. Nor does spontaneous reversal occur.

A second converging operation: If I view the successive figures in Figure 8.4A, each of which maintains one tridimensional orientation, in sequence, one direction of apparent tridimensional motion appears to occur; if the figures each show the other tridimensional orientation, Figure 8.4B, the other direction of motion appears to occur. I have indicated the motions in profile at the bottom in each column. If these successions of figures are presented by any of the three procedures described above (including our modified Parks method, that is, by moving a succession of stereograms behind a binocular slit while the succession itself is proceeding), the appropriate directions of tridimensional motion are reported (although with the Parks procedures the motion—which is taking place largely "offstage," *behind* the slit—appears to me to be qualitatively different from normal *phi*, being "paler" and less compelling).

It seems reasonable, therefore, to accept subjects' ratings of relative tridimensionalities of ambiguous figures as obtained with these displays on the same terms as their ratings obtained with normal displays. If these relative tridimensionalities reflect organizational factors, Gestalt or otherwise, such organization must be characteristic of the way in which successive glimpses are stored in the nervous system, rather than (or perhaps in addition to) being a characteristic of the interactions between simultaneously entered

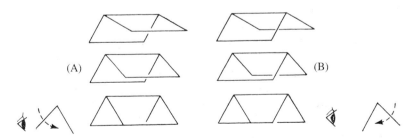

Figure 8.4. Direction of apparent motion as a function of depth "cues." A: Motion away from the observer. B: Motion toward the observer.

sensory processes—that is, Gestalt organization may be a characteristic of immediate memory, rather than of sensory projection (a point that Attneave, 1959, and I, 1957, have suggested for other reasons, anyway).

Before we consider this matter of organization and storage, however, let's turn to a curious class of figures which I think are very relevant to this question.

"Impossible Pictures" and Their Implications

Figure 8.2A is an "impossible picture" published by Penrose and Penrose in 1958. Modified as in Figure 8.2B, C, D, the pattern permits parametric study, by keeping constant the informative regions while varying the distance over which the integration proceeds. Since the corners are inconsistent in three dimensions, any reasonable application of the Hochberg and Brooks algorithm or, in fact, of Kopfermann's Gestalt formulation, should predict that the figure would appear flat. As we reported in 1962, with small distance between inconsistent corners (Figure 8.2C), the figures do appear inconsistent and, relatively often, as a flat nested pattern. However, with increased distance (Figure 8.2B), tridimensionality judgments are about as high as with completely consistent figures of the same dimensions.

Such figures have been "explained" as being examples of the inherent difficulties of presenting tridimensional objects by two-dimensional drawings, but this misses some very important implications: First, in what sense is Figure 8.2B "impossible"? In one sense: as an integrated three-dimensional object, line x must be seen (discontinuously, one would think) as the apex of one dihedral angle at the left corner, and as the apex of a different dihedral at the right corner. As a flat pattern, on the other hand, it involves us in no such inconsistencies. Nevertheless, we see a tridimensional picture and, with sizable intercorner distance, do not even initially note its impossibility. Our perceptual systems seem more tolerant of inconsistency than they would if they mirrored faithfully the couplings found in the real world. To me, this phenomenon suggests one minor point and two major ones.

The minor point: Our algorithm for ambiguous pictures (and Kopfermann's, as well) doesn't fit inconsistent pictures. In Figures 8.2B and 8.2C, apparent tridimensionalities change merely with changing separation between inconsistent corners, leaving unaltered the criteria of simplicity— for example, number of angles, number of line segments, and so on.

Next, two major points: (A) The stimulus determinants of depth are not given by the whole configuration, but only by certain features (in Figure 8.2, by the corners) which act as *local depth cues* and which exert their effects only over some limited distance. (B) Form perception must be broken down into at least two very different components of processing: one, the input of a single glance; the other, the perceived structure or *schematic map* (which has only limited interresponse coupling or consistency constraints) within which the separate glimpses take their place. I shall propose that the former components are relatively independent of learning, or of set, or of knowledge, while the latter are more susceptible to, and dependent on, such factors.

I shall try to explicate these two points in turn.

Local Depth Cues: Indirect Evidence

The idea of local depth cues is, of course, the more difficult to incorporate in any Gestaltist model. I suggest that, at least with line-drawn figures, any indication of depth affects the relevant lines only in its immediate neighborhood. I cannot prove this point, but I can bring a number of indirect arguments to bear.

First. As we've already seen, it's perfectly possible to incorporate two incompatible depth cues in a single picture and, if they're not too close to each other, each continues to maintain its appropriate depth in its immediate vicinity. This is probably related to the fact that line-drawn depth cues are ineffective away from the fovea (perhaps because of the detail loss in the periphery). This isn't surprising. But consider what it implies about your normal viewing of such a drawing: Not all of the potential indicators of depth are simultaneously effective, and the uniformly tridimensional appearance that the object seems to present must result from the integration of the various cues as they are successively fixated.

Second. Consider the stimuli in Figures 8.5A and 8.5B. Each total pattern is presented to the observer by means of a succession of strips, as indicated by the vertical dotted lines that show how the pattern is "cut up" for successive presentation. (The second and third strips of Figure 8.5A are shown at Figures 8.5C and 8.5D, respectively.) In the lower patterns appearing in Figures 8.5A and 8.5B, each local depth cue is presented as a unit, simultaneously, for parallel processing; in the upper patterns, the cuts are made so as to minimize the depth cues in each strip. Note that these patterns are presented to adjacent regions of the retina, so that the eye knows where each strip falls relative to the adjacent strips. We have sidestepped the question of whether retinal "painting" is responsible for any effects we obtain—the opportunity for such "painting" is provided for in both conditions of "cutting up" the pattern.

If we present all of the strips simultaneously, or in such rapid succession that they fall on adjacent regions of the retina with dwell times below 120 msec, the upper and the lower patterns appear about equally tridimensional. This is not surprising, of course, since the information contained in the total assemblage of strips is the same, regardless of where the pattern is cut.

With slower succession, however—with rates of the order of 300 to 960 msec per strip—the two methods of cutting have different results. Although the shapes are identifiable in both cases, the upper patterns look flat, and no spontaneous depth reversal occurs, while the lower patterns

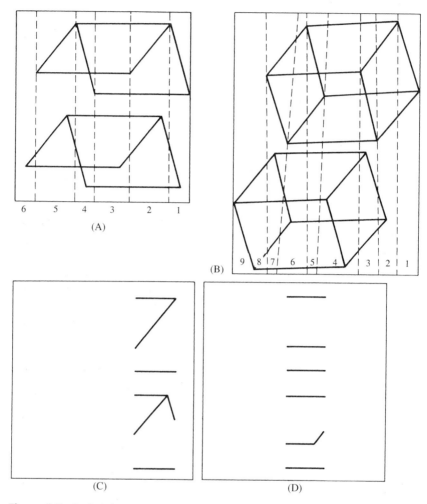

Figure 8.5. Analysis by successive presentation. A, B: Reversible-perspective figures presented in single vertical slices (as numbered). C: Slice 2 of display (A). D: Slice 3 of display (A).

look tridimensional and often display appropriate spontaneous depth reversal despite their fragmented presentation. I think the reversal may be keyed to the presentation of certain cues, but I am not sure.

What I think we have in this demonstration is a display of the action of local depth cues as minimum chunks or features. Figures can be subdivided into these features and still display appropriate tridimensionality. But the features themselves cannot be subdivided, or entered serially, and still maintain perceived depth. Although the technique is reminiscent of McFarland's (1965), we are not concerned, as he was, with judgments of simultaneity, but with obtaining a method for isolating local depth cues—and this one looks promising. Parenthetically, this phenomenon is also obtained binocularly with Julesz patterns, as well as with the line contours of Figure 8.5.

These then are my arguments for *local depth cues*: that different parts of a figure, when fixated, can elicit different depth responses; that the effects of (outline) depth cues are spatially restricted; and that breaking up a pattern so as to prevent parallel processing of the local depth cues, as in Figure 8.5, makes those cues relatively ineffective.

Now, let us consider the other question raised by the Penrose figures—how successive glances are integrated into a single perceptual structure.

The Integration of Successive Glimpses: Perceptual Storage and Schematic Maps

I will first describe a technique currently being used to study the stored structure of impossible pictures, and some preliminary findings; I will then discuss more general questions about perceptual structure.

Consider the pair of patterns in Figures 8.6A and B. Figure 8.6A is a Necker cube; Figure 8.6B is a very simple sort of "impossible" figure derived from it. Move this pattern around behind a hole whose diameter is such that we can see at most one *corner at a time* through the hole. With the pattern moved through positions 1–7 in Figure 8.7, with about ½ sec dwell time at each of the corners (that is, at fields 4 and 7), five of five adult observers correctly reported the figure as "impossible." (Note that the subjects were set to detect inconsistency, not like the naive subjects who cannot initially pinpoint what's wrong with the Penrose figure.) How do they do this?

Look at the corner in field 4, Figure 8.7. Its orientation is ambiguous: either the apex of a convex dihedral (Figure 8.8A) or a concave one (Figure 8.8B). After the sequence fields 1 through 3 (Figure 8.7), the corner in field 4 looks concave; starting at the other end of the sequence, it appears convex. In looking at the sequence 1–7 (Figure 8.7), given this kind of aftereffect, the observer will have to reverse the depth relationships between the upper and lower edge of the cube's side when fields 6–7 appear. This depth reversal can reveal to the observer that the pattern is inconsistent. But does this imply visual storage of the entire pattern? If it is merely the effect of one local depth cue on a successively viewed local region, then we should be able to interfere with this restricted form of storage by an equally restricted kind of visual confusion. I think we can, by merely interposing the convex dihedral, shown in Figure 8.8A, in the sequence of views immediately after

Figure 8.6. A: Reversible-perspective cube. B: Inconsistent cube.

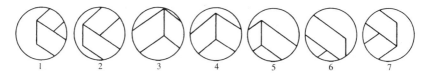

Figure 8.7. Views of Figure 8.6B being moved around behind an aperture.

field 4 in Figure 8.7. Since there is no conflict between the convex corner and the subsequent view of the next corner in fields 6 and 7, the local cue to inconsistency has been removed. Of course, that in turn introduces a noticeable reversal between the previously determined orientation of corner 4, and the interposed convex corner, but we can cause the subject to lose track of these simply by alternating, at random, some number of times, between the two nonambiguous views of the corner shown in Figures 8.8A and B. When we do this (cf. Figure 8.9), the ability to detect whether the figure is possible or impossible seems to disappear for a while. But the observer has other resources. He can, for instance, ignore the corner at field 4 entirely, and merely encode the corner at field 1 as "down" and then remember that verbal cue until he gets to field 7, which he might encode as "up." These verbal crutches can, in turn, be interfered with. For example, I tried having one subject solve an imaginary visual maze which required responses of "up" and "down" in an irregular order, imposing this task while the sequence (abbreviated in Figure 8.9) was presented. Performance again dropped, until still another encoding strategy was devised.

These are preliminary findings with few subjects and limited by the fact that I have not yet been able to devise a suitable control for any possible effects due to sheer distraction. The subjects' resourcefulness, and the multiplicity of possible cues and strategies, makes this a messy line of research, reminiscent of the old work on objective tests of imagery (Woodworth, 1938). Yet the technique does seem to have some promise, and it raises two substantive points to which we can bring other evidence. (1) We can interfere with the detection of inconsistency by visual means, interfering with the continuity of depth-meaning attributed to an ambiguous line. (2) We can interfere with the detection of inconsistency by verbal means, interfering with the way in which the subject stores the two critical corners.

Figure 8.8. Unambiguous corners.
A: Convex. B: Concave.

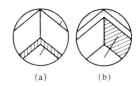

(a)   (b)

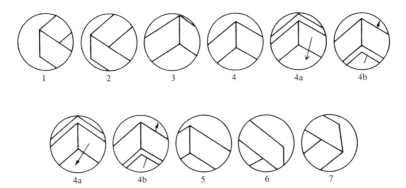

Figure 8.9. Visual interference with the storage of orientation in Figure 8.7.

Are there two kinds of storage providing the integration of successive glances in normal form perception, visual and verbal?

One simplifying assumption would be that, aside from a rapidly fading afterimage, there is no visual storage, only verbal coding, and that the visual interference described above functioned merely as a distractor, or via the medium of the verbal encodings that accompanied the alternations between corners 4*a* and 4*b*. Conversely, we might argue that, normally, the succession of glimpses is almost continuous, and that the context of such succession removes the need for most or all of the "verbal loop" storage, in Glanzer's term, by which gaps in visually determined integration seemed to be bridged, when necessary (and by which the inadequate glance presented by tachistoscopic exposures is eked out), that is, we might argue that the "verbal loop" determines perceptual organization (cf. Glanzer and Clark, 1963, 1964) only under the abnormal demands of tachistoscopic recognition experiments (and perhaps under the normal demands of rapid reading saccades; cf. Hochberg, 1970).

Of these two alternatives, I think the first one—that organization rests solely on verbal storage—quite unlikely. There is clearly also something visual that the subject stores, as we will see when we consider how he builds up a schematic map of a cross (Figures 8.10–12).

Two types of visual storage have received attention recently, but neither would seem to account for the integration of successive views into perceived objects or scenes. (1) Eidetic imagery seems to be complete visual storage of the world and the result of successive integration, since it apparently preserves the distribution of spatial relationships between objects, not their retinal traces (Haber and Haber, 1964). This ability is not widely available and most probably doesn't explain normal form perception. (2) The short-term storage demonstrated by Sperling (1960) and Averbach and Coriell (1961): essentially an afterimage, tied to retinal locus. This certainly contributes to retrieval of tachistoscopically presented material, by prolonging the effective

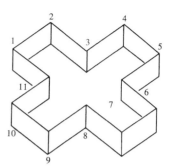

Figure 8.10. Form showing the mind's eye, using the same elements as those of Figure 8.7.

duration of any momentary glimpse, but it cannot normally help and should more usually hinder the integration of successive glimpses of forms and scenes. Look from corner 1 to corner 2 on the square in Figure 8.13B, C. Since retinally tied persistence could not discount the eye movement (or the figure's traverse, if the eye is stationary and the figure moves), what we should perceive in consequence is a stick cross (Figure 8.13D).

What we need is a set of operations for defining and studying the kind of visual storage that will build up the structures of perceived forms out of momentary glimpses, not simply add them up in overlapping persistence.

If we move the block outline crosses shown in Figures 8.10 or 8.12 around behind a hole at a reasonably slow pace and with good cues as to the motion (ca. 500 to 1000 msec between corners), and follow the order indicated in each case by the small numbers, we have no difficulty in recognizing the shape as a cross. In fact, when the sequence reaches the gaps—the blank spaces between corners 6 and 8 in Figure 8.11, and between corners 8 and 9 in Figure 8.12, most uninstructed subjects (13 of 15) *report the arm of the cross as moving behind the window, even though the view is blank at the moment.* A more objective measure of this "jump" is perhaps this: angles 8 in Figure 8.10 and 9 in Figure 8.12 are seen appropriately as 270° rather than 90°, even though the same view is seen as 90° in the first field in each sequence.

This looks much more like visual than verbal storage (although I think that some formal statements of the properties of each had best be worked out and agreed on); certainly the times involved place it beyond the short-term storage of Sperling and others. How might we study such visual *schematic maps*, as I will tentatively call them, and determine their properties?

Figure 8.11. Part of the sequence in Figure 8.10. A: Corner 6. B: Blank (view 7), seen as motion across the southeast arm. C: Corner 8.

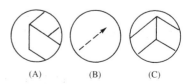

(A)   (B)   (C)

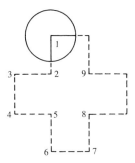

Figure 8.12. Form presented to the mind's eye by sequential views of right angles.

We can build different shapes out of the corners and lines shown in Figures 8.12 to 8.15 by varying the sequence in which we present these elements in *direct* succession (that is, with *no* actual intervening motion or motion cues) through the stationary hole. With very rapid succession of the corners in Figure 8.12, of course, sensory fusion occurs, producing a "+"; with somewhat slower rates (such as 8 cps), a pretty straightforward set of apparent motions occur (such as an "L" flipping over in space or a pair of clock hands skipping from one quadrant to another). Presented at moderate rates, for example, with dwell times of ca. 140 msec and ISIs of 45 msec, a most peculiar kind of *phi* may result. I usually perceive a square moving around behind the window with whatever motions are appropriate—along a lateral between corners 6 and 7 in Figure 8.12, or a diagonal between corners 1 and 2; cf. Figure 8.13C, D. This effect does not seem to be subject to set or to knowledge. Views taken successively around the cross, in the order shown in Figure 8.12, start out with the mask transparent so that the cross is initially entirely visible, then make the mask opaque so that the occluded parts of the cross gradually fade out as we continue to move it around behind the hole. When only the part seen through the hole remains visible, the motion again becomes that of a square. This effect is new to me, and I know next to nothing about it. But whatever it is, the important point here is that set and knowledge do not seem to contribute to what is seen when the succession of views is rapid.

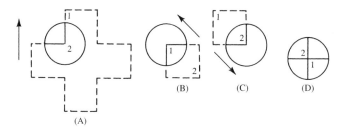

Figure 8.13. Succession of two right angles. A: Second view in Figure 8.12. B, C: Sampling a square. D: Results of persistence of the first view.

Figure 8.14. Successive views of Figure 8.12. A: Corner 1. B: Vertical side. C: Corner 2. D: Horizontal side. E: Corner 3.

Let us now slow down the presentation rate to a dwell time of about 400 to 1000 msec duration. This will also help to introduce a line, as shown, between the presentation of the corners, as in the sequence of views shown in Figure 8.15. What we see then *is* a function of set and knowledge. Told that he is being shown a square, the subject recognizes a square, making the appropriate motions; told he is being shown a cross, and he reports a cross, again with the appropriate motions.

Thus, with rapid succession, set seems incapable of eliciting the perception of the cross; with slow succession, set and knowledge do appear more capable of affecting which shape, executing its appropriate motions, is seen.

This suggests to me something about the mechanism by which such factors normally influence form perception, and I shall explore this suggestion in the next section of this paper.

But first, as I have tried to ask throughout this paper, how do I know that the subject really perceived what he says he does? Let us return to what the defining characteristics of such visual storage, of such a schematic map, should be. In Figure 8.12 if I have such a map, when I look at point 1, I should expect to see a 90° angle, and when I look at point 9, I should see a 270° angle. *The program of possible samplings of an extended scene, and of contingent expectancies of what will be seen as a result of those samplings*, is what I mean by a schematic map.

With this in mind, the obvious measurement technique suggests itself: If we *did* perceive the sequence of views in Figure 8.15 as the successive glimpses of a square, the individual displacements that would appear to connect the views would not fall into any simple pattern (cf. Figure 8.14). Since they exceed in number what we can hold in immediate memory span, we shouldn't be able to distinguish that sequence from another sequence which begins and ends similarly but which is very different in between. But when told the object is a cross, we see that the sequence forms a simple

Figure 8.15. Part of the sequence in Figure 8.12. A: Corner 8. B: Blank, seen as motion across the right-hand arm. C: Corner 9.

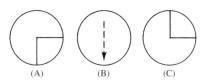

predictable pattern, and it is then easy to tell, on the very first trial, that some other sequence which does not follow a simple path around the cross, is different. (I have tried this demonstration on some dozen observers, and the effect seems to be clear and usable; but I have not yet undertaken formal experiment and there may be unforeseen difficulties with the method.)

"To apprehend a pattern is to discern the principle on which its elements are ordered. To see the elements only will not suffice, for the pattern does not reside in the elements . . . [but] in the rule which governs their relations to each other. . . . Stereotyped vision sees only those patterns which its stereotypes have permitted it to anticipate." I'm quoting from *Design and Expression in the Visual Arts* by J. F. A. Taylor (1964). For "apprehended pattern" say "schematic map," and we are talking about the integrative component in visual processing, the "glue" by which successive glimpses are joined into a single perceptual structure. If I have the right schematic map, successive glimpses fit together so well into the perceptual structure that the stable form is easy to see and the component glances are difficult to detect. With the wrong schematic map, I have only momentary glimpses, erratic and disorganized *sensations*, and no *perceptual* structure emerges, no form is *perceived*. The schematic map is thus not merely a variety of visual storage, or aftereffect; the passive aftereffects, like the familiar afterimage, are tied to retinal locus and, except in the special conditions of tachistoscopic information retrieval (cf. Sperling, 1960), can only degrade and confuse the perceptual process. In contrast, the storage effected by these schematic maps is contingent on direction of gaze, or on the *clearly indicated motion of an object, viewed by a stationary eye, that apparently can be substituted for the exploratory movements of the glance over a stationary object in building up a perceived structure.* These facts place the map's locus much higher in the nervous system than anything like an afterimage.

(A) Schematic maps have local visual consequences, that is, they contain visual information or structure. A schematic map is a matrix of space-time expectancies (or assumptions).

These expectancies are revealed by the couplings or constraints which they impose on otherwise ambiguous shapes and motions, but I presume them to be responsible for the integration of successive glimpses, and for perceptual structure in general, *whether the stimuli are ambiguous or not.*

(B) A schematic map is not a completely detailed counterpart of the total pattern—it is not like an eidetic image (cf. Haber and Haber, 1964)—else the "impossible picture" problem would not arise. Remember that verbal encoding was used to detect the "impossibility" in Figure 8.7. Perhaps such directional information can be added to the schematic map by practice, so that unmediated visual detection of "impossibility" could be made despite the interference between frames 4 and 5 of the sequence in Figure 8.9, but I have no evidence to this point at present.

(C) I have not been able to produce the "cross" response, in Figure 8.12, by furnishing appropriate set or knowledge, with *rapid* succession of inputs. There might well be several reasons for this; for example, perhaps with rapid succession, stimuli might be present that produce unambiguous *phi*, that is, that produce an apparent motion peripherally determined and resistant to central intrusions. But I propose that the explanation is at least partly that schematic maps are ways in which successive sensory input is stored, and storage probably takes substantial time for read-in and read-out, so that *rapid succession rates prevent retrieval of the relevant expectations in time to affect the next glimpse.*

These schematic maps seem closely related to what Hebb calls "phase sequences" (1949). It seems most plausible to me that they are built up not only from the successive views of a given object or scene, but from *previous* experiences as well. I say this only because it seems most unlikely that the completion phenomena involved in the perception of crosses in Figures 8.10 and 8.12 (that is, the "filling in" of the gap where the cross's arms were jumped over) are innate, rather than learned. If schematic maps, which are a form of short-term storage, are thus also vehicles of long-term storage, they suggest a very simple approach to one of the fundamental questions of perceptual learning.

Clear-cut examples of the effects of learning on visual form perception are not easy to come by. But one seems clear enough at first glance—the effects of *having learned to read* on the tachistoscopic recognition of letters. Such effects *must* be the result of learning and, what's more, they seem to affect rapidly presented displays, which here seemed to be resistant to the effects of knowledge. Let us consider this research area, therefore, in the context of the preceding discussions.

Short-Term Storage as the Site of Perceptual Learning: Maps and Plans

While only a few unrelated letters can be recognized in a brief tachistoscopic exposure, a great many more can be recognized if they form some familiar or pronounceable word. After we learn to read, the letters in familiar words are processed in larger chunks (cf. Miller, 1956). These old observations seem to offer clear evidence of learning in perception, as does the fact that legible letters have lower tachistoscopic thresholds for recognition than do their illegible mirror images (Henle, 1942). But does learning affect the way we *see* the words—that is, the way we pick up their forms initially—or does learning to read only alter the ways in which those forms are stored and remembered? There are two extreme alternatives to this issue:

(1) The basic receptive processes themselves might alter, and thereby the nature of what will be an adequate visual stimulus might change. That

is, I think, characteristic of such otherwise diverse theorists as Hebb, Hayek, and J. J. Gibson.

(2) The receptive processes, and at least some associated *perceptual* phenomena, might remain untouched by perceptual learning (there might be basic and relatively unalterable form-perception mechanisms, inherited or established early in the individual's life; surely, today, the facts of sensory physiology can no longer be marshaled to oppose such a proposal—cf. Hubel and Wiesel, 1962). Any changes in form perception that do occur through learning would then consist, on the one hand, only of changes in the organism's deployment of attentional eye movements; on the other hand, of changes in the ways in which each glimpse of the world is remembered and integrated with other glimpses into schematic maps.

I shall argue here that what little evidence there is more closely supports the second alternative, that is, that *the effects of perceptual learning consist of changes in where you look, and of how you remember what you saw, but not of changes in what you see in any momentary glance.*

The proposal is not a really new one, of course; it is an aspect of the old and complex nativism-empiricism issue and, characteristic of that domain of problems with its multiple goals and criteria (Hochberg, 1962), it is not clear how it could be put to direct test. But as a general strategy one can try to show two things: first, that phenomena very similar to those effects that others have offered as examples of the influences of learning on perception can be obtained by what looks more like manipulations of memory. Second, that other form-dependent phenomena normally accompanying the recognition of a particular form with a given display remain unaffected by the presumed effects of learning or past experience on that form.

Thus, several of us argued some years ago that most of the New Look attempts to demonstrate the effects of motivation and of set on perception, usually by means of tachistoscopic recognition experiments, were memorial rather than perceptual. For example, the perceptual defense findings (that negative words require longer tachistoscopic exposures to recognize than do neutral ones) could be explained this way: Emotional response to the momentarily presented word interferes with the fragile memory of what has just been seen and, since all perceptual report has to be retrospective to a greater or lesser degree if it is to be made at all, the subject is left with nothing to report (Hochberg, Haber, and Ryan, 1955; Hochberg and Brooks, 1958). The classic work on the effects of set on tachistoscopic recognition stems from Kulpe's finding that subjects seemed to see better, under tachistoscopic exposures, those stimulus attributes which they had been set to attend. Harris and Haber showed recently that these effects could well be accounted for as the results of encoding processes, rather than as effects on sensitivity (1963; cf. also Haber, 1964; Haber, 1966). What all these explanations have in common is their stress on the strong involvement of short-term memory processes in perceptual reports and, thereby, the possibility that the effects of emotion, needs, set, and so on might be mediated entirely by the memorial processes.

Let us return to the interpretation of the effects of learning on the tachistoscopic recognition of letters and words. Henle (1942) had shown longer exposures to be needed for unfamiliar (reversed) letters than for familiar ones; is this changed sensitivity a result of perceptual learning? Not if Hayes, Robinson, and Brown (1961) are right, because they reported that when subjects' task was to report whether two tachistoscopically presented forms were the same or different—that is, when the task didn't by its very nature require that the subject compare his fading memory of the vanished stimulus display with his memories of how the various letters appeared—then no difference was obtained between normal and reversed letters. Is it, therefore, the same with the effects of having learned to read as with the effects of set, that in both cases the change is due to having a set of encoding responses by which the observer can better store the fading trace left by the momentary glance (cf. Haber, 1966)? I have two series of demonstrations to this point, done with Robert Keen and Virginia Brooks. The first series does for words pretty much what Hayes et al. did for letter forms—it sets up a condition under which a form-dependent phenomenon, namely same-difference judgments, is no better for familiar words than it is for unfamiliar or illegible ones. The second series shows that with the same procedures, but with more involvement of short-term memory, the characteristic differences between familiar and unfamiliar material reappears. These experiments were performed in two different versions. The first time through, the stimuli were all printed on pages which were handed to the subject, who responded "same" or "different" to each pair of words in turn; here the dependent variable was the total time taken to read each page of word pairs (cf. Hochberg, 1966). The findings by this method were, for the most part, replicated in a completely new set of experiments with Robert Keen (cf. Hochberg, 1970), using tachistoscopic exposures (ca. 1 sec) of each word pair, with the dependent variable being the number of times the exposure had to be repeated to make the same-difference judgment of that pair. In all of these experiments, adequate numbers of subjects were used, and the differences that I shall describe were statistically significant at the .05–.01 level.

Direct or Simultaneous Comparison

In this condition, the two words were close together in a double column, the corresponding letters in each word being immediately adjacent. This demanded least of subjects' memories, and minimized possible responses to overall familiar word forms. Each word might be either meaningful or pronounceable or meaningless and unpronounceable, printed in normal orientation, or in reversed or inverted arrays (cf. Figure 8.16A, B, C). Both members might be in uppercase, or one in upper- and one in lowercase, as in

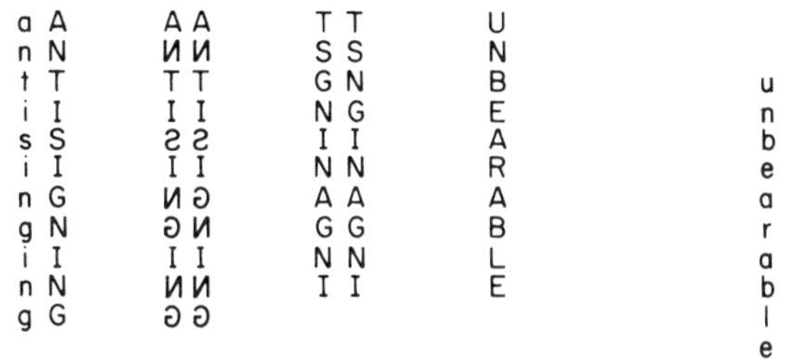

```
a A      A A      T T      U
n N      И И      S S      N                    u
t T      T T      G N      B                    n
i I      I I      N G      E                    b
s S      ᒒ ᒒ      I I      A                    e
i I      I I      N N      R                    a
n G      И ᴅ      A A      A                    r
g N      ᴅ И      G G      B                    a
i I      I I      N N      L                    b
n N      И И      I I      E                    l
g G      ᴅ ᴅ                                    e

(A)      (B)      (C)              (D)
```

Figure 8.16. Simultaneous and successive comparison of legible and illegible words. A: Meaningful, legible, simultaneous. B: Meaningful, illegible, simultaneous. C: Meaningless, legible, simultaneous. D: Successive.

Figure 8.16A. (This last condition has not yet been replicated via tachistoscopic exposure.)

In this direct condition, familiarity has no measurable effect. Whether the words were meaningful or not, whether in illegible mirror images or in normal type, the comparison time and the number of tachistoscopic glances needed in order to decide whether the words were the same or different, both measures were unchanged. (Only one condition made a difference in performance: When one word was printed in capitals, the other in lowercase—as in Figure 8.16A—performance time increased. That is, if the two words differed in *form*, even though they had the same spelling, the comparison task took longer [as noted above, this last condition has not yet been replicated]. The letters now had to pass through a decoding stage, in which different shapes have equivalent meaning, before the subject could decide whether they were the same or different, and *now* familiarity helped.)

Indirect or Successive Comparison

Subject compared two words which were separated horizontally, as in Figure 8.16D, by about 20°. Both words could not now be seen foveally with one fixation, so the subject had to consult his memory of at least one of them. Otherwise, procedures were as before. Now, however, the effects of familiarity were evident: When the words were illegible or unfamiliar and unpronounceable they took more time to judge. With familiar words, one or two fixations suffice to decide whether the words are the same or different; with illegible or unpronounceable stimuli, subjects must compare the two words piece by piece. As we would predict, it makes no difference whether the words are of the same shape (both capitals) or of different shape (capitals and lowercase); comparison times remain essentially unchanged.

These two sets of experiments, simultaneous and successive comparison, thus have diametrically opposite results. This is what we would expect if the learned ability to recognize letter-groups as chunks, and to recognize legible letters better than illegible ones, is due to the formation of appropriate units in encoding and storing momentary glimpses, and not to changes in the immediate processing of form.

If this is true—if the components of visual form picked up in the momentary glance remain unchanged by perceptual learning—then we should be able to demonstrate that some appropriate phenomenon which depends on form pick-up, other than the same-difference judgment, also remains unchanged. The results obtained in the following pilot study on apparent motion are fully consistent with the above conclusions; subjects are still too few in these experiments for appropriate significance tests, but this now seems to me almost an armchair issue. I cannot believe, after seeing how it looks, that when the following experiments have more trustworthy data, they will turn out otherwise.

Successive Comparison with Variable ISI

In these experiments, two 12-letter words were projected, in repeated succession, for 1 sec each, on the same spot on the projection screen, separated temporally by a variable interstimulus interval (ISI). Subjects had to say whether the two words were the same or different. At a short ISI (say, 40 msec), spelling (and shape) differences produced apparent motion, detected in one or two cycles, regardless of whether the words were familiar or unfamiliar, upright or inverted. However, with one word in uppercase and one in lower, apparent motion occurred even when the two words had the same spelling (since the words' forms were now different, regardless of spelling), so from three to twelve cycles were required to make a judgment. With increased ISI (say, to 1000 msec), it made no difference whether the words were in the same typeface or not, but their familiarity and their legibility became crucial: subjects needed one or two cycles to make the same-difference judgments for familiar words, while for a meaningless or illegible word pair, they required as high as a dozen cycles, as they observed, stored, and compared the first word, piece by piece, with the second. Increasing the ISI past the point at which form differences produce apparent motion has made the task dependent on memory, and now the effects of having learned to read are clearly manifested.

The results of all of these experiments with word recognition are consistent with the idea that perceptual learning produces changes in the way in which momentary glimpses are stored, not changes in the form as registered in those glimpses.

What is stored? Here, unlike the schematic maps we probed earlier, the results show no compelling evidence of visual storage (and in this sense, experiments in reading may be very poor tools for the study of visual perception). With words (or displays easily encoded in words), a simple means of storage is, of course, at tongue's tip—repeated auditory rehearsal (Glanzer and Clark, 1963; Levin, 1965; Sperling, 1963). The superiority of pronounceable material in our successive-comparison conditions is certainly consistent with this storage mechanism (cf. Conrad, 1964). If purely auditory rehearsal storage mechanisms were all we had, however, then the difference between *homonyms* (words that are spelled differently but sound alike) should be undetectable under successive-comparison conditions, yet we have found no differences in the same-difference judgments of homonymic and non-homonymic pairs.

Perhaps it is not an auditory storage but one of *articulatory intentions*, or of the *programs* to initiate the visual-vocal behaviors, that translate graphemes into speech.

One would expect such programs to be somewhat different for homonyms, since the grapheme-phoneme correspondence, and hence the translation rule, would be different. I cannot develop this point here, but I urge anyone interested in this question to obtain George Sperling's 1966 International Congress paper, in which a similar proposal, independently developed and more completely thought through, is very clearly presented and defended (Sperling, 1967).

This is not the time, however, to pursue this intriguing question. I would like instead to examine one more experiment in recognition, and then summarize what I have discussed.

There is one other easy demonstration of perceptual learning: If we rotate human faces, and transform them from positives to photographic negatives, their expressions become unreadable. This certainly would seem to be the result of perceptual learning. Unlike the effects of learning to read, however, expressions might be learned very early. Therefore we might find changes in sensory processing demonstrable in recognizing different facial expressions, where we didn't do so with text recognition.

This hypothesis once seemed plausible to me, but no longer. The successive-comparison procedure using drawn faces instead of words (Figure 8.17) seems to give the same pattern of results as with words: With short ISIs, it doesn't matter whether the faces are inverted negatives or upright positives, since even small differences in disposition of the facial features produce apparent motion that is easy to detect within a couple of presentation cycles. With increased delay times, however—ca. 1000 msec—it takes many cycles to detect differences between the inverted negative faces; upright and positive faces are still discriminated, when different, in one or two cycles, even when separated by the long ISIs.

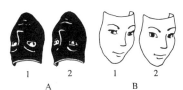

Figure 8.17. Immediate and delayed succession, faces. A: Inverted negatives. B: Upright positives. In both (A) and (B), pattern 2 is projected after a variable interstimulus interval on the place previously occupied by pattern 1.

Figure 8.18. Elements of an expressive sequence.

As in printed text, learning to perceive facial expressions apparently means acquiring ways of storing the expressions, not changes in the reception process. And here, it seems to me, there is *finally an area of perception from which it is reasonable for the social and clinical psychologist to borrow, an area at which the New Look should have been looking, instead of at tachistoscopic word recognition and psychophysical size matching.* Something like the way in which schematic maps seemed to bring the otherwise meaningless sequences of Figure 8.15 into manageable chunks, or in which linguistic meaning codes phonemes into phrases, must surely be found in the perception of social movements and events. In *Potemkin*, Eisenstein cut from face to face, building up *across* their diverse physiognomies a single expressive sequence; drawn facial expressions can be set in sequences (cf. Figure 8.18) that are distinguishable from each other by their timing differences when viewed as upright positives, and that are very difficult to distinguish as sequences of inverted negatives. Upright, they express a single familiar facial event but, inverted, the sequence of successive patterns is meaningless and beyond span.

Until now I have talked about how successive glimpses are organized into perceived stationary forms, or *schematic maps*, and about techniques for studying such stored structures. But these last remarks are to a different point: that successive glimpses can also be organized into and stored as perceived temporal events, or *schematic sequences*; that these schematic sequences can, as a start, be studied by similar techniques; and that they suggest similar but more socially interesting questions. How are such sequences stored—as programs for arranging one's own features in some well-encoded order? How do set, experience, stress, motivation affect expressive schematic sequences? How standard are such sequences? What are the dimensions of individual differences?

These questions run far afield, and I do not have preliminary observations with which to guide speculation. Let me summarize what I've covered today.

Summary

(1) There is a sense in which it is meaningful and useful to ask whether a subject "really" perceives the structure he is naming, and to use the appropriate form-dependent phenomena both to define and to test the point.

(2) Analyses of the perceived forms of reversible-perspective figures and of "impossible pictures" suggest the operation of local depth cues of limited effect, which determine apparent local spatial arrangement more than they suggest effects of an overall perceptual organization dependent on the total configuration of the stimulus pattern. Indirect methods intended to reveal the action of such local depth cues seem to do so.

(3) The perceived structure of an object may consist of two separable components: (a) the features glimpsed in momentary glances, and (b) the integrative *schematic map* into which those features are fitted. I have offered a technique for studying the structure of such schematic maps, at least for certain kinds of scenes and objects, and it may be applicable to other kinds of perceived structure as well.

(4) The contents of the momentary glance may be relatively immune to the effects of set and learning, and it is in the storage structure—the schematic map, in the case of form perception—that the effects of learning are to be found. Form-dependent phenomena in the areas of recognizing text and recognizing facial expression are consistent with this proposal. Recent data by Posner (1966) are very much to this point, and those of Anne Pick can be similarly interpreted (1965).

If you try translating the above terms into the old words, momentary glance into "sensation," schematic map into "image," and perceptual structure into "perception," the fit is very good indeed. The units and measures have changed, but the main features are surprisingly close to those outlined by Helmholtz, Wundt, and Titchener.

References

ATTNEAVE, F. *Applications of information theory to psychology.* New York: Holt, Rinehart and Winston, Inc., 1959.

AVERBACH, E., and A. CORIELL. Short-term memory in vision. *Bell System Tech. J.*, 1961, *40*, 309–328.

CONRAD, R. Acoustic confusions in immediate memory. *Brit. J. Psychol.*, 1964, *55*, 75–83.

GARNER, W., H. HAKE, and C. ERIKSEN. Operationism and the concept of perception. *Psychol. Rev.*, 1956, *63*, 317–329.

GLANZER, M., and W. CLARK. Accuracy of perceptual recall: An analysis of organization. *J. Verb. Learn. Verb. Behav.*, 1963, *1*, 289–299.

GLANZER, M., and W. CLARK. The verbal loop hypothesis: Conventional figures. *Amer. J. Psychol.*, 1964, *77*, 621–626.

HABER, R. N. The effects of coding strategy on perceptual memory. *J. Exp. Psychol.*, 1964, *68*, 257–362.

HABER, R. N. Nature of the effect of set on perception. *Psychol. Rev.*, 1966, *73*, 335–351.

HABER, R. N., and R. B. HABER. Eidetic imagery: I. Frequency. *Percept. Mot. Skills*, 1964, *19*, 131–138.

HARRIS, C., and R. N. HABER. Selective attention and coding in visual perception. *J. Exp. Psychol.*, 1963, *65*, 328–333.

HAYES, W., J. ROBINSON, and L. BROWN. An effect of past experience on perception: An artifact. *Amer. Psychologist*, 1961, *16*, 420 (Abstract).

HEBB, D. *The organization of behavior.* New York: Wiley, 1949.

HENLE, M. The experimental investigation of past experiences as a determinant of visual form perception. *J. Exp. Psychol.*, 1942, *30*, 1–22.

HOCHBERG, J. Perception: Toward the recovery of a definition. *Psychol. Rev.*, 1956, *63*, 400–405.

HOCHBERG, J. Psychophysics and stereotype in social perception. In Sherif, M., and M. Wilson (Eds.), *Emerging problems in social psychology.* University of Oklahoma Press, 1957.

HOCHBERG, J. Nativism and empiricism in perception. In L. Postman (Ed.), *Psychology in the making.* New York: Knopf, 1962.

HOCHBERG, J. Reading pictures and text: What is learned in perceptual development? *Proc. 18th Int. Congr. Psychol.*, 1966, Sympos. *30*, 18–26.

HOCHBERG, J. *Components of literacy: Speculations and exploratory research.* In H. Levin and J. Williams (Eds.), *Basic studies on reading.* New York: Basic, 242–251, 1970.

HOCHBERG, J., and V. BROOKS. Effects of previously associated annoying stimuli (auditory) on visual recognition thresholds. *J. Exp. Psychol.*, 1958, *55*, 490–491.

HOCHBERG, J., and V. BROOKS. The psychophysics of form: Reversible-perspective drawings of spatial objects. *Amer. J. Psychol.*, 1960, *73*, 337–354.

HOCHBERG, J., and V. BROOKS. "Edges" as fundamental components of the visual field. Paper read at the 1962 meeting of the Psychon. Soc.

HOCHBERG, J., S. HABER, and T. RYAN. "Perceptual defense" as an interference phenomenon. *Percept. Mot. Skills*, 1955, *5*, 15–17.

HUBEL, D., and T. WIESEL. Receptive fields, binocular interaction and functional architecture in the cat's visual cortex. *J. Physiol.*, 1962, *160*, 106–154.

JULESZ, B. Binocular depth perception of computer-generated patterns. *Bell System Tech. J.*, 1960, *39*, 1125–1162.

KOPFERMANN, H. Psychologische Untersuchungen über die Wirkung zweidimensionaler Darstellungen körperlicher Gebilde. *Psychol. Forsch.*, 1930, *13*, 293–364.

LEVIN, H. Studies of various aspects of reading. *Project Literacy Reports*, 1965, no. 5, 13–25.

MCFARLAND, J. The effect of different sequences of part presentation on perception of a form's parts as simultaneous. *Proc. 73rd Annual Conv. Amer. Psychol. Assoc.*, Wash., D.C.: A.P.A., 1965.

MILLER, G. The magic number seven, plus or minus two. *Psychol. Rev.*, 1956, *63*, 81–97.

PARKS, T. Post-retinal visual storage. *Amer. J. Psychol.*, 1965, *78*, 145–147.

PICK, A. Improvement of visual and tactual form discrimination. *J. Exp. Psychol.*, 1965, *69*, 331–339.

POSNER, M., and R. MITCHELL. A chronometric analysis of classification. Mimeo. publ., University of Oregon, 1966.

POSTMAN, L. Experimental analysis of motivational factors in perception. In *Current theory and research in motivation.* Lincoln, Nebr.: University of Nebraska Press, 1952.

SPERLING, G. The information available in brief visual presentations. *Psychol. Monogr.*, 1960, *74* (11, Whole No. 498).

SPERLING, G. A model for visual memory tasks. *Human Factors*, 1963, *5*, 19–31.

SPERLING, G. Successive approximations to a model for short-term memory. *Acta Psychologica*, 1967, *27*, 285–292.

TAYLOR, J. *Design and expression in the visual arts.* New York: Dover, 1964.

WOODWORTH, R. *Experimental psychology.* New York: Holt, Rinehart and Winston, Inc., 1938.

9

Attention, Organization, and Consciousness

Julian Hochberg

Two major features of consciousness are these: it is selective, and it is organized. All three of the terms that I have just used have many alternative meanings, so I shall have to define them for the purposes of this paper.[1]

By *consciousness*, I mean what we can report having been aware of; by *selective*, I mean that when we are asked what we have seen or heard, we can normally report only some very small part of what potentially we could describe. By *organized*, I mean that what we perceive usually has internal constraints—that is, that some features of what we say we see can be predicted from other features of what we say we see.

Perceptual organization is usually explained in terms of speculations about electrical fields in the brain or in terms of imaginary nerve nets. *Selective attention* is usually explained by proposing that there are essentially filters or sieves that are interposed between our sense organs and our mind, which screen out what we don't want attended to. In this paper, I shall outline a theory of focal consciousness in which both sets of phenomena—the phenomena of *attention* and the phenomena of *perceptual organization*—result from the normal exercise of well-practiced skills that are fundamental to the perceptual process, rather than from the intervention of special faculties.

Specifically, I will suggest first that focal conscious experience consists of testing anticipated sensory events, i.e., "If I move my eyes over there, I will see a corner facing to the left" or "If I check the speaker's voice two sounds from now, I will hear a hard 'd'." Second, that selective attention consists of testing and remembering one set of anticipations rather than another; and third, that perceptual organization arises predominantly from the ways in which such sets of anticipations, such anticipatory schemas or maps, are structured.

Both the statement about attention and that about organization must be qualified because a mix of processes normally contributes to both functions. Many orienting behaviors contribute to selective attention, behaviors that maximize one kind of sensory input as against others, i.e., turning your head and eyes toward the source, cupping your ears, etc.; holding yourself rigid to prevent rustle-producing body movements; covering your ears when you're trying to read, etc. There are probably even internal ways of reducing a sense organ's input (cf. Hernández-Péon et al., 1961; Fry, 1936). But these means of increasing what we may metaphorically (and with great caution) call the signal-to-noise ratio are, in principle, simply orienting behaviors, and their explication offers no challenge beyond those already posed in abundance by adaptive responses in general. It is the set of problems posed by the effects of selective attention *within* a given sense modality that offers the primary challenge to any psychological theory, and it is to such problems that this paper is addressed.

A complex mix of processes also produces the organizational phenomena. Thus, when perceptual theorists seek to induce the "laws of organization," or other formal rules about the perceptual interactions that appear in response to patterned stimuli, they include in the domain of data some unknown number of phenomena that are really sensory or peripheral in nature (e.g., those attributable to specialized receptor units), and these peripheral factors must be removed from the mix before we can confront the psychologically interesting problems of perceptual organization (Hochberg, 1969).

One classic example illustrates both points: The most striking attribute ascribed to attention is that we can think of only one thing at a time, and retinal rivalry is one traditional manifestation of this: "... if we look with each eye upon a different picture ... sometimes one picture, sometimes the other, or parts of both, will come to consciousness, but hardly ever both combined" (James, 1890). One can attend voluntarily to one or the other picture, and wherever one is visible, the other vanishes (Helmholtz, 1962; Breese, 1909). This alternation between the two appearances is, therefore, often taken to express fluctuations in the observer's attention, or to depend on his conscious or unconscious desires (cf. Ittelson, 1962). When we interpret the results of such experiments, however, we should consider the following three points:

(1) Voluntary control of the fluctuation seems to be mediated by the observer's indirect control of uniocular changes in the sharpness of visual focus, since drugs and artificial pupils which eliminate such focus changes also eliminate the voluntary control (Fry, 1936).

(2) The uncontrolled fluctuation itself seems to consist of a piecemeal replacement of one eye's view by the other's, determined mechanically by the sharpness, relative contrast, and geometry of the contours that fall in the small, local, corresponding regions of each eye's view (cf. Asher, 1953; Crovitz, 1967; Hochberg, 1964; Kaufman, 1964; Verhoeff, 1935; Whittle, 1963).

(3) Minute changes in convergence permit the observer to change the pattern of piecemeal rivalry at will, by bringing different parts of the two half-views in conflict with each other. There are thus more than enough purely peripheral responses, by which the observer can select what he sees, to explain any effects that his instructions (or his personality) may have on the way in which he resolves this perceptual puzzle.

This paper is concerned with problems of selective attention for which peripheral adjustments are *not*—at least at first glance—plausible solutions.

The model that I will apply to this purpose is extremely close to that of Neisser (1967), especially in its treatment of selective listening; it is also similar in various features to those of Egeth (1967), Glanzer and Clark (1962, 1963), Haber (1966), Stroud (1956), and Sperling (1960, 1967); in its general outline, it owes most to Miller, Galanter, and Pribram (1960).

I shall examine, in order, demonstrations of selective perception in (1) single momentary (tachistoscopic) presentations of figures, words, and multidimensional arrays of symbols; (2) the perception of speech in conflict with other speech; and (3) the perception of normally presented ambiguous visual displays.

Selective Perception in Tachistoscopic Presentations

The Effects of Set and Motivation on Shape and Word Recognition

To the engineer concerned with pattern-recognition or shape-detection, words are as good a set of stimuli as any with which to start an investigation of the effects of attention on recognition. From the standpoint of the perception psychologist, the figure-ground phenomena come first, since there are, in theory, at least two alternative shapes that can be seen with any given contour pattern. After looking at Figure 9.1C for a while, for example, the shape first seen disappears from view and is replaced by an alternative one.

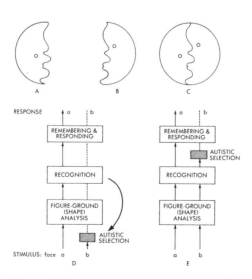

Figure 9.1.

Which shape predominates in prolonged viewing seems to be subject to voluntary control, a point to which we shall return. The theoretically exciting selective effects, however, were those reported to occur with only momentary viewing; Murphy and his coworkers (Schafer and Murphy, 1943; see Solley and Murphy, 1960, for a general review) had reported that rewarding the perception of one alternate shape, say, Figure 9.1A, and punishing the other, Figure 9.1B, or vice versa, led to the perception of the rewarded shape in tachistoscopic exposures in which both shapes shared a common contour, Figure 9.1C, *even though the exposure times were too short to permit reversal to occur.* This appeared to demonstrate that the processes that effect perceptual selection precede those of contour-formation: that is, the rewarded shape must have been the one which was *first* seen, since once a shape emerged in the brief time of exposure, the subject presumably had no way of knowing what the other shape was. The question then inevitably arises of how the observer knew that the rewarded shape was in fact the rewarded one, before it was recognized at all. The assumption that subjects can only report one alternative in such a tachistoscopic presentation is, however, probably wrong (Wallach, 1949; Smith and Hochberg, 1954), so the effects of reward on shape perception may well rest, not on which way a figural process develops but, instead, on how the subject remembers or reports the two figural alternatives after having seen fragments of both (Smith and Hochberg, 1954). These two models are schematically represented respectively in Figures 9.1D and 9.1E; the diagrams are adapted from those of Treisman and Geffen (1967).

By far the greater amount of research on the effects of differential motivation on tachistoscopic recognition has been performed with words, rather than pictorial shapes. The "New Look" procedures were, typically, to show that words or nonsense syllables that are negatively valued (through either normal usage or prior experimental punishment) require longer exposure—have higher tachistoscopic recognition thresholds—than words that are positively valued or neutral (Bruner and Postman, 1949; see Natsoulas, 1965, for a methodological review).

Once again, a question of processing order seems to be raised by the data. In order to have an effect on the conscious recognition threshold, doesn't the word first have to be recognized? And doesn't this imply that some pre-perceptual observer, some Freudian censor, first recognizes the word and then defends the subject from its nastiness? Not necessarily; there are two alternative explanatory models to handle such phenomena, even were the phenomena more fully established than they are. They are *response bias* (the effect may be at least in part at the response end, rather than at the perceptual end of the flow chart, as in Figure 9.2B; cf. Goldiamond, 1958) and *immediate memory loss.*

To explain the point about *immediate memory loss,* consider what a subject has to do, in a tachistoscopic word-recognition experiment (see Figure 9.2C).

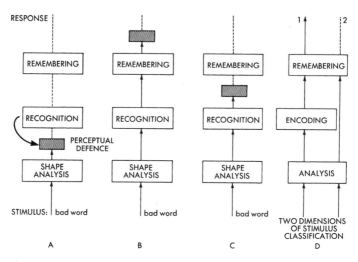

Figure 9.2.

(i)   The word is flashed on a screen, and withdrawn long before he can respond.

(ii) After the exposure is over, the subject must consult his memory of that brief flash (eked out by his afterimages of it, unless they are masked by a post-exposure field) and prepare the appropriate verbal response.

(iii) Finally, he must make the appropriate overt verbal response.

Such experiments are by their nature experiments in retrospection, experiments in which the subject is unable to check his memory of the stimulus because the stimulus is no longer available for consultation.

Short-term memory is notoriously fragile, however, and stimuli that have been associated with trauma in the past (such as those associated with electric shock, the typical punishment) are equally notorious as producers of disruptive emotional responses. Perhaps, therefore, a "...weak and labile memory trace, newly laid down by the brief tachistoscopic exposure, might be eradicated by the violence of almost-simultaneous response... [that is] the startle response [which may be aroused by fractional recognition of the stimulus] 'automatically' interferes with recognition and recall of briefly presented material" (Hochberg, Haber, and Ryan, 1955, p. 17). If this hypothesis is correct, a given nonsense syllable should show a raised tachistoscopic threshold even if it, itself, has never been associated with shock; all we should need to do, in order to raise its threshold, is present some other signal, such as a buzzer, that has been paired with shock and which therefore elicits a startle response, at the same time that the subject is viewing the nonsense syllable. These are the results that we obtained (1955).

According to this analysis, the chief feature of the tachistoscopic experiment is that it is an experiment in retrospection or immediate memory, and immediate memory may be vulnerable to disruption and loss. With this in mind, let us consider the research aimed at demonstrating the direct effects of selective attention on tachistoscopic perception.

The Effects of Instructions on the Description of Multidimensionally Varying Arrays

Külpe's classic experiment (1904), designed to demonstrate the selective perception of sensory attributes, underlies most of the subsequent inquiry. Subjects who were instructed to note one attribute of a tachistoscopically presented display, such as the number, color, or spatial locations of a set of letters, could report more accurately those attributes for which they had been set than those for which they had not been set. From the standpoint of structuralist psychology, this was a particularly critical experiment, since it seemed to destroy the integrity of the units of experience, the sensations, and to dissolve them into abstract attributes. There has since been a great deal of research devoted to this class of experiment, directed to the questions of whether the effect is a perceptual one (in which case the model is similar to that of Figure 9.1A); whether the limitation is on the response (which would be like Figure 9.2B); or whether the limitation on the report of the non-attended attributes is due to effects on memory (Wilcocks, 1925; Lawrence and Coles, 1954; Lawrence and Laberge, 1956). This field of literature was recently well reviewed by Haber (1966) and by Egeth (1967). Both reviewers were brought to a set of conclusions close to those with which we left the perceptual defense literature in the previous section, by the experiments of Harris and Haber (1963) and Haber (1964a, b). All of the measured effects of set on tachistoscopic recognition may be attributable to the fact that while the visual memory of the tachistoscopic presentation fades very rapidly, it takes time for the subject to encode in more permanent form all the things he might be asked to report about the stimulus. Therefore, the subject has the most information available to him about those aspects of the display that he encodes first, and by the time he comes to the encoding of the features that he has not been specifically set to report, his immediate (unencoded) memory of the stimulus display is too degraded to be of much use. As in our analysis of the perceptual defense experiments, the primary characteristic of the tachistoscopic experiment appears to be that it forces the subject to respond to a memory that he cannot refresh, whose validity he cannot check, and whose detail he cannot extend because the stimulus is no longer present. And again, the fragility of immediate memory plays a heavy role in the explanation of the selective effects of attention. But something new has been added, for here the selected material is the material that resists being lost because it has been encoded in a more permanent form (Figure 9.2D).

This is clearly an important contribution to the model of how selective attention works with tachistoscopic recognition. Let us see how such a model helps us to explain the effects of selective attention once we leave the tachistoscopic experiment behind.

Attention to Embedded Speech

From the tachistoscopic presentation, which mimics in some respects the single momentary glance, it would seem natural to consider next the normal nontachistoscopic inspection of an object or scene, which is usually perused by a succession of momentary glances. The sequential nature of the normally viewed scene is extremely hard to dissect, however, and it may be easier to conceptualize this difficult task after we have tried to account for selective attention in speech.

Suppose a subject attends to one of two simultaneous and fairly rapid monologues that differ from each other in some manner that is easy to keep track of—say, one is in a male and the other in a female voice, or the two messages each enter into a different ear. One method that will both force the subject to attend to the primary message and test his reception of it, is to have him "shadow" the primary or attended message while it is being presented. Under such conditions, the subject appears to fail to hear the contents of the secondary message.

Many research workers in this field have explained this kind of selective attention by positing a filter (Figure 9.3A) that passes the primary signal to which one is attending and that attenuates or blocks the other signal so that

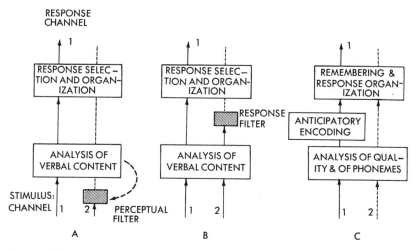

Figure 9.3.

the subject never analyzes the secondary signal to determine its meaning (Broadbent, 1958; Broadbent and Gregory, 1963; Treisman, 1960; Treisman and Geffen, 1967). The filter's exclusion of the secondary message cannot be complete, however, as at least two striking pieces of evidence show: (a) If the two voices are speaking the same message, but the message in the secondary channel is lagging behind that in the primary channel, after a while most subjects realize that both messages are the same (Treisman, 1964); (b) moreover, subjects can usually hear their own names even when those are presented on the secondary (nonattended) channel (Moray, N., 1959). Note that this gives the filter a strong formal similarity to the censor in the perceptual defense diagram of Figure 9.2A. The filter must decide what will be consciously heard, not simply in terms of some relatively simple variable, to which we should expect to be able to tune a filter (e.g., frequency or ear-of-entry), but in terms of the analyzed verbal meaning of the sound. For this reason, Deutsch and Deutsch (1963) suggested, it might be better to place the filter *after* all channels have been analyzed for meaning, as in Figure 9.3B. In this model, the effects of selective attention would be due to selection of responses (or of memories), not of preanalyzed heard sounds. Treisman and Geffen (1967), in a set of experiments that should prove to be a gold mine of detailed information about selective auditory attention, had subjects perform two tasks simultaneously. The main task was to "shadow" the primary message, which was given to one ear, while a secondary message was given to the other ear. A second, subsidiary task was to *tap* whenever certain target words were heard in either of the two messages. The results were clear-cut—the target words elicited the tapping response far less often when they appeared in the secondary message than when they appeared in the attended message; since the actual tapping response was identical, regardless of which message carried the target word, the authors conclude that the effects of selective attention must be due to perceptual selection (Figure 9.3A) rather than to response selection (Figure 9.3B).

At first glance, therefore, selective attention to sequential auditory input would seem to operate prior to perception (as in Figures 9.1A, 9.2A, and 9.3A) rather than as a process subsequent to perception (as in Figures 9.1C and 9.2C). But I think that we should take a closer look at what's probably involved in listening to speech. Suppose there is *no* filter. Suppose, instead, that when we have a continual flow of sounds, we rapidly forget those that are not encoded into verbal structures, or at least, that we forget their *order* of occurrence. What would the model look like?

Consider Figure 9.3C, which is developed out of the models offered by Deutsch and Deutsch (Figure 9.3B) and by Harris and Haber (Figure 9.2C), and which is very close to Neisser (1967). Here, a word or a phrase is presented on either the primary or the secondary channel. The first instant or two of auditory input contains certain immediately available information: about the spatial location of the source, which will be different with different ear-of-entry; about the voice quality (male vs. female); and so forth. Each such sound should then elicit a set of expectations about other sounds to follow, for example, the next set of sounds will be unchanged as to source and voice quality. These are high-probability expectations. But there are other high-probability expectations about the next moment's sounds for speech. Because the number of different recognizable phonemes is small compared to the single sounds that can be discriminated, I'm assuming that intraphonemic expectancies are extremely high, and that speech sounds are analyzed to the phonemic level as soon as they enter the auditory machinery (1, in Figure 9.3C).

So much for "passive listening." Now, let's ask the subject to reproduce the sounds that he hears, and let us feed the sounds to him slowly enough that he doesn't have to store more than, say, nine phonemes at any time while waiting to respond. No active attention is required. But this is not the rate at which speech normally proceeds, and, when we feed in two speeches at the same time, paralleling in the laboratory the kind of distraction that we probably face continually in our daily life, the rate of phonemic input is too high, and the subject must rely on the less certain redundancies of speech (semantic, syntactic, paralinguistic, etc.) to reduce the high phonemic information rate of auditory conversational input to manageable chunks. How can he do this?

Without making any more general commitments to a motor theory of speech perception (Liberman et al., 1962; Lane, 1965), let us assume that there is at least one form of active listening that consists of a special sort of covert speech, in which the listener does the following:

(a) he identifies a heard phoneme;
(b) he selects an articulatory command program that would produce a well-practiced morpheme, choosing a program that starts out with the appropriate phoneme(s);
(c) he only listens for the later occurrence of one or two distinctive phonemes in order to check whether or not he really heard the anticipated morpheme, thereby drastically reducing the load on short-term memory;
(d) if that morpheme checks out, he chooses programs to articulate a string of as many relevant words as he can predict ahead.

Obviously, we have to push this sort of extrapolation of speech contingencies even further, since individual morphemes are probably often quite ambiguous, and the listener must already have considerable practice at guessing the nature of the rest of a phrase in order to identify the ambiguous morpheme. This implies that the active listener must formulate a speech "plan" (Miller, Galanter, and Pribram, 1960) for what he is hearing, meaning that he must have in store a hierarchical program that controls the order in which the sequence of individual morphemes will be generated and tested. When such a plan for one's own speech is formulated, it must be stored while the sequence runs off in real time, so that the speaker can check his utterances for appropriateness, can see where he is in the program, and so that he can upon its completion initiate the next one. In active listening, the "plan" is an "analog," to be checked against another speaker's utterances, rather than a schema against which one's own utterances are checked. This sketchy analysis implies three things:

(a) The active listener often (perhaps usually) tests an entire analog, instead of testing an individual morpheme-generating program, so he need only check actual phonic input very occasionally.

(b) What he stores as having heard is the confirmed analog (which enables him to regenerate the set of received morphemes, on request) rather than the original morphemes themselves, so he should be deaf to departures from the analog that he did not happen to test.

(c) Storage, even of purely verbal material, cannot be restricted to purely verbal encoding alone (in the sense of verbal rehearsal), since the listener must be storing the analog of what the speaker said even while he, the listener, organizes and performs his own "shadowing" responses.

Let us now try to explain the phenomenon of selective auditory attention. The subject makes an active anticipatory response to the initial phonemes that are tagged as the primary message (by spatial source or by voice quality). Meanwhile, a set of sounds (a secondary morpheme) enters the secondary channel while the listener is still actively encoding the morpheme in the primary channel. The secondary morpheme will be stored as a sequence of phonemes, and in most cases will have faded from immediate memory by the time the subject reproduces, or otherwise responds to, the primary morpheme. Now suppose that the secondary morpheme was a target word, one to which the subject was instructed to respond by, say, tapping, as in the Treisman and Geffen experiments. In this case, the tapping response has been assigned to an identifiable morpheme, not to the individual sounds, nor even to the coded phonemes; therefore, further processing (based either on anticipation or on retrieval from immediate storage) would be needed before the tapping response could be elicited, and such processing would not normally be undertaken for words in the secondary channel while there are competing words in the primary channel to be actively anticipated. Another way of saying this is that even though the tapping response does not compete directly with the repeating response, some sizable component of the repeating response is necessary to mediate the tapping response and that this is where the interference occurs in Figure 9.3B.

Do any predictions follow from this model of "shadowing," and of active listening in general, that differ from those readily offered by the concept of a filter? Since we are talking about time-dependent processes, the model in Figure 9.3C should be able to generate some reasonably precise quantitative predictions, whereas it is not clear that a filter model can do so, aside from specifying some level of attenuation of the unattended signal. But there are a number of qualitative predictions, flowing naturally from the present active-listening model, that are supported by existing data, and that do not follow, without *ad hoc* amendments, from a filter model. First, as to the assumption that shadowing (and active listening) depends on linguistic extrapolation—this means that contextual redundancy should be necessary for the shadowing to occur at all, and it is (Moray and Taylor, 1958). Second, as to the assertion that the failure to respond to the target words in the nonattended channel is not a failure to hear any sound at all, but rather a failure to process the phonemes into morphemes—if the experiments of Treisman and Geffen were repeated, using *tones* as the signals to tap, rather than target words, the difference in tapping response between primary and secondary messages should disappear, and in fact it does (Lawson, 1966). Third, if the contents of the first channel lead the listener to anticipate a word that actually occurs on the second channel, that word should then have a better chance of being encoded as a confirmed expectancy (since the observer is already actively rehearsing it regardless of the fact that its initial phonemes were not the initiators of that rehearsal), and just these intrusions seem to occur (Treisman, 1960, 1964; Treisman and Geffen, 1967, p. 7). Fourth, if the secondary morpheme were one's own name, it would have extremely high internal transition probabilities for the listener; additionally, even the first few phonemes of one's own name probably serve as an overlearned instruction to listen actively to whatever channel carries it.

The filter theory can be altered to handle these data, of course, and Treisman (1964) and Treisman and Geffen (1967) have done this by describing the filter as an attenuator which raises the noise level in the unattended channel; by taking speech recognition to depend on a hierarchy of tests (of as yet unspecified nature) that are performed on all sounds in both channels; by assuming that the subject can attach responses to whatever testing level is required by the task; and by making the test criteria (equivalent to response thresholds in the Deutsch and Deutsch model?) dependent on context and other extrinsic factors. As far I can see, the distinction between "perception" and "response" has essentially disappeared, and by the time all of these addenda to the filter model are taken into account, I can see no difference between such a modified version of the model in Figure 9.3A and that in Figure 9.3B, and the only difference between it and the model in Figure 9.3C is that it continues to rely on the notion of a filter. If the listener has to choose one set of sounds to encode (whether by rehearsal or otherwise) I cannot see what this notion adds, because the loss of another set of sounds that has remained unencoded does not seem to call for any special agency.

Perhaps, then, we don't need to posit a filter that either attenuates or suppresses sensory inputs in order to explain the phenomenon of selective attention to simultaneous spoken messages. What is encoded as a confirmed expectation is recalled long enough to be reproduced; what is not encoded is lost. Whether or not this model can compete successfully with the other explanations that have been offered, it does contain some interesting features that can be applied to the problems of both nontachistoscopic and tachistoscopic visual perception, to which I shall now return.

Visual Attention with Normal and Fixed Viewing

In the first section, I held (with Haber, 1965; Egeth, 1967; and Neisser, 1967) that the effects of selective attention on the perception of tachistoscopic displays are due to the selective encoding of the rapidly fading visual trace that is characteristic of briefly presented material. So far, of course, all of the examples of visual selection that we have talked about were gathered tachistoscopically, using a procedure that is quite foreign both to the continuous search-and-test procedures to which our perceptuomotor systems are best suited and to the reading habits upon which the experimental tasks usually depend.

When the observer is set to search displays that are before him for more than one fixation (say, for as long as it takes him to detect, under time pressures, the presence or absence of a member of one class of letters amidst an array of other letters), Neisser finds phenomena that fit the same model of attention very closely. Thus, the items for which the subjects were searching seemed to jump out at them, whereas the irrelevant items appeared to be "blurred," and the irrelevant items were not recognized as having been seen before when they were presented in a recognition test after the search was completed. Neisser presents a model of active perceptual synthesis, in which what he calls "preattentive" processes more or less passively separate out one figure (the one for which the subject is searching) from among an entire field of figures, in terms of some relatively global features, after which an active synthesis of the attended visual figure occurs, based on the fragments that are offered by more detailed feature-analyzers (1963, 1967). Again, the items that have been encoded by active synthesis can be recalled; the other items, never having had this benefit, are lost. I shall try later to spell out something of the nature of what Neisser calls "figural synthesis," and of its relationship to the "preattentive" process, but here let's merely note that the preattentive analyses are most probably extrafoveal, although Neisser does not go into the matter, and occur before the irrelevant items are actually fixated (hence, in part, their blurred appearance), while the attended items were brought more closely to the fovea.

Eye movements are, of course, the most massive instrument of visual attention. In normal vision, in which the eye is free to move, the direction of gaze offers so obvious and powerful a source of perceptual selection that it seems almost unnecessary to look any further in explaining the phenomenon of attention. What doesn't fall within your field of view, you can't perceive at all, and what doesn't fall on the fovea, you can't see clearly. But this is not all there is to the matter of selective visual attention. Aside from the problems of what guides the eye movements, and how the contents of successive glances are combined, there is a set of attentional phenomena that do not appear, at first inspection, to be at all related to the kinds of search procedures that we have been discussing. Thus, the most clear and striking examples of selection in vision are the figure-ground phenomena, in which, as described in the first section, the subject reports that he can see one or another, but not both, of two apparently exclusive shapes that share the same contour.

In such experiments, the observer knows very well what shapes are before him. The point is that under prolonged viewing he can decide which one he will attend to, and somehow keep that alternative clearly visible (and keep the other alternative invisible) for a longer period than would occur in such "fluctuations of attention" without such instructions. Now it is easy to explain how the observer can exert voluntary control on the appearance of at least certain ambiguous pictures if he is permitted to move his eyes, since he can then bring to his fovea those regions of the display that most strongly elicit one response or the other. Thus, if he glances at the region marked i in Figure 9.4A (which is an adaptation of a "puzzle picture" of Boring's, 1930), and looks at region ii only briefly, if at all, he can "encode" the picture as an old lady, and the region at ii is encoded simply as the general curve representing her nose, with inconsistent details being unencoded and therefore

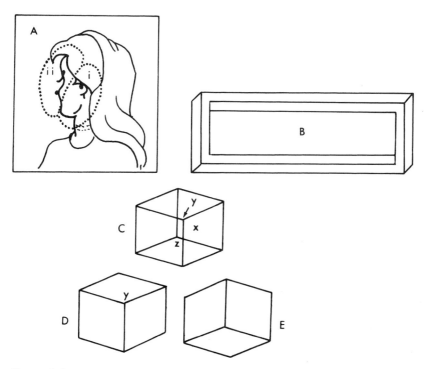

Figure 9.4.

forgotten between glances (we have yet to take up what might be involved in *visual* encoding as opposed to the verbal processes discussed in the previous section). Contrariwise, if he looks at region *ii* predominantly, the detailed shape clearly visible is that of a young lady's cheek, chin, and eyelashes, and the general blur of lines at region *i* may then be encoded as an ear and earring. To switch attention here, the subject need merely change his predominant fixation point. Again, in the "impossible" picture at Figure 9.4B, the subject can switch from seeing a picture frame open to the right, to one that opens to the left, merely by looking predominantly at one side or the other. Particularly if we assume that it takes some minimum looking time for a line to develop, or to change, its representationally meaningful function (i.e., which way it will face as the apex of a dihedral angle, or which way it will function as an edge), the voluntary control of such "attention fluctuations" is not different in principle from any other effects on what one sees of where one looks.

But these phenomena appear to occur, as well, where eye movements will not provide any clear explanation of such voluntary control of figure-ground organization. Thus, a reversible-perspective figure (Figure 9.4C) that is presented to the eye as a stabilized retinal image, displays its characteristic change from one orientation (Figure 9.4D) to the other (Figure 9.4E), even though its projection to the eye is so coupled to the eye's movements that its retinal image appears on the same part of the retina regardless of what the eye does (Pritchard, Heron, and Hebb, 1961). This might be so because the reversals express some "satiation" process, in which the neural events associated with one alternative percept become "fatigued" or otherwise build up resistance to their own continuation, thus permitting the other competing and mutually exclusive alternative process to occur (Howard, 1961; Orbach et al., 1963). The subject can exert voluntary control over the perspective reversal even under conditions of stabilization, however (Zinchenko, 1966), thus exhibiting perceptual selection as well as satiation, and we cannot explain such selection in terms of how the subject directs his foveal vision because the retinal image is stabilized.

Even though eye movements could have no direct effect on the relative clarity of the different parts of the stimulus when the image is stabilized, Zinchenko reports that the subject makes eye movements while he attempts to exert control, and Zinchenko explains the control of attention as due to the effects of the eye-movement behaviors on the sensitivities of one set of receptive fields (which might, for example, favor orientation 9.4D) as against another (which might favor orientation 9.4E). A direct route by which sensitivity changes might occur is offered by the fact that the contact lenses used in image stabilization permit slight shifts of image position on the retina, and the eye movements might be exerting their effects through the mediation of just such minute shifts of the retinal image.

Accordingly, Hochberg and Brooks (in preparation, a) produced an after-image of a Necker cube (Figure 9.4C) by momentarily illuminating a white-on-black drawing of the cube with an intense flash of light. Immediately after painting the afterimage in the eye, the subject was instructed to report the durations of the two alternative appearances (Figure 9.4D, E) by pressing either of two telegraph keys, for the space of 60 secs., while he projected the afterimage on a flickering postexposure field. This was done under two conditions of fixation and two conditions of instruction. The conditions of fixation were these: (F1) The subject fixated the region marked "x" in Figure 9.4C during the placing of the afterimage, but could move his eyes freely while inspecting the afterimage; (F2) the subject fixated the point "y" during painting of the afterimage, and then kept that point superimposed as steadily as possible on a fixation point in the postexposure field when inspecting the afterimage. The two instructions were these: (I1) hold the orientation of Figure 9.4D and (I2) hold the orientation of Figure 9.4E.

The results were clear-cut: (a) The subject can change the durations of appearance of each apparent orientation of the cube in accordance with instructions; and he can do this when *no* shift in retinal image is possible (cf. Washburn et al., 1929). (b) He can maintain one or the other appearance for extended durations while his fixation is held constant. Because of the procedure used, we can't be sure that momentary eye movements did not accompany the actual change in apparent orientation, but we can be sure that different postexposure eye positions were not necessary to maintain each of the two versions.

Does this finding send us back to something like the model in Figure 9.1A? Perhaps so. It appears that selective attention can indeed operate to determine in which of two alternative appearances a reversible-perspective figure is seen, without any mediation by peripheral sensory mechanisms. I think, however, that it is worth trying to imagine what mechanisms might underlie this phenomenon, because the effort to do so will extend the model of Figure 9.3C, which was devised for handling selective speech perception, into the much richer area of visual shape and form perception.

What I shall argue is that (a) the mature observer has a vocabulary of sequential visuomotor expectancies (e.g., "If I look along this edge to the left, I will see a corner concave to the right"), and that some of these expectancies (like phonemes in hearing) span a small period of time and space, whereas others (like morphemes and phrases in hearing), span longer intervals of time and require multiple spatial fixations to encompass; (b) the perception of form over multiple fixations demands active looking (like active listening in speech perception), and it is the plan for such active looking-and-testing that is stored over successive fixations, not the myriad details that are glimpsed with each independent fixation; (c) as the structure of linguistic expectancies provides the basis for selective perception of speech, the structure or organization of visuomotor expectancies provides the basis for the selective perception of visual form. There is, thus, a vocabulary and a grammar of vision to be found, and both attentional and organizational phenomena arise as that visual language is applied to mapping and remembering the world to which we are exposed.

The primary characteristic of visual sequence is this: Shapes that fall on the periphery of the retina, with its low acuity and unknown mix of receptive fields, are brought to the fovea, and vice versa; and the primary determinant of this visual sequence is the sequential distribution of eye movements. Such eye-movement distributions appear to be lawfully dependent on features of the stimulus display (Hochberg and Brooks, 1962; Brooks, 1961), so it is tempting to try to find the compositional laws that govern them and to expect that the phenomenon of visual attention will then be easier to comprehend. However, even if we knew enough about attentional eye movements to predict what their distribution would be for any given display, we would still need some theory of how the momentary glimpses they provide are built up into a single perceived scene before we could make predictions about selective perception. There is, of course, a set of well-worked-out theories of visual direction that seem to offer a starting point, but we shall see that they are more important here for what they leave out of account than for their direct value.

The problem that such theories are designed to handle is this: Imagine some point, $s1$, fixed in space in front of the observer. With his eye in one position, that point will fall on some retinal receptor, $r1$. The image of a second point, at some other locus $s2$ to the left of $s1$ in space, will fall on another receptor at some different place on the retina, $r2$. If the eye now rotates to the right by some visual angle θ so that the image of point $s1$ falls on retinal receptor $r2$, how does our visual system know that the fixed position of point $s1$ in real space—what I will call its *distal address*—has remained unchanged? The obvious answer is that we must somehow take into account the extent of the eye's rotation, i.e., that we must assign distal addresses on the basis of some function of $r1$, $r2$, and θ. Theories differ as to the precise nature of this function; currently, some version of Lotze's local sign theory (that the relative locations of $r1$ and $r2$ are given by the memories of the rotation needed to bring each to the fovea) and of Helmholtz's "sense of innervation" (that the visual system keeps track of the commands that have been issued to the oculomotor apparatus) seems to be in the ascendancy (e.g., Festinger et al., 1967). Since the head, trunk, and body move in the world while the eyes move in the head, those other motions also have to be taken into account in assigning each point on the retina to a distal address in space, and the models that attempt to incorporate explicit provision for all of the simultaneous changes in the relationship between successive glimpses of the world become, of necessity, very cumbersome (cf. Taylor, 1962). Regardless of the details or validity of any of these theories as models of space perception, however, they are both unnecessary and insufficient for our present purpose, which is to account for the integration of successive glimpses into an extended object or perceived scene.

Unnecessary, because a scene can indeed be comprehended by a searching eye that scans the world with a sensitive fovea, but it can also be built up by a stationary eye that receives information from a changing scene. I can

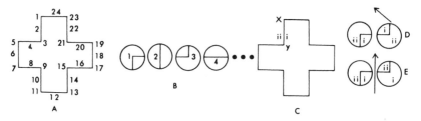

Figure 9.5.

learn that Figure 9.5A is a cross by fixating different points on it in succession or, conversely, I can move the cross around behind an aperture while my eye remains stationary. And this, of course, is no mere laboratory curiosity; ever since the motion picture camera was freed from its fixed-station point, movies and TV have used this integrative ability of the visual system to portray objects and scenes that are many times larger than the projection screen itself.

Insufficient, as well, because the number of independent visual events that would have to be handled by any such means of keeping track of successive glances would be well beyond the capacities of immediate memory. The immediate memory span is about seven to nine items. Suppose that I move my eyes from point to point around the cross in Figures 9.5A, B, and attempt to build up my picture of its form by keeping track of where I looked each time. If each corner and each side is an individual item, I'm beyond the upper limit of immediate memory span, yet there's no difficulty in describing or recognizing the pattern (Hochberg, 1966). Similarly, with my gaze fixed on an aperture, behind which there is a moving figure (9.5B) I can tell without any question when the cross has come back to the same point. I'm sure that I don't have to proliferate examples to make the point that the separate glances are not stored as independent items but are encoded (by the experienced observer) as part of a remembered spatial structure or image, what I have called a *schematic map* (1966). In order to say anything about how it is that successive fixations make their separate contributions to the perceived scene, therefore, we'll have to make a stab at assigning some properties to these schematic maps.

To function at all, these structures must have the following properties:

(a) They tell me what to expect if I look at some distal address, and, conversely, they permit me to enter information about what to find at such an address (and to add amendments or more detail there later, if needed).

(b) It must be possible to recognize a given place on an object, or within a scene, even though the eye has come to it by different routes, and even if it is the object or scene that has moved.

(c) Some features of the scene must be stored at least for the duration of the visual inspection of the scene, so that each time the eye returns to them they are familiar and do not get reentered as new information.

(d) The visual system must be able to recognize which features of an object that are being seen only in peripheral vision contain no information not already recorded and which, therefore, do not require specific foveal fixation (for example, unless I am searching for specific details, I don't fixate each and every point of a multipointed star or notary seal before letting my eyes desert that region of the display).

There may be other things that we can say about these schematic maps, but these last two points are the most important for our present purposes. Point (c) is important, because even a scene that requires only seven quick fixations has already exceeded the *duration* of primary visual memory (cf. Sperling, 1960) and has entered some more permanent storage. Point (d) is important because it implies for the case of continuous visual inspection the same kind of encoding into a limited visual vocabulary that we have already invoked to explain the effects of selective attention in the cases of tachistoscopic viewing and of selective listening.

Active reading is an instructive example to consider first, since it superimposes on the normal perceptuomotor skills, with which the observer translates successive fixations, over time, into a perceived spatial structure, another (and initially contradictory) set of skills with which the reader translates an array of shapes, laid out in space, into a sequence of verbal structures in time. Although the child may learn to read by putting together groups of one or two letters that are fixated one after the other, the practiced reader must sample a text, rather than look closely at each grapheme (or even at each word or at each phrase), and it looks as though the skilled reader is "picking up" many more letters in each fixation. What is he picking up that permits him to make fewer fixations? To me, this requires a minimal extension of the model in Figure 9.3C. He cannot now see more letters at a single glance than he did before having learned to read, else "proofreader's error" would not be as easy to demonstrate. Instead of seeing more letters, he is more ready to make the response that would be appropriate had he brought all of the letters to the fovea and made the correct phonemic response to each grapheme. That is, the experienced reader responds (a) with a readiness to emit one or another spoken word or phrase, as a preplanned *motor* unit, on the basis of only a few features that fall within clear vision; and (b) with the attempt to confirm the programmed verbal sequence by fixating the array of text at some place as much further along as his anticipatory span will permit. When the active reader moves his eye from one fixation point to the next, he is, of course, picking up graphemes from the lines above and below the one he is attending, but these are like the secondary channel in one of the selective listening experiments we discussed in the previous section (or like what he must receive when passively looking at a page of print rather than actively reading it). They were not anticipated from previous context and peripheral cues, they do not confirm any expectation, so they are not encoded. It should be possible to do something like the Moray experiment here, and by suitable presentation of the subject's own name in the next line, to produce intrusions into his normal linear progress. That is, the task in active reading is to fixate only those parts of the visual array that the reader expects (on the basis of previous semantic and syntactic constraints and on the basis of how words and spaces appear to peripheral vision) and which will enable him to check his guesses about what is being said and will help him to formulate further anticipations. The better the reader, the more widespread the fixations by which we should expect him to sample the text, and the more likely that morphemes with shapes having only a superficial resemblance to a highly probable word will be encoded as that word. After the eye has passed on, of course, the visual memories of the unencoded graphemes will quickly fade, and the "proofreader's error" alone will remain to reveal the nature of the task he was pursuing.

Let us now turn to the perception of objects and events in space. How much of this speculative description of the reading process might also apply to the perception of surfaces, shapes, and forms?

Clearly, there are differences between perceiving objects and reading text. Our expectations of what we shall see when we look directly at some form that is now seen only in peripheral vision, or that is otherwise not yet in sight, as in the aperture-viewing situation of Figure 9.5B, are given not by linguistic convention, but by ecological contingencies (Brunswik, 1943), i.e., by the ways in which the world is put together. Some of these contingencies are very high and are probably learned very early indeed, or they may even be prewired. These high-contingency expectations are subject to continual overlearning and, like phonemes, are probably encoded even to passive inspection. Let us consider one set of such short, high-probability visuomotor sequences first, then some longer and less ubiquitous sequences that will include the case of the reversible-perspective figures.

One high-probability relationship is that between contours and edges. We should expect to find, with very high frequency, that a brightness-difference

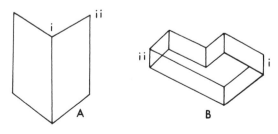

Figure 9.6.

contour in the periphery turns out to mark a corner or an edge when it is brought to the fovea, or when other testing action is applied to it. That is, a contour, when fixated, usually either marks an *edge* (which is a division to one side of which accommodation, motion parallax, etc., defines a surface, and to the other side of which there is only empty air) or a *fold* (i.e., the crease or crest of a dihedral angle that is either convex or concave toward the observer).

When one runs one's eye around a scene, a profusion of such elements must be moved around the retina in an apparently disordered and incomprehensible succession of views. If nothing else is done with such a meaningless succession, it will soon be forgotten, and will have no effects on further anticipations. But we have acquired a vocabulary of *schematic maps* by which (if a real scene confronts the observer so that there really is some underlying order to the sequence) at least the main features of the successive views can be encoded and stored by anticipating and testing what kind of edge or angle will meet one's gaze next (cf. Figure 9.5).

And this brings us back to our reversible-perspective figures. Like a brightness-difference contour, a line seems to be encoded almost automatically as an edge or a fold (cf. Hochberg and Brooks, 1962). But this is not a one-to-one relationship because I can anticipate two completely different outcomes as I look at some point i in Figure 9.6A. The first is this: that when I move my eyes out to point ii, I will have to accommodate and converge my oculomotor system for closer vision in order to keep it clear, i.e., the figure appears to be *concave toward me*. The second expectation is that the figure is *convex toward me* and that ii is *farther away* than i.

And this explains the figure-ground phenomenon, the fact with which we opened the entire discussion of selective perception in the first section of this paper. We seem to be able to see only one shape at a time whereas the contour really divides two areas of complementary shapes; it is because there are two different perceptuomotor expectancies, two different *schematic maps* that can be fit to the same contour, that the figure-ground phenomenon occurs.

Where two alternative (self-consistent) maps fit a single reversible pattern, any given line segment serves a different function (as edge or fold) in each map. When I fixate the top corner (x) of the cross in Figure 9.5C, I see the vertical line as an edge between a surface at i and ground (or air) at ii. If I anticipate moving my fixation from corner (x) to corner (y), I expect that the vertical line in (y) will continue to function (since it appears to contain no discontinuities between x and y) in the same way when it is brought to the fovea, as does the section presently being fixated at (x)—that is, that the vertical line at (y) also marks an edge that is surface at i and ground at ii. Within limits, such expectations are self-fulfilling: If I expect to see the vertical line in (y) as the edge of a surface at i, that's what I do see. Thus, if I am told that the sequence of views in Figure 9.5D is a square moving around behind the aperture, I see two convex corners and the motion shown by the arrow; if I am looking for a cross, I see one corner as convex and the other as concave, as shown in Figure 9.5E (Hochberg, 1966). If the stimulus is only an outline drawing, whichever expectation I test will be partially confirmed. With outline drawings, after all, there are no cues of accommodation, microtexture, or motion parallax to disconfirm the expectation. Selective attention has led to selective perception, all right, but it has done so in a very special way, under very special circumstances—with such reversible figures, we have two mutually exclusive schematic maps, each of which can generate sequential expectations about which of two mutually exclusive edges will be seen in each subsequent glimpse, and the stimulus display itself permits a line to be encoded in accordance with the expectation with which it is approached. The selection is between two maps or sets of expectations, therefore, not between any sensory responses.

Why, then, does reversal ever occur, and how does voluntary attention effect such reversal? There are probably several factors that bring about reversal, some of which may be local and relatively peripheral; e.g., local satiational processes may cause intersections of lines, which we have said act as ambiguous depth cues, to reverse their local depth functions. But there is another possibility that is suggested by our previous analysis of how schematic maps guide our visual search patterns. Suppose when actively looking at the Necker cube in Figure 9.4C, we test and confirm the orientation shown in Figure 9.4D (to the extent that confirmation is possible with outline drawings); then no further active search is needed, and the entire figure is encoded as a "cube." Now suppose further that this encoding (i.e., a "cube") normally does not carry with it the details of orientation that determine, at every point, which function each line will serve. The fact that no discontinuity is obvious in Figure 9.4B suggests this same point on other grounds anyway, i.e., the details of orientation of each line are not stored, only the generating programs for how to get either to the orientation shown in Figure 9.4D or to that in 9.4E, depending on the orientation of the edge with which one happens to start (cf. Hochberg, 1966). In effect, having established that the figure is a cube, the *nonencoded directional details are forgotten*, and only the overall orientation is preserved, e.g., that Figure 9.4D "faces right." Since the figure remains before the eye, now idly, passively, looking at different corners and lines, these will be fixated without any expectation of which way the edge should face, and, if only by chance, but perhaps by local satiation as well, one or more of these will be encoded as an edge facing in a direction consonant with Figure 9.4E, not with Figure 9.4D. After a short period of such "idling," an active analog test program will again be undertaken to fit the pieces together and, if that program starts from an edge that is now consistent with the alternative map, reversal will occur.

In short, reversal occurs when active looking is relaxed and attention falters.

To the extent that this hypothetical factor really contributes to figural reversal, such reversal should be subject to voluntary attentional control, i.e., as long as the subject continues to test one map, the figure should maintain the same orientation until satiational processes wrest control from the anticipatory process.

And now we can try to explain how the observer seems to be able to select which alternative he will see, even when his retinal image is fixed. Suppose the image is fixed on my retina with my gaze centered on point (x) in Figure 9.4C, and I wish to hold the orientation shown in Figure 9.4D. I can *intend* an eye movement toward point (y) in 9.4C with the expectation that I will be fixating a fold that has the orientation of point y in 9.4D when the move is completed. Whether or not I actually execute such an eye movement, of course, my retinal-image will not change. After having made this attempt, I can attempt another test (e.g., intending an eye movement toward point (z) in 9.4C with the expectation of seeing something like point z in 9.4D). And as long as I keep on making such attempts with definite expectations, the orientation should hold.

This model of the reversal process explains why Zinchenko found that eye movements tend to occur with perspective reversal of stabilized images, even though they can have no direct effect on the image. But it also makes a different kind of prediction about normal (unstabilized) viewing of such figures. If figural reversals occur in part as the result of "losing track" of which way a particular edge must face within a map, this implies that, in passive viewing, local regions may be assigned inconsistent orientations. Thus, fixing the direction of one edge (Figure 9.6B.*i*) should not fix the direction of another edge in the same figure (9.6B.*ii*), and in fact reversal continues to occur in such locally ambiguous pictures (Hochberg and Brooks, in preparation, b).

In this third section, then, I have attempted to explain the effects of selective visual attention, and especially the effects of attention on reversible figures using an active-looking model analogous to the active-listening model developed in the earlier section.

Conclusion

I have tried to defend the proposition that the perceptual effects of selective attention are either the results of purely peripheral adjustments (like covering your ears with your hands, or like looking in one direction rather than another) or, where they are not, that they are the results of testing the perceptuomotor analogs which encode, in one structure of expectations, what would otherwise be a larger set of perceived events than can be remembered. Whatever is not so encoded is likely to be lost. The structure of any set of expectancies generates the facts of perceptual organization; the loss of unencoded sensations (or of smaller encoded units) generates the facts of selective attention. I am not pretending that this approach solves the problems of organization or of attention, but I do suggest that those problems can be rearranged to form a more economical and interrelated package.

Note

1. Supported by National Science Foundation Grant No. GB 5270. A somewhat shorter version of this paper was presented as a Pillsbury Lecture at Cornell University in May 1968. I am indebted to Murray Glanzer, Eugene Galanter, and Daniel Kahneman for discussions of the problems to which this paper is addressed.

References

ASHER, H. Suppression theory of binocular vision. *Brit. J. Opthalm.*, 1953, *37*, 37–49.

AVERBACH, E., and CORIELL, A. C. Short-term memory in vision. *Bell Systems Tech. J.*, 1961, *40*, 309–328.

BORING, E. A new ambiguous figure. *Amer. J. Psychol.*, 1930, *42*, 444.

BREESE, B. B. Binocular rivalry. *Psychol. Rev.*, 1909, *16*, 410–415.

BROADBENT, D. E. *Perception and communication.* London: Pergamon, 1958.

BROADBENT, D. E., and GREGORY, M. Division of attention and the decision theory of signal detection. *Proc. Roy. Soc. B.*, 1963, *158*, 222–231.

BROOKS, V. *Attention.* Unpublished master's thesis, Cornell University, 1961.

BRUNER, J. S., and POSTMAN, L. Perception, cognition and behavior. *J. Personal.*, 1949, *18*, 14–31.

BRUNSWIK, E. Organismic achievement and environmental probability. *Psychol. Rev.*, 1943, *50*, 255–272.

CROVITZ, H. F., and LOCKHEAD, G. R. Possible monocular predictors of binocular rivalry of contours. *Percept. & Psychophysics*, 1967, *2*, 83–85.

DEUTSCH, J. A., and DEUTSCH, D. Attention: Some theoretical considerations. *Psychol. Rev.*, 1963, *70*, 80–90.

EGETH, H. Selective attention. *Psychol. Bull.*, 1967, *67*, 41–57.

FESTINGER, L., BURNHAM, C., ONO, H., and BAMBER, D. Efference and the conscious experience of perception. *J. Exp. Psychol.*, 1967, *74*, 1–36.

FRY, G. A. The relation of accommodation to the suppression of vision in one eye. *Amer. J. Ophthal.*, 1936, *19*, 135–138.

GLANZER, M., and CLARK, W. H. Accuracy of perceptual recall. An analysis of organization. *Journal of Verbal Learning and Verbal Behavior*, 1963, *1*(4), 289–299.

GOLDIAMOND, I. Indicators of perception: I. Subliminal perception, subception, unconscious perception: An analysis in terms of psychophysical indicator methodology. *Psychol. Bull.*, 1958, *55*, 373–411.

HABER, R. N. Nature of the effect of set on perception. *Psychol. Rev.*, 1966, *73*, 335–351.

HABER, R. N. The effect of coding strategy on perceptual memory. *J. Exper. Psychol.*, 1964, *68*, 257–362.

HABER, R. N. A replication of selective attention and coding in visual perception. *J. Exper. Psychol.*, 1964, *67*, 402–404.

HARRIS, C. S., and HABER, R. N. Selective attention and coding in visual perception. *J. Exp. Psychol.*, 1963, *65*, 328–333.

HELMHOLTZ, H. v. *Physiological optics.* Vol. 3, transl. from the 3rd German ed. In J. P. C. Southall (Ed.). *Treatise on physiological optics.* New York: Dover, 1962.

HERNÁNDEZ-PEÓN, R. Reticular mechanisms of sensory control. In W. A. Rosenblith (Ed.), *Sensory communication*. New York: Wiley, 1961, 497–520.

HERNÁNDEZ-PEÓN, R., SCHERRER, H., and JOUVET, M. Modification of electric activity in cochlear nucleus during "attention" in unanaesthetized cats. *Science*, 1956, *123*, 331–332.

HOCHBERG, J. *Perception*. Englewood Cliffs, N.J.: Prentice-Hall, 1964.

HOCHBERG, J. Contralateral suppressive fields of binocular combination. *Psychon. Sci.*, 1964, *1*, 157.

HOCHBERG, J. In the mind's eye. Address read at the Sept. 1966 meeting of the American Psychological Association, Div. 3. In R. N. Haber (Ed.), *Contemporary theory and research in visual perception*. New York: Holt, Rinehart and Winston, 1969, 309–331.

HOCHBERG, J. Components of literacy: Speculations and exploratory research. In H. Levin and J. Williams (Eds.), *Basic studies on reading*, in press.

HOCHBERG, J. Units of perceptual analysis. In J. Mehler (Ed.), *Handbook of cognitive psychology*. Englewood Cliffs, N.J.: Prentice-Hall, in press.

HOCHBERG, J., and BROOKS, V. The prediction of visual attention to designs and paintings. Paper at APA 1962 (Abstract) *Amer. Psychol.*, 1962, *17*, 7.

HOCHBERG, J., and BROOKS, V. Pictorial recognition as an unlearned ability: A study of one child's performance. *Amer. J. Psychol.*, 1962, *75*, 624–628.

HOCHBERG, J., and BROOKS, V. Perspective reversals in fixed images. In preparation. (a)

HOCHBERG, J., and BROOKS, V. Perspective reversal and intercue distance. In preparation. (b)

HOCHBERG, J. E., HABER, S. L., and RYAN, T. A. "Perceptual defense" as an interference phenomenon. *Percept. Mot. Skills*, 1955, *5*, 15–17.

HOWARD, I. An investigation of a satiation process in the reversible perspective of revolving skeletal shapes. *Quart. J. Exp. Psychol.*, 1961, *13*, 19–33.

ITTELSON, W. A. Perception and transactional psychology. In S. Koch (Ed.), *Psychology: A study of a science*, Vol. 4. New York: McGraw-Hill, 1962.

JAMES, W. *Principles of psychology*, Vol. 1. New York: Holt, 1890, 402–458.

KAUFMAN, L. Suppression and fusion in viewing complex stereograms. *Amer. J. Psychol.*, 1964, *77*, 193–205.

KÜLPE, O. Versuche über Abstraktion. *Bericht über den Ie Kongresz für Experimentale Psychologie*, 1904, 56–58.

LANE, H. The motor theory of speech perception: A critical review. *Psychol. Rev.*, 1965, *72*, 275–309.

LAWRENCE, D. H., and COLES, G. R. Accuracy of recognition with alternatives before and after the stimulus. *J. Exp. Psychol.*, 1954, *47*, 208–214.

LAWRENCE, D. H., and LABERGE, D. L. Relationship between recognition accuracy and order of reporting stimulus dimensions. *J. Exp. Psychol.*, 1956, *51*, 12–18.

LAWSON, E. A. Decisions concerning the rejected channel. *Quart. J. Exp. Psychol.*, 1966, *18*, 260–265.

LIBERMAN, A. M. Some results of research on speech perception. *J. Acoust. Soc. Amer.*, 1957, *29*, 117–123.

MILLER, G. A., GALANTER, E., and PRIBRAM, K. *Plans and the structure of behavior*. New York: McGraw-Hill, 1960.

MORAY, N., and TAYLOR, A. The effect of redundancy in shadowing one of two messages. *Language & Speech*, 1958, *1*, 102–109.

NATSOULAS, T. Converging operations for perceptual defense. *Psychological Review*, 1965, *64*, 393–401.

NEISSER, U. *Cognitive psychology*. New York: Appleton-Century-Crofts, 1967.

NEISSER, U. Decision time without reaction time: Experiments in visual scanning. *Amer. J. Psychol.*, 1963, *76*, 376–385.

ORBACH, J., EHRLICH, D., and HEATH, H. A. Reversibility of the Necker cube: I. An examination of the concept of "satiation of orientation." *Percept. Mot. Skills*, 1963, *17*, 439–458.

PRITCHARD, R., HERON, W., and HEBB, D. Visual perception approached by the method of stabilized images. *Canad. J. Psychol.*, 1960, *14*, 67–77.

SCHAFER, R., and MURPHY, G. The role of autism in figure-ground relationship. *J. Exp. Psychol.*, 1943, *32*, 335–343.

SMITH, D. E. P., and HOCHBERG, J. E. The effect of punishment (electric shock) on figure-ground perception. *J. Psychol.*, 1954, *38*, 83–87.

SOLLEY, C. M., and MURPHY, G. *Development of the perceptual world*. New York: Basic Books, 1960.

SPERLING, G. A model for visual memory tasks. *Human Factors*, 1963, *5*, 19–31.

SPERLING, G. The information available in brief visual presentations. *Psychol. Monogr.*, 1960, *74* (No. 11, Whole No. 498).

STROUD, J. M. The fine structure of psychological time. In H. Quastler (Ed.), *Information theory in psychology*. Glencoe: The Free Press, 1956, 174–207.

TAYLOR, J. G. *The behavioral basis of perception*. New Haven: Yale University Press, 1962.

TREISMAN, A. M. Monitoring and storage of irrelevant messages in selective attention. *J. Verb. Learn. Verb. Behav.*, 1964, *3*, 449–459.

TREISMAN, A. M. Contextual cues in selective listing. *Quart. J. Exp. Psychol.*, 1960, *12*, 242–248.

TREISMAN, A., and GEFFEN, G. Selective attention: Perception or response? *Quart. J. Exper. Psychol.*, 1967, *19*, 1–17.

VERHOEFF, F. H. A new theory of binocular vision. *Arch. Ophthalmol.*, 1935, *13*, 151–175.

WALLACH, H. Some considerations concerning the relation between perception and cognition. *J. Pers.*, 1949, *18*, 6–13.

WASHBURN, M. F., KEELER, K., NEW, K. B., and PARSHAL, F. M. Experiments on the relation of reaction-time, cube fluctuations, and mirror drawing to temperamental differences. *Amer. J. Psychol.*, 1929, *41*, 112–17.

WHITTLE, P. A. Binocular rivalry and the contrast at contours. *Quart. J. Exp. Psych.*, 1965, *17*(3), 217–226.

WILCOCKS, R. W. An examination of Külpe's experiment on abstraction. *Amer. J. Psychol.*, 1925, *36*, 324–340.

WOODWORTH, R. S. *Experimental psychology*. New York: Holt, 1938.

ZINCHENKO, V. Perception as action. *Proc. Int. Congr. Psychol.*, Moscow, 1966, Symposium, *30*, 64–72.

10

Components of Literacy

Speculations and Exploratory Research

Julian Hochberg

We must learn about the wide world that confronts us in installments, by very narrow glances in different directions, for our eyes register fine detail only within a very small region of the visual field. The integration of these serial glimpses into a single, apparently stable perceived world, with fine detail apparently equally distributed throughout, is usually very good, and the perceived world normally contains little hint of the continual changes of retinal image that occur as the eye sweeps the optic array confronting it. In consequence, the psychologist can often ignore the sequential nature of the sensory input by choosing the outer environment as his starting point when he analyzes the perceptual process (the optic array, the "picture plane," the distal world itself). Where one is concerned with looking behaviors per se, however, this simplification is impossible. Especially in the case of the reading process, the limits of the single glance, the nature and determinants of the succession of glances, and the rules by which the contents of successive glances are integrated into a single perceptual structure are questions that cannot be disregarded.

To put together the information obtained by the eye in successive glances, the effects of all of the following must be taken into account by the integrating mechanisms of the visual system: the direction in which the eye is pointed during each glance; the order in which the glances occur; and the station point of the head and body as a platform for the eye throughout all these glances. Thus, if the reader fixates in turn each of three letters, *a, b, c,* he must be able to register and to store the visual data both about shape gained in each fixation and about the shapes' relative locations in outer space—that is, their "distal addresses"—if he is to perceive the spatial array as *abc* rather than as *cba* and so on. He must also be able to treat as completely equivalent the various different sequences of successive glances by which he arrives at a given distal address, so that regardless of how his eye arrives at a given fixation point (for example, whether he fixates in the ordered sequence *abc, cba, acb,* and so on) and regardless of that fixation point's position relative to the shape to which some distal address must be assigned, the same spatial array is perceived.

The spatial framework within which a distal address is assigned to any given shape by the visual system need not be at rest with respect to the reader—for example, at least in some circumstances, the various points on a sheet of paper, which is itself in random short-excursion movement, are nevertheless assigned to fixed and rigid distal addresses on that paper, as when one reads a mildly fluttering newspaper. This point is sufficient to distinguish that property of a shape that I am here calling its "distal address" from the similar term of "visual direction."

The sequential fixations must be guided by the distributions of information within each visual display if any economy of search is to be achieved. Such guidance of the search pattern by the visual display itself can only be of two kinds:

1. The low-acuity information picked up in the periphery of the eye can suggest to the optic search system where it must move its point of clearest vision in order to get detailed view of some potentially interesting region; call this "peripheral search guidance," or PSG.
2. Knowledge about what he has seen so far should provide the observer with some hypotheses about where he should look in order to obtain further information; call this "cognitive search guidance," or CSG. I'm not talking about real or consciously reported hypotheses, but about *constructs*—the observer acts *as though* he had hypotheses.

Visual perception requires such complex directional guidance and record keeping in a very general way that we should expect to find the implied visuomotor abilities to be highly developed even in early childhood. Because CSG will in general depend heavily on both the immediate and the long-term personal history, looking-sequence patterns should vary from one observer to the next, and perhaps from one time of perusal to the next (Buswell, 1935). However, because the number of points of informational value in the view is determined by the display, as well as by the observer's own patterns of CSG, we should expect that the general selection of regions that will be fixated, if not the order of their fixations, should be similar from one observer to the next, and this also seems to be the case (Brooks, 1961; Hochberg, 1962).

I know of no studies in which eye movements were recorded in normal environments without the subjects' knowledge. In fact, I do not know of any practical method by which this can be done without either fettering the head and trunk in an exquisitely unnatural manner or generating records that are extremely laborious and expensive to read. However, it seems reasonable to believe that something like the following occurs.

First, the major potentially informative points of the scene are scanned, probably with as much information gathered from one position of head and trunk as possible, that is, with as small a ratio of head movements to eye movements as possible. Then, where small detail is needed to determine some aspect of the scene's meaning, saccades will bring the appropriate regions to the fovea, followed by whatever small excursions may be needed to answer questions raised by the major glimpses and to confirm conclusions thus formed about the contents of the array.

This should produce a high ratio of large saccades to small ones, with successively more detailed expectations being tested by smaller saccades, up to the limits dictated by the task and by the stimulus display. The mechanism for keeping track of distal addresses over large excursions should be well practiced; the mechanism for keeping track of small, sequential excursions need not be, because these are merely filling in forms that have already been surveyed roughly by large movements.

There is nothing at all in this posited ability, however, as we have discussed it so far, that should make it possible for a subject to keep precise track of the order in which any search course has been traversed, mapping spatial order into temporal sequence. The mechanisms have been developed to keep track of spatial structures regardless of the sequence of glimpses by which that structure has been sampled. Keeping track of the temporal order of letter-by-letter fixations should not be an easy task with this set of skills. Yet this is just what beginning readers have to do, and, I shall argue, it is only much later, when the reader becomes expert at traversing a large spatial array of text by a relatively small number of fixations, that he can apply to the perusal of the printed page the habits of eye movements practiced so long and continually in looking at the world.

The first new task introduced by reading is the necessity of translating spatial into temporal order. Assume that the reader starts by learning to put together groups of one or two letters into the sequences comprised by words. Whether or not the reader actually learns this way, or by some more "molar" method of instruction, seems to me to be largely immaterial; even if he started with a visual vocabulary in which each word had been learned as a unique pattern, he would still have to put together the successive glances necessitated by words and phrases that are longer than can be encompassed in a single glance. Assume next that such small sequential fixation movements are very difficult and tiring to execute and to keep track of because they run counter to the normal demands that the visual environment has trained the oculomotor system's search functions to fulfill. Common usage has it that children need to learn with large letters and words because these are easier to discriminate. Why are they easier to discriminate? Certainly not in terms of visual acuity, of which the child has plenty to spare. My explanation is that if larger letters are in fact easier for beginning readers, it is at least in part owing to the difficulties in hobbling the eyes to make shorter and more systematically sequential saccades than those to which they are accustomed and suited.

The advanced reader, on the other hand, should need much less in the way of short saccades, making relatively long sweeps directed by PSG and CSG. That is, the practiced reader should learn to sample a page or text (rather than to "read it" in the strict sense of the term), moving his eyes in ways much closer to those used in viewing the normal world, therefore closer to the long and irregular excursions of normal vision. Skilled, directed reading should be a process closer to an open-ended expectancy testing than to decoding a string of symbols.

What has the skilled reader learned that makes fewer fixations and longer eye movements possible? Originally, with one letter or letter group as a stimulus, and with an overt vocalization or subvocalization as his response, the beginning reader must make many fixations. After skill in directed reading has been achieved, far fewer fixations per block of letters are made, and it looks as though the reader is "picking up" many more letters per fixation. What makes it possible for the skilled reader to do with fewer fixations?

For one thing, the skilled reader has acquired strong response biases, or guessing tendencies. Given a few cues, he will respond as though the entire word, or perhaps an entire phrase, had been presented. Does this mean that he now can see more letters at a single glance? Hardly, else "proofreader's error" would not be so prevalent and so easy to demonstrate. Instead of seeing more letters, what this implies is that the reader is more ready to make the response that would be appropriate were a whole word seen clearly, when in fact only a portion of it falls on the fovea. Why should he have been reinforced for doing this? Because under meaning-retrieval conditions, the reader is always concerned, not with what particular stimulus pattern momentarily confronts his eye, but with the provisional information that this fixation brings to him about the substance of what he's reading and about where it tells him to look next. This careless and premature response must be the very heart of what is learned in directed reading.

What I'm arguing here, in short, is that there are a number of very different response systems that change as a result of acquiring skill at directed reading, but that there's no reason to believe that there's any change in what the reader actually sees at any glance. What responses change with the acquisition of reading skill? The answer, one would think, would be found in the three response systems that are most important to speed of sampling for meaning:

1. The experienced reader must respond with a readiness to emit one or another spoken word or phrase, as a preplanned motor unit, that is, with an articulatory program appropriate both to some features of the printed word that falls within clear vision where he happens to be fixated and to the various meaningful expectations that his previous fixations have built up with respect to that text. Because vocalization is rarely called for, and because reading speed greatly exceeds articulation speed anyway, I envision such verbal responses as being more in the nature of programs to speak a given word—perhaps merely the preparatory set to vocalize the initial sounds—rather than actual verbal responses. I shall return to this point shortly. This response bias will not

only produce informed guesses about partially glimpsed stimuli; it will also help encode, store, and retrieve the contents of even fully grasped fixations.

2. The experienced reader must treat each important printed cue, each distinctive visual feature of word or phrase, as a confirmation or disconfirmation of some class of expectations and must respond with a set of expectations concerning what should follow the particular material he's reading. (This is a psycholinguistic problem, and I have no idea how one would go about studying this aspect of the reading process.)

3. The experienced reader must respond to the contents of one fixation by making plans as to where he will look next. At the very lowest level, he must pick up with his peripheral vision cues that tell him where regions of high informational value lie in the field. (I shall present some research to this point, too.)

But in addition to all of these responses, which obviously must change as reading skill develops, the subject should also be able to see the forms of the letters and words he looks at. Is there good reason to believe that this ability has changed?

Much of the relevant evidence has been obtained by tachistoscopic research. Let us briefly consider whether such research findings really imply perceptual change.

A major argument in favor of the thesis that familiarity has increased the ability to receive a greater number of letters during a single exposure is the long-attested fact that it takes fewer (and/or shorter) exposures to report familiar textual material (for example, letters, words) than to report unfamiliar material (for example, reversed letters, nonsense syllables). In tachistoscopic presentation, the subject looks very briefly at a particular stimulus pattern. Presumably, the reason tachistoscopic exposures are treated as being relevant to the reading process is that they simulate the momentary fixations that occur between saccades in normal reading. However, because they appear out of context, are usually not programmed by the subject's eye movements, and demand a response (namely, *What word do you see?*) that is very uncharacteristic of the reading process, the relevance of any tachistoscopic experiment to the normal reading process must always be questioned. What I'm saying may be a commonplace, but it means that the good reader—certainly the student who survives to become a college freshman, and provides our major subject population in tachistoscopic experiments—is trained to do all sorts of things with briefly glimpsed letter groups, but saying with precision the letters that he actually sees is not one of them. However, there is good evidence that under tachistoscopic exposure, familiar graphic material is reported better than unfamiliar material (Henle, 1942; Solomon and Howes, 1951). It is not clear, however, whether this advantage of familiar over unfamiliar words is owing to improved reception, that is, to an increased sensitivity to the forms of letters or letter groups, or to response bias, either as expressed in a simple guessing tendency or in a greater capacity to encode and to remember meaningful rather than unmeaningful material.

Consider Henle's demonstration that familiar letters can be identified under briefer presentations than their unfamiliar mirror images. This advantage of familiar over unfamiliar letters disappears when subjects are asked to make a same-different judgment (SD) between pairs of letters or of mirror images presented simultaneously (Hayes, Robinson, and Brown, 1961). What about words? We know that familiar words can be recognized at briefer exposures than unfamiliar words. But tachistoscopic recognition experiments require the subject to compare his memory of the letter group he has just seen with some word memory. R. Keen, V. Brooks, and I adapted the procedure of Hayes et al. to demonstrate that the effects of familiarity appear when subjects have to make same-different judgments between words that they cannot view simultaneously, but that the effects may disappear when the displays permit simultaneous shape comparison (Hochberg, 1968).

In the set of experiments I shall describe here, pairs of words or pairs of paralogs were arranged in double columns of letters, with each member of any pair of corresponding letters falling within foveal distance of each other. Columns were used, instead of horizontal displays, to minimize distance between corresponding letters and to minimize responses to familiar word shapes. One member of each double column (that is, one word or paralog) was either the same as or different from the other member, in that a difference in two letters appeared in half the presentations. Each such member might be either meaningful and pronounceable by both adults and children (for example, *cowboy*); it might be pronounceable only by adults (for example, *bierre*); or it might be meaningless and unpronounceable. There were six different pairs; each appeared twice with the two members of each pair the same, and twice different, for a total of twenty-four pairs. Pair members consisted of sets of letters varying in length from four letters (for example, *idol*) to six letters (for example, *serial*). Pairs were spaced with a one millimeter within-pair horizontal spacing. There were six such pages with a total of twenty-four different pairs per page. Order of presentation of pages was counterbalanced between subjects (sixteen adults; sixteen children of from five years eleven months to seven years of age). Subjects were instructed to say as quickly as possible whether the two members of each column pair were the same or different.

Some pairs of columns were pronounceable, some were unpronounceable; one whole set of column pairs was printed in mirror-image letters, so that reading would normally be delayed.

No differences could be found, either for adults or for children, among any of these conditions. Adults averaged approximately 1 second per column pair (including response time and transfer of their attention to the next column), with an SD of 0.33 second; the children averaged about 3.5 seconds.

On one page, one member of each pair was in capitals, whereas the other member was in lowercase. These pairs took longer for fourteen of the sixteen subjects (averaging about 2 seconds per column pair, and SD of 0.64 seconds), whereas the remaining two subjects, for whom the order of the tasks was such that the effects of practice worked to counteract the difference otherwise manifested, showed no difference for this condition.

In summary, when each pair of words was simultaneously fixated, the findings were these: Whether the words were meaningful or not, pronounceable or not, mirror image or normal—none of these factors resulted in longer times to perform the task. Only one condition hindered discrimination: a difference in form (letter case) between the two column pair members. These findings suggest two things.

First, within the obvious limitation that the subject had to be able to know at what level of detail he could consider two letters to be identical (that is, and not continue to search for changes below some detail size, which he might do in the case of some completely unknown alphabet or other arbitrary form-matching task), perceptual learning and experience did not enter into this performance. The judgment seemed to be one of symmetry, not "reading."

Second, when corresponding letters differed in shape (capitals and lowercase), performance time increased because the letters had to pass through a decoding stage, one in which different shapes were equivalent in alphabetic or auditory meaning, in order to decide the sameness or difference of any given letter pair. This point is underscored by the results of the next set of experiments.

In the second set of experiments, the procedure was unchanged, except that the words were now not arranged in columns, but in horizontal tiers, so that subjects could not now read both members of any pair at one fixation (separation between words was now about 20 degrees). Because both words could not now be read at one fixation, comparison had to involve a memory of at least one of them. Otherwise, procedures were as in the previous experiment.

In this procedure, the effects of learning and familiarity became very evident. For all sixteen adult subjects (and for four of the children), comparison of the word pairs when they were in mirror-image form took longer (mn = 1.7 seconds, SD = 0.5 second) than when they were in normal orientation (mn = 0.8 second, SD = 0.3 second). The twelve children who showed no differences took as long with the normal orientation as the others took with the mirror images—that is, they were not yet able to store the words in larger units. No differences were obtained between word pairs in which one member was in upper- and one in lowercase, on the one hand, and those in which both were in the same case (mns = 0.8, 0.8 second), on the other. But now age level and reading skill made a difference, because those words that were unpronounceable to the particular subject took significantly longer in the case of each of those four children who could otherwise handle the words as units (p's ranging from < .08 to < .005).

To summarize the successive-comparison condition, no increase in average comparison time attended the difference in letter shape (uppercase vs. lowercase) between the two words to be compared, but comparison time did increase significantly for all subjects when the two words to be compared were printed in reversed letters (mirror image) and also tended to increase for words the subject couldn't pronounce.

In the first experiment then, a direct form-dependent judgment is being made (something like a response to symmetry), whereas in the second experiment, in which words had to be viewed successively, at least one of the two words must be compared as an encoded and stored memory. The effects of word legibility appear in the second and not in the first experiment, whereas the effects of the differences in configuration between letters appear in the first and not in the second experiment. Moreover, in the second experiment, the reader was required to compare successively viewed words, whereas the first experiment permitted comparisons to be made within a single fixation. These facts suggest that learning to read long words is a function of encoding and storage, not of changes in immediate input processing. I assume that, in the first experiment, subjects could detect form differences in one or two fixations, as long as each letter pair was made up of same-case letters. However, with different-case letters, each pair had to be compared letter by letter, decoding them to a common form of storage. In the second experiment, all comparisons had to be made in terms of stored material anyway, and here the longer times obtained in certain conditions reflect the greater number of fixations required to compare material for which no larger storage units were available.

Several factors were uncontrolled in these experiments and offered possible sources of artifact. First, when a difference was introduced into a meaningful word pair, that difference usually made one of the two words meaningless. Second, the use of columns in the first condition, and of rows in the second, permitted subjects to rely on familiar word forms and on reading habits more in the second experiment than in the first, and we cannot therefore separate the effects of delay from those of word-form familiarity. Third, because subjects regulated their own looking behavior, we cannot be sure that the differences in comparison times are an expression of fixation rather than, say, of decision times. Accordingly, these experiments have been replicated by R. Keen and myself, using tachistoscopic presentation conditions and more controlled stimuli, with essentially the same results.

All subjects were adults. Viewing times were approximately 1.5 seconds, and subjects called for as many presentations as were needed to decide whether the two columns were the same or different. Stimuli were pairs of nine-letter or ten-letter columns, with the two members of each pair being either identical or different in only one letter at the same place in each letter string. Both members of each pair were either meaningful or meaningless, either pronounceable words or unpronounceable anagrams of those words.

As in the previous experiments, no differences were obtained in the number of exposures that subjects needed in order to make the same-different judgment for the pairs of nonsense words as compared to the pairs of real words, when the members of each pair were immediately adjacent. On the other hand, when successive comparison was enforced by lateral separation of the two columns, a significantly greater number of exposures was required to obtain correct same-different judgments for nonsense strings than for real words.

What do such findings imply about the question of why experienced readers require fewer fixations? They do *not* prove that familiarity does not increase the number of letters actually sensed during each fixation, because our technique might mask such an effect. But they do show that the characteristic effects of familiarity that are obtained in tachistoscopic recognition experiments may be explained, economically, as being the result of having available a library or repertory of well-practiced responses, each of which encodes the entire set of letters into a single response, thereby enabling the subject to store the whole set of letters without loss before his overt verbal response can be completed. This, of course, raises the question of what the attributes of such storage mechanisms are like. There is seductive evidence to the effect that tachistoscopic visual presentations leave a primary visual image that can be read off for about 0.33 second, after which the information is encoded in the form of auditory or subvocal rehearsal (Glanzer and Clark, 1963; Sperling, 1963; Conrad, 1964; Biemiller and Levin, 1965). I believe that good arguments can be made (Hochberg, 1966; Sperling, 1967) that such encoding is neither auditory nor subvocal but consists, instead, of articulatory programs, that is, of the plans that, if executed, would result in the translation of printed graphemes into spoken words. However, I do not think this question is an important one to the understanding of normal reading, because in reading the continual, if saltatory, nature of the visual stimulation and its speed of intake change the conditions very substantially from that of the single tachistoscopic presentation. The primary visual image (or afterimage) then becomes an annoyance rather than a source of information, because it can only interfere with the contents of the next fixation. Auditory rehearsal or subvocalizations would similarly either slow down reading speed or interfere with the encoding of subsequent fixations and, in turn, be interfered with by any auditory storage they might produce. Surely the reader's storage of a 150-page novel is not a constantly expanding subvocal recitation of what he has read, and it is not necessary for him to listen to what such auditory rehearsal tells him in order to know what to expect next. Even if sheer subvocal rehearsal plays a role in tachistoscopic recognition, actual reading must demand something like the articulatory programs, contingent expectations, and whatever other mechanisms mediate the laying down of cognitive structure.

But this is a side issue. What is relevant here is the argument that the skilled reader makes fewer fixations not because he can process letters faster, but because he has better response availabilities. And this in turn means that his greater reading speed has to be explained in terms of sampling the text, not in terms of greater "graphemic sensitivities." Let us now consider some requirements of, and some evidence for, such guided sampling.

In order for sampling to be effective, that is, in order for anything less than step-by-step reading of each letter, word, or phrase to suffice, some degree of redundancy must be present. In fact, redundancy is impressively great in printed English. Resistance to spelling reform has been attributed to the fact that redundancy is pretty close to 100 percent (in the middle of long sentences) with our present spelling and syntax. But redundancy has virtues only in conditions of transmission that are "noisy" in some sense—conditions in which parts of the message are likely to be lost.

Why do we need redundancy in printed English? What is the noise? Why should part of the message be lost, with good type on white paper in decent light? Because it is hard to make small and systematic saccades, and because it is easy and rewarding to make information-retrieving guesses that are confirmed—to sample as lightly as possible here and there in the text, putting the pieces together with as little actual reading as possible. Orthographic redundancy is the price of a weak grammar and the adult's substitute for large type. But it is also more than that. The length of a word, or of a phrase, or even of a paragraph is informative, and unlike a mere enlarging of letters (which permits the eye to make large excursions instead of small ones), the use of a spelling system that can be sampled at relatively widely separated strategic places also provides information that the periphery of the eye can use for guidance in the rapid perusal of type.

Normal practiced reading, then, is an active process, involving the continual generation and testing of hypotheses, not an automatic sequential decoding process. On the other hand, it should also be an extremely variable process. It would depend on the task of the reader, that is, what he is reading for; on his knowledge of the language and of its contingencies; on his knowledge of the world about which that language is talking; and on his memory and understanding at one moment of what he has read in previous moments. Thus, receiving instructions to read aloud would change the pattern of search in the mature reader, forcing him to do much closer sampling. Instructions to find spelling errors would change the nature of the task almost completely. Because such differences in recorded eye movements with differences in task have indeed been reported by Judd and Buswell (1922), the question of the implicit instructions in any reading experiment becomes particularly important. One must interpret very cautiously the results of any procedure in which the subject knows that eye movements are being recorded or that the experiment involves the quality of his reading.

In general, one would expect that the longer-span search tasks, which involve expectancies that may not be confirmed for paragraphs or even for pages of reading, would provide the main impetus to continuing a book. Tell someone the contents of its last pages and you terminate his interest in the who-done-it. This kind of expectancy, which demands knowledge about the world, is clearly dominated by cognitive search guidance (CSG) and requires more knowledge about subject matter than about orthographic and syntactic redundancies. However, short-term CSG, exercised within sentences and even within words, demands some knowledge about the structure of the language. The reader cannot sample economically unless he is able to fill in the spaces between the points he samples and proceed to further sampling.

Yet, this kind of reading sampling cannot proceed under CSG alone. The reader also needs some degree of peripheral guidance from the stimulus display. What kinds of redundancy might be sampled on the basis of such PSG, and how would these differ at different stages of reader sophistication?

The first letter in any word probably carries the most information, for at least two reasons. Being next to a blank space, which can be picked up readily even by the low-acuity vision of the periphery, the fixation point can be programmed to center on or near the initial letter more readily than on any other letter except the last one, and the last letter is probably too subject to constraints to be as informative. Second, the first letter's shape offers a more characteristic and invariant pattern than does the same letter with its sides masked in the middle of a word. In fact, there is evidence (Marchbanks and Levin, 1965) that readers do pay more attention to the initial letters in words, as determined by the errors of confusion in reading when words are presented singly. If what I have just argued is true, we should also expect readers to tend to look at or near letters that immediately follow any blank space. Peripheral search guidance should be well able to accomplish this task.

There is another, more sophisticated function that PSG would seem likely to assist. Words differ greatly in length and the smaller ones are usually functors: *on*, *in*, *to*, *up*, and so on. In many cases, these words are probably redundant, because their meaning is completely recoverable from context once you know where they are in the sentence. In other cases, what the particular functor is may be critical. In either case, it should be possible for the reader to detect that a functor lies at some distance out along the line of text in the periphery, and then decide either to look at the word or, if it's likely to be redundant, to look at the word after it. I have tried casually to determine the average information value of each common functor over a variety of common sentences, by determining reading time (1) with the functors present and clearly legible; (2) with the functors present but partially obscured; and (3) with *xx*'s substituting for functors which had been deleted. In the last two cases, a list of functors was printed at the head of the page to help the reader. On the basis of data from a few readers of widely disparate reading ability, this technique does seem to be workable and might make it possible to test the assumption that word length operates as a fixation cue in accordance with the average uncertainty of that word length.

Although it seems plausible to me that PSG should be able to mediate CSG in reading sampling, as suggested above, the wherewithal must first exist. A child who is unable to guess what a word may be on the basis of its first letter or two will have to spell out more of the word in order to read it correctly. If the functors do offer peripheral information via their character-istic word lengths, fixation deployment can only capitalize on that informa-tion to the extent that the reader has acquired expectancies conforming to those contingencies. And so, if all the preceding is close to the truth, we should be able to test the stage of development of the component skills of a given reader by noting the effects of interference with each kind of redun-dancy sampling.

I shall sketch briefly a recent attempt at this indirect form of mea-surement of the search patterns. Short stories, graded roughly as to reading difficulty, were prepared in two typographical versions (Hochberg, Levin, and Frail, 1966). In the unfilled, or U version, normal spaces were left between words. In the filled, or F version, the spaces between all words were filled with a meaningless symbol made by superimposing an x on a c, each typed at half pressure, so that the resulting contrast of the two characters together was roughly that of the surrounding letters. Seen in peripheral vision, the F version of the text looked like an unbroken line of type. Which story appeared in which version was balanced between two groups of sub-jects, who were matched in reading ability. The material was presented for silent reading. Two age levels of subjects were used, twenty-four subjects from first and second grades, and twenty-four subjects from fifth and sixth grades. The dependent variable was reading time per character. The F version took significantly longer to read. Of primary interest, however, were the results of the following analysis. The eight slowest and the eight fastest first- and second-graders, as determined by their base rates, t_U (reading speeds on the U stories), were compared with respect to the difference in reading time, t_F minus t_U, divided by the base rate, t_U. The beginning readers, who are still looking from letter to letter, with sparse knowledge of orthographic and syntactic redundancies, should be little affected by filled-in spaces. The more advanced readers, deprived of the blank spaces as cues about where to look, should show a marked deficit. In fact, the poorer readers did show little drop in reading rate induced by the F condition. On the other hand, we expected that the better readers, who normally direct their gaze more selectively, would show much more loss, and they did. We have since replicated this experiment (with slightly different conditions) and obtained essentially the same results. The slow, beginning reader shows significantly less deficit when the blank spaces are filled than does the fast. The better reader makes the poorer showing in response to interference with PSG.

These findings are consistent with the present argument that one of the components of skilled, rapid reading is the use of peripheral stimulus pat-terns to guide the eye in sampling the text. This set of experiments is very primitive and nonselective and does not permit us to distinguish the possible points of interference with the sampling process (for example, orthographic, syntactic, or semantic redundancies). Our future plans are to interfere more selectively with the spaces between words while they are still in the reader's periphery, keeping ahead of where the subject is fixated at any moment and, hopefully, making the kind and locus of interference contingent on the subject's performance.

In summary, reading is a mix of many different kinds of activities sustained by different goals and mediated by different skills. It is not clear that learning to read is related in any simple way to changes in form perception as such. I have argued that the main task in skilled, literate reading is to extract information about some subject from an array of redundant and often irrelevant graphic symbols and that this ability is very different in goal, in methods, and in mechanism from the task of translating graphemes into speech.

With respect to goals and incentives, some of these must depend on readers' needs external to the reading material itself, and some must be generated by the interest-arousing and expectation-confirming characteristics of the stimulus display itself.

With respect to the perceptuomotor tasks and abilities implied by such rapid processing of graphemic material, it was argued that no present evidence strongly supports any hypothesized improved letter-form sensitivity. The fact that familiar words can be recognized at shorter exposures than can nonsense words may be explained in terms of more available encoding responses for the former. Experimental findings consistent with this explanation were described. Rapid reading was therefore ascribed to effective sampling abilities, resting on hypothetical processes of cognitive search guidance and peripheral search guidance. The theory implies that poor beginning readers should be less affected than faster ones by interference with peripheral guidance cues, an implication supported by experimental findings.

References

BROOKS, V. *Attention.* Master's thesis, Cornell University, 1961.

BUSWELL, G. T. *How people look at pictures.* Chicago: University of Chicago Press, 1935.

CONRAD, R. Acoustic confusions in immediate memory. *British Journal of Psychology,* 1964, *55,* 75–83.

GLANZER, M., & CLARK, W. Accuracy of perceptual recall: an analysis of organization. *Journal of Verbal Learning and Verbal Behavior,* 1963, *1,* 289–299.

HAYES, W., ROBINSON, J., & BROWN, L. An effect of past experience on perception: an artifact (abstr.). *American Psychologist,* 1961, *16,* 420.

HENLE, M. An experimental investigation of past experiences as a determinant of visual form perception. *Journal of Experimental Psychology,* 1942, *30,* 1–22.

HOCHBERG, J. The psychophysics of pictorial perception. *A-V Communication Review,* 1962, *10,* 22–54.

HOCHBERG, J. Reading pictures and text: what is learned in perceptual development? *Proceedings of the Eighteenth International Congress of Psychology,* 1966, *30,* 18–26.

HOCHBERG, J. In the mind's eye. In R. N. Haber (ed.), *Contemporary theory and research in visual perception.* New York: Holt, Rinehart & Winston, 1968, pp. 309–331.

HOCHBERG, J., LEVIN, H., & FRAIL, C. Studies of oral reading:VII. how interword spaces affect reading. Mimeographed, Cornell University, 1966.

JUDD, C. H., & BUSWELL, G. T. Silent reading: a study of various types. *Supplementary Educational Monographs,* no. 23, 1922.

LEVIN, H., & BIEMILLER, A. J. Studies of oral reading: I. words vs. pseudo-words. In H. Levin, E. J. Gibson, & J. J. Gibson (eds.), *The analysis of reading skill,* Cooperative Research Project No. 5-1213, Final Report to the U.S. Office of Education, 1968.

MARCHBANKS, G., & LEVIN, H. Cues by which children recognize words. *Journal of Educational Psychology,* 1965, *56,* 57–61.

SOLOMON, R. L., & HOWES, D. H. Word frequency, personal values, and visual duration thresholds. *Psychology Review,* 1951, *58,* 256–270.

SPERLING, G. A model for visual memory tasks. *Human Factors,* 1963, *5,* 19–31.

SPERLING, G. Successive approximations to a model for short-term memory. *Acta Psychologica,* 1967, *27,* 285–292.

11

Reading as an Intentional Behavior

Julian Hochberg and Virginia Brooks

To the perception psychologist, reading is not an isolated behavior that can be understood adequately by itself. Depending as heavily as it does on the language skills and on directed visual search, reading text, as a perceptuo-motor activity, has certain characteristics in common with listening to speech and with viewing scenes. The first characteristic shared by these three activities, which is more obvious in the case of reading than in the other two, is that these behaviors do not consist of automatic responses to the array or sequence of patterned stimulation that confronts the subject. The reader does not merely regard a block of text and immediately realize its message. He must *intend* to read the display, must "pay attention" to its meaning, if he is to be able to respond to its contents. What a phrase like "pay attenton to" might mean in this context has not received much thought or experimental research, but it would seem to be of fundamental importance to any understanding of what the reading process is all about.

Let us consider briefly some of the more obvious ways in which intention affects reading: (1) As noted, if a person looks idly at a page of text, with no intention to read, he may recognize only those few words on which his gaze may rest. (2) An efficient reader may read text for meaning at up to 4,800 letters per minute, but at that rate he is very likely not to notice minor spelling errors or omissions; therefore, this figure certainly does not mean that each letter is actually looked at, even though comprehension scores may be very high. (3) In fact, if the task requires the reader to look at or near each letter—for example, if he is checking for misspellings or broken letters, as in proofreading—then his reading rate will slow down and his comprehension score will drop. Here, then, are two clearly separable reading tasks: one with the intention to extract meaningful content from the printed page; the other with the intention to pay attention to the letters and the spelling of the words that make up the printed page. These and other tasks, set either by the goals given the reader, or by the relative

Supported by NICH and HD R01HD04213-01.

difficulty or unfamiliarity of the material, affect the reader's visual search patterns and performances (18, 2). Normally, of course, the subject is required neither to skim as lightly as possible nor to attend to each serif on each letter. Instead, his behavior is probably determined by the changing demands imposed by what he is reading—at one point, casting his eye far ahead; at another, looking at almost each individual letter. *Reading* is thus a very general term, covering a wide range of behaviors, involving diverse purposes and skills.

Skills in reading can be arranged in a logical hierarchy: the ability to discriminate letters and letter groups, the ability to form grapheme-phoneme correspondences, and to spell out (1). In general, one might expect that these "lower" skills are to some degree necessary to the acquisition of higher ones—some minimum ability at letter discrimination and at syllable and word recognition is needed in order for reading-for-meaning to proceed. Thus, it seems extremely likely that every practiced reader has had to acquire these lower skills at some stage in his career toward literacy, and that he can fall back upon them when the task requires it; for example, he can dissect some unfamiliar word or passage into its component letters, and then put it together again. But, these lower skills are probably used only occasionally. When the skilled reader reads normally, that is, when he uses his eyes to retrieve linguistic meaning from the printed page in as natural and content-oriented a way as he uses his ears to listen to speech, he probably looks at the text infrequently, compared to when he proofreads or compared to a less skilled reader. He "samples" the text in order to develop hypotheses about what the next string of symbols consists of and to test those expectations at appropriate places further along in the text. This, of course, sounds more like what we think of as "skimming" than what we consider to be reading, but no hard distinction is really possible: "Skimming" and "reading" represent points on a continuum of intention; they are not basically different activities. In fact, skimming is much closer to what the subject has learned to do when he is listening to speech or when he is looking at scenes, long before he comes to the special task of learning to read, that is, to the special task of using his eyes to "listen."

Before we consider how the various components of literacy might fit together in the intentional activity of normal reading, let us first examine in turn the prior behaviors of active listening and looking.

The first thing we should note about listening is that it, too depends on the subject's attention. As a great deal of research has shown (7, 3, 21, 27), if a subject is asked to attend to one of two fairly rapid monologues that are being presented to him simultaneously, but in two different "channels" (e.g., one in a male voice and one in a female voice, or one in the right ear and one in the left ear), he *seems* to fail to "hear" the content of the unattended message; at least, he cannot recall it. Nor will the subject respond to some sets of words to which he has been instructed to respond, if they have been embedded in the unattended channel.

Such selective attention is often explained as being the result of a "filter" that passes the signals that are presented on the attended channel, but which attenuates or even blocks the other channel's signals. On closer examination, however, the filter analogy requires too many unlikely and complex properties to be very helpful. And in fact it is not true that we can say, *as a general statement*, that the content of the unattended message is unheard. For example, if both channels contain the same message, but the unattended one is delayed so that it lags behind the attended one, after a while most subjects realize that both messages are the same (27). As another example: If the subject's own name is presented in the unattended channel, he will tend to hear it even though it is not in the channel to which he has been instructed to attend. Now, while it is easy to see how one could "tune" a filter to select one frequency rather than another, or to select one ear rather than the other, it is hard to see how to construct a filter to work in terms of analyzed verbal meaning (9). For these and other reasons, Neisser (22) and Hochberg (14, 16) have argued that it is not necessary to invoke any filter at all in order to explain selective attention in listening; instead, we need to consider more closely what is really involved in attentive listening to speech.

The study of which sounds listeners confuse with each other, and which they can discriminate, lends some support to the proposition that we do not normally do much with the raw phonic elements of speech (20). We usually respond, instead, to larger packets of sounds, judging them to be one phoneme or another on the bases of certain distinctive features—distinctive features which tend to be those which distinguish the listener's own speech-producing actions, for example, tongue placement. The perception of word sounds may be accomplished, therefore, by a process of "analysis of synthesis," that is, by matching certain features of the sensory input against corresponding features of one's plans to articulate speech.

Neisser (22) and Hochberg (16) propose that listening to speech follows the same outline as listening to word sounds: In active listening, the subject has available to him in his own speech-generating repertory organized strings of language, that is, speech-generating plans which may be of the order of words, phrases, or even sentences in length, depending on the cliché content of the language habitually used. The listener unfolds or reviews these units as he listens, checking the stimulus input relatively infrequently to confirm or revise his hypotheses. Speech sounds that were not anticipated in this fashion, nor encoded and stored as part of some such higher speech structure, present too much unorganized material to retain, exceed the memory span for such unorganized and independent material, and cannot be recalled. This would explain what happens in the two-channel experiments, without recourse to any concept of a filter: The subject makes active anticipatory responses to the initial phonemes that he receives in the channel to which he is attending and stores the results of his testing of those expectations. Sounds that were uttered on the nonattended channel may be briefly stored as unrelated sounds and will usually fade from memory while the subject reports the message received on the attended channel. As we should expect from our analysis of the situation, the experiment cannot be performed unless the verbal material presented is organized into redundant and predictable sequences (19). This argument is presented in more detail elsewhere (16). What is important to us here is that if listening to speech rests upon anticipating the results of having sampled redundant trains of sound, then something like this hypothesis testing should also occur in reading, which is rooted in the listening and speaking processes.

Let us now turn to the skills that the subject must have acquired from his experiences in looking at scenes—skills which also antedate by many years his acquisition of reading abilities. Because our eyes register fine detail only within a very small region of the retina (the fovea), we must learn about the visual world by a succession of glances in different directions. Hence, like listening to speech, looking at scenes must occur by a temporal sequence of patterned stimulation. But whereas the listener only has the redundancy of ordered speech or music to guide his anticipations of what the next moment's stimulation will bring, the subject viewing a normal world has two sources of expectations: (1) Like the listener, he has learned something about the shapes to be expected in the world, and their regularities (14, 17); (2) the wide periphery of the retina, which is low in acuity and therefore in the detail that it can pick up, nevertheless provides an intimation of what will meet his glance when the observer moves his eyes to some region of the visual field. And because such changes in fixation point are executed by *saccadic movements*, whose endpoints are decided *before* the movement is initiated (i.e., saccades are *ballistic* movements), the content of each glance is always, in a sense, an answer to a question about what will be seen if some specific part of the peripherally viewed scene is brought to the fovea.

We do not know too much about the strategies and tactics of free eye-movement deployment in viewing scenes, but it seems safe to say that the major potentially informative parts of the scenes are scanned. This is followed by making whatever small excursions are necessary to fill in the detail needed to decide what is being looked at. There is, in general, a relatively high number of large saccades, a great deal of recursion, and nothing at all that should make it easy for a subject to keep precise track of the temporal order in which any search of the visual field has been executed, that is, no mapping of spatial order into temporal sequence. But this is just the task that faces the child when he first learns to read: He has to put together letters into words by a sequence of small adjacent fixations. Surely this is an un-accustomed task for the visuomotor system.[1] It is one which needs whatever assistance can be provided and is one which the reader will try to escape as soon as he can (Hochberg, 1964).

The task of reading text, which requires the child to make many small, sequential, adjacent saccades, can be made easier in various ways. The strain can be reduced by using large type or by moving one's finger under the type, letter by letter; above all, and most useful to the attainment of literacy, by "guessing" at what some syllable, or some word, or even phrase would turn out to be. This last point is particularly important. Normal text is highly redundant in many ways, so that the subject does not have to *see* every part of a letter clearly, or every part of a word, in order to know what is being said. In short, the subject will—and *should*—tend to "guess" at what is vaguely seen in peripheral vision—and the more he knows about the re-dundancies of spelling, grammar, and idiom employed by the text, or *the more the text approaches the patterns of speech that he is normally prepared to generate*, the more he can correctly anticipate the message, the more likely that his guesses will be right, and the fewer the fixations that he actually needs to make. But the knowledge is essential: Training for fewer fixations can be of little use if the anticipations are not correct to begin with and if consequent reinforcement stemming from the correctness of the guess and from the relief of the onerous necessity for small saccades does not occur.

This reminds us of what is, of course, one of the primary characteristics of skill in reading: the fact that the practiced reader needs shorter and fewer fixations in order to identify letters, to recognize words, to read text. How is this skill acquired, and on what psychological processes does it rest? Much of the research to this point has used the method of *tachistoscopic presentation*, in which the subject is shown letters or other stimulus patterns at some short exposure. In some ways, though with many reservations (15), we may con-sider the tachistoscopic presentation as being analogous to a single fixation that is made in the course of the reading process. Many years ago, Cattell (5, 6) showed that the exposure required to identify each of a tachisto-scopically presented set of unrelated letters increased as the number of letters increased. The exposure time required to recognize some familiar word or phrase is, however, no longer than that for a single letter. In other words, the skilled reader is "picking up" as a unit what the unskilled reader would have to identify by multiple fixations. Since then, it has been amply shown that subjects can recognize words and shapes with which they are familiar at shorter exposure times than are needed for material with which they are unfamiliar (13, 25). Here, then, is one obvious reason that the skilled reader can make fewer and shorter fixations in reading text. This does not mean, however, that he *sees* the letters any differently, that is, that his sensory processes have been affected. There are reasons to believe that these effects of familiarity occur because of the subject's *response bias*: He is more ready to respond with a given letter, word, or phrase even when only partial or no sensory basis for that response is actually present (10), and he can better *recall* familiar material. That is, as with speech sounds, we would expect that the arrangement of the letters of a completely unfamiliar word would soon be forgotten, whereas once the skilled reader has identified the stimulus as being a familiar word, he can generate all the individual letters in sequence whenever he is called upon to do so (assuming he can spell it), regardless of the number of letters involved. In support of this suggestion, we should note that it is possible to demonstrate effects of familiarity on tachistoscopic word recognition under conditions in which those effects are almost certainly due to the differential availability of memory units by which the strings of letters may be encoded and subsequently regenerated, and not due to differential sensory processing (12, 14). And the demonstration by Graf and Torrey (11) that comprehension scores are higher for written material that is broken at major linguistic boundaries than are comprehension scores for material broken at minor boundaries might be interpreted as the effect of greater ease of storing the material in the former condition.

By responding to the few features seen in clear foveal vision with an entire word or phrase, the skilled reader, then, has largely relieved himself of the necessity of looking closely at the text. He therefore needs to fixate only those parts of the array, further along the page, that will enable him to make new guesses and to check his previous ones. The better the reader, the more widespread can be the fixations by which he samples the text—just so long as the text provides him with contextual redundancy and as long as his task permits him to attend to the meaning or content, rather than to spelling or to individual letters.

The question then becomes, what guides the skilled reader's fixations? How does he decide what the text in question is, without looking at each letter?

As in listening to speech, of course, the skilled reader's expectations of what he will find when he looks further along the page are based in part on the syntax and on the meaning of what he has just read. In order for sampling to be possible, and for anything less than letter-by-letter reading to suffice, some redundancy, of course, is needed. With our present spelling and syntax, redundancy in the middle of long sentences is close to 100 percent. Like the listener, therefore, the reader can formulate and test speech fragments. He need not look at each letter because he can guess at the next n letters, and he knows enough about the constraints of language to make a profitable guess at how much further along he should look next in order to test these fragments and formulate new ones. Thus, it has been found that reading errors are influenced by associative factors and by language habits based on syntactic framework (8, 23, 24), which is what we would expect if readers' hypotheses are only intermittently tested. Call this determinant of fixation CSG for "cognitive search guidance" (15). Unlike the listener, however, the reader is not restricted to previous content as the source of his extrapolations because he can, in addition, use the information given in peripheral vision, as modified by his linguistic expectancies, to select the places at which he should seek successive stimulus input. Thus, at the very least, he should be able to anticipate, through the use of interword spaces that appear in the peripheral vision, where he must look in order to fixate the most informative portions of words (that is, their termini), and which words are likely to be short functors. Call such determinants of fixation PSG for "peripheral search guidance." The practiced reader must move his eyes under the combined control of CSG and PSG.

The beginning reader, who really must look at most or all of the letters, probably makes little use of PSG. He is, therefore, less hampered than is the better reader when the information available in peripheral vision is interfered with, for example, by filling in the interword spaces so as to make the word boundaries indiscriminable when viewed peripherally (15). Readers with "tunnel vision," that is, lacking peripheral vision, have very low reading rates. But, the discovery of what actually guides a skilled reader's fixations and how these can be improved calls for more than a simple demonstration of the importance of peripheral vision. One possible avenue of research, which we are currently exploring with Roger Nelson and Murray Glanzer, is to present the reader cinematically with a paragraph of text in which a simulated fixation point, that is, an area of clear vision containing four or five letters, appears successively at various places in the text. This procedure provides the reader with an incomplete sample of the page. The independent variables in this investigation are these: how the samples are taken; how the simulated fixation points are presented throughout the text; and the amount of information, if any, that is transmitted in the periphery of the field, that is, outside of the simulated fixation point. When the reader performs at or near his normal reading rate, we may assume that we have simulated his sampling procedure. In other words, we have given him the information he normally employs in terms of the units by which he normally reads.

This picture of skilled reading is one of successive extrapolations, not of information processing, letter by letter. If it is an accurate picture, it will explain why it appears as though really skilled readers are processing a tremendous amount of information per second, whereas, in fact, they are not—they merely know a great deal about the language and about writers. If we are to attempt to teach readers to make such extrapolations and to use them, we shall have to keep two things in mind: First, we must fit the text—which we are teaching them to anticipate—to the anticipations that their speech habits already provide; second, we cannot expect them to transfer such skilled reading habits to less idiosyncratic text until the appropriate habits of speech and knowledge have been built up.

But, are we talking about skimming or reading? In view of the fact that visual perception almost always entails a procedure of sampling from a display of stimulus information that is redundant for the perceptual task at hand—another way of saying this is that it is very hard to present the adult with a perceptual task to which none of his previous visual experience is relevant—it is hard to see how the distinction between skimming and reading can be maintained as an absolute one. That is, the distinction must be referred to the size of the units that the task requires the subject to process. For example, if the task is to detect blurred or broken serifs in the text, each letter must be fixated more than once; anything less is skimming. But this is not how people normally read, whether for entertainment or for information. It is plausible that children should be encouraged to predict and anticipate what is coming next in reading. The exact methods for so encouraging them, however, should be the subject for empirical study and not for speculation. Empirical studies are also needed to determine what the goals and the appropriate units are for the different intentions that initiate and maintain reading behavior, if reading behavior—as opposed to symbol recognition, orthography, or tachistoscopic perception—is to be understood in a way that is theoretically satisfying or socially useful.

Note

1. Adjustment to this task is not always satisfactorily achieved. Thus Taylor and Robinson (1963) found that inefficient early ocular motor activity may result in final motor habits which inhibit efficient reading after the original causes (difficulty with word identification and recognition) no longer exist.

References

1. BETTS, E. A. "Reading: Perceptual Learning," *Education*. Indianapolis: Bobbs-Merrill, 1969.
2. BRANDT, H. F. *The Psychology of Seeing*. New York: Philosophical Library, 1945.
3. BROADBENT, D. E. *Perception and Communication*. London: Pergamon, 1958.
4. BUSWELL, G. T. *How People Look at Pictures*. Chicago: University of Chicago Press, 1935.
5. CATTELL, J. McK. "The Time It Takes to See and Name Objects," *Mind, 11* (1886), 63–65.
6. CATTELL, J. McK. "The Inertia of the Eye and Brain," *Brain, 7* (1886), 295–312.
7. CHERRY, E. C. "Some Experiments on the Recognition of Speech, with One and Two Ears," *J. Acoust. Soc. Amer.*, 25 (1953), 975–979.
8. CLAY, M. "A Syntactic Analysis of Reading Errors," *Journal of Verbal Learning and Verbal Behavior, 7* (1968), 434–438.
9. DEUTSCH, J. A., and D. DEUTSCH. "Attention: Some Theoretical Considerations," *Psychological Review, 70* (1963), 80–90.
10. GOLDIAMOND, I. "Indicators of Perception: I. Subliminal Perception, Subception, Unconscious Perception: An Analysis in Terms of Psychophysical Indicator Methodology," *Psychological Bulletin, 55* (1958), 373–411.
11. GRAF, R., and J. W. TORREY. "Perception of Phrase Structure in Written Language," *Proceedings of the 74th Annual Convention of the American Psychological Association*, 1966, 83–84.
12. HAYES, W., J. ROBINSON, and L. BROWN. "An Effect of Past Experience on Perception: An Artifact," *American Psychologist, 16* (1961), 420 (Abstract).
13. HENLE, M. "The Experimental Investigation of Past Experiences as a Determinant of Visual Form Perception," *Journal of Experimental Psychology, 30* (1942), 1–22.
14. HOCHBERG, J. "In the Mind's Eye," in R. N. Haber (Ed.), *Contemporary Theory and Research in Visual Perception*. New York: Holt, Rinehart and Winston, 1968, 309–331.
15. HOCHBERG, J. "Components of Literacy: Speculations and Exploratory Research," in H. Levin and J. Williams (Eds.), *Basic Studies on Reading*, New York: Basic, 1970.

16. HOCHBERG, J. "Attention, Organization, and Consciousness," in D. Mostofsky (Ed.), *Attention: Contemporary Theory and Analysis* pp. 99–124, 1970. New York: Appleton-Century-Crofts.

17. HOCHBERG, J. "Units of Perceptual Analysis," in J. Mehler (Ed.), *Handbook of Cognitive Psychology*. Englewood Cliffs, N.J.: Prentice-Hall, forthcoming.

18. JUDD, C. H., and G. T. BUSWELL. "Silent Reading: A Study of the Various Types," *Supplemental Educational Monographs, 23* (1922).

19. LAWSON, E. A. "Decisions Concerning the Rejected Channel," *Quarterly Journal of Experimental Psychology, 18* (1966), 260–265.

20. LIBERMAN, A. M. "Some Results of Research on Speech Perception," *J. Acoust. Soc. Amer., 29* (1957), 117–123.

21. MORAY, N., and A. M. TAYLOR. "The Effect of Redundancy in Shadowing One of Two Messages," *Language and Speech, 76* (1958), 376–385.

22. NEISSER, U. *Cognitive Psychology.* New York: Appleton-Century-Crofts, 1967.

23. ROSENBERG, S. "Associative Factors in the Recall of Connected Discourse," *Psychonomic Science, 4* (1966), 53–54.

24. SAMUELS, S. J. "Effect of Word Associations on Reading Speed and Recall," *Proceedings of the 74th Annual Convention of the American Psychological Association,* 1966.

25. SOLOMON, R. L., and D. H. HOWES. "Word Frequency, Personal Values, and Visual Duration Thresholds," *Psychological Review, 58* (1951), 256–270.

26. TAYLOR, S. E., and H. A. ROBINSON. "The Relationship of the Ocular-Motor Efficiency of the Beginning Reader to His Success in Learning to Read," paper presented at the *American Educational Research Association Conference,* February 13–16, 1963.

27. TREISMAN, A. M. "Monitoring and Storage of Irrelevant Messages in Selective Attention," *Journal of Verbal Learning and Verbal Behavior, 3* (1964), 449–459.

12

The Representation of Things and People

Julian Hochberg

The study of pictures and the study of psychology as a scientific inquiry have long been intertwined. As our understanding of the processes of perception and learning has increased, we have had to alter our view of how pictorial communication takes place; conversely, various pictures and sketches, ranging from the early experiments with perspective drawing, through the Gestaltists' explorations of the laws of grouping, to the inconsistent drawings of Escher and Albers, have had profound implications for the study of visual perception.

In this paper, I shall try to bring current perceptual theory to bear on some of the issues that have been raised in the context of pictorial theory. First, however, we shall go back to da Vinci's early experiments on pictorial representations, and to the ways in which the two classical schools of perceptual theory dealt with the problems posed by those experiments. Leonardo offered the following method to discover the techniques by which pictures could be made:

> ... place a sheet of glass firmly in front of you, keep the eye fixed in location and trace the outline of a tree on the glass. . . . Follow the same procedure in painting . . . trees situated at the greater distances. Preserve these paintings on glass as aids and teachers in your work.

One of the reasons why Leonardo's window becomes a picture is because the pane of glass (Figure 12.1a, c), if perfectly prepared, would provide the eye with much the same distribution of light as would be produced by the scene itself (Figure 12.1b), and it is on the basis of the light reaching our eyes that we learn about the surfaces and distances in the world around us. This is one way of making a picture, then, if we define a picture as a flat object with a pigmented surface whose reflectance varies from place to place, and which can act as a substitute or surrogate for the spatial arrangement of an entirely different set of objects.

This paper was written with the support of NICHHD Grant 5-R01-HD04213.

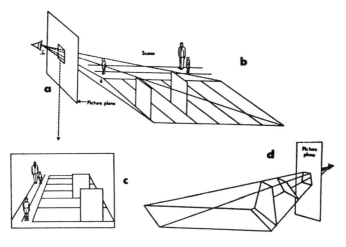

Figure 12.1.

In effect, when viewed from the same position as that at which the painter stood when he traced the scene, one of Leonardo's windows is a surrogate for the scene simply because it affects the viewer's eye in a way that is similar to that in which the scene itself does. Now, such pictures will not always cause us to see tridimensional depth, but then we will not always correctly perceive the nature of a real three-dimensional scene, either, if that scene is itself viewed with a fixed head from one position in space. But by examining the pictures produced by this method (or by functionally analogous but more sophisticated procedures) that do successfully portray depth, Leonardo took note of almost all of the depth and distance cues that can be utilized by the painter. That is, he noted those characteristics of the painted window that seemed to occur in conjunction with differences in the distance—characteristics that in fact would seem of necessity to occur frequently whenever one traces the projection of a three-dimensional world onto a two-dimensional surface.

The implications of this "experiment"—and of the prescriptions that follow from it—have been much debated (Gibson, 1954, 1960; Gombrich, 1972; Goodman, 1968; etc.). I believe that the extreme positions that have been taken in this controversy, and in fact the debate itself, are rooted in an erroneous assumption. This is the assumption, usually implicit and unrecognized, that a single domain of perceptual operation is involved in the processing of visual information and that a single set of rules will explain the relationship between the stimulus that confronts the eye and our perception of the scene.

This argument has centered mainly around one of the depth cues—*perspective*—and has come to rest heavily on this point: The pattern on the picture plane produces the same distribution of light and shade at the eye as does the original scene *only* when the observer regards the picture from the same viewpoint and from the same distance as that at which the picture was traced. Under these conditions the picture should in principle produce the same experience as does the scene itself. The problem arises for four reasons.

Why Is Only One Scene Represented by a Picture?

The picture, on the one hand, and the scene, on the other, can both produce the same pattern of light at the eye. This fact is an example of a very familiar and very general statement: There are infinitely many objects that can produce the same two-dimensional distribution of light.

It is also true, therefore, that there are infinitely many collections of objects and surfaces and distances that can be represented by any given picture, regardless of whether or not that picture is being viewed from the proper station point (Figure 12.1d). However, in most cases we see each picture as representing only one (or two) scenes, and because an infinity of scenes *could* be perceived, but only one *is* perceived, this means that we must consider more than the stimulus itself: We must consider the nature of the observer, who only responds to the picture in that one of the many possible ways. This is a good point at which to see how each of the two classical schools of perceptual psychology deals characteristically with this problem.

The Classical Perceptual Theories.   The older version, which we may call "structuralism" in order to identify it later on, was an *empiricist* theory: It asserted that the fact that we see the football field stretching into the distance in Figure 12.1, rather than the upright trapezoid, must be the result of our having learned to assume that things are square, that lines are parallel and not converging, etc. More specifically, this explanation proposed that our visual experiences consist of (i) *sensations* of different colors—light, shade, hue—and (ii) *images*, or memories of those sensations. Neither in viewing a scene itself nor in viewing the object that we call a picture are there any direct *visual* experiences that relate to the spatial characteristics of the scene. Space, it was contended, is a nonvisual idea, a *tactual-kinesthetic* idea (composed of the memories of touch and of muscle action) which our past experiences have taught us to associate with the visual depth cue. By careful analysis of the scene when we look at it, we note that we can indeed see the depth cues themselves—i.e., we can see that the lines converge—and we can note that there is no direct knowledge of space. This kind of observation makes the theoretical position plausible. It is also an example of introspection, that is, of the examination of our experience in order to identify its components, and what I can only call the causal relations between those components.

Aspects of this approach can still be found in uncritical analyses of the art of pictorial representation, for example, I see this object as being farther away *because* the perspective lines appear to be converging; I see this object as larger *because* it appears to be farther away; I see this man as angry *because* I see him scowling. Let us say right now that whether or not we really must learn to react to spatial differences (and there is good reason to doubt whether that is universally and necessarily true), there is one feature of structuralism that has clearly been discarded in psychology: It is the assumption that we can, by introspection, identify the elementary components of experience and that we can observe their causal interaction.

Because we cannot now accept conclusions based on introspection, much of what goes on in art theory—and aesthetic criticism—is on very dubious ground indeed. (This is why Gombrich's emphasis on artistic *discovery*, rather than insight, is particularly salutary.)

Structuralism, then, considered all *depth cues* to be symbols: the results of learned associations that have been formed between particular patterns of visual sensations and particular tactual-kinesthetic memories. What makes each of the depth cues effective (Figure 12.1c) is merely the fact that it has been associated with the other depth cues and with movement, touching, etc., in the prior history of the individual.

When we try to predict specifically what a particular picture will look like, whether it will in fact successfully portray the scene or object that it is supposed to represent, structuralism is not particularly useful. Here, it was *Gestalt theory*—the second of the classical perceptual approaches—which seemed to offer the more attractive account of the relevant processes. Instead of viewing perceptual experience as composed of individual, isolatable sensations of light, shade, and color—sensations to which images or memories of prior experiences become associated—Gestaltists proposed a "field theory": Each pattern of light stimulation which falls on the retina of the eye presumably produces a characteristic process in the brain, a process that is organized into overall fields of causation and that changes with each change in the stimulus distribution. Individual sensations are not determined by the stimulation at any point in the visual display (and in fact are not really to be observed in perceptual experience). In order to know what some stimulus pattern (e.g., any picture) will look like, therefore, we have to know how the observer's underlying brain fields will organize themselves in response to that pattern. In general, the brain fields will (presumably) organize themselves in the simplest (most economical) way possible, and knowledge of this fact permits us to predict how any picture will be perceived. Particular rules of organization can be extracted, for example, that we will see those shapes that are as symmetrical as possible (e.g., *x* rather than *y* in Figures 12.2a.*i, ii*; the "law of symmetry"); that we will tend to see lines and edges as uninterruptedly as possible (e.g., we see a sine wave and a square wave in Figure 12.2b.*i*, rather than the set of closed shapes shown in black at *ii*; the "law of good continuation"); that we will tend to see things that are close together as belonging together (the "law of proximity"; Figure 12.2d). We experience tridimensionality when the brain-field organization that is produced by a given stimulus distribution on the retina is simpler for a tridimensional object than it is for a bidimensional one. Thus, in Figure 12.2c.*ii* we see a

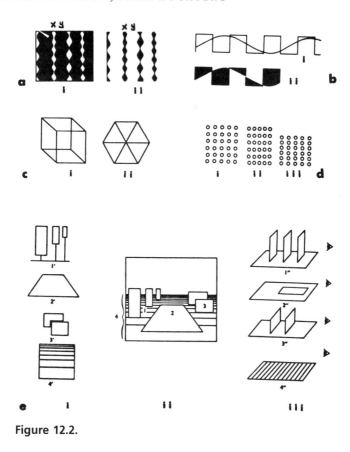

Figure 12.2.

flat pattern rather than a cube because we would have to break the good continuation of the lines in order to see the latter; in Figure 12.2c.*i*, the situation is reversed, and we see a cube. In Figure 12.2e, we see a dissection of the depth cues that had been identified in Figure 12.1. Note that in each case, the three-dimensional arrangement that we can see (*iii*) is simpler than the two-dimensional one (*i*), and it is (presumably) because the brain processes also are simpler in three-dimensional organization in these cases that these patterns act as depth cues. In short, to Gestalt theory, whether or not the depth cues are learned, they are not arbitrary, nor do they in any sense depend on memories of past tactual and kinesthetic experiences. What we see depends on the organizational characteristics of the brain field.

Arnheim is probably the chief exponent of this viewpoint today, in art theory. In perceptual psychology proper, exceedingly little adherence can now be found for the general approach, and the idea of brain fields as an explanatory principle seems to be just about totally defunct. The laws of organization, however, may still turn out to be gross but useful prescriptions for designing pictures so that they will be comprehended as we want them to be comprehended—although we should note that these "laws" have never been adequately formulated nor measured as objective and quantitative rules.

These are the two major classical theories of perception, and they have had their effects on theoretical discussions of art and pictorial representation. The last decade has seen vigorous and at least partially successful attempts to combine positive features of both of these classical approaches, and it will be to one such class of theory, and its relevance for pictorial representation, that we shall return. But first, let us continue with the other problems that are raised by Leonardo's experiment, and with which any adequate theory will have to cope.

Resistance of Pictures to Perspective Distortions; Tolerance of Inconsistencies

The second problem with taking Leonardo's window as the prescription for making good pictures is this: Pictures can be viewed from one or the other side of the proper point, or from another viewing distance, without destroying their efficacy as pictures and without offensive distortion (or even distortion that is noticeable) being reported. When viewed from an incorrect position, of course, the picture can no longer offer the same light to the eye as did the scene being represented: It now coincides with the light that is produced by a different "distorted" family of scenes (Figure 12.3). Nevertheless, it is frequently asserted that pictures can be viewed from various angles without any perceptual distortion. And, although I do not believe that such sweeping statements have any experimental support, it does seem to be quite clear that one can view pictures in an art gallery, or on the pages of a book, from viewpoints that are quite different from the proper point (the projection center i in Figure 12.1a) and not experience a noticeable distortion of the represented scene. In fact, as a loose corollary to this, we shall soon see that adherence to correct perspective is not always sufficient in order for things to look right. An even more telling point in this connection is that the discrepancy between the light produced by the picture and the light produced by the scene itself becomes even more drastic as the observer moves with respect to the picture. If he moves his head with respect to the *scene* itself, objects in the observer's field of view will shift their relative positions in accordance with the geometry of *movement parallax*; on the other hand, the parts of a *picture* retain their relative positions unchanged, lying as they do on the same plane. Because movement parallax is traditionally the strongest of all depth cues, it would seem that the picture as normally viewed (i.e., by the reader of a book or by the viewer in a gallery) must bear only a conventional and essentially arbitrary relationship to the scene being portrayed. For these reasons, and for others that we shall consider shortly, it has been strongly argued that the use of linear perspective must be considered an arbitrary,

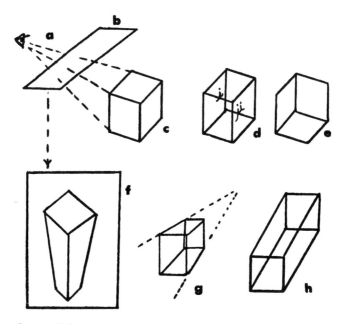

Figure 12.3.

learned convention—a "language of vision" invented by Western painters and accepted by dint of Western viewers' experience with perspective paintings. This argument receives some support from the fact that natives who have had little or no contact with Western pictures appear to be unable to interpret pictorial perspective; however, we should note that in such cases the perspective in question was conveyed by sketchy outlines, in pictures of very problematic fidelity. Even if it should prove true that the efficacy of such minimum sketches does indeed depend on the viewer's pictorial sophistication, that would not mean that the same would necessarily be true of more detailed and finished representations.

And the argument that grows out of the fact that we normally view pictures from some angle must also be rejected: Whether or not perspective is learned, it is in no sense arbitrary, and the fact that pictures can be accepted as representations of scenes even when they are viewed from an inappropriate station point has other explanations that are both plausible and interesting:

   a. Shapes and extents are usually determined more by the framework in which they appear than by the image that they present to the eye. Because the distortions that result from any displacement in viewpoint are imposed equally on the frame and on the major lines within the picture, as well as on any particular shape within the picture, the shape/frame ratio remains intact. The apparent shapes of building facades, arches, etc., should then also remain unchanged to the degree that framework is important in shape and size perception.

b. We don't really know how much perceptual distortion does indeed result from changing the viewpoint. In 1972, Gombrich suggested (and there is independent experimental evidence to support him) that distortions *do* appear in pictures that are viewed from an improper station point. When viewed from a slant, for example, the square facade on a pictured building may indeed continue to "look square," but its apparent slant toward the observer changes. This means that the scene that is being portrayed has changed, of course, in that the relative orientation between its parts have changed. Gombrich observes that the parts of a pictured scene do indeed appear to move and deform in their spatial relationships as the viewer moves relative to the picture—if the viewer pays close attention to these details. These changes are simply not noticed under normal conditions, which is part of the more general problem of *attention*, to which we shall have to address ourselves shortly.

Such distortions of the represented scene can, of course, be made noticeable by increasing their magnitude sufficiently. The perspective inconsistencies of a de Chirico are immediately evident. Also, the projection of the cube in the slanted picture plane in Figure 12.3b is clearly distorted if the picture is viewed normally (Figure 12.3f), whereas it becomes an acceptable cube if it is viewed from the central projection point (Figure 12.3a).

A closely related issue arises when we discuss the accuracy of projections of regular objects, like cubes. Consider the two cubes shown in Figures 12.3d and 12.3e: They cannot truly be pictures of cubes, although they may at first be taken as such. If they were indeed the projections of cubes, they would, of course, display some degree of linear perspective, as in 12.3g.

This fact has been used to support the argument that perspective representations are really only arbitrary conventions: If we are willing to accept the parallel lines of Figures 12.3c, d, e as *perspective*, then it must be as a mere convention that we do so—or so the argument runs. But this argument may rest on a false premise. Suppose the objects pictured in Figures 12.3c, d, e are not cubes, but are instead truncated pyramids whose sides *diverge* away from the observer, and whose farther face is larger than the nearer face. Perspective convergence then would just balance each object's divergence, and Figures 12.3c, d, e are thus perfectly good pictures. They are pictures of truncated pyramids, rather than of cubes, and we simply don't notice that fact. Farfetched? Consider Figure 12.3h, in which the distance between the front and back face has been increased, making the effect more noticeable.[1]

The object in Figure 12.3h can be seen in either of the two orientations shown in Figures 12.3c and 12.3e. When the object changes its apparent orientation, the two faces appear to change their relative sizes also, with the nearer face always the smaller. There is thus a *coupling* between perceived size and perceived distance: With a given pattern of lines confronting the eye, if the apparent distances change, the apparent sizes, angles, etc., also change correspondingly. (This is the clearest example of "perceptual causation" that I know, in which one aspect of what one perceives—i.e., orientation—seems to determine other aspects of what one perceives—e.g., size. And as such, it offers one of the few exceptions to the inutility of introspection: In this class of situations, it is meaningful to say, "X appears larger than Y *because* the cube appears to be oriented with side X farther away than Y.") In structuralist terms, this coupling occurs because we make unconscious inferences, that is, because we have built up strong perceptual habits in the course of our experience with the world.

In any case, however, we see that the fact that such nonconvergent perspectives as those of Figures 12.3c, d, e produce impressions of pictorial depth does not necessarily mean that linear perspective (and pictorial depth, for that matter) are arbitrary artistic conventions. Instead, such *non*convergent perspective drawings may be viewed as perfectly good *convergent* perspective drawings: drawings of objects whose sides diverge instead of being parallel.

Moreover, it is not safe to say that depth is portrayed as well by the nonconvergent perspective of Figure 12.3d as it is by the convergent perspective of Figure 12.3g, and that therefore both pictures rely equally on an arbitrary convention. As we adjust the angles and sides of the cube to make its representation consistent with the rules of perspective (making 12.3d into 12.3g), its apparent extension out of the picture plane and into the third dimension increases (Attneave and Frost, 1969). Thus, both aspects of the attempt to use nonconvergent-perspective pictures to prove that convergent perspective is merely an arbitrary convention must be seriously questioned. The pictures may really be perceived as convergent-perspective pictures of divergent objects, despite the artist's intentions; and the pictured depth may in fact decrease, as the picture departs from being a true convergent-perspective projection of a true (nondivergent) cube.

Lest this rebuttal lead us to discard too much, let us note that it leaves us with the necessity of explaining why (and how) we can so often fail to notice that the objects portrayed in Figures 12.3c and e are not cubes, and why we can tolerate the inconsistencies that must arise between the parts of any accurate picture when it is viewed from any point other than the projection center. In fact, as Pirenne has pointed out (1970), inconsistencies must often be introduced in pictorial perspective if the picture is to look right. An example of this is the use of circles in Figure 12.4a, instead of the ellipses that would have been consistent with the rest of the perspective used in that painting. That our eye tolerates, and may even demand, such inconsistency is a fact which makes Leonardo's window a poor model of what a picture is and how it works, regardless of whether or not perspective is a learned and arbitrary pictorial convention.

Let us attempt to account for why inconsistency is tolerated, by considering pictures with far greater amounts of inconsistency built into them.

b   **c**

Figure 12.4.

Consider the inconsistent pictures of Escher, and of Penrose (Figure 12.4b). Two kinds of inconsistency are patent which are both revealed more clearly in Figure 12.4c.

I think that these pictures are truly important for understanding perceptual processes. It is very hard to explain, in terms of any Gestalt analysis, why they appear to be tridimensional. Gestalt theory, it should be remembered, would say that the pictures will look solid only if the organizations are simpler in three dimensions than in two. In order for the represented object to look tridimensional, however, the line that is continuous—*as a line*—at x must in fact represent a *discontinuous* corner between two planes (i.e., a discontinuous dihedral angle). This is not the place to dissect out all of the implications of this sort of figure, but note these facts:

First, that the way in which the object appears to face depends on where one is looking (i.e., at i or at ii), and on the local depth cues that one finds there.

Second, that the tridimensional inconsistency between the two halves of the figure causes the figure neither to look flat, nor to appear to be broken in the middle, which tells us that the *good continuity* of a *line* (see Figure 12.2b) is a separate phenomenon from the *good continuity* of an *edge*. (I will argue later that this is because the two—line and edge—reflect two different tasks that can be pursued by the perceptual system.)

Third, the nature of the inconsistency is not immediately evident when the observer peruses Figure 12.4b, or even when he glances at the inconsistent "frame" of Figure 12.4c, unless the two inconsistent parts are brought close together. This suggests that certain aspects or features of the object are simply not *stored* while the observer looks from one corner to the other.

In other words, the explanation of why inconsistencies of pictured space can go unnoticed, may in part be this: The inconsistent regions of the picture are not normally compared to each other directly. This brings us to a major point, almost completely ignored by Gestalt theory: Any object is usually examined by a succession of multiple glimpses, and the various regions that are looked at each fall in turn on the same place in the eye. That is, the separate parts of the figure all have to be brought at different times to the central part of the retina, the fovea, if they are to be seen in full clarity of detail. Let us consider what this fact suggests about the perceptual process, and about the nature of pictorial representation.[2]

It is evident that when we read a line of type, the action depends on the movement of our eyes (Figure 12.5a), and that the same thing occurs when we look at a picture (Figure 12.6). From such successive glimpses, we must construct an integrated scheme that encompasses the whole scene. Mere persistence of vision is of course no explanation for the fact that we see a coherent picture, rather than a set of discrete views: Persistent vision would result only in the kind of superposition that we see in Figures 12.5b and 12.6c. Nor is successive vision merely a matter of having looked everywhere in the field, as does the scanning raster of a TV camera. The fact is that we do not look everywhere in the field, and the looking process is both an active and selective one. What we perceive of the world is determined therefore both by the processes that guide fixation, and by those that determine what we retain from a sequence of fixations.

These processes, in turn, depend on the observer's attention (and on his perceptual *intentions*), so that it is now evident that we cannot make a full accounting of pictorial representation in terms of Leonardo's window alone (nor in terms of any other analysis that restricts itself to discussions of the

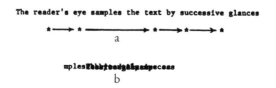

Figure 12.5.

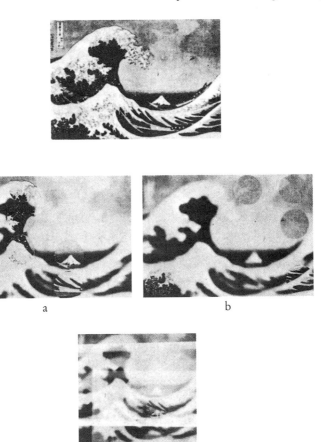

Figure 12.6.

stimulation of the visual system). This is so regardless of whether or not we take Leonardo's depth cues to be mere pictorial convention.

Perception as a Purposive Behavior

A frequent criticism of the classical perceptual theories was that they ignored the purposive nature of perception (Brentano, 1924; Brunswik, 1956; Bruner, 1957), and in examining perception with a view toward remedying this deficiency it will be helpful to consider first some of the main characteristics of purposive behaviors in general.

Analyses of skilled sequential behaviors (whether they be maze learning, skilled motor acts like typing or piano playing, or language production and perception) all suggest the existence of guiding structures: of "expectations," "cognitive maps," or "deep structure." From such cognitive structures, quite different specific detailed response sequences may be generated, all of which are equivalent only in that they produce the same end result. There is a long and continuing argument to this point that recurs at various junctions in psychological theorizing (cf. Tolman, 1932; Miller et al., 1960). I add here only that *most or all visual perception also involves highly skilled sequential purposive behaviors* and that some large component of the perceptual process in the adult is best understood in terms of the "expectations" and "maps" that underlie these skilled behaviors.

Skilled purposive activities are run off in accordance with organized plans, and their progress must be tested at appropriate points. That is, although such acts may initially consist of individual, more-or-less simple responses to individual stimulus situations, a very different kind of behavior emerges with continued practice: Entire *sequences* of actions are run off smoothly, with no need for an external stimulus to initiate each act. Moreover, such sequences are not merely "chains" in which each response has become the stimulus or "trigger" that sets off the next response. In playing the piano, in typing, or in speaking, responses are executed with such rapidity, and the interval between any two successive responses is so short, that there simply is not sufficient time for the nerve impulse that arises from the response in one set of muscles to travel to the muscles that execute the next response (Lashley, 1951). What then determines the sequence of muscular actions—e.g., what makes the fingers strike the keys in one order rather than another, or coordinates the sequence of tongue and lip movements in one order rather than another?

It is clear that our nervous systems can generate, store, and execute what in a computer would be called a *program*—that is, a series of orders, or *efferent commands*, that go out from the central nervous system to the musculature, that can be run off in sequence. The possession of skill depends on having a working repertory of such programs, such prearranged sequences of efferent commands. Such sequences have *goals*—i.e., states of affairs in the world that are to be brought about by these actions. This means that each program must also contain provisions for obtaining sensory information about the world at critical points in the sequence and for comparing that information to some desired state of affairs. This function was filled by the "image" in structuralist psychology: In that view, behavior was guided by sensory images, so that both the thought that guides the act and the information that terminates it were held to consist of sensory experiences, and of memories of these.

In fact, there is no necessary implication of consciousness in such behaviors, any more than there is in the response of a thermostat that governs the behavior of an automatic heating system by sampling the temperature of the room.[3]

Note that such purposive behavior programs have several characteristics of present interest: They are *selective*, in that only certain specific aspects of the environment are relevant to them (e.g., the thermostat is built to respond mainly to temperature differences and will usually be unaffected by musical notes). They are goal-directed, in that the programs are executed only in order to achieve some specific state of the world. These two characteristics will reappear under the names of *attention* and *intention* (those hitherto mysterious properties), when we turn to consider the behaviors that are specifically designed to gather information, i.e., the perceptual behaviors.

Perceptual behavior.   How one casts his gaze around the world depends therefore both upon his knowledge of the world and on his purposes—i.e., on the information that he seeks.

It is well known that we can only remember a small number of unrelated items in immediate memory—somewhere in the neighborhood of five to seven items. In order to remember a larger number of items, they must be committed to more permanent storage in an encoded form (i.e., in an abstracted, reduced, or symbolic form). Because the succession of our eye movements is often quite rapid (about four per second), an observer will normally make more fixations during the inspection of a single scene than he can hold in his immediate memory. Some part of his perception of the scene therefore must draw on encoded recollections of his earlier glimpses. We must next inquire, therefore, how the separate glimpses are put together over time into a single perceived scene, and how they are retained over a series of many discrete glances.

Because our eyes register fine detail only within a very small foveal region of the visual field, we must learn about the visual world by a succession of glances in different directions. Such glances are made by *saccadic* eye movements, whose endpoints are decided before the movement is initiated (i.e., saccades are *ballistic* movements): Where one looks is decided in advance. Therefore, the content of each glance is always, in a sense, an answer to a question about what will be seen if some specific part of the peripherally viewed scene is brought to the fovea. In viewing a normal world, the subject has two sources of expectations: (*i*) He has learned something about what shapes he should expect to meet with, in the world, and about their regularities; and (*ii*) the wide periphery of the retina, which is low in acuity and therefore in the detail that it can pick up, nevertheless provides an intimation of what will meet his glance when the observer moves his eyes to some region of the visual field.

The fact that looking at static pictures is a temporal process has always been evident to students of composition, who discuss "leading the eye" in some obligatory sequence over the layout of the picture. In fact, however, the actual *order* in which the parts of a picture are regarded is probably not well enforced under normal viewing conditions (cf. Buswell, 1935).

This freedom makes it difficult to begin our functional analysis of what we may call *active looking* (as opposed to passive or abstract staring) with the study of the skills that are involved in pictorial perception itself.

Let us therefore look first at the *reading skills*, in which the order of encoding is not free, but is enforced by the nature of language. These skills are acquired relatively late in childhood, moreover, so that we can examine their acquisition with relative ease (whereas many of the skills that underlie the perception of people, objects, and events are probably acquired largely before the age at which we can profitably study infants). This is partly due to the arbitrary nature of the symbols that are used in reading. (This is a good point at which to forestall a misunderstanding: I am not equating reading with picture perception. The symbols of art are not, in general, arbitrary; they are not learned in the same sense that we learn to read; and while the concept of a "language of vision" is not meaningless by any means, it is sometimes used in a very misleading sense in drawing unjustified analogies between reading and pictorial perception.)

Reading text letter-by-letter, as a child must do when he decodes words whose pattern he has not yet learned to recognize, requires the reader to make many small adjacent fixations in a fixed sequence. This is probably a very unnatural way of using one's eyes and quite contrary to the skills that we acquire in the cradle and that we maintain throughout our active visual exploration of an extended three-dimensional world. Small wonder that the task of letter-by-letter reading is aversive.

The task can be made easier in various ways, most simply by printing in a very large typeface, with a lot of space between the letters. But the best way is to outgrow the need for letter-by-letter (or even word-by-word) fixations.

Normal text is highly redundant in many ways, so that the subject does not have to look at every part of a letter clearly (nor at every part of a word) in order to know what is being said. In short, the subject will—and *should*—tend to "guess" at what is vaguely discerned in peripheral vision. The more he can correctly anticipate the message (by his knowledge of the spelling, grammar, idiom, and substance of the text), the more likely that his "guesses" will be right, and the fewer the fixations that he actually needs to make. But *knowledge* is essential: Training the reader to make fewer fixations can be of little use if his anticipations are and remain incorrect.

The skilled reader thus can largely relieve himself of the necessity of looking closely at the text, by responding with an entire word or phrase to the few features that he sees clearly in the foveal vision. He therefore needs to fixate only those parts of the text, further along the page, that will enable him to make new guesses and to check his previous ones. His expectations of what he will find when he looks further along the page are based in part on the syntax and meaning of what he has just read. In order for sampling to be possible, and for anything less than letter-by-letter reading to suffice, some redundancy is therefore needed. Given the redundancy of connected discourse, the reader formulates and tests speech fragments, and he knows enough about the constraints of language to make a profitable guess at how much further along he should look next in order to test those fragments and to gain information to formulate new hypotheses. In addition, he can use the information given in peripheral vision to select the places at which he should seek successive stimulus input.[4] The better the reader, the more widespread can be the fixations by which he samples the text—just so long as the text provides him with contextual redundancy, and so long as his task permits him to attend to the meaning or content, rather than to attend to the spelling or to the shapes of individual letters. Note that the skilled reader does not simply look at a block of text and automatically apprehend its message. He must *intend* to read the display, must "pay attention" to its meaning by developing hypotheses about what the next string of symbols consists of and by testing those expectations at appropriate places in the text further along. He must generate the material at which he has not yet looked on the basis of whatever fragments he has in fact seen. Any contents of his glances that were not anticipated in this fashion, and that were not encoded and stored as part of some such speech structure, will soon exceed the memory span for such unorganized and independent material. We would expect therefore that a completely unfamiliar word or passage would soon be forgotten, whereas once the subject has identified the stimulus as being some particular familiar word or phrase, he can generate all the individual letters in sequence whenever he is called upon to do so (assuming he can spell), regardless of the number of letters involved.

Let us now extend this analysis of an active, purposive, searching perceptual system, which we have examined in the context of the reading process, into the much richer area of the visual perception of objects and space.

The first point to remember is that the array of stimulation that is presented to the eye from a picture (as from the scene itself) is not simultaneously available to the brain: Only what falls within the eye's field of view is visible at all, and only what falls within the narrow span of the fovea is clearly visible. During a single glance at the Great Wave, in Figure 12.6, for example, the experience might be roughly like that obtained by looking at any one of the clear areas in Figure 12.6a. Successive glances will bring other parts of the picture into clear vision. These glances are not randomly distributed, but rather are directed to bring the most informative parts of the picture to the fovea (Buswell, 1935; Brooks, 1961; Pollack and Spence, 1968). For example, Figure 12.6a shows the five most frequent fixations that subjects make when they look at that picture (according to Buswell's eye-movement records), and it is clearly a more complete sampling of the picture's content than are the five least frequent fixations (Figure 12.6b). As in skilled reading, therefore, where we direct our foveas when we look at pictures is guided by the hypotheses that are generated by what we see in peripheral vision. And also as in reading, the integration of the successive glimpses that we receive when scanning a picture must depend on our ability to fit each view into some "mental map," into a cognitive structure that stores the information that each glance brings, in a form that enables us to return our gaze to any part that we may wish to reexamine. A mere persistence of vision, a merely passive storage of the successive glimpses, will not do: It would result only in a superposition such as that of Figure 12.6c, as different regions of the picture fall successively on the same parts of the eye. Instead, each eye movement tests an expectation, and what we perceive of the picture is the map that we have actively fitted together from smaller pieces in this way.

"To apprehend a pattern is to discern the principle on which its elements are ordered. To see the elements only will not suffice, for the pattern does not reside in the elements... [but] in the rule which governs their relations to each other.... Stereotyped vision sees only those patterns which its stereotypes have permitted it to anticipate" (Taylor, 1964). This is the basis of visual integration, the "glue" by which successive glimpses are joined into a single perceptual structure. If I have grasped the right "apprehended pattern," or *map*, my successive glimpses fit together into the perceptual structure so well that the stable form is easy to see and the component glances are difficult to detect. With no map (or with the wrong one), on the other hand, I have only momentary glimpses, erratic and disorganized.

So we see that at any given time most of the picture as we perceive it is not on the retina of the eye, nor on the plane of the picture—it is in the mind's eye (see Hochberg, 1968). And in that as yet mysterious domain, the scene being portrayed is stored in encoded form, rather than as a mental mirror of the scene. What is in fact encoded, as well as how it is encoded, depends on the observer's task, on what he can anticipate and store, and on where he looks. Unfortunately, we know very little about what is encoded and stored in the process of putting together a picture in our minds out of successive glimpses. The violations of perspective consistency that we discussed earlier seem to show that we do not normally encode and store all the metric aspects of a scene. Moreover, from Figure 12.4c, we learn that—even within the span of a single object—what we do not encode and store is lost to perception.

It is here that our familiarity with the artist's discoveries of how to portray the world must have its greatest effect (and perhaps its only effect) on our perception of pictures. But although Gombrich's point that such conventions are *discoveries* appears to be widely accepted, there seems to be little recognition that discoveries are *not* inventions, i.e., that the conventions are not necessarily arbitrary, that the artist is not free to design just any old language of vision that strikes his fancy. Let us here consider the use of lines on paper, which has been advanced as strong evidence of the arbitrary nature of the "language of pictures." Lines, which are merely ribbons of pigment, will fulfill the following functions in pictorial representation: They will act as the edges of surfaces (Figure 12.7a), as a sharp corner or *dihedral* (Figure 12.7b.*i*), as a rounded corner or *horizon* (Figure 12.7c.*i*), etc. Now,

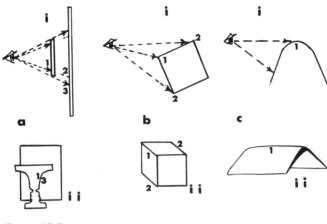

Figure 12.7.

a line on a piece of paper is really quite different from any of these edges and corners. So it certainly seems reasonable—at least at first glance—to assume that the use of lines for this purpose must be the use of an arbitrary convention. But the fact is that outline pictures are not, in principle, anything like a learned language: A nineteen-month-old child who had been taught his vocabulary solely by the use of solid objects, and who had received no instruction nor training whatsoever concerning pictorial meaning or content (and indeed, had seen practically no pictures) recognized objects that were portrayed by two-dimensional outline drawings as well as photographs (Hochberg and Brooks, 1962). Thus, if the ability to understand outline drawings is entirely learned (and it may not be; it may be innate), the learning must occur not as a separate process, but in the normal course of whatever learning may be needed in order to see the edges of objects in the world. In line drawings, the artist has not invented a completely arbitrary language: Instead, he has discovered a stimulus that is equivalent in some way to the features by which the visual system normally encodes the images of objects in the visual field and by which it guides its purposive actions.

Let us speculate about how such "conventions" must be learned by experience with the world of objects. Consider a real object's edge: If you move your eye across it, there is an abrupt increase in distance past that point. This fact has very considerable consequences for oculomotor behaviors. As long as you intend to move your eye from one point to another, there are no adjustments that the eyes have to make other than the move itself. Moreover, if the eyes are to fixate any point on the surface during or after the head has changed position, then the positions of all the points on the surface, right up to the object's edge (Figure 12.7a1), are *determinate* (i.e., each of them can be fixated by some definite eye movement), whereas each change in the head's viewing position should cause the object's edge to change the part of the background (Figure 12.7a2) that it hides from view. Thus, the *shape* (or set of fixatable positions) is determinate to one side of the object's edge, but not to both. Now these are the very figure-ground properties to which, as we have seen, the Gestaltists look for the new units of experience, and it seems very plausible in terms of the analysis that I have just described (cf. Hochberg, 1970, 1968) that these properties reflect, not the actions of "brain fields," but rather the existence of "expectancies" about the consequences of making eye and head movements while looking at an object's edge. Why do we have such expectancies? Because eye movements are programmed in advance of their execution (they are ballistic, remember). They must therefore be guided by expectations, based on peripheral vision, of what the fovea will confront. But why should such expectancies be aroused by lines on paper? Perhaps because much of the time that an edge between two surfaces appears in the visual field, it is accompanied by a brightness difference: that is, because of lighting, because of surface-texture differences, etc., a brightness-difference contour should provide a *depth cue* that can furnish guidance as to where in the periphery an object's edge will be found.[5]

This analysis, if it is taken seriously, contains at least two points that are of interest to our general discussion of pictorial representation. First, the efficacy of line drawings can tell us something about the ways in which we perceive and encode the world itself, not only about the art of pictorial representation. It is a possibility such as this, of course, that makes the study of pictorial art important to the perceptual psychologist.

But lines are merely part of the medium, as it were, and "artistic conventions" are much more matters of *pattern.* And for patterns, the only powerful generalizations still seem to be the laws of organization that Gestaltists demonstrated largely by means of line drawings. We can easily reach conclusions about the laws of organization that are similar to the conclusions we reached about outlines. First we note that the laws of organization are probably not merely arbitrary artistic conventions. The protective colorations by which animals camouflage themselves and render themselves invisible to predatory animals seem to depend on the same principles of organization that conceal familiar shapes from human eyes, and surely the predators have not been exposed to our artistic conventions (cf. Metzger, 1953). To the extent that such determinants of organization are learned, therefore, it must be chiefly by way of commerce with the objects in the real world. Next, let us see why the Gestalt laws of organization help us to perceive objects correctly, and might therefore be acquired (ontogenetically or phylogenetically) in the course of dealing with the world. We have noted that brightness-difference contours offer our peripheral vision cues to where the edges of objects lie. Of course, not all brightness changes mark objects' edges, horizons, or corners. Some are caused by shadow, some are due to layers of pigment, etc. There are, however, certain characteristics that tend to distinguish the brightness differences that are produced by edges and corners. For example, it is very improbable in nature that the edges of two surfaces that lie at different distances from the observer will by chance be so oriented to his line of sight that they will form a single continuous contour in his visual field. A continuous contour is a good indication of an object's edge. It is not surprising, therefore, that we are very sensitive to discontinuities of contours (Riggs, 1965) and that we tend to organize our perceptions in such a way that continuous contours are seen as being the edge or corner of a single surface (law of good continuation, already mentioned).

This is not to deny that the patterns by which we represent shapes in outline drawings are ambiguous, because they surely are: Figure 12.2c.*i* can be seen as a heptagonal flat pattern; the line at Figure 12.7c 1 *can* be seen as a flat curve (instead of a hemicylinder's horizon); etc. This is not to deny that these means of portraying objects and space must be *discovered*: After all, lines and flat patterns are not themselves the objects that they are used to portray (and, as we have seen, introspection will not in general serve to identify for us the features in a scene that cause us to perceive it as we do). Nor is it to deny that these methods of representation are very low-fidelity surrogates, in that they do not project to the eye an array of light that is identical (or even closely similar) to that produced by the scene portrayed.

Nevertheless, their ambiguity does not make such drawings arbitrary. I can identify, say, Moshe Dayan, by a variety of stimuli: (1) by printing his name in type (which *is* arbitrary, and does not involve the same perceptuomotor plans that I use when I see his picture); (2) by drawing an eye patch (which also is arbitrary as a label, but which does involve as well some of the visual features by which his face is encoded as a shaped object); (3) by a high-fidelity surrogate (a painting or photograph that offers the observer's eye the same light as Dayan does—surely nonarbitrary); or (4) by a drawing, which is composed of lines and is distorted so as to make sure that we encode the drawing—a flat, static pattern of pigment—as a solid, mobile face. Far from arbitrary, this last method permits us to bypass the accidental patterns and textures that are presented to the eye from any specific viewpoint of the object itself, and to select only those features that the viewer will encode and store in ways that we want him to. This is, of course, most clearly exemplified in the process of deliberate *caricature*. In attempting to understand that process, the study of visual perception must set aside its reliance on purely geometrical analyses of stimulation and start to confront the more refractory problems of how form, movement, and character are encoded and stored.

Caricatures of Objects

Let us note first that caricatures, in the sense of pictures that capture the "essence" of some represented object, are not restricted to the portrayal of people or animals. In fact, it will be easier to approach the problem of what is meant by "capturing the essence" if we examine first the caricaturization of objects' physical properties, in which essence is more readily described, and then return over the same ground in a discussion of the portrayal of such "nonphysical" properties as expression and character.

The two patterns in Figure 12.2c.*i, ii* are both equally good (or equally bad) projections of a cube, but it is surely the case that Figure 12.2c.*i* is closer to the *canonical form* of a cube—i.e., to the features by which we encode and remember cubes. It is hard to remember where and how the lines break, even while you are looking at Figure 12.2c.*ii* with every intellectual conviction that it is a cube. Figure 12.2c.*i* has caught more of the essence of a cube. In this sense, most of the demonstrations by which Gestalt laws of organization were studied (and especially those in which reversible-perspective figures were employed) represent experiments on, and prescriptions for, the caricature of tridimensional objects. In general, however, more attention has been paid to camouflage—that is, to making objects harder to perceive—which is in a sense the inverse of caricature.

I know of only one experimental study directly concerned with caricature. Ryan and Schwartz (1956) compared four modes of representation: (a) photographs; (b) shaded drawings; (c) line drawings that were traced from the photographs, and thus were projectively accurate; and (d) cartoons of the same objects (Figure 12.8). The pictures were presented for brief

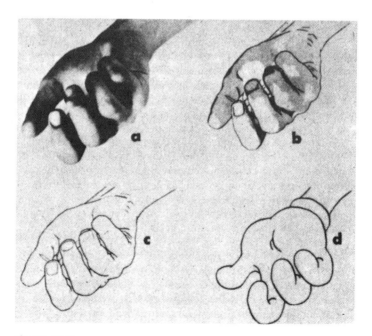

Figure 12.8.

exposures, and the subject had to specify the relative position of some part of the picture—e.g., the positions of the fingers in a hand. The exposures were increased from a point at which they were too brief, until they were sufficient for accurate judgments to be obtained, with this finding: Cartoons were correctly perceived at the shortest exposure; outline drawings require the longest exposures; and the other two were about equal and fell between these extremes.

Why is the cartoon drawing correctly grasped at more rapid exposure than the high-fidelity photograph? The contours that have been retained, for one thing, have been "simplified." That is, smooth curves have been substituted for complex and irregular ones. Information about the anatomy of the hand is lost in the process (the picture is thereby made more redundant); it now requires fewer fixations to sample it and to make predictions about unsampled portions; those features that have been retained require fewer corrections to be applied to our encoded schemas (cf. Hebb, 1949; Hochberg, 1968), or canonical forms, of these objects. Moreover, the portrayed object is probably recognizable further out into the field of peripheral vision. For this reason also, fewer fixations are required, and these are probably executed with firmer expectations of what will be seen.

Although no one has actually tested the peripheral recognizability of these stimuli, the following reasons underlie the above assertions: (1) Increasing the smoothness and redundancy of the curves in Figure 12.8d must increase the efficacy of peripheral vision, which is poor on small detail and "noisy." (2) Wherever contours intersect in the cartoon drawing, the artist has deliberately rearranged them so that they meet at right angles; whether because of good continuation, or as the depth cue of "interposition," this arrangement should make unambiguous to the observer which edge is the nearer one, perhaps even in peripheral vision. (3) Wherever the contours in the cartoon represent the boundaries of "holes" or spaces, their relative separation has been increased. This in turn has two consequences: (a) Each contour is more clearly separable from its neighbors, even in peripheral vision; (b) as we have seen, the factors of contour proximity and enclosedness tend to make a region become figure (i.e., to be seen as object). Increasing the separation between two fingers, for example, increases the size of the regions which we are intended to see as empty space and thereby keeps the spaces from being seen as objects.[6] (Note that the process that we have been talking about is the *inverse* of camouflage, in which the laws of organization are used to make objects seem like spaces and to make local pigmentation on one object look like other objects' edges.)

The caricature has thus been made better than the more accurate pictures by accentuating those distinctive features (cf. E. J. Gibson, 1969) by which the tridimensional nature of objects is normally apprehended. It seems plausible that as a particular caricature of an object is picked up and used by other artists (see Gombrich, 1956), the pattern *as a two-dimensional design* may, by progressive simplification in passing through the eyes and hands of successive artists, entirely lose its projective relationship with the object. When that happens, we are left with only an arbitrary relationship between the symbol and its referent. But because the distinction between arbitrary symbol and a distorted, simplified caricature may not be a sharp one, this does not mean that the latter is just as arbitrary and as conventional as the former. Consider the differences between learning to read text and learning to "read" comic strips: Very few children learn to read text of their own accord, i.e., without undergoing formal instructions and a great deal of paired-associates learning (learning what sounds go with what graphic symbols). Comic strips, on the other hand, may contain many graphic symbols that are indeed arbitrary, but they must also have so many features which they share with the real world in a *nonarbitrary* fashion[7] that no formal education, nor paired-associates learning, is required: Once the viewer grasps the nature of the idiom, no further instruction seems to be needed.

The problem with what I have just said, however, is this: What can the object that is portrayed in the caricature in Figure 12.8d have in common with the hand (i.e., the object that is accurately projected) in Figure 12.8a? Two possible answers apply here.

The first answer is one which we have already considered in passing, that various objects with which we are familiar have *canonical forms* (i.e., shapes that are close to the ways in which those objects are encoded in our mind's eye). Throughout history, for example, artists have tended to draw certain familiar objects from standardized positions. Pirenne has argued (as we noted) that the use of such shapes, whether or not they are appropriate to the perspective of the scene in which they are embedded, helps us to perceive the objects in undistorted form, even when the observer views the picture from some position other than the projection center. As I understand Pirenne's argument, when the observer automatically corrects for the slant of the picture's surface, the object being represented will quite naturally still be seen in its canonical form (because that is the way it is projected on that surface). Whether or not this particular explanation will survive quantitative experimental inquiry (to which it is susceptible, but to which it has not yet been subjected), the selection of canonical views—and the violation of projective fidelity in order to keep the views canonical—makes of each such picture a caricature of a scene. Why is the violation, the projective inconsistency, not noted by (or not bothersome to) the spectator? Because those features of the picture are not encoded, nor stored from glance to glance, any more than are the directions of sides *i* and *ii* in Figure 12.4c in the absence of special instruction. This may also be the case with Figures 12.8d and 12.8a; the sausages of the one, and the digits of the other, may both be stored in terms of the same visual features.

The second answer is this: In addition to the *visual* features of the represented object, there are also *non*visual features that might be encoded, or that might offer a partial basis for encoding. In the experiment of Ryan and Schwartz, the task of the subjects was to reproduce the position of the fingers in the picture by placing their own fingers in the same position. As far as the task of reproducing the hand position is concerned, the accurate drawings, in which the fingers of rigid sections bend at the joint, may be less like what we actually *feel* that we do (muscularly) when we curl our fingers. Thus, the caricature might in fact not only be as informative as is the accurate drawing: It might even be more directly informative for the task that the subject is to perform. This, then, is a second way in which such visually disparate patterns as Figures 12.8d and 12.8a might be alike, i.e., in the bodily response that we make to them. This is not a novel idea: It rests at the heart of an old theory of Theodor Lipps', the *empathy theory*, that has recently resurfaced in somewhat different proposals by Gombrich and by Arnheim (1969), and we shall return to it shortly.

Little research (and not much more speculation) has been devoted as yet to the nature of the perceptual encoding and storage of such physical caricatures. We cannot judge, therefore, whether either or both of these answers are even partially true. The general question of how visual forms are encoded has recently begun to receive a great deal of attention, however, and the next few years may bring us relevant information. For the present, we shall see that the same issue arises again in connection with the perception of faces, whether they are pictured veridically (i.e., in perfectly accurate projection) or in caricature, and in that context we shall be able to add a little to the discussion of the issue.

The Representation of Faces: Likeness and Character

The world of rigid objects is full of physical regularities. Some of these are manmade (e.g., the prevalence of right angles and parallel edges); some are natural (e.g., the relationship between image size and distance that generates linear perspective). For this reason, it is usually easy to ask whether a picture looks distorted, because the subject has some idea of what any scene is likely to look like even if he has never seen it before: A de Chirico looks distorted, though the landscape portrayed may be completely unfamiliar. But what of *nonrigid* objects or, more specifically, what of that class of semirigid objects, *faces*, of which portraits are made?

Gombrich has recently focused attention on three problems of long standing. Two of these are posed by the fact that faces as objects differ both because persons differ in their permanent physiognomies, and because any person differs from one moment to the next as the features deform in nonrigid transformations (Gibson, 1960). How, then, can we tell whether or not a portrait is a good likeness or distorted, if we don't know the sitter? Again, how do we know whether a particular configuration of a pictured face (e.g., flared nostrils) represents the resting state of a person with that particular physiognomic endowment, or presents instead a momentary expression that is temporarily deforming the resting state (e.g., a sneer)?

Obviously, in both cases, there are limits to what we are prepared to accept as accurate likenesses. No one really ever looked like an El Greco or a Modigliani portrait, and surely nobody considers these paintings to be accurate projections of freakishly elongated sitters. There must also be some limits to the degree to which any picture is ambiguous about expression and endowment: Surely no one takes the anguished pictures of Munch or Goya as the resting states of deviant physiognomies.

The third problem is related to the other two. Why do we seem to attribute expression to stimulus patterns which in some cases seem appropriate to elicit such responses (i.e., human faces that have their features disposed in some familiar emotional display), but which in other cases seem remote from both expression and affect? Among the cases that seem difficult to explain are those in which people seem to agree about the affective qualities of what appear to be meaningless "doodles" of line on paper (Arnheim, 1966). And if such doodles evoke affective or emotional responses in their viewers, does it not seem reasonable and economical to regard our responses to portraits as being special cases of this more general "aesthetic" or "expressive" response to visual patterns? The Gestaltists' solution was that the same brain fields were produced by the doodle, by some portrait's pattern of pigment on canvas, and by our own affective state, but such a solution is much too general to be useful.

Partly in response to these problems, Gombrich has proposed that faces are encoded by expressive content and that this encoding is not so much in visual as in muscular terms. This idea lay at the heart of Lipps' theory of empathy. Lipps attempted to explain aesthetics in terms of the emotional or reactive response that the observer makes when he looks at even relatively simple stimuli. What makes this idea attractive is that it seems to explain the affective qualities that are so frequently attributed to even abstract and nonrepresentational art, and to explain the expressive response that we seem to make to faces that we do not know, or even to the barest caricatures.

To say that we encode our fellow humans in terms of our own muscular response may be treated as a poetic statement. However, it can also be given specific meaning, and can be used to predict which aspects of people we cannot distinguish or remember—that is, those aspects to which there is no appropriate empathic muscular response. For example, Gombrich has suggested that this is why we may not be able to describe the eye color or nose shape of someone even though we can recognize him with no hesitation at all. This suggestion might imply a very strong form of the muscle-movement encoding explanation: that *only* muscular programs are stored. But surely the strong form is neither plausible on a priori grounds nor is it supported by the results of experiments on face recognition and on expression recognition.

The problem is really one for which psychologists have devised techniques of varying efficacy to study, attempting to determine the nature of the imagery used in some psychological process (or, more accurately, the dimensionality of storage).

In general, as we have seen, introspective discussions are not very useful, and this is as true of imagery as it is concerning perception in general. Techniques have been worked out to give us more objective measures of the kinds of information that are being encoded and stored, however, and, although these measures do not in general correlate well with subjects' own ratings about their strengths of imagery, they do have their own validity. Three general kinds of methods have been used. The first is to show that the information in question is better acquired by one sense modality than by another—say, by visual presentation rather than by auditory presentation. This technique is probably not directly applicable to the kinds of imagery that we have been discussing. The second is to show that the subject can perform tasks that are more appropriate to one sensory modality than to another. For example, if we flash an array of numbers briefly on a screen, and then ask the subject to read off the diagonal numbers from his memory, it seems more likely that he can do this if his memory is visual than if his memory is verbal in its structure. Gombrich's point about our inability to remember eye color offers support for the reality of nonvisual storage, according to the logic of this second method. We might also expect, applying this logic to the strong form of the empathy theory, that after having viewed pictures of strangers, we would not be able to identify them when intermixed with pictures of other strangers if the first set of sitters wore different expressions on the second presentation than they had on the first occasion. But the fact is that we can recognize them under these conditions (Galper and Hochberg, 1971), so it is not easy to maintain that we encode and store people only in terms of their expressions (whether muscularly or otherwise).

The third method for measuring imagery is by introducing interference of one sensory kind: If I can disrupt the observer's performance by visual distraction and not by auditory distraction, then the memorial machinery involved is in that sense more visual in its structure than auditory. Kowal and I have addressed an experiment of this kind to the hypothesis that expression is encoded in terms of kinesthesis or muscular plans. We have recently been presenting subjects with a set of pictures of a single face, in a sequence of different expressions, presented at a rate of three per second. The subject's task is to identify the order in which the expressions occur, by pointing to a set of still pictures of the same faces. Because the sequence occurs too rapidly to permit the subject to respond between any two presentations, he must encode and store the entire sequence and then review it in deciding the order of occurrence. Because too many different expressions are presented for the subject to retain in his immediate memory, he must look at the sequence several times before he is able to do it correctly. During one of the conditions of viewing, the subject is required to execute a rapid series of different facial expressions himself; in this condition, both his motor plans and his kinesthetic imagery might be expected to interfere with his recognition of the sequence of faces, to the degree that expressions are encoded muscularly. Unfortunately, we have not been able to demonstrate any interference with the subject's encoding of the set of expressions, nor with his ability to report the order of their occurrence.

The evidence against the strong form of the empathy theory is by no means definitive, but it certainly does not urge us to accept the theory. The empathy theory in its strong form would have provided a set of constraints concerning our responses to faces, and a repertory within which the effects of any portrait could be explained. In order to find a new basis for explaining how we perceive and depict faces, let us reexamine the problem.

The problem is to explain the affective and expressive response that we make to faces, and to explain how we can distinguish good likeness from bad and distinguish temporary expression from permanent facial structure. The empathy theory explains at most why we make expressive responses to visual patterns. It is, in the following ways, very much like the early empiricist explanation of depth perception. Because there seemed to be no way of accounting for perceived space purely in terms of the properties of those pictorial patterns that are called depth cues, and because the perceptual attribute of *space* itself seemed so clearly characteristic of the tactual-kinesthetic memories of actions made in the tridimensional world, the spatial properties of pictures were attributed to the tactual-kinesthetic imagery they presumably aroused. The empathy theory, for very similar reasons, offers a similar explanation of face perception. As in the case of the depth cues, neither the logic nor the evidence is compelling. When we examine the perceptual habits that the observer is likely to bring to the contemplation of portraits— habits evolved in the service of actively looking at faces to extract information that is needed to anticipate others' behavior and to guide one's own—the nature of facial representation takes on a different form.

In the case of space and object perception, we had both a general rule about how we would see a given picture (i.e., that we perceive the arrangement of objects in space that would most usually project the same stimulation to the eye as the picture does), and one or two plausible theories to explain the origin of the rule.

What is there to represent in pictures of faces? First, of course, if we know the sitter, we might ask whether the picture is a good likeness in the sense that we can recognize the picture as his portrait. But even if the portrait is of some unknown person, it still communicates some information, just as does a landscape of some particular scene which we have never actually confronted, and we can notice whether the information is consistent. Some of the information is about the sitter's physical characteristics, such as the configuration and coloring of the head as a semirigid object, and information about gender, age, and race. Some is about the sitter's temporary state, for example, his emotional expression. And some seems to be about his character. How can all of this be represented by one and the same set of features?

When I first mentioned the problem of how it is that we can tell whether the picture represents a transient expressive deformation or a permanent physiognomic endowment, I noted that there are limits to what we might be willing to accept as physiognomic endowment—nobody will take Munch's *The Shriek*, for example, as a face in repose. This point becomes very much more important when we consider the *patterns* in which expressive deformations must normally occur.

Temporary expression and permanent endowment are not necessarily antonyms. It is not an all-or-none matter that we see the feature *either* as temporary expression *or* as permanent endowment,[8] and part of the problem can be resolved by considering this point in some detail. In particular, the problem dwindles when we note that the features of the face are not usually viewed in isolation any more than single words are read with no context. Consider: A *momentary* widening of the mouth is clearly an expression—say, a fleeting smile. But a widened mouth can also be a much more protracted deformation, without being a truly ineradicable physiognomic feature, for example, it might be a characteristic *stance* of that person, indicating his willingness to be obliging. Of course, it might indeed be an ineradicable physiognomic endowment, having nothing to do with either a momentary emotion or with any more long-term readinesses (i.e., it may offer the viewer a label by which to identify the person being portrayed, not a signal about his probable behavior).

Is it true that we cannot tell these apart? I don't think so. Physically, the facial muscles move in gross expressionlike patterns in response to simple innervation (Duchenne, 1876), and the stretching and contracting of the tissues of the face, across its rigid substructure, offer redundancy to the eye of the observer. In a simple and genuine smile, for example, the mouth is stretched, *and* the eyes will be "crinkled" (Figure 12.9a.*i*). In a voluntarily assumed smile, in which the actor innervates the muscles that pull his mouth wide, a much smaller set of local deformations will be involved; for example,

Figure 12.9.

the eyes may remain undisturbed (Figure 12.9a.*ii*). In order to distinguish these two states—which have different meanings in social interaction—the viewer must learn to note the relationship between mouth and eye as a feature that distinguishes between the two states; this would seem to be a task no harder than his learning the phonemes that separate one set of speech sounds from another (e.g., *r*attle from *c*attle).[9]

The fleeting smile will engage the eyes and cheeks, as well as mouth, in a pattern of tensions that cry out their transience and imminent resolution. Such a portrait will seem to catch a frozen moment and may tell us little about the sitter save that he or she is capable of that human action. One can, of course, use the fleeting expression to identify the picture itself, or to identify the moment, but it would clearly not do to identify the person: It signals its own change and disappearance.

In the case of a prolonged or habitual smile, on the other hand, the tensions must be minimal (e.g., the eyes may be attentive or grave, but not crinkled up), and we see a state that may last for some time. Note that a picture, unless otherwise marked so as to indicate its momentary and un-characteristic nature, will probably be taken as being the typical state of the object or scene depicted, inasmuch as it would be a statistical improbability that the picture would have been taken at some uncharacteristic moment. (This is similar to the reason why *good continuation* is such a powerful organizational determinant.) The picture then allows us to predict (perhaps wrongly) the nature of the person's response-readinesses. Or it shows the face with several local deformations, which we can identify as being *some* stance, but we may not know what the behavioral consequences are (as in *La Giaconda*). In both cases, the portrait has more-or-less obvious "character." That character will also serve to identify the sitter, as well as to help predict his social responses, to the degree that the pattern of features is clearly a habitual or nonmomentary expression. (Many habitual expressions probably have their own signs that identify them as such.) Thus the apparent paradox of how we can judge whether or not the portrait of someone we have never seen has captured his character is resolved. The answer to whether we choose to regard a given feature as being an expressive deformation, or a relatively permanent characteristic, may be "both."

Before we turn to the last case, the deviant physiognomic feature (as opposed to the momentary expression or the habitual stance), there are two questions that we should consider with respect to the stimuli for "charac-ter": (a) *Can* we respond to such "higher-order variables" (Gibson, 1950, 1960, 1966) that involve not one, but several different features (e.g., wid-ened lips, slightly indented mouth corners, noncrinkled eyes) with a single unitary response (e.g., "calm amiability")? And, if so, (b) *why* do we do so?

With respect to whether we can so respond: The answer seems to be a qualified yes, with the qualification being that it may take somewhat longer to do so than it does for single features. Consider the features that go into identifying the age of a sitter whom we have never seen. We can tell whether his hair is prematurely gray, or whether his face is prematurely wrinkled, or whether he simply has sunken jaws, etc. Although not one of these cues, taken alone, defines the sitter's age, we can make quite finely graded estimates of how old he is, and recognize him as the same sitter that we have seen in another portrait. The problem, as Gombrich here recognizes, is very close to that of how expression is perceived, and the solution seems to me to be the same: We have learned the local and higher-order features of age that are common to all men (and unadorned women), and there are features of physiognomic endowment that do not normally vary much either from one age group to another or from one expressive deformation to another.

There is a qualification that should be appended: The distinction between "higher-order" and "local" features that I am making here is based on whether a given stimulus feature can be detected during a single glance, in which case it is a local feature (i.e., it may be a compact pattern that falls entirely within the field of foveal vision in a single glance, or a pattern that is sufficiently gross to be recognizable even when much of it falls in peripheral vision); or conversely, it may require several glances to sample the characteristic pattern of stimulation (e.g., mouth corners, cheeks, and eyelids), and as a higher-order feature it will therefore take longer to apprehend (at least 250 msec per glance) and will require facilities for encoding, anticipating, and storing the widespread pattern between glances.

The next question to consider is *why* we respond to such cues about the temporary, habitual, and permanent characteristics of the sitter.

The momentary emotional expressions (and some of the more protracted stances, such as *vigilance*) have been with the species a long time. They have probably served as signals that, when manifested by one actor, demanded attention and responses (of vigilance, attack, flight, sexual approach, etc.) from all observers, long before our present facile human speech developed. Given the neural mechanisms for emitting these facial (and bodily) behaviors as signals to the other members of one's group, it seems very likely that *partial* gestures are soon learned to help us in less emotional communication. Understanding speech (like reading) probably places very high demands on one's anticipations and expectancies, and the speaker's stances will help reduce the listener's uncertainty about a verbal message, or about the general nature of the speaker's intentions (e.g., truculent, attentive, amiable, deferential). Such distinctive features of the social interaction should be as subject to learning as are the phonemes by which the listener learns to distinguish one word from the next. And this should be true not only about anticipating speech messages per se, but in steering the complex but finely tuned "interaction rituals" by which social contact is shaped and maintained (Goffman, 1967).

Bear in mind both the fact that it takes time (and several glances) to survey the higher-order expressions and the argument just made that facial expressions serve as signals to guide social interaction (and active listening) by shaping the participants' anticipations. We should then expect that, in general, even a single local part of a higher-order expression will come to serve as a signal and will have *some* expressive effect on the viewer, for example, a widened mouth, even without confirmation from the eyes, will be a tentative basis for assuming a smile (Figure 12.9a.*ii*). Local cues (that is, departures from the norm of what features should look like in their resting state) are like initial syllables in words: They may be disconfirmed or confirmed by subsequent events, but meanwhile they probably affect the observer's expectations. This brings us to the final case, the deviant physiognomic feature.

The person with the wide mouth has one of the local features of a smile—but it is only one feature, and all of the other confirming cues will most likely be missing (i.e., it is improbable that he will also just happen to be so endowed that his eyes, in resting state, are crinkled up as they would be in a genuine smile). If the rest of the face is merely neutral (Figure 12.9a.*ii*) and does not actually disconfirm the smile, the face will probably be encoded as having a smiling stance. After long acquaintance with the sitter, I should be able to identify those specific and idiosyncratic signs that would enable me to disconfirm the stance that is (spuriously) signaled by his wide mouth. But otherwise, the wide mouth should affect my expectations about him. And, of course, a person's physiognomic endowments *do* affect our judgments of his expression, even though (or especially because) we cannot tell *precisely* what his resting state is. There is a great deal of experimental evidence supporting the obvious fact that perfect strangers, even with their features "in repose" (if features are ever fully in repose while the subject lives), appear to have discernible character traits. Thus subjects show a great deal of consistency in their judgments when they are asked to evaluate, from photographs, the characters or personalities of persons whom they have never seen before (see Secord, 1958), and when they are asked to decide what a person intended to convey by an ambiguous statement that was included in a briefly described social situation (Hochberg and Galper, 1974).

My argument here is very close to those I have proposed earlier to explain the efficacy of outline drawings and of the Gestalt laws of organization (i.e., that lines serve as cues about the object's edges that we should expect to find when we sample the visual field), and to explain the reading process (i.e., that the letters and word forms that we glimpse in one fixation serve as cues about those that we can expect to find when we sample the text further on). My present proposal is that a person's expressive features serve to signal what that person will do next (Hochberg, 1964), thereby serving primarily to reduce the observer's uncertainty about what the other person intends to say or do. If a local feature has the shape it would have in one of the common paralinguistic gestures, and if it is not disconfirmed by other features, it will therefore evoke an "expressive expectation" on the part of the observer. Features that do not have any place in an expressional deformation (e.g., a high forehead) may also have affective connotations for two reasons: (1) They may present a relationship that is also presented by some expressional deformation (e.g., raised eyebrows); or (2) they may deviate from the norm in the direction of some well-established model that carries its own set of expectations with it (e.g., being babyish).

Thus we can account for the fact that faces, even in repose, have expressive effects on the viewer, and we can do so without necessarily calling on the empathy theory. Furthermore, even isolated lines will usually share some feature of their shape with some expressive stance, as long as the viewer approaches them as expressive features. This is especially so when there is no way to check any other features in the (nonexistent) face (Figure 12.9a.*iv*). This is then one of the powers of the caricature: By eliminating disconfirming features, it can present the sitter's wide mouth, which is characteristic and which everyone recognizes, as an expressive stance instead of as the physiognomic endowment that it may in actuality be.

This explanation assumes that the lines and patterns of a caricature have the effects they do because they are encoded in the same way as the expressive gestures to which we must normally attend in dealing with people. Thus, the symbols of cartoon iconography are not arbitrary in the sense that they have to be learned by experience with the artist's repertoire of expressive elements. Although we have no research to the point, it does seem that at least some minimum content of the comic strip can be comprehended without specific instruction: Even untutored children recognize (and revel in) cartoons and comic strips.[10] In most cases the cartoon is "wrong" in the sense that it does not produce the same sheaf of light rays to the eye that the object does. What features of Mickey Mouse can be made to coincide with those of a real mouse? or with those of a human? Nevertheless, the way in which the physiognomy and expression of Mickey Mouse is encoded and stored *must be identical in some fashion* to the way in which those of a mouse—and a human—are stored. Inasmuch as it is very likely that these similarities are not merely the result of having been taught to apply the same verbal names to both sets of patterns (i.e, both to the features of caricatures and to the features of the objects that they represent), what we learn about caricature will help us understand how faces themselves are perceived.

One way we might discover the features of caricature is by exploiting what Gombrich has called "Toepffer's law": making systematic variations in drawings of faces and discovering their effects on the viewer. Some work has been done on this, mostly by using very simplified drawings such as those of Figure 12.9b (Brunswik and Reiter, 1937; Brooks and Hochberg, 1960). Subjects seem to agree about the relative mood, age, beauty, intelligence, etc., of such pictures, and as aspects of the stimulus pattern are changed, subjects' judgments of entire sets (or "packets") of traits follow suit. Pictures in which the mouth was high were judged as being gay, young, unintelligent, and unenergetic (Brunswik and Reiter, 1937; Samuels, 1939). There is some reason to doubt whether such simple drawings can really be treated as a set of caricatures of faces and whether the results of such inquiry can be applied to more complex and veridical pictures and photographs (Samuels, 1939), but that is a matter for empirical inquiry in any case, and it seems abundantly clear that fruitful research is possible with such tools.

I know of no research addressed to the relative comprehensibility of caricatures of people versus veridical portraits and photographs, but it seems very likely that recognition would be faster for good caricatures than for nondistorted pictures. In addition to the factors adduced in connection with the Ryan and Schwartz experiment, there are three other reasons why caricatures may be more effective than photographs, reasons specific to the caricatures of people.

As a first point, we should note that caricatures make possible a more compact visual vocabulary. That is, caricatures use a relatively small number of features by which to represent a much larger set of faces. (Remember that we are using the word "features" in a general sense that applies to text, to speech, and to objects and not solely to the gross anatomical parts of the face that are frequently intended by that term.) There are at least three reasons why a relatively small set of features will suffice:

1. Although the anatomical parts of human physiognomies may differ from each other in very many ways, and in very many gradations, some of these differences are effectively imperceptible.
2. More important than the fact that some of the ways in which faces differ from each other are imperceptible is the fact that *we do not need to notice all of the ways in which faces differ from each other in order to tell them apart.* For any set of faces, each of which we may wish to be able to identify rapidly and with assurance, the set of features that we must have if we are to identify any individual face can probably be considerably smaller in number than the set of features that actually varies from one person to the next. That is, the differences between people in any group are probably *redundant* in the technical sense of that term (Garner, 1962). Thus the observer need only identify the population of faces being used (e.g., heads of state, stage celebrities, the cast of characters of a particular comic strip), and for this task a small visual vocabulary will suffice. This implies what Garner and his colleagues have demonstrated to be true for the recognition and storage of abstract patterns (1963, 1966): that the qualities (and identifiability) of a particular stimulus depend on the total set of stimuli to which the viewer attributes it. (I believe that the same applies to what is usually meant by "aesthetic value," but that is another story for another time.) In illustration of this point: An eye patch can identify Moshe Dayan only in the context of politicians; in children's tales, the eye patch might signify Old Pew; and in a company of pirates, it identifies no one.
3. Finally, we have seen that inconsistencies are tolerated in pictures that simply would not be possible in physical reality, and this means that

the caricaturist is free to choose features so that each is close to its canonical form (i.e., so that each feature is approximately in the form in which it is remembered), and so that the pattern formed by the arrangement of the features is also close to *its* canonical form, even though no face could ever be seen in this way from a single viewpoint.

These factors should all contribute to making the caricature more readily comprehensible than the veridical picture or the perfect photograph that stimulates the eye in exactly the same way as does the person being portrayed. If, in addition, an "accidental" feature of physiognomic endowment that is so characteristic of the person as to identify him can be presented in a way that is also characteristic of some expressive stance (which, in turn, is germane to the context in which we must think of that person—see Gombrich, 1956, p. 344), it might well be that the caricature can change our attitudes toward that person. Research on the nature of caricature may thus be as central to the study of how we perceive and think about people as research on Leonardo's depth cues was central to the study of space perception.

Summary

In the simplest sense, an object may be "represented" by replacing it with any other object that projects the same pattern of light to the viewer's eye. The problems here are predominantly geometrical ones, and Leonardo's prescriptions were to this point. But why we see pictures as represented scenes, rather than as patterned canvases, and why we not only tolerate but require major "distortions" or departures from projective fidelity in scenes and portraits alike—these are predominantly psychological problems, often taken as demonstrating the symbolic and arbitrary nature of "pictorial language." Even our perception of a static picture, however, requires that successive glances be integrated over time (just as when we read text or watch motion-picture montages) and consists therefore mostly of memories and expectations that reflect a much more rapid and intimate interaction with the world, and with its signals about what the next glance may bring, than is connoted by the concept of "symbols." The fundamental features of pictorial representation are probably learned by commerce with the world itself (where learned at all, and not innate), not established by arbitrary convention that the artist is free to devise at will.

Notes

1. There are several reasons why the effect might be expected to be more striking in Fig. 12.3h than in Fig. 12.3d: Thus, in 12.3d, it is harder to overlook the

fact that faces *i* and *ii* are of equal size on the printed page, because the lines that describe their edges fall simultaneously within the clear foveal region at the center of the retina; again, because the front-to-back distance is increased in Figure 12.3h, the amount of divergence needed to compensate for perspective convergence is also greater, etc.

2. In passing, let us note that this means that we simply cannot retain the Gestaltists' model of the nervous system, in which object properties are explained in terms of simultaneous interactions that occur within some hypothesized field within the brain.

3. That is, the program may be concerned with one or more kinds of information—e.g., photic (visual), phonic (auditory), thermal, etc.—but that does not, by itself, require that the effective device (e.g., the heating system) have conscious images of visual, auditory, or thermal experience. All we can say is that the *dimensionality of an expectation* is given by the sensory modality against which it is checked. A program that is checked against one predominant modality will thus have the characteristics of being guided by one kind of imagery.

4. For example, he should, by noting where the interword spaces fall in peripheral vision, be able to anticipate where he must look in order to fixate the most informative portions of words (i.e., their beginnings and ends), and he should be able to anticipate which words are likely to turn out to be articles and prepositions.

5. But still—why *lines*, which are probably not, after all, the kinds of contour that we most frequently encounter? Perhaps the answer is this: There are structures in the visual nervous system that respond to the contour between regions of different brightness, and the same mechanisms probably respond to lines as well. And so, unless the viewer has had much more experience with lines on paper than he has had with the brightness differences that arise at objects' edges, lines that fall in the periphery of his eye should serve as stimuli appropriate to objects' edges. This poses an interesting contrast to the more traditional proposal that our responses to line drawings are learned from pictures. From the present viewpoint, if we could really expose people to outline pictures of the world more than they are exposed to the world itself, the pictures would cease to "work" as representations.

6. Here we may note one source of "aesthetic value," in passing: It has been suggested over and over again, in visual art as in other art forms, that economy is a (or even *the*) cardinal virtue. Economy must be distinguished from *simplicity*, which we discussed earlier: One and the same pattern may be either more or less economical, depending on whether it is taken as representing a simple or a complicated object (cf. Figs. 12.2c. *i* and *ii*). But for a pattern of given complexity, the more economical it is as a pictorial representation, the more satisfying it may be to recognize the object in the picture. This will interact with another source of satisfaction. Because simplicity of representation can be achieved in different ways, we can expect that different artists will find characteristically different ways of doing so; and the recognition of the artist's "signature" will help the viewer to perceive the represented object and will also give some tangible value to this cultural expertise (i.e., to the ability to identify the artist).

7. Or, more accurately, stimulus features to which the visual system responds in the same manner as it does to stimulus features frequently encountered in the normal (nonpictorial) environment.

8. A tempting analogy to the expression/endowment problem is offered by the depth cues illustrated in Figure12.2e. In the case of the depth cues, it is true in one

sense that they cannot both be flat patterns and layouts in depth: The railroad cannot both be parallel and converging. Of course, they are not both, in space: The railroad tracks themselves are parallel; it is their projection in the picture that converges. To some degree, it is true that this physical coupling of *exclusion* is mirrored in perceptual experience: At any time, we tend to see either the flat pattern *or* the spatial layout. But even here, as we have seen, we respond to both in the sense that the judgments of pictorial depth are usually a compromise.

9. Note that it is the overall inherent (and inherited) simplicity of innervation of some facial expressions that makes them difficult to mimic. This is what makes it easy to produce stances that will *not* be confused with spontaneous expressions and makes it easy to detect insincerity—an ability that it should be very profitable to investigate.

10. We don't know how much (and what kind of) pictorial education underlies the ability to recognize cartoons, but it is clearly not of the paired-associates variety (e.g., man=*l'homme*) that is involved when adults learn new languages; moreover, as we have seen, some features of normal perception must also be tapped by cartoon recognition.

References

ARNHEIM, R. *Toward a Psychology of Art.* Los Angeles: University of California Press, 1966.

———. *Visual Thinking.* Los Angeles: University of California Press, 1969.

ATTNEAVE, F., and FROST, R. "The Discrimination of Perceived Tridimensional Orientation by Minimum Criteria." *Perception and Psychophysics 6*(1969): 391–96.

BRENTANO, F. *Psychologie von Empirischen Standpunkt.* Leipzig: Felix Meiner, 1924–25.

BROOKS, V. An Exploratory Comparison of Some Measures of Attention. Master's Thesis, Cornell University, 1961.

BROOKS, V., and HOCHBERG, J. "A Psychological Study of 'Cuteness'." *Perceptual and Motor Skills 11*(1960): 205.

BRUNER, J. S. "On Perceptual Readiness." *Psychological Review 64*(1957): 123–52.

BRUNSWIK, E. *Perception and the Representative Design of Psychological Experiments.* Los Angeles: University of California Press, 1956.

BRUNSWIK, E., and REITER, L. "Eindrucks Charaktere Schematisierter Gesichter." *Zeitschrift f. Psychol. 142*(1937): 67–134.

BUSWELL, G. T. *How People Look at Pictures.* Chicago: University of Chicago Press, 1935.

DUCHENNE, G. *Mécanisme de la Physionomie Humaine.* Paris: Baillière et Fils, 1876.

EPSTEIN, W., PARK, J., and CASEY, A. "The Current Status of the Size-Distance Hypothesis." *Psychological Bulletin 58*(1961): 491–514.

ESCHER, M. *The Graphic Works of M. C. Escher.* New York: Duell, Sloan and Pearce, 1961.

GALPER, R. E., and HOCHBERG, J. "Recognition Memory for Photographs of Faces." *American Journal of Psychology 84*(1971): 351–354.

GARNER, W. R. *Uncertainty and Structure as Psychological Concepts.* New York: Wiley, 1962.

———. "To Perceive Is to Know." *American Psychology 21*(1966): 11–18.

GARNER, W. R., and CLEMENT, D. E. "Goodness of Pattern and Pattern Uncertainty." *J. Verb. Learn. Verb. Behav. 2*(1963): 446–52.

GIBSON, E. J. *Principles of Perceptual Learning and Development.* New York: Appleton-Century-Crofts, 1969.

GIBSON, E. J., OSSER, H., SCHIFF, W., and SMITH, J. *Cooperative Research Project No. 639.* U.S. Office of Education.

GIBSON, J. "A Theory of Pictorial Perception." *Audio-visual Communications Review* *1*(1954): 3–23.

———. *The Perception of the Visual World.* New York: Houghton Mifflin Co., 1950.

———. "Pictures, Perspective and Perception." *Daedalus 89*(Winter 1960): 216–227.

———. *The Senses Considered as Perceptual Systems.* Boston: Houghton Mifflin Co., 1966.

GOFFMAN, E. *Interaction Ritual.* Garden City: Anchor, 1967.

GOMBRICH, E. H. *Art and Illusion.* Princeton: Princeton University Press, 1956.

———. "The 'What' and the 'How': Perspective Representation and the Phenomenal World." In *Logic and Art: Essays in Honor of Nelson Goodman*, ed. Richard Rudner and Israel Scheffler. Indianapolis: The Bobbs-Merrill Co., Inc., 1972. Pp.129–49.

GOODMAN, N. *Languages of Art: An Approach to a Theory of Symbols.* Indianapolis, Ind.: The Bobbs-Merrill Co., Inc., 1968.

HEBB, D. *The Organization of Behavior.* New York: Wiley, 1949.

HOCHBERG, J. "Attention, Organization, and Consciousness." In *Attention: Contemporary Theory and Analysis*, ed. D. I. Mostofsky. New York: Appleton-Century-Crofts, 1970.

———. *Perception.* New York: Prentice-Hall, 1964.

———. "In the Mind's Eye." In *Contemporary Theory and Research* in *Visual Perception*, ed. R. H. Haber. New York: Holt, Rinehart and Winston, 1968.

———. "Nativism and Empiricism in Perception." In *Psychology in the Making*, ed. L. Postman. New York: Knopf, 1962.

———. "The Psychophysics of Pictorial Perception." *Audio-Visual Communications Review, 10*(1962): 22–54.

HOCHBERG, J., and BROOKS, V. "The Psychophysics of Form: Reversible-Perspective Drawings of Spatial Objects." *American Journal of Psychology 73*(1960): 337–54.

———. "Pictorial Recognition as an Unlearned Ability: A Study of One Child's Performance." *American Journal of Psychology 75*(1962): 624–28.

HOCHBERG, J., and GALPER, R. E. "Attributed Intent as a Function of Physiognomy." *Memory & Cognition, 2*, 39–42, 1974.

LASHLEY, K. S. "The Problem of Serial Order in Behavior." In *Cerebral Mechanisms in Behavior: The Hixon Symposium*, ed. L. A. Jeffress. New York: Wiley, 1951.

METZGER, W. *Gesetze des Sehens.* Frankfurt: Waldemar Kramer, 1953.

MILLER, G. A., GALANTER, E., and PRIBRAM, K. *Plans and the Structure of Behavior.* New York: Henry Holt and Company, 1960.

PIRENNE, M. H. *Optics, Painting, and Photography.* London: Cambridge University Press, 1970.

POLLACK, I., and SPENCE, D. "Subjective Pictorial Information and Visual Search." *Perception and Psychophysics, 3* (1-B)(1968): 41–44.

RIGGS, L. A. "Visual Acuity." In *Vision and Visual Perception*, ed. C. H. Graham. New York: Wiley & Sons, 1965.

RYAN T., and SCHWARTZ, C. "Speed of Perception as a Function of Mode of Representation." *American Journal of Psychology 69*(1956): 60–69.

SAMUELS, M. R. "Judgments of Faces." *Journal of Personality, 8*(1939): 18–27.

Secord, P. F. "Facial Features and Inference Processes in Interpersonal Perception."
    In *Person Perception and Interpersonal Behavior*, ed. R. Tagiuri and L. Petrullo.
    Palo Alto, Calif.: Stanford University Press, 1958.
Taylor, J. *Design and Expression in the Visual Arts.* New York: Dover, 1964.
Tolman, E. C. *Purposive Behavior in Animals and Men.* New York: Century, 1932.

13

Higher-Order Stimuli and Inter-Response Coupling in the Perception of the Visual World

Julian Hochberg

Gibson's most intriguing and most powerful concept, and one that unites and underlies many of his far-flung interests and proposals, is his idea that there exist higher-order variables of stimulation to which the properties of the objects and events that we perceive are the direct and immediate response. His proposal is that many or most of the properties of the perceived world are evoked directly by the variables of stimulation that the sensory system receives from the normal ecology and are not the end products of associative processes in which kinesthetic and other imagery come to enrich two-dimensional and meaningless visual sensations with tridimensional depth and object meaning.

This proposal appears in various forms.[1] But it is with distance and the distance-related properties of objects and scenes that Gibson has been most concerned, because these properties confront us with the most general of the traditional problems in perception and cognition. Gibson, while a revolutionary in some respects, must be understood in terms of the traditional psychological concerns and methods. I shall therefore first review very briefly the context in which Gibson's proposals are both radical and promising, and then consider the major issue that I see must be faced in order to profit from those proposals.

The Theoretical Context

The Task and Terms   The general problem of perception is to explain (account for) the perception of objects and events. We must distinguish the following domains of measurement and phenomena: (1) *the physical property of the object*—for example, the object's size, S, in inches; (2) *the proximal stimulus*, that is, the physical effect of that object property on the sensory organ—for example, the size, s, of the object's retinal image, in degrees of visual angle; (3) *the percept*, that is, the apparent size, S', of the object; this cannot be measured directly, of course, but is inferred from (or sometimes identified with) some set of responses, R_s, that the subject makes to the object. Note that S is usually measured directly; s is calculated (although in principle it could be measured directly); and S' is a *construct*, which may, if we are lucky, bring a more elegant and parsimonious structure to our description of the relationship between stimulus and response than we can otherwise obtain (Hochberg, 1956). Disregarding many fine distinctions, the following main alternative ways of accounting for the perception of the world can be and have been proposed:

(1) The distal stimulus causes (determines, accounts for) what we perceive, and as we perceive, so we act and respond. A diagram of this primitive account is this:

$$ S \;\text{---}\!\!\!\!\dashv\; S' \;\dashv\!\!\!\!\text{---}\; R_S \tag{1} $$

The dotted lines enclose the "mental" events of "perceptual experience." If you decide that S' doesn't add much to the account, make it $S \rightarrow R_s$. Neither the original formulation, nor the behaviorist elision, will do, however. Two very different objects will be indistinguishable if they produce the same proximal stimuli, so that objects and their physical properties simply are not the adequate stimuli for predicting either perception or behavior.[2]

One reason why the object doesn't *determine* the percept is, of course, because the object affects the sense organ only by way of the proximal stimulus (for example, by way of the retinal image). But the proximal stimulus doesn't determine the final percept either, because the two different proximal stimuli may produce the same receptor response. For example, a mixture of light made up of components of 640 and 550 nm and a pure light of 580 nm both produce the same effect on the end organs of the eye. So the next approximation of Formula 1 expands the first one to become:

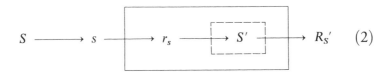

$$ S \longrightarrow s \;\text{---}\!\!\!\!\rightarrow r_s \;\text{---}\!\!\!\!\dashv\; S' \;\dashv\!\!\!\!\text{---}\; R_S' \tag{2} $$

The solid line encloses the processes that occur within the organism; as before, the dotted line encloses "perceptual experience." We can in theory extend the analyses of physiological processes deeper into the sensory system, a flourishing field of research by which the perception psychologist must not be seduced but which he cannot fully ignore. But, as it is, the main players are now on stage, and the main problems of perception can now be displayed. The father of this inquiry is, without question, Helmholtz, whose system and analyses comprise the heart of the theoretical context of present inquiry.

Helmholtz's "Atomistic" Solution.   Objects and scenes differ from each other in a vast number of ways, and any explanatory system must account for these differences. Johannes Müller explained the modality differences (sound, sight, touch) in terms of specific sensory receptors that are attuned to the specific kinds of proximal stimulation (e.g., to pressure waves, to photic energy, to skin deformation). His pupil Helmholtz accounted in similar manner for *all* discriminable differences, even those within modalities, for example, each discriminable and indivisible point of color is attributed to the stimulation of a specific visual receptor. The visual receptor is stimulated by photic energy; thus, a particular receptor might be most affected by light of 580 nm, but it can also be stimulated in other ways, such as by mechanical pressure, or by photic energy at other wavelengths. In any case, its response, r_s, remains the same. And the experience, S', that accompanies the receptor response, also remains the same, regardless of what the stimulus was; in the case of the receptor that is maximally responsive to 580 nm the experience would be a dot of "yellow light." Thus, in Formula 3, any object S_1 is perceived as an ensemble of separate primitive sensations $(s_a', s_b', \dots)$ corresponding to each receptor response. (The other features of that formula will be discussed later.)

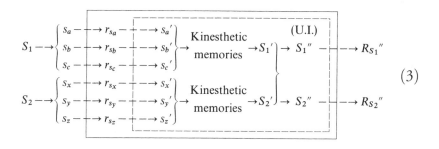

$$(3)$$

For vision, this would mean analysis of the field of view into points of color. This analysis may be *sufficient* to describe the proximal stimulus field as a flat field, but it leaves out, of course, most of the apparent object properties that we started to explain—solidity, distance, size, and so on. These properties of the apparent world can theoretically be constructed, however, from the points of color by processes of perceptual learning: The entire weight of empiricist philosophy has it that the world we know is built up by associations of such simple ideas as color and direction. Such associations are presumably formed between any frequently encountered set of visual sensations and the proprioceptive sensations that are experienced in consequence of the organism's reaching, touching, turning its eyes, and so forth, in its commerce with the real world.

No "naive realism" here. Philosophy has yet to extricate itself completely from this essentially idealist and solipsistic position (cf. Ayer, 1972). But the system has an appearance of lean elegance: A finite set of specific nerve energies (r_i) and of elementary experiences (s_i') provide the elements from which the vast rich world we know is built up by our experiences with the real world itself. And before we abandon this viewpoint completely, as impatience with history impels us to do, let us note that this approach survives, with minor modifications, in much more modern thought and in many current "models" of pyschological process.[3]

Elegance suffers on closer inspection, however: It is now perfectly clear that the *sensations*, s_i', have no observable existence; local spots or small patches of color are simply not elements of experience; how some small region in a scene looks is not predictable from its appearance when it is presented alone. Moreover, the spatial properties of the various regions of the retinal image (e.g., the size and shape of a particular patch of light) are not well reflected in the experience; these interactions are variously known as *contrast, illusions*, etc. The sensations thus become unobservable constructs rather than observable elements. Presumably they have become swamped by the weight of our experience with objects (Mill, 1869; Helmholtz, 1925) and are no longer consciously available because we have no call to respond to them as such (Helmholtz, 1925).

But then what *do* we perceive, given some set of objects (distal stimuli, S)? Helmholtz proposed (in essence) that we perceive the object, scene, or event that would *normally* fit the proximal stimulus distribution. This follows reasonably from the general empiricist position. And in fact this rule would be expected to follow from a nativist position, as well, if "normally" is defined by the ecology of the species rather than by that of the individual. In more detail, Helmholtz proposed that the perceiver performs something like a calculation based on his sensations in order to estimate what the object characteristics would be—but that both the sensations that are drawn upon, and the calculations that are made, are not consciously noted, and only the perceptual "conclusions" are experienced. This is the famous doctrine of "unconscious inference," and in the case of the example that we have been following—namely, object size, S_1—it would work as follows. The proximal stimulus subtended by the object elicits the set of sensations of adjacent similar color, $s_a' + s_b' + s_c'$. Because of past experiences with the eye movements that would traverse such an extent of the proximal stimulus, these sensations of color, in conjunction with their associated kinesthetic memories of those movements, produce a percept of size, S_1'. But this percept is so far one only of extensity in two dimensions, i.e., it corresponds to the proximal projection of the object—what Gibson has called the "visual field" (Gibson, 1952). At the same time that the observer is receiving the proximal stimuli, $s_a + s_b + s_c$ from the object, S_1, however, he is also receiving proximal stimuli $s_x + s_y + s_z$ from other parts of the proximal stimulus field, or *optic array* (Gibson, 1957). These other stimuli allow the observer to establish the object's distance, S_2, from the observer. For example, S_2 might refer to the perspective of the ground plane on which the object stands (although before Gibson, few theorists paid particular attention to the ground plane as a source of information about distance). And the sensations, $s_x' + s_y' + s_z'$, coupled with their associated kinesthetic memories (such as those of reaching, accommodating, and converging), are added up to form the percept of distance, S_2'.

We are now almost through, but we have still to take distance into account in order to be able to infer object size, S_1'', from perceived extent, S_1'. In the real world of physics and Euclid, an object's distal size, S_1, will be proportional to its distance, S_2, if it is to maintain a given proximal extent. That is, for a given proximal stimulus (and a given retinal excitation), object size $= k$ (object distance). If this knowledge has been incorporated into the observer's visual system through commerce with the physical world, and the appropriate calculation is performed on S_1' and S_2', then we finally arrive at S_1''—the perceived object size. We have labeled this unconscious process of computation as U.I. in Formula 3; all of the contents of the dotted box are now to be viewed as unconscious events as well as mental ones and hence not directly measurable.

If this is too complicated to use for purposes of actual prediction—and it usually is—remember that its outcome is relatively simple: What we perceive is the physical event that would most normally fit a given proximal stimulus distribution (or a given retinal excitation).

This is a very powerful principle. It explains why we see the world correctly, in those very many cases in which we indeed do so (the "perceptual constancies"); it explains why we see the world incorrectly, in those relatively few cases in which our perceptions are incorrect—in those cases (the "illusions") in which the proximal stimulus elicits a perceptual "habit" that is more frequently produced by some common distal layout than by the distal layout that happens to be producing it at the moment; and it may even explain perceptual properties, such as the figure-ground distinction, that do not at first thought seem to inhere in *either* the proximal stimuli, the distal stimuli, or the receptor apparatus.[4] But this principle, too, becomes a less-than-satisfactory answer when we examine it at close range:

(a) How do we know what the specific nerve energies really are if we can't observe the sensations directly?

(b) What is "normal"?

(c) And inasmuch as we are now asked to consider the context of the local spot of light in the proximal stimulus in order to predict and explain the appearance of that spot, we must ask: How large a context in space and time must be weighed in the calculation?

(d) Finally, inasmuch as the (unconscious) calculations are usually ones that involve *relationships*, like $S_1'' = kS_2''$, we must ask: How does an aggregate of discrete sensory responses ever add up to a generalized *function*, not itself composed of specific sensations, but into which specific values can be "plugged in"?[5]

The answers to these questions engage the major lines of traditional and modern perceptual inquiry.

What Are the Physiological Mechanisms That Mediate Perception? The task of analyzing the receptive system has of course continued. Gestalt theory proposed a neural structure that responds innately in an organized way to the *entire* stimulus input. Hebb and others have speculated about how a neural network that is initially unorganized and unstructured might develop organized responses to the patterned stimulation that is offered by the uniformities of the physical world; such structures, once developed, would not require the intermediate integrative steps that are inserted between r_i and S'' in Formula 3. And physiologists have identified structures in the peripheral and central nervous system that respond directly (and innately) to patterns of stimulation that are sufficiently complex as to destroy the once-elegant simplicity of Helmholtz's analysis. These physiological discoveries have not, of course, been ignored by perceptual theorists. But no clear-cut replacement for Helmholtz's proposal has emerged from these that has more power, specificity, and generality, and surely none that proposes to deal with object characteristics (S) as opposed to proximal stimulation (s).

What Is "Normal"? That question cannot be answered by examination of, or speculation about, the organism. We must turn instead to an examination of the organism's habitat, its visual ecology (Gibson, 1958, 1961, 1966); and we shall do that in a moment, when we consider the relationship between Brunswik and Gibson. As to *what is the appropriate grain size* for the analysis of stimulation, let us defer that question. I don't think that a satisfactory answer can yet be given, but we shall see that Gibson takes much larger portions of the stimulus array, and longer periods of time, as the unitary stimulus to which response is made, than traditional psychologists did, and that this increase in the size of his analytic grasp enables him to bypass the entire question of how *"relationship" is added to nonrelational stimuli*. In Gibson's formulation the relationships between distal object characteristics are to be found in the proximal stimuli, not in any contribution by the organism.

Emptying the Organism and Filling in the Ecology: A Comparison of Brunswik and Gibson

If our introspective analysis of conscious experience into its elementary sensations will not serve to reveal the atoms of perceptual response, nor the corresponding specific nerve energies, then we must find other bases for filling in the details of the perceptual process and for predicting response from stimulation. Within the Helmholtzian tradition, only Brunswik has really followed up these implications fully: Associationism is a predictive theory only if we know the frequencies with which various proximal stimulus combinations (s_i) have confronted the organism. If the perceived structure of attributes, S'', is formed by the observer's experiences with his environment, the associations that determine S'' can mirror the environment no better than the consistency of the environment itself permits. Brunswik has defined various measures of environmental consistency; the most relevant here is *ecological validity*, which measures the degree with which one stimulus variable is coupled to (or predicts) another (Brunswik, 1956).

In order to use this kind of theory, derived from the analysis of perceptual processes represented in Formula 3, we really don't have to know any of the steps that intervene between proximal stimulation (s_i) and perception (S'' or R_s): Because those processes presumably mirror the contingencies of the real world, we need only measure the ecological validities as they occur in the environment to which the individual has been exposed. Because in the empiricist tradition the world is probabilistic, ecological validities will generally be less than 1.0 (if the degree of association is expressed as a correlation), although physical laws may provide some exceptions. The task of perceptual research is therefore to assemble a catalog of the interstimulus correlations, a catalog that is representative of the ecology in which our perceiver will have formed his perceptual habits and in which we hope to predict his responses. Whatever those perceptual habits are, they will reflect the strength with which each "packet" of stimuli occurs together in a representative survey of the ecology.

Brunswik's program rests on two assumptions: first, that representative sampling is needed because of the "inevitably probabilistic" relationships between proximal stimuli (s_i) and distal properties (S_j); second, that "representative sampling" can adequately tell us what association between proximal stimuli and distal properties will have confronted the individual perceiver. These assumptions were strongly challenged by the work of Gibson, who otherwise shares certain formal similarities with Brunswik.

Gibson himself has evidenced even less concern with the intermediate processes than Brunswik, if that is possible. But because he has examined the relationships within the proximal stimulus array, and discovered therein stimulus properties that are (in general) likely to be highly correlated with distal objects' attributes, ecological validities are assumed to approach 1.0 in Gibson's world—*if* we have attended to the right variables of stimulation. The relevant variables are the higher-order invariants and stimulus gradients that confront the normal observer—usually an observer-in-motion (Gibson, 1959). These proximal stimulus variables are, practically speaking, in perfect correspondence with the distances, sizes, and so on of the distal objects in the world. Such variables presumably offer determinate, rather than probabilistic, information about the size and distance of the distal objects. We do not yet know the degree to which real observers do in fact make use of this potentially usable information, and because situations differ in the availability of these "higher-order" cues, some kind of ecological sampling will be needed before Gibson's proposals can be fully assessed or applied (Johnston, 1972; Kaufman, 1968; Smith and Smith, 1966). But a fundamental difference remains between Brunswik and Helmholtz, on the one hand, and Gibson, on the other: Gibson has shown that, counter to the probabilistic bias that has dominated empiricism since Hume, it is possible to undertake a psychophysical approach to perception in which statistics is used only to deal with errors. It must be stressed that this is really an "in principle" argument, not an assertion of empirical fact: We do not now have such a psychophysics in hand. Although there is ample evidence that some of the stimulus variables that Gibson and his colleagues have considered do indeed affect and effect perception, there is also evidence that some of those variables do not (cf. Johnston, 1972) and that many environments simply do not provide sufficient *effective* information, regardless of the fact that, to mathematical analysis, potential information exists in the proximal stimulus pattern sufficient to specify the distal object or scene (cf. Smith and Smith, 1957, 1966; Kaufman, 1968; Johnston, 1972). But *in principle* it remains true that in those cases in which perception does correctly reflect the distal state of affairs, there must be features of the proximal stimuli which convey the information being used, and the response to those features may be as direct as the response to, say, wavelength or intensity in Formula 1. (Of course, the simpler the features we propose for that status, and the less arbitrary their connection with the distal properties, the more convincing their candidacy.)

Although Gibson's higher-order variables do depend on some assumptions about the nature of the ecology (that texture distributions are usually homogeneous, for example, and that surfaces are usually continuous and rigid), the proximal-distal relationship is basically a determinate one in his system, so that his program doesn't demand enormously expensive (and perhaps impossible) ecological surveys in order to obtain *representative* ecological information, as Brunswikian empiricism requires.

At present, we have three components for a "complete" theoretical explanation of how we perceive space and objects: the Gestalt proposals of a *minimum principle* that selects the simplest object for us to see, from among the various objects that *could* be seen (and the various modern attempts to explicate what such a proposal might mean; cf. Attneave, 1954, 1959, 1972; Hochberg et al., 1953, 1960, 1968; Vitz and Todd, 1971); Brunswik's *representative functionalism*, which focuses on the distal stimulus and on the cues by which the perceiver "achieves" the distal stimulus in the face of supposed ambiguity (cf. Brunswik, 1952, 1956); and Gibson's *higher-order psychophysics*, which discards the supposedly simple elements of Helmholtzian analysis and attempts instead to discover such dimensions of proximal stimulation as are in correspondence both with properties of the distal world and the perceptual responses made to it. To Gibson, these dimensions (and not points of color) are the stimulus characteristics with which analysis of the perceptual process should start; they first must be cataloged as to their potential informativeness about the distal world, and then examined as to whether they are indeed used by the perceiving organism; and only then can we search intelligently for specific nerve energies (or for their higher-order equivalents).

Gibson's proposal seems to me to be the most important one since Helmholtz's. Let us examine it in specific operation in a problem area that Gibson has tended to avoid (the area of illusions and of ambiguous figures), because we can there press it to its limits.[6]

Gibson's Solution: Object Size, a Concrete Example

Consider an object (A or B in Figure 13.1) that stands on the ground plane at some distance Z from the observer. The extent (E_1, E_2) of the texture-density gradient in the proximal stimulus is usually well correlated with the object's distance (Z_1, Z_2). In Helmholtzian terms, E offers a potential distance cue which the observer may use in conjunction with the visual angle subtended by the object's retinal image (X_1, X_2) to "infer" the object's distal size (S_1, S_2). But, as Gibson points out (1950, 1959), in addition to providing potential information about distance Z, the texture-density gradient also provides information, just as directly, about the object's size, S. The number of texture-density units that the object subtends where it is in contact with the ground plane (in a given gradient) remains constant, regardless of the object's distance. If this *texture-scale size cue* is a direct stimulus to which the organism responds directly with a perceived size, either innately or by experience, then we can omit the bulky machinery of unconscious inference (the steps between S_i and S' in Formula 3).

This is a specific and powerful example of what Gibson means when he says that the organization is not provided by the perceiver, but that it is in the stimulus: If by organization we mean inter-response constraint, or couplings, and the size-distance relationship is an example of such coupling, we

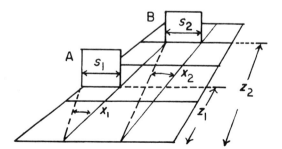

Figure 13.1. Size, distance, and texture-density gradient.

see that apparent size and apparent distance may vary together because the stimuli which determine them vary together. With such analyses, the nature both of perceptual learning and of the sensory mechanisms that underlie size perception take on a very different cast.

If the information about object properties exists in encoded form within the visual proximal stimulus array itself, then the processes of association or "enrichment" (all of the enclosed steps in Formula 3) need not be involved in order to explain the subject's perceptual responses to object properties. Such responses can be made directly to the *informative features* of the optic array once the subject has learned to differentiate those features (e.g., once he has learned that the *ratio of occluded texture gradient* is the feature that identifies distal object size). Of course, the fact that information exists in the stimulus array does not by itself preclude the association or enrichment model of perceptual learning. In fact, an enrichment model requires that such information be present in the stimulus, or there would really be nothing to learn. But if we can find relatively simple invariant features or cues to which one could plausibly hypothesize that the organisms might merely learn to attend, then the differentiation model is more economical—unless we have some independent reasons to believe in enrichment; as we shall see, such reasons may in fact exist.

Let us turn then to examples of size-distance covariation in which it is difficult to see how the coupling can be *in* the stimulus, and in which it seems, consequently, that the coupling must be provided by the perceiver. We shall see that Gibson's approach may be applied to such examples as well, and to the entire realm of ambiguous stimuli, but that the implications of doing so have not been fully worked out.

Nonstimulus Coupling and Its Implications

In fact there is evidence to suggest that the coupling between perceived size and perceived distance (and between other apparent object attributes) cannot be attributed entirely to separate responses made to stimulus information. Such evidence is offered by instances in which the stimulus (S) remains the same, yet the responses (S_1', S_2') change (that is, the stimuli are ambiguous and reversible), and as one perceived attribute (S_1') changes so does the other (S_2'). The coupling between size of face and apparent orientations in the Sanford figure (Sanford, 1897) is an illustration of this point: As the pattern in Figure 13.2a appears to reverse in depth, the near face (whichever it is) appears smaller, although we should note that the conditions for obtaining the effect, and its reliability, are not yet clear. The phenomenon has been reported by some observers (Hotopf, 1966; Hochberg, 1968; Mefferd and Wieland, 1968; Hochberg, Farber, and Stern, 1974), and not by others using similar figures (cf. Gregory, 1966). The reversal of direction in the Ames trapezoidal window and in similar rotating figures is another

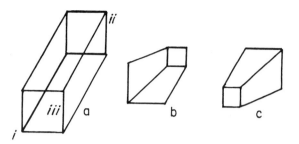

Figure 13.2. A reversible-perspective figure and two different objects it can represent (size-distance effects are exaggerated).

example of this critical phenomenon. What coupling exists in these cases cannot be attributed to the conjoint variations in the stimulus pattern, inasmuch as the stimulus doesn't change as the figure reverses.

The nonstimulus coupling between apparent size and apparent distance (or between apparent slant and apparent shape) assumes a significance far beyond the magnitude of the effects themselves when we consider that they appear to offer us something very rare. They seem to be clear-cut instances of "enrichment," of "mental process," and of phenomena in which there is a purpose that is served by asking the subject what he perceives. If these implications are sustained, then the potential information in the optic array, regardless of its richness and specificity, cannot be the whole story; nor can a differentiation model of perceptual learning be a sufficient account of perceptual learning, because the nonstimulus coupling seems to offer direct evidence of enrichment.

Consider the Sanford figure, which is simpler to analyze than the Ames window (although the phenomenon seems to be less robust): When the right side looks nearer, it also tends to look smaller, as is shown in vastly exaggerated form at Figure 13.2b. When the left side looks nearer, it in turn looks smaller. The effect is small and, as we noted above, its reliability is still in question. If we stipulate its reality, however, it is very important. (No great harm will be done even if the coupling turns out not to be a reliable one, inasmuch as the same analysis applies in principle to the Ames window, which *is* reliable, but which is not as simple a platform for the argument that I wish to present.)

Note that the Sanford effect presents us with a very different situation from that of Figure 13.1. In Figure 13.2a, one and the same proximal stimulus pattern elicits two very different judgments of apparent size. There is no way that we can tell which judgment the subject will make, simply from our knowledge of the proximal stimulus pattern (nor from our knowledge about the state of the receptors). We must know whether a given face appears the nearer, at any time, to know whether it appears to be the larger or the smaller one. And because the stimulus remains unchanged, we cannot attribute the response change, when it occurs, to the proximal stimulus. We must therefore know both the stimulus pattern and at least one response which is an acceptable index[7] of the perceived orientation of the cube in order to predict what the response of apparent size will be. Nor can we conclude that such packets of inter-response couplings are obtained only with static line drawings on paper (which are inherently equivocal artifacts). The same argument applies to the multiply coupled aspects of the trapezoidal window illusion: Rotation, direction, and shape are all mutually constrained so that even though the stimulus remains unchanged, when one aspect of the object's appearance changes, the others change, as well. These nonstimulus inter-response couplings therefore seem to imply at least this limited form of "perceptual causation": that we can better predict the subject's response about one aspect of the object's appearance if we know or can infer other aspects of how it appears to the subject, than if we don't know.[8]

Dissecting "Perceptual" Causation.   To say that one perceived attribute determines another demands explication (and, hopefully, some thought about underlying physiological mechanism, because many of us remain metaphysically queasy with a formula in which one "mental" event is the "cause" of another event, even if the second event is also "mental"). In the case of nonstimulus couplings like the Sanford and Ames phenomena, we have several approaches open to us if we are willing to discuss intraorganismic additions or enrichments. As far as an explanation is concerned, we can first try the general Helmholtz-Brunswik solution: that we see the most ecologically probable object that will fit the proximal stimulus. For Figure 13.2a, that means either of the two objects 13.2b and 13.2c. As overall forms or objects, however, they do not appear at all familiar, nor common, so that we must assume that it is in some features other than their overall forms that they are to be considered ecologically probable—and those features remain to be specified. Perhaps the intersections (i, ii) are most often encountered as objects' three-dimensional corners. But then why do we not see the faces as being equal? Such a percept would preserve the rectangularity that is required by those theories in which the illusions are explained as being perceptual habits formed by our experiences in a "carpentered world" (see Segall et al., 1966; Gregory, 1966); it would also preserve the equality of solid angles and of lengths of sides that is required by an application of a minimum principle (see Attneave, 1973, for a recent and elegant attempt to make this work). So it cannot be to either of these that we look for an explanation of the size-distance coupling. But we should note that Attneave and Frost (1969) did find that the angles and proportions that made a picture of a cube appear most three-dimensional were those that would be appropriate if the cube were being viewed from a distance at least approximately that of the picture plane. If we assume that the object is seen as being reasonably near the picture plane, and that one face is seen as being nearer than the other, then—in order to fit the proximal stimulus pattern that is actually presented to the eye—the nearer end must be smaller (Figures 13.2b, 13.2c). This is, of course, another aspect of Helmholtz's general solution, one of the many variants of the "internalized law of visual angle" that we discussed in connection with Formula 3.

As for speculation about possible mechanisms, it is not difficult to imagine physical events that might underlie these "mentalistic" couplings. For example, the coupling might be one between the programs that guide the depth-dependent visuomotor behaviors and those that guide direction-dependent (depth-independent) visuomotor behaviors. Let us see why this is so. When the head moves, the eyes are programmed to make compensatory pursuit movements in order to keep a steady view of some stationary object, and any residual displacement of the object in the field of view is perceived as object motion (Hay, 1968).[9] Note that *such compensatory programs must not be independent of the object's distance from the observer*, if they are to be general: For a given translatory head movement (M, in Figure 13.3) and a given initial retinal image, a more distant object (O_2 in Figure 13.3) will require a slower pursuit. So a single correlation between eye movements and head movements is not enough to keep objects visually fixated. Different correlations are needed for objects at different distances.

More generally, the correlations between the array-sampling perceptuomotor behaviors (saccades and pursuit eye movements and rotational head movements), on the one hand, and those perceptuomotor behaviors that produce predictable changes in the array as a function of objects' distance (for example, translational head movements, binocular vergence changes, accommodation, and so on), on the other hand, may reflect and in fact may *comprise* our perceptions of size and distance: An eye movement that is directed from i to ii in Figure 13.3 must be guided by the proximal stimulus extent, E, not by object size, S, if the movement is to arrive at its goal; the "knowledge" that guides such behavior is knowledge only about the *visual field*. With a moving (or binocular) observer, the different dis-

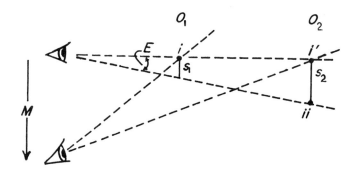

Figure 13.3. A larger eye movement is needed to fixate a near object while the head moves than is needed to fixate a far one.

tances between *i* and *ii* become important in maintaining any up-to-date plan to look at them. Information about visual field and about distance from the observer is sufficient to define the attributes of the *visual world* (I am using these terms as in Gibson, 1950, 1952, and in part offering an explanation of why we have these two apparently disparate kinds of experience; cf. Hochberg, 1971, 1972).

What we may mean by perceived object size, then, is the packet of correlated plans (e.g., pursuit rate $\div$ head movement rate, saccade rate $\div$ convergence angle, and so on) that are readied by the depth cues that are provided by the object's visual environment. When the eye fixates one of the "local cues" (Hochberg, 1968) that are provided by Figure 13.2a, and the remainder of the figure is viewed by the relatively poor vision of the periphery, the distance of the peripherally viewed portion is probably indeterminate. Assume (cf. Hochberg, 1970) that when some point *i* is fixated, the brightness-difference contours that fall in peripheral vision, outside the fovea, act as *ambiguous edge cues*. That is, assume that a contour like *iii* of Figure 13.2a is taken as marking the occurrence of what Gibson has called depth-at-an-edge (Gibson 1950–1966; I have previously discussed various aspects of this contour-depth proposal in other papers; Hochberg 1962, 1970, 1972). Because both the local depth cues and the peripheral contours are ambiguous, two quite different and mutually exclusive sets of distance plans are readied, in alternation, and the same peripheral extent takes on in turn two different perceived object sizes because the denominator in the packet (for example, planned convergence angle in the ratio saccade/convergence angle) has changed.

This seems to me to be a possible underlying mechanism, with several testable features, and I have been making some attempts to test it. But need we introduce speculations about such intraorganismic processes, physiological or otherwise, in order to explain these phenomena, or can some version of Gibson's approach encompass them?

Perhaps it can, but at a cost: Gibson has on occasion adopted Koffka's idea of the *invariant* (itself a modification of Helmholtz's proposals that we discussed previously). An object's shape is *always* perceived as a shape-at-a-slant, so that the two variables are therefore always coupled. We should note, however, that although a shape is always at *some* slant, the stimulus may specify several different shapes-at-slants equally well. This is a weaker form of specification than Gibson usually expects from the stimuli in which he is most interested, of course, but it is specification nevertheless. The Ames rotating "window" specifies both of the sets of rotation directions that subjects do in fact report, if the information about the actual direction of rotation is below threshold (cf. Graham, 1963; Day and Power, 1965) or is ineffective for some other reason. And a similar argument can be made to account for the Sanford effect.

Let us assume that lines on paper share some critical stimulus features with objects' edges and corners, as discussed above. Let us assume further that the observer can somehow set himself to "ignore" the information that tells him that the lines really lie on the plane of the paper, perhaps by carefully keeping his fixations on the picture and away from the edges of the paper (so that the latter fall only in low-acuity peripheral vision), and that what "learning to see pictures" might mean, therefore, is learning to do this deliberately and efficiently.[10] Thus, lines are automatically attributed depth: either the figure-ground phenomenon, as flat silhouettes (cf. Hochberg, 1970, 1972) if no other features characteristic of slant to the frontal-parallel are provided by the pattern; or the ambiguous shape-slants pointed out and examined by Attneave (1968) in the case of triangles, which can be read as alternating among any of the three slants that would be given by having each vertex as most distant in space. In like fashion, a single face of the Sanford pattern, Figure 13.4a, is like the triangles: It can be "read" equally well as a shape at any one of the four sets of slants, 13.4b–4e. Figures 13.4b and 13.4c correspond to the "readings" in Figures 13.2b and 13.2c, respectively, and display the appropriate size differences. By this kind of analysis, the Sanford pattern possesses features that will specify both objects shown in Figures 13.2b and 13.2c, which are truncated pyramids with one face smaller than the other.

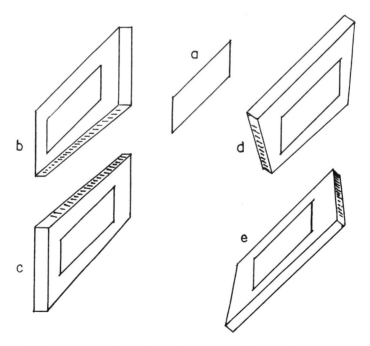

Figure 13.4. A rhombus (a) and four different ways of "reading" the same rhombus.

In both the Ames window and the Sanford pattern, then, the information that would normally specify an object or event, and rule out alternative readings, is missing. And because there are mutually exclusive sets of alternative objects that will fit the proximal stimulus distribution, both kinds are seen (but not simultaneously). By this analysis, however, in both cases, the stimulus does *not* produce a response of size and a response of distance, coupled by some additional Helmholtzian process or minimum principle— the response is a single one of shape-at-a-slant (and hence, size-at-a-distance) that is as unitary as any other response, such as color or temperature, that we can dissect out of the flux of perceptual experience.

This kind of explanation seems feasible as a preliminary sketch, but it leaves a host of questions to be answered, foremost of which is this one: What are the conditions and limits under which the perceiver obtains effectual information from the optic array? The fact that the Ames trapezoid is ambiguous even though it is a real moving surface viewed under normal conditions means that potential information is only potential; it need not be used nor usable, and even when it is usable, there are thresholds which must be exceeded before even those variables of stimulation which the organism is in principle capable of picking up are in fact effective. And until we know these limits, we must be prepared to find that any given scene at all will turn out to be as ambiguous as the reversible-perspective patterns that we have been discussing.

Moreover, the reversible-perspective patterns are not arbitrary symbols nor can they be dismissed as ecologically unrepresentative artifacts: After all, the perceptual learning process (e.g., the differentiation, if such it is, that isolates the features of the proximal-stimulus array that are relevant to and serve to specify such exclusive and alternative objects as those in Figures 13.2b and 13.2c) must itself have occurred in the process of dealing with such solid objects in the real world, not by dealing with drawings on flat paper. And this means that the proximal stimuli produced by such line drawings must share some features with the proximal stimuli that are produced by real objects themselves.

Our analysis of the Sanford effect thus leads to the following alternatives: Either we have to posit an enrichment (i.e., an adding of distance, given size, or vice versa) as in Formula 3; or we have to assert that line drawings are not merely arbitrary symbols, but are themselves stimuli for the perception of objects and are unusual only in the sense that they may more readily specify several mutually exclusive objects than is true of the visual fields that we normally encounter.[11] These two alternatives are not, of course, mutually exclusive but neither are they merely different ways of saying the same thing. There would seem to be ways of separating them, for example, the enrichment or addition hypothesis of Formula 3 may (but doesn't have to) imply a *sequence* of processes—for example, *first* a distance reversal, *then* a size change. The addition hypothesis would therefore be better able to explain a finding that longer latencies are associated with apparent size changes in patterns like Figure 13.2a than are associated with orientation reversal; absences of such a lag would leave open the application of a version of Gibson's psychophysical approach.

But in any case, the application of a global psychophysical approach to such problems requires the recognition that potential stimulus information is not necessarily effectual stimulus information; that the kinds of "higher-order variables of stimulation" that do in fact comprise the distinctive features that actually determine our perceptions of objects and events are not necessarily large in extent and iterative in nature, like texture-density gradients, but maybe also comprise relatively small patterns, like the intersections of a Sanford pattern; and that as we make the transition from potential information to effectual information, the differences between peripheral and central vision, and the differences in the ways in which the perceiver can deploy his gaze, are not inconsequential and will be the next necessary area of inquiry to demand our attention.

Notes

Supported by a grant from the National Science Foundation (GB-5270).

1. E.g., Gibson argued that the curvature and slant aftereffects that he had discovered (Gibson, 1933) were the result of an adaptation to shape, analogous to the more familiar aftereffects of temperature and color that follow adaptation to heat and light, respectively, and that the response to an object's shape or configuration is thereby shown to be just as "sensory" and direct as are the temperature or color responses.

2. A point persistently ignored by behaviorists who are impatient to get to real objects and to their behavioral consequences; Gibson has discussed the inadequate usage of the term "stimulus" in some detail (1960).

3. E.g., as Don Hood has pointed out to me, the assumption of point-to-point correspondence between perceived local brightness (s') and local retinal response (r) can be found in proposals as recent as those of von Bekesy (1968).

4. For recent discussions of these points, see Hochberg, 1972.

5. Helmholtz implied (1925) that what we are really talking about in such cases is a large repertory of specific associations. This is certainly the traditional empiricist solution of Berkeley and Mill. But Helmholtz also wrote as though rules or principles are being applied in the course of "unconscious inference," and it is not clear how the specific-association explanation applies when we are looking at unfamiliar objects of unknown size at some distance at which we never happen to have seen an object of just that size.

6. To the degree that Gibson wishes to discover those features of proximal stimulation that are informative about distal layout, he seems perfectly justified in ignoring "illusions" or nonveridical perception, his critics (cf. Gregory, 1964) notwithstanding. But that does not mean that the study of illusions has nothing to contribute to a Gibsonian approach to the perceptual process.

7. We cannot however simply identify the percept as being one or the other cube, 13.2b or 13.2c, and assume that its orientation defines the relationship between the faces, as would be the case if the percept were a real, rigid cube. An analysis of the

"impossible figures" of Penrose and Escher argues, as we shall see, that the grain of coupling (or inter-response consistency) is surely smaller than an entire object.

8. The point has apparently been generally accepted that "converging operations" are needed in order to decide what a subject perceives, in any instance, but the only clear prescription that I know of for choosing appropriate sets of different measures with which to "converge" is to select different members of a single packet of coupled responses. Only thus do we simultaneously make use both of stimulus information and of information about what the subject perceives, when we attempt to explain and predict the subject's responses—to me, a reasonable set of requirements to impose on any discussion of "perception" (Hochberg, 1956).

9. Hay doesn't actually assert this, but it seems to me to be strongly implied by his very important findings: After a subject has adapted to fixating a point that moves leftward whenever he raises his head vertically, and rightward whenever he lowers his head, a spot that actually remains stationary will appear to move rightward and leftward when he raises and lowers his head, respectively. The existence of the aftereffect argues that the compensatory eye movements that are made when the head moves are *programmed* and are not the results of executing just those movements that will null retinal motion.

10. Perhaps it is this skill that makes urban Africans more susceptible to the geometrical illusions than are rural Africans, in such studies as that of Leibowitz and Pick (1972), rather than any specific experience with perspective representation as such, or with "carpentered environments" (as Segall et al., 1963, 1966, maintain).

11. The point has other support: The finding that subjects totally untrained in pictorial perception appear to recognize objects that have been drawn in outline (Hochberg and Brooks, 1962; Zimmermann and Hochberg, 1971) implies that the features in line drawings that are shared with three-dimensional objects must be learned by the subject (if they are learned at all, and not innate) in the course of the subject's normal commerce with the world of objects, and are not acquired by learning to associate object properties with lines on paper as a set of arbitrary symbols.

References

ATTNEAVE, F. Some informational aspects of visual perception. *Psychological Review*, 1954, *61*, 183–193.

———. *Applications of Information Theory to Psychology*. New York: Holt, Rinehart and Winston, 1959.

———. Triangles as ambiguous figures. *American Journal of Psychology*, 1968, *81*, 447–453.

ATTNEAVE, F., and FROST, R. The discrimination of perceived tridimensional orientation by minimum criteria. *Perception and Psychophysics*, 1969, *6*, 391–396.

AYER, A. J. *Bertrand Russell*. New York: Viking, 1972.

BRUNSWIK, E. The conceptual framework of psychology. In *International Encyclopedia of Unified Science*. Vol. I, No. 10. Chicago: University of Chicago Press, 1952.

———. *Perception and the Representative Design of Psychological Experiments*. Berkeley, Calif.: University of California Press, 1956.

DAY, R. H., and POWER, R. H. Apparent Reversal (oscillation) of rotary motion in depth: An investigation and a general theory. *Psychological Review*, 1965, *72*, 117–127.

GARNER, W. R., HAKE, H. W., and ERIKSEN, C. W. Operationism and the concept of perception. *Psychological Review*, 1956, *63*, 149–159.

GIBSON, J. J. Adaptation, aftereffect and contrast in perception of curved lines. *Journal of Experimental Psychology*, 1933, *16*, 1–31.

———. *The Perception of the Visual World.* Boston: Houghton Mifflin, 1950.

———. The visual field and the visual world: A reply to Professor Boring. *Psychological Review*, 1952, *59*, 149–151.

———. Optical motions and transformations as stimuli for visual perception. *Psychological Review*, 1957, *64*, 288–295.

———. Visually controlled locomotion and visual orientation in animals. *British Journal of Psychology*, 1958, *49*, 182–194.

———. Perception as a function of stimulation. In S. Koch (ed.), *Psychology: A Study of a Science.* Vol. I. New York: McGraw-Hill, 1959.

———. The concept of the stimulus in psychology. *American Psychologist*, 1960, *15*, 694–703.

———. Ecological optics. *Vision Research*, 1961, *1*, 253–262.

———. *The Senses Considered as Perceptual Systems.* Boston: Houghton Mifflin, 1966.

GRAHAM, C. H. On some aspects of real and apparent visual movement. *Journal of the Optical Society of America*, 1963, *53*, 1019–1025.

GREGORY, R. L. Human perception. *British Medical Bulletin*, 1964, *20*, 21–26.

———. Visual illusions. In B. M. Foss (ed.), *New Horizons in Psychology.* Harmondsworth, England: Penguin Books, 1966.

HAY, J. C. Visual adaptation to an altered correlation between eye movement and head movement. *Science*, 1968, *160*, 429–430.

HELMHOLTZ, H. VON. *Treatise on Physiological Optics.* Trans. from the 3rd German ed. (1909–1911) by J. P. Southall (ed.). Rochester, N.Y.: Optical Society of America, 1924, 1925.

HOCHBERG, J. Perception: Toward a recovery of a definition. *Psychological Review*, 1956, *63*, 400–405.

———. The psychophysics of pictorial perception. *A-V Communication Review*, 1962, *10*, 22–54.

———. In the mind's eye. In R. N. Haber (ed.), *Contemporary Theory and Research in Visual Perception.* New York: Holt, Rinehart and Winston, 1968.

———. Attention, organization, and consciousness. In D. I. Mostofsky (ed.), *Attention: Contemporary Theory and Analysis.* New York: Appleton-Century-Crofts, 1970.

———. Perception: I. Color and shape; II. Space and movement. In *Woodworth and Schlosberg's Experimental Psychology*, J. Kling and L. Riggs (eds.). New York: Holt, Rinehart and Winston, 1971.

———. The representation of things and people. In E. H. Gombrich, J. Hochberg, and M. Black (eds.), *Art, Perception, and Reality.* Baltimore: The Johns Hopkins University Press, 1972.

HOCHBERG, J., and BROOKS, V. The psychophysics of form: Reversible-perspective drawings of spatial objects. *American Journal of Psychology*, 1960, *73*, 337–354.

HOCHBERG, J., FARBER, J., and STERN, F. Size-distance coupling in the Sanford figure. Unpublished manuscript, 1974.

HOCHBERG, J., and McALISTER, E. A quantitative approach to figural "goodness." *Journal of Experimental Psychology*, 1953, *46*, 361–364.

Hotopf, W. H. N. The size-constancy theory of visual illusions. *British Journal of Psychology*, 1966, *57*, 307–318.

Johnston, I. R. *Visual judgments in locomotion*. Doctoral dissertation, University of Melbourne, 1972.

Kaufman, L. *Research in visual perception for carrier landing: Suppl. 2. Studies on the perception of impact point based on shadowgraph techniques*. Report SGD-5265-0031. Prepared by Sperry Rand Corp., Great Neck, New York, for Physiol. Psychol. Branch–ONR for Contract # Nonr 4081, 1968.

Leibowitz, H., and Pick, H. L., Jr. Cross-cultural and educational aspects of the Ponzo perspective illusion. *Perception and Psychophysics*, 1972, *12*, 430–432.

Mefferd, R. B., and Wieland, B. A. Apparent size–apparent distance relationship in flat stimuli. *Perceptual and Motor Skills*, 1968, *26*, 959–966.

Mill, J. *Analysis of the Phenomena of the Human Mind*. Vol. I. Ed. by J. S. Mill. London: Longmans, Green, Reader, and Dyer, 1869.

Sanford, E. C. A. *A Course in Experimental Psychology. Part 1: Sensation and Perception*. London: Heath, 1897.

Segall, M. H., Campbell, D. T., and Hershkovits, M. J. Cultural differences in the perception of geometric illusions. *Science*, 1963, *139*, 769–771.

———. *The Influence of Culture on Visual Perception*. Indianapolis: Bobbs-Merrill, 1966.

Smith, O. W., and Smith, P. C. Interaction of the effects of cues involved in judgments of curvature. *American Journal of Psychology*, 1957, *70*, 361–375.

———. Development studies of spatial judgments by children and adults. *Perceptual and Motor Skills*, 1966, *22*, 3–73.

Vitz, P. C., and Todd, T. C. A model of the perception of simple geometric figures. *Psychological Review*, 1971, *78*, 207–228.

Von Bekesy, G. Mach- and Hering-type lateral inhibition in vision. *Vision Research*, 1968, *8*, 1483–1499.

14

Film Cutting and Visual Momentum

Julian Hochberg and Virginia Brooks

Introduction

We perceive the world by means of successive sensory samples. In vision, this means by sequences of views. Most view sequences are obtained by the viewer's own perceptuomotor acts. Some view sequences are given to the viewer by a filmmaker, and these often consist of sequences of nonoverlapping views.

There are two general kinds of answers to the question of how we combine our successive glances into a coherent perceptual world: These are (1) the *compensatory*, or subtractive, explanations, whether based on extraretinal signals (cf. Martin, 1976; Sedgwick & Festinger, 1976; Skavenski, 1976) or on the transformations of the visual image (Gibson, 1954, 1957, 1966; Johansson, 1974); and (2) the inferential, expectancy-testing, or schema-testing explanations (Hochberg, 1968; Neisser, 1967; Piaget, 1954).

The compensatory explanations may or may not be fully adequate to explain how we combine view sequences that we obtain by our own perceptuomotor acts, but they simply cannot account for our perception of motion pictures in which scenes are built up by a succession of *nonoverlapping* views.

The inferential or schema-testing theories seem capable in principle of explaining both how we combine our own glances and how we perceive motion-picture sequences, but these are still remarkably vague, and we have only rudimentary psychological research on the question of how subjects integrate successive views (Girgus, 1973, 1976; Girgus & Hochberg, 1972; Farley, 1976; Hochberg, 1968; Murphy, 1973). The psychologist is not the first to be concerned with this question, however; the filmmaker has been here before him.

The work reported here was supported by a grant from the National Institute of Education, NIE G 74-0099. Paul Roule assisted greatly in the preparation, execution, and analyses of the experiments. Programming and final design and construction of the controlling circuitry were done by Ted Hills.

Most cinematic sequences are made up of nonoverlapping views, and that makes the filmmaker's purposes in using such sequences, and his techniques in dealing with them, of interest to us. Conversely, we may be in the position of providing the filmmaker with quantitative information that may be of considerable use to him.

In nonoverlapping sequences of views such as *montages*, or rhythmic series of discontinuous shots, the filmmaker relies on the viewer's knowledge of the world, or on "establishing shots" (e.g., longshots) to provide the "glue" that joins the successive views. This motion-picture procedure must draw on the abilities that we normally use in guiding and interpreting our normal purposeful perceptual inquiries. Film editors have, in fact, said that what makes a cut good and rapid to comprehend is the successful effort of the filmmaker to provide the viewer with the visual answer to a question that he would normally have been about to obtain for himself at that time, were he able to change the scene by his own perceptuomotor acts (as he normally can, of course, but as he cannot do in the movies).

Once the viewer's visual question is answered, there is no further reason for him to explore the scene, and the scene goes "cinematically dead." To the filmmaker, this is a challenge that he can meet by changing to a new camera position, even when there is no need to do so in order to tell the story. To the psychologist, this phenomenon (if he can measure it) is a potential tool for studying how we go about posing and answering visual questions. Such cutting from one view to another merely for the purpose of keeping the screen "alive" is most blatantly evident in television, when a news commentator faces one camera, then another, in order to relieve the viewer's visual boredom or habituation.

This same factor is a central ingredient in the widespread use of montage sequences. These sequences are of interest to us here because this motivating factor, which we will call *visual momentum*, should reflect the course of the viewer's perceptual inquiry—the momentary state of his development and testing of schematic maps. This simple form of cutting provides a baseline to study visual momentum; further complexities and varieties will be discussed elsewhere.

When a viewer is first shown a static picture, he looks at the most informative regions (Antes, 1974; Brooks, 1961; Hochberg & Brooks, 1962, 1963; Loftus, 1976; Mackworth & Morandi, 1967; Pollack & Spence, 1968). The glance rate is initially high, and declines rapidly (curve W, in Fig. 14.1B, from data of Antes, 1974). In our terms, the viewer takes a few glances to establish the main features or landmarks of the scene, and then his impetus to schema formation wanes: He knows what he will see, in a general way, wherever he looks, if the scene is a normally redundant one (Biederman, 1972; Loftus, 1976; Reed & Johnsen, 1975). When the eye is exploring a scene at its most rapid rate—say, at four to five glances per sec—there is clearly no time between glances in which the viewer can sum up what he has seen up to that point, and decide how many more glances are needed.

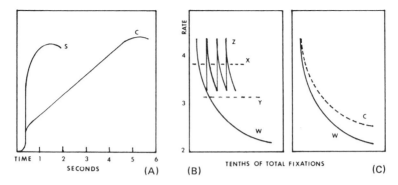

Figure 14.1. (A) Curves S and C depict Spottiswoode's (1933/1962) introspective account of glance rate or aesthetic arousal for simple and complex scenes, respectively. (B) and (C) Models of glance rates of subjects looking at static pictures. Curve W is from data obtained by Antes (1974).

Something like a rate regulator sounds plausible, perhaps even a mechanism similar to the one recently proposed for reading by Bouma and deVoogd (1974) and Kolers (1976).

If visual momentum is the impetus to obtain sensory information, and to formulate and test a schema, it should be reflected by the frequency with which glances are made and by the viewer's tendency to keep looking within one display *when he is free of external demands to do so*. Visual momentum should, presumably, decline with the length of time that the viewer has been looking at the display and should increase with the number of different places at which he can look to receive nonredundant information (i.e., to apprehend or comprehend the scene to some level of awareness, which should be task-dependent). These functions ascribed to visual momentum are very similar to those Spottiswoode (1933/1962) attributed to an aesthetic arousal variable which he called *affective cutting tone*. Based on the introspective account of his own cinematic experience, he proposed that simple and striking scenes would have their maximum effect early, and then fall off as shown in curve S of Fig. 14.1A, whereas more complex and unexpected scenes would take longer to reach their maximum effect as in curve C of Fig. 14.1A. Sequences of simple scenes would sustain high affective cutting tone when presented at a fast cutting rate and would be reduced at slower rates, whereas the reverse would be true with the more complex scenes.

We do not know whether these semiquantitative but wholly subjective aesthetic functions can be made more objective, but they seem to be sufficiently close to what we have called *visual momentum* that we will return to the question of aesthetic judgment. We will present and discuss first a set of eye-movement experiments designed to provide data on which to base a model of visual momentum; and second, experiments on the ways subjects distribute their glances when they are free to look at one or another (or neither) of two displays.

The Course of Looking at Sequences of Successive Views

If we assume that curve W in Fig. 14.1B is a rough guide to the course of looking at a single scene, then by repeatedly changing the scene before the glance rate has had a chance to fall very much, we could repeatedly return the glance rate to its peak, and increase the mean rate of looking as represented by line X in Fig. 14.1B. Again, if *attentional complexity*—the number of places to look at—is increased, the curve should not fall sharply, as represented in curve C in Fig. 14.1C.

Two kinds of experiments using similar apparatus and measurement procedures were performed to test whether these functions in Fig. 14.1 do indeed obtain. Experiment 1 used sequences of arbitrarily generated abstract pictures as its stimulus material; Experiment 2 used montages constructed of meaningful, representational photographs assembled in arbitrary orders.

Experiment 1: The Course of Looking at Sequences of Abstract Views

In this experiment, subjects' eye movements were recorded while they watched sequences of abstract pictures on a rear-projection screen. The frequency with which eye movements occurred was a function of the attentional complexity of the views in the sequence, and of the rate at which views were presented. In the first experiment (Hochberg and Brooks, 1974), three degrees of complexity and two cutting rates were used. This was intended as a replication and extension of Brooks and Hochberg (1976), in which sequences of two degrees of view complexity were used at three cutting rates. Results were substantially the same in both experiments, and in accord with the model in Fig. 14.1B and 14.1C. The details of the first experiment are as follows.

Stimuli

To pursue research with sequential views, we need a procedure for generating stimulus sequences by some arbitrary process that provides different numbers of places to which the subject's gaze will be drawn. To do this, we drew on an inelegant formula that had been found in earlier research (Hochberg & Brooks, 1962) to account, at least roughly, for where subjects assigned their judgments of "prominence"; it had already been shown (Brooks, 1961; Hochberg & Brooks, 1962) that such prominence judgments were, in turn, correlated with eye-movement recordings of where subjects looked (Buswell, 1935). Estimates of prominence may be achieved if a picture is divided into cells, and all of the

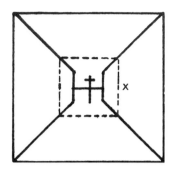

Figure 14.2. Typical unit pattern used to construct stimuli for Experiment 1. (The dotted rectangle [X] did not appear in the actual stimuli.)

lines and contours are of approximately equal thickness and contrast; then a simple count of the number of points of inflection and intersection which fall within any cell is an approximate predictor of the mean prominence ratings given that cell. A more cumbersome formula, which provided a better empirical fit to prominence distributions, included a reference point called a *sink*, which is a point having the greatest number of real or *extended* lines passing through it. We drew upon the notion of a sink at the center of the pattern in constructing the present designs.

The unit pattern is shown in Fig. 14.2. From this, a set of 12 abstract patterns was constructed. Each pattern used four units, located according to a random decision process. The outer dimensions of each unit were also randomly determined, as was the choice among a set of 12 small details, one of which was placed in the center of each unit. When a decision was needed as to which unit would continue and which would end at any intersection, that too was randomly determined.

The set of 12 patterns generated in this way was intended to contain four attention centers per view. Again, using a random decision procedure to retain two and one centers per view, two more sets of patterns were generated from the first set. Examples of the 36 patterns are shown in Fig. 14.3. These three sets of views were each made into motion-picture sequences on high-contrast 16mm film, with a 50% random dot matrix inserted before and after each sequence. The sequences were ordered as follows: $1CL_1$, $4CL_1$, $4CS_2$, $2CS_2$, $4CS_1$, $1CS_1$, $2CL_2$, $4CL_2$, $1CL_2$. The notation $1CL_1$ refers to a set of six of the single-center patterns presented for long durations (4 sec/view); $1CL_2$ refers to the remaining set of six of the single-center patterns presented at 4 sec/view; $2CS_1$ refers to a set of the two-center patterns presented at 1 sec/view (i.e., short presentation); and so on.

Subjects and Instructions

Subjects were 10 paid volunteers, graduates and undergraduates, who were naive as to the purpose of the experiments. They were told that we were concerned with their pupillary diameters and other responses in relation to

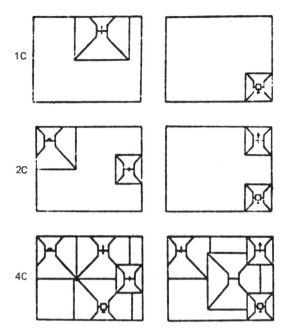

Figure 14.3. Representative stimuli for one, two, and four attention centers per view used in Experiment 1.

their aesthetic preferences, on which they were to report after the entire series had been viewed. (The pupil diameter data were, in fact, both noisy and uninformative, and the aesthetic reports obtained under these conditions were too sketchy to use but, of course, they were not our primary interest.)

Apparatus and Procedure

Stimuli were presented to each subject on a rear-projection screen in a semi-darkened room. Each subject sat with his head in a headrest while his eye movements were recorded by a system built around a Gulf & Western Eye View Monitor (formerly known as the Whittaker, as described by Young & Sheena, 1975) and a computer-coupled 16mm motion-picture camera. Stimulus sequences were projected by a modified L & W 16mm Optical Data Analyzer motion-picture projector so arranged that the dimensions of each view were 15.9° horizontal by 12.0° vertical. Subjects viewed the screen from a distance of 65 cm; the direction of the left eye's gaze was monitored by a Gulf & Western Eye-Tracker. A 16mm Bolex camera, driven by a synchronous motor at four frames per sec, recorded the monitor's screen. In addition, in some of the experiments the online computer calculated eye position data 60 times per sec and identified an eye movement as a change taking less than 100 msec (to prevent inclusion of drifts and pursuit movements) and of more than 1.5° magnitude.

Results and Discussion

The course of looking at each view in each sequence was obtained as follows: The subject's gaze was sampled with a 150 msec photograph four times/sec. Starting with the first frame in which a new view was sampled, a change in fixation greater than 1.5° was recorded as an eye movement in the 1/4 second sample in which it first appeared. The 4 sec/view, 2 sec/view, and 1 sec/view sequences were therefore recorded as 16, 8, and 4 samples, respectively. These data are shown in Fig. 14.4. Note that these graphs are time-locked to the start of each view. Means of the frequencies of eye movements in all samples of each sequence, averaged across views and then across subjects, with the standard deviation of the subjects' means, are given for each cutting rate, and each complexity, in Table 14.1. This was done for entire sequences and, for the 4 sec/view sequences, was also done for the first four views and for the remaining views (5–16) separately.

Differences between each subject's mean glance rate for long and short sequences were significant ($t = 4.3$, $df = 9$, $p < .01$), with no interaction effect of complexity ($F < 1.0$); while effects of complexity on glance rate were significant ($F = 8.7$, $df = 2, 18$, $p < .01$), pooling cutting rates.

The number of fixations falling within $2° \times 4°$ of the center of each unit (cf. the area marked off by the dotted line in Fig. 14.2) was obtained, and the proportion of fixations falling within those central areas is also listed under *Accuracy* in Table 14.1 and did not vary with number of centers per view ($F < 1.0$). In order to determine how the actual fixations correspond to subjects' prominence judgments, copies of the four-center views were given to two additional groups of subjects, for a total of 27, who marked and ranked

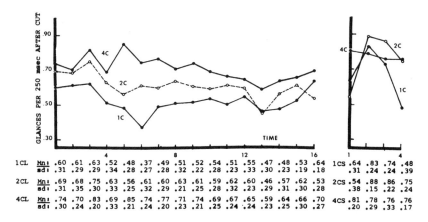

1CL	Mn:	.60	.61	.63	.52	.48	.37	.49	.51	.52	.54	.51	.55	.47	.48	.53	.64	1CS	.64	.83	.74	.48
	sd:	.31	.29	.29	.34	.28	.27	.28	.32	.22	.28	.23	.33	.30	.23	.19	.18		.31	.24	.24	.39
2CL	Mn:	.69	.68	.75	.63	.56	.61	.60	.63	.61	.59	.62	.60	.46	.57	.62	.53	2CS	.54	.88	.86	.75
	sd:	.31	.35	.30	.33	.25	.32	.29	.21	.25	.28	.32	.23	.29	.31	.30	.28		.38	.15	.22	.24
4CL	Mn:	.74	.70	.83	.69	.85	.74	.77	.71	.74	.69	.67	.65	.59	.64	.66	.70	4CS	.81	.78	.76	.76
	sd:	.30	.24	.20	.33	.21	.24	.20	.23	.21	.25	.24	.24	.23	.25	.30	.27		.20	.29	.33	.17

Figure 14.4. The means and standard deviation for each time sampled for each view, averaged across subjects for Experiment 1.

Table 14.1.
Sequences of Geometrical Patterns

Attentional Complexity		1 Center			2 Centers			4 Centers		
Samples		1–16	1–4	5–16	1–16	1–4	5–16	1–16	1–4	5–16
Glance rate, 4 sec/view *Mn*		.53	.59	.51	.60	.69	.59	.66	.73	.70
	sd	.09	.11	.10	.12	.18	.10	.10	.10	.05
Glance rate, 1 sec/view *Mn*			.64			.76			.77	
	sd		.14			.11			.13	
Accuracy, 4 sec/view	*Mn*	.62			.59			.67		
	sd	.13			.14			.15		

what they judged as the most prominent regions in each view. In terms of total area of each view that was included in the designated centers, the proportions were .08, .16, and .32 for the one-, two-, and four-center view sequences, respectively. The proportions of glances that fell in these regions were greater than expected by chance: $t = 11.4$, 9.7, and 8.5, respectively, all with $df = 9$. In obtaining the prominence judgments, 15 subjects scored each of the 12 four-center views used, and 12 scored the mirror images of those views. Subjects were asked to indicate at least 6 and no more than 10 points in each view that were prominent, that is, that attracted and held their attention the most. (Although there might be some doubt as to precisely where within the region indicated by the dotted lines in Fig. 14.2 subjects may have placed their marks, there was never any doubt as to whether the point lay within the demarcated region; the dotted lines did not appear, of course, on the stimuli that were shown to the subjects.) The sum of the number of subjects who included each designated region in their first four rankings was obtained for each of the 12 views. The mean of the number of such judgments for each view (which with perfect agreement would be $15 \times 4 = 60$) was 40.50, with a standard deviation of 4.54. This result is significantly greater than the 20 markings one would expect ($t = 15.7$, $df = 11$, $p < .01$). The same analysis performed on the mirror-image views (using 12 additional subjects) yielded essentially the same results; in fact, the correlations between the most frequently chosen 10 points in the two groups for each picture ranged from .82 to .98, with a mean $r = 0.95$ (and a mean rho $= 0.86$), averaging z transformations. In short, the first four judgments agreed significantly with the points that we had intended to be the attentional centers, and on the average each view had only four points about which subjects agreed.

Discussion and Conclusions

As we expected from the earlier research on single static displays, fixations within the individual views of a sequence are emitted neither randomly nor in a systematic raster, but are directed to points that are also rated as being the most prominent. (Incidentally, this shows that the procedures by which we generated pictures of four attention centers were at least approximately successful.) The course of looking, within each view of the sequence, is much as Antes (1974) found: *The initial response to each view was initially high, followed by a declining glance rate.* The curve derived from Antes' graph in Fig. 14.1B cannot be directly compared to those obtained here: The abscissa in the former is in tenths of total fixations, whereas the abscissa in the latter is in 250 msec intervals of time so as to allow the course of looking to be time-locked to regular sequences of various frequencies.

As we expected from the simple considerations discussed previously, the rate of active looking is maintained at a higher level when there are more places at which to look, and when the cutting rate is higher. There was no strong interaction between cutting rate (4 sec/view and 1 sec/view) and attentional complexity in these experiments. Because the interaction between complexity and affective cutting tone is an important feature of Spottiswoode's model, and because a decline in glance rate at high cutting rates has been incidentally reported before (e.g., Potter & Levy, 1969), a replication of Experiment 1, including higher cutting rates, was performed (Brooks & Hochberg, 1976) with the same absence of interaction; at 4, 2, 1, and .5 sec/view, respectively, four-center sequences evoked glance rates of .70 (s.d. = .14), .74 (.13), .78 (.18), and .82 (.17), and one-center sequences evoked glance rates of .48 (.10), .50 (.12), .67 (.18), and .80 (.18).

Within the range in which it applies, the relationship demonstrated here between cutting rate, attentional complexity, and glance rate may make it possible, in principle, to "titrate" cutting rate against attentional complexity, in order to measure the latter. However, we cannot tell from Experiment 1 whether the same kinds of functions will appear when sequences are used that consist of meaningful views instead of abstract arrangements. Experiment 2 was directed to that question.

Experiment 2: The Course of Active Looking at Sequences of Meaningful Pictures

Two populations of pictures were obtained by cutting up old magazine illustrations, appliance catalogs, and college yearbooks. From these, sequences of views on 16mm film were assembled. When projected, they had the format shown in Fig. 14.5A, B, and C. One population (set *NC*) was chosen to have what appeared to be many centers of attention (one such photograph is represented by the outline drawing in Fig.14.5A), whereas the other population (set *SC*) had what we hoped would be a single center (Fig. 14.5B, C). In set *SC* two sequences consisted of views that occupied the entire format (Fig. 14.5B), and in which the center of attention might appear to one side or centrally; two other sequences were constructed in which either

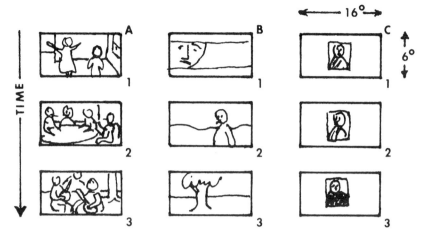

Figure 14.5. Line drawings of typical stimuli, in varying complexity, used in Experiment 2.

a series of faces from a yearbook (Fig. 14.5C) or a sequence of pictures of small household appliances appeared at the same place in each view.

Sequences were all six views in length and were presented at a rate of either 4 sec/view (*Long*) or 1 sec/view (*Short*). These sequences were presented to each of six naive subjects using the same instructions, apparatus, and procedures that had been used in Experiment 1. The order of the sequences for all subjects was as follows: SCL, NCL, SCS, NCS, NCS, SCS, NCL, SCL, SCL, NCL, SCS, NCS, NCS, SCS, NCL, and SCL.

Data were analyzed as they were in the previous experiments. Graphs of the time course of glance rate are shown in Fig. 14.6; the glance rate data, corresponding to those in Table 14.1, are summarized in Table 14.2. As with the abstract pictures, glance rates increased with both cutting rate and attentional complexity. Means and standard deviations of intrasubject differences are as follows: NCL–SCL = .31, s.d. = .08, t = 9.9, df = 5 (p < .01); NCS–SCS = .36, s.d. = .15, t = 5.99, df = 5 (p < .01); (NCL–SCL)–(NCS–SCS) = −.05, s.d. = .12, t = 1.02. No interaction of complexity and cutting rate were found here, either.

One other aspect of these data should be considered: We can separate two components in the time course of looking, the early peak and the later sustained glance rate. As the graphs suggest, the effects of the difference in cutting rate is significantly greater in the average of the last 3 sec than it is in the first sec, with mean intrasubject differences of $[(SCS–SCL) + (NCS–NCL)]_{1-16} - [(SCS–SCL) + (NCS–NCL)]_{1-4} = .11$, s.d. = .07, t = 3.6, p < .02.

Various explanations can be suggested for this difference. One that follows naturally from the approach we are pursuing is that the initial movements are made to points about which the subject has only the very

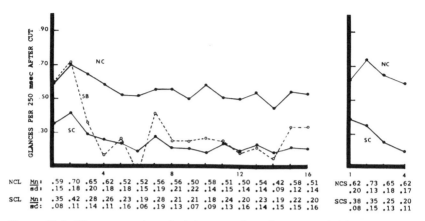

		4			8			12			16					1			4
NCL	Mn:	.59 .70 .65 .62 .52 .52 .56 .56 .50 .58 .51 .50 .54 .42 .58 .51														NCS	.62 .73 .65 .62		
	sd:	.15 .18 .20 .18 .18 .15 .19 .21 .22 .14 .15 .14 .14 .09 .12 .14															.20 .13 .18 .17		
SCL	Mn:	.35 .42 .28 .26 .23 .19 .28 .21 .21 .18 .24 .20 .23 .19 .22 .20														SCS	.38 .35 .25 .20		
	sd:	.08 .11 .14 .11 .16 .06 .19 .13 .07 .09 .13 .16 .14 .15 .15 .16															.08 .15 .13 .11		

Figure 14.6. The means and standard deviations for each time sampled for each view, averaged across subjects for Experiment 2.

general information that he can gain by peripheral vision. These movements occur under what we have called elsewhere *peripheral search guidance* (Hochberg, 1970a, b; Hochberg & Brooks, 1970). After the initial eye movements have established the general nature of the peripherally visible *landmarks* (Hochberg & Gellman, 1977), subsequent saccades are directed to the answers of more cognitively driven questions (*cognitive search guidance*, in the case of meaningful pictures), which sustain inquiry about details near the landmarks. This is similar to suggestions made by Antes (1974) and Loftus (1976). Note, however, that it might be argued, at least as well, that the sustained parts of these curves might arise from an ahistorical recycling, with perturbations, through the points of highest salience (cf. Baker, 1977; Senders, Webb, & Baker, 1955). It is hard to believe that the geometric "scenes" of Experiment 1 can hold much that is of cognitive interest to the viewer after 1 or 2 sec of looking. We will return to this point later, noting here that it makes glance rate, alone, an inadequate index of cognitive search.

Table 14.2.
Sequences of Meaningful Views

Attentional Complexity		S Center			N Centers		
Samples		1–16	1–4	5–16	1–16	1–4	5–16
Glance rate, 4 sec/view *Mn*		.24	.33	.21	.55	.64	.53
	sd	.10	.09	.11	.11	.13	.12
Glance rate, 1 sec/view *Mn*			.30			.66	
	sd		.08			.13	

It will be remembered that we employed two kinds of simple sequences, that is, views like those in Fig. 14.5B and in Fig. 14.5C. In Fig. 14.5C, successive views all fell in much the same place, so that no large peripheral movements were needed in order to observe succeeding objects or faces. In the sequence of views like Fig. 14.5B, on the other hand, the viewer would need one or two large initial saccades in order to locate the region at which he might look for the remainder of his viewing time. Compare the graphs of a sequence of views like those in Fig. 14.5B to those of the whole set of SCL sequences (Fig. 14.6): The average glance rate is higher (.13) with samples 1–4 than samples 5–16 (.03), $t = 3.2$, $df = 5$, $p < .05$, but this difference is restricted to the first few moments of looking. This raises another difficulty in the use of glance rate to assess perceptual inquiry: The amount of eye movement is strongly dependent on where attentional foci fall in successive views; and a subject might gaze in rapt but immobile attention at successive views that are all most informative at the same place (cf. Potter & Levy, 1969).

We need another measure of visual momentum or tendency to keep looking at a view sequence. We discuss a subjective preference measure in the next section, and turn to a more successful objective measure later.

Aesthetic Preference and Visual Momentum

These experiments, described elsewhere in more detail, were quite straight-forward attempts to determine whether the sequences of views used in the previous experiments would elicit judgments of preference (other than by chance), and how such preference judgments relate to the variables being investigated. Small groups of two or four subjects, naive as to the hypothesis being tested, were shown the sequences. In each experiment, they were initially shown one sequence to which they were to assign the number 100 as a measure of its *pleasingness*. Tables 14.3A and 14.3B show the geometric means of the preferences for the sequences of Experiments 1 and 2, respectively. The effect of complexity is significant, but the effect of cutting rate is not, despite what we expected from Spottiswoode's (1933/1962) model.

It may be that subjects are merely displaying the well-known correlation between aesthetic judgments and complexity (cf. Berlyne, 1958; Faw & Nunnally, 1967), without regard to cutting rate, that is, they may simply be reporting the structure they perceive, and the higher cutting rate may merely be an interference—that would certainly be consistent with the *lower* pleasingness of the higher cutting rates. We have not yet run this experiment on subjects steeped in motion-picture analysis, and we may yet obtain different results with them. But in any case, we cannot use pleasingness judgments to measure visual momentum. A more objective procedure for measuring the impetus to keep looking was explored in the remaining set of experiments.

Table 14.3.
Pleasingness Judgments (Geometric Means)

Attentional Complexity	A Sequences of Experiment 1		
	1C	2C	4C
Short views	88.0	104.2	131.7
Long views	78.7	97.2	124.2

Attentional Complexity	B Sequences of Experiment 2	
	SC	NC
Short views	74.2	88.7
Long views	84.4	125.0

Preferential Free Looking: Split-field Measures of Momentum

The following experiments are intended to test a measure of the moment-by-moment impetus to look at an extended sequence of views.

Experiments 3–5

The following experiments all have the same basic procedure: Two sequences were displayed simultaneously, one above the other, with the dimensions shown in Fig. 14.7. We will call these the upper and lower channels. After a relatively small number of pairs of views, a different short typed word appeared briefly in each channel. The sequences of pictorial views in each channel then continued, as shown schematically in Fig. 14.7B.

Each subject was told that we were concerned with his eye movements under cognitive load and that he was to attend to the word that would appear in the particular channel specified before each presentation began.

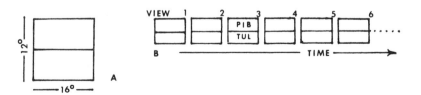

Figure 14.7. (A) Schematic of display with upper and lower channels. (B) Typical view sequence used in Experiments 3–5.

He was to note the word and press a key as quickly as possible as soon as he had read it. After that, he was free to look wherever he wished until the experimenter told him that the next trial was about to begin and in which channel the next target word would appear. When the subject pressed the key, an LED signal was recorded on the motion-picture film.

Each pair of sequences was shown twice during the course of each experiment. The channel that had contained the target word on one presentation was the nonattended channel on the other presentation. In all cases, target channels were alternated on initial presentation between subjects. The measure that we were concerned with in each case was the proportion of time spent looking at the nontargeted channel during the "free-looking" period (i.e., after the word). Thus, no task required him to look at that channel, but the distracting or attractive effect of the alternate channel with which it was paired was controlled within subjects, while order was controlled across subjects. Because the looking time for one channel was necessarily affected by the attractiveness of the alternate channel, however, comparisons were made only between sequences that were members of the same pair.

Experiment 3: Preferential Looking at Montages of Geometrical Patterns

The procedure and subjects (N = 10) were as described above. The stimulus sequences were those used in Experiment 1, paired so that the two channels were matched in duration and phase of the view sequences, that is, both were 1 sec/view or 4 sec/view, or paired so that the two channels were equal in complexity but differed in view duration (cutting rate) for a total of 24 possible combinations. A sample of the sequence pairs is as follows: 1CS/4CS, 4CS/4CL, and 1CL/1CS, with the slash (/) separating upper/lower channels.

The means and standard errors of the average proportions of the posttarget time that subjects looked at each category of sequence when it was the nontargeted channel are given in Table 14.4. When four centers are pitted against one center, it is clear that subjects look longer at the four centers. And when short views (fast sequences) were pitted against long views (slow sequences), the former prevails. Most proportions are less than .50 because there is a tendency to keep looking at the target channel even after the word has been removed. The mean of the differences between each subject's mean of A and B and his mean of C and D, in Table 14.4, was .23, s.d. = .22, t = 3.21, df = 9, p < .01, indicating a significant effect due to complexity. The mean of the differences between means of E and F–G and H was .24, s.d. = .13, t = 6.03, df = 9, p < .01, indicating a significant effect due to cutting rate. The interaction between complexity of the scene and cutting rate is not significant.

Table 14.4.
Preferential Looking: Sequences of Geometrical Views[a]

	Proportion of Time Spent Looking at Nontargeted Channel							
	Short Versus Long				1 Center Versus 4 Centers			
	A: 4CS	B: 4CL	C: 1CS	D: 1CL	E: 1CL	F: 4CL	G: 1CS	H: 4CS
Mn	.41	.50	.20	.25	.21	.17	.39	.46
s.d.	.27	.14	.13	.09	.17	.13	.16	.16

[a]N = 10 in all cases

Experiments 4A, B, and C: Preferential Looking at Montages and Connected Sequences of Representational Views

The procedure in these experiments was that of Experiment 3, using meaningful pictures (primarily, those of Experiment 2).

Experiment 4A: Effect of Cutting Rate

Two kinds of sequence pairs were presented here, either complex (NC) or simple (SC) views in both upper and lower channels. In each case, the views in one channel were short (.5 sec/view) whereas those in the other were long (3 sec/view). The means and standard deviations for preferential looking (the time spent looking at a channel when the other channel was targeted) are shown in Table 14.5. Analyses of intrasubject differences showed that cutting rate clearly affects looking time (pooled t [S/L] = 3.9, df = 7, p < .01), while the effect of cutting rate was not significantly different for the NC and SC view sequences.

Experiments 4B, C: Effect of Attentional Complexity

In Experiment 4B (N = 10), two kinds of sequence pairs were presented; in both, one channel contained complex views (NC) and one contained simple views (SC), taken from Experiment 4A. One set of paired sequences was presented at .5 sec/view and the other set was presented at 3 sec/view. In Experiment 4C (N = 10), the same sequences were used as in Experiment 4B, except that (a) what had been in the upper channel in Experiment 4B was in the lower channel in Experiment 4C, and vice versa; and (b) Experiment 4C contained several additional paired sequences as preliminary inquiries for future research, some of which will be referred to later. An ANOVA of subjects' mean scores on NCS, SCS, and SCL for the two groups of Experiments 4B and 4C showed no difference between the two groups

Table 14.5.
Preferential Looking: Sequences of Meaningful Views

	Proportion of Time Spent Looking at Nontargeted Channel			
	Experiment 4A. Effect of Cutting Rate			
	NCS	NCL	SCS	SCL
4A				
Mn	.65	.40	.65	.33
s.d.	.22	.20	.16	.24	N = 8

	Experiments 4B and 4C. Effect of Attentional Complexity			
	NCS	NCL	SCS	SCL
4B				
Mn	.28	.53	.22	.34
s.d.	.27	.14	.18	.13	N = 10
4C				
Mn	.46	.66	.31	.25
s.d.	.27	.18	.25	.15	N = 10

($F = 1.47$, $df = 1$, 54), an interaction between group and sequence which approached significance ($F = 2.31$, $df = 3$, 54, $p < .10$), an effect of complexity which was significant ($t = 3.12$, $df = 18$, $p < .01$), and an effect of the interaction between complexity and cutting rate which was significant ($t = 6.40$, $df = 18$, $p < .01$). It is clear (Table 14.5) that attentional complexity affects looking time and that the effect is greater at lower cutting rates.

Discussion. Experiments 4A–4C give the concept of visual momentum, as a hypothetical construct over and above the measured glance rates obtained in Experiments 1–3, some plausibility. They do not show, however, that cognitive inquiry, as distinct from stimulus factors such as change and complexity per se, contribute substantially to the sustained component of looking—this is essentially an extension of the question we raised in the course of discussing Experiment 2. That is, movement in the channel that one is not looking at might capture the gaze and account for the greater visual momentum of the channel having the higher cutting rate; and greater complexity might act to hold the gaze simply by increasing the intrachannel transitional probabilities, regardless of any questions of perceptual inquiry.

With respect to the possibility that mere change in pattern accounts completely for visual momentum differences, we have two examples to the contrary, neither of them completely convincing, within the data of the experiments we have already described. If "peripheral capture" were the sole basis of the looking-preference measures, a sequence in which the center of attention was in a different place in each view should be looked at more frequently than one in which such displacement did not occur. We have some indication that effects attributable to displacement per se are not a major factor. First, note that the sequence in Fig. 14.5B, which elicited a higher glance rate during the first second of viewing time, presumably due to the greater displacement from view to view, did not differ from Fig. 14.5C when the data of Experiment 4C are analyzed specifically with respect to these two sequences, and no differences on the basis of rate were found. We cannot make too much of this point, however, because they had no occasion to be pitted against each other in the same two-channel pair, and we noted that cross-pair comparisons cannot really be made. Second, consider the two sequence pairs in Fig. 14.8A and 14.8B. These were designed to induce more eye movements in one channel than in the other, and they were successful in this regard. In sequence A, each channel had a story in the sense that the successive views were designed to represent parts of the same scene, the same "characters" appeared throughout, and the sequence could readily be described in terms of a continuous action narrative. The attention center in the upper channel was designed to fall close to the center on each view; the attention center in the lower channel fell on alternate sides of the view, in successive views. Mean of the momentum differences between upper and lower channels was 0.18, s.d. $= .52$, t $= 1.09$, df $= 9$.

In sequence B, the upper channel was a stick-figure animation of the apple-shooting scene in the William Tell story, with occasional cuts and small amounts of continuous movements in the actions of walking, lifting the apple, etc. The movement of the swing in the lower channel was 8°/sec, with a .17 sec pause at each end of the arc. Mean of the differences between momentum for the upper and lower channels was 0.28, s.d. $= .35$, t $= 2.57$,

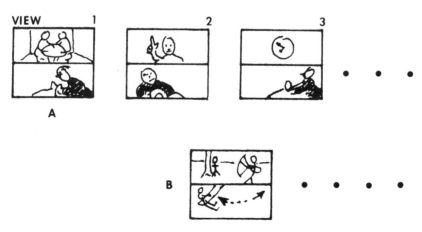

Figure 14.8. Line drawings of typical stimuli used in Experiment 5 to induce more eye movements in one channel than the other.

df = 9, p < .05. No differences were found in favor of looking at the lateral eye movement–inducing channel in either of these two sequence pairs.

If these results are generally reliable, they have some practical importance to filmmakers, who often cut in such a way that the two different foci of attention fall in essentially the same place in two successive views (and maintain the same velocities, if the objects are in motion). This should result in an effectively lowered cutting rate, and in less impetus to keep looking, if peripheral capture were a major component of visual momentum. But if peripheral capture is not the main factor in visual momentum (which is what we are arguing here), then the filmmaker's practice is probably sound for a rather subtle reason: It should delay the viewer's comprehension by several hundred msec (because he lacks the signals that would indicate, rapidly and noncognitively, that changes have occurred), and this delay should sustain visual momentum over a slower cutting rate (cf. Fig. 14.1A).

This assumes, of course, that cognitive inquiry contributes substantially to visual momentum, an assumption for which we have so far provided only weak support. The next experiment provides better support. The second way in which noncognitive factors might account for visual momentum is by having complexity capture the gaze in the split-field experiments regardless of the viewer's experience. This is addressed by Experiment 5.

Experiment 5: The Effects of Repetition on Preferential Looking

This experiment is addressed to the same question, within sequences, that Flagg discusses in regard to between-sequence effects. In order to test the possibility that change and complexity per se determine preferential looking, regardless of the viewer's history with the stimuli, new sequences were made from those used in Experiment 4B, with these changes: (1) The sequence length was extended to a total of 18 views past the target word, and (2) the attentionally complex (NC) sequence consisted only of the same two views, alternating repetitively with each other. Eight new subjects were used with these stimuli presented at 1.5 sec/view. Eye movements were recorded and analyzed only during the presentations of the pairs in which the simple sequence (SC) consisted of the extended views (Fig. 14.5B) as distinguished from the view sequences of single items (yearbook faces, appliances) centered in each successive view.

Eye-movement records were divided into segments corresponding to each cycle (i.e., pair of repeated views) of the NC sequences, and the duration each subject spent in looking at the nontargeted channel within each of the nine cycles was obtained for the presentation in which the NC sequence was the nontargeted channel and that in which the SC sequence was the nontargeted channel. The difference in response among the nine cycles is significant (F = 3.83, df = 8, 56, p < .01); momentum is significantly greater for SC than for NC in the second half of the sequence: The

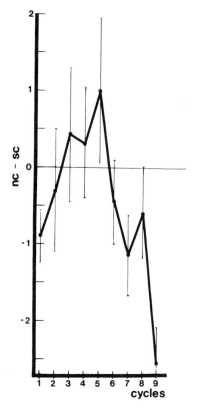

Figure 14.9. Time course of differences in visual momentum for a repeating complex view sequence (NC) paired with a nonrepeating simple view sequence (SC). The heavy line is the graph of the differences between durations of looking at the NC and at the SC sequences when each is the nontargeted channel. Thin lines indicate standard errors. The abscissa is the number of the cycle of the repeating NC pair of views after the presentation of the target word; the ordinate is the mean difference in looking times for NC and for SC for that cycle, in terms of number of 250 msec samples.

mean of subjects' differences is .25, s.d. = .17, t = 4.18, df = 7, p < .01. The difference in visual momentum (NC–SC), averaged across subjects for each cycle after the target word, is graphed in Fig. 14.9. The effect of history is clear and, having seen that the two alternating NC views were the same (to some criterion) from cycle to cycle, subjects reversed the looking preferences they had displayed in the other experiments.

Summary and Conclusions

The ways in which people move their eyes while they are watching sequences of changing views and the proportions of time that they spend in looking at one sequence rather than another are lawfully related to the characteristics of the views and to the rates at which they are changed (cutting rates).

We have seen that in general the outcome of experiments on glance rate and experiments on preferential looking at sequences of abstract and representational views (montages) are consistent with the notion of an impetus to gather visual information, which we have called *visual momentum*. The time course of visual momentum as a function of complexity and of cutting rate is quite similar to Spottiswoode's semiquantitative introspective model of what he called affective cutting tone. There are some results that suggest that the course of active looking, and of the visual momentum that presumably impels it, can be partitioned into components: a fast component that brings the eye to those peripherally visible regions that promise to be informative or to act as landmarks, and a more sustained component that directs the eye to obtain more detailed information about the main features that have already been located.

Both of these components of momentum should have theoretical as well as practical interests: practical, because they are important in such applications as film editing; theoretical, because the fast component may be informative about the uses of peripheral vision, and the slow component may reveal the momentary state of schema formation, using cutting rate (for example) to "titrate" the loss of visual momentum that occurs after the view is comprehended. Such research is now in progress.

Discussion

LAWRENCE W. STARK: Do you think you could put your test words in such a way as to see if the subject was in this peripheral guidance mode or the central schema testing mode and really test out your various hypotheses?

HOCHBERG: We could do that by adding additional probes in the body after the test words have appeared. The initial test words are "covers"; they're used simply to give the subject some task and to mark the start of his free period; after he sees the word he can do what he wants. We can indeed put probes into the free-looking period. It is definitely something to do. I have some reservations; that is, I think that will change the mode of the subject's looking. I try to keep the subjects unconstrained, and that's the point of all this elaborate secrecy. For example, the glance-rate experiments were presented as experiments in aesthetics. We actually did gather some aesthetic data, because we're constrained by NIH regulations not to lie to our subjects and some of those data are interesting—unlike the pupillary reflex data, but I can't report them now.

So, the answer is: yes, it can be done, and my guess is that the early component is so robust and probably sufficiently resistant to instructions that using additional probes would work. We haven't tried it.

CALVIN F. NODINE: You've indicated that the early component has to do with peripheral guidance and the later component is more concerned with attention to detail.

HOCHBERG: Maybe, but it would be very possible that there's also a stochastic component as well.

NODINE: Where does expectancy come into this?

HOCHBERG: You set the stage for a paragraph that I had cut out because I didn't have time.

Yes. We've given peripheral search guidance here a new function, namely, because of the nature of unconnected views, it has to bring the viewer to some meaningful fixation point to begin with. Now, one of the reasons we use disconnected montage is that it gives us a baseline against which we can refer sequences of views in which the subject does carry over information and expectations from one view to the next.

References

ANTES, J. R. The time course of picture viewing. *Journal of Experimental Psychology*, 1974, *103*, 62–70.

BAKER, M. A. *A model for predicting duration, location, and sequence of eye-fixation for metric polygons*. Paper presented at US Army Human Engineering Laboratory Conference, Eye Movements and Psychological Processes II: The higher functions, Monterey, Ca., February, 1977.

BERLYNE, D. E. The influence of complexity and novelty in visual figures on orienting responses. *Journal of Experimental Psychology*, 1958, *55*, 289–296.

BIEDERMAN, I. Perceiving real-world scenes. *Science*, 1972, *177*, 77–80.

BOUMA, H., & deVOOGD, A. H. On the control of eye saccades in reading. *Vision Research*, 1974, *14*, 273–284.

BROOKS, B. *An exploratory comparison of some measures of attention*. Unpublished master's thesis, Cornell University, 1961.

BROOKS, V., & HOCHBERG, J. Control of active looking by motion picture cutting rate. *Proceedings of the Eastern Psychological Association*, 1976, *49*. (Abstract).

BUSWELL, G. T. *How people look at pictures*. Chicago: University of Chicago Press, 1935.

FARLEY, A. M. A computer implementation of constructive visual imagery and perception. In R. A. Monty & J. W. Senders (Eds.) *Eye movements and psychological processes*. Hillsdale, N.J.: Lawrence Erlbaum Associates, 1976.

FAW, T. T., & NUNNALLY, J. C. The effects on eye movements of complexity, novelty and affective tone. *Perception and Psychophysics*, 1967, *2*, 263–267.

GIBSON, J. J. The visual perception of objective motion and subjective movement. *Psychological Review*, 1954, *61*, 304–314.

GIBSON, J. J. Optical motion and transformations as stimuli for visual perception. *Psychological Review*, 1957, *64*, 288–295.

GIBSON, J. J. *The Senses Considered as Perceptual Systems*. Boston: Houghton Mifflin, 1966.

GIRGUS, J. A developmental approach to the study of shape processing. *Journal of Experimental Child Psychology*, 1973, *16*, 363–374.

GIRGUS, J. A developmental study of the effect of eye movement on shape perception in a sequential viewing situation. *Journal of Experimental Child Psychology*, 1976, *22*, 386–399.

GIRGUS, J. & HOCHBERG, J. Age differences in shape recognition through an aperture in a free-viewing situation. *Psychonomic Science*, 1972, *28*, 237–238.

HOCHBERG, J. In the mind's eye. In R. N. Haber (Ed.), *Contemporary theory and research in visual perception.* New York: Holt, Rinehart, and Winston, 1968.

HOCHBERG, J. Attention, organization and consciousness. In D. I. Mostofsky (Ed.), *Attention: Contemporary theory and analysis.* New York: Appleton-Century-Crofts, 1970. (a)

HOCHBERG, J. Components of literacy: Speculation and exploratory research. In H. Levin & J. P. Williams (Eds.), *Basic studies on reading.* New York: Basic Books, 1970. (b)

HOCHBERG, J. & BROOKS, V. The prediction of visual attention to designs and paintings. *American Psychologist*, 1962, *17*, 7. (Abstract)

HOCHBERG, J. & BROOKS, V. Geometrical vs. directional factors in the prediction of attention distributions. *American Psychologist*, 1963, *18*, 437. (Abstract)

HOCHBERG, J. & BROOKS, V. Reading as intentional behavior. In H. Singer (Ed.), *Theoretical Models and Processes of Reading.* Newark, Delaware: International Reading Association, 1970.

HOCHBERG, J., & BROOKS, V. *The maintenance of perceptual inquiry: Quantitative tests of some simple models.* Paper read at the Spring 1974 meetings of the Society of Experimental Psychologists.

HOCHBERG, J. and GELLMAN, L. Feature saliency, "mental rotation" times, and the integration of successive views. *Memory and Cognition*, 1977, *5*, 23–26.

JOHANSSON, G. *Spatio-temporal differentiation and integration in visual motion perception.* (Report #160). Uppsala, Sweden, Department of Psychology, 1974.

KOLERS, P. A. Buswell's discoveries. In R. A. Monty & J. W. Senders (Eds.), *Eye movements and psychological processes.* Hillsdale, N.J.: Lawrence Erlbaum Associates, 1976.

LOFTUS, G. R. A framework for a theory of picture recognition. In R. A. Monty & J. W. Senders (Eds.), *Eye Movements and Psychological Processes.* Hillsdale, N.J.: Lawrence Erlbaum Associates, 1976.

MACKWORTH, N., & MORANDI, A. J. The gaze selects informative details within pictures. *Perception and Psychophysics*, 1967, *2*, 547–552.

MARTIN, E. Saccadic suppression and the stable world. In R. A. Monty, & J. W. Senders, (Eds.), *Eye movements and psychological processes.* Hillsdale, N.J.: Lawrence Erlbaum Associates, 1976.

MURPHY, R. Recognition memory for sequentially presented pictorial and verbal spatial information. *Journal of Experimental Psychology*, 1973, *100*, 327–334.

NEISSER, U. *Cognitive Psychology*, New York: Appleton, 1967.

PIAGET, J. *The construction of reality in the child.* (Margaret Cook, trans.) New York: Basic Books, 1954.

POLLACK, I., & SPENCE, D. Subjective pictorial information and visual search. *Perception and Psychophysics*, 1968, *3* (1-B), 41–44.

POTTER, M. C., & LEVY, E. I. Recognition memory for a rapid sequence of pictures. *Journal of Experimental Psychology*, 1969, *81*, 10–15.

REED, S. K., & JOHNSEN, J. A. Detection of parts in patterns and images. *Memory and Cognition*, 1975, *3*, 569–575.

SEDGWICK, H. A., & FESTINGER, L. Eye movements, efference and visual perception. In R. A. Monty, & J. W. Senders (Eds.), *Eye movements and psychological processes.* Hillsdale, N.J.: Lawrence Erlbaum Associates, 1976.

SENDERS, J. W., WEBB, I. B., & BAKER, C. A. The peripheral viewing of dials. *Journal of Applied Psychology*, 1955, *39*, 433–436.

Skavenski, A. A. The nature and role of extraretinal eye position information in visual localization. In R. A. Monty, & J. W. Senders (Eds.), *Eye Movements and Psychological Processes*. Hillsdale, N.J.: Lawrence Erlbaum Associates, 1976.

Spottiswoode, R. *A grammar of the film*. Berkeley, Calif.: University of California Press, 1962. (Originally published, 1933.)

Young, L., and Sheena, D. Survey of eye movement recording methods. *Behavior Research Methods and Instrumentation*, 1975, *7*, 397–429.

15

Pictorial Functions and Perceptual Structures

Julian Hochberg

Pictorial Representation and Perceptual Theory

Realistic representation has been one of the avowed goals of Western art for millennia. Moreover, realism has always been and continues to be a popular value in the pictures that are produced for mass consumption. There have repeatedly been significant departures from this goal, however, and it has not been even a discernible purpose of modern painting for most of the past century.

In pursuit of realistic representation, artists have investigated the nature of light and pigments, the laws of optics, the physical structures that are to be represented (e.g., anatomy and botany), and the psychology of visual perception. There is therefore a rich set of problems that are shared by the perception psychologist and the studious or innovative artist.

Representation as a Problem for Theories of Perception

Because pictorial representation appears to entail the use of illusion as its central fact—that is, the perception of scenes and objects that are not actually presented to the viewer—it is easier for some theories to deal with than for others. Let us see why.

The Picture Is Not the Thing It Represents

Realistic representation is not a simple term. A common but very restricted meaning is illusionistic in its definition: One object (e.g., a painting) represents another very different object or set of objects (e.g., a person or a scene) perfectly if it is completely indistinguishable from the object or scene, that is, if it is optically identical or equivalent to that scene. By *optical identity*, I mean that the light to the eye from scene and from surrogate are physically identical, as with a mirror, a hologram, or with some trompe l'oeil pictures viewed from a great distance. By *optically equivalent*, I mean an array of light that is physically very different (e.g., having an entirely different spectral distribution) that nevertheless elicits the same visual response from the viewer, point by point, as does the original scene; this distinction is important in discussing paintings from the standpoint of their apparent color and shade (Hochberg, 1979b). The conditions for achieving such indistinguishability of surrogate and scene by either means are rarely attained. In general, the light transmitted to the eye from picture and object are not alike in any way that can readily be defined in terms of the physical stimulus alone. It is only because of the sensory and perceptual characteristics of the viewer that the object and picture appear to be similar in certain respects, that is, the picture *simulates* part or all of the object it represents. I have discussed the picture as it simulates object color and scene luminances in a companion paper (Hochberg, 1979b); here, I attempt to discuss the picture as it simulates the form and space of the scenes and objects that are represented.

The represented scene is a set of surfaces at different distances; the picture is a single flat, mottled, lined, or dappled plane surface. When viewed monocularly from a single place, the scene (Figure 15.1A) and its picture (Figure 15.1B) present similar patterns of light to the eye. Figure 15.1 illustrates Leonardo's famous prescription to painters that they should trace scenes on sheets of glass and then study the latter in order to learn about representing the former. Some of what Woodworth (1938) called the *cues* to depth that are provided by flat pictures are listed in the caption. But Figures 15.1A and B are very different physical arrangements, and the patterns and sequences of light that each offers a normal binocular observer who is free to move his or her head and eyes, and free to change the direction and focus of his or her gaze, are obviously different too.

If the viewer rotates his or her head while looking at the picture (Figure 15.2Aii) or the scene (Figure 15.2Ai), different motion parallax will result in each case (Figure 15.2Bi, ii), because the eye is not located at the center of rotation of the head. And the convergence and disparity of the binocular gaze is likewise different in the two cases. Moreover, pictures often use outlines—which are mere ribbons of pigment—to represent edges, dihedrals, and horizons (Figure 15.2C), although the latter are physical situations that present no lines to the eye. We must certainly concede that the picture and the scene may physically be very different, both as events in the world and in terms of the stimulation they provide the eye of the unfettered viewer.

Indeed, the differences between pictures and their objects are usually so great that it has been tempting to philosophers, psychologists, and artists alike to consider pictures to be a learned and arbitrary language, with the relationship between a picture and an object being just as discretionary as that between a word and its object. As we will see, however, that is not true: The "language of pictures" may or may not be learned, but it is certainly not arbitrary, nor is it learned only from our experiences with pictures themselves.

The fact that pictures *appear* to the viewer to be so similar to the things they represent, although they are so different physically, is a major fact that any theory of perception must confront.

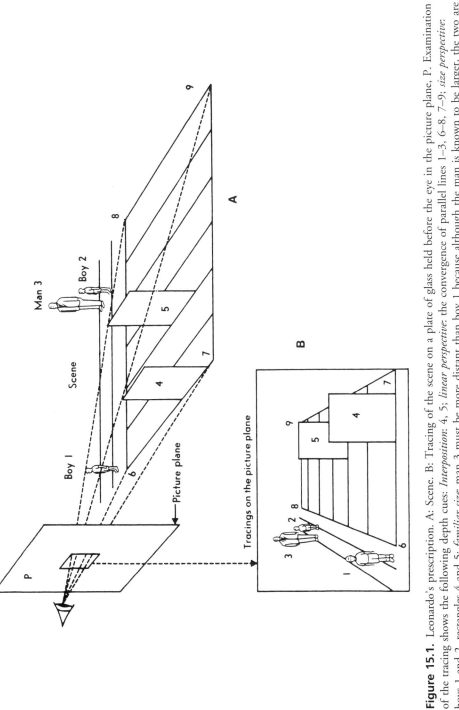

Figure 15.1. Leonardo's prescription. A: Scene. B: Tracing of the scene on a plate of glass held before the eye in the picture plane, P. Examination of the tracing shows the following depth cues: *Interposition:* 4, 5; *linear perspective:* the convergence of parallel lines 1–3, 6–8, 7–9; *size perspective:* boys 1 and 2, rectangles 4 and 5; *familiar size:* man 3 must be more distant than boy 1 because although the man is known to be larger, the two are drawn to the same size; *texture-density gradient:* The horizontal stripes between 6–7 and 8–9 are progressively closer in spacing from bottom to top, in B, though homogeneously spaced in A. (From Hochberg, 1978a.)

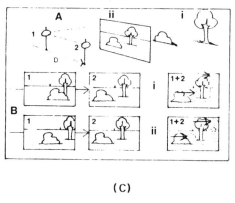

(C)

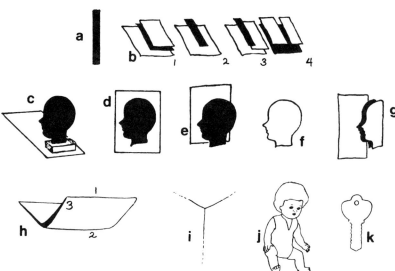

Figure 15.2. The picture is not the scene that it represents.

A: An eye, moving distance D from position 1 to 2, gazing at either a scene in depth (i) or a picture of that scene (ii).

B: i (1, 2). Views of the scene that the eye receives from each location; 1 + 2. The two views superimposed. ii. Views of the picture that the eye receives at each location; 1+2. The two views superimposed.

C: Lines and represented objects. a: A short line, itself a narrow ribbon of pigment on paper, having both a left and a right edge. b: Four different ways in which surfaces' edges could produce the same stimulus pattern as the ribbon of pigment. c: A solid black, featureless head. d: A surrogate for c, consisting of pigment on paper, which is also a surrogate for a flat cutout, e. f: A line of pigment on paper, which can serve as a surrogate for g (see Figure 15.2Cb1) and therefore for c–e as well. h: Three representational functions of a line: 1. a surface's edge (as in Figure 15.2Cb1); 2. a horizon, where a curving surface is tangent to the line of sight; 3. a far surface edge occluded by a near one. i. The three corners or apices of dihedral

232

The Implications of Pictorial Representation

If the perception of surfaces and their arrangements in space were a direct and automatic response to the information presented to the eye, a picture of a playing field (Figure 15.1B) must be directly perceived as an upright flat surface with converging lines drawn on it, not as a rectangular surface receding into distance. What is specified by the information in the viewer's changing retinal image as he or she moves relative to the picture (i.e., what is invariant throughout the transformation) is the flat plane and converging lines. To proponents of a direct theory of surface perception, therefore, these considerations have suggested that pictures need a separate and special theory of perception: that is, that pictures may be subject to unconscious inference, etc., but that does not mean that all perception requires such assistance (Gibson, 1951).

Is a Special Theory Needed for Picture Perception?

I see only two possibilities for such a special theory: (*a*) The perception of pictures is in its entirety a special learned ability, acquired by experience with pictures as manmade artifacts; (*b*) the perception of pictures draws at least in part upon the same mechanisms, whether learned or innate, by which we perceive the world itself.

We can reject the first alternative for two quite different and equally important reasons. First, the most theoretically critical aspects of picture perception can be demonstrated to occur with no prior training with pictures: The recognition of objects represented as outline drawings does not require prior instruction or substantial pictorial experience of any kind (Hochberg & Brooks, 1962a). Second, the fact that motion parallax is insufficient to overcome the static pictorial depth cues on the canvas is not unique to pictures: Pictures may be the most salient and widespread demonstrations that stimulus information is insufficient to determine perception, but other demonstrations are well known, as we see next.

Stimulus Information Is Insufficient to Determine What We Perceive

In Figure 15.3A, the diagrams illustrate a demonstration by Kopfermann (1930), which I have replicated, in which the continuous edges of a cube are in fact represented by fragments at different distances from the eye. The fragments align with each other to form the outline cube at ii when viewed from precisely the right place in space. What is important to our present

---

angles formed by three surfaces meeting. j: A picture of a doll, in which the lines serve as horizons (cf. Figure 15.2Ch2); and k, a picture of a key, in which the lines serve as surface edges (cf. Figure 15.2Ch1); both of these were recognized by a child who had received no prior pictorial instruction whatsoever (Hochberg & Brooks, 1962a), a fact that must be confronted by any theory of picture perception that is impressed by the differences between pictures and the scenes that they represent. (Figure 15.2C is adapted from Hochberg, 1962.)

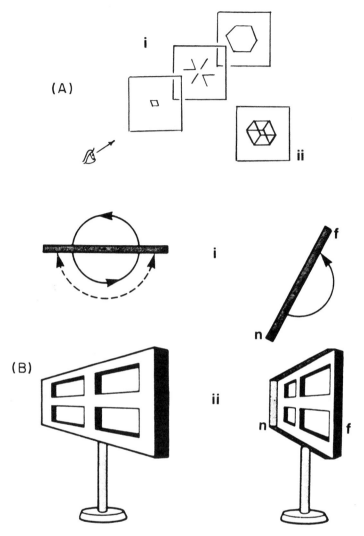

Figure 15.3. Pictorial cues can overcome parallactic information about spatial layout.

A. At i, fragments of a cube drawn on three glass plates at different distances in space from the viewer. At ii, what the viewer sees when properly stationed. What is important here is that when the viewer makes small head movements, the cube appears to deform rather than to be perceived in its true spatial separation, as at i (Kopfermann, 1930).

B. The Ames trapezoid: This is a trapezoidal cutout of cardboard or metal with converging lines painted on it as shown. At left: top view (i) and bottom view (ii) show the object to be rotating (solid arrow). When looked at monocularly from a distance of a couple of meters, the object appears to oscillate (dotted arrow), almost certainly because the small side appears farther away (see Figure 15.1) even when it is nearer (n, at right). (This figure is adapted from Hochberg, 1978a.)

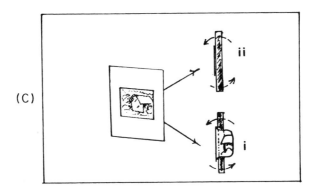

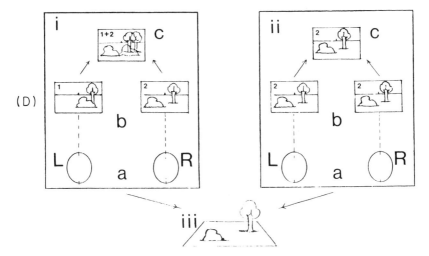

C. At i, a model of a house, recessed in a white cardboard frame and covered with clear celluloid which is lightly textured to match the texture of the cardboard. At ii, a picture of the model, similarly covered with textured celluloid. When the two objects are oscillated as shown by the arrows, the uninstructed viewer does not notice that only one of them is a picture. The model at i serves as a deep surrogate for a flat picture (Hochberg, 1962).

Di. Binocular parallax: When the left eye (L) and the right eye (R), both at (a), receive appropriately different views (1, 2) of a deep scene, the scene itself is perceived, three-dimensional and deep. The parallactic difference between the views is shown by the superimposition (1 + 2) at c. ii. Two identical views when presented in a stereogram also look deep, if they contain pictorial depth cues (Schlosberg, 1941), despite the fact that the absence of disparity (as shown by the superimposition at c) specifies to the visual system of the viewer that he or she confronts a flat object. (This does not imply that i and ii look equally deep.)

purpose is that movements of the viewer's eye away from that one place—movements that are sufficient to exceed the normal thresholds for non-alignment—do not break up the apparently continuous cube into its real components. In Figure 15.3B, the famous Ames trapezoid is shown from above at i and from in front at ii: Even when edge n is near the viewer, the image it presents the eye is smaller than that of edge f, so in accordance with the static pictorial depth cues of relative size and linear perspective (Figure 15.1B), it is always perceived as farther away. The trapezoid therefore appears to oscillate rather than to rotate (which is what it is actually doing, as shown by the solid arrow). Figure 15.3C is a demonstration that I once set up consisting of a model of a house, recessed into a cardboard mat and covered by a textured, transparent piece of celluloid to provide a simulation of a picture plane; at ii is a picture of the same model. Whether presented to the naked eye of a naive observer who is free to move his or her head as in normal viewing or with both i and ii in motion recorded by a motion-picture camera and projected on a screen, the casual observer, asked after a brief presentation (ca.1 sec) to guess which of the two was flat and which was solid, performed at chance.

What is true of motion parallax—thus far studied only in these qualitative demonstrations—is true of binocular parallax as well: Viewed in a stereoscope which relaxes the accommodation of the eyes' lenses and makes the pictures' margins less obtrusive than they normally are, two identical pictures (Figure 15.3Diib) look tridimensional and depthlike because of the pictorial depth cues alone (Schlosberg, 1941), even though the absence of disparity in the two views (Figure 15.3Diic) *specifies* to the viewer that he or she is looking at a flat plane. Indeed, Schriever (1925) has shown that pictorial depth cues can overcome binocular parallax when the two are in conflict, and it is well known from classroom demonstrations that a pseudogram of faces (that is, a pair of pictures of a person taken from the positions of the viewer's two eyes, in which the two disparate views are switched right for left) will usually look convex and not concave, which is what the reversed binocular parallax should effect.

Part of what the artist learns from the Leonardo exercise in Figure 15.1 (or from such equivalent procedures as measuring the relative visual angles subtended by objects in the field of view by comparing them to a brush or ruler held at arm's length) is to hold his or her head still and to fit an imaginary plane, B, to the array of light that reaches the eye from the scene. To the degree that fitting a flat projection to a deep scene succeeds (and it must be more difficult with some aspects of the scene than with others, cf. the section of this chapter entitled "Real and Represented Objects Differ Mostly at Their Edges"), the artist need only copy that flat projection onto canvas. What is learned, however, cannot consist merely of a set of specific tracings or shapes, but must consist rather of calling the artist's attention to the combination of elective acts that will allow the array of light to the eye, coming from the scene, to be perceived more or less as a flat pattern. Even the untrained viewer must be able to fit a flat projection to portions, at least, of the light that comes from a deep scene, that is, to perceive those parts of the scene as flat. The ability to respond to either visual angle or projective information about depth is implied by our everyday abilities to execute saccadic eye movements to any point in the visual field regardless of the relative distances of the objects being looked at, and by the ability to move one's head enough to disocclude some far object that is presently being hidden by some nearer one (Hochberg, 1961, 1972a). I believe that what Gibson calls the *visual field* (1950) is perceived whenever the viewer attempts to fit a flat projection, like an imaginary Leonardo plane, to a deep scene, and that verifiable quantitative predictions follow from knowing the distance at which that imaginary plane lies (Hochberg, 1961).

The point of these demonstrations is not that motion parallax and binocular parallax are unavailable in stimulation to distinguish a picture from the scene it represents, but that such information is not automatically used, and that it can be overcome by other kinds of static pictorial information, or depth cues, as to the spatial arrangement. (Incidentally, the distinction between "cues" and "informative variables of stimulation" is real as long as the latter are considered to be automatic and preemptive in their use and effectiveness; as soon as the use of such variables by the viewer's perceptual system is shown to be a matter of option and degree, I see no reason not to use Woodworth's earlier term, *cue*, which I find more accurate in its connotations.)

Stimulus Information Is Unnecessary to Pictorial Representation
Figure 15.4A shows two views of the same square; Figures 15.4B and C show a house and a box, respectively, using a method of partial presentation devised by Bradley and Petry (Bradley, Dumais, & Petry, 1976). Something must be added to the stimulus, which by itself is not optically equivalent to either a house or a box. The viewer must fit some imaginary object to the fragmentary stimulus display. The process can be made more evident by using patterns to which several very different alternatives can equally well be fit. Thus, Figure 15.4D represents a sentry behind his box, a soda and drinking straw, or a gopher entering its burrow.

I have to be very careful here: I am not saying that we perceive the complete object that is represented in these pictures in the same sense that the object would be perceived if full information were present. The difference between the two cases is discussed later (in the sections of this chapter entitled "Perceptual Testing of Real and Represented Objects" and "Unavoidable Conflict in 'Distributed' Pictures and Scenes"). The point that I want to make here is this: In these examples, we are clearly engaged in fitting objects to incomplete stimulus projections of them. The ability to do so thus exists in our perceptual repertory. Whether we draw upon that ability in less minimal representations, and in our perceptions of the real world—and why we should find need to do so in the real world—remain to be addressed.

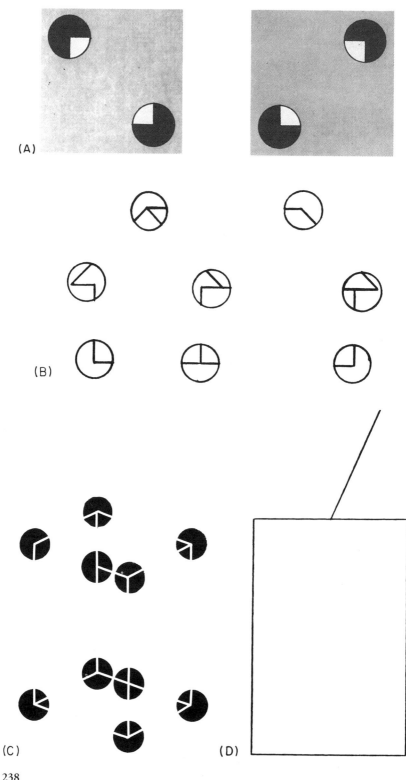

(A)

(B)

(C)

(D)

238

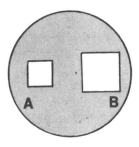

Figure 15.5. The mental structure of the size-distance relationship.

The Role of Mental Structure in Normal and Pictorial Perception

There is in fact a close connection between the notion of a representation as a projection of a given object (Gibson, 1951, p. 407) and Helmholtz's notion of unconscious inference. The latter can be paraphrased as a process of fitting the most probable physical object of our experience to the sensations we receive. The phrase "unconscious inference" requires stress on both terms in order to use it as Helmholtz intended—*unconscious*, because neither the "raw" sensations nor the inferences as to what the likely object is, are consciously experienced; *inference,* because various factors not usefully provided by the stimulus information must be taken into account, in some sense, in "reaching the decision" as to what object or scene in fact fits the stimulus pattern. For example, if object A in Figure 15.5 is at the same distance as object B, it cannot be the same physical size: It is constrained by the laws of optics to be a smaller object. If it *is* the same physical size, it must be at a greater distance, by the same reasoning. These internal constraints, which are not given by any information in the stimulus pattern itself, comprise a *mental structure* to perception. We noted other evidence of mental structure in connection with Figures 15.3B and 15.4A–D. What is important to us here is that it is not easy to find areas in which to study such mental structure. Indeed, most of the substance of the direct theory of Gibson (1950, 1966) and his colleagues is the effort to show that one can so

---

Figure 15.4. Fitting mental structures to incomplete pictures. A: Two views of the same square. B: A house viewed through holes in a near surface. C: A three-dimensional outline picture presented by a method devised by Bradley and Petry (Bradley, Dumais, & Petry, 1976). This figure will be important to us in connection with Figure 15.8. Its ambiguity is not a consequence of the fragmentary mode of presentation, as the preceding figure (which is not ambiguous as to three-dimensional organization) shows. D: Many different objects can be fit to this figure which, however, fits only one of them at a time. See text.

formulate analyses of the stimulation that is provided to the eye by natural scenes that it is sufficient to talk about the information that specifies some layout of objects, and neither unconscious inference nor its associated notion of mental structure are then necessary.

There is no question that pictures display the operation of mental structures: that is, of visual knowledge, not given in the stimulus display, about the physical properties of objects and of their spatial relationships (e.g., that of size and distance). If that is true, where do the structures come from? Why should we have these abilities, if direct response to information in the visual stimulus array that is presented by the world normally suffices for veridical perception?

The answer to that puzzle, I believe, is that pictures are not unique in being ambiguous and incomplete: The objects of the world, as they are glimpsed within each momentary glance, are usually partially hidden from sight, and are ambiguous and incomplete as far as usable stimulus information is concerned. I believe that the *usable* stimulus information in each momentary glance is inadequate to determine a truthful perception of the world in terms of that stimulation alone; I believe that mental structures of sensory expectation are developed to bridge the successive glances at the world; that the differences between realistic pictures and many of the scenes they represent may be negligible to the momentary glance; and that pictures therefore draw on mental structures normally developed in the service of seeing the real world.

The reason that we cannot simply ignore the limits on the information that can be picked up in a single glance, as is often in effect proposed (cf. Gibson, 1966; Turvey, 1977), is that the eye movements and head movements by which we gather stimulus information about the world, and about pictures, are *elective*. That is, *whether or not the information is obtained, and what is done with it, depends on the viewer's perceptual purpose or intention.* I believe that an understanding of the elective nature of the perceptual process, in its fine structure, is essential to an understanding of pictorial representation.

Elective Perceptual Inquiry and the Fine Structure of Looking at Pictures and at the World

Perception depends on the viewer's purposive activity, not simply on the presence of an array of informative stimulation. That is not a metaphor: In each momentary glance, only a tiny part of the field of view is clearly visible, and detailed information about the rest of the scene can only be obtained by successive glances (Figure 15.6). *These glances are elective.* We cannot simply analyze the array of light and let it go at that: The viewer must decide *whether* he or she wants any more information than has already been obtained, and *where* to look in order to obtain that information. In looking at

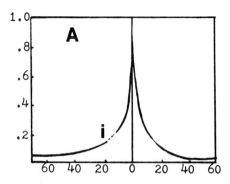

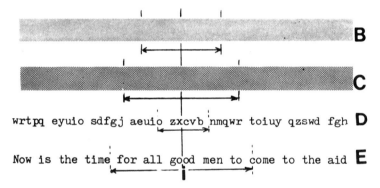

Figure 15.6. The distribution of acuity. A: The relative ability of the eye to detect separation between two contours (i.e., twoness versus oneness). Taking 1.0 as the maximum acuity (shown on the ordinate), the ability to resolve detail falls off as a function of the distance from the center of the fovea in degrees of visual angle (abscissa). In this graph, the acuity distribution of the right eye is shown; i is the blind spot. B–E: Estimates of the limited distance to which you can detect that the gray stripes are composed of dots (B, C); recognize individual letters (D); and recognize words (E). It is assumed that in each case your eye is fixed on the point in each row that is marked by the line i.

pictures, and presumably in looking at the world, the viewer may stop looking after a few small glances. If the viewer stops, it is because the undetailed view of the whole scene that is obtained with the wide span of peripheral vision, combined with the narrow regions of detail given by the fovea in each of the glances that the viewer has taken, inform him or her in a general way what detail would be brought by any further glances. Both expectation and storage are needed to bridge the successive glances. The same is true a fortiori when we consider the viewer's head and body movements: In general, parts of more distant objects will be hidden from view by nearer ones. The viewer may elect to move so as to disocclude the hidden parts, when such movement is necessary; the disoccluding movement is unnecessary when the viewer's mental structure provides reasonable certainty about what those movements would disclose. In either case, in the viewer's perception of the world, he or she must draw on mental structures corresponding to contingent visual knowledge about what would be seen if either the viewer or the object moved one way or another.

On the Permanent Possibilities of Sensation

I have argued elsewhere that it is these abilities, necessary in dealing with a world that is ambiguous and incomplete *in each momentary glance,* that are drawn on in perceiving pictures (Hochberg, 1972b, 1978b). Helmholtz and J. S. Mill both defined perception in general in just this way—as both the result and the goal of active perceptuomotor exploration of and experiment on the world: We perceive the most likely arrangement of objects that would fit the pattern of sensations that we receive, and the perception itself consists of our expectations of the sequences of sensations that we would obtain if we performed various perceptuomotor explorations—moving our heads and eyes this way or that, etc.—that is, the *permanent possibilities of sensation* that are entailed by perceiving a given object. (I must stress that in this formulation the sensations are *not* directly experienced: Criticisms of Helmholtz that accuse him of believing that we experience the momentary sensations more "immediately" or directly than the objects that we perceive are simply wrong and derive their apparent significance from berating a straw man.) Implicit in this view is the notion that we stop exploring once we have solved the perceptual problem and have tested our solution, that is, that we elect to keep looking only until we are satisfied that we know what any additional search would reveal about the structure (scene and objects) that we are testing for fit to the stimulus array.

I believe that this general view of perception encompasses the facts of picture perception, and profits from the study of those facts. Gibson too has emphasized the importance of exploration in perception, but his account contains no explanatory mechanisms other than that exploratory movement is one way to expose the viewer to informative stimulus sequences. Helmholtz's theory of elementary sensations and what they were was surely wrong (Hochberg, 1979); and theorists like Mach, Hering, and Gibson, all of whom stress the need to discover aspects of stimulation that vary *directly* with object properties rather than with the changing seeing conditions, were surely right. Nevertheless, the second aspect of Helmholtz's and Mill's theory—that of mental structures—also seems to me to be clearly right and required. That theory, to which I subscribe, is also shared with variations by a great many contemporary psychologists (e.g., Hebb, Piaget, Neisser). Let us next see in more specific detail how this approach applies to pictorial representation.

Perceptual Testing of Real and Represented Objects

Consider a color photograph, or a photographically realistic painting. The perceptual actions that would show the viewer that such a picture is not the object it represents are mostly elective. Nothing forces the viewer to move his or her head nor to direct his or her gaze in such a way as to provide the information that the picture is flat and not tridimensional. When making those elective movements, of course, the telltale information would be available in the stimulation reaching the viewer's eye—although even such information can be ignored, or can be overridden by the pictorial static cues (Figure 15.3A–E).

If the viewer elects to keep his or her gaze away from represented objects' edges, where as we shall see in the following section entitled "Real and Represented Objects Differ Mostly at Their Edges," the information about relative distance between objects in the real world is concentrated, and to store only the tridimensional scene of objects and surfaces that is represented, the contradiction between flat surface and tridimensional scene need not be confronted. The spatial arrangement of the represented scene or object will of course change somewhat with each movement past the scene (Figure 15.7). As the viewer moves from point i to point ii in Figure 15.7B, the same picture represents different scenes (i′, ii′). If the viewer attends to the expected change that the stationary objects in a scene undergo (Figure 15.7A), and fails to find at the completion of the movement the change that he or she expected would result from that movement, the viewer can *either* perceive that the relative locations of marks on a flat picture have remained unchanged, or that the represented directions of the objects in represented space have changed. Apparently viewers can elect to apply either of these tests (Goldstein, 1976), but tests of spatial location and orientation do not appear to be generally mandatory: Pictures like those in Figure 15.8 show that we do not necessarily (or even normally) store the details of represented spatial orientation, nor test them for consistency (although we can of course deliberately do so, and with some effort determine that the object is "impossible").[1] The changes in a represented scene that should be provided by a change in the position from which one views the picture, therefore, may simply not be noted, nor re-membered from one glance to the next.

Limited Span of Pictorial Consistency

The argument just made in connection with Figure 15.8A implies that the picture is not normally treated as a whole. That implication, which is only suggested by Figure 15.8A, is clearly demonstrated by Figure 15.8D: When you fixate the intersection marked 1, the orientation is like that of Figure 15.8F. If you keep your gaze fixed at point 2, after a short while the orientation will reverse, alternating between those of Figures 15.8E and 15.8F. Where you look therefore determines whether or not the figure is am-biguous, and what *local depth cues* will determine its appearance (Hochberg,

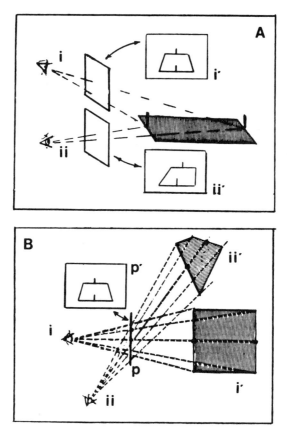

Figure 15.7. The different effects of viewers' movements on pictures and scenes. A. The different views (i', ii') of a deep scene that the viewer should expect to receive when moving from point i to point ii (see Figure 15.2A, B). B. The different scenes (i', ii') that would fit the same picture (p') as the viewer moves from point i to point ii.

1968, 1970). Figures like these, and like those of Escher (1960) and Albers (1973), tell us that, in general, perspective and the other depth cues need not be consistent from one place to another within an object or a scene in order to have some local effects on apparent depth or orientation.

Thus, if the viewer is not led to test consistency any more than he or she does with, say, the adjacent panels in a comic strip, pictures of people or things can be scattered around a loosely figured field of view with an eye to the "pleasingness" of the design that they present, or to their relative social status, ignoring whether they are represented consistently with a single projection viewpoint and geometry. The drawings on a vase or frieze, a Chinese scroll painting, a Gothic or Byzantine panel, fall into this class to which central perspective is simply irrelevant.

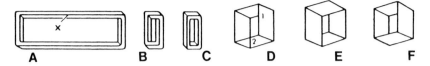

Figure 15.8. Inconsistencies are tolerated in representation: The importance of where one looks and the involvement of visual memory (mental structures) in assembling the percept across successive glances.

A. The representation of left and right sides is inconsistent, for example, the line marked x must change its function as the corner of a dihedral angle (cf. Figure 15.2Ci) somewhere between the two sides. This drastic inconsistency is not immediately evident to the viewer and does not interfere with the figure's apparent tridimensionality because the two sides cannot be encompassed by foveal vision in a single glance, as is shown by the next two figures.

B. Here the left and right sides are close enough to be encompassed in a single glance, and the figure appears much more flat and inconsistent. That this is not due to some principle that makes all compact figures look flat is shown by the next figure.

C. This figure is as compact as B, but is not inconsistent and does appear tridimensional.

D–F. The figure in A cannot be read as an object that is both tridimensional and consistent. D, on the other hand, can be read as a perfectly consistent object, that is, a partly transparent box oriented as in F. Nevertheless, with the gaze directed at point 2 in D, perspective reversals will be perceived to occur, and the orientation of the figure in E will alternate with that of F, even though only the latter is consistent with the local depth cue at point 1 in D.

This set of figures seems to me (Hochberg, 1968, 1974b) to argue very strongly that only those lines that fall near the fovea act as cues in the representations of objects' corners and depth, and that the full structure of the represented physical object and its orientation is not preserved in the mental structure that is fitted to the successive foveal glimpses.

Outlines and Their Multiple Ambiguities

Pictures represent objects or scenes in the sense that we can fit an object to the drawing or painting. As is well known, we can fit an infinite number of objects to a given picture because we cannot specify three dimensions in two. As we saw in Figure 15.8A, the ambiguity is greater than is simply implied by the fact that we can fit different planes or objects to a single picture—we see that the objects need not even be consistent, overall, in order for us to fit them locally.

Real and Represented Objects Differ Mostly at Their Edges

In looking at an object in the world, if an edge of the object's surface lies near the fovea, that edge offers the gaze good monocular and binocular information (accommodation, convergence, and disparity, respectively) that one side is a near surface and that the other is empty air or a more distant surface (i and ii in Figure 15.9A). If the object is more than a few yards

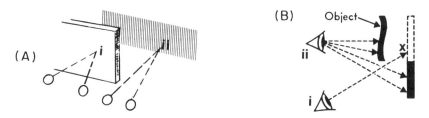

Figure 15.9. Depth at an object's edge and the probable basis of the figure-ground phenomenon.

    A. To bring any point on the surface of a near object, i, to sharp focus on the foveas of both eyes, neither the accommodation of the lenses nor the angle of convergence between the two eyes need be changed. In order to move one's gaze across the object's edge, however, and to gaze at some point on the far surface (ii), both accommodation and convergence must be changed appropriately, processes that take much more time than is needed merely to switch the eyes from one point to another at the same distance.

    B. To maintain fixation of any point on a surface while the head is rotating or moving laterally, as from i to ii, or to switch fixation to another point on that surface under those conditions, requires only simple eye movements that are appropriate to the head movements. To cross the object's edge during such a head movement, however, or to maintain fixation on some background point x while the head moves from point i to point ii, is more complicated, and impossible, respectively (adapted from Hochberg, 1978b).

    These figures show why the perceptual system must "decide" before executing eye and head movements which side at an edge is near and which is far. The set of perceptuomotor expectations that accompanies that decision comprises, I believe (Hochberg, 1962, 1970, 1972b), the figure-ground phenomenon. In any case, it is clear that information about the spatial arrangement of objects is particularly strong at their edges.

away, however, *or if the gaze is not directed near its edge,* the information about which side of the edge is near is probably lost or unusable, for reasons concerned with the structure and function of the eye.

    Crucial Importance of the Inhomogeneity of Retinal Acuity. I have in mind here the following facts: The acuity for detail falls off rapidly each side of the fovea (Figure 15.6). Acuity for relative motion also probably falls off with a similar curve, although I know of no direct measures.[2] Accommodation or focus of the eye is apparently correct only for the retinal image in the region of the fovea, so that not only is the retinal pick-up of information progressively coarse in terms of the receptor arrangements themselves, but the retinal image itself is degraded outside of the region being fixated (cf. Johnson et al., 1968; Leibowitz & Owens, 1975). For these reasons, relatively small amounts of disparity in the two eyes' views (binocular information) and of motion parallax at the objects' edges should not be salient or even detectable while the eye is directed away from the edge. If we assume that the acuity of parallax falls off in parallel with acuity for detail, and take as our highest value for both binocular and motion parallax resolution of 2 sec of arc, Figure 15.10 shows how much depth at an edge could go undetected 50% of the time at different distances between the edge and the fixation point.[3]

At objects' edges, of course, and for features like the nose in a frontal portrait that extends toward the viewer, the represented object offers parallax (both binocular and movement parallax) that the picture cannot. The picture must fail to provide the parallax that the viewer expects to obtain with such features *if* he elects to test them. There has been no research as to whether

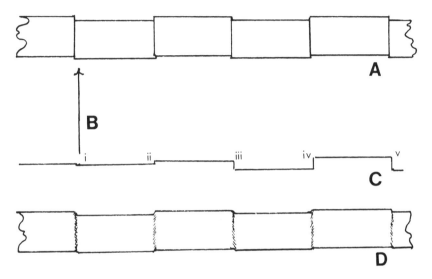

Figure 15.10. The real depth that a flat edge could represent without conflict at different distances from the fixation point.

A. A represented strip with five folds or edges.

B. The edge at which the gaze is directed.

C. If the fovea is kept fixed on edge i, even a very slight real depth would be detected, and its absence would limit the effectiveness of the line as a surrogate for edge depth. At increasing distances from the fovea, however, greater amounts of real depth could go undetected. The depths shown at ii–v would not be detected (50% of the time) if the fovea remained fixed at i.

D. *Sfumato*, a technique introduced by Leonardo da Vinci, involves blurring the edges of represented objects in a way that is simulated here. I believe that such blurring serves at once to make the discrepancy between picture and real edge less determinate; to simulate the blurring that must normally prevail in the retinal image of a horizon (Figure 15.2Ch2) when the eye is focused on the near bulge of a convex object; and most important, by tending to keep the viewer from looking directly at the blurred edge, to obtain the advantage of reducing the conflict between real and represented edge depth as outlined in A–C above. Leonardo's *sfumato* thus anticipates Rembrandt's more massive use of focal chiaroscuro to a similar purpose (see section of this chapter entitled "Rembrandt's Solution: Separate Painting for Foveal and Peripheral Gaze").

pictures' apparent flatness actually depends on where the viewer fixates relative to objects' represented edges, as this analysis suggests it to do, but if the analysis is correct it shows that the stimulation provided to the exploring eye of the viewer need not be so tremendously different for picture and scene that separate theories are needed to account for the ways in which we perceive them.

Sfumato is a device introduced by Leonardo da Vinci in which objects' edges are blurred, as approximated in Figure 15.10D. I believe that the use of this technique has three consequences: First, it leaves the viewer a completion task, a perceptual puzzle to work at (Gombrich, 1956) and to sustain visual interest (see the chapter section entitled "On the Permanent Possibilities of Sensation"). Second, because the blur presents no sharp line either to foveal vision, when the viewer looks directly at it, nor of course to peripheral vision, when the viewer looks away, the viewer must store from glance to glance the general area or volume bounded by the blurred outline, not a clear set of sharp lines on canvas. Third, and most important: Because *the blur does not look different from what an object's sharp edge or horizon (Figure 15.2 Ch2) would look like when glimpsed peripherally, the viewer can obtain a realistic picture in view only by keeping his or her eyes away from the blurred outlines.* Sfumato is a form of microcomposition, therefore, controlling the viewer's gaze in a way that directly presages Rembrandt's use of specialized focal regions (see the section entitled "Rembrandt's Solution: Separate Painting for Foveal and Peripheral Gaze") and the later inversion of this device by the impressionists (see the section of this chapter entitled "The Impermanence of Impressionist Representations").

Many Identifying Features in Represented Objects Are in Low Relief. Viewed from a distance of a few feet, many of the most important identifying and interesting details by which we recognize objects, and distinguish one from another—an eye, a mustache, an eyebrow, a fingernail— do not extend significantly less in the case of a flat picture of the same feature than they do in the case of the object itself. With flat representation and represented feature not substantially different in their effective stimulation, the fact that we can recognize the objects that those pictorial features identify (and endow with verisimilitude) is no surprise. Surely we can recognize that a flat-faced, small-featured person is a person, or that a hand with unindented fingernails is a hand.

We can now see why and how the flat canvas or paper can represent three-dimensional objects or scenes, and do so without losing their two-dimensional appearance.

Outline Drawings, Figure-Ground, and Tridimensional Organization: Representation of Surfaces and Volumes
Gestalt Phenomena Are Fundamental to Pictorial Representation

Because the same line can serve so many different pictorial functions (Figure 15.2C), outline drawings are multiply ambiguous. Many different objects, and different kinds of objects, can be fitted to the same pattern of lines. If there were no way of controlling their representational functions, lines could not be used in pictures.

A host of Gestalt demonstrations, and millennia of graphic art, prove that lines' representational functions are lawfully and reliably controlled by a finite set of determinants. Three of the more important determinants are illustrated in Figure 15.11. To Gestalt psychologists, these were known as laws of organization. Their importance to pictorial representation is made

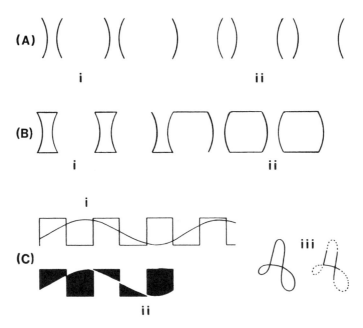

Figure 15.11. Taming the wild ambiguity of outline pictures: The Gestalt determinants.

A. Proximity: Concave "apple cores" tend (rather weakly) to be figure at i, convex "spindles" tend to be figure at ii.

B. Closedness: The apple cores are strongly figure as opposed to ground, at i; closedness overcomes proximity at ii to make the convex "barrels" figure. Note that the proportion of cores and barrels depends on whether you fixate the top or bottom of the set, showing a local determinacy similar to that shown in Figures 15.8A and 15.8D.

C. Good continuation: The strongest of the static Gestalt laws. At i, a sine wave superimposed over a square wave is perceived in accordance with good continuation, here overcoming the factor of closedness (which, by itself, would lead to the perception of the closed shapes shown in black at ii). At iii, a highly familiar shape is concealed (at left) by good continuation.

An explanation for these representational determinants in terms of general theory is given in the section of this chapter entitled "Gestalt Phenomena and Determinants Are Cases of Helmholtz's Rule."

clear by two examples, that is, the way in which the Gestalt "laws" control the *figure-ground distinction* and the way they summarize the facts of *tridimensional representation*.

Figure and Ground.   A thin line divides the picture area into two regions. If that line is perceived as being the edge of a surface corresponding to one region, that region as *figure* has a recognizable shape, whereas the other region, as *ground*, has no boundary but seems to extend indefinitely behind the edge of the figure, and therefore has no recognizable shape. Figure is thinglike and shaped; ground is more like empty space, amorphous and unshaped.

There are three things to notice about this phenomenon, of which the phenomenological descriptions were originally made by Rubin (1915, 1958), and the theoretical implications were worked out by Gestalt psychologists (for example, Koffka, 1935); an alternative description and explanation in a quite different context, as an example of interposition (Figure 15.1) has been provided by Helmholtz (1857).

First, this phenomenon can determine whether or not an object is perceived at all. In Figure 15.12B, one effortlessly perceives a vase but must

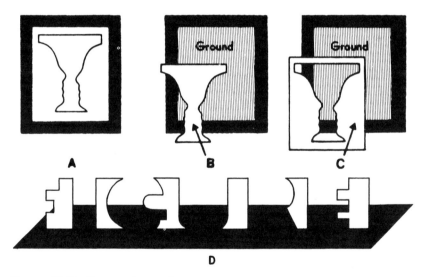

Figure 15.12. Figure and ground.

A–C. A is an ambiguous picture, which may be perceived either as a vase (B) or as two faces (C). In each case, the figure has a well-defined and recognizable shape, whereas the ground appears to extend to some indefinite extent behind the figure and therefore to lack a definite shape.

D. The spaces between the letters of the word FIGURE have been themselves made figure, and the letters made ground, by applying the laws of closedness (Figure 15.11B) and good continuation (Figure 15.11C) (adapted from Hochberg, 1978a).

The properties of figure and ground are therefore the properties that an object's edge normally provides a viewer's eye (cf. Figure 15.9).

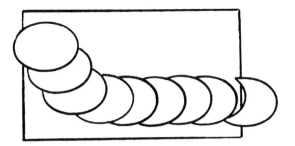

Figure 15.13. Figure and ground are not absolute.

search in order to discover a pair of faces; this relationship is reversed in
Figure 15.12C. In Figure 15.12D, the spaces between a set of letters has
been made figure, so that the letters themselves are hard to perceive.[4]

Second, the figure-ground distinction is not necessarily absolute. In
Figure 15.13, the line that is figure one way at one point is ground at another; both vase and faces can be seen in Figure 15.12A, although probably
not both alternatives at the same place at the same time. The degree of
figure-ground dominance (i.e., the ambiguity with which an edge is represented by an outline) is controlled by the way lines are arranged.

Third, definite laws or rules seem to be at work in these demonstrations.
That is also true in the ways in which lines are perceived as representing
solid objects and scenes, which we consider next.

Tridimensional Organization of Objects and Scenes.   Figure 15.14 shows
two equally accurate (or inaccurate) drawings of a wire cube. In order to
perceive B as a flat pattern of adjacent triangles and quadrilaterals, or to see
A as a "wire cube," the continuity of the lines must be broken in each case.
Additionally, as a flat pattern, B is less symmetrical than A, and is more
complex in terms of line segments than A is, so that the concurrence of the
"law of good continuation" (i.e., that we perceive that organization which
best preserves the continuity of lines and contours), the "law of symmetry"
(i.e., that we perceive that organization which is the more symmetrical), and
the "law of simplicity" (i.e., that we perceive the simplest organization that
fits the stimulus pattern) works to make A a flat pattern. The law of simplicity
comes closest to being a single general law (Attneave, 1954; Hochberg &
McAlister, 1953). In Figure 15.14C, a scene containing what were termed
"monocular depth cues" in Figure 15.1 can be viewed as the working out of
the law of simplicity, in that it is simpler for example to perceive a homogeneous texture on the ground, or two rectangles one behind the other, as in
the tridimensional scene, than to perceive a gradient of texture and an inverted letter L adjacent to a rectangle on the plane of the page.

The Application and Nature of these "Laws."   Because the phenomena
that I have described comprise the heart of pictorial representation, and

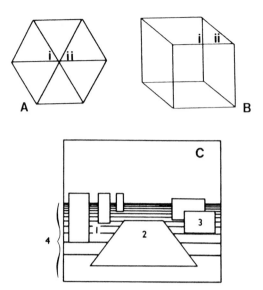

Figure 15.14. Outline representations of depth.

A and B. Two projections on the picture plane of a wire cube. A looks flat and B looks three-dimensional because (among other things) in each case the good continuation (cf. Figure 15.11C) of the lines marked i and ii would have to be broken in order to perceive the alternative organization. See text.

C. A picture of a scene, like that in Figure 15.1B. It is in some measurable sense simpler to perceive the rectangles at 1 as the same in size but at different distances; the shape at 2 as a rectangle (i.e., with equal internal angles) in depth rather than as an upright trapezoid; the pattern at 3 as two rectangles in depth rather than as a rotated letter L and an adjacent rectangle in the same plane; and the horizontal stripes as a homogeneously textured ground at a slant rather than as a set of line segments in the picture plane, irregularly fragmented and separated by 11 different spacings. (For attempts to measure simplicity objectively, see Attneave, 1954, and Hochberg & McAlister, 1953.)

cannot be avoided in any serious account of pictures, they are surely at least as important as the study of central perspective, which is of limited use outside of Western art in any case. Any theoretical account of picture perception that does not attempt to deal with the Gestalt phenomena is necessarily trivial; any practical account of representation must start with those phenomena or assume that the practitioner knows them intuitively.

As to the origin or nature of the Gestalt factors, they cannot be dismissed as being an arbitrary "language of vision" any more than can the pictorial response to outline drawings of objects (cf. the chapter section "Is a Special Theory Needed for Picture Perception?") or the use of central perspective. The same laws of organization that allow us to represent recognizable objects by use of ambiguous outlines can be discerned in the principles of protective coloration by which real, solid animals conceal themselves from the eyes of

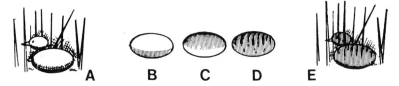

Figure 15.15. Gestalt determinants in protective coloration.

predators who must be quite unschooled in pictorial conventions. In Figure 15.15A, a solid and visible schematic white bird; in Figure 15.15C, the lighter ventral surface, characteristic of most animals, *flattens* the bird by canceling the inhomogeneity of illumination that makes the body in Figure 15.15A and B simpler as a tridimensional than as a flat object; in Figure 15.15D, stripes are added, which, by good continuation with the grass in the background (Figure 15.15E) destroy the animal as coherent figure, and make the bird invisible. (For more examples, see Metzger, 1953.)

In the application of these laws, so far as I can tell by inspecting pictures and designs from various cultures and periods, the artist who wishes to stress the represented object deploys the Gestalt factors so as to maximize an unambiguous figure-ground distinction, whereas the artist or craftsman concerned with flattening the canvas (for reasons I discuss in the final section of this chapter, "Why and How to Flatten a Painting of a Deep Scene"), as in Figures 15.16A, B, and stressing the design and interplay of figure and ground forms (cf. Figure 15.17A, B) uses precisely the same Gestalt determinants to increase figure-ground ambiguity.

Gestalt Phenomena and Determinants Are Cases of Helmholtz's Rule

In my opinion, the Gestalt laws are merely previously unnoticed examples of Helmholtz's rule (that we perceive the object or scene that would most likely fit the effective stimulus pattern); that is, the Gestalt laws are cues as to which side of an outline is likely to be near surface and which is likely to be far—factors equivalent to the depth cues that were originally identified by Leonardo in Figure 15.1. In Gestalt theoretical terms, the law of good continuation is responsible for the cases illustrated in Figures 15.11C, 15.12B, C, and 15.14A, B, C3: that is, we perceive the object(s) which will best preserve the identity of continuous lines. As a descriptive principle, this is a reasonable rule of thumb for artists and designers, but it is not explanatory in any way. As I see it (Hochberg, 1972a, 1974), if the segments in each case were parts of different separated objects in space, it would be very unlikely that the viewer would be at just that one place in space from which they fall into alignment. It is therefore most likely that they are parts of single continuous and colinear edges or corners. This is essentially the depth cue of interposition in Figure 15.1, and Helmholtz (1874, p. 284) anticipated in those terms its use as the law of good continuation in figure-ground formation by some half-century.

Figure 15.16. Flattening the picture: Good continuation and symmetry.

A. A tracing of main lines of *The Blue Window* by Matisse (painted in 1911). It has often been noted that Matisse wanted to "bring the outdoors into the room." The techniques used to achieve that purpose all seem to be straightforward applications of the factor of good continuation (Figure 15.11C). The tree and mullion at 1 and 2, respectively; the ways in which interposition (Figure 15.1B, Figure 15.2Ch3) is avoided where one object occludes the line of another and instead the interrupted line is rounded to continue into the interrupting line (3, 4, etc.; note also how the outline of the foliage, 10, is rounded to continue into the sculpture at 9 and the lamp chimney at 1); the coincidence of lines and edges which lie at different distances and thus would not by chance alone be expected to line up as they do (5, 6, 8; 1, 2); the alignment of the vase and pincushion (6, 7)—all of these must contribute to making the canvas look like a flat pattern (as in Figure 15.14A, B), with no new principles involved.

B. A sketch from memory of the main lines of *Woman in Black* by Vuillard (painted in 1891) in the National Gallery, Washington, D.C. Clock and head (1), skirt and table (2), door frame and woman's back (3)—all are brought into two dimensions by good continuation.

Neither of the pictures sketched in A and B draw on perceptual discoveries not already discussed in this paper. Note however that the dates of the painting B considerably antedate the writings of the Gestalt psychologists, although the painting does not antedate Helmholtz's observations on interposition.

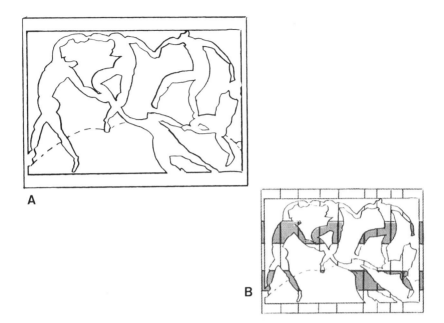

Figure 15.17. Making ground figure.

A. A tracing of the main outlines of *The Dance* by Matisse (painted in 1910). The Gestalt determinant of closedness (Figure 15.11B) here contributes to the tendency of the space between the dancers to become figure, so that the shapes of those spaces enter as recognizable components into the design of the painting.

B. Good continuation has been added to increase that tendency, and to make more salient the *hidden* organization of the picture.

The other Gestalt laws yield readily to similar analysis in Helmholtzian terms. Thus, consider the Gestalt law of symmetry: The angles in Figure 15.14A are more symmetrical as a flat object than those in 15.14B, so the law of symmetry can account for the relative tridimensionality of the two figures. But it is also true that only from one viewpoint out of very many would the different angles formed by the intersections of the parts of a wire cube fall into such complete symmetry, making it highly unlikely on the basis of that fact alone that B is a view of a cube.

We perceive what is most probable, given the effective stimulus pattern: Perfect alignment and symmetry of angles is more likely with a single object than it is likely to be provided by a randomly chosen view of objects or parts that lie at different distances.

This principle sounds reasonably compact and testable, but it cannot be applied as it stands. The "impossible" patterns in Figure 15.8 and the inconsistent pictures of Albers and Escher should be perfectly flat in appearance, according to a literal application of this principle, and the apparent orientation of Figure 15.8B should be completely fixed. These figures tell us that the features through which Helmholtz's principles should be applied to drawings are in fact relatively local, and that the mental structures that are fitted to them are likely to be more tolerant of inconsistency than the physical structures that are represented by the drawings could be.

Consequences of This Analysis: Constituents of Effective Representation and Canonical Form

Three aspects of this analysis are particularly important to the study of pictorial recognition—the fact that not all representations that are equally good projections, geometrically speaking, are equally good representations, perceptually; the argument that pictorial features are anchors for mental structures; and the argument that the mental structures are complexes of sensory expectations. We consider these in turn.

Canonical Forms of Representation

The term *canonical form* has been used to describe the most readily recognized and remembered view or "cleaned-up" version of some form or object (Culbertson, 1950; Hochberg, 1972b; Neisser, 1967). The term is important, and particularly important to the ways in which an artist can surpass a camera, but it has too many disparate meanings to be of much use without separating those components.

The camera has competed with the graphic artist, and changed the purpose of nonphotographic pictorial art, in ways discussed later (cf. "Paintings as Objects and Subjects" in this chapter). Primarily, the camera can surpass the most skilled artist in making an absolutely accurate surrogate for a scene of objects *when viewed from the correct station point*—surpass in amount of detail and subtlety of rendering gradations, surpass in precision of foreshortening, etc. There is no guarantee, however, that the camera will reproduce each object from its most recognizable position, nor even that any single view will present the object in a way that will make it most distinguishable from other objects. The artist, however, is free to chose a view of an object which displays those features by which the object is readily recognized or distinguished from other objects (Gibson, 1969; Gombrich, 1956). Moreover, the kind of flexibility of mental structures that we noted in connection with Figure 15.8 makes it possible for the artist to combine within a single view features that could normally not be seen together, something that is much more difficult for the camera to do. Egyptian art, for example, combines profile views of face, hands, and feet with frontal views of shoulders (cf. Gombrich, 1956). In caricatures originating in all cultures, some features are exaggerated, and others may be deleted entirely.

The very fact that the artist can do what the camera cannot is reason enough for the artist to do it, as we will see. But such deliberate pictorial distortions and selection are not merely a response to photography: They long antedate the camera, and even antedate the formulation of the laws of perspective that made it possible to be mechanically realistic, in a sense, before the camera. We can separate at least four different reasons to use such distortions.

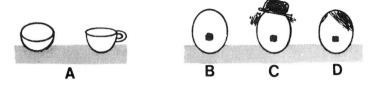

Figure 15.18. Canonical form and distinctive features.

Inclusion or Emphasis of Identifying or Distinctive Features. The first reason for using distortion is to help distinguish one object from others with which it might be confused, for example, the two views of the teacup in Figure 15.18A are equally good projections, speaking both mathematically and in terms of the Gestalt determinants, but only one of them is clearly not a sake cup or a soup tureen. The function of a feature, in this analysis, depends on the other potential members of the set. Among celebrated movie stars, the mustache in Figure 15.18B suffices, whereas among wearers of toothbrush mustaches additional features are needed (Figures 15.18C, D). This point, which is by no means a new one (cf. Gibson, 1963; Gombrich, 1956; Hochberg, 1972a), is concerned with distinguishing one object from others. But that object must first be perceived as a shape or form, and that itself may require selection or distortion.

Optimal Representation of Form. Most of the discussion of distinctive pictorial features and related questions of visual recognition have dealt with features that logically pick the object out from the possible set of objects with which it might be confused. Identification and perception are not the same, however: Knowing that Figure 15.14A is the projection of a cube does not really make it any more tridimensional in its sustained appearance; "breaking" the continuous lines in imagination and thereby seeing the figure as a cube is clearly a conceptual and not a visual act. This component of the general notion of canonical form is the more fundamental one, it seems to me; it reduces to the Gestalt phenomena that were discussed in connection with Figures 15.11–14, and I do not see how our understanding of this important constituent of canonical form can progress any faster than our understanding of the largely neglected Gestalt phenomena.

Departures from Central Projection. In general, objects' projections on the picture plane will not have the same shape as the objects themselves. From the single appropriate viewpoint, of course, they will provide the same retinal image. When the represented object or scene has a highly specific shape (e.g., a square or a circle) from which even slight departures would be recognizable, any movements that the viewer makes (and the other cues to the actual surface of the picture) define for the viewer the recognizably *non*congruent projected shape, recognizably different from the object that was to be represented (Figure 15.7B). One way to handle this is to make the picture of the object the same shape as that of the object itself, so that the perceived similarity between picture and object will be clear to the viewer from all except extreme viewing positions (such as those used with anamorphic pictures); Pirenne (1970) has discussed the relationship between the perception of the picture's plane and the departures from central projection perspective at length. Other departures from strict projective fidelity are made in the service of representation: The parallel sides of buildings, for example, do not look right if they are allowed to converge within the picture in accordance with linear perspective: in fact, viewers judge rectilinear objects drawn in parallel perspective (Figure 15.14B) to be more realistic than when they are drawn in the converging central projection that would be appropriate to the viewer's distance (Hagen & Elliott, 1976), and other anomalies arise as a function of the distance between picture and viewer (Hagen, Jones, & Reed, 1978).

I do not agree with Goodman (1968) and Wartofsky (1979) that such phenomena in any way show central projection to be an arbitrary tool for the representation of depth. What makes such departures from central projection necessary, as I shall show, is the difference between the depth of field of view in picture and scene; what makes such departures effective is the elective nature of the perceptual testing procedure and the tolerance for inconsistency that is displayed in Figure 15.8A, B.

With respect to the depth of field: When looking at the real object, the eye's limited depth of field, combined with its limited span of acute vision, restrict the effective, sharp momentary glance to a small section of the perspective gradient. *Each section of the converging road or of the building's facade, receding into the horizontal and vertical distance, respectively—each depth plane of the scene or objects—is viewed in detail at different times, and these separate views are connected only by elective eye movements that make provision for the different distances.* Between looking at the base of the building and at its apex, a succession of changes in focus and convergence, and a change in head position, must normally occur, so that the entire pattern of convergence is not simultaneously present in the eye. In the picture, on the other hand, the entire pattern that it bears upon its surface is simultaneously in focus, and the consequences of perspective foreshortening, noncongruent with the shapes of the objects themselves, are softened only by the limits on the viewer's parafoveal and peripheral vision.

The compromise, therefore, is to use central projection sparingly, as a *setting* within which frontal views of characteristic shapes appear. The perceptual tolerance and the elective nature of perceptual integration that this ready use and acceptance of pictorial inconsistancy implies has already been demonstrated in connection with Figure 15.8. Much research is needed to fill in the relationship between perceptual intention, stimulus information, and perceptual integration, and the study of picture perception seems ideally suited for such inquiry.

Canons of Execution. A high-bridged nose distinguishes its bearer's face from others equally well in full face and in profile. It is probably easier to recognize in profile than in full face, however, because in the latter only shading testifies to the nose's prominence; in full face, the precise extent of the prominence remains ambiguous, and the extension toward the viewer is itself in conflict with the flatness of the picture. In profile, the congruence of portrait and subject can be unambiguous and unopposed. This is the point to which the discussion of the Egyptian pictorial conventions are usually addressed.

There is another reason to use the profile, however: It requires much less skill, and no knowledge of foreshortening, to execute. A tradition in which faces are always dealt with in profile does not depend critically on artists and craftsmen with high native ability, nor on workers with uniformly good training in drawing. I am not implying that the Egyptians were either poor artists or untrained, but that there are distinct economic advantages to some modes of representation where a high rate of production is to be maintained, a point to which I return in the section of this chapter entitled "Obtrusiveness of Impressionist and Post-Impressionist Paintings and Painters."

Pictorial Features Are Anchors for Mental Structures: Attention Laid Bare
Figures 15.4A–C all suggest to me that in pictorial recognition, mental structures are (or can be) fitted to features of the picture, and that the fit is piecemeal rather than whole structure to whole pattern (Figure 15.8). In each case, the perceptual act is obviously an elective one: We are free to fit any of several very different mental structures to the stimulus patterns.[5]

With such figures, what I have taken to be the process of selective attention (Hochberg, 1970) is laid bare: You cannot simultaneously see the "sentry" and the "gopher" in Figure 15.4C. The selection occurs not because there is some selective "filter" that you can draw upon to exclude the other alternatives but because you can only fit one or the other to the stimulus pattern. If the processes that are revealed in recognizing such fragmentary and minimal pictures are also those used in filling out and completing our narrow glances at the world, then we should value such minimal pictures as a research tool precisely because they leave so much to the imagination.

Nor should it be thought that these graphic cues to which I fit mental structures are abstract or arbitrary symbols. For example, although it is almost impossible to draw a squiggle that will not represent *some* facial expression (Gombrich calls this "Toepffer's law"; 1956, p. 342), any given squiggle cannot represent just any expression at all: If Figure 15.19A is a

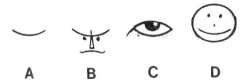

Figure 15.19. Not just any line can represent any expression (or thing).

human mouth, and neither the curve of the eyebrows, as in Figure 15.19B, nor a lower eyelid (Figure 15.19C), it must be a smile (as in Figure 15.19D).

Nor should it be thought that we *perceive* the missing forms in Figure 15.4C in the sense that the sentry is actually seen behind the box: No mere glance that I can actually execute can tell me the color of the hidden sentry's uniform, nor the shape of his hat. But there are many elective actions that I could take, were these in fact real objects or scenes, actions that would bring those hidden parts into view and that would allow me to test my expectations about the permanent possibilities of sensation that comprise my mental structures of those objects. The Gestalt assertion is correct, then, that we perceive the table extending behind some object that rests on it, but correct only in this very restricted and probabilistic sense: We expect that the disocclusion of the table by the object would reveal a complete table and not a *coincidentally concealed hole.*

Testing the Reality of Pictures and of the Scenes That They Represent
Features and details are usually encountered in some context which both reduces the ambiguity of the individual lines and allows the viewer to test his or her mental structure by seeking out expected corroboratory detail. If I look at the mustache in Figure 15.18C and guess that the sketch is one of Charlie Chaplin, I find that the blob that falls in the upper periphery of my field of view during my first glance will, when brought to foveal vision, fit quite nicely to my image of a bowler hat.

To the constructivist viewpoints of J. S. Mill and Helmholtz, this testing process that I have just described is precisely what we normally do when testing the reality of our perceptions of the world. When Van Eyck and Bruegel provide a minute detail, just where it should be, the admiring viewer who discovers it marvels at the "realism" of the painting because the latter has met his or her normal criteria of perceptual reality, despite the knowledge that the scene is not really real, but is only flat, painted canvas.[6]

Flat Canvas and Deep World: Evolving Solutions and Shifting Intentions

Unavoidable Conflict in "Distributed" Pictures and Scenes

Whether by nature or by nurture, we are ready to see objects' edges at each contour (Figure 15.2) and to read areal or voluminous depth into gradients and discontinuities of color and shade. It may be that some of these spatial responses to flat pictures are preemptive, in a sense analogous to the Stroop phenomenon in reading (i.e., if asked to name the color in which the word *green* is printed, and the word is printed in red ink, subjects will have difficulty in saying "red" because of the strong tendency to respond "green"): After all, as we saw earlier (Figure 15.3A–E), pictorial depth cues can overcome small but detectable amounts of movement parallax and binocular parallax.

On the other hand, in order to look from one place to another on a canvas, the viewer must either make those eye-muscle adjustments that will maintain appropriate convergence and fixation on a flat surface, or continually lose sight of the picture. Moreover, as we saw in the section entitled "Real and Represented Objects Differ Mostly at their Edges," each fixation at or near the edge of a represented object, especially if made with free head movements, can provide the viewer with information that both sides of the pictured edge lie at or near the same distance from him. Unless the picture is trompe l'oeil on an architectural scale, and lies at a great distance from the viewer, therefore, it both requires that the viewer treat it as a flat surface and provides the information needed to do that. In addition, *to the degree that the picture is illusionist, it requires the viewer to anticipate and store his or her successive glances at the represented three-dimensional scene of objects as a three-dimensional scene (else the viewer could not remember and combine the contents of each glimpse), and the picture normally provides that information,* too.

It has been repeatedly suggested that what is characteristic about pictures is this conflict between their two-dimensional and three-dimensional perceptual implications, and that this provides a source of their visual interest. It seems to me that the novelty of a hologram does wear off with astonishing rapidity, and that my purely visual interest in viewing one is substantially less than that of viewing a picture, but research to this point is lacking.

In any case, the discrepancy is relatively little for low relief at a moderate viewing distance, and a frieze of individual objects or people against an unfigured background provides little difference between picture and low-relief sculpture. Within a single detailed scene in deep relief, with sharply delineated objects that occlude each other, and with consistent central perspective, the two alternative percepts—those of solid objects and flat painting—must alternate continually, depending on what expectancy is being tested at any given moment. In a Van Eyck or a Bruegel painting, the conflict must be very real indeed. Rembrandt found a way out of the conflict that is applicable to normal viewing distance.

Rembrandt's Solution: Separate Painting for Foveal and Peripheral Gaze

Focal Chiaroscuro and Differential Detail

Chiaroscuro, the distribution of light and dark for purposes of composition, emphasis, and contrast, was brought in many of Rembrandt's paintings to a form of spotlight treatment that I will call *focal chiaroscuro* because it provides a very few regions of the canvas—focal regions—to which the viewer is almost forced to pay particular attention. Rembrandt's use of chiaroscuro served several perceptual functions, such as permitting the painter to simulate luminance ranges far beyond the reflectance range of the painter's palette; it also served in several important paintings to separate focal from nonfocal regions of the picture. I have discussed his probable purpose and the consequences elsewhere (Hochberg, 1979b). The point I want to summarize briefly here is this: A few areas of the picture are provided with relatively sharp detail and with reflectances in the middle range, whereas the remainder of the painting is either very dark or very light, and is executed in a blurred and sketchy way that *looks natural only to peripheral vision.* This procedure, and the composition of the painting, constrains the viewer's gaze predominantly to the focal regions.[7] When the gaze is in fact restricted to a focal region, the entire picture looks uniformly detailed, inasmuch as the focal regions are executed with normal detail, and the parts that are sketchy, outside those regions, are not brought to foveal vision, which alone could show them to be sketchy.

There is an important aspect of this use of focal chiaroscuro (as opposed to the distributed chiaroscuro of, say, El Greco) that can be developed only in the context of our discussion in the section of this chapter "Real and Represented Objects Differ Mostly at Their Edges": The amount of relief within any focal region is generally small, so that little conflict between flat canvas and the three-dimensional scene arises as long as the viewer's gaze indeed remains within such a region. When the viewer's eye does stray outside a focal region, which will probably be a relatively infrequent occurrence, the sketchy execution and the heavy impasto and painterly brushwork offer no sharply represented edges to the viewer, nor any anchor for the viewer's prolonged inspection. Only after the viewer's eye returns to a focal region, and the outer regions of the picture are returned to peripheral vision, do the blobs and brush strokes disclose themselves—miraculously— as being just those marks that will merge to look like normal objects and surfaces when viewed by the corner of the eye.[8] When properly viewed, such a picture is highly illusionistic. Its construction and composition help assure that it will in fact be properly viewed.

Composition of the Painting Versus Layout of the Represented Scene: Control of Gaze and Imposition of Order

Although there has been an enormous amount written by perception psychologists about pictorial perspective, and there exists some scanty literature and research on the Gestalt phenomena in the service of representation, practically nothing has been written by perception psychologists about composition. Artists and art theorists (and the occasional phenomenologist) have, however, written heavily about composition, because, in essence, the composition of the painting *is* the design of the work of art. Indeed, in the case of representational art, the layout of the scene in space, which is what the viewer is invited to perceive through the medium of the canvas (considered as a transparent window), is in fact determined more by the design that the artist desires to achieve on the flat canvas than by the event or scene to be represented, because both rearrangement and distortion are tolerated or even unnoticed in the latter (see the section of this chapter entitled "Limited Span of Pictorial Consistency").

Several interrelated goals appear in discussions of composition (cf. Taylor, 1964): to provide balance to the design; to provide evidence of purposive order for the viewer to discern; to direct the focus and sequence of attention. Although artists have traditionally felt that composition leads the eye in a controlled sequence (cf. Poore, 1967, 1976; Taylor, 1964), and phenomenological reports have supported these assertions (cf. Gaffron, 1962), objective records of how viewers direct their eyes at paintings are less supportive. Whereas there is a great deal of agreement between viewers in their selection of regions at which they look most or longest (Antes, 1974; Buswell, 1935; Hochberg & Brooks, 1978b), there is little agreement as to the sequence in which they look. In addition, even this modest agreement in where viewers look has been obtained under conditions in which the subjects know that their gaze is being recorded, a fact that may well affect the outcome of the experiments.

Nevertheless, there are some aspects of composition about which we can be reasonably confident: In normal viewing, the eye is not directed just anywhere or everywhere, but to places that depend on the composition (Antes, 1974; Buswell, 1935), and on the objectively (Loftus & Mackworth, 1978) and subjectively judged informativeness (Brooks, 1961; Hochberg & Brooks, 1962b, 1978a; Parker, 1978; Pollack & Spence, 1968). These facts imply that the gaze is directed by what was seen in peripheral vision. We know that small detail is not available to peripheral vision (Figure 15.6); enough is picked up in even a single peripheral glimpse of a natural scene to provide a context for individual, indistinctly viewed shapes which in isolation would be ambiguous to peripheral vision (Biederman, 1972). Unless particular pains are taken to avoid it, *some* overall pattern or design will be provided to peripheral vision in any case by almost any random arrangement of objects into a scene, but the viewer can legitimately assume that the artist had some purpose for the arrangement that was in fact chosen and the gist and emphases that it provides. These facts, by themselves, place substantial constraints on what composition the artist may use. For example, a canvas that is homogeneously covered by small detail does not direct the viewer's gaze to any particular regions, and a canvas in which the features that are salient to peripheral vision all lie in one place directs the gaze only to that place. How and why eye movements should be sustained, and how that question interacts with the task of fitting mental structures to the picture (see the chapter section "Elective Perceptual Inquiry and the Fine Structure of Looking at Pictures and at the World") are issues that are, I believe, extremely important to any theoretical understanding of aesthetic judgment

(Hochberg, 1978a) and to any practical application of our knowledge about visual interest maintenance (Hochberg & Brooks, 1978a, b). I cannot pursue those issues here, other than to note that by affecting where the viewer looks, the composition determines what will be seen in foveal vision and what will be predominantly seen only by peripheral vision.

The artist has many reasons, of course, for which he or she may re-arrange or distort forms and change the viewpoints from which they are depicted, reasons quite unrelated to the problem of representation: Blake and El Greco do not rearrange their people into swirling or elongated patterns in order to keep one set of depicted volumes from being confused with some other set. But distortions and choices of viewpoint for repre-sentational purposes do have design consequences, and vice versa: If we want a radially symmetrical shape, we cannot also have a readily comprehensible cube (Figure 15.14A, B). If we want the picture's flatness emphasized, and the shapes of the spaces between objects to be almost as salient as those of the objects themselves, then the normal depth cues of interposition (i.e., the law of good continuation) must be avoided (Figures 15.16, 15.17). Why anyone should ever think this desirable is considered shortly.

Paintings as Objects and Subjects

One solution to the discrepancy between the flatness of the painting and the depth in the represented scene, I proposed above, is that provided by Rembrandt's focal chiaroscuro, or by any other equivalent compositional device that provides separate paintings to foveal and peripheral vision and that keeps the fovea away from represented deep edges.

The Impermanence of Impressionist Representations

This relationship between foveal and peripheral vision is exploited in a different way, and in a sense inverted, by impressionist painters: Wherever the fovea rests in impressionist paintings, only patches of paint can be seen. It is only in peripheral vision, or when viewed from a great distance, that the represented scene is perceived, not as fragments and patches of color, but as continuous uninterrupted shapes and objects.[9] Those depth cues that are normally discernible only to detailed foveal vision have been removed, and the canvas has been decomposed into discrete, visible patches. The tridi-mensionality of the represented scene is available only to peripheral vision, whereas the flatness of the canvas is conveyed by the brush strokes and patchwork that fill much of the central field of view at the normal distance from which such pictures are regarded. The objects represented therefore dissolve into a formless fog of shreds and patches when looked at directly, only to be recaptured when the viewer looks away from them. Imperma-nence and continued rediscovery and loss of the represented scene are built into the method.

Obtrusiveness of Impressionist and Post-Impressionist Paintings and Painters

The patchwork and pointillist technique has important advantages, of course, for representing the luminance range in outdoor scenes, and for simulating the freshness of the momentary glance. But the price is heavy: The impressionist canvas can never be trompe l'oeil, and the flatness of the canvas can never be ignored. The painter, and the act of painting, are made so obtrusive by this technique that there is simply no chance of mistaking the painting for the represented scene viewed through a window. The painting can be "read" as the scene; it can simulate the scene to peripheral vision or when viewed from a great distance; but, when viewed from a normal distance, it is simply not possible for the picture to be "transparent" to the three-dimensional set of objects in a way that leaves the picture itself, and its devices, unobtrusive.

From this point on, serious perceptual analysis of Western art is almost nonexistent, although post-impressionist artists repeatedly claim (with justification, I believe) that their art is itself a form of perceptual research, although it has been repeatedly announced that such art teaches us "new ways to see," and although it is such puzzling art that leads the average viewer to be at all interested in what the perception psychologist has to say about art. (Surely no layman feels the need to ask the perception psychologist to explain what Van Eyck or Vermeer was up to.)

I don't believe that we can understand the vicissitudes of representational art without taking into account the perceptual purposes for which paintings are made, used, and collected. The following point, elaborated elsewhere (Hochberg, 1979b), is an attempt in that direction.

Once the Techniques for Simulating Depth Were Perfected and Widespread, Their Use Became a Hindrance to Artistic Success

Since the Renaissance, artistic innovation has been increasingly a path to economic comfort and social mobility; the evolution of the modern international art market has made the recognition and development of an individual painter's characteristic style a matter of great financial importance to the dealer, collector, and investor, even more than to the painter. Two paintings of the same scene that are both perfect simulations and that are both unobtrusive and transparent to the represented scene cannot be very different from each other in many ways. Given these constraints, the painter can demonstrate superior or unique ability by the way in which he or she selects the literary content of the paintings and by the way in which their subject matter is staged or mounted (dramatic gesture, thoughtful arrangement, mood lighting, etc.)—surely restrictive and time-consuming arenas for competition. And the technical background necessary to produce high-fidelity visual surrogates for any scene had indeed been established by the end of the nineteenth century: the development of reliable pigments, understanding of the laws of optics, and the existence of a vast number of relatively cheap photographs that any painter could consult when in doubt about how a particular object should be drawn. (Note that by augmenting the number of existing masters' sketchbooks that were previously available to fledgling artists, photography must have had as devastating an effect on the scarcity value of realistic pictures as it had in its more direct capacity of producing such pictures.)

To say that some artist *can* paint realistically and chooses not to do so does not necessarily imply that the choice is dictated by purely aesthetic and expressive considerations. Other strong reasons to abandon realistic representation exist and should not be overlooked. Foremost among these are such considerations as speed of execution and signature or manifest identity.

With respect to speed of execution: It takes time to use the devices that achieve realistic representation and to put in the thought and planning (and the trial and error) that are needed to combine realistic representation with a coherent and purposive composition. It takes many years of unpaid practice to achieve a speed in these skills that might make "photographic" realism economically feasible, and the days in which the artist's atelier was staffed by cheap apprentice help are long gone.

These considerations work against the large, realistic painting. So, paradoxically, does the fact that a high level of realism became more accessible to more painters. More realistic representation was a goal worth pursuing for social and economic reasons, and for personal satisfaction, only so long as each step toward that goal made the artist who took it unique. Once the secrets of achieving realistic representation under limited light conditions (e.g., indoors, twilight, etc.) became well known, the artist who wished to be outstanding and to achieve a recognizable signature had to pass on, first to the task of capturing impressions of scenes that could not in fact be simulated "realistically" (e.g., the strong light of Turner and of the impressionists; see Hochberg, 1979b), and then look beyond that goal.

The goal of achieving uniquely realistic representation had to be abandoned and surpassed once the limits of the medium were reached in the late nineteenth century. Each artist has in essence been required to devise his or her own art form since then, and the response to the protests of the layman who fails to perceive the painter's pictorial intent, and therefore to appreciate the painter's abilities to execute that intent, is that each new wave of visual art teaches us new ways to see.

New Art Teaches Us to See Art, Not the World, in New Ways

It cannot be true that art changes the fundamental ways in which we perceive objects and events in the real world. The ways in which painters depart from representational realism and the methods employed to do so (Figures 15.16, 15.17) display only a reliance on perceptual laws that we already know (although compare the dates of Rubin's paper with those of Matisse's paintings!) and which, when operating on the things of the real world, will result only in the kind of perception with which we are already familiar.

What the new painters do teach us is how to perceive pictures that were executed with different premises, and they thereby open to public acceptance new areas of painting within which the individual painters are free to find their own individual signatures in greater numbers, and are able to produce paintings at a faster rate without maintaining an entire atelier of apprentices to help turn out their pictures. This latter point is probably not trivial, in that high productivity both encourages a demand for such individually identified work and makes it possible to meet the demand (i.e., to earn a living at painting).

The key to the new line of development hinges on the flattening of the picture.

Why and How to Flatten a Painting of a Deep Scene

The impressionists' methods provided depth cues only in peripheral vision, allowing illusionistically represented forms to dissove with each foveal glance. Cézanne restored the stability or permanence of the represented forms, providing them with firm outlines so that they remain visible to the fovea, but they still appear solid only to peripheral vision and appear flat to foveal vision by virtue of those very outlines, as well as for other reasons. That is, like the impressionists in this regard, Cézanne retained and developed the massive, undetailed volumetric forms that are all that peripheral vision can see, and he retained the painterly surface that looks uncompromisingly flat to foveal vision. And in fact he took active steps to keep the canvas perceptually flat in foveal vision. For example, he often repeated the color of the background for a short distance within the object's outline; although we have no research directly to the point, this procedure should have little effect on peripheral vision but should flatten the picture to foveal vision. Additionally, he modified central perspective not for purposes of enhancing depth, nor even for purposes of design, but to help flatten the picture plane.

The representation of objects and scenes as geometric volumes was itself adopted as the subject matter by subsequent painters (the cubists and other post-impressionists, like Seurat), providing to sharp-edged foveal vision no more than the shapes that peripheral vision can discern (see especially Léger for an extreme example). Most widely adapted were techniques for flattening the picture, now a goal in its own right and not merely a by-product of the impressionistic brushwork.

Reversed and inconsistent perspective (Figure 15.20) has been judged in perceptual experiments to reduce the degree of apparent depth or volume (Attneave & Frost, 1969; Hochberg & Brooks, 1960), and it is reasonable to assume that the same effect is obtained in an artistic context. Other techniques for flattening pictures were discussed in connection with Figures 15.16 and 15.17.

No longer a transparent window on the world, the picture proclaims to the viewer that it is the purposive creation of an individual painter and that it cannot be considered mainly in terms of the scene it presents. The

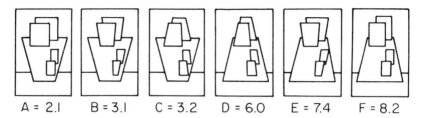

A = 2.1   B = 3.1   C = 3.2   D = 6.0   E = 7.4   F = 8.2

Figure 15.20. Flattening the picture through inverted and inconsistent perspective.
Mean subjects' ratings of apparent tridimensionality, on a scale of .0 (flat) to
10.0 (highly tridimensional). Figures A–F differ in the consistency of the linear
perspective with which the cards and the table are depicted and in whether the
perspective is normal (i.e., surface viewed from above) or inverted (i.e., surface
viewed from below). (From Hochberg & Brooks, 1963; reprinted with permission
of publisher.)

techniques, devices, and tasks of painting have themselves become the
subject matter and the design elements of paintings. This transformation of
the medium at once frees the painter from the tyranny of central perspective,
provides a vastly wider subject matter, and permits an almost unlimited
choice of artistic signatures. The flattening of the picture contributes immensely to this process: The devices of color contrast and modeling become
visible as adjacent patches of color, rather than being totally transformed
into perceived volumes and illumination, and therefore become accessible to
use for other pictorial purposes—a line of descent that traces from the
colored shadows of early impressionism through the fauves and expressionism to abstract expressionism. Similarly, the converging lines of linear
perspective that are encoded by the viewer as a receding road with parallel
sides in the deep scene become visible as a triangle when the painting is
viewed as a flat surface. Attention to the depth cues as such, to the shapes
formed by the figure as well as the ground, to the gestures implied by the
artist's brush strokes, to the order and balance of the pigment pattern—all of
these characterized the good painter in previous centuries. But these components are thoroughly concealed in a successful trompe l'oeil painting, in
which the viewer is almost forced to fit three-dimensional objects and layouts to his or her successive glances. The reason that the viewer cannot
perceive the projected shape of the foreshortened object, or the design of the
composition, is not because the flat pattern cannot be perceived—obviously
it can, in the sense that the viewer can accurately focus his or her eyes on, or
touch, the plane of the canvas. *But although the viewer already has mental
structures about the represented deep scene which enable him or her to store
successive glances and anticipate what will be seen in those terms, the viewer does
not know enough about the two-dimensional structure of the scene to store it
either as an abstract design or as a set of devices that contributes to the representational function.* Given the painting as a scene composed of objects and

people in what is called a realistic style, the viewer is inevitably led to attend to that represented scene, and to enter his or her successive glances at the painting into a perception of the scene of depicted objects and depth. It is therefore by the arrangement and substance of the *depicted* scene, and of how well it is done, that the viewer arrives at a judgment of the picture. That is not what the present artists want.

The painting should *not* be fully transparent to the scene, nor should it be construed as the scene itself. It is an object, which is to be viewed in a history of such objects, that is, earlier paintings. Most of those earlier objects were in fact more transparent as represented scenes, but they are only being referred to as *objects* in the contemporary pictures. What such paintings "represent" therefore are previous paintings, in a sequence of variations and successive steps of development radiating from the original pictorial functions in what David Levine called "the begats."

According to my understanding of the perceptual process, it is impossible to experience completely meaningless sensations, visual or otherwise. In vision, we primarily perceive and remember objects, or parts of objects, and their spatial arrangements. A patch of paint may be in fact perceived as merely a blob of pigment on the canvas, as a Rorschach blot may be perceived as a blot on a piece of paper, but that is neither memorable from one glance to the next nor evocative as such. If the blot is presented to the viewer for his or her attention—whether as found art or as purposeful construction—the viewer is being asked to relate the blot to something. To perceive and remember it at all, from one glance to the next, the viewer must be able to fit some structure to it. That structure can be of represented objects and scenes, or fragments of them, or the elements of previous paintings; or it can be perceived as a film of pigment deposited in a pattern that is not related to the appearance of any object but that represents the trace left by the painter's expressive movements. Or, with experience in art, and particularly as a result of experience with the obtrusive surfaces that have comprised the body of art in this century, the viewer can fit several alternatives to the pattern, that is, the viewer can perceive that the brush marks that are traces of the artist's agitated gestures also serve as the projective outline to which he can fit an agitated face or wind-torn sky (e.g., Munch or Van Gogh).

If new art teaches us new ways to look at art, it is because we need that instruction. A realistic picture needs no tradition to make it comprehensible to the naive viewer: His or her experience with the world of things provides the viewer with all of the repertory of perceptual structures that is needed in order to perceive pictorial representations of those things. In a line of pictorial endeavor that takes other pictures as its references, as much or more than it does the things of the world, the viewer necessarily needs a more or less extensive pictorial education, and needs to know the premises of that endeavor before its products can be appreciated, enjoyed, or evaluated. If perception psychologist and artist are to be of any use to each other, it is essential to spell out what it is that art "teaches us to see," because the phrase is not as metaphorical, I believe, as it sounds.

Acknowledgments

The theoretical inquiries underlying the sections of this chapter entitled "Perceptual Testing of Real and Represented Objects," "Outline Drawings, Figure-Ground, and Tridimensional Organization: Representation of Surfaces and Volumes," "Consequences of This Analysis: Constituents of Effective Representation and Canonical Form" were undertaken in connection with NSF BNS77-25653. Chapter sections entitled "Unavoidable Conflict in 'Distributed' Pictures and Scenes," "Rembrandt's Solution: Separate Painting for Foveal and Peripheral Gaze," and "Composition of the Painting Versus Layout of the Represented Scene: Control of Gaze and Imposition of Order" were done under NIE 74009 and 80-0029.

Notes

1. Note too that the unbroken line that connects the corners cannot in fact represent the same dihedral all along its length, although in the normal course of commerce with the world such a contour would normally do so. We may regard the impossible figure in Figure 15.8A as a conflict between good continuation, on the one hand, and the local depth cues at each of the corners, on the other. Viewed in these terms, breaking the lines at x should make it easier to detect whether the left and right sides of the frame are or are not compatibly oriented, but no evidence to that point has yet been gathered.

2. In any case, if the detail cannot be discerned, the relative movements between the elements of the detail cannot be discerned either (Hochberg, Green, & Virostek, 1978).

3. Assuming a viewing distance of 18 inches, a foveal acuity for parallax detection of 2 seconds of arc, parallax of 1 inch, and a tenfold decrease in acuity (in terms of visual angle) at a distance of 20° from the fovea. I know of no research directly to the point of these assumed parameters, but they seem reasonable ones to make in terms of the distribution of separation acuity.

4. There may be something of a puzzle here: There are a number of such demonstrations available in which by turning letters into spaces, or "holes," they appear to be rendered invisible. On the other hand, in an experiment designed to conceal letters and numbers by embedding the lines of which they are composed, so as to make them the edges either of cavities or of protuberances, subjects judged the letters and numbers to be more effectively concealed when they were embedded in the edges of the cavities or holes (Hochberg & Brooks, 1963).

5. One can, of course, talk about these phenomena and those of Figures 15.2C, 15.4A, 15.4B, 15.11, 15.12, 15.18, and 15.19 in terms of "tuning" or "invariants," but I don't see how that is better or more natural than talking about cues and mental structures. The latter terms more adequately reveal that our knowledge is quite rudimentary about how such phenomena work, a fact concealed by the former terms. There is, in addition, a substantive difference between the theory that

underlies the present paper and that of Gibson and his colleagues: *To Gibson, the function of exploration is to generate the sequence of overlapping stimulus samples that result from the exploratory eye movements or head movements, and that sequence—the sensory consequences of exploration—provides the information to which the perceptual system is directly tuned.* To the position from which this paper is written, the exploration consists of the testing of mental structures—of alternative sensorimotor expectancies that can be generated and compared to segments of the sequence of sensory input—that are themselves elective. I find the latter much more compatible with the facts of picture perception in general and the phenomena displayed in these figures in particular.

6. Very similar descriptions can be offered for the figure-ground phenomenon (Figures 15.9–12), for the demonstrations of selective attention to motion pictures (Hochberg, 1968, 1970; Neisser & Becklen, 1975), for attention to speech (Hochberg, 1970; Neisser, 1967), for the perception of scenes containing a great deal of redundant detail by means of a few elective glances that could only provide incomplete samples of the scene (Hochberg, 1968), and for the perception of scenes containing substantial amounts of overlap or occlusion (Figure 15.4A, B, C). Considering the similarity of these completion and attentional phenomena, some of which cannot be expressed in terms of the Gibsonian position mentioned in note 5 (e.g., selective listening to speech), I think it is prudent and reasonable to assume that the perception of fragmentary pictures taps a general ability, and does not require a special theory.

7. Eakins also provides striking examples of the use of focal detail as a compositional device: In his larger compositions, I believe that it is often the case that the overall design of the canvas, and the distribution of viewers' attention, would be much less satisfactory if sharp edges and detail had been distributed throughout the canvas, thus providing places outside the focal regions at which the eye might tarry.

8. Expressed in terms of spatial frequencies, the high-frequency information in the light from the scene has all been filtered out, while additional and irrelevant high-frequency information has been provided by the edges of the brush strokes and patches of color that cover the canvas. The latter must in turn be removed if the scene is to be recognized, and the viewer can remove the irrelevant high-frequency information by relying only on peripheral vision or by viewing the picture from a distance that makes that information too fine to resolve (cf. Hochberg, 1979b).

9. For a more formal statement of this, see n. 8 above.

References

ANTES, J. R. The time course of picture viewing. *Journal of Experimental Psychology*, 1974, *103*, 162–170.

ATTNEAVE, F. Some informational aspects of visual perception. *Psychological Review*, 1954, *61*, 183–193.

ATTNEAVE, F., & Frost, R. The discrimination of perceived tridimensional orientation by minimum criteria. *Perception and Psychophysics*, 1969, *6*, 391–396.

BIEDERMAN, I. Perceiving real-world scenes. *Science*, 1972, 77–80.

BRADLEY, D. R., DUMAIS, S. T., & PETRY, H. M. Reply to Cavonius. *Nature*, May 1976, *261*, 77–78.

BROOKS, V. An exploratory comparison of some measures of attention. Master's thesis, Cornell University, 1961.

BUSWELL, G. T. *How people look at pictures.* Chicago: Univ. of Chicago, 1935.

CULBERTSON, J. T. *Consciousness and behavior.* Dubuque, Iowa: William C. Brown, 1950.

ESCHER, M. C. *The graphic work of M. C. Escher.* New York: Duell, Sloan, and Pearce, 1960.

GAFFRON, M. Phenomenal properties and perceptual organizations. In S. Koch (Ed.), *Psychology: A study of a science: II. Empirical substructure and relations with other sciences (Vol. 4). Biologically oriented fields: Their place in psychology and in biological science.* New York: McGraw-Hill, 1962.

GIBSON, E. J. *Principles of perceptual learning and development.* Englewood Cliffs, New Jersey: Prentice-Hall, 1969.

GIBSON, J. J. *The senses considered as perceptual systems.* Boston: Houghton Mifflin, 1966.

GIBSON, J. J. What is a form? *Psychological Review,* 1951, *58*, 403–412.

GIBSON, J. J. *The perception of the visual world.* Boston: Houghton Mifflin, 1950.

GOLDSTEIN, E. B. The rotation of objects in pictures viewed at an angle: Evidence for two types of pictorial space. *Journal of Experimental Psychology: Human Perception and Performance,* 1976, *2*, 130–138.

GOMBRICH, E. *Art and illusion.* Princeton, New Jersey: Princeton Univ., 1956.

GOODMAN, N. *Languages of art: An approach to a theory of symbols.* Indianapolis: Bobbs-Merrill, 1968.

HAGEN, M. A., & ELLIOTT, H. B. An investigation of the relationship between viewing condition and preference for true and modified linear perspective. *Journal of Experimental Psychology: Human Perception and Performance,* 1976, *2*, 479–490.

HAGEN, M. A., JONES, R. K., & REED, E. S. On a neglected variable in theories of pictorial perception: Truncation of the visual field. *Perception and Psychophysics,* 1978, *23*, 326–330.

HELMHOLTZ, H. *Treatise on physiological optics,* Vol. III. New York: Dover, 1962. Originally published, 1857.

HOCHBERG, J. *Visual world and visual field: Perception, sensation and pictorial observation.* Mimeographed report, Cornell University, Ithaca, New York, 1961. Available from author, Columbia University.

HOCHBERG, J. The psychophysics of pictorial perception. *Audio-Visual Communication Review,* 1962, *10*, 22–54.

HOCHBERG, J. In the mind's eye. In R. N. Haber (Ed.), *Contemporary theory and research in visual perception.* New York: Holt, Rinehart, Winston, 1968.

HOCHBERG, J. Attention, organization, and consciousness. In D. I. Mostofsky (Ed.), *Attention: Contemporary theory and analysis.* New York: Appleton-Century-Crofts, 1970.

HOCHBERG, J. Perception: I. Color and shape. II. Space and movement. In J. W. Kling & L. A. Riggs (Eds.), *Woodworth and Schlosberg's experimental psychology* (third edition). New York: Holt, Rinehart, Winston, 1972(a).

HOCHBERG, J. The representation of things and people. In E. H. Gombrich, J. Hochberg, & M. Black (Eds.), *Art, perception and reality.* Baltimore: Johns Hopkins, 1972(b).

HOCHBERG, J. Higher-order stimuli and interresponse coupling in the perception of the visual world. In R. B. Macleod and H. L. Pick (Eds.), *Perception: Essays in honor of James J. Gibson.* Ithaca: Cornell Univ., 1974, 17–39 (a).

HOCHBERG, J. Organization and the Gestalt tradition. In E. C. Carterette & M. Friedman (Eds.), *Handbook of perception* (Vol. 1). New York: Academic Press, 1974(b).

HOCHBERG, J. Art and visual perception. In E. Carterette & M. Friedman (Eds.), *Handbook of perception* (Vol. 10). New York: Academic Press, 1978(a).

HOCHBERG, J. *Perception* (second edition). Englewood Cliffs, New Jersey: Prentice-Hall, 1978(b).

HOCHBERG, J. Sensation and perception. In E. Hearst (Ed.), *Experimental psychology at 100.* Hillsdale, New Jersey: Lawrence Erlbaum, 1979(a).

HOCHBERG, J. Some of the things that pictures are. In C. Nodine & D. Fisher (Eds.), *Views of pictorial representation: Making, perceiving and interpreting.* New York: Praeger, 1979(b).

HOCHBERG, J., & BROOKS, V. The psychophysics of form: Reversible-perspective drawings of spatial objects. *American Journal of Psychology*, 1960, *73*, 337–354.

HOCHBERG, J., & BROOKS, V. Pictorial recognition as an unlearned ability: A study of one child's performance. *American Journal of Psychology*, 1962, *75*, 624–628 (a).

HOCHBERG, J., & BROOKS, V. The prediction of visual attention to designs and paintings. *American Psychologist*, 1962, *17*, 7 (Abstract) (b).

HOCHBERG, J., & BROOKS, V. Compression of pictorial space through perspective reversal. *Perceptual and Motor Skills*, 1963, *16*, 262 (a).

HOCHBERG, J., & BROOKS, V. Graphic symbols: Things or holes? *American Journal of Psychology*, 1963, *76*, 326–329 (b).

HOCHBERG, J., & BROOKS, V. Film cutting and visual momentum. In R. A. Monty and J. W. Senders (Eds.), *Eye movements and psychological processes, II.* Hillsdale, New Jersey: Lawrence Erlbaum, 1978(a).

HOCHBERG, J., & BROOKS, V. The perception of motion pictures. In E. C. Carterette & M. P. Friedman (Eds.), *Handbook of perception* (Vol. 10). New York: Academic Press, 1978(b).

HOCHBERG, J., GREEN, J., & VIROSTEK, S. Texture occlusion requires central viewing: Demonstrations, data and theoretical implications. Paper delivered at the APA Convention, Toronto, 1978. Available from the senior author.

HOCHBERG, J., & McALISTER, E. A quantitative approach to figural "goodness." *Journal of Experimental Psychology*, 1953, *46*, 361–364.

KENNEDY, J. M. *A psychology of picture perception.* San Francisco: Jossey-Bass, 1974.

JOHNSON, C. A., LEIBOWITZ, H. W., MILLODOT, M., & LAMONT, A. Peripheral visual acuity and refractive error: Evidence of two visual systems? *Perception & Psychophysics*, 1976, *20*(6), 460–462.

KOFFKA, K. *Principles of Gestalt psychology.* New York: Harcourt, Brace, 1935.

KOPFERMANN, H. Psychologische untersuchungen uber die wirkung zweidimensionalar darstellunger körperlicher gebilde. *Psychologische Forschung.* 1930, *13*, 293–364.

LEIBOWITZ, H. W., & OWENS, D. A. Anomalous myopias and the intermediate dark focus of accommodation. *Science*, 1975, *18*(3), 162–170.

LOFTUS, G. R., & MACKWORTH, N. H. Cognitive determinants of fixation location during picture viewing. *Journal of Experimental Psychology: Human Perception and Performance*, 1978, *4*, 565–572.

METZGER, W. *Gesetze des sehens.* Frankfurt-am-Main: Kramer, 1953.

NEISSER, U. *Cognitive psychology.* New York: Appleton-Century-Crofts, 1967.

NEISSER, U., & BECKLEN, R. Selective looking: Attending to visually specified events. *Cognitive Psychology,* 1975, *7,* 480–494.

PARKER, R. E. Picture processing during recognition. *Journal of Experimental Psychology: Human Perception and Performance,* 1978, *4,* 284–293.

PIRENNE, M. *Optics, painting and photography.* Cambridge, England: Cambridge Univ., 1970.

POLLACK, I., & SPENCE, D. Subjective pictorial information and visual search. *Perception & Psychophysics,* 1968, *3,* 41–44.

POORE, H. R. *Pictorial composition and the critical judgment of pictures* New York: Sterling, 1967. (Reprinted as *Composition in art,* New York: Dover, 1976.)

RUBIN, E. Figure and ground (M. Wertheimer, trans.). In D. C. Beardslee & M. Wertheimer (Eds.), *Readings in perception.* New York: Van Nostrand, 1958. (Originally published, 1915.)

SCHLOSBERG, H. Stereoscopic depth from single pictures. *American Journal of Psychology,* 1941, *54,* 601–605.

SCHRIEVER, W. Experimentelle Studien über das Stereoskopische Sehen. *Zeitschrift für Psychologie,* 1925, *96,* 113–170.

TAYLOR, J. *Design and expression in the visual arts.* New York: Dover, 1964.

TURVEY, M. T. Contrasting orientations to the theory of visual information processing. *Psychological Review,* 1977, *84,* 67–68.

WARTOFSKY, M. Picturing and representing. In C. F. Nodine & D. F. Fisher (Eds.), *Perception and pictorial representation.* New York: Praeger, 1979.

WOODWORTH, R. *Experimental psychology.* New York: Holt, Rinehart, Winston, 1938.

16

Levels of Perceptual Organization

Julian Hochberg

Abstract

Perceptual organization refers to constraints on what is perceived (e.g., with visual angle held constant, apparent size and apparent distance covary; apparent figural quality varies with apparent simplicity of configuration). Three major classes of organizational phenomena (space, shape/form, and movement) have been important to perceptual theory. Theories of organization differ in the roles assigned to *stimulus structure* (intrastimulus constraints) and to *mental structure* (interresponse constraints) and on the degree of *wholism* posited (i.e., the size of the structure within which constraints are strong). The major perceptual theories are analyzed in these terms. Phenomena are reviewed that very sharply limit the tenability of any theory to which spatial or temporal wholism is important and that clearly demonstrate mental structure in the absence of stimulus structure.

The class of theory proposed by J. S. Mill and Helmholtz—that we perceive by fitting the most likely or expected (global) object or event to the sampled (local) sensory components—remains the one best suited to the widest range of organizational phenomena (including the Gestalt phenomena). Mental structure does not simply reflect physical (stimulus) structure, however, and the different levels of organization must be separated before such theories can be seriously considered and developed.

Introduction

Organization has meant very different things to different theorists and to the same theorists at different times. In the first part of this chapter, I try to classify the major ways in which organization has been used in the study of perception and to place the major theories in the appropriate cells of this classification scheme. In the second part, I review a body of recent data that, to my mind, rule out some of the cells and strongly support others (mostly

275

the one that I have come to occupy, along with other right-thinking psychologists). Two points in preview:

1. The phenomena of perceptual organization cannot be encompassed by a single rubric, for a nontrivial reason: The interactions that are responsible for organization occur at different levels and involve different processes. To try to fit a single function to the disorderly mixture and interaction of these different kinds of organization can only be done by ruling out every exception to that function on increasingly ad hoc grounds. The domains within which relatively compact explanatory systems can be applied must first be isolated by experiment, not by definition.

2. Many of the sources of organization contribute only indirectly, accidentally, or even serve as impediments to what I consider to be the most important subject matter of "visual" perception—namely, *schematic maps* (which are contingent expectations of what one will see if one looks here or there) and *schematic events* (contingent expectations of what one will see *when*, in a changing visual world). Even so, we must try to identify such sources, because their contribution contaminates what we take to be the data of perceptual organization, and because they offer opportunities to rule out some classes of theory.

Classification of Theories of Organization

First, we consider classes of phenomena to which theories of organization have addressed themselves.

Classes of Organizational Phenomena

Historically, there have been three main classes of organizational phenomena in visual perception: organization of space, of shape/form, and of movement. In each, the organization consists of constraints on what will most likely be perceived—that is, on what the appearance of one aspect of a perceived object or event implies about the appearance of other aspects. I sketch them very briefly in turn.

Space. The major constraints in spatial perception are those of size/distance, slant/shape, and distance/velocity. That is, for a given retinal image, when cues to size or distance, shape or slant, and distance or velocity are varied, apparent size is found to vary with apparent distance, apparent shape varies with apparent slant, and apparent velocity varies with apparent distance. It is usually assumed that these constraints are exhibited by proximal stimulation. That is, in the normal physical environment, the proximal stimulation specifies invariants between its terms (e.g., for an object that subtends a given visual angle, the ratio of the distal object's size to the object's distance is a constant). Note that *all theories, from at least Berkeley's on, assume that the proximal stimulus pattern normally contains enough information to account for the adult viewer's response.* That is, no clairvoyance or other ESP is invoked by any theory. The theories differ only in their predilections about how that information is used.

According to some of the theories discussed, responses like perceived size and perceived distance vary together because they are subject to constraints internal to the organism that comprise a mental structure, so that the responses covary even when the constraints are not given in the stimulus pattern. For example, if the viewer is led somehow to perceive an object as changing its distance although the stimulus pattern itself remains unchanged, the object's apparent size then changes as well.

From the point of view of theories that propose and deal with mental structure (which means the interresponse constraints already described), it is necessary to introduce abnormally impoverished stimulus patterns if we are to show the existence and nature of mental structure, because in normal circumstances there is enough information in stimulation to make it theoretically uneconomical to introduce such constraints as mental structures. To rule out of consideration either impoverished (ecologically unrepresentative) stimulus situations or abnormal perceptions (e.g., illusions) makes mental structure (i.e., organism-furnished organization) unstudyable. That is, it prejudges the question of whether mental structures exist and precludes their study if they do exist.

Shape/Form. By a shape, I mean a silhouette or projected pattern; by a form, I mean a solid or volume. Both are classifications of some set of spatial points or regions into one class (object, group, and so forth) rather than another. Not all possible classifications that are permitted by the physical stimulus are equally available as perceptions. First, for example, there are the flip-flop figure-ground phenomena, in which it is partially true that only one object will be given shape by a contour at one time or place: That is, at any point on the contour of Fig. 16.1A, we see a vase or faces, but usually not both. Second, there are the similar "grouping" phenomena that occur when subjects are asked which dots belong together. In both cases, the relative strengths of the alternative perceptual outcomes appear to be affected by the configuration of the stimulus pattern. How wholistic the constraints exerted by such an overall configuration of object or scene may be and which rubric

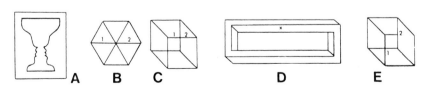

Figure 16.1. Organization, impossible figures, and local depth cues.

best summarizes these phenomena of organization are empirical questions. They are not questions to be answered either by fiat or by definition.

Movement. I mentioned under "space," earlier, that there are distance/velocity constraints. In addition to these constraints, there is a set of problems that arises from the fact that depending on what the viewer takes to be stationary, the same pattern of retinal motions can be perceived in quite different ways. In normal viewing conditions, we usually perceive the invariant world as in fact invariant under a transformation that is provided by our own head or eye movements. In abnormal (impoverished) conditions, hierarchical vector-extraction principles have been offered (Johansson, 1950, 1977) that seem to subsume the normal case under a single organizational rubric. Whether there is a single domain of phenomena to be fit under such a rubric (rather than multiple determinants of different levels of processing that happen to produce perceptual phenomena that approximate vector extraction under Johansson's conditions and that may combine very differently under more normal conditions) is still very much an empirical question. If the Gibsonian position is that we should not study artificial situations, it is hard to see how the Johansson experiments are to be exempted from that injunction.

The three kinds of organization I have sketched are those of spatial organization (e.g., size/distance), Gestalt organization (e.g., shape/form constraints), and Johansson's hierarchical movement organization. The list is surely not exhaustive (e.g., it does not include color, to which it could easily be extended), but it suffices to show that there is a large area of phenomena and relationships to which the major theories were intended to apply. In the next section, I remind you how each was tried.

Theories of Organization

I distinguish three attributes of an organizational theory—whether it is (1) a *stimulus structure theory*, (2) a *mental structure theory*, and/or (3) a *wholistic theory* (I myself have been +, +, and – on this checklist for the past decade; Hochberg, 1968). Note that in general any theory will fall into more than one classification and will be + on more than one attribute.

The term *stimulus structure*, as I use it, refers to the intrastimulus constraints in the stimulation that are normally provided to our sense organs by the world. For example, an approaching object projects an expanding retinal image, so that cues in the stimulation as to the object's distance are correlated with the visual angle that the object subtends at the eye; for another example, apples are roughly spheroidal, so that the shape of a portion of one that is partially hidden from view can be predicted better than chance.

The term *mental structure*, as I use it, refers to the interresponse (or intraperceptual) constraints that can be attributed neither to structure in the present stimulation nor to the characteristics of sensory response to that stimulation (Hochberg, 1956, 1974a). Thus, mental structure involving size/distance constraints would (as already noted) be manifested if an object's perceived size and perceived distance are found to covary even when the entire retinal image remains unchanged in any way.

The term *wholistic*, as I use it, refers to the size of the structure within which constraints are strong. In Helmholtz's infamously "atomistic" sensory theory, each fundamental point sensation was taken to be independent of its neighbors; in Gestalt theory, the whole form of a configuration constrains the appearance of the parts, so that those appearances were not thought to be free to vary independently. In Gibson's theory, the constraints over a spatially and temporally extended stimulus structure (e.g., the gradient of texture density over a sector of the optic array) comprise a unitary source of stimulus information about the layout of surfaces in the world. In general, the bounds over which wholistic theories extend their analyses have not been well defined.

Stimulus Structure Theories.   The physical nature of the distal objects that we are likely to encounter and the probabilistic "laws" of environmental or ecological physics place constraints on the patterns of proximal stimulation that we are likely to receive under normal conditions.

1. The theories of Helmholtz, Brunswik, and Hebb (in principle, though not in practice) represent variations of the *classical approach to perception* (Hochberg, 1979). According to this approach, we perceive those objects or events that would, under normal conditions, most likely produce the sensory stimulation we receive. With normal seeing conditions, therefore, and an ecologically representative sample of the world, the viewer's sensory systems are "transparent" to the physical world. To Helmholtz and Hebb, who were also concerned with what the organism contributes to structure, it is important to know what structure is contained in the proximal stimulation and to know, too, the constraints imposed by our sensory limitations, inasmuch as these are the starting point of whatever contribution the organism may make. Helmholtz therefore placed great emphasis on the dynamic, movement-based information about objects and scenes that is available to active perceivers in the proximal stimulus distributions that they receive over time. Cassirer (1944) showed that Helmholtz's notions, when expressed in group theory, concern invariance under transformation; and Hebb (in his phase sequences argument, 1949) attempted to devise neural schemes for dealing with such transformations over time.

   Because the perceiver would normally learn to perceive as veridically as possible, Brunswik considered proximal stimulation and neural mechanisms as "merely mediating variables"; if our perceptions are normally so distally focused (1956), what need is there to study the proximal stimulus except when perceptual achievement is poor?

The psychologist's first task evidently is to survey the world and to find out, by experiments that are ecologically representative of conditions in that world, how good perception is in what circumstances. By contrast, Gibson, in his "global psychophysics" days (1950), proposed to turn the problem around and ask what stimulus information might exist in the light at the eye that would permit the organism to achieve perfect veridical perception; the answers to that question would provide the starting point for more adequate theories of perceptual processing. I discuss that proposal shortly; I do not address the neo-Gibsonian position on this matter because I have not yet grasped why "direct realists" are concerned with proximal stimulus information in the first place. That is, unless they undertake to explain the mechanisms that achieve distal focus from proximal stimulation, I cannot see why they do not, with Brunswik, concern themselves primarily with distal focus and ecological achievement.

To Helmholtz, Brunswik, and Hebb, the physical organization of stimulation is reflected in mental structure. For example, corresponding to the physical size/distance constraints in stimulation, the perceiver has acquired (through perceptual learning) internal constraints that link perceived size and perceived distance. These internal constraints are in turn evidenced in our perceptions, so that our perceptions are in this sense—the sense that intervening mechanisms are involved—"indirect." The constraints in space perception, shape perception, and movement perception reflect and reveal the structure that the perceiver brings to each stimulus pattern, by these theories. All of these theories are +, +, − on my checklist.

Note that there are two distinct components to this approach: First, there is *local sensory input.* Helmholtz's (forgivable) first assumption was that punctiform sensory input would be the simplest basis for the system to work upon, but that assumption is not viable today; nor do Hebb and later proponents of this type of approach rely on such small receptive channels. (Read almost any issue of *Vision Research* to find retina-wide schemes for processing "local" input.) Second, there is *integrative mental structure.* Helmholtz's theory of space and motion perception, empiricist though it is, should be read with Kant's "schemata" in mind (Helmholtz's teacher Müller and his father were both Kantians); perceivers perform unconscious calculations or inferences upon their sensory data, with the constraints of size/distance, distance/velocity, and so on as their premises.

2. The Gestalt psychologists announced that the major phenomena of shape/form perception were completely beyond any possible Helmholtzian account, but we will see shortly that this claim was a premature, self-proclaimed victory. In fact, Brunswik countered that the Gestalt laws were merely aspects of stimulus organization, reflecting the probability that any parts of the visual field belonged to the same object. We see later

that this Helmholtzian argument becomes more plausible, the more we learn about Gestalt organization. Gestalt theory is +, +, + on my checklist.

3. To Gibson, the information in the proximal pattern (or optic array) potentially supplies the perceiver with a direct basis for any attribute of the physical world he or she can perceive. The organization of the stimulus information is therefore sufficient to account for perception.

This approach has come to be called a *direct theory* of perception, because its proponents often claim that our sensory systems respond directly to the information about the permanent properties of objects and layouts that is offered by the flux of stimulation that the active perceiver receives from the world. It is asserted that we pick up the size, shape, and more evolutionarily important characteristics afforded by the objects in our environment as directly as Helmholtz thought we picked up brightness or hue. (In fairness to Helmholtz, however, and to some degree depriving subsequent theoreticians of a straw man, we should note that Helmholtz did not believe that the basic sensations of brightness and hue were directly consciously experienced; indeed, with most philosophers and psychologists since James Mill, Helmholtz argued that it is the invariant properties of objects that are important to our survival and that comprise our conscious experience [cf. Hochberg, 1979], so that the issue seems to me to reduce to questions of specific receptive mechanisms, which the direct theorists have not yet provided.)

The viewer must be active in order to perceive, as in Helmholtz's theory, and the kinds of stimulus structure described by the theory are those presaged by Cassirer and Helmholtz. Because for Gibson there is no room for mental structure—indeed, what is unique to him is his rejection of mental structure—we need not consider impoverished, abnormal stimulus situations. In fact, there are positive injunctions to avoid such ecologically unrepresentative traps. Analyses of stimulus "information" compatible with this approach have been carried out for space perception, for those aspects of movement perception that meet these requirements of loosely defined ecological representativeness, and (largely by Johansson, whose views are somewhat similar to Gibson's) for those aspects of movement organization that fit easily under an invariance/transformation or vector-extraction treatment. Figure-ground, grouping, the Gestalt laws, and the illusions, however, are not only not addressed—they are ruled out of court.

To anticipate, Gibson is +, −, + on my checklist.

Mental Structure Theories.   Helmholtz and his successors (e.g., Brunswik and Hebb) assume mental structure to exist and to be important *in addition to* physical stimulus structure. This means that they assume that size/distance, shape/slant, and distance/velocity invariances are manifested in perception even when they are not given directly in the stimulus information.

Let me define this by contrast. To Gibson, for example, apparent size and apparent distance covary because the information that specifies each of them will normally covary in the proximal stimulus pattern. To mental structure theorists, on the other hand, the appearances will covary even if there is no stimulus basis for either apparent size, apparent distance, or both. Let us note here that such mental structure has been demonstrated to occur in impoverished situations, in which stimulus information cannot account for the coupling (e.g., the coupling of perceived size and distance) between appearances. Because the situations are impoverished, and perhaps are neither commonplace nor ecologically valid, the direct theorist can therefore question whether such structure plays an important role when stimulus information *is* present. The mental structure theorist's rebuttal is this: Although it is true that we can only study mental structures in their pure state in such impoverished situations (and in others that we discuss later), we can show mental structure at work even in cases in which there is good stimulus information to contradict the organization that is in fact perceived. For example, in the Ames trapezoid, the purely presumptive relative size cue or the viewer's assumptions about the rectangular shape of the rotating object overcome the information about the invariant trapezoid undergoing the transformation that should specify its true shape and rotation, and so we perceive a rectangle oscillating. This, of course, is an illusion, and like most of the illusions, it is readily accounted for in terms of Helmholtzian mental structure (cf. Gregory & Harris, 1975). It is hard to see how this phenomenon can be dismissed or ignored. One might say that the movement information lies below the thresholds required by a "direct" or Gibsonian theory. That rebuttal opens a wide range of problems, however, because as we will see, the question of limits is in fact a vital one to any such direct theory and a question that has not been seriously addressed.

Helmholtzian mental structure is (at least qualitatively) well designed to deal with perception in the impoverished and abnormal (e.g., illusory) situations that the direct theories (e.g., Gibson's) cannot handle. There has been little thought devoted by Helmholtzians to the organizational phenomena in shape/form and in movement perception, although Helmholtz does have an interesting discussion of the cue of *interposition* that reads very much like a Gestaltist description of the factor of *good continuation*, to which we return later.

Gestalt theorists also invoke mental structure in the form of a *Prägnanz*, or *minimum principle*: We perceive just that organization (shape, scene, or movement) that is simplest (according to some specification). The internal relationships that must be taken into account to decide what is simplest are not a feature of the proximal stimulation but of the alternative imaginary objects that might be fitted to the proximal pattern. Gestalt principles, couched either in terms of simplicity or in terms of the specific "laws of organization," can be used to explain all of the depth cues (except for *familiar size*, which by definition must be learned), as I have demonstrated elsewhere

(Hochberg, 1978a, pp. 139–140); they can explain most of the shape/form phenomena (except for the figure-ground phenomenon itself; see the later subsection entitled "Evidence of Mental Structure"); and they can explain many of the phenomena of movement organization. The notion of slant/ shape, size/distance, and distance/velocity invariances, however, are not explained but are merely taken over from the Cassirer-Helmholtz formulation.

Let us contrast these two rubrics of mental structure, *likelihood* and *simplicity*. To Helmholtz and his successors, the major rule runs something like this: *We perceive whatever object or scene would, under normal conditions, most likely fit the sensory pattern we receive.* In principle, likelihood can be measured by the objective frequency with which particular aspects of stimulation occur in the course of our interacting with the world. Nothing was said about how large a piece we try to fit at one time or about what practical methods might be found to measure "likelihood" and so forth, however.

To Gestalt theorists (and to their diverse successors), *we perceive whatever object or scene would most simply or economically fit the sensory pattern.* Note that this rubric has great difficulty in specifying simplicity or economy. Even without that difficulty, there is what I now consider to be a fatal problem to this approach. There is a specific implication that *some* overall measure of simplicity can be found and that it is to be applied to some *overall* unit (e.g., an object); otherwise, there is no proposal at all. Either the "whole determines the appearance of the parts," or there is no Gestalt theory. And I believe that this judgment applies as well to Gestalt theory's successors (e.g., Attneave, 1954, 1959; Attneave & Frost, 1969; Garner, 1962, 1970a; Hochberg & Brooks, 1960; Hochberg & McAlister, 1953).

In other respects, we would expect the Helmholtzian and the Gestalt rubrics to be roughly similar, because the constraints in the ecology are subject to the same laws of thermodynamics as are used to model a Gestaltist nervous system. The size of the unit—the "grain size," as Attneave has put it—is central to any attempt to apply either rubric, but it is crucially important to the theoretical viability of the Gestalt position. I do not know of any serious and successful attempts to specify a size of unit (details, objects, or scenes) within which the Gestalt principles apply, and I do not now believe that any such attempt could work. Grain size is also important to any "global psychophysics" of "higher-order variables." Let us consider the matter of grain size next.

Wholistic Theories. Here we complete the round. Gestalt theory and Gibsonian direct theory occupy this niche. We consider them in turn and contrast them with Helmholtz and Hebb in this regard.

It is often stated that a shape remains perceptually unchanged despite transposition (rotation, translation) on the retina. This "fact," sometimes called *the* Gestalt problem, was "explained" by saying that the form itself remains unchanged after transposition—for example, after an eye movement has moved the object to a new part of the retina—so there is presumably no problem about why the form can be perceived despite its being transferred to a totally new set of receptors. Studies of inversion, reversal, rotation, and so on have made this argument a very weak one today: Transposition is simply not immediate or instantaneous, wholistic, or complete.

As to Gibson's approach, there is nothing inherent in global psychophysics that requires us to assume that the viewer responds to large-scale and extended variables of stimulation, but the specific variables that Gibson has in fact considered require that the user have access to information over a relatively wide expanse of the field of view, if not over the entire optic array. A texture-density gradient, for example, or an optical flow pattern is by its nature an extended source. If we remember that acuity outside of foveal vision is very poor for small details, we can see why the variable of texture-density gradient (for example) as it is stated is a wholistic one: Depending on the size of the texture grain and the slope of the gradient, the eye may need several fixations to determine the gradient. Gibson is not concerned with such acuity questions, because he takes the entire array as the stimulus and the movement of the fovea over the array as a form of active exploration, like that of a moving hand exploring a form: The stimulus is the invariant under transformation (in this case, the transformation that unites the successive views of the moving eye). Until (or unless) explicit provision is made for bridging successive partial glimpses, Gibson's theory is wholistic in nature.

Helmholtz, of course, assumed very small units (cones) as the first level of peripheral sensory organization, but we should note that he allowed for something like larger units or substructures to be built up by learning. In Hebb's theory, in fact, there is nothing to limit the spatial extent of a cell assembly; it might include a pattern of light over most of the retina plus a touch on the back of the knee and an efferent command to wiggle the left ear, all as a single unit. Although the line of thought that descends from Helmholtz is surely not wholistic, it can tolerate the demonstration of wholistic phenomena.

In the next section, I describe research and demonstrations in each of the three classes of organizational phenomena (space, shape/form, and movement) that argue strongly against any theory that rests on wholistic stimulus structure or wholistic mental structure. These put quietus to any form of Gestalt theory and make it necessary to consider alternative explanations of the Gestalt phenomena, of which at least one explanation appears to be viable. Strong limits are placed on a stimulus organization theory (i.e., one that denies the need for mental structure), and it is shown that mental structure can, under proper circumstances, contribute to perceptual organization, although we have not proved that such mental structure contributes to perception under conditions in which full stimulus information is available.

Research, Theory, and Demonstrations

Gestalt Explanations of Form and
Why They Must Be Rejected

Figures 16.1B and 16.1C provide good examples of how Gestalt theories explained perceived solidity without recourse to past experience or depth cues: Fig. 16.1B appears flat because one would have to break the good continuation between 1 and 2 in order to see those lines as the rear and front corners of a cube, whereas in Fig. 16.1C, 1 and 2 form a continuous edge of a cube—an edge that would have to be broken in order for the figure to appear flat. Alternatively, in terms of a minimum principle, Fig. 16.1B is simpler as a flat object than Fig. 16.1C, whereas the two are equally simple as cubes, so that Fig. 16.1B appears the more two-dimensional (for a discussion of this, see Hochberg & Brooks, 1960). The impossible picture in Fig. 16.1D is disturbing to this viewpoint because (as I argued in 1968) both good continuation and simplicity should cause us to perceive it as a flat pattern, whereas we quite obviously do not. When the distance between the right and left corners is reduced, such figures look flat, whereas consistent figures continue to look tridimensional under such conditions (Hochberg, 1968), strongly suggesting that the corners fail to conflict in Fig. 16.1D only because of their separation.

Figure 16.1D is an "impossible" figure and for that reason—or others—may represent a special case. Figure 16.1E, however, is perfectly possible and is of precisely the same size and kind as those in Figs. 16.1B and 16.1C, with which the Gestalt case has been made. It differs from Fig. 16.1C only in that it is made unambiguous in orientation at point 2. As long as you fixate point 2, the orientation is indeed relatively unambiguous. When you fixate point 1, however, the horizontal line does not remain in front of the vertical line as it must in order to be consistent with point 2; after a moment or two, the orientation will reverse, and the horizontal line will appear behind the vertical line in an organization that is inconsistent with the good continuation at point 2.

I think this clearly shows the operation of local depth cues and that the whole does not in any simple sense determine the appearance of its parts. Where one looks in figures like 16.1B, 16.1C, and 16.1E determines what one sees; it is simply the consistency or homogeneity of the first two that have concealed this important fact. This demonstration is important because spontaneous appearances of the organization in which the horizontal line appears to lie behind the vertical line are incompatible with any object-wide definition of simplicity that I know of, and because it argues very strongly that the figures that the Gestaltists chose to study (e.g., 16.1B and 16.1C) appear unified only because they provide consistent local depth cues to the successive glances that one executes in looking at them. So we have to take into account the differential effect of foveal and peripheral vision and of the storage of information from glance to glance—that is, the laws that govern the integration of successive views—in any attempt to describe and explain the phenomena of organization.

There really is very little of the Gestalt theory, as proposed by Wertheimer, Köhler, and Koffka, that survives the facts shown by these demonstrations: I cannot see how either a brain-field theory (no matter how metaphorical), parallel processes, or laws of organization much larger in scope than a couple of degrees in extent can accommodate these particularistic or neoatomistic implications.

The Gestalt phenomena themselves—figure and ground, the demonstrations of the so-called laws of organization, the purported demonstrations that the whole organization determines the appearance of the parts, and so on—remain to be explained; and I try to do this later in terms of the perceptuomotor expectancies that the peculiarities of the human gaze, taken together with the ecological probabilities of objects' characteristics, provide in the way of integrative mental structure. Note that any such explanation is more than the Gestaltists ever got around to offering (i.e., their brain fields never did explain either the figure-ground phenomenon or the laws of organization that presumably constrained figure formation—they only promised to do so).

A Direct Stimulus Organization Theory and Why It Must Be Strongly Circumscribed

What Figs. 16.1D and 16.1E tell us is that for line drawings, we must take into account the limitations of the momentary glance. Line drawings are surely not the best examples of the normal objects of perception. Can we show similar limits in the pick-up or processing of the information available to the moving observer in the real world?

The two kinds of information discussed by Gibson and his colleagues are the *optical flow pattern* (Gibson, Olum, & Rosenblatt, 1955; Lee, 1974; Purdy, 1958) and the occlusion of texture that occurs in the optic array when one textured surface moves behind another surface's edge (Kaplan, 1969)—that is, *kinetic occlusion.* The Ames trapezoid, discussed earlier, is strong evidence that acuity factors limit the effects of the optical flow pattern. We will now see that differences between foveal and peripheral vision limit the effectiveness of kinetic occlusion information within the momentary glance as well. Figure 16.2 represents the stimuli and data of a study by Hochberg, Green, and Virostek (1978). A textured surface moves behind a window cut in a similarly textured surface. No brightness difference betrays the edges of the window, which is therefore defined only by the relative motion gradients of the two sets of dots. The leftmost column of dots on the rear surface disappears when the surface moves to the left and

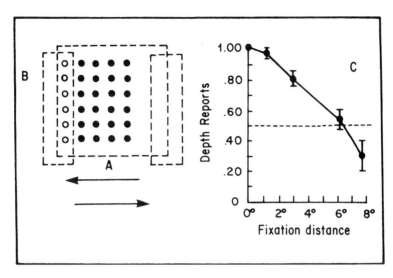

Figure 16.2. Kinetic occlusion as a function of fixation distance (after Hochberg, Green, & Virostek, 1978).

reappears when the surface moves to the right. As Kaplan (1969) has shown, this elicits the perception that the enclosed moving surface is behind the stationary enclosing surface. When subjects fixate points at progressively greater distances from the critical leftmost column of the rear surface, however, their ratings of the rear surface's depth are progressively less affected by the kinetic occlusion of that column (as shown by the graph at right).

This experiment does not, of course, show that peripheral information about spatial layout is, in general, useless. For one thing, we would expect that with larger texture elements, the effects of kinetic occlusion would be manifest at greater distances from the fovea; for another, we as yet have no direct evidence about the importance of fixation to other forms of kinetic depth information (e.g., motion perspective). These data do tell us that the momentary gaze shows limits for kinetic, as well as for static, depth information and that therefore it is of general importance (not merely of importance in explaining the perception of drawings) to deal explicitly with the problems of how we combine the information from successive glances, or the *integration of successive views.*

Gestalt theory, which held that the form per se, regardless of its retinal location, is *the* stimulus to which we respond "directly," never really confronted the problem of how we combine the momentary glances except to introduce the terminology of *invariance* to the problem (Koffka, 1935). Gibson (1966) and Johansson (1977) have somewhat similar theoretical ways of handling this problem—essentially by denying that it exists (cf.

Turvey, 1977). Their formulation is as follows: An eye movement consists of a translation. Our perceptual systems somehow extract the invariant undergoing that translation and relegate the transformation itself to information about a change in viewpoint. Information indicating the fact that the object has not changed its place in space during the eye movement—and perhaps information about the relationship between successive partial glimpses of the object—is directly given as stimulus information. (In Johansson's terms, we extract the common vector as framework and perceive only those stimulus motions that are residual to such extraction.)

With this formulation, we might sidestep the problem of the limitation of the information that can be picked up in a single glance by taking the optic array as sampled by the actively moving eye to be the unitary stimulus. It is not clear, however, whether this approach would in fact allow us to disregard the differences between foveal and peripheral vision, nor whether the approach could really be fleshed out into a systematic theory without introducing mental structure in the form of the integration of successive glances. Further, we should note that there is no evidence whatsoever to support this argument: Its plausibility depends solely on that of the more general doctrine that we can extract invariant information from transformations, and that in turn has very little empirical support. Good analyses of proximal stimulation show mathematically that the "information" may, under some conditions, be there to extract (Gibson et al., 1955; Hay, 1966; Lee, 1974; Purdy, 1958), but there is practically no evidence to show if it is used or, if so, how it is used. Warren (1977), it is true, attempted to demonstrate that two successive views must be "ecologically transformable" into each other if they are to be seen as a single object in apparent motion; this demonstration would, if generalizable, comprise evidence very much to the point, but counterexamples are extremely easy to demonstrate (Hochberg & Brooks, 1974; Kolers & Pomerantz, 1971; Navon, 1976; Orlansky, 1940; Ullman, 1977).

In any case, however, the formulation faces a much more serious problem when it is applied to the processing of information from discrete, successive views: Regardless of the fact that the perceptual psychologist may discern "mathematical information" that relates two views to each other, the perceptual system of the viewer does not appear to be capable of using this information (unless perhaps it is packaged in ways that have not yet been specified). As we will see, the immediate perceptual response to such a sequence does not in fact use the correlated information in the two views that relates them to each other, and the immediate response may well be incorrect in consequence of that fact. Slower or more delayed responses that are in fact based on seeking information that relates the views can be executed and used to judge the views' relationship. But these responses do not use the information from the brief interval of time that includes the transition itself, and they necessarily take us out of discussions about the invariant information in the stimulus transformation and into discussions about how that interval is bridged—that is, into questions of identification, "landmarks" (Hochberg & Gellman, 1977; Lynch, 1960), and so forth. This point is spelled out in the following discussion.

The primary problem in applying a direct theory to the transition between two views is occasioned by a "low-level" phenomenon of apparent motion, which is as likely as not to result in the incorrect perception of the relationship between two views if the displacement between them is at all large relative to the appropriate units (e.g., local features) or grain size of the scene (a factor that is at present entirely missing from the vocabulary of the direct theory), if the field of view is at all cluttered, and if there is no extraretinal (e.g., proprioceptive) information about the relationship. The following two examples make that point.

Figures 16.3a, 16.3b, and 16.3c are successive views of a scene composed of five geometric objects, the views being related by discontinuous transformations to the right (i.e., like saccadic traverses to the left). Because the places at which objects fall in successive views are displaced slightly in the direction opposite to that in which the objects themselves are being displaced, there are *two* transformations to consider—the actual transformation, which the viewer can identify only by correctly identifying the objects in each view, and an illusory transformation, occurring between two different objects that lie near each other's places in successive views. At moderate to high rates of presentation (stimulus onset asynchronies, or SOAs, of

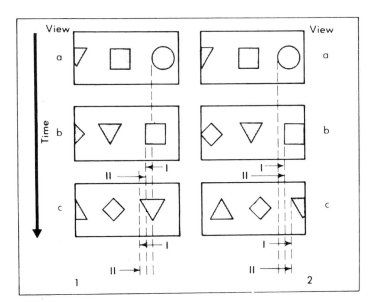

Figure 16.3. Anomalous apparent movement between noncorresponding objects (after Hochberg & Brooks, 1974; reproduced from Hochberg, 1978a).

1000 milliseconds or less), the wrong translation is perceived (translation to the left), and after viewing the sequence, subjects' descriptions of the layout of the objects are incorrect. At very slow rates (SOAs of 1500 to 3000 milliseconds or more) and with the viewer's active effort to identify and label corresponding objects in successive views, the correct translation and layout are reported (Hochberg & Brooks, 1974). Kolers (1972) describes a similar case in which subjects completely fail to perceive the lateral displacement of an entire set of shapes from one view to the next, and instead each shape appears to change smoothly into the figure that replaces it on the same place on the screen. Navon (1976) also describes similar phenomena. A direct theorist might argue that the artificiality of the situation produces transients, which are normally masked by saccadic eye movements, and that once the transients die down, the actual transformations will prevail. (That is, one might suppose that it is the information in the transformation that provides for correct identification of motion and layout at the slow rates, rather than any process of purposive identification of specific objects.) The following experiment argues against that possibility.

In Fig. 16.4A is a set of views of a maze, with 50% overlap between successive views. Sequences of views were shown with different amounts of overlap between views, moving in one or the other direction. At the smallest displacement between successive views (85% overlap), the correct translation is perceived; at larger displacements, performance drops to chance. The stimulus information is there, but the viewer cannot use it. Note that it is not the amount of overlap that is important but its relation to grain size: If we remove some of the maze to reduce the clutter and produce "large grains,"

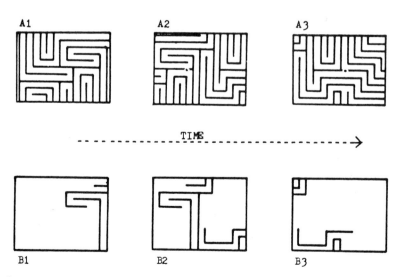

Figure 16.4. Translatory view sequence of cluttered (A) and uncluttered (B) mazes (after Hochberg, Brooks, & Roule, 1977).

"low-frequency information," and "large or global features" that are visible at some distance into peripheral vision and/or are processed faster, and (we have not separated these possibilities) if we remove the local features that should clutter up a succession of views like those at Fig. 16.4A with spurious local apparent movements, we get sequences like those in Fig. 16.4B. Such sequences are correctly perceived at all the displacements tested.

Demonstrations of the kind described in connection with Figs. 16.1 through 16.4 convince me that Gestalt-like approaches to the organization of shape and form must be abandoned in favor of some enlightened (more or less Hebbian) kind of atomism. But the examples in Figs. 16.2 through 16.4 show as well that a Gibsonian approach to the organization of space will have to attend to matters of threshold, time limits, parafoveal visibility, and the distinctions between high- and low-frequency information. Alternatively, Gibson's approach might go the whole route toward Brunswik's position, at which point it must both confront the horrendous problem of defining ecological representativeness in precise and quantitative terms and explain why it is studying proximal stimuli at all. If one is interested in predicting the appearance of some object or scene under representative circumstances, and if the perceptions of the world are generally correct under those circumstances, then the proximal stimuli are an unnecessary diversion. On the other hand, if the proximal stimulation is of interest because the information it contains is the first stage of processing, then sensory limitations on the pickup of such information become critically important.

We have one class of theory of organization left to consider. We have (I maintain) ruled out Gestalt-like approaches by demonstrating the efficacies of parts versus those of wholes. We have yet to explain the Gestalt phenomena and the apparent importance of wholes, and we must still decide whether stimulus structure alone suffices to account for organization or whether mental structure is also needed. Research to that point appears in the next section.

Evidence of Mental Structure

The myriad examples of figural completion, of which the Bradley, Dumais, and Petry figures (1976) and Kanizsa's subjective contour patterns (1955) are the most dramatic instances, are clearly cases of "something contributed by the viewer" that is not in the stimulus, but they do not necessarily demand explanation in terms of mental structures. Sensory factors might be responsible: The fact that the fragments to be connected in such patterns are simultaneously present in the field of view makes some kind of low-level explanation at least conceivable, if farfetched (e.g., lateral inhibitory networks of greater complexity and extent than have yet been seriously considered or investigated). The following two examples, representative of research and demonstrations I have described elsewhere (Hochberg, 1968, 1978b), seem to me to be unassailable instances of mental structure in form perception, and they allow us to study processes of fitting and testing a global schematic map or other mental structure to a set of local features presented over time.

The first example is the kind of aperture-viewing situation I have been belaboring for the last 10 years: A series of what look like unrelated right angles are all presented at the same place in space (Fig. 16.5). Two such series, which differ only in the orientation of one of the angles in the middle of the series, will not be reliably detected as being different if the series length exceeds memory span (i.e., about 8 to 10 angles), regardless of the rate of presentation. (Suitable precautions must be taken, of course, to use enough different series that the viewer cannot learn them "by rote.") If, however, the viewer is first shown an entire geometrical figure of which one corner is the angle viewed through the aperture (e.g., a cross whose upper right-hand corner is the first view in the series), it then is easy for that individual to detect whether the rest of the series of angles is "correct" or "incorrect," as long as the presentation rate allows an SOA of more than 375 milliseconds. The schematic map into which he or she fits each successive view permits the adult viewer to determine whether or not each view belongs to the sequence of views of that figure and, therefore, to judge whether or not two sequences (one of which may be "incorrect") are the same.

The second example addresses what Gestaltists and non-Gestaltists alike have long taken as a fundamental property of shape or form perception: figure-ground differentiation.

Note first that no satisfactory Gestalt theoretical explanation was suggested, much less established, for either the figure-ground phenomenon itself or for the phenomena illustrating the laws of organization. Köhler offered "steady-state" direct-current speculations in 1920 and 1958 b and in his papers with Wallach (Köhler & Wallach, 1944) and Emery (Köhler & Emery, 1947), in which a denser DC current was thought to flow through the cortex in a region that corresponds isomorphically to figure as opposed to ground. That theory seems to me only an embodiment of what Helmholtz proposed as a parody or *reductio ad absurdum* of the nativist position

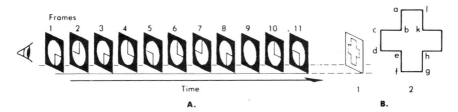

Figure 16.5. Successive views of the corners of a cross. If the viewer is first shown a longshot of the cross (B1), and is shown or told that the first frame (A1) is the corner marked a in B2, the sequence of views is comprehensible, and the viewer recognizes that the sequence has taken a shortcut from h to k on the cross (after Hochberg, 1968; reproduced from Hochberg, 1978a).

(1856/1962, p. 23). In any case, it is totally inapplicable to a world in which viewers are free to move their eyes four times each second. Let us note also that the aperture-viewing task that I have described requires a series of piecemeal decisions about figure and ground if the viewer is to treat a 90-degree outside corner and a 270-degree inside corner appropriately. I have found in discussions of this kind of experiment and its implications that the involvement of figure and ground in piecemeal shape perception is by no means self-evident; the following experiment may make that involvement and its implications more clear.

Each frame of the motion picture schematically shown in Fig.16.6A contained two subviews, thus providing an upper and a lower visual channel. Each channel showed a segment of a Rubin vase-faces pattern. The same segment was shown in each channel. The sequence of views in each channel was essentially what would have been given by moving the outline of the figure systematically behind the aperture, circumnavigating the entire contour. Although the same section of contour was shown in each channel, a stationary black disc (stationary with respect to the aperture) was partially occluded by the "faces" side of the contour in the upper channel and by the "vase" side of the contour in the lower channel. Both channels together subtended less than two degrees of visual angle. The spacing between channels and the size of the represented pattern were such that the contents of the two channels were in conflict in this sense: If there really were an object moving behind the two apertures, the top of the object would be showing in one channel at the same time the bottom would show in the other.

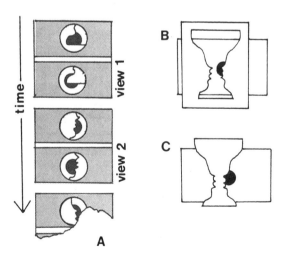

Figure 16.6. (A) Two-channel piecemeal presentation of Rubin faces and vase. (B) Visualization of what is perceived when attending the top channel. (C) Visualization of what is perceived when attending the bottom channel (Hochberg, 1978b).

When asked to attend the upper channel in such a display, all viewers report seeing the faces aspect of the Rubin figure; when attending the lower channel, they see the vase aspect. This is true even though the instructions were to fixate the line between the channels, and the entire display is so small that both channels surely fall in foveal vision.

This demonstration is, of course, just the figure-ground relationship that Gestalt theory took as its starting point, and with effort the viewer can temporarily reverse it. (For example, the upper channel can be perceived as a moving vase, with a changing portion of a black disc moving over its surface at a rate that keeps the disc steady within the aperture.) This demonstration makes several points:

1. It illustrates with a familiar example that the figure-ground phenomenon is implicated in the perception of shape under piecemeal aperture viewing.

2. Because of the piecemeal presentation procedure, with all parts presented in the same (foveal) region, we can be sure that *this figure-ground phenomenon (if that is what it is) does not depend on the overall configuration of the stimulus as a source of parallel processing* (i.e., no "brain-field organization" of the sort proposed by Köhler and his colleagues, nor anything remotely like it, can be invoked in an explanation of these findings).

3. Neither can we say that the stimulus information in the sequence over time *specifies* vase or faces (as the direct theory might have it); although both channels are simultaneously present and near the fovea, only the object "specified" by the attended channel is perceived. (Note that because of the size of the represented objects and the proximity of the two channels, no single object could be specified by the display.) Only when the viewer undertakes to fit a coherent object to the sequence of views given in one channel or the other does a percept result.

Such experiments show us that when the task requires viewers to draw on mental structure to fit their successive fragmentary views together, they can do so. I would like to believe that this is so because they normally draw on such structure in the course of fitting their saccadic glances together. Can we say anything about the mental structure that is fitted to the stimulus sequence in such demonstrations? As I have argued elsewhere (1962, 1970), the characteristics of the structure—the phenomenal properties of figure and ground—are those of objects' edges as fitted to the momentary glance. There are good perceptuomotor reasons for the viewer to make such "decisions" about what points lie in the same plane before executing any eye and head movements (e.g., saccadic response times are long—around 200 milliseconds—and the parallax produced by head movements will change the location of, or even occlude, the points that lie on the further plane before a planned move to fixate them can be consummated; see Hochberg, 1971a, 1971b, 1974a, 1978b). The Gestalt laws, in fact, are very easy to think of as cues on which to base that decision. For example, the law of good continuation is probably only an aspect of the depth cue of interposition: It is very unlikely that the eye should be (and stay) at just that place in space that will bring into precise alignment the edges of two objects that lie at different distances. A continuous line most likely identifies the edge of a single object (Helmholtz, 1856/1962; Hochberg, 1971a, 1971b, 1974b).

The mental structures of the Gestalt phenomena are therefore better subsumed under the general Helmholtzian rubric than they were explained by Gestalt theory. But it is not the physical world per se that is reflected by such mental structure; it is the constraints on perceptuomotor expectancies, not the constraints on the physical world itself. *Ecological validity* (Brunswik, 1956), *will not do: We cannot ignore the "merely mediating variables" of eyeball and oculomotor apparatus, of acuity differences and saccadic response times. These contribute to the characteristics of mental structure as much as do the properties of the world they mediate.*

Levels of Mental Representation: Mental Structures Simply Do Not Reflect Proximal or Distal Physical Organization

This seems to me to be an extremely important point and a very difficult problem. Most of the major perceptual theories, from unconscious inference through Gestalt organization, Brunswik's probabilistic problem solving, and Gibsonian direct theory, have been designed to avoid confronting it. But there are, I think, no shortcuts. We cannot disregard mental structures, but we cannot encompass them within a single explanatory principle, either, nor consider them within one causal domain.

Take the figure-ground example (although we could pursue this point just as well with distance, color, or movement): The properties of figure and ground surely can be attributed neither to the present proximal stimulus distribution nor (because the stimuli are lines on paper and not usually object's edges) to the present distal layout. Figures comprise structures that are evidently mental. Demonstrations like those in Figs. 16.1 through 16.6 show that the properties of figure-ground organization do not fit the who-listic prescriptions of Gestalt organization, but neither do they reflect the constraints of objects in the physical world. In fact, these demonstrations show that we can separate at least two levels of mental structure. Each intersection in Figs. 16.1D and 16.1E acts as a local depth cue. I have previously (1968) given my reasons for considering such local depth cues to be irreducible, organized, elementary features not subject to further subdivision nor to piecemeal presentation. The structures into which they fit, however, appear to have different characteristics entirely: As the aperture-viewing experiments that I already described show, piecemeal presentation is no obstacle for constructing these larger structures. In Figs. 16.1C and 16.1D, moreover, we see that such larger structures do not impose strong constraints on the local features and, as the other side of that coin, are not constrained to be consistent with them.

In short, some aspects of mental organization (mainly local regions that correspond to what central vision can grasp in a single glance, I believe) are closely constrained; others (mainly the larger layouts into which we must place them) are not. The way I have separated them is of course consonant with Hebb's speculations about cell assemblies (local, closely constrained) versus phase sequences (more extended in time and space and less closely constrained). This approach is close to Neisser's (1964, 1967). It is even closer to the classical proposals of J. S. Mill and Helmholtz that I discussed in earlier parts of this chapter—that is, that we perceive by fitting the most likely or expected (global) object or event to the sampled (local) sensory components. The process of fitting the more global and elective structures to the more local and obligatory ones must offer major opportunities for the effects of perceptual learning (Hochberg, 1968) and of set or attitude (Hochberg, 1970) to emerge, with such contextual structures to some degree determining the role or function of the part in the whole but not the part's purely local appearance. I am afraid that I cannot do much to sharpen these speculations at present, nor offer a more specific model as yet, although I have been fumbling at the task for some years. In any case, we must separate these levels of mental organization from each other and from the effects of lower-level organizational processes (cf. Figs. 16.3 and 16.4) and examine separately the rules that govern each before any concept of organization can be useful. Organization is not *a* thing.

Conclusions

If we agree to consider the Gestalt phenomena to be part of the mental structure of space and object perception, it seems to me that the neo-Helmholtzian position, with its intrinsic notions about mental structure, becomes by far the most economical position. Mental structure is not only manifested in such serial tasks as aperture viewing; it can be demonstrated (albeit not in so readily measurable a form) in connection with the perception of both spatial organization and movement. As to spatial organization, there are several compelling examples in which size and distance, or slant and shape, are coupled in an invariant relationship even when there is no information in the stimulus array to specify either. The most striking of these is probably the Ames window, in which such a mental slant/shape relationship (or interresponse constraint) not only can be obtained in the absence of any stimulus information; it is obtained *against* the information given by the differential optical flow pattern that is given in the optic array. This robust phenomenon makes it clear that the pick-up of such higher-order stimulus information is subject to threshold considerations. That is, when viewed from nearby, the trapezoidal shape and rotary motion of the object are correctly perceived. As viewing distance increases to a few yards, however, the information in the flow pattern clearly falls below threshold, inasmuch as the object is very strongly perceived as an oscillating rectangle. The fact that oscillation is just what one should perceive, given that one perceives the trapezoid as a rectangle, is a strong argument for mental structure. (But an even more important fact is the demonstration that the optical flow pattern information can easily fall below threshold, and if it does so in this case, it surely must do so in others as well. The question of the nature and distribution of thresholds for the higher-order informative variables of the direct theory offers a central challenge—a challenge that has not yet been taken up, to my knowledge, by either Gestalt theorists or direct theorists, central though it would appear to the application of the former and to any real meaning of the latter.) In the case of movement, similar couplings have been shown; a particularly striking phenomenon recently reported by Farber and McConkie (1977) shows a strong coupling between apparent distance and apparent velocity, using planes of random dots that offer no stimulus information to support such coupling. In the constancies, in the illusions, and in the Gestalt organizational phenomena, therefore, as well as in the new field of research on the integration of successive views, the same sort of Helmholtzian mental structure provides at least a qualitative description of most of the findings.

When full stimulus information is present for the observer to use "directly," it is possible of course that mental structure is not in fact activated or used. I know of no evidence one way or the other to this point. But the position so closely approaches special pleading that it seems completely unwarranted to argue that one should only study situations in which full stimulus information is indeed available, in order to avoid "unnatural" perceptual tasks. In a similar vein, one might hold that when no inconsistencies exist between parts of objects or scenes, and when all the parts are harmonious in some sense *yet to be defined* that is violated by Fig. 16.1E, then wholistic determination prevails. But again, the same caution about arbitrary exclusion of subject matter must be raised. Of the three systems into which I forced my classification of organizational explanations, some variety of Helmholtzianism comes off best by far. Overall, it takes some kind of tunnel vision to maintain that mental structure is unnecessary or even an unparsimonious construct, and the Gestalt alternative—a wholistic mental structure—appears to be untenable as a general proposition.

This does not mean that all is well with Helmholtz, despite a significant upswing in his popularity (cf. Rock, 1977). Punctiform receptors as the sole basis of visual analysis look pretty silly today, of course, and a great deal of organization clearly takes place in the peripheral reaches of the nervous system. That organization (which encompasses opponent processes, feature detectors, frequency channels, and so forth) is not the product of a single cognitive arena to which Helmholtz's rubric might be applied—the rubric that holds that we perceive what would be most likely to cause any given sensory excitation under normal conditions. Before we could hope to apply that rule, we would have to be able to identify the more peripheral and noncognitive contributions to organization. Even after that, it is hard to see, in fact, how that rubric can be used to either theoretical or practical profit without specifying what the "given sensory excitation" refers to (i.e., what is the grain size; is it scene-wide, object-wide, or intersection-wide?) and without some way of knowing what is "likely." That is, to apply Helmholtz's rule we must first discover the relevant structure of the world as it is filtered through the proximal stimulus information and the characteristics of the sensorimotor apparatus. I know of no shortcuts. *To talk about perception as probabilistic problem solving is not much use unless we know the "premises" and the "inference rules." We do know that they are not merely the rules of physics; that much is guaranteed by Figs. 16.1D and 16.1E.*

Let me stress that point: Both Helmholtzians and Gibsonians agree that perception should and does (at least to some degree) reflect the structure of the environment, but neither offers us a method for determining what the relevant structure actually is. For example, although a convincing case can be made that the Gestalt phenomena, as well as the geometrical illusions (Gregory & Harris, 1975), comprise a set of expectations about the structure of the world, as already mentioned, we should note that neither Helmholtz nor anyone else deduced either the Gestalt phenomena or the illusions from the nature of the world. These explanations arose only after the puzzling phenomena themselves had been explored and worried over, and the explanations are still far from established. And only after such explanations are devised do we know what to look for in our studies of the perceptual ecology.

In short, I think that the study of stimulus organization is indeed essential, but that in order to know what aspect of stimulation we should be studying, we must first investigate precisely those perceptual phenomena that do not, at first glance, appear to be veridical. They set the problems to which a direct theory must be addressed. They provide the occasion for rendering unto physiology and anatomy what is rightfully theirs and what is not the consequence of either stimulus information or constructive cognitive processes. Most interesting to me are those cases in which neither stimulus organization nor peripheral processes can possibly account for perceptual organization (most notably in the combination of successive glances); those cases provide windows through which the central processes of psychology— the cognitive workings, or their cast shadows—can occasionally be glimpsed.

Mental structures do contribute to perceptual organization. They seem to me to comprise the most important problems that the student of organization can confront, whether or not the circumstances in which they are manifest are ecologically representative. They are best observed in experimental circumstances that require the viewer to fill out partial presentations, like those that study how we integrate successive piecemeal glimpses of objects and scenes. They do not simply reflect the regularities of the physical world. They cannot be summarized by a single organizational rubric, because there appears to be more than one level of mental structure. Those levels must be separated empirically before general principles can be fitted to them.

References

ATTNEAVE, F. Some informational aspects of visual perception. *Psychological Review,* 1954, *61,* 183–193.

ATTNEAVE, F. *Applications of information theory to psychology.* New York: Holt, Rinehart & Winston, 1959.

ATTNEAVE, F., & FROST, R. The determination of perceived tridimensional orientation by minimum criteria. *Perception & Psychophysics,* 1969, *6,* 391–396.

BRADLEY, D. R., DUMAIS, S. T., & PETRY, H. M. Reply to Cavonius. *Nature,* 1976, *261* (May 6), 77–78.

BRUNSWIK, E. *Perception and the representative design of psychological experiments* (2nd ed.). Berkeley: University of California Press, 1956.

CASSIRER, E. The concept of group and the theory of perception. *Psychologia,* 1944, *5,* 1–35.

FARBER, J., & McCONKIE, A. Linkages between apparent depth and motion in linear flow fields. *Bulletin of the Psychonomic Society,* 1977, *10,* 250. (Abstract)

GARNER, W. R. *Uncertainty and structure as psychological concepts.* New York: Wiley, 1962.

GARNER, W. R. Good patterns have few alternatives. *American Scientist,* 1970, *58,* 34–42.

GIBSON, J. J. *The perception of the visual world.* Boston: Houghton Mifflin, 1950.

GIBSON, J. J. *The senses considered as perceptual systems.* Boston: Houghton Mifflin, 1966.

GIBSON, J. J., OLUM, P., & ROSENBLATT, F. Parallax and perspective during aircraft landings. *American Journal of Psychology,* 1955, *68,* 372–385.

GREGORY, R. L., & HARRIS, J. P. Illusion-destruction by appropriate scaling. *Perception,* 1975, *4,* 203–220.

HAY, J. Optical motions and space perception: An extension of Gibson's analysis. *Psychological Review,* 1966, *73,* 550–565.

HEBB, D. O. *The organization of behavior.* New York: Wiley, 1949.

HELMHOLTZ, H. VON. *Treatise on physiological optics* (Vol. 3) (J. P. Southall, Ed. and trans.). New York: Dover, 1962. (Originally published in German, 1856.)

HOCHBERG, J. Perception: Toward the recovery of a definition. *Psychological Review,* 1956, *63,* 400–405.

HOCHBERG, J. Nativism and empiricism in perception. In L. Postman (Ed.), *Psychology in the making.* New York: Knopf, 1962.

HOCHBERG, J. In the mind's eye. In R. N. Haber (Ed.), *Contemporary theory and research in visual perception.* New York: Holt, Rinehart & Winston, 1968.

HOCHBERG, J. Attention, organization and consciousness. In D. L. Mostofsky (Ed.), *Attention: Contemporary theory and analysis.* New York: Appleton-Century-Crofts, 1970.

HOCHBERG, J. Perception: I. Color and shape. In J. W. Kling & L. A. Riggs (Eds.), *Woodworth & Schlosberg's experimental psychology* (3rd ed.). New York: Holt, Rinehart & Winston, 1971(a).

HOCHBERG, J. Perception: II. Space and movement. In J. W. Kling & L. A. Riggs (Eds.), *Woodworth & Schlosberg's experimental psychology* (3rd ed.). New York: Holt, Rinehart & Winston, 1971 (b).

HOCHBERG, J. Higher order stimuli and interresponse coupling in the perception of the visual world. In R. B. MacLeod & H. L. Pick (Eds.), *Perception: Essays in honor of James J. Gibson.* Ithaca: N.Y., Cornell University Press, 1974 (a).

HOCHBERG, J. Organization and the Gestalt tradition. In E. C. Carterette & M. P. Friedman (Eds.), *Handbook of perception* (Vol. 1). New York: Academic Press, 1974 (b).

HOCHBERG, J. *Perception* (2nd ed.). New York: Prentice-Hall, 1978 (a).

HOCHBERG, J. *Motion pictures of mental structures.* Presidential address given at the meeting of the Eastern Psychological Association, Washington, D.C., March 29–April 1, 1978 (b).

HOCHBERG, J. Sensation and perception. In E. Hearst (Ed.), *The first century of experimental psychology.* Hillsdale, N.J.: Lawrence Erlbaum Associates, 1979.

HOCHBERG, J., & BROOKS, V. The psychophysics of form: Reversible perspective drawings of spatial objects. *American Journal of Psychology,* 1960, *73,* 337–354.

HOCHBERG, J., & BROOKS, V. The integration of successive cinematic views of simple scenes. *Bulletin of the Psychonomic Society,* 1974, *4,* 263. (Abstract)

HOCHBERG, J., & GELLMAN, L. The effect of landmark features on mental rotation times. *Memory & Cognition,* 1977, *5,* 23–26.

HOCHBERG, J., GREEN, J., & VIROSTEK, S. *Texture-occlusion as a foveal depth cue.* Paper presented at the meeting of the American Psychological Association, Toronto, August 28–September 1, 1978.

HOCHBERG, J., & MCALISTER, E. A quantitative approach to figure "goodness." *Journal of Experimental Psychology,* 1953, *46,* 361–364.

JOHANSSON, G. *Configurations in event perception.* Uppsala, Sweden: Almqvist & Wiksell, 1950.

JOHANSSON, G. Spatial constancy and motion in visual perception. In W. Epstein (Ed.), *Stability and constancy in visual perception: Mechanisms and processes.* New York: Wiley, 1977.

KANIZSA, G. Margini quasi-percettivi in campi con stimolazione omogenea. *Rivista di Psicologia,* 1955, *49,* 7–30.

KAPLAN, G. A. Kinetic disruption of optical texture: The perception of depth at an edge. *Perception & Psychophysics,* 1969, *6,* 193–198.

KOFFKA, K. *Principles of Gestalt psychology.* New York: Harcourt Harbinger Book, 1963. (Originally published, 1935.)

KÖHLER, W. *Die physischen Gestalten in Ruhe und im stationären Zustand.* Braunschweig: Vieweg, 1920.

KÖHLER, W. The present situation in brain psychology. *American Psychologist,* 1958, *13,* 150–154.

KÖHLER, W., & EMERY, D. A. Figural after-effects in the third dimension of visual space. *American Journal of Psychology,* 1947, *60,* 159–201.

KÖHLER, W., & WALLACH, H. Figural after-effects: An investigation of visual processes. *Proceedings of the American Philosophical Society,* 1944, *88,* 269–357.

KOLERS, P. *Aspects of motion perception.* Oxford: Pergamon Press, 1972.

KOLERS, P. A., & POMERANTZ, J. R. Figural change in apparent motion. *Journal of Experimental Psychology,* 1971, *87,* 99–108.

LEE, D. N. Visual information during locomotion. In R. B. MacLeod & H. L. Pick (Eds.), *Perception: Essays in honor of James J. Gibson*. Ithaca, N.Y.: Cornell University Press, 1974.

LYNCH, K. *The image of the city*. Cambridge, Mass.: M.I.T. Press, 1960.

NAVON, D. Irrelevance of figural identity for resolving ambiguities in apparent motion. *Journal of Experimental Psychology: Human Perception and Performance*, 1976, *2*, 130–138.

NEISSER, U. Visual search. *Scientific American*, 1964, *210* (June), 94–102.

NEISSER, U. *Cognitive psychology*. New York: Appleton-Century-Crofts, 1967.

ORLANSKY, J. The effect of similarity and difference in form on apparent visual movement. *Archives of Psychology*, 1940 (Whole No. 246), 85.

PURDY, W. C. *The hypothesis of psychophysical correspondence in space perception*. Unpublished doctoral dissertation, Cornell University, 1958.

ROCK, I. In defense of unconscious inference. In W. Epstein (Ed.), *Stability and constancy in visual perception: Mechanisms and processes*. New York: Wiley, 1977.

TURVEY, M. T. Contrasting orientations to the theory of visual information processing. *Psychological Review*, 1977, *84*, 67–88.

ULLMAN, S. Transformability and object identity. *Perception & Psychophysics*, 1977, *22*, 414–415.

WARREN, W. H. Visual information for object identity in apparent movement. *Perception & Psychophysics*, 1977, *22*, 264–268.

17

How Big Is a Stimulus?

Julian Hochberg

Introduction

The last few years have seen a great increase in the popularity of organizational approaches to the study of perception, more or less explicitly indebted to Gestalt theory, and of direct or stimulus-informational approaches, explicitly indebted to the work of Gibson (1950, 1979). The mere fact that the appearance of a pattern cannot in general be completely predicted from the appearances of its parts presented in isolation does not by itself provide a basis for reviving anything like Gestalt theory. And the mere fact that what has been called higher-order stimulus information about distal (object) properties are normally provided by the environment, and that such information is sometimes used by the normal viewer, by itself implies nothing whatsoever about the processes of perception. Helmholtz discussed quite explicitly what later was taken by the Gestaltists as the law of good continuation; he discussed at length the importance of motion-produced stimulation and of active exploration in vision and in touch as providing what was later to be called the invariant information in the stimulus transformations (Cassirer, 1944; Gibson, 1950, 1979). Moreover, Helmholtz stressed that as far as our perceptions are concerned, the distal properties are usually directly perceived (i.e., we are not aware of the activities of the individual receptors, nor of the processes by which the percepts are constructed). If one is to go beyond (or oppose) Helmholtz in these respects, therefore, it will have to be in terms of evidence about the ways in which larger spans of stimulus information are used, not merely by showing that they are present in stimulation, or that they are used.

That has not yet been adequately done.

I do not see how one can discuss perceptual organization until the phenomena in Figs. 17.1 and 17.2 are dealt with; I do not see how one can discuss any theory of direct response to invariant spatial information until the phenomena of Figs. 17.3 and 17.4 are dealt with; nor do I see how the problem of integrating the information in successive glances can be discussed seriously until the phenomena in Figs. 17.6 and 17.7 are dealt with.

Figure 17.1. Although inconsistent as a tridimensional object (i.e., line x must be discontinuous as a dihedral although continuous as a line), A looks tridimensional. The same inconsistent features, in closer proximity (B) look flat, whereas consistent features, equally close (C), look tridimensional (Hochberg, 1968).

In each case, the phenomena show strong limits on the size of the stimulus pattern that is effective at any time and imply similar limitations on the duration over which an event can be considered to be a single stimulus. Such limits clearly determine what we can mean by the terms *stimulus information* and *perceptual organization*: If we knew that our visual systems were directly responsive to the changes in light at only one small point over some very short interval of time, it would not seem like much of an explanation to say that "configuration is itself a stimulus," nor that various aspects of the extended visual stimulus (such as gradients of texture and motion) *directly* elicit our perceptions of the world of space and movement. In fact, I believe that many current attempts at perceptual theory seem explanatory and intelligible only because they ignore the question of limits and all of the associated issues that naturally accompany that question.

It seems to me, therefore, that the prudent scientist who is interested in stimulus information or perceptual organization would welcome any indications of relevant sensory limitations, inasmuch as these must help to define the nature of both phenomena and theory. Evidence and arguments to this point abound, but they have been almost totally without effect on those concerned with either organization phenomena or extended stimulus information. The fact is that the general shape and emphases of any theory of perception and of information processing depend strongly on this matter of the size of the effective stimulus. Gibson at least recognizes that occasions for appeal to enrichment (i.e., occasions in which the organism must contribute what I have called mental structure) arise when stimulus information is inadequate (Gibson, 1951, 1979) or is inadequately picked up, that is, is subthreshold. A substantial change in the way in which we think of

Figure 17.2. The intersection at point 2 is reversible despite the interposition at 1 (Hochberg, 1978a; Peterson & Hochberg, in preparation).

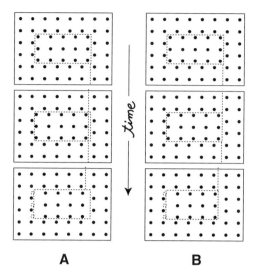

Figure 17.3. Kinetic occlusion defines a textured moving surface behind a rectangular aperture in a similarly textured surface, at A, and a moving rectangle in front of an occluded surface, at B (Kaplan, 1969). The two different arrangements are here distinguished only at the left-hand edge and only during the leftmost moment of the cycle of back-and-forth horizontal motion. If the viewer's gaze is not very near that edge at those times, the viewer cannot distinguish A from B (Hochberg, Green, & Virostek, 1978; Hochberg, Virostek, & Green, in preparation).

perceptual process—that is, a substantial departure from the constructivist theory of J. S. Mill and Helmholtz—can be achieved only if information in an entire extended stimulus array is picked up in some sense to which the word "direct" can be meaningfully applied (cf. Hochberg, 1979b). It is precisely to this point that my present questions are addressed.

The Gestaltists' criticisms of the primitive view of specific nerve energies with which Helmholtz started, and of the list of "primary" sensations of early associationism, were perfectly well founded, but the physiological speculations and the philosophical edifices that they built on these criticisms were unjustifiable. Gibson's attempt to seek out and measure the higher-order variables of stimulus information, and the responses that they determine, was probably the most important new attempt since Helmholtz, but is still largely a proposal, with little empirical foundation. Furthermore, even the most inclusive of direct theories will not make the problem of mental structure go away: Even if the limits of direct determination by higher-order variables are broad, there still remains the question of where the mental structure comes from that is used beyond those limits, and the acquisition and nature of that structure would not be a minor question in any case. But if the limits of direct pick-up are severe—if for much of normal perception the effective stimulus span in space and time is so small that mental structure

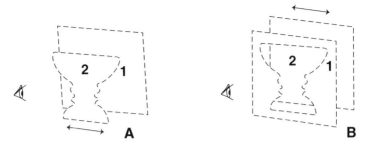

Figure 17.4. Kinetic occlusion defines the two alternatives of a Rubin figure. In each case, reversal is easier with fixation away from the edge (2) than near it (1) (Hochberg, Virostek, & Peterson, in preparation).

must comprise a substantial part of the perceptual process—then studying the nature and mechanism of that component becomes the most urgent task that psychology must undertake.

I briefly review some old and some new demonstrations showing that each individual glance is severely limited in the amount of information that can be picked up, and that these limitations affect the information that can be picked up in sequences of freely initiated and directed glances; then I discuss the implications of these demonstrations for wholistic theories of perception.

The Whole Does Not Determine the Appearance of the Part: Local Depth Cues and Other Local Features

Figure 17.1A looks three-dimensional even though its corners are inconsistent; figure 17.1B looks much more flat. Is this merely a matter of proportion? Not so: Fig. 17.1C looks solid, in the same proportions (Hochberg, 1968). These figures are modified from one of the now-classical Penrose and Penrose (1958) impossible objects. When Jacob Beck called the latter to our attention in 1960, they capped the grave doubts that Virginia Brooks and I had developed about the attempt to devise quantitative models of figural organization (Hochberg & Brooks, 1960). Such attempts continue, but not in my hands, because I now think them misguided: Figs. 17.1A and 17.1B should both look equally (and highly) flat, by any reasonable encoding theory or minimum principle, and they simply do not do so. If this argument seems strained, and insufficient to set against the rich tradition of Gestalt psychology, consider Fig. 17.2 (Hochberg, 1978a). *This is not an impossible object.* The orientation in which the horizontal line looks nearer than the vertical at point 2 is specified by the intersection at point 1 (by the depth cue of interposition, or by the Gestalt law of good continuation, terms which I believe to mean the same thing; Hochberg, 1972). In fact, however,

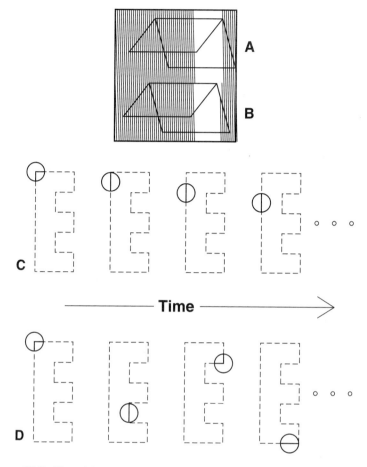

Figure 17.5. Viewed in successive vertical apertures behind an opaque mask (here shown as a grey screen), the pattern is recognizable in both A and B. At A, however, in which intersections are dissected by the aperture viewing procedure, the object looks flat, whereas at B, in which the intersections are left intact, the object looks tridimensional (Hochberg, 1968). In C and D, aperture views are of the same shape in different orders (Girgus, Gellman, & Hochberg, 1980).

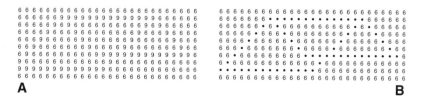

Figure 17.6. The same shape is delineated by nines in A and in B, but the nines are filled in, in B, to increase their parafoveal visibility (Hochberg, 1968).

306

if you look at point 2 for a few moments, the perspective will reverse, and the vertical line will look nearer. (Perspective can also be reversed even while you attend point 1, especially if you try to see it that way, but not as much as at point 2 [Peterson & Hochberg, 1981].)

It is conceivable, of course, that the piecemeal perspective reversals implied by Fig. 17.2 do not occur when both intersections 1 and 2 are ambiguous, that is, when both are unsigned depth cues as they are in the fully ambiguous Necker cube. I cannot think how to test that possibility: Note that if the orientation at intersection 1 had not been fixed in Fig. 17.2, the fact that independent reversals occur at intersection 2 could probably not have been detected. Once we recognize that organizations can indeed reverse piecemeal (Fig. 17.2) and that inconsistencies are not immediately evident (Fig. 17.1A), the question of what a perceptual response entails is not clearly answerable. (So the behaviorist's distrust of introspection or phe-nomenology has yet another good grounding.) I return to this point in my conclusions, in discussing some of the recent experiments that have been taken as evidence for wholistic perceptual process. For now, the point is that the prudent man, faced with this indeterminacy, would assume that if such at least partial independence of part from whole is manifest when that independence *can* be tested, than it is also true of conditions in which it cannot be tested.

Figure 17.1A provides evidence that the corners (as local depth cues) are at least partially independent of the whole configuration in the sense that an impression of their tridimensionality is maintained despite their mutual inconsistency. In Fig. 17.2, the orientation of the ambiguous and unsigned local depth cue at point 2 changes in at least partial independence of the signed depth cue at point 1. And in both cases, where one looks or attends affects what one perceives. I don't see how it is possible, therefore, to sub-scribe to any theory of perceptual organization that is even remotely like that of Gestalt theory, because these demonstrations reject either the rule that the organization of the whole determines the appearance of the parts, the rule that we perceive the simplest organization that can be fitted to the stimulus, or both rules (see Hochberg, 1981). And I do not see how any alternative organizational theory can be formulated which does not take demonstrations like these into account in some way.

The Limits on Any Direct Theory of Surface Perception

Figures 17.1 and 17.2 dealt with static line drawings, the primary subject matter of Gestalt theory. Figures 17.2, 17.4, 17.6, and 17.7 pertain as well to limitations on any more "ecologically oriented" direct theory of surface perception.

At the heart of such theories lies the fact that as the relative position of viewer and object change, the invariance of a rigid object or scene will result in invariant relationships within the transformations in the light to the eye that are imposed by the relative motion of viewer and object. This point was first explicitly developed by Helmholtz; the terms of set theory (e.g., invariance and transformation) were introduced to Helmholtz's theory by Cassirer; and the far-ranging discussion of such invariances, and their implications, was of course pursued by Gibson. The nature of one's theory of perceptual organization in particular and of psychology in general vary greatly, depending on whether, how, and with what limits one takes such information to be actually used by the organism. No matter how much information there may be in the light reaching the eye, if the organism does not use it, or does not respond to it directly, the psychological consequences remain moot.

Despite the fact that an extraordinary amount has been written about such information, and about how it changes the way in which we must view psychology, the fact is that as yet we know very little about the pick-up of such invariances. One particularly simple invariance is the stimulus for surface reflectance. The luminance ratio of object and surround, under changing illumination of both, is essentially invariant. Whether this invariance indeed determines lightness perception has been pursued for well over a century (Hochberg, 1979; Hurvich & Jameson, 1966). A ubiquitous stimulus invariant, one would surely expect it to be a good test case. In fact, it has been almost completely ignored by direct theorists, and what research there is to this point does not clearly support the contention that reflectance perception is a direct response to luminance ratios (Beck, 1972; Epstein, 1977; Hochberg, 1972).

With respect to the perception of the shapes, movements, and spatial disposition of surfaces, we know from the evidence of the robust Ames trapezoidal illusion that kinetic depth information is not exempt from threshold considerations: Viewed from a few feet, the rotating and invariant trapezoid, undergoing a continuous and informative transformation in full view of the subject, is nevertheless perceived as an oscillating rectangular surface. Clearly, if thresholds limit the pick-up of such higher-order information, the very first task is to explore those limits, and the Ames trapezoid should be a matter of considerable importance to the direct theorists. Instead there has been a remarkable lack of concern with this matter among advocates of this position.[1]

The fact is that higher-order variables are particularly vulnerable to the question of thresholds, inasmuch as there are two separate levels at which such questions can arise, as I will now attempt to spell out.

Carrier Elements and Their Modulations by Higher-Order Variables

In general, higher-order variables are imposed as what we may consider *modulation* on what we may call *carrier elements*, and each of these has its own characteristic thresholds. I will make this point with respect to a particularly simple higher-order variable, that of *texture-density gradient* (Gibson, 1950), but it applies as well to any of the information that is carried by the textures and contours of the visual field.

Imagine each element of texture, for example, each grain on a sheet of sandpaper. If its contrast with the background is too low, or its size is too small, it cannot be individually detected. That is, each texture element has a set of thresholds which must be exceeded if it is to have any effect. Of course, the threshold for the detection of an element in a repetitive or otherwise ordered array will be different from the threshold for the element in isolation, and the threshold for the array of elements will be different from that for each of the elements, but there will nevertheless surely be such thresholds for carrier elements to be effective at all. Now consider the density gradient of the set of textural elements: If the change in density per unit of distance is too small, the texture-density gradient will go undetected, and so will the slant of the surface to which it normally corresponds, that is, the modulation can be below threshold even if the carrier elements are above threshold. This is of course not a new point (cf. Hochberg & Smith, 1955; Smith & Smith, 1963), but it has not been seriously considered by direct theorists. It should be. With this analysis in mind, I will now try to show that the problem of thresholds is indeed a general one—perhaps a critical one—for the question of how, or even whether, such higher-order variables of stimulus information are used at all. The problem is not restricted to such exotic phenomena as the Ames trapezoid.

In the real world of objects and surfaces, information about where one object's surface ends, and a farther surface begins, is not carried by lines, but by color differences and by changes in moving texture distributions as well. It is conceivable that the limitations noted in the peripheral use of the line-drawing information noted in connection with Figures 17.1 and 17.2 simply do not apply to the motion-produced patterns of texture flow that define surfaces and their edges. A primary fact in defining objects visually is that nearer surfaces potentially overlap or occlude parts of farther ones. What Gibson calls kinetic occlusion then specifies which surface is nearer. In A and B in Fig. 17.3, a textured surface moves leftward behind an aperture in a nearer surface or moves as a small rectangle in front of a farther surface, respectively. Note that in the third view of both A and B, a column of texture elements is deleted; this information specifies that the physical arrangement is one of a near window and a far surface, respectively. In both A and B, the occlusion and subsequent disocclusion at the left-hand edges specify the tridimensional arrangement of the surfaces, and George Kaplan (1969) showed several years ago that this condition elicits the appropriate perception. A recent series of experiments (Hochberg, Green, & Virostek, 1978; Hochberg, Virostek, & Green, in preparation) was designed to discover whether this class of edge formation is less well picked up in peripheral than in foveal vision, or whether the visual system is so attuned to kinetic occlusion that we can afford to ignore the fact that the scene is sampled by a finite number of glances.

In all of these experiments, the display was such that kinetic occlusion might occur only at the left edge (as it does in Fig. 17.3), at the right edge, or at neither. In the last case (and at the unoccluded edge in all cases), the depth information is ambiguous or *unsigned*. When the depth information was signed, the central region could be either nearer or farther than the surround. The only depth cues in any cases were those of kinetic occlusion and shear (the latter occurring along the horizontal edges that bounded the central moving set of dots, comprising an unsigned depth cue); of course, no outline between center and surround existed in the displays actually used. In some experiments of the series, fixation points were assigned at different distances from the active edge (e.g., at 0, 1.4, 2, 8, . . . 12.8 degrees from the active edge). Highly significant effects of where one looked were found in several experiments in which task and conditions were varied slightly; detection of depth direction dropped to chance by about $4°$ from the active edge.

Lest it be thought that the results are not ecologically representative because a stationary eye was used in these experiments, let me hasten to add that the same phenomenon holds when the display is viewed by a moving eye executing voluntary saccades: In one of the experiments, whether the active edge specified the central region to be a near or a far surface was changed periodically, in a regular cycle. Above the moving region, a letter was shown at one corner or the other, and what the letter was (e.g., an X or a Y) changed on an erratic schedule. The letter was near the active edge only when that edge specified the center region as being far, whereas at other times the letter was near the corner above the unsigned edge. Below the moving region of the display was a similar moving letter, out of phase with the upper one and following a schedule that placed it near the active edge only while the latter specified that the center region was near. Subjects were given two tasks: to count the number of changes in either the upper or the lower letter, and to note whether the center region was near or far. When monitoring the changes in the upper letter, all subjects reported the center region to be far; when monitoring the lower letter, the center region appeared near.

It is clear that *the pick-up of depth information can depend strongly on where one looks, even with a freely moving gaze.*

There are other ways of talking about these findings, especially in terms of the viewer's intentions (which I discuss later), but none of them that I can think of set aside the main points of this conclusion.

These facts place an upper limit on the extent over which a higher-order variable can be picked up: Whenever the higher-order variable that defines perceptual structure is carried by moderately small elements (e.g., by surface texture), the effective radius of pick-up of those variables, within each glance, may be so small that perceptual overlap between successive views will not serve as even a *possible* direct basis for perception. We know from research with aperture viewing (Hochberg, 1968) and motion pictures (Hochberg & Brooks, 1979; Hochberg, 1978c) that people can build up scenes in their mind's eye from views that do not overlap at all. In such cases, the integration of successive glances simply *must* rest on mental structures that bridge the individual glances. Higher-order variables may indeed contribute to our perception of the world through successive glances when the glances overlap, as they normally do. It is clear, however, that mental structures and lower-order variables are important, too, and the perception psychologist's first priority must be to determine the limits of these different levels of determinants, and to discover the mechanisms by which the subject matter of old and new psychophysics work together.

Concern with molar factors is no license for ignoring the molecular.

A last experiment should be considered before leaving this series. The question is whether the dependence of depth judgment on gaze direction pertains only to perceived edge depth per se, which makes it of limited importance, or pertains as well to the closely associated question of the perceived shapes of the objects that comprise the content of our field of view.

Several years ago, I proposed that the figure-ground distinction arose as a result of "decisions" as to which side of a peripherally viewed edge was the near surface (figure), and was therefore potentially available to the gaze over its entire extent, and which side of the edge was occludable and background (Hochberg, 1970a); the "laws of figure-ground organization" should then be construed as cues to that decision (Hochberg, 1970a, 1972). This perceptual assumption could not be considered to be merely a single-level matter of perceived depth, however, because figure-ground reversals could occur even when shapes like the vase or faces (alternatives in the Rubin pattern) were so produced as to be unambiguous figures in depth, for example, by using Julesz patterns or by using kinetic occlusion to make one or the other alternative be seen as near surface and the other as occluded background (Hochberg, 1968). For this reason, I argued that the figure-ground phenomenon was not a unitary one, but concealed several separate processes. Julesz (1971) later reported that such figure-ground patterns are nonreversible, but we will now see that that is not true in general and that the circumstances under which they are relatively nonreversible are directly relevant to the question of the size of a stimulus, and of the inferred response to it.

In the experiment represented in Fig. 17.4 (Hochberg, Virostek, & Peterson, in preparation), an inner set of moving dots defines either a moving vase (Fig. 17.4A) or a moving background as space between two faces (Fig. 17.4B). The stimulus displays actually used dot fields, of course, and not outlines. Subjects were asked to try to see the vase, or to try to see the faces, while they kept their attention and gaze fixed on one of the two fixation points (1 or 2). Summarizing the vase responses: When subjects are holding fixation 1, they can see the vase much more readily while watching stimulus A than stimulus B, and when watching stimulus A, they are *forced* by the stimulus information to see the vase more of the time, even when they are instructed to try to see the faces—but this is true only as long as they are fixating point 1. When, conversely, subjects fixate point 2, which is farther from the active edge of the moving region, they are more free to see stimulus A as B and vice versa: The edge still defines a potential shape, inasmuch as both alternative responses are still obtained, but the direction of the depth is apparently unsigned at fixation point 2 because of its distance from the edge.

What is important to my present argument in this experiment is the fact that gaze direction and the associated sensory limits determine not only which edge is perceived as nearer, but which *shape* is perceived, even with unambiguously specified stimulus displays. I think these demonstrations (Figs. 17.3 and 17.4) clearly show that there are important limits of pick-up of higher-order stimulus information within the individual glance.

Next, I wish to discuss the matter of temporal limits, and how they relate to the spatial limits that I have described.

Direct theorists argue thus. Granted that the momentary glance is limited, and that the effective stimulus is smaller in any one glance than the whole configuration or the whole optical expansion pattern being considered, what difference does that make as long as the viewer is free to obtain information from any point in the entire field by shifting his gaze? Indeed, Gibson completely sidesteps the question of the limitations of the momentary glance by considering the entire optic array, subject to a freely exploring gaze, as the relevant stimulus situation. Is this a viable alternative?

I consider that point next, and conclude that such an attempt can only successfully solve the problem under a special set of assumptions that have not been tested.

Implications of Spatial and Temporal Limits on the Pick-up of Higher-Order Variables

Imagine first the contrafactual case of an eye having only a fovea—say, an effective field of vision of about 2°. If a larger shape were presented—say, one of 6°—the eye would have to make several successive fixations in order to encompass the entire pattern, and the viewer's information about the entire shape would have to be integrated from the information obtained from the successive discrete glances. Because these glances are spread out over time, one would think that any account of the perception of the entire shape would have to include some mechanism of memory, storage, or expectation—some *mental structure*. An alternative treatment has been offered both by Gestaltists and by direct theorists, however, and we consider it next.

The Notion of Stimulation Over Time
(and of Timeless/Formless Invariants)

To Wertheimer, the configuration of an entire melodic sequence of notes, or of a succession of visual stimuli in stroboscopic movement, provides the single stimulus event to which the melody or perceived movement, respectively, is the unitary response. The form of the event over time was taken as the direct and essential stimulus for the perceived auditory or visual event. Gibson has similarly taken visual information over time, picked up by the eye in free and active exploration of the optic array, as the direct and essential basis of perception.

The Different Meanings of the Distinction Between Active
and Passive Stimulation, in Constructivist Versus Direct
Theories, and Their Relation to the Question
of Effective Stimulus Size

Helmholtz envisioned perception (as distinct from sensation, which was not thought by him to be part of conscious experience) as active and as the result of exploration and expectation. One of his most striking examples is that of active touch: how little can be discerned in response to passive contact, but how the same shape, actively explored by the hand, becomes an organized, perceived object. Gibson and his colleagues have similarly emphasized the importance of active versus passive exploration, indeed using the same example of haptic perception (1962). A different meaning attaches to the two uses of the term "active," however. This difference is important, is often obscure to those who use the term, and is very closely related to the limits of a direct theory and to the question of the size of the effective stimulus.

To Helmholtz, the purpose of perceptuomotor exploration was to provide the viewer with occasions for mobilizing a schema of expectations about what the results of the next perceptuomotor action would bring, and for testing those expectations (Helmholtz, 1962). Helmholtz, like J. S. Mill, was an early formulator of what is currently called a constructivist theory of perception, and in such theories the function of sensory activity is to test a set of sensorimotor expectations.

To Gibson (the most explicit of the direct theorists in the field of perception), the purpose of sensory activity is to provide for motion of the viewer relative to the object, so as to provide the transformations of the light received which will, by their invariances, provide information about the invariant objects and scenes and layouts in space. Note that by this account, *no* mental structures—no hypotheses, schemas, or models of the world—play a role in normal perception. (That is what makes this theory different from Helmholtz's.) The activity has as its purpose the elicitation of informative stimulation, to which the response is direct. Although Gibson may on some occasions distinguish between active and passive presentation of the same stimuli, on other occasions, he does not do so, and *the distinction is in any case without theoretical content in his explanatory system.* I cannot see how in fact the distinction could be maintained without making the direct theory identical to the indirect or constructivist theory (or if it can be done, I have not come across it).

It seems clear to me that the Wertheimer/Gibson theory is at least partially correct: With respect to apparent movement, as early as Exner it was proposed that the entire visual event occurring over some (short) time is the stimulus for the perception of motion; and it is hard to believe that the interval between two or three notes is not indeed a significant stimulus event in the perception of melody. That is, direct sensory responses to stimulus events are surely not restricted to a single point in time any more than they are to points in space. The recent hectic quest for feature detectors, pursued with some success in the field of motion as well as in pattern vision, is testimony of a widespread belief in that point among physiologists and sensory psychologists of varied theoretical persuasions. But questions of temporal limits are as important as those of spatial limits, and indeed as we see later, the one implies the other. In any case, at one extreme, we have the Helmholtzian view of the function of exploratory activity, which by its emphasis on the prediction of sensory events to come, stresses the finite temporal extent of present sensory stimulation; on the other, we have the wholistic approaches, to which a stimulus event that stretches over some unspecified duration comprises the adequate information to which the visual system responds directly. To assume the lower span (i.e., a very brief sensory moment) is, I think now, clearly wrong. Let me try to show why it is also reasonable to assume that there are also upper bounds, and why it is important to determine what they are.

Can the Notion of Temporally Extended Stimulation Replace the Notion of Storage (That Is, of Mental Structure) in Bridging the Limited Momentary Glance?

There are two strong limits that must be placed on the notion of temporally extended stimulation.

The Elective Nature of Ballistic Saccades. Exploration glances are highly elective both as to occurrence and direction, and saccades are programmed in advance and in discrete steps as to when, where, and how far the eye will next be sent. That is, after a first glance, the viewer might well elect not to look at other parts of the stimulus display. The act of glancing at some place that has not yet been brought into the field of foveal view requires a very specific decision. In normal vision, in which we are not restricted to a single $2°$ of foveal vision but enjoy some $180°$ of total peripheral vision as well, our eyes are moved neither randomly, repetitively, nor endlessly: After a few glances at specific places, the perceptual act is normally complete. Visual questions are asked by looking, but are asked only until they are answered to the satisfaction of the viewer acting under some specific perceptual task. I cannot see how we can discuss when the viewer elects to look, where he elects to look, and when he elects to cease looking without conceding that he possesses some form of mental structure about what he is looking at (some schema, expectation, storage) that guides, sustains, and terminates that activity. The activity of the eye is not determined either by the stimulus array, nor yet by the information that the array contains, but by the interaction between these and the viewer's perceptual questions, and by the point at which the latter are answered to his or her satisfaction. The occurrence and duration of pick-up thus depends on task and on mental structure, and cannot be defined merely in terms of an array and the free looking that is devoted to it. The point is that the act of exploration is self-limited, and those limits determine both the duration of the temporal event that is considered as a single stimulus and the kind of theory that we bring to the question of stimulus size.

When Do "Cue" and "Information" Have Different Implications?   What if the viewer does *not* execute the saccade that brings the next transformation of the field of view, or does not execute the head movement that would disocclude a partially hidden object? Such actions are, after all, elective. (The same question arises, of course, if the effective temporal span of stimulation does not extend beyond the period of the single glance.) These limits are of course imposed by pictures, and Gibson's description of what must then be drawn on is apt (1979, 271f.):

> When the young child . . . sees the family cat at play, the front view, side view . . . and so on are not seen, and what gets perceived is the *invariant* cat. . . . Hence, when the child first sees a picture of a cat he is prepared to pick up the invariants. . . . When he sees the cat half-hidden by the chair, he perceives a partly hidden cat, not a half-cat, and therefore he is prepared to see the same thing in a drawing.

The preparation "to see the same thing in a drawing" in response to a picture of a partly obscured cat makes the latter what Woodworth (1938) called a "cue," rather than what Gibson has seemed to imply elsewhere by "information," because it depends upon the past experiences of the child (see the word "hence") and because it is a response to a selected and restricted part of the visual field. (Elsewhere in the same paragraph, Gibson proposes that the child "pays no attention to the frozen perspective of the picture," and it is hard to see how the interposition of the cat can arbitrarily be selected out from the entire array of information about space of which it is a part unless it is also so used, on sufficient occasions to make an impression, in the course of normal perception of the real world.) The invariant that underlies the transformation that would be produced by a disoccluding head movement is simply not present in the frozen array of a picture, and the only sense in which it can be talked about as being available to the viewer is in terms of what is clearly *mental content* (i.e., "preparation to see") and not in terms of stimulus information in any defined or implied use of the latter phrase; the elicitation of that mental content is attributed to the child's prior experiences with the world ("Hence...") in the paragraph quoted above. Moreover, Gibson's use of the notion that the child perceives the invariant cat and not the momentary views, and that the perception of the cat from the frozen view consists in the child's readiness for that invariant to emerge in the course of potential transformations, is identical in content to Helmholtz's view that we do not perceive our momentary sensations but instead perceive the object that generates some anticipated set of orderly sensory consequences to any perceptuomotor exploration we undertake (Helmholtz, 1962, p. 22f.) and to J. S. Mill's argument "On the permanent possibilities of sensation":

> The conception I form of the world existing at any moment, comprises, along with the sensations I am feeling... the whole of those which past observation tells me that I could, under any supposable circumstances, experience at this moment.... My present sensations are generally of little importance, and are moreover fugitive: the possibilities, on the contrary, are permanent.... These possibilities, which are conditional certainties, need a special name to distinguish them from mere vague possibilities, which experience gives no warrant for reckoning upon. (Mill, 1965, p. 185)

Gibson had already conceded, in 1951, that in the case of pictures, mental structures in the classical sense (e.g., unconscious inference) might be called upon, so his reliance upon what amount to cues and mental structure in the above quotation is no surprise. The question of where these abilities come from, that is, of the circumstances in which the viewer has been called upon to use them outside of the pictorial situation, and of how widespread their use may be, becomes important in assessing the meaning of stimulus information and the content of a direct theory.

The "frozen array" of the picture provides a limiting case of the question that I have been concerned with, i.e., how long a temporal span is needed to convey usable transformation-carried information about the spatial invariants? We know that for some kinds and instances of information, very short bursts of motion will suffice (e.g., Johansson, 1977), but anecdotal descriptions of experiences with distant mountains, rotating radar antennas, and so on suggest that in other cases longer times—and specific directed effort—are required.

There is another sense in which the succession of glances can be considered as a single stimulus, and that is by taking the sequence (regardless of the fine structure of where the glances have gone, and the number of glances taken) as a single four-dimensional stimulus input. I consider that next.

The Incomplete Nature of Visual Storage.   Only if all of the information provided by the first views of a sequence of views survives through the entire sequence in a form that will affect the final perceptual outcome, could we ignore the limitations of the momentary glance. After all, if the spacing of the texture in the first glance at a sparse gradient, or the direction of a corner in the first glance at some complex pattern, is not retained by the time the next piece of information with which it must be integrated is received (e.g., the spacing of the texture in another glance at the gradient, or the direction of a second corner in the pattern, respectively), then the content of those glances will not have been part of the effective stimulus. Of course, *to the degree that a single invariant is defined over that interval, and to the degree that the perceptual response is indeed based on that invariant, we could ignore the limitations of the momentary glance and ignore as well the question of how well the information is stored between glances.* In other words, *if* we knew of a set of conditions within which perception was both veridical and predictable from some temporally extended invariant, then we could afford to ignore these questions of momentary limits and interglance storage. We do not, however, have that knowledge, nor do we know that such conditions are at all general. On the other hand, we do know that viewers cannot encode and store all features of each glimpse from one glance to the next, as we see in Fig. 17.1A, and as we will see even more strongly in connection with Fig. 17.7. The prudent man should therefore question the assumption of perfect retention of information between glances as a general rule, and therefore should assume that the span of the event that can be considered to be a single stimulus must depend on the way in which it is sampled, processed, and stored over time (which may indeed in certain cases cover a relatively large duration).

In the previous discussion, I have frequently relied on the limited spatial span of the fovea. One can, however, argue with perfect justice that the fovea is not the sole source of information, that the periphery serves essential functions in perception, and that therefore the argument about perceptual exploration with a small (ca. 2°) fovea is misleading.

Let us consider that point next.

Fovea Versus Periphery and the "Elementarism" Their Differences Impose

I do not want to argue that the periphery of the eye is useless. Indeed, Fig. 17.6 (Hochberg, 1968) was designed to show that the periphery is as important to the perception of form as I have long believed peripheral vision essential to skilled reading (Hochberg, 1970b). But the fact is that our acuity for the detection of two points, for the recognition of letters, and for the resolution of gratings and texture differences *is* drastically lower at increasing distances from the center of the eye. We do not have to believe in punctiform receptors to recognize this fact. The information carried by specific letters, for example, is detectable in the course of reading text to a distance of about four letter spaces from the fixation point (McConkie & Rayner,

1975). We have seen that there are functional differences in the pick-up of signed and unsigned pictorial depth cues (Figs. 17.1 and 17.2) and of kinetic occlusion as signed information about surface depth (Figs. 17.3 and 17.4), as a function of where one looks.

It is true that we have not as yet separated the factor of attention from that of gaze, in this research, and that we do not know whether the differences between fovea and periphery are all due to failures of acuity, to the greater degree of interference between contours in peripheral than in foveal vision (Bouma & Andriessen, 1973), or to other differences between the two kinds of vision. (There is reason to believe that at least certain kinetic as well as static cues remain unsigned as to which of two regions is nearer until those cues are brought to foveal or near-foveal vision, even though they act to indicate that *some* depth exists even when viewed only peripherally).[2]

In any case, moreover, we know that pick-up of most kinds of visual information is poorer in peripheral than in foveal vision, and that the image is not even correctly focused on the retina for normal peripheral vision (Leibowitz & Owens, 1975). To the degree that the pick-up of higher-order information depends on resolution, focus, or other factors in which peripheral vision is deficient, we indeed have only an exploring fovea (or small region around the fovea) to pick up those aspects of stimulus information. And we next see that this means not only that higher-order information may be limited but that in fact it may be totally unusable under a set of circumstances whose generality and importance are unknown. That is, we have as yet absolutely no knowledge about the set of conditions under which higher-order information can be directly used.

Why the Previous Considerations Might Make Gradients (and Other Extended Stimulus Variables) Generally Unusable

Apply the previous considerations to a texture-density gradient produced by a surface that is slanted horizontally away from the viewer (i.e., with the bottom nearest, as in the ground plane). Some minimum difference in spacing between the top and bottom elements in the field of view must surely be exceeded before the texture-density gradient can provide usable information about slant. Furthermore, it surely must be true that there is some minimum field of view needed to detect that difference, for a given gradient and a given texture-element size, as the following exaggerated limiting case shows: Consider a sparse, fine texture, composed of carrier elements that are (a) so small that the usable field of view is only about 2 to 4 degrees, and that the carrier elements become too small to detect except in the region where they are nearest to the viewer (i.e., at the bottom of the optic array); and (b) so sparse that within that region, only two elements fall within a 2- to 4-degree portion of the retina. Under such conditions, more than one fixation would necessarily be needed in order to determine the sense and extent of the difference in texture density between a lower and upper adjacent sample of the optic array.

Now, we do not know whether, and how well, such spacing information is stored from one glance to the next. If such storage is not adequate (and we have no reason at present to think that it generally is), or if the necessary but elective glances are not appropriately sequenced, directed, and executed, then the gradient information cannot be used, even with free vision.

Are the considerations evidenced in this exaggerated limiting case so general that they provide a serious obstacle to the use of texture-density gradients and optical flow patterns in real life? I do not know, nor have I seen reason to believe that anyone else does. What research there is, is not particularly encouraging (Gogel, 1977; Johnson, 1972; Smith & Smith, 1977). Certainly, the prudent man would worry somewhat about the matter before either making practical prescriptions to the designers of aircraft displays and landing strips, or building theoretical and philosophical structures on the assumption that such information from extended stimulus arrays is in fact the predominant basis of normal perception.

And in any case, the relevant stimulus questions tend to be obscured by insisting that we ignore the carrier elements and discuss only the modulating information; by ignoring the pick-up limitations of the momentary glance; and by disregarding the elective nature of eye movements and of other perceptuomotor behaviors that need motivation and guidance.

Perceived Shapes and Objects Are Not Merely Loci of Points, But They Are Not Themselves Forms or Objects, Either

To Gestalt theory, the entire configuration determines all of the attributes (solidity, shape, etc.) of the perceived object, with no clear limits on this assertion (cf. Petermann, 1932). As we noted in connection with Figs. 17.1 and 17.2, this primary claim (that configuration is unitary in the sense that it determines the appearance of the parts) cannot be sustained in view of the effects of gaze direction. There is another part to this claim, however, which requires separate consideration: that when the form falls on different parts of the retina with each change in fixation, the perceptual response remains the same because it is the form of the stimulus to which we are directly responsive and that form has remained invariant regardless of retinal locus (see Koffka, 1935). No provision was made for the limitations and inhomogeneities of the momentary glance. In fact the problem of how the information from successive views is combined, and of how we keep track of the relationship between the successive partial glimpses of any object, has not been directly addressed in a systematic manner by the Gestaltists,[3] nor by anyone else that I know of, save for Hebb (1949), whose view is essentially a physiological phrasing of the constructivist one we discuss later.

A related problem that has received considerable attention, however, is that of compensation for the viewer's eye movements and head movements. This topic has been considered mostly in terms of the perception of motion, and of the partitioning of perceived motion (e.g., into gaze-direction changes, framework motion, object motion, etc.). Two general methods of compensation for viewer's movement have been proposed. The first, which goes back to Helmholtz, is that we take the efferent eye-movement commands into account. The second, best developed in Gibson's (1957, 1966b) theory of optical kinesthesis and in Johansson's closely related vector-extraction model of motion perception, is that uniform transformations of the entire field of view are extracted as a framework against which any residual vectors provide the stimulus for perceived motion. Although these are basically discussions of perceived motion, the relationships between features (or parts of shapes) glimpsed in successive glances can be assigned their relative locations by simple extension: If one feature of the object is centered on the fovea in one glance, and another is centered on the fovea after the eye has made an excursion of, say, $5°$ to the left, and if that excursion is fully taken into account (i.e., is compensated for either by keeping track of the efferent commands or by pick-up of the invariant locus underlying the uniform optic transformation, as Helmholtz and Gibson, respectively, would have it), then the second feature must lie in space $5°$ to the left of the first.

If we were to stop here in our account of shape perception as integrated across successive glances, however, a great deal of the story would be left out. What these analyses have done *at best* is to preserve the information about the shape as a locus of points in the field, under the transformations supplied by perceptuomotor exploration, but they have nothing more to say. And there is more to the perception of shape than these compensatory mechanisms for getting the pieces in the correct relationship to each other by canceling the changes in gaze direction, or by knowing where one is looking at each moment. Let me expand this point briefly.

Form and Shape Are Not Merely Matters of Spatial Specification

Form and shape are often treated merely as matters of specification: the locus of points in space for which the viewer has different readinesses, that is, that he is prepared to fixate or point to (Festinger, Ono, Burnham, & Bamber, 1967); the invariant distribution of edges and surfaces that comprise an object or scene as they are provided by the changing optic array of a moving viewer (Gibson, 1966b). The specifiable stimulus pattern is just the first step, however, and we do not know the irreducible unit for the various disparate properties that depend on configuration. The following examples show that the perceptual attributes of forms and shapes are not all encompassed by the specifiable locus that comprises such geometrical definitions.

Figure 17.5 shows demonstrations (Hochberg, 1968) that the reversible-perspective figures appear tridimensional only if their intersections are presented in intact form: If the pattern is revealed by successive presentations, either in ways that subdivide the local depth cues (as in A) or that preserve them intact (as in B), the pattern is recognizable as a pattern in both cases, but it looks three-dimensional only in B. That is, adjacent egocentric order of small segments is sufficient for shape recognition to occur but not for perceived tridimensionality; for the latter, the intersections are needed as irreducible features. In Fig. 17.5C (adapted from Girgus, Gellman, & Hochberg, 1980), a moving aperture shows contiguous portions of a concealed pattern (here shown by the imaginary dotted line), whereas in Fig. 17.5D the aperture reveals parts of the same pattern in noncontiguous (random) order. Note that *the shape is equally well specified mathematically as an egocentric locus of small segments in both cases.* Nevertheless, recognition of the shape is much better in condition C than in condition D.

In interpreting the result of the experiment sketched in Figs. 17.5C and D, it should be noted that in both conditions the locus of aperture presentations is such that any eye movements that are made in order to fixate the individual presentations of the aperture would produce strongly overlapping fields of view, and therefore would provide the adjacent order and continuous transformations that are needed in Gibson's theory to specify the locus of points (i.e., the aperture in view 4 of Fig. 17.5C is within $5°$ of that in view 1). As far as an efference-readiness theory is concerned, condition D is such as to elicit saccades, whereas condition C is more likely to elicit pursuit movements, and the former are often thought to be at least as well compensated as the latter, if not substantially better. What condition C has that condition D lacks is adjacent order in the presentation of the shape per se, and not in its specification of the spatial locus, because the latter is present by any theory in both conditions. This outcome is what one would expect from schema-testing theories of object perception (e.g., Hebb, 1949; Hochberg, 1968, 1970a, 1974a, b; Neisser, 1967), in which shape is viewed as a structure that must be considered in addition to specifying locus.

These arguments may seem abstract, and the demonstrations that I described to support them may be hard to visualize. In any case, the demonstrations lie sufficiently outside what one would take to be the normal conditions of perception that their generality may be questioned. Not so with the next set of demonstrations and experiments.

In both Figs. 17.6A and 17.6B (Hochberg, 1968), a reversible-perspective pattern is delineated by sixes in a matrix of nines. The carrier elements of the pattern (i.e., the set of sixes) are almost indistinguishable from the background elements (nines) when viewed in peripheral vision. In Fig. 17.6B, we have by filling in the nines introduced gross contrast differences that make the carrier elements of the shape visible outside of the fovea. *Note that the shape is mathematically equally well specified in A and in B.*

In A, we have approximated an aperture-viewing situation that removes much of the effectiveness of peripheral vision, but otherwise preserves the viewer's totally free gaze. That is, in A the viewer is given a glimpse of some portion of the figure only in the center of his vision, but he can receive such a glimpse wherever he elects to direct his eye. Even though the shape is fully specified, and even though free visual exploration is available to the viewer, the shape is not clear: The viewer can with effort (i.e., undertaking the task of tracing out and identifying the shape) recognize and reproduce the pattern as such, but the figure does not look tridimensional, nor do spontaneous perspective reversals occur. In B, the shape is clearly perceptible, with or without effort, and is sufficiently tridimensional in appearance for spontaneous perspective reversals to be reported.[4]

For our present purposes, the main point of this demonstration, which is similar in its basis to those in Figs. 17.3, 17.5C, and 17.5D, is that full stimulus specification and an absolutely untrammeled gaze are not sufficient in themselves to account for shape perception. The next pair of experiments shows that the same is true of object perception.

The next experiments (Hochberg & Klopfer, 1981) show that full visual information about surface layout, presented to free gaze, does not automatically assure the perception of layout and its relationships. First, I describe an experiment with line pictures, to introduce the problem and method. Subjects were shown figures like those in Figs. 17.7A and 17.7B, with different numbers of panels and twists in different figures. They were asked to judge as quickly as possible, but as correctly as possible, whether the free ends (marked 1 and 2 in the figures shown here, but not in the actual presentations) were the same or different sides of the surface. (They are the same side in A, opposite sides in B.) Judgment times are shown in Fig. 17.7C: The solid points show the mean judgment times for pictures of the stimuli having different numbers of panels; note that the times increase fairly regularly with the number of panels. This procedure was repeated in a second experiment, using tridimensional versions of the same kinds of twisted objects that had been portrayed in the pictures of the previous experiment. The objects were made of rigid plastic "ribbon," with two different numbers of panels; they were viewed binocularly, and the subjects had free head movement and consequently had full visual information about the corners and edges of the objects before them. The entire visual angle subtended by any object was never more than about 9 degrees. The two empty circles on the graph in Fig. 17.7C show the decision times for the two classes of solid objects used; the results obtained with outline pictures (the solid points) clearly hold as well for freely viewed tridimensional objects.

The point of these experiments is this: Although each intersection is fully open to the viewer's gaze, and the stimulus is so compact that one or two glances at most are needed to bring all parts of the entire pattern within foveal vision, whether the two ends are the same or different sides of the surface is not immediately evident. Apparently the viewer needed to parse

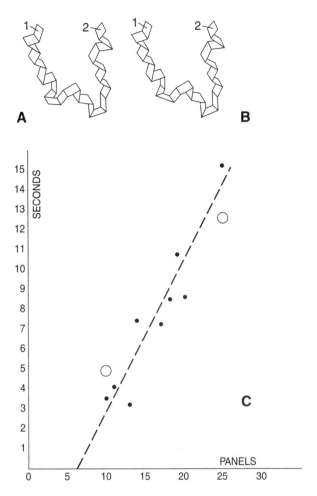

Figure 17.7. The relationships between an object's surfaces (i.e., its form) are not necessarily directly perceived even when all of the component surfaces are fully visible (Hochberg & Klopfer, 1981).

the figure (perhaps using the fovea much as the unskilled reader uses his finger to "keep his place"; eye-movement measurement has not been done with these figures, however, so this description may only be metaphorical).

It is difficult to see what one might mean by the direct perception of the object's form or surfaces' layout when the time needed to decide so simple a question as surface orientation increases with increasing number of panels. This point becomes clearer still when we realize that the perception of whether the end panels are the same or different, in these figures, is fully elective: If the viewer were to stop at any point short of the final judgment, the relationship between the surfaces, and therefore the specific form of this fully exposed, freely explored suprathreshold object, mathematically speci-fied as it is and invariant under all of the transformations provided by head and eye movements, would go undetermined.

Form is not a unitary response. A perceived object is not a thing. This point needs some expanding.

Percepts Are Not Objects, Either: The Implications of These Demonstrations for Wholistic Theories of Mental Structure

As the opposite side of the tendency to consider that the perception of an object is explained once the locus of points that define its place in space have been specified, the perception of an object is often "explained" in terms of the physical properties of the object being perceived. The temptation is understandable: If we could not count on at least *some* relationships to hold between the potential responses that can be made to any stimulus pattern that elicits the perception of some object, nothing would be gained by concluding that the subject perceives the object. For example, knowing that the subject perceives the leftmost edge of a reversible prism to be nearer, we may predict that the edge will also be judged to appear smaller; the fact that the subject says the left-hand facet appears nearer in Fig. 17.2 would seem to imply that the bottom facet is seen from above. But such interresponse constraints between two parts or attributes of an object, such as the cou-plings that are often manifest between perceived size and perceived distance, need not be obligatory, nor need we assume that an object must have a definite perceived size during the same perceptual moment that it has some definite perceived distance.

It is true that there has been a resurgence of "wholistic" discussions about shapes and objects, based on demonstrations of context effects (see Cooper, 1980, for a recent review) and on the more demanding mental ro-tation experiments, but those demonstrations and experiments have not been designed to test how much of the stimulus is effective at one time, nor how consistent and obligatory the interresponse couplings may be. Indeed, the same kinds of limits as were discussed in connection with Figs. 17.3–17.7 in the present chapter can be shown to apply to the mental rotation task (Hochberg & Gellman, 1977).

One must therefore not slide into the implicit assumption that the perceptual response to an object is in any sense an object. Kolers and Smythe (1979) have recently stressed this point with respect to controversies about the nature of imagery, and it is clearly appropriate to the case of perception itself. Figure 17.7 tells us that the perceptual implications of the impossible objects in Fig. 17.1 are not restricted to those anomalous figures: Unlike objects themselves, our perceptions of objects are not everywhere dense, and the attributes that we perceive do not in general exist in some internal model of the object, waiting to be retrieved. They are the results of our intention to perceive, and they appear in the context of the perceptual task that calls upon them.

There is a very old theory to this point, that fits all of the demonstrations that I have been describing. I construe these and other demonstrations as providing evidence for the use of local depth cues, and of other local as well as nonlocal features (e.g., gross size or shape), to which we fit schematic maps of objects and events. By schematic maps and events, I mean expectations of what one will see if one looks over there, or moves one's head so as to disocclude whatever is behind that edge. This of course is the approach of J. S. Mill and Helmholtz (see Hochberg, 1979b, 1981, for reviews to this point). This theory can make provision for most of the facts of psychophysics and perception, can explain the figure-ground phenomena and the Gestalt laws in a more plausible fashion than Gestalt theory ever did (Hochberg, 1972, 1974a), and can embrace Gibson's direct theory without being embarrassed by the existence of limits. All of this may well be too good to be true, however, and should not be taken too seriously until we can specify better what is meant by schemas (i.e., by what in Helmholtzian terms would be the premises of unconscious inference), and until we can put limits on this theory as I have been trying to put limits on the other theories of perceptual organization.

Acknowledgment

The new research described in this chapter was assisted by NSF BNS 77-25653.

Notes

1. The only reference by any direct theorist to the Ames trapezoid, that I know, is an acknowledgment by Gibson (1979). In the Ames trapezoid, of course, not only does the static depth cue of linear perspective override the higher-order information specifying an invariant trapezoid undergoing rotation that must be provided by the object's edges, but a bar thrust through the window and allowed to rotate with it will be perceived to undergo rubbery deformations appropriate to the perceived oscillation that is in turn consistent with the static depth cue. All of this has been known for decades, and immediately raises the question about where such powerful mental structures come from if they are not drawn upon the normal course of perception. The same sorts of questions arise as soon as we think about picture perception (Hochberg, 1978a, 1981b; see the section of this chapter entitled "When Do 'Cue' and 'Information' Have Different Implications?").

2. I say this because in the studies connected with Figures 17.3 and 17.4, it is clear that the subjects can detect that occlusion is occurring, and the direction in which the occlusion occurs, even at distances from the fixation point at which their depth responses fall to chance levels.

3. Köhler and Wallach (1944) do suggest that retinal anisotropies will be self-correcting as a result of differential satiation, but that explanation could in no way replace the information that is missing in peripheral vision.

4. It is possible that with sufficient practice, these differences might be overcome, but no hint of that has occurred in our experience with these patterns. In any case, I cannot see how these demonstrations and the other related work with reading and aperture viewing can be construed as arguing that peripheral vision is unimportant, as it has sometimes been taken to do (cf. Parker, 1978).

References

BECK, J. *Surface color perception.* Ithaca, N.Y.: Cornell University Press, 1972.

BOUMA, H., & Andriessen, J. J. Eccentric vision: Adverse interactions between line segments. *Vision Research*, 1973, *16*, 71–78.

CASSIRER, E. The concept of group and the theory of perception. *Philosophical and Phenomenological Research*, 1944, *5*, 1–35.

COOPER, L. A. Recent themes in visual information processing: A selective review. In R. Nickerson (Ed.), *Attention and performance, VII.* Hillsdale, N.J.: Lawrence Erlbaum Associates, 1980.

EPSTEIN, W. (Ed.) *Stability and constancy in visual perception.* New York: Wiley, 1977.

FESTINGER, L., ONO, H., BURNHAM, C. A., & BAMBER, D. Efference and the conscious experience of perception. *Journal of Experimental Psychology Monograph*, 1967. Whole No. 637.

GIBSON, J. J. *The perception of the visual world.* Boston: Houghton Mifflin, 1950.

GIBSON, J. J. What is a form? *Psychological Review*, 1951, *58*, 403–412.

GIBSON, J. J. Optical motions and transformations as stimuli for visual perception. *Psychological Review*, 1957, *64*, 288–295.

GIBSON, J. J. Observations on active touch. *Psychological Review*, 1962, *69*, 477–491.

GIBSON, J. J. *The senses considered as perceptual systems.* Boston: Houghton Mifflin, 1966.

GIBSON, J. J. *The ecological approach to visual perception.* Boston: Houghton Mifflin, 1979.

GIRGUS, J. S., GELLMAN, L., & HOCHBERG, J. The effect of spatial order on piecemeal shape recognition: A developmental study. *Perception and Psychophysics*, 1980, *2*, 133–138.

GOGEL, W. C. The metric of visual space. In W. Epstein (Ed.), *Stability and constancy in visual perception.* New York: Wiley, 1977.

HEBB, D. *The organization of behavior.* New York: Wiley, 1949.

HELMHOLTZ, H. VON. *Treatise on physiological optics, Vol. 3.* Originally published 1857. Translated from the third (1909–1911) German edition by J. P. C. Southall. New York: Optical Society of America, 1924, reprinted, New York: Dover, 1962.

HOCHBERG, J. In the mind's eye. In R. N. Haber (Ed.), *Contemporary theory and research in visual perception.* New York: Holt, Rinehart & Winston, 1968.

HOCHBERG, J. Attention, organization, and consciousness. In D. I. Mostofsky (Ed.), *Attention: Contemporary theory and analysis.* New York: Appleton-Century-Crofts, 1970. (a)

HOCHBERG, J. Components of literacy: Speculations and exploratory research. In H. Levin & J. Williams (Eds.), *Basic studies in reading.* New York: Basic Books, 1970. (b)

Hochberg, J. Perception: I. Color and Shape, II. Space and movement. In J. W. Kling & L. A. Riggs (Eds.), *Woodworth and Schlosberg's experimental psychology.* 3rd ed. New York: Holt, Rinehart & Winston, 1972.

Hochberg, J. Organization and the Gestalt tradition. In E. C. Carterette & M. Friedman (Eds.), *Handbook of perception, Vol. I.* New York: Academic Press, 1974. (a)

Hochberg, J. Higher-order stimuli and interresponse coupling in the perception of the visual world. In R. B. Macleod & H. L. Pick (Eds.), *Perception: Essays in honor of James J. Gibson.* Ithaca, N.Y.: Cornell University Press, 1974. (b)

Hochberg, J. *Perception.* Englewood Cliffs, N.J.: Prentice-Hall, 1978. (a)

Hochberg, J. Art and visual perception. In E. Carterette & M. Friedman (eds.), *Handbook of perception, Vol. X.* New York: Academic Press, 1978. (b)

Hochberg, J. *Motion pictures of mental structures.* E.P.A. Presidential Address, 1978. (c) (Available from author.)

Hochberg, J. Some of the things that pictures are. In C. Nodine & D. Fisher (Eds.), *Views of pictorial representation: Making, perceiving and interpreting.* New York: Praeger, 1979. (a)

Hochberg, J. Sensation and perception. In E. Hearst (Ed.), *Experimental psychology at 100.* Hillsdale, N.J.: Lawrence Erlbaum Associates, 1979. (b)

Hochberg, J. Levels of perceptual organization. In M. Kubovy & J. Pomerantz (Eds.), *Perceptual organization.* Hillsdale, N.J.: Lawrence Erlbaum Associates, 1981. (a)

Hochberg, J. Pictorial functions and perceptual structures. In M. Hagen (Ed.), *The perception of pictures, Vol. II.* New York: Academic Press, 1981. (b)

Hochberg, J., & Brooks, V. The psychophysics of form: Reversible-perspective drawings of spatial objects. *American Journal of Psychology,* 1960, *73,* 337–354.

Hochberg, J., & Brooks, V. The perception of motion pictures. In E. C. Carterette & M. P. Friedman (Eds.), *Handbook of perception, Vol. X.* New York: Academic Press, 1979.

Hochberg, J., & Gellman, L. The effect of landmark features on mental rotation times. *Memory and Cognition,* 1977, *5,* 23–26.

Hochberg, J., Green, J., & Virostek, S. *Texture occlusion requires central viewing: Demonstrations, data and theoretical implications.* Paper delivered at the A.P.A. Convention, 1978. (Available from the senior author.)

Hochberg, J., & Klopfer, D. Seeing is not perceiving: Schemas are needed even when visual information is complete. *Proc. Eastern Psychological Association,* 1981, 148 (Abstract).

Hochberg, J., & McAlister, E. A quantitative approach to figural "goodness." *Journal of Experimental Psychology,* 1953, *46,* 361–364.

Hochberg, J., & Smith, O. W. Landing strip markings and the "expansion pattern." I. Program, preliminary analysis and apparatus. *Perceptual and Motor Skills,* 1955, *5,* 81–92.

Hochberg, J., Virostek, S., & Green, J. *Texture occlusion depends on gaze direction: Fixed and moving eye.* In preparation.

Hochberg, J., Virostek, S., & Peterson, M. A. *Figure-ground ambiguity and unsigned depth cues.* In preparation.

Hurvich, L. M., & Jameson, D. *The perception of brightness and darkness.* Boston: Allyn & Bacon, 1966.

Johansson, G. Spatial constancy and motion in visual perception. In W. Epstein (Ed.), *Stability and constancy in visual perception.* New York: Wiley, 1977.

JOHNSON, I. R. *Visual judgments in locomotion.* Doctoral dissertation, University of Melbourne, 1972.

JULESZ, B. *Foundations of Cyclopean perception.* Chicago: University of Chicago Press, 1971.

KOFFKA, K. *Principles of Gestalt psychology.* New York: Harcourt Brace, 1935.

KAPLAN, G. A. Kinetic disruption of optical texture: The perception of depth at an edge. *Perception and Psychophysics,* 1969, *6,* 193–198.

KÖHLER, W., & WALLACH, H. Figural after-effects: An investigation of visual processes. *Proceedings of the American Philosophical Society,* 1944, *88,* 269–357.

KOLERS, P. A., & SMYTHE, W. E. Image, symbols and skills. *Canadian Journal of Psychology,* 1979, *33,* 158–184.

LEIBOWITZ, H. W., & OWENS, D. A. Anomalous myopias and the intermediate dark focus of accommodation. *Science,* 1975, *18,* 162–170.

MCCONKIE, G. W., & RAYNER, K. The span of the effective stimulus during a fixation in reading. *Perception and Psychophysics,* 1975, *17,* 578–586.

MILL, J. S. *An examination of Sir William Hamilton's philosophy,* 1865 (On the permanent possibilities of sensation). Reprinted in R. J. Hernstein & E. G. Boring (Eds.), *A source book in the history of psychology.* Cambridge, Mass.: Harvard University Press, 1965.

NEISSER, U. *Cognitive psychology.* New York: Appleton-Century-Crofts, 1967.

PARKER, R. E. Picture processing during recognition. *Journal of Experimental Psychology: Human Perception and Performance,* 1978, *4,* 284–293.

PENROSE, L., & PENROSE, R. Impossible objects: A special type of visual illusion. *British Journal of Psychology,* 1958, *49,* 31–33.

PETERMANN, B. *The Gestalt theory and the problem of configuration.* New York: Harcourt Brace, 1932.

PETERSON, M. A., & HOCHBERG, J. Perspective reversals that refute both Gestalt and direct theories of object perception: Measures of local cue strength and attention. *Proc. Eastern Psychological Association,* 1981, 148 (Abstract).

SMITH, O. W., & SMITH, P. C. On motion parallax and perceived depth. *Journal of Experimental Psychology,* 1963, *65,* 107–108.

SMITH, O. W., & SMITH, P. C. Developmental studies of spatial judgments by children and adults. *Perceptual and Motor Skills,* 1966, *22,* 3–73.

WOODWORTH, R. S. *Experimental psychology.* New York: Holt, Rinehart & Winston, 1938.

18

Form Perception

Experience and Explanations

Julian Hochberg

Form Perception: Mental Structure or Direct Sensory Experience?

My concern in this chapter is the perception or experience of visual form, and with the kinds of proposals that have been offered to explain the phenomena of form perception. Such explanations fall in two general classes: one which involves (unconscious) inference-like or computational processes, based on premises about the world (i.e., mental structure), and one in which our perceptions of form and other object properties are direct responses to the stimulation received by the visual system. Depending on how they are fleshed out, the two alternative approaches may in fact be indistinguishable, or they may be very different in their psychological and physiological implications.

In the first kind of approach, form perception must be explained in terms of unobservable events (mental structures) that are difficult to specify and study. In the other, perceived form is taken to be a direct response, either to the actions of specifiable neural structures (or their abstract theoretical representations) or to specifiable aspects of sensory stimulation. On the face of it, the latter class of explanations seems the less nebulous and the more promising scientifically. That is true, however, only if the "direct" explanations can in fact free us from the need to define and study mental structure in form perception. I do not think they can. The first part of this chapter briefly presents the context of the problem, and the kinds of phenomena that seem most refractory to any explanation that seeks to sidestep the problem of mental structure; the second part considers the most difficult of such phenomena (form perceived in response to piecemeal sequence) at greater length; the third section considers the limitations of each kind of theory; and the last section is concerned with how we may study mental structure in form perception.

First, a word about the definition of terms that will keep reappearing in this paper. "Mental structure" and "direct" are defined in their contexts, but consider the opening sentence: The critical terms in this sentence are "form" and "experience." "Form" is not easy to define exhaustively, but a more or less adequate effort can be made. I cannot however define the crucial term in that first sentence, "experience," in a satisfactory way. An important achievement of any adequate theory of form or shape perception would be a definition or set of definitions of the relevant experience. Despite this fundamental difficulty, however, we cannot abandon the problem because it is nevertheless a real one of great importance not only to the psychologist, but to the sensory physiologist and neurologist as well. There is an important substantive problem here (not merely the philosophical mind-body issue) that cannot really be ignored.

Two extreme positions have been taken with varying degrees of militancy and smugness: The first, of course, is to make a show of dismissing the notion of experience; the second, opposite but closely related, is to accept experience as an obvious given, and discuss "phenomenological report" as a datum like any other, with no further critical analysis.

Some sensory physiologists take the first position, and the issue of experience then does not arise: They propose to trace physical information transfer from proximal stimulation at the receptor to motor response at the effector.

Fine. Taken seriously, this approach neither draws on visual experience, *nor can it contribute to an account of visual experience.* It maintains sensory physiology and perceptual psychology as two orthogonal domains of discourse.

Most sensory physiologists are more relaxed in this regard and, with suitable linking hypotheses (Brindley, 1960), will accept help from threshold psychophysics. Still, they will have no commerce with the *appearances* of things. It wasn't always thus.

Past and Present Context of the Mental Structure/Direct Response Issue

Helmholtz and Mill: Form as Mental Structure, Opaque to Physiology

From Hartley to Johannes Mueller, the attempt was to formulate ways of analyzing experience and to discover the physiological bases of experience. To Mueller, of course, specific nerve energies analyzed the total world of sensory experience into different qualities. To Helmholtz, his student, specific fiber energies analyzed each sensory quality or modality into elementary sensations. In principle, the linkage remained clear: for each physiological channel, a corresponding experience, and vice versa.

From the beginning of this scheme, however, the linkage of physiology and experience was in trouble: As Maxwell noted, introspection might *sometimes* serve to reveal the components in a mixture—e.g., the blue and green in aqua—but even more often would not: yellow (red plus green), white (red plus green plus blue), etc. How can we tell when it *will* serve?

Indeed, J. S. Mill and Helmholtz argued that experience is not transparent to physiology, in the general case, because we adults do not perceive our *sensations*—we *perceive* those properties of objects, like their relatively permanent distal reflectances and sizes, that would in each case be most likely to generate the flux of fleeting, impermanent sensations that we receive. The object's size and reflectance are stable; the size of the retinal image, and its luminance, vary as *our* distance and *its* illumination change (Mill, 1865; Helmholtz, 1911).

Let us consider in more detail how form perception is explained in such theories.

Perception as Expected Contingencies.   In addition to color, the receptors of the classical theory must offer spatially coded information that serves to distinguish different patterns of the same color. The most powerful way to do this, permitting the greatest range of discriminable shapes, is a coordinate system giving each receptor a separate spatial identity. Those are the "local signs" of Lotze (1896). This does not mean that the perception of form results from, or is to be equated with, the pattern of local signs.

The meanings of the descriptors "shape" and "form" can arise from *any* set of contingencies associated with a particular retinal pattern: It is these contingencies that comprise what we must mean by shape and form perception, and that any theory of shape and form must address. We consider them next; the important point here is that it is those contingencies and not the distribution of local signs themselves that provide the content of the Helmholtz-Mill theory of object perception.

For example, to perceive a given object is to be prepared for the different views that would be obtained if one changed one's viewpoint of it (Helmholtz, 1911).

That example—"knowing" in advance what some presently occluded or obscured view of an object would be—comprises *one* meaning of what it means to perceive an object's *form*. It is that meaning that is most directly addressed by the aperture-viewing research, discussed in the next section. But there are many other meanings: The same properties of the object provide different contingencies to different behaviors that are also included in the perception of an object's form as registered by the eye (at least, given the Mill-Helmholtz position, that assertion is true for a mature perceiver)—e.g., how the object will feel if one runs one's hand over it. Given the constraints of the normal physical world, therefore, other sensory properties are also necessarily coupled with each other, and come in packets. For example, the tridimensional object presents to the viewer's eye a projected contour that comprises the set of directions that the eye must take to bring each point to the fovea; that set comprises a flat silhouette that it shares with a line drawing, with a cutout that the finger can trace, etc. Note that both the flat shape and the solid form are equally *perceptions*, only indirectly occasioned by the pattern of light in the eye. It is not true that the Mill-Helmholtz account of form perception begins with flat shapes and adds inferences to these to achieve the perception of tridimensional form or layout. That "snapshot" theory (e.g., Gibson, 1966, 1979; Turvey, 1977) is a straw man: In the classical account, the retinal image (which is indeed flat) is itself inaccessible to experience, and neither flat shape nor solid form are direct or primitive.

Other contingent properties of the world will also be reflected in the perception of shape and form. For example, changing one's gaze direction changes the retinal pattern that would result from a stationary object in the world. Perceiving a particular shape or form implies, therefore, the knowledge of where to move one's gaze so as to bring some particular part of it into clear vision; it also includes the perception of the same (stationary) form despite the fact that a new set of receptors has been stimulated. The translation or rotation may occur because the eye has moved, because the object has moved, or both. In each case, because we have learned what to expect from such transformations, the actual fulfillment of our expectations— i.e., the transformed stimulus pattern—results in the perception of an invariant object.

The Theory Is Qualitatively Powerful, but Frighteningly Complex and Indirect. Qualitatively, this is a powerful story. It accounts for the constancies.[1] It accounts for the illusions.[2] It will even account for the phenomena of Gestalt organization.[3] And all of these are the kinds of things that perception psychologists want explained, inasmuch as these arise at the first attempt to relate sensory information to performance in, and experience of, the world.

That was one generation after Mueller set the business up. Helmholtz still has adherents, of differing degrees of sophistication. More about them later. In this theory, however, experience is not in general transparent to physiology. Note the following:

> That you can't discern the first stages of perceptual processing (the *sensations*), free of contamination by cognitive and interpretive processes.

> That most of the properties of the perceptual world are *indirect*—that is, they draw upon learned constraints, or *mental structure*, such as the relationships among reflectance, luminance, and illuminance, or among image size, object size, and object distance.

> That in consequence the prediction of what we will perceive is an incredibly complex affair: We must take into account the sensory physics, the physiology, the "ecological physics" (i.e., what the physical relationships are that provide the regularities we will learn to use), and the mental structure that a viewer effectively brings to any perceptual situation.

Given this distance between measurable stimulus characteristics and perceived attributes, it might seem only prudent to avoid basing physiology on appearance.[4] But these complex factors intervening between stimulation (or physiology) and appearance are, at least in part, theoretical consequences of what we take to be the primitives of neural analysis. More direct alternatives were proposed almost as soon as the Helmholtzian explanation had been provided, and those are introduced next.

The Phenomenological Theories of Hering and Mach, and Their Modern Descendants

Hering (1878/1964) and Mach (1886/1959) *started* with perceptual experience (or "phenomenology"); they sought physiological mechanisms that would account for such experience, and between them they achieved a triumphant array of vindicated speculations: interconnected neural networks or sensory structures that provide for lateral inhibition in contrast, constancy, and contour formation; binocular channels of stereoscopic responses; and—most spectacularly—opponent-process color theory.[5] Even with respect to color vision, which seems the simplest of sensory problems, by not considering how things look, the conservative sensory physiologist now seems to have backed the wrong horses for about half a century.

So the question of whether and under what conditions experience is transparent to physiology is not an empty one. It deserves much more thought than it has received, either by those who avoid any concern with appearances or by those who seem eager to duplicate the Hering/Mach successes.

In any case, we now know that in fact the nervous system is interconnected in ways that make for response to fields of stimuli that are more general than the response to localized points acting on single receptors. Such neural networks are now the model for numerous attempts to explain the sensory basis of our perceptions of such physical properties as depth and form as direct responses to aspects of the distribution of light entering the eye. The new approaches are, like those of Hering and Mach, seeking for analytic sensory mechanisms other than those of Helmholtz's specific fiber energies. In general, however, these modern efforts do not start with perceptual experience, as Hering and Mach did, nor is it claimed that the elementary sensory responses are themselves evident in our perceptions of form or shape. For example, none of those who argue that spatial-frequency channels mediate form perception by means of something like a two-dimensional Fourier analysis also propose that we are able to discern the constituent frequencies in any scene or object.

This means that in order to explain or predict how things appear, these new theories must make more explicit provision for linking perceptual experience to the responses of their proposed analytic mechanisms than they have yet done. More critical to me is that even if any of these theories is right as far as it goes, it cannot hope to "explain" form perception in any general sense, a limitation that I have never found acknowledged in their presentations. I cannot see how such mechanisms can possibly deal with the central fact, known for most of this century, that the same form can be perceived in response to very different stimuli. What that means is discussed next.

The Challenge to Direct Response Theories: The Same
Forms Perceived With Very Different Stimuli

As noted above, perceived form cannot be equated with a response to the distribution of local signs because form appears to remain unchanged even though a different set of receptors is stimulated whenever the eye or the object moves. This poses what is often considered as *the* Gestalt problem (e.g., Rashevsky, 1948)—the supposed fact that (under certain conditions) the viewer does not perceive that the form is changed even though it falls upon a totally new set of receptors. A considerable amount of inquiry has been devoted to whether and how the nervous system might "discount" the eye movements that have been ordered and executed (von Holst, 1954; see Matin, 1972), and considerably less inquiry has addressed the case in which the eye is stationary but the object moves (Hochberg, 1968; Fendrich, 1982). In what sense does the perceived form then remain unchanged? More than anything else, this idea—that perceived form remains constant under transformation—has encouraged the recent search for mechanisms that will respond *directly* to the form that has remained invariant under the transformation.

The first such attempt was, of course the main thrust of Gestalt psychology. To the Gestalt theorists (see Hochberg, 1981a), an object's perceived form or shape remains invariant because the configuration of the object's retinal image is the essential stimulus for perceived form, and that configuration remains essentially invariant regardless of its displacements within the field of view. The sense in which configuration is itself a stimulus was to be answered by a new approach to the relevant processes in the central nervous system, topologically isomorphic in some sense to stimulus configuration, and to which perceptual experience in turn was presumed to be isomorphic; that approach has since been abandoned, except for a persistent assumption, made by some of the intellectual descendants of the Gestalt attempt, that the proper unit of analysis is the entire form or shape of a coherent object.

If it is our aim to explain phenomena of form constancy without invoking mental structure, it is a reasonable strategy to propose as the effective stimulus some feature that remains invariant under transformation, as the Gestaltists tried to do, and we will see later that this is still a frequent task. But in the attempt to deal with the textbook statements about constancy, it is important to set the problem in perspective. Such explanations may be attempting to explain both too much and too little in order to allow us to dispense with mental structure. Too much, because (a) constancy of form under displacement is not complete (and indeed it is not clear what is meant by the term), and (b) forms are not unitary responses, so they do not by themselves demand unitary explanation; too little, because (c) there are other forms of shape and form constancy in addition to those that these explanations can encompass, and it may be misleading to suggest that *the* problem of form perception is solved by solving the set of phenomena that is being addressed by the proposal in question.

We next consider each of these points briefly.

Shape and Form Constancy Are Not Complete

In fact, perceived shapes are not completely invariant under transformation. A square may not be recognized when it is transformed into a diamond by being rotated 45 degrees; faces and their expressions become unrecognizable when inverted or reversed in contrast (Galper, 1970; Hochberg & Galper, 1967). Indeed, with careful research, even translation to another retinal location can be shown to have an effect on recognizability (Wallach & Austin, 1954). With very simple shapes, the constancy under translation or rotation may be substantial, but that should not be taken as evidence that the invariance of the perceived form is as perfect as the invariance of the physical object in the physical environment.

It is true that there are experimental conditions, such as the mental rotation tasks, in which the perceiver's responses are similar to what they would have been if an invariant physical object were rotating in physical space (Cooper, 1976; Shepard & Metzler, 1971), but it is also clear that the shape that is perceived is not invariant in all ways—or even in any important ways—under all of the transformations of orientation and location that can be provided.

One critical problem in such research—I think, *the* critical problem—is that of response criterion: In what sense do we say that the same shape or form is perceived after transformation?

What It Means to Say That a Form Has Been Perceived

Viewers very often give an object the same label (using that term loosely) on the basis of very different features; examples that will be important in the present discussion are given in Fig. 18.1. Many other examples, of many different kinds, can be found. The point is that without exhaustive introspection (of dubious validity) and testing (of what may conceptually prove to be a moving target), we cannot tell exactly what a subject perceived at any time—even if that phrase can be given some well-defined meaning (which many psychologists doubt). It is only on a very few occasions that any inquiry has been directed to this point; the fractionation experiments comprise one of the few areas in which a substantial attempt was made, with consequences that are not encouraging for the uncritical acceptance of subjects' names for the shapes and forms that they perceive.[6]

More recently, the issue has surfaced in the mental rotation literature: When a subject reports that shape 18.2a is the same as (and not a mirror image of) shape 18.2b, does that imply that the entire shape is used in

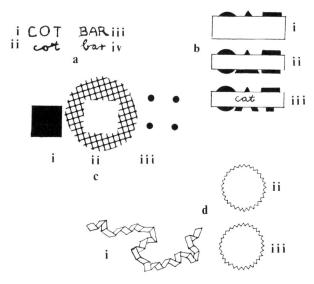

Figure 18.1. (a) At i and ii, two patterns to which the same verbal label is given rapidly and reliably, and which evidently have stimulus features in common. At iii and iv, two patterns that also elicit a common verbal label, probably as rapidly and reliably as in i and ii, but which do not have any evident stimulus features in common.

(b) Partially occluded geometrical shapes are perceived in i. Looked at with that set, the figures at i and ii are perceived as the same shapes, although surely not as identical patterns. Given the set provided by the handwritten word in iii the partly occluded word is perceived there and, with that as reference, the same shapes can also be perceived in i. Note that the demonstrations here, and in Figures 18.1c and 18.4B, can be so designed as to produce definite subjective contours; in order to avoid the question of whether or not such contours can be explained peripherally, I have used figures where these are weak or nonexistent.

(c) Three ways, out of thousands, by which a square shape may be presented. In all of these, the shape remains the same qua shape, but there is no likelihood of confusing the patterns by which it is carried. The shapes remain recognizably the same even though the carrier pattern changes radically.

(d) Even with identical carrier patterns, one cannot recognize whether or not two ribbons like that in i are the same, nor whether ii and iii are identical—e.g., do they have the same number of cusps? (Yes.)

reaching that decision? Cooper and Podgorny (1976) have made an effort to ensure that it would be, using distractor shapes that were designed to rule out the use of any obvious local features. On the other hand, with naive subjects, and with stimuli that look grossly the same (i.e., have no distinguishing landmark features: Figs.18.2d and 18.2e), it is easy to show that something less immediate and more feature-dependent can go into such decisions (Hochberg & Gellman, 1977). One cannot explain the recognition of rotated forms, therefore, simply by appealing to the detection and a   b   c   d   e

Figure 18.2. Are (a) and (b) the same or enantiomers (mirror images)? (Answer: same.) Cooper and Podgorny (1976), using similar figures, found that judgment times were proportional to angle of transformation (as in other mental rotation research) and unaffected by complexity. (c) A distractor figure. Are (d) and (e) the same? (Answer: no, they are enantiomers.) Using naive subjects and patterns similar to these, that may differ only in local detail, complexity becomes important (Hochberg & Gellman, 1977).

removal of a rotational transformation operating on just any informative shape (i.e., one that is sufficiently asymmetrical to reveal the rotation).

One might argue that these phenomena occur only in naming shapes, or in discriminating outline drawings of peculiar objects, i.e., that both stimuli and responses lack "ecological validity." With respect to the issue of naming or discriminating, we should note that other criteria for whether one perceives (or merely reports) a shape have been proposed. These rest upon the notion, incompletely worked out, of "convergent definitions" (Garner, Hake, & Eriksen, 1956; Hochberg, 1956; Postman, 1954). More specifically, they rely on deciding what we want from a definition—what would make it informative to learn that the viewer had "really" perceived a form, rather than merely reported it—i.e., what can we better predict about the viewer given that he or she perceives the form (Hochberg, 1956, 1968)?

What that must mean in the case of form perception is that the convergent definition should include at least some of the perceptual couplings that we have been describing, i.e., that the viewer can retrieve information from the perceived form other than merely its name or label. This means that the couplings that prevail in the physical world, with respect to the constraints on the properties of any distal object, also prevail at least to some degree in the constraints on subjects' responses: For example, a subject who is really confronted by the object depicted in Fig. 18.3b, and who can retrieve the distal information it presents, should be able to report not only that it is a cube-like shape: He or she should also report the horizontal "wire" to be nearer than the vertical, at intersection 2, given that intersection 1 constrains the cube's orientation as shown in Fig. 18.3c. Or a subject should perceive that tab 2 is the same surface as that of 1, in Fig. 18.3f, whereas in e it is not.

When there are no probes applied to test for perceptual consistency (e.g., in the familiar Necker cube), or when the form is determined according to some ruling principle or schema that the viewer knows and can consult, as in the staircase at Fig. 18.3d, neither viewer nor experimenter can

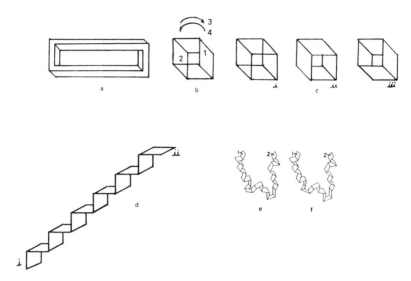

Figure 18.3. (a) A modified version (Hochberg, 1966) of the Penrose and Penrose (1958) impossible figure, which allows the inconsistent corners to be separated by a variable distance.

(b, c) A possible object (e.g., as in ciii, but with a transparent lower panel): a Necker cube (as at ci) fixed at intersection 1. Despite the fact that the orientation is fixed at 1, if you regard intersection 2 for a few moments, the intersection there will be seen to reverse between the orientations at cii and ciii. When the object in b rotates clockwise (3), and intersection 2 reverses, so that the vertical wire appears the nearer, the apparent rotation becomes counterclockwise (4) (Peterson & Hochberg, 1982).

(d) Given a schema that relates the parts of the objects to each other, the layout of the surfaces within it appears to be immediately given: E.g., it seems directly evident that tabs i and ii (and the horizontal and vertical surfaces visible here in general) are opposite sides, and not the same surface.

(e, f) Without a schema which specifies the layout of the component surfaces, the relationship between two nonadjacent surfaces must be arrived at by parsing the intervening dihedrals: Are e and f the same? (No.) In which are panels 1 and 2 part of a single continuous surface? The phenomenon demonstrated here with outline drawings holds as well for freely viewed tridimensional objects (Klopfer & Hochberg, 1981).

tell immediately whether or not such figures are perceived consistently. In Figs. 18.3e and 18.3f, where no familiar or simple scheme is known to the viewer with which to decide on the basis of the *local* regions near i and ii themselves whether they represent the same or different surfaces, the viewer must examine the information that is distributed over the form, bend by bend, to reach that decision (Klopfer, 1983; Klopfer & Hochberg, 1981). Even though all of the information is given to the eye at once, the facts about the layout and the relationship between the surfaces must be parsed piecemeal. (It should be stressed that the phenomenon described here is obtained as well with freely viewed 3D objects as with line drawings.)

And indeed, in the version of the cube shown in Fig. 18.3b, when the viewer fixates intersection 2, perspective reversals occur there despite the fact that the cube's orientation should be fixed by the intersection at 1 (Hochberg, 1970, 1981a). This is true not only of such outline drawings, but of actual objects as well, whether stationary, undergoing a slight rotation (Peterson & Hochberg, 1983), or even when viewed by a moving observer (Peterson & Hochberg, 1982).

In short, what it means to say that a subject perceives a given form is not clear. Not clear, because the subject may use quite different criteria and features to identify a form from one situation to the next, and not clear because the consequences of having perceived a form are not all coupled as their corresponding physical properties are coupled in the physical object, and indeed are to some unknown degree task-dependent. In the case of the ribbon figures (Figs. 18.3e, f), the viewer clearly does not make the effort to parse the figure except when required to judge the surface relationship between tabs 1 and 2. In the case of the cube depicted in Fig. 18.3b, which orientation is perceived depends on the intersection fixated, but it also depends on which alternative the viewer *attempts* to perceive (Peterson & Hochberg, 1983). And we are not merely talking about response bias: Viewer motion relative to the object produces the perceived direction of parallax that is appropriate to the perceived orientation of the object (Fig. 18.3b). *Some* couplings hold.

As a general theoretical problem, this is awesome. The term *representation*, which is currently in favor in cognitive psychology, is empty of meaning unless the set of coupled properties to be expected on any occasion is spelled out. In a concrete case, as in asserting that forms remain constant despite transformations like translation and rotation, it means that *what* remains constant must be spelled out, together with the evidence for the assertion.

Neither phenomenally, nor in terms of the coupled consequences of perceiving a form, do such responses as "I see an _____" or "Stimulus A and B have the same form" mean the same thing from one situation to the next, nor serve a useful function without further explication. And the fact is that when such explication is done, and suitable criteria employed, the observed interresponse constraints do not support the notion that a form is perceived as a whole (except in the sense that some gross pattern and distribution provides a detectable aspect).

Other Kinds of Form and Shape Constancy

The literature tells us that perceived shape also remains invariant (to some degree) under the following transformations:

> When the retinal image changes *its* shape in consequence of changes in the slant of the object to the line of sight (e.g., in Fig. 18.4A, the rectangle at a slant provides a trapezium in the retinal image);

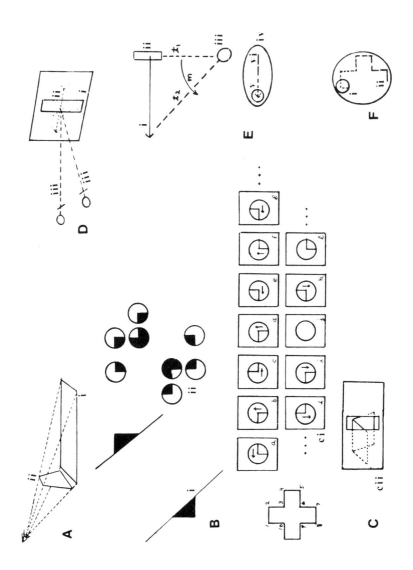

Figure 18.4. (A) "Shape constancy": The rectangle at a slant provides the eye with a trapezoid projection in the optic array and in the retinal image, but the shape perceived usually remains close to rectangular. (B) In the normal, cluttered environment, objects are usually partially occluded. The square revealed by upper right and lower left corners at i remains the same square when partially occluded in another way, e.g., so as to reveal its upper left and lower right corners. The eight discs in ii are also apertures behind which a cross is partially disclosed, as it could also be disclosed by a quite different set of apertures. (C) Shapes can also be disclosed piecemeal by being moved around behind a stationary aperture, so that all of the parts are displayed successively at the same place in space. (The following are from Hochberg, 1968.) i. Successive views of an outline cross. Directions of motion as indicated by arrows. ii. Reversible-perspective figure being moved left and right behind a slit. (D) The shape can be made even less dependent on brightness-contrast retinal contours: Looking through polaroid spectacles (iii) at a random-dot stereogram being moved left and right behind an aperture (i), the subject perceives a Mueller-Lyer pattern presented piecemeal (through the slit) as a raised or recessed region of the dot matrix (Hochberg, 1968). Even with aperture's width such that no two "fins" are visible simultaneously, the illusion is obtained. (E) When the slit is narrow, the shape is small, and the motion is fast, retinal painting can spread the image out on the retina: The arrow (i) pulled from right to left through the slit (ii) will, if the eye moves (m) so as to keep the (occluded) arrowhead aligned with the fovea (v), project a narrow image to successive places on the retina (iv). Given sufficient visual persistence, the retinal image of the arrowhead on the fovea (v) may still produce a detectable effect when the tail end of the arrow is presented through the aperture and falls in the retinal periphery (vi). (F) In the case of a large figure and slit, and long duration of movement, painting becomes implausible (Hochberg, 1968): In the kinds of displays summarized in Figure 18.4Ci, above, even if the eye executed all of the movements shown by the arrows in that figure, the image of the seventh view (ii) would fall some 20 degrees away from the fovea (i) and as much as 2 seconds after the first view.

341

when some or most of the area of different color, or of the contour, is occluded in some fashion (Fig. 18.4Bi, ii);

when the contours that define the shape are presented piecemeal by aperture viewing (18.4C) or even by piecemeal random-dot stereogram (18.4D).

Not only does the subject report perceiving the appropriate form in all of the situations, but some of the appropriately coupled consequences are manifest: For example, viewers can detect shortcuts from one arm of a cross to another in Fig. 18.4Ci, perspective reversals occur in Fig. 18.4Cii, and the Mueller-Lyer illusion is obtained under the conditions of Figs. 18.4C and 18.4D.

It is possible to find *some* examples of each of the traditional constancy phenomena for which some form of stimulus equivalence can be offered: Thus, we can offer to explain size constancy in terms of an invariant relationship of extension to texture density (Gibson, 1959), in terms of ratios of spatial frequency ensembles (Blakemore & Campbell, 1969), and in terms of ratios relative to adjacent objects (Rock & Ebenholtz, 1959), and we consider some of these later. But it is also possible to choose conditions that make those stimulus (or peripheral) explanations implausible, or even impossible, and the aperture-viewing situation of Figs. 18.4C and 18.4D provide clear examples of the latter. We discuss the phenomenon in the next section.

Aperture Viewing: Forms Perceived by Piecemeal Presentation

Retinal Painting, Mental Maps, and Other Explanations

When a pattern is moved more-or-less rapidly behind an aperture, if the eye itself moves with the same velocity, as shown in Fig. 18.4E, and if the visual stimulus has some persistent effect, it is evident that the entire pattern would be laid out sequentially on the retina much as if it were presented to the eye simultaneously. The presentation would then be spatially equivalent to a normal one, and no special function to integrate form need be posited. That is, with such retinal painting, a form is perceived on much the same bases as it normally is, arising from differences in color and brightness that are simultaneously visible at different points in the visual field. Forms perceived in this way are merely somewhat exotically achieved afterimages.

Given that retinal persistence exists, and that most subjects probably *can* execute the appropriate pursuit movements, it must be that painting can occur in some of the cases of what Zollner (1862) called *anorthoscopic perception*, if slits are narrow and the excursions are short and brief, and may then account for certain findings (Hochberg, 1968, 1971), e.g., some of the compression that is characteristic of the phenomenon at higher speeds, and mirror-image reversals that can sometimes occur (see Anstis & Atkinson, 1967). Because painting raises no new questions about form perception, however, the important question for the perception psychologist is whether there is any aspect of form perception under successive piecemeal presentation that is *not* attributable to painting. For over a century, there has been an intermittent debate about whether painting fully accounts for the perception of the entire shape under such circumstances.[7] It is my belief, however, that the entire issue was effectively sidestepped in 1966 by the following demonstrations (Hochberg, 1968, 1971) shown in Fig. 18.4F.

In such displays, the partially hidden or "virtual shapes" that are presented piecemeal through the aperture may, were they fully disclosed, subtend visual angles of 23 degrees (changing directions of motion many times in the process). In order to paint the entire image of the cross on the retina in Fig. 18.4Ci, the viewer would have to have executed the set of movements in Fig. 18.4F, which would place some parts of the figure 20 degrees into the periphery (slit width was 3 degrees), over a duration of 1.5 seconds. This seems exceedingly far-fetched, for retinal painting. In order for the picture in Fig. 18.4D to be painted on the retina, the viewer would have to be detecting the dots, which act as the carriers for the stereodisparity, and define the form being presented, at 15 to 20 degrees outside of the fovea.

Although retinal painting clearly must contribute to the phenomenon under some conditions, it is thus also clear that a constructive process, by which the successive views are integrated in the mind's eye, must exist as well (Fendrich, 1982; Fendrich & Mack, 1981; Hochberg, 1968, 1971; Morgan, 1981). In any actual case of aperture viewing, it is likely that some degree of painting and a considerable amount of constructive processing *both* occur, and it would be valuable to separate their contributions. Using stabilized images, Fendrich and Mack (1980, 1981) and Fendrich (1982) have been able to set some of the limits on the two contributing sources. By stabilizing both the slit and its moving contents within one retinal region, they showed that a simple shape could be recognized in the total absence of retinal painting. But painting also contributes: Fendrich's recent demonstration (1982) that the moving pattern is seen in mirror-image reversal when presented by retinally locked counterphase retinal motion, seems conclusive evidence to this point.

Both painting and constructive processes must participate under some conditions of aperture viewing. If one is interested in sensory processing, the limits and nature of retinotopic painting—and perhaps the actions of a mixed population of direction-sensitive cells which, I suspect, might produce much the same results—are the important fruit of such inquiry. Short and rapid excursions favor painting (Fendrich, 1982; Hochberg, 1968). But the constructive component is of far more general importance to psychology— and indeed in the long run to physiology and neurology as well. By the *constructive component*, I mean the fact that the same form that is perceived and defined in terms of a specific distribution of stimulation on the retina can be perceived as well when no plausible sensory basis can be found.

That leaves us with a reasonably strong example of a constructive process in the perception or recognition of form, under conditions in which no direct explanation seems plausible. And that provides a clear challenge to *any* theory which attempts to base form perception on specific analyzing mechanisms.

This is not to say that the appearances obtained with large-shape, long-duration excursions are the same in every way as those obtained with brief, small shapes. Quite the contrary: The former are clearly perceived as moving shapes seen piecemeal through a window, and the latter tend to appear more *simultaneous* (and often, paradoxically, larger than, yet within, the aperture). This returns us to the question, raised earlier, of what it means to say we perceive a form.

What Do We Mean by "Form Perception" in Aperture Viewing?

What does it mean to say that we see the entire form when it is moved piecemeal behind the slit? As noted in the discussion of Fig. 18.1, the problem of specifying what is meant by form perception is general, and not unique to aperture viewing. If we tried to apply Brindley's criterion here, we would be restricted to situations in which the viewer could detect no difference between the two different stimulus presentations. I know of no one who has attempted an experiment in which the viewer would be unable to discriminate successive from simultaneous presentation. Present technical constraints would restrict such research to a very narrow range of conditions (indeed, those in which painting processes would likely predominate). And in any case the aspects of aperture viewing that are most theoretically interesting in terms of the "final common path" argument are just those which could not possibly deceive the viewer into believing that the entire shape had been simultaneously presented.

What one experiences under conditions like those in Fig. 18.4Ci is *not* a moving shape entirely open to view, but the conviction that a specific shape is moving behind an aperture. We see the same form in normal and in aperture viewing, but an impression of simultaneity is generally missing in the latter case. Can we still say that we *perceive* the same form, rather than merely apply the same verbal label? To answer that question meaningfully, I think we have to ask what purposes the question and its answer are intended to serve (Hochberg, 1956, 1968). A general answer therefore cannot be given. Let us try a less general question.

How much can we strip from the surplus meaning of saying that the viewer has perceived a form and still leave the statement informative about the viewer's experience?

Note that the attributes of a perceived form arise at different levels, and comprise different domains within which perceptual couples may be expected to be manifest. Some of these are what Helmholtz called "subjective sensations" that can be viewed as side effects of the processing system: e.g., afterimages, FAEs (figural aftereffects), etc. These are not usually experienced by the viewer as being part of the physical world, because there are tests that will show him or her that these sensations are internal in origin (e.g., after-images persist with eyes closed). These side effects of form perception can be used to study the structure and function of the processing system: Just as the Purkinje shift is used to study the color system, FAEs have been used in support of various speculations about the pick-up of form (Blakemore & Campbell, 1969; Gibson, 1937; Köhler & Wallach, 1944; Wundt, 1902). Some of these subjective sensations have occasionally been used as criteria of whether the viewer *really* perceived some object, but they are in general too tied to a specific mode of presentation to serve as general criteria. Thus, the time course of afterimages critically depends on luminance differences and state of adaptation, not on the characteristics of the form itself. Perspective reversal is a criterion for perceiving depth (Hochberg, 1956; Wallach, O'Connell, & Neisser, 1953), and it does occur under some conditions of aperture viewing (Hochberg, 1968), but perspective reversal can also be a clearly local affair, specific to a given intersection (Hochberg, 1970, 1981a; Peterson & Hochberg, 1982), and therefore can provide no strong implications concerning the perception of the entire form.

The irreducible minimum that one would want to be entailed by saying that a viewer perceives some form or shape is that he or she displays some minimum of spatial information concerning its identifiable features. Let us consider the set of such possible responses as a *map.* (I do not mean to imply *any* kind of isomorphism here, whether of "first" or of "second" order.) It is clear from the discussion of Figs. 18.1–18.3 that such maps are *schematic* and leave attributes unconstrained in perception that are fully constrained in the physical world.

The availability of a schematic map is manifest in the aperture viewing of shapes, e.g., if the viewer is provided with sequential views of a moving outline figure of a cross, with good cues as to the changing directions of motion that are indicated by the arrows in Fig. 18.4C, adult viewers readily recognize the shapes by name or by matching tests (Girgus & Hochberg, 1972; Murphy, 1973). Indeed, viewers recognize that the left arm was omitted if the views jump from 2 to 10 as in Fig. 18.4C. If the motion cues are eliminated and only a sequence of static corners is presented, the viewer has no basis for constructing a map from the sequence. Once given such a basis, the static sequence behaves perceptually in the same way.

This last point makes it clear that the information that the viewer contributes is not specified by the stimulus sequence itself. The maps themselves are surely "cognitive" rather than sensory in nature, in the sense that the viewer can apply them to sequences of stimuli that are grossly different in terms of stimulus energy or information. Indeed, what is special about aperture viewing, by this account, is that there is *no* plausible way to speak of mechanisms of direct response that will apply to the overall form that is fitted to the successive views. But note that the phenomenal experience is of a *perceived* form, only one part of which can actually be seen at each moment. This is presumably so because the map is supported by the sensory contributions of the successive views in the sequence. Each individual view is part of the experience as well and indeed displays figure-ground properties that depend on the role assigned each by the map to which it is being fitted: The view which is perceived as a 90-degree corner of a surface at 1 in Fig. 18.4C is perceived as a 270-degree corner at 6.

Is all of this strained and artificial, and unrelated to the conditions of normal perception? One could say with Gibson (1951, 1979) that when stimulus information is sufficient to specify the object and its layout (i.e., its form), the latter is perceived directly, whereas when information is insufficient to that end, the viewer may draw on what I have been calling mental structure. There are serious reasons to doubt, however, that stimulus information is in fact normally sufficient in Gibson's terms (Hochberg, 1981b, 1982). But even were that information normally sufficient for direct perception, we must then explain the origins of the abilities demonstrated in Figs. 18.1b, 18.4C.

Precisely when will mental maps be manifest and intrude on the direct responses (if such exist)? How were they acquired and brought into correspondence with the direct response to shape and form (if we grant such)? What sorts of processes do they comprise? What are their limitations and constraints?

With respect to when such structures are manifest: I submit that they must be ubiquitous. Occlusions and partial glimpses are surely the norm, in our perceptual ecology, and if the viewer moves to disocclude some part of the field of view, it is unlikely that retinal painting could then connect the successive glimpses. And even when they lie in full view, objects of any complexity must be treated serially (Fig. 18.3; Hochberg, 1981b), and draw on mental structures. Do we have any basis in theory or data to exclude the latter from *any* kind of perceptual response, other than assertions by direct theorists to the effect that it would be parsimonious and nonmentalistic to do so? I will return to this point.

How mental structures are acquired and related to whatever direct responses exist, and what sorts of processes they comprise, are closely related problems about which we can only speculate at present. It seems inescapable that the schematic maps depend on some irreducible degree of learning.[8]

I know of no convincing perceptual evidence that any of the proposed direct response mechanisms, larger than punctate local signs, contribute in any necessary way to form perception (except in the way of side effects, as mentioned earlier). It is surely true, however, that neural structures abound which *can* respond differentially to significant elements of form (see Braddick, Campbell, & Atkinson, 1978), and it seems extremely likely that many such networks, differing in sophistication, in degrees of abstraction, and in response speed, contribute to the experience of form perception. At some point, our perceptual systems must get all of these processes together with each other, and with the schematic map; again, some irreducible degree of learning seems inescapable.

As to the limitations and constraints on schematic maps, these are unfortunately still largely unexplored. Some of them have been touched on, and we discuss the point below.

The Two Classes of Theory and Their Present Inadequacies

Mental Structures and the Premises of Unconscious Inference

This general description of the perceptual process is not new. In its broad features, it is very much that of J. S. Mill and Helmholtz, as I summarized it earlier. So are the positions also offered by Hebb (1949), Gregory (1970), and Rock (1977). The most important reason for noting the indebtedness to the classical theory is that the latter has been severely criticized for decades, and by not facing up to the indebtedness one can too easily avoid facing up to the criticisms as well. The most important criticisms were these: The theory of unconscious inference is unparsimonious, it is mentalistic, and it is vague.

Let us briefly consider those criticisms as they apply to the notion of schematic maps.

Unconscious Inference Is Unparsimonious

The entire structure of unconscious inference and unnoticed sensations, its critics held (Köhler, 1929), was erected to save the ideas of independent sensations and specific nerve energies. By bringing the units of psychological and physiological analysis more into correspondence with perceptual experience, unconscious inference could be made an unnecessary notion. And even more important, following the examples of Hering and Mach, it was to be hoped that explanations would be found that would account for perceptual experience—for the appearances of things.

As far as the present achievements of its competitors are concerned, however, the classical theory explains a wider range of phenomena (Hochberg, 1981a, b), at least in qualitative terms, which is often all that the theory can do. And if we have reason to retain the notion of unconscious inference (or computation) and mental structure for *any* phenomena, then the argument about parsimony becomes a muddy one indeed. This is what lends importance to any demonstration that seems to demand mental structure.

The Theory Is Mentalistic

That is surely true: In this formulation, mental events have mental causes—i.e., they cannot be anchored in the stimulus information, nor in neural structures. They depend on the viewer's mental maps, and on his or her intentions to mobilize and use them. One can of course attempt to obscure this fact by constructing circumlocutions, but if we do espouse any version of this theory we had best recognize its mentalistic core and be careful of the nontrivial dangers and consequences.

The Theory Is Vague

It is easy enough to fault the classical theory for being vague and meta-theoretical. Those faults are obvious. (That's one of the reasons to keep history straight—by being presented as though it were new, a proposal can evade for a time the most well-known objections to the old phrasing.)

Consider the essential form of this explanation: We perceive by solving a sensory problem, which is to find the set of objects or events that would, under normal conditions of seeing, produce the pattern of stimulation and resulting sensations.

To say "problem solving" and let it go at that is both uninformative and misleading, for at least two reasons. First, it is too general, and all modes of presentation are not alike. When a "wire figure" like that in Fig. 18.3ci is presented all at once, it appears in depth, and the depth is spontaneously seen to reverse—*if* the viewer knows the perceptual alternatives (a condition that Girgus, Rock, and Egatz, 1977, demonstrated using normally viewed figures). Presented for aperture viewing in such a way that the intersections are present as wholes, both depth and reversal are seen; but if the piecemeal presentation is so arranged that the intersections are never present as simultaneous units, the pattern looks flat, and reversals do not occur (Hochberg, 1968). To me, this phenomenon implicates "local depth cues," as does the phenomenon discussed in connection with Fig. 18.3b. In any case, how the perceptual problem is solved depends on the details of presentation in a way that is eluded by merely saying "problem solving."

Second, it is also misleading to present problem solving or "unconscious inference" as an explanation because the premises which would make these terms meaningful are unknown. The critical case is posed by the impossible figures of Penrose and Penrose (1958). These have received a great deal of attention as curiosities, but the important lesson that they teach us has largely been ignored: The consistency constraints of the physical world are not automatically reflected in those of perception (Hochberg, 1962). The relative independence of the local depth cues evidenced in the impossible figures, in the partially transparent cube of Fig. 18.3b, and in Gillam's reports of piecemeal reversal of shadow-cast objects (1972), are of course other warnings to this same point: We do not know the premises of unconscious inference, nor the rules of mental structure.

Helmholtz (1925) did in fact offer a few premises (e.g., the relationships between distal size and distance for a given retinal extent, distal reflectance and illuminance for a given retinal illuminance, etc.). This is all right as far as it goes, but it falls short on two counts which reveal its vagueness, and a third which results from its oversimplified (and therefore unconstrained) local-sign theory of form perceptions: (a) It didn't *predict* the illusions and organizational phenomena (although it can explain them in retrospect); (b) it has no limits, e.g., why don't we see things *exactly* as they are in the world (cf. impossible figures; cf. Figs. 18.3a, b); (c) what the mind has to supply depends on the limitations of what the sensory apparatus (feature detectors, frequency channels, etc.) presents directly, and that is not now known.

What these examples show to me is that the vagueness of the Helmholtzian position is not to be cured by careful formulation: It rests on ignorance that can only be remedied by research.

Direct-Response Alternatives to Mental Structure and Their Limitations

The direct theories have been proposed to avoid this formidable set of criticisms and because observed physiology seems to invite them.

The first disappointment is (as I noted earlier) that few if any of these theories offer in any explicit fashion to explain the perceptual experience of forms and shapes. The precedent for replacing the analytic units of Helmholtzian theory is clear: In the field of color *perception*, the opponent-process model appears to have supplanted the Young-Helmholtz model. It has done so, however, not because it is so powerfully supported by physiological evidence; what made it compelling is its precise and specifiable relationship to the *appearances* of colors—their similarities, their differences, and the results of their mixtures. I have yet to see anything in the various attempts to deal with form perception that starts with even the possibility of such powerful persuasion.

Consider the proposal that we perceive form by means of a Fourier analysis of the stimulus (Blakemore & Campbell, 1969; Ginsburg, 1971; Kabrisky, Tallman, Day, & Radoy, 1970). There is no claim, for example, that we experience a particular grating whenever a particular frequency channel is activated. The primary arguments that have been offered have been the demonstrations of lowered detection thresholds after exposure to a particular stimulus (which says very little about suprathreshold phenomena) and the demonstrations of negative aftereffects to such exposures, arguing by analogy to other adaptation aftereffects (like chromatic afterimages) that the fatigue of a particular channel is thereby established. This argument is an old one (Gibson, 1937; Wohlgemuth, 1911). But there is nothing inherent in the facts of aftereffects per se that necessarily implicate sensory channels—indeed, Wundt (1902) used very similar demonstrations of shape aftereffects to prove that shape is learned! Only when such phenomena are integrated into a mechanism that helps us to understand suprathreshold appearances do they take on significant theoretical meaning for the perception of form.

There are a number of such proposals, but they are as yet quite unconnected to the general phenomena to be explained, nor is it clear how they could be expected to add up to an explanation of form perception. One example: Blakemore and Campbell proposed that the visual system extracts frequency *ratios* and that this explains how we recognize the same shape, regardless of its size. This proposal illustrates a common flaw in the genre: There are very many other stimulus features that are invariant with size; by what criterion is this explanation a better one than any of the others?[9]

Another example (out of many): Beverley and Regan (1980) proposed that mechanisms which detect size change provide for the direct perception of shape. But they also claim to have shown that changing-size detectors have a span of about 1.5 degrees. *For shapes that are larger than 1.5 degrees, therefore, we would need some quite different mechanism of shape recognition.* Not to mention the fact that we can, after all, recognize shapes even when they are stationary, and that means that we would need still another mechanism for that. Whether or not there do exist changing-size detectors, and whether they are in some circumstances involved in the perception of shape, is to me an open question. But it is surely evident that they cannot be responsible for direct shape perception in any reasonable sense: The explanation of shape perception must encompass the other means of recognizing the same shape—the final common path of shape recognition—which cannot possibly inhere in 1.5-degree changing-size detectors alone, and we would need in addition some means of bringing together the responses of the different mechanisms in order that we could recognize them as being the same.

It is not clear what these theories propose as an explanation of form perception, or to what extent they can do away with inference and mental structure even when dealing with the common constancy phenomena. These theories suffer, in a sense, by being too particular, and leaving the major problems in form perception, which they purport to address, totally untouched. Let us turn next, therefore, to the most general of direct theories.

By far the most general proposal to explain form perception as a direct response, and the least trammeled in terms of specifying possible underlying mechanisms, is the "ecological optics" approach of J. J. Gibson (1966, 1979). It is, quite simply, that our perceptual systems pick up directly whatever invariants underlie the transformations of the optic array (*not* of the retinal image, as Regan and Beverley, 1982, would have it). The limits of what the Gibsonian system is able to encompass, therefore, will lie beyond those of any more specific analysis in terms of proposed physiological channels.

Even this most general formulation, however, fails to apply to significant phenomena of form perception—it is hard to see how the class of completion phenomena that was described in connection with Figs. 18.1b, 18.4C can be attributed to a direct response by any sensory mechanism (as Gibson admits; 1979, p. 271f.). So we are again left with two different explanations for perceived shape: In some cases, the process is direct, and in others it rests on mental structure.

Both the specific and the general direct theories are clearly incomplete in a crucial way, in that the completion and aperture-viewing phenomena are not accommodated within those frameworks, making something like the central component of the Helmholtzian theory necessary in any case. For these reasons, I think that the current vaguenesses of the Helmholtzian theories are better viewed as challenges, not as condemnations.

Taking these points together, it becomes clear that the most important task for the perception psychologist is to start from the other end—to try to find those aspects of perception that cannot be attributed to sensory analysis, and to attempt to remedy our ignorance about the characteristics of mental structure. The "unconscious inference," "problem-solving" rubric cannot be used in any meaningful way unless the nature and limitations of mental structure can be specified.

Exploring the Characteristics of Mental Structure

The demonstrations that I have surveyed in this chapter should be considered in any attempt to describe the nature of schematic maps and models of mental structure. I very much doubt that they provide the complete set that must be taken into account, but they do raise a set of questions and guidelines to which other demonstrations can be addressed—what is the nature of the spatial limits implied in Figs. 18.3a, b (i.e., retinotopic, spatiotopic, or some variable depending on the way the viewer's maps are chunked)? Are the mental structures organized according to hierarchies or other arrangements that can be formalized, or are they completely at the mercy of the user's intentions? What are the time scales for retrieval? How does learning effect changes and merges in maps?

Questions of this sort rapidly become quantitative, and demonstrations will not suffice for their study. There is no reason that we are restricted to demonstrations of such phenomena. The following experiments provide two paradigms for quantitative study.

Figure 18.5A represents the first six views of a sequence of static, non-overlapping views of an outline cross. The first view is on the left, and time runs from left to right. Each view shows one corner behind an aperture. When presented in sequence, this row looks like a right angle jumping from one place to the next, or a square jumping erratically around behind the aperture. Given two such sequences, and asked whether they are the same or different, the subject's performance is, understandably enough, at chance. (We must, of course, take the appropriate precautions not to make the sequences different in more than one or two places, and to keep the differences away from the endpoints of the sequences.) These results are quite

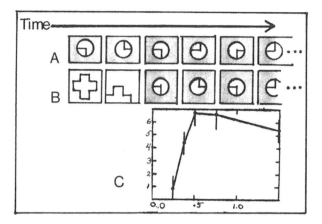

Figure 18.5. (A) Sequence of 6 static successive corners of a cross, presented without prior information of starting point or direction. (B) Same sequence, introduced by "longshots" which provide information about starting point (and hence direction). (C) Subjects are shown two sequences (under conditions A or B), one of which may be different in one view in the middle part of the sequence, and given the forced choice of "same" or "different." Ordinate is mean "rights minus wrongs"; abscissa is dwell time per view. Sequence A judgments fall on the abscissa; sequence B judgments are shown (Hochberg, 1978).

understandable: There are simply too many views for the subject to re-member as *independent* items, and to compare between sequences. If the pair of "longshots" in row B are shown before the rest of the sequence, however, these inform the viewer that the structure is a cross (an already-familiar schematic map), and what the first corner is. Now, when the subject is shown two sequences introduced by their longshots, in this manner, and a single view somewhere in the middle of one sequence is changed (and is there-fore inconsistent with the mental map that the subject is consulting), it is much easier for him or her to detect that the two sequences are different. In the graph at C, 0.0 on the ordinate represents chance (the ordinate rep-resents right judgments versus wrong judgments). The abscissa represents the dwell time per presentation of each view within the aperture. At dwell times of 333 msec or greater, the viewer is able to draw upon and test the mental map provided at the beginning of each sequence, and error rates drop ac-cordingly.

This experiment was undertaken to measure the time that it takes the viewer to access and test the map (Hochberg, 1978a). As a method, it obvi-ously can be adapted to answer other questions, e.g., are more-unfamiliar shapes stored and chunked, and how do their maps reflect any learning process that may be attempted?

It is also important to find methods of studying how viewers mobilize and apply mental structures to real objects, freely viewed, in the real world,

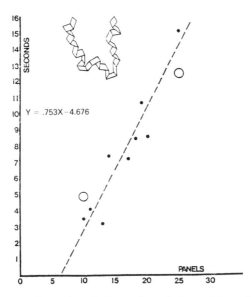

Figure 18.6. Required to judge whether ends marked 1 and 2 are the same or opposite surfaces in objects like those of Figures 18.3e, f, subjects' response time is a reasonably tight linear function of the number of panels (the points are line drawings, the unfilled circles are freely viewed 3D objects; Klopfer & Hochberg, 1981; Klopfer, 1983). The data suggest parsing by fixation of the intervening dihedrals, and glance records support that hypothesis (Klopfer, in progress).

inasmuch as it must be here that the viewer acquires the completion abilities demonstrated in the more artificial laboratory settings. Research on the class of objects in Figs. 18.3e, f shows that that is possible.

Those objects, as noted earlier, show that even with free access to full visual information about surface layout, the relationship between the parts of an object takes time to parse. Subjects who were shown objects (whether real or merely drawn) like those in Figs. 18.3e, f required more time to decide whether the two ends of the figure were the same or different sides, depending on the number of panels, as in Fig. 18.6 (Klopfer & Hochberg, 1981). This was reflected in the number of glances taken (Klopfer, 1983), even though the objects are so compact that only a glance or two will bring all of their parts into foveal vision. If there is no schema by which to decide the relationship between parts of the object on an assumptive or generated basis, the perceptual inquiry must be handled as a successive process, similar to that in aperture viewing, even when the entire object is fully and simultaneously displayed. It would be desirable to apply this technique to more-familiar objects, as well, to explicate the constraints provided by established schemas and the rates with which such information can be accessed and applied.

Acknowledgment

Part of the preparation of this paper and the research connected with Figures 18.3b–f were supported by NSF grant BNS-82-9470.

Notes

1. E.g., starting with such direct sensory responses as retinal intensity or extension, we use cues to illumination and distance to solve the regularities or structures we have learned from the world, such as (luminance = reflectance × illumination) and (object size = k [image size × distance]) to arrive at perceptions of objects' lightnesses and sizes, respectively.

2. I.e., our visual system applies the corrections that would normally lead to the constancies, in a case to which such corrections are inappropriate. Such explanations in terms of "unconscious inference" have always been popular and have recently gained in adherents in reaction to the more extravagant claims of the direct theorists and of their counterparts in sensory physiology.

3. Briefly, by regarding the figure-ground phenomenon as an inference as to which side of a contour is an object's surface and which side is further space, and by regarding the "laws of organization" as perceptual cues on which that inference is based; cf, Hochberg, 1981a.

4. Brindley (1960), echoing Fechner nearly a century before, asserts that the only perceptual response that we can use as information about physiology is the fact of failure to discriminate, i.e., that two stimuli have exactly the same appearance and must therefore have the same effects on the nervous system.

This position has some apparent plausibility when applied to what can be construed as "simple" attributes like those of homogeneous patches of color (although even then, I don't think that it will bear close inspection; see Boynton & Onley, 1962). In connection with form perception, it seems totally inapplicable: It is hard to see how we could undertake the study of form perception at all, given the fact that two displays which look very different in many ways (see Figure 18.1C4) may yet have indistinguishable shapes or forms, and it is the latter fact that will concern us. In the classical theory, this causes no problem, because form was considered a derived and "cognitive" property.

5. Note that the psychophysiological linkage was built directly into these proposals, in that the physiology was designed to account for the perceptual experience, and the experience is therefore automatically transparent (or at least translucent) to the physiology. Hering's appearance-based color theory led to the development by Hurvich and Jameson of a new form of color psychophysics in 1957 (e.g., "adjust this color until it is neither yellowish nor bluish"), and to Svaetichin's recognition that cells in the goldfish eye were behaving just as opponent-process cells should (1956), and with that guidance DeValois could find the same kinds of records in the neural activity of the monkey (1968). And Mach's description of the appearance of contours (1886) led him to lateral inhibition 50 years before Hartline (1949).

6. In those experiments, stabilized image technique, or other less heroic methods, were used to obtain the piecemeal disappearance and reappearance of a

figure that characterizes an image that is held almost stationary on the retina. The most theoretically interesting perceptual aspect of the phenomenon was that the parts of any pattern seemed to come in or go out in meaningful, geometrically "good" or familiar units (Donderi & Kane, 1965; Pritchard, Heron, & Hebb, 1960), which would be consistent with (although not required by) Hebb's conceptions of "cell assemblies" and "phase sequences." On the other hand, we cannot be sure exactly *what* fragments were perceived, inasmuch as we can only expect reports of those forms which the viewer could readily name, given that he or she experienced only a fleeting and irregular set of fluctuating appearances which would not stay for more careful description. Some attempts have indeed been made to settle the issue (Schuck & Leahy, 1966; Tees & More, 1967), but work in the area has effectively ceased without doing so.

7. Constructive, integrative, or "postretinal storage" explanations of the phenomenon, of varying descriptions, have been maintained by Zollner (1862), who discovered the phenomenon, and by Vierordt (1868), Hecht (1924), Parks (1965), Hochberg (1968), Rock (1981), and Fendrich (1982). Retinal-painting explanations were maintained by Helmholtz (1911), Anstis and Atkinson (who rediscovered the history of this problem in 1967), Vierordt (1868), Hecht (1924), Parks (1965), Hochberg (1968), Rock (1981), Fendrich (1982), Haber and Nathanson (1968), and Morgan (1981). In fact, as discussed in the text, Morgan argues that, for simple shapes, both a painting and a postretinal process must be at work; I have maintained that both processes must be at work, depending on the parameters of presentation (Hochberg, 1968, 1971); and Fendrich and Mack (1980, 1981) and Fendrich (1982) have now shown conclusively that the latter is true and have begun to establish the parameters.

8. Simplicity principles have been proposed which might account for some of the grouping and completion of Figs. 18.1b, 18.4B. I don't myself believe that any of the simplicity-encoding schemes can be sustained in the face of Fig. 18.3b, or its predecessors, the impossible figures (Hochberg, 1981a), and in any case the completion and grouping phenomena of Figs. 18.1a, b necessarily depend on some form of learning.

9. There are other flaws: The theory does not tell us at all how shape attributes are related to the power spectrum. In fact, a given set of frequency ratios is neither necessary nor sufficient for the perception of a particular form, e.g., in Figs. 18.1, 18.4, the display draws upon the viewer's ability to complete, spatially and temporally, shapes of which only part are present; in others, the frequency spectrum is greatly altered by placing additional shapes in the scene without interfering with the recognizability of a particular local shape. One solution is to think of multiple channels in each locality, rather than a retina-wide frequency spectrum analysis (see Graham, 1981), but I have not seen that spelled out so as to explain the perception of even a single object, let alone of a scene. But in any case, we are then back to something approximating Helmholtzian pieces, eked out or even superseded by global "ideas" of shape or form (see especially Fig. 18.1b) that provide the structure that frequency channels themselves are inadequate to provide. This explanation can at best offer just one more form-responding mechanism, but not even a partial solution to the general problem.

References

ANSTIS, S. M., & ATKINSON, J. (1967). Distortions in moving figures viewed through a stationary slit. *American Journal of Psychology, 80*, 572–585.

BEVERLEY, K. I., & REGAN, D. (1980). Visual sensitivity to the shape and size of a moving object: Implications for models of object perception. *Perception, 9*, 151–160.

BLAKEMORE, C., & CAMPBELL, F. W. (1969). On the existence of neurons in the human visual system selectively sensitive to the orientation and size of retinal images. *Journal of Physiology, 203*, 237–260.

BOYNTON, R. M., & ONLEY, J. W. (1962). A critique of the special status assigned by Brindley to "psychophysical linking hypothesis" of "class A." *Vision Research, 2*, 383–390.

BRADDICK, O. J., CAMPBELL, F. W., & ATKINSON, J. (1978). Channels in vision: Basic aspects. In R. Held, H. W. Leibowitz, & H. L. Teuber (Eds.), *Handbook of sensory physiology* (vol. 8). Heidelberg: Springer.

BRINDLEY, G. S. (1960). *Physiology of the retina and the visual pathway.* Baltimore: William & Wilkins.

COOPER, L. A. (1976). Demonstration of a mental analog of an external rotation. *Perception & Psychophysics, 19*, 296–302.

COOPER, L. A., & PODGORNY, P. (1976). Mental transformations and visual comparison processes: Effects of complexity and similarity. *Journal of Experimental Psychology: Human Perception and Performance, 2*, 503–514.

DEVALOIS, R., & JACOBS, G. (1968). Primate color vision. *Science, 162*, 533–540.

DONDERI, D. C., & KANE, E. (1965). Perceptual learning produced by common responses to different stimuli. *Canadian Journal of Psychology, 19*, 15–30.

FENDRICH, R. (1982). *Anorthoscopic figure perception: The role of retinal painting produced by observer eye motions.* Ph.D. dissertation, New School.

FENDRICH, R., & MACK, A. (1980). Anorthoscopic perception occurs with a retinally stabilized image. *Supplement to Investigative Ophthalmology and Visual Science, 19*, 166 (Abstr.).

FENDRICH, R., & MACK, A. (1981). Retinal and postretinal factors in anorthoscopic perception. *Supplement to Investigative Ophthalmology and Visual Science, 20* (Abstr.).

GALPER, R. E. (1970). Recognition of faces in photographic negative. *Psychonomic Science, 19*, 207–208.

GARNER, W. R., HAKE, H. W., & ERIKSEN, C. W. (1956). Operationism and the concept of perception. *Psychological Review, 63*, 149–159.

GIBSON, J. J. (1937). Adaptation with negative aftereffect. *Psychological Review, 44*, 222–244.

GIBSON, J. J. (1951). What is a form? *Psychological Review, 58*, 403–412.

GIBSON, J. J. (1959). Perception as a function of stimulation. In S. Koch (Ed.), *Psychology: A study of a science* (Vol. 1). New York: McGraw-Hill.

GIBSON, J. J. (1966). *The senses considered as perceptual systems.* Boston: Houghton Mifflin.

GIBSON, J. J. (1979). *The ecological approach to visual perception.* Boston: Houghton Mifflin.

GILLAM, B. (1972). Perceived common rotary motion of ambiguous stimuli as a criterion for perceptual grouping. *Perception and Psychophysics, 11*, 99–101.

GINSBURG, A. (1971). *Psychological correlates of a model of the human visual system.* Master's thesis, Air Force Institute of Technology.

GIRGUS, J., & HOCHBERG, J. (1972). Age differences in shape recognition through an aperture in a free-viewing situation. *Psychonomic Science, 28*, 237–238.

GIRGUS, J., ROCK, I., & EGATZ, R. (1977). The effect of knowledge of reversibility on the reversibility of ambiguous figures. *Perception & Psychophysics, 22*(6), 550–556.

GRAHAM, N. (1981). Psychophysics of spatial-frequency channels. In M. Kubovy & J. Pomerantz (Eds.), *Perceptual organization.* Hillsdale, N.J.: Lawrence Erlbaum Associates.

GREGORY, R. L. (1970). *The intelligent eye.* London: Weidenfeld.

HABER, R. N., & NATHANSON, L. S. (1968). Post-retinal storage? Some further observations on Parks' camel as seen through the eye of a needle. *Perception & Psychophysics, 3,* 349–355.

HARTLINE, H. K. (1949). Inhibition of activity of visual receptors by illuminating nearby retinal elements in the *Limulus* eye. *Federation Proceedings, 8,* 69.

HEBB, D. O. (1949). *The organization of behavior.* New York: Wiley.

HECHT, H. (1924). Die simultane Erfassung der Figuren. *Zeitschrift für Psychologie, 94,* 153–194.

HELMHOLTZ, H. L. F. VON. (1924–1925). *Treatise on physiological optics* (Vols. ii and iii). (Trans. from the 3rd German ed., 1909–1911, J. P. C. Southall, ed. and trans.). Rochester, N.Y.: Optical Society of America.

HERING, E. (1964). *Outlines of a theory of the light sense* (L. Hurvich & D. Jameson, trans.). Cambridge, Mass.: Harvard University Press (originally published in 1878).

HOCHBERG, J. (1956). Perception: Toward the recovery of a definition. *Psychological Review, 63,* 400–405.

HOCHBERG, J. (1962). The psychophysics of pictorial perception. *Audio-Visual Communication Review, 10,* 22–54.

HOCHBERG, J. (1968). In the mind's eye. Invited address, Div. 3, A.P.A., 1966. In R. N. Haber (Ed.), *Contemporary theory and research in visual perception.* New York: Appleton-Century-Crofts.

HOCHBERG, J. (1970). Attention, organization, and consciousness. In D. I. Mostofsky (Ed.), *Attention: Contemporary theory and analysis.* New York: Appleton-Century-Crofts.

HOCHBERG, J. (1971). Perception: Color and shape. In J. A. Kling & L. A. Riggs (Eds.), *Woodworth and Schlosberg's experimental psychology.* New York: Holt, Rinehart and Winston.

HOCHBERG, J. (1978a). *Motion pictures of mental structures.* Presidential address of the Eastern Psychological Association. Washington, D.C., April.

HOCHBERG, J. (1978b). *Perception.* Second edition. Englewood Cliffs, N.J.: Prentice-Hall.

HOCHBERG, J. (1981a). Levels of perceptual organization. In M. Kubovy & J. Pomerantz (Eds.), *Perceptual organization.* Hillsdale, N.J.: Lawrence Erlbaum Associates.

HOCHBERG, J. (1981b). On cognition in perception: Perceptual coupling and unconscious inference. *Cognition, 10,* 127–134.

HOCHBERG, J. (1982). How big is a stimulus? In J. Beck (Ed.), *Organization and representation in perception.* Hillsdale, N.J.: Lawrence Erlbaum Associates.

HOCHBERG, J., & GALPER, R. E. (1967). Recognition of faces: I. An exploratory study. *Psychonomic Science, 9,* 619–620.

HOCHBERG, J., & GELLMAN, L. (1977). The effect of landmark features on mental rotation times. *Memory & Cognition, 5,* 23–26.

HURVICH, L., & JAMESON, D. (1957). An opponent-process theory of color vision. *Psychological Review, 64,* 384–404.

HOLST, E. VON. (1954). Relations between the central nervous system and the peripheral organs. *British Journal of Animal Behavior, 2,* 89–91.

KABRISKY, M., TALLMAN, T., DAY, C. H., & RADOY, C. M. (1970). A theory of pattern perception based on human physiology. In A. T. Welford & L. Houssiadas (Eds.), *Contemporary problems in perception.* London: NATO Advanced Study Institute, Taylor and Francis.

KLOPFER, D. (1983). *Perception of unfamiliar complex objects and their drawings.* Ph.D. dissertation, Columbia University.

KLOPFER, D., & HOCHBERG, J. (1981). Seeing is not perceiving: Schemas are needed even when visual information is complete. *Proceedings of the Eastern Psychological Association, 148* (Abstr.).

KÖHLER, W. (1929). *Gestalt psychology.* New York: Liveright.

KÖHLER, W., & WALLACH, H. (1944). Figural after-effects: An investigation of visual processes. *Proceedings of the American Philosophical Society, 88,* 269–357.

LOTZE, R. H. (1852). *Medizinishe Psychologie oder Physiologie der Seele.* Reprinted, Göttingen: L. Horstmann, 1896.

MACH, E. (1959). *The analysis of sensations and the relation of the physical to the psychical* (Trans. by S. Waterlow from the 5th German ed., 1886). New York: Dover.

MATIN, L. (1972). Eye movements and perceived visual direction. In D. Jameson & L. M. Hurvich (Eds.), *Handbook of sensory physiology,* vol. 7 (4): *Visual psychophysics.* Heidelberg: Springer.

MILL, J. S. (1865). *An examination of Sir William Hamilton's philosophy.* London: Longman, Green, Longman, Roberts and Green.

MORGAN, M. J. (1981). How pursuit eye motions can convert temporal into spatial information. In D. F. Fisher, R. A. Monty, & J. W. Senders (Eds.), *Eye movements: Cognition and visual perception.* Hillsdale, N.J.: Lawrence Erlbaum Associates.

MURPHY, R. (1973). Recognition memory for sequentially presented pictorial and verbal spatial information. *Journal of Experimental Psychology, 100,* 327–334.

PARKS, T. E. (1965). Postretinal storage. *American Journal of Psychology, 78,* 145–147.

PENROSE, L., & PENROSE, R. (1958). Impossible objects: A special type of visual illusion. *British Journal of Psychology, 49,* 31–33.

PETERSON, M. A., & HOCHBERG, J. (1982). Attention and local depth cues affect the perception of (and not merely the reports about) real objects. *Proceedings of the Eastern Psychological Association, 97* (Abstr.).

PETERSON, M. A., & HOCHBERG, J. (1983). Opposed-set measurement procedure: A quantitative analysis of the role of local cues and intention in form perception. *Journal of Experimental Psychology: Human Perception and Performance, 9,* 183–193.

POSTMAN, L. (1954). The experimental analysis of motivational factors in perception. *Current Theory and Research in Motivation, 28,* 59–108.

PRITCHARD, R. M., HERON, W., & HEBB, D. O. (1960). Visual perception approached by the method of stabilized images. *Canadian Journal of Psychology, 14,* 67–77.

RASHEVSKY, N. (1948). *Mathematical biophysics.* Chicago: University of Chicago Press.

REGAN, D., & BEVERLEY, K. I. (1982). How do we avoid confounding the direction we are looking and the direction we are moving? *Science, 215,* 194–196.

Rock, I. (1977). In defense of unconscious inference. In W. Epstein (Ed.), *Stability and constancy in visual perception.* New York: Wiley.

Rock, I. (1981). Anorthoscopic perception. *Scientific American, 244,* 145–153.

Rock, I., & Ebenholtz, S. (1959). The relational determination of perceived size. *Psychological Review, 66,* 387–401.

Schuck, J., & Leahy, W. R. (1966). A comparison of verbal and non-verbal reports of fragmenting visual images. *Perception and Psychophysics, 1,* 191–192.

Shepard, R. N., & Metzler, J. (1971). Mental rotation of three-dimensional objects. *Science, 171,* 701–703.

Steinbach M. (1976). Pursuing the perceptual rather than the retinal stimuli. *Vision Research, 16,* 1371–1376.

Svaetichin, G. (1956). Spectral response curves from single cones. *Acta Physiologica Scandinavica, 39* (Suppl. 134), 17–46.

Tees, R. C., & More, L. K. (1967). Effect of amount of perceptual learning upon disappearance observed under reduced stimulation conditions. *Perception and Psychophysics, 2,* 565–568.

Turvey, M. T. (1977). Contrasting orientations to the theory of visual information processing. *Psychological Review, 84,* 67–88.

Vierordt, K. (1968). *Der Zeitsinn Nach Versuchen.* Tübingen: Laup.

Wallach, H., & Austin, P. (1954). Recognition and localization of visual traces. *American Journal of Psychology, 57,* 338–340.

Wallach, H., O'Connell, D. N., & Neisser, U. (1953). The memory effect of visual perception of three-dimensional form. *Journal of Experimental Psychology, 45,* 360–368.

Wohlgemuth, A. (1911). On the aftereffect of seen movement. *British Journal of Psychology,* Monograph Supplement, 1.

Wundt, W. (1902). *Outlines of psychology* (4th German ed.). Trans. by C. H. Judd. Leipzig: Englemann, 1902.

Zollner, P. (1862). Ueber eine neue art anorthoskopischer zerrbilder. *Annalen der Physik und Chemie, 117,* 477–484.

19

The Perception of Pictorial Representations

Julian Hochberg

Pictures are flat pigmented objects, very different from the objects and spaces they represent. Nevertheless, pictures must in some sense be like the things they depict, else they could not represent them. This is what has made pictorial representation of interest to generations of philosophers, psychologists, and art theorists.

The ways in which a picture can be like its object are not fully understood. We consider first the most direct way in which a picture and object might be alike: They might present the eye with the same pattern of light, or *optic array*.

Pictures as Optical Surrogates

The *picture plane* is a surface interposed between an observer and the scene that is to be represented. Light travels in straight lines. If straight lines are drawn to the viewer's eye through that plane from each point in the scene, the intersections of those lines with the picture plane provide a pattern that can (under certain ideal circumstances) be substituted for the scene without changing the pattern of light that the eye receives. The "artificial perspective" introduced or reintroduced by Brunelleschi in 1420 and codified by Alberti in 1435 provided a picture plane that could approximately meet this requirement. In Figure 19.1A (modified from a sketch by Leonardo), the picture plane (P) and three columns as viewed from above in cross-section provide the eye (E) with the same patterns of light.[1]

Two sets of theoretical issues center on this fact: (a) what it implies about the nature of knowledge and perception, and (b) what it implies about the nature of pictorial representation. These two issues must be separately considered.

Because a flat picture plane can (under certain conditions) provide the eye with approximately the same optic array as does a layout of surfaces at different distances in space, it has often been concluded that we cannot sense distance directly,[2] that we do so only by inferences drawn from characteristic

360

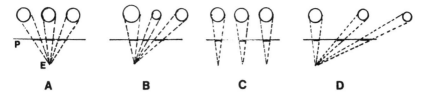

Figure 19.1.

signs, now called "depth cues," that can be provided just as well by flat pictures as by real space: Our sense data are not foolproof. Historically, this belief in turn provided an important part of the philosophical empiricist view that all our ideas about the world are learned associations of elementary sense data.

As to whether our sense data are inherently ambiguous, the answer is clear: It is indeed inescapable, and true by definition, that one cannot specify three dimensions in two (or four in three, etc.). Sense data cannot therefore provide a foolproof basis for the correct perceptions of space.

The closely related psychological question is not firmly answered: Whether space perception is wholly learned and inferred, or is at least in part a direct and innate response to the light in the eye (ambiguous though it is), is by no means settled. For the more extreme "direct theorists" in psychology, notably Gibson, Johansson, and their followers,[3] who maintain that the moving viewer perceives space and distance directly, the fact that flat, static pictures can convey three dimensions necessarily constitutes a stumbling block, as we will see. To these psychologists, pictures require special explanation, which has not yet been explicitly attempted except to suggest that children learn by experience with pictures to identify the information about objects that they contain. There are also philosophers (Goodman, Wartofsky),[4] whose views are otherwise diametrically opposed to the views of the direct theorists, to whom pictorial representation stands as a specifically acquired learned skill, because of the necessary differences between picture and object.

We consider next the similarities and differences between pictures and the things they represent.

Pictures and Their Objects

Centuries before chemistry-based photography was achieved, Leonardo discussed a discipline more general than artificial perspective that would teach the artist the devices needed to provide a surrogate of any scene: By tracing the outlines of the objects in a scene on a pane of glass interposed between the scene and his eye, the artist can discover and learn the characteristic pictorial

Figure 19.2.

depth cues. These include linear perspective, but they also include such features as interposition (Figure 19.2a–c), modeling through shading (19.2d), and aerial perspective.

These are discoveries, rather than inventions, because they are found in the optic array that is presented by real scenes in the normal world, as well as by pictures of those scenes. In this sense, pictures are like their objects. But it must always be remembered that the depth cues do not exist in the scene itself: Railroad tracks do not in fact converge to a point, far objects are not in fact interrupted by nearer ones, and paving stones are not progressively smaller with increasing distance. In this sense, pictures are very unlike their objects.

Although the depth cues are not arbitrary, and in the limiting case the picture can serve as an optical surrogate for its scene (providing the same optic array to the eye), that is not normally true: Because pictures as physical objects differ so greatly from the things they represent, it should not be surprising that they usually differ also in the light they provide the eye. Let us review some of the major differences.

If the viewer moves even slightly while viewing a real scene, near objects move more in the field of view than far ones. All the parts of the picture, on the other hand, move together. Moreover, even if the viewer remains stationary, but is not standing at the proper station point, the picture will no longer fit the scene: In Figure 19.1B, a different set of columns would be needed to provide the same optic array as does the picture plane of 19.1A when viewed from a different position. A picture can be a perfect surrogate for a scene, therefore, only if the viewer's eye is held precisely at the apex of the pyramid of rays from the thing being represented. Nevertheless, aside from a relatively few examples that use peepholes or otherwise constrained viewpoints,[5] paintings are not made to be viewed from a single place.

Second, even when the picture is viewed by a stationary observer, the degree to which the two eyes are converged and the focus of the eyes' lenses (or *accommodation*) usually provide information to the viewer that the picture is flat.

These differences between picture and scene are inherent. The resulting differences in their optic arrays can be mitigated by restricting the station point from which the picture is to be viewed (which minimizes the first set of factors) and by increasing the distance from which the picture is to be viewed (which minimizes the second set of factors). Such efforts are made only occasionally, and the differences are therefore usually substantial. Indeed, other major differences between picture and scene are usually deliberately introduced by the artist.

Of these, violations of perspective have received the most attention: Perspective violations or inconsistencies are made necessary by the fact that it is impractical to display pictures from a single viewpoint. For this reason, artists usually construct their pictures from more than one viewpoint. The most widely used method was diagrammed by Leonardo in the 1490s and is sometimes called "synthetic perspective";[6] simplifying slightly, what it amounts to is that people and familiar objects are each painted from a viewpoint perpendicular to the canvas they occupy (Figure 19.1C). The picture cannot then be optically equivalent to the scene it is intended to represent from any position of viewing, nor can the views of the objects be consistent with any unified linear perspective of walls, floors, etc. Thus the three columns must be of different cross-section when the representation on the picture plane of Figure 19.1C is viewed from any single position, as in 19.1D.

With such facts in mind, some philosophers argue, as we will see, that perspective is essentially a conventional and arbitrary device. We should add that some cross-cultural studies have reported that natives who lack schooling with Western pictures are unable to comprehend perspective information. But we should also note that in those studies (which are flawed in any case)[7] the same natives usually have no difficulties in recognizing the outline sketches of people and animals.

Perhaps the most obvious violation of the optical similarity of picture and object is the use of brush strokes, cross-hatching, and, above all, outlines. Outlines are merely ribbons of pigment on flat canvas or paper. They are routinely used to represent objects' edges, the horizons of curved surfaces, and even the modeling of form in light and shade.[8] The outline drawing is totally unlike its object, and the light that it provides is also very much unlike that provided by the object.

Are Pictures Learned Through Pictorial Experience?

Because of such differences between pictures and objects, philosophers and art theorists have argued that we must learn a language of pictures from specific experience with pictures. Given the appropriate culture, any picture can then represent any thing. This is the position maintained by Wartofsky and by Goodman, and by art theorists (such as Kepes): that there is a "language of vision" or a "language of pictorial art" that must be learned from commerce with pictures.[9] Pictures would then tell us much about pictorial culture, and something about the learning process, but not much that is general about how we perceive the world itself.

We have seen that in a strict sense the major pictorial depth cues are not arbitrary, and that in the limiting case pictures can provide the eye with the same light as the scene being represented. But because it is also true, as we have seen, that in practice most pictures are *not* optically equivalent to their objects, the argument that picture perception is a specially acquired skill must be directly faced.

First, we should note that those arguments are poorly reasoned: The fact that picture and object provide different light to the eye but elicit the same response simply does not itself imply that we must learn to perceive pictures per se. One example should suffice.

Objects have different colors because the light they provide the eye varies in its mix of wavelengths. To simplify only slightly, by means of a picture that uses only three wavelengths we can match the appearance of some scene that provides any or all of the different wavelengths in the spectrum. This is of course what the television screen does, with its palette of red, green, and blue phosphors. The scene and its picture may have no wavelengths in common yet may be indistinguishable in appearance.

This does not mean that our color responses are learned. Our response to wavelength is channeled through three types of receptors, and the different mixtures of wavelengths presented by the scene and by its picture are equivalent only because they both affect those three types of receptors in the same ways.

Thus pictures and objects that provide different light to the eye may look alike simply because they affect the sensory-perceptual system in the same ways. Considered alone, the differences between object and picture prove nothing.

The second point is not a matter of logic but of fact. Pictorial learning implies that some *pairing* of a picture (or a pictorial feature, e.g., an outline or a depth cue) and an object, or a pairing of a picture and a name, has occurred. Although such pairing of pictures and names occurs very often in the course of teaching children about the world, it is not essential to the perception of pictures. The empirical fact, known for at least twenty-two years (and known long before that to anyone who bothered to question people who had been raised in a strictly nonpictorial Orthodox Jewish village) is that even mere line drawings can be recognized on the child's first contact with them, and with no prior training whatsoever in pairing pictures with their objects or with the names of such objects.[10]

If it is in fact learned at all, therefore, the fundamental ability to perceive objects as represented by line drawings (and a fortiori, to perceive objects that are represented by other and less impoverished techniques) must be learned as an untutored result of the viewer's interaction with the world itself, and not as the result of a process even remotely like learning an arbitrary language of pictures. It follows that flat pictures must share *some* essential features with the three-dimensional world, and that in turn must tell us something about how we perceive the latter.

Any theory that holds picture perception to be a culturally acquired skill, and that does not confront this fact, can only be considered frivolous.

We are left with the question of how we recognize three-dimensional objects from their flat pictures when they differ both as objects and in the optic arrays that they provide. Before appealing to more specialized drawings, I will use the following discussion of two actual paintings to try to frame an answer to that question.

David's Sabine Women *and Cézanne's* Father

On commercial exhibition for many years,[11] David's *Sabine Women* (Figure 19.2) was designed to be viewed from many standpoints, but also to appear as realistically three-dimensional (or *illusionistic*) as possible. It sidesteps the problem of distortion that is inherent in viewing linear perspective from an eccentric station point by avoiding its use almost completely—a common solution.[12]

Other problems of station point and viewing distance were minimized by making the frontal figures approximately life-size (the warrior on the right is approximately 1.9 meters in height). This is important in an illusionistic picture for the following reason: The human figure has long been used to provide scale and distance in pictures.[13] If the picture of the human is substantially smaller than life-size, in order that it be perceived in its true size it must appear to be substantially farther from the viewer than the picture plane itself. Because the viewer's eyes must be converged and focused (accommodated) for the distance of the picture plane if the picture is to be seen at all, there would then be an inherent conflict between the latter adjustments and the indicated distance of the human figures if they were other than life-size.

Although linear perspective is virtually absent from the picture, other pictorial depth cues are used with great care to provide solidity to the foremost figures. Three classes of cue predominate: (1) Although not reproduced in Figure 19.2, shading is used to model the three-dimensional volumes of the figures (d). (2) The shading also forms contours that bound the figures (a, d) and provides *interposition* as a depth cue: In T-junctions, such as those in the circles marked (a), (b), and (c), the contour which is interrupted is shown thereby as belonging to the farther, occluded surface. (3) Aerial perspective, indicated in Figure 19.2 by making the farther figures lighter, separates the front figures from the rear expanse.

None of these cues offers strong indications as to the *amount* of depth (which helps to avoid contradictions): Interposition only shows which surface is nearer, not how much nearer it is. Although the figures represented are solid ones, the space being represented could almost be a bas-relief set against a painted background, which limits further the difference between the flatness of the picture and the depth in the scene. This is clearly not accidental: The design of the composition, and the frontal orientations both of the main figures and of geometrically familiar objects (e.g., circular and oval shields, the spear on the ground, the walls in the background, etc.) are all designed to keep the viewer's attention in the frontal plane.[14]

The frontal orientations of such geometrical forms as the circular shield serve another perceptual function as well: When the viewer stands in front of some other part of the canvas, and the round shield is therefore viewed at an angle, the ellipse that the latter then provides the eye is of course just that ellipse that would be provided by a circular shield from that viewpoint.

Contrast this with human figures, which are essentially cylindrical. If the figures were accurately painted from a single station point, their images on the canvas at greater distances from the perpendicular would have to be distorted in order to provide the viewer with the correct pattern of light at the eye (see Figures 19.1A, B). But as is standard in most paintings, the figures are painted in each case as though viewed from straight ahead. The painting employs multiple station points.

There are two reasons for that practice. The first is that viewers normally view paintings from various positions; this is particularly true in a painting on public exhibition, as this one was, with large numbers of viewers. The second, and theoretically more interesting, reason is that we normally perceive the plane of the picture, as such, perfectly well, and we can therefore perceive the shape that is in fact drawn or painted on that plane. (This is sometimes discussed in terms of "discounting" the slant of the surface,[15] but that term implies more about the process than is now known.) There is a famous sphere in Rafael's *School of Athens* that is drawn as a circle on the canvas even though it is to the right of the central ray and should therefore be painted non-circularly (cf. Figure 19.1A), but it looks spherical nonetheless, regardless of the viewer's station point.

The depth cues used in this painting (modeling, interposition, and familiar size) are not arbitrary inventions of artists or culture. They are, as noted earlier, to be found in the light to the eye that is used in seeing the scene itself; they are found in almost any photograph; and when viewing conditions are right, they should act as optical surrogates, providing the viewer with a true depth experience. (Indeed, the kinds of elements circled in 19.2a–c are proposed in computer science as the elements with which machines that are to recognize scenes in the world can parse the contours that they extract from those scenes.)[16] We even have some experimental evidence that the first two cues—modeling and interposition—operate innately in animals' spatial behaviors.[17]

Unlike linear perspective, *the depth cues used here remain largely unaffected by changes in station point*; for example, when viewed at a slant, the intersection at (c) remains a T-junction, and its spatial significance remains the same. The discrepancies between the pictorial depth cues in the optic arrays that are provided by this painting and by the scene it represents cannot be great, given the large viewing distance, the nature of the depth cues used, and the restriction of the main figures (and of the viewer's attention) to a zone close to the picture plane. The differences between picture and scene must be very largely those of form and of the nonpictorial cues (e.g., binocularity).

The forms, as in all pictures in synthetic perspective, deviate from what they should be if the picture were painted from a single viewpoint (cf. Figure 19.1D), but while such distortion might be noticeable, especially since it increases in a systematic gradient each side of the straight ahead, the solid forms that are to be depicted by those images are not thereby changed past recognition. Nearby distortions, which are minimal, should not be noticeable. Only the larger distortions of the more peripheral figures should be. Thus, if one is standing about twenty-five feet away and directly in front of the circular shield, the flat picture of the thigh of the bearded figure on the left is only slightly narrower than it would have to be to present the same outline as would a cylinder (it is approximately 98 percent of what it should be).

So far as binocular cues to the picture's flatness are concerned, a complex picture emerges. At twenty-five feet, a small feature, about one inch in depth (a nose, an ornament, etc.), would provide the two eyes with views that differ only slightly, and the failure of the picture to provide that difference would probably not be noticeable. The depth of a head or a limb is another matter, however: That should provide a difference of about 4 seconds of arc, which under good seeing conditions should be detectable, and the absence of that difference could reveal that the limb is really a flat pattern and that its apparent modeling is only a painted gradient from light to dark.

To stationary viewing, the painting is therefore *locally* equivalent to a tridimensional scene in some places but not in others. What I in fact perceive, when I look at the painting itself, supports this analysis very closely. Viewed from approximately twenty-five feet, with one eye closed and the other's field of view restricted by a short tube to about one foot of picture area, the figures do not appear flat, just so long as I do not attend to some edge that should provide a large depth difference if it were real (e.g., the top edges of either shield). That is true even without the tube, and with binocular vision, so long as I keep my attention focused on a small region near some convincingly modeled but shallow depth.

To the extent that my personal observation will serve, David's technique has provided a surrogate for solid tridimensional figures. Under restricted conditions, the devices serve to produce a circumscribed but patent impression of depth.

Can we say, then, that in general we recognize the figures represented in this (and other) pictures because the cues lead us to perceive those figures as solid people and objects, in three dimensions, rather than as the flat patterns that they are?

That is not a reasonable description of the process. Even in this illusionistic painting, the apparent tridimensionality that I can maintain with fixed head and careful deployment of my attention dissipates entirely under normal viewing, yet the represented forms do not become one bit less recognizable when the picture then looks flat. Although the depth cues are capable of providing a depth impression, therefore, the latter does not seem to be instrumental in the representation process: So far as I am aware, the picture need not look three-dimensional in order to represent three-dimensional things.

Perhaps awareness is a poor informant here: It might be that three-dimensional perception is going on even though the picture overall looks flat. That might happen as follows: In unrestricted viewing, the eye moves in brief glances or *fixations*. The eye itself is sensitive to fine detail only in the fovea, which is a small region in the center of the retina (the receptive tissue, at the back of the eye, on which the image is focused); in the surrounding peripheral regions, only large features can be discerned. Within each glance, therefore, only foveal vision can register the smaller patterns of interposition and modeling, and the visual situation is therefore momentarily similar to that in which I looked fixedly through a tube at a good cue to shallow depth. One might propose, therefore, that narrow and fragmentary depth impressions occasioned by these foveal glimpses are embedded in the overwhelmingly flat perception of the picture and, although not noticed as such by the viewer, serve as the basis by which the solid figures are recognized.

Might we say, therefore, that we normally recognize the tridimensional figures in a picture because pictures are like their objects in what the fovea retrieves from the momentary glance?

That does not seem to me to be a reasonable description of the process, either. A comparison with Cézanne's painting of his father, which deliberately attempts to make most of the pictorial depth cues unavailable to foveal viewing, will help me to make the point.

Cézanne's painting is similar to David's in many ways. It too is composed so as to emphasize the frontal plane; it too avoids perspective and draws on interposition and modeling as its depth cues; it too is clearly intended to represent its object in an immediately accessible form. But it is unlike the David in an extremely important way: Painted sixty-seven years after the David, and over a decade after photographs began to establish their pictorial hegemony, the Cézanne is obviously not intended to be perceived as a three-dimensional object. Viewed from approximately eighteen feet, the painting looks unassailably flat wherever I rest my gaze. This is of course what Cézanne wanted, and it is useful to compare his depth cues with those in the David.

The flatness is achieved in several ways, the most important being the manner in which modeling and interposition are used. Modeling is restricted to a few critical regions (e.g., left side of face, newspaper, trousers), and in those regions is produced by salient patches of paint rather than by smooth gradients from dark to light. Such gradients are absent by decision, not from ignorance: They had been practiced for centuries, were central to such illusionistic paintings as David's, and were made evident in exquisite if automatic rendering by the many photographs that had become widely available since the 1850s.

Interposition is deliberately avoided in some places in which its use would be natural. Cézanne aligns the edges of areas that lie at different represented distances, not only thereby avoiding interposition but also using what Gestalt psychologists later called the "law of good continuation" in order to make the two areas appear to lie in the same plane (Figure 19.3a–c). (That "law" states that we tend to organize our perceptions so as to avoid interrupting smoothly continuing lines or curves.)[18] In the most salient example of this, the edge of the doorway is not quite aligned with the figure's shoulder at (d). Regardless of Cézanne's reasons for keeping these contours slightly offset in this way, it is clear that he also wanted to achieve good continuation between them, which was done by inserting a thin section of intermediate color to fill the gap at (d).

Where interposition is actually used in this painting, it is often carefully neutralized. The abrupt interruption of the rearmost line is avoided by carrying it around in an arc which continues along, and merges with, the nearer contour (e, f). This was half a century before Gestalt psychologists formulated this "law," and Cézanne's painstaking use of it to overcome interposition is further support (but not certain proof, of course) of the view that neither good continuation nor interposition is a learned convention. It should be noted that in his efforts to flatten the canvas, Cézanne did not invent a new set of visual terms: The flattening is accomplished by specific, nonarbitrary, and understandable modifications of the very same depth cues that David had employed to provide depth.

I believe that the scale in which these flattening devices are painted shows them to be aimed primarily at foveal vision. In the impressionist paintings that preceded Cézanne, because the picture consists of discrete dabs of paint, objects' forms are discernible in peripheral vision but dissolve into flecks of color in foveal vision. (By disarming the fovea in this way, the impressionist painting shows the viewer only what he or she would have seen in the first moment of inspection of some scene, before the accumulation of

Figure 19.3.

successive foveal glances at the world would fill in the details that are missing in the first impression.)[19] In the present painting, the arcs of good continuation that are used to neutralize the cue of interposition, and the patches of paint that provide the modeling, are generally too small to be seen in peripheral vision, so the depth cues retain some effect when viewed peripherally. In foveal vision, however, the depth cues lose their spatial significance, and it seems clear to me when looking at the canvas that Cézanne intended to make the canvas look flat wherever the gaze is directed.

Unlike many of his successors, Cézanne provided a perfectly accessible picture of a recognizable, solid person and his surroundings. Given his successful intention to keep the canvas looking flat within the momentary foveal glance, we can reject the notion that it is the latter that provides the three-dimensional content for recognizing solid figures in flat paintings. The modeling and interposition in the painting do work in peripheral vision to provide some impression of solidity to the newspaper, trousers, and shoes when these are not looked at directly, however, so perhaps another version of that notion might be entertained. But the depth cues in the drawing of Figure 19.3 itself are still more depleted, and that drawing looks perfectly flat all over, both to foveal and peripheral vision, yet Cézanne's *Father* is clearly and easily recognizable as representing a solid figure.

A picture need not look at all three-dimensional in order to represent a three-dimensional object. But this is not because it draws upon a learned "language of pictures." It is my knowledge about trousers, shoes, and newspapers that allows me to recognize their representations in so impoverished a sketch; it is my knowledge about the world, and not my knowledge about pictures, that enables me to perceive the former as represented by the latter.

In order to see how such knowledge about the world can be applied to pictures, we must consider the processes by which we perceive the world itself, and then speculate about what they might share with picture perception.

Glances at the World and at Pictures of It

In the direct theories of perception, mentioned at the beginning of this paper, the perception of surfaces in space (their distances, slants, and forms) are held to be direct responses to the changing patterns of light that are received by a moving observer. The static two-dimensional optic array (and the resulting image on the retina) is held to be irrelevant to the perception of objects and their forms. Objects are perceived directly (and therefore recognized) in terms of their three-dimensional structure. This belief is what makes the direct theories unable to deal with picture perception (despite occasional claims to the contrary). The forms of the flat pigmented patches on the canvas are not those of the objects being represented; how then are they recognized?

In fact, the two-dimensional array is *not* unimportant in perception: It is the field in which eye movements occur. Eye movements are the most ubiquitous of the behaviors that are guided by vision (more than 10,000 guided movements per day). They occur for an important reason: The eye must be directed at new places in order to glimpse details from more than one tiny part of the world or picture. The eye does not merely glide at random: It jumps "ballistically" to some definite place about which the viewer has some visual question. Four things that are important to our present discussion follow from this.

First, no matter how flat the picture looks, and how solid the scene it represents, the two-dimensional relations that determine what any eye movement will disclose—its beginning and end—are essentially the same if they subtend the same angle at the eye. *The picture and scene are very similar,* so far as the gross aspects of this fundamental process of perceptual inquiry are concerned.

Second, we do not see everything in detail at once. Consider then the argument that picture perception is a specifically learned skill: That argument rested on the unstated assumption that the picture necessarily comprises a perceptual whole, and that unless pictures were arbitrary, inconsistencies in perspective (for example) should have strong perceptual consequences. The fact is, however, that inconsistencies do not necessarily have any perceptual consequences, drastically weakening that argument. We have known since the so-called impossible figures of Penrose and Penrose, however, and since Escher's graphic preoccupation with them,[20] that we have great tolerance for certain pictorial inconsistencies. In Figure 19.4A, for example, the object at 1 looks three-dimensional, and its inconsistency is not evident[21] until we break the good continuation at 2.

Nor is this tolerance true only for picture perception. The interposition that is shown at intersection 2 in Figure 19.4B should completely fix the orientation of the cube; nevertheless, if you gaze at intersection 1 for a moment, you will see the vertical line—which must be to the rear, in order to be consistent with intersection 2—reverse its position in depth and appear in front of the horizontal line. Moreover, what is true of this picture is true as well of real cubes of wire and cardboard constructed in this way.[22] Because

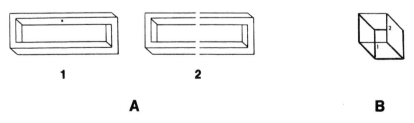

1   2

A   B

Figure 19.4.

the physical world itself is usually consistent, our perceptual tolerance of inconsistency is not normally made evident to us as it is in these figures.

Third, the process of integrating information from successive glances is an *elective act*. The viewer is in no way compelled to look at all parts of any picture (or at a real scene in the world) or to test its consistency. This point, taken with the last one, vitiates the conclusions that such philosophers as Goodman and Wartofsky draw from the facts of pictorial inconsistency. The viewer need not even be aware of them, or take them into account if he is.

Last, given the fact that eye movements are made in order to answer visual questions, the viewer must keep some account of the body of "questions and answers." Such an account comprises a "schema" of the object or scene. When looking at intersection (a) in Figure 19.2, I know that a rightward glance would probably disclose a hand; the parallel contours that I find there then fit that expectation, and I can marvel at how every detail of shape and shade that I might look for in a hand is in fact available to be seen. In general, the schemas that are brought to the integration of successive glances at a picture are expectations about objects in the world. In some cases, the schemas are of specific and familiar objects; in others, they are such more general expectations of how straight edges and smooth curves of drapery, limbs, or walls continue, and how shadows grade on curved or angled surfaces. In addition, such shadow gradients are depth cues, whether innate or learned from the environment. When viewed with the constraints I outlined in connection with the David painting, therefore, they are capable of providing restricted impressions of depth, embedded in the overall perception that the canvas is flat, which characterize illusionistic pictures.

I must admit that there are arbitrary graphic symbols and patterns that one learns from experience with heraldry, say, or from electrical circuit diagrams. But these are not generally accessible representations. What makes the pictorial representation accessible and nonarbitrary is that it draws on the characteristic cues that are provided to all viewers by the two-dimensional optic array within which we direct our glances when we seek to obtain detailed information about different parts of the three-dimensional world.

Our act of fitting the visual schemas we have learned from the world to the nonarbitrary patterns that are presented by the pictures themselves is what enables a picture to fulfill its specifically pictorial function.[23]

Otherwise, it's not a picture.

Notes

1. Figure 19.1 is adapted from part of a diagram presented by Leonardo in 1492. That, and the contributions of Brunelleschi and Alberti, are discussed at length by John White, *The Birth and Rebirth of Pictorial Space* (Boston: Boston Book and Art Shop, 1967).

2. Alhazen, 1572, and Peckham, 1504, as discussed by White, *Pictorial Space*, pp. 126–129. The most systematic treatment, of course, was by George Berkeley, *Essays Towards a New Theory of Vision* (Dublin: Rhames, 1709). For a recent review of the subsequent perceptual consequences of that treatment, see Julian Hochberg, "Sensation and Perception," in Eliot Hearst, ed., *The First Century of Experimental Psychology* (Hillsdale, N.J.: Lawrence Erlbaum Associates, 1979).

3. James J. Gibson. *The Ecological Approach to Visual Perception* (Boston: Houghton Mifflin, 1979); Gunnar Johansson, "Visual Space Perception Through Motion," in Alexander Wertheim, Willem Wagenaar, and Herschel Leibowits, eds., *Tutorials on Motion Perception* (New York: Plenum, 1982).

4. Norman Goodman, *Languages of Art: An Approach to a Theory of Symbols* (Indianapolis: Bobbs-Merrill, 1968); Marx Wartofsky, "Picturing and Representing," in Calvin Nodine and Dennis Fisher, eds., *Perception and Pictorial Representation* (New York: Praeger, 1979).

5. Brunelleschi's first demonstration, using a peephole, is discussed at length by White, *Pictorial Space*: a detailed treatment of Pozzo's ceiling in the Church of St. Ignatius in Rome, which is designed to be viewed from a single place on the floor, is to be found in M. H. Pirenne, *Optics, Painting and Photography* (Cambridge, England: Cambridge University Press, 1970).

6. See White, *Pictorial Space*, pp. 209–215.

7. These studies are cited and criticized in the following reviews: Julian Hochberg, "Perception: II. Space and Movement," in J. W. Kling and Lorrin Riggs, eds., *Woodworth and Schlosberg's Experimental Psychology* (New York: Holt, Rinehart & Winston, 1971); Rebecca K. Jones and Margaret A. Hagen, "A Perspective on Cross-Cultural Picture Perception," in Margaret A. Hagen, ed., *The Perception of Pictures*, vol. 2 (New York: Academic Press, 1980).

8. Julian Hochberg, "Pictorial Functions and Perceptual Structures," in Hagen, *Perception of Pictures*.

9. Goodman, *Languages of Art*, and Wartofsky, "Picturing and Representing," are fairly straightforward here, as is Georgi Kepes, *Language of Vision* (Chicago: Theobald, 1944).

10. Julian Hochberg and Virginia Brooks, "Pictorial Recognition as an Unlearned Ability," *American Journal of Psychology* 75 (1962): 624–628.

11. Anita Brookner, *Jacques-Louis David* (London: Chatto & Windus, 1980), p. 139.

12. Ingrid Söström, "Quadratura: Studies in Italian Ceiling Painting," *Acta Universitatis Stockholmiensis, Stockholm Studies in the History of Art* 30 (1978).

13. Of all of the depth cues, the known size of a familiar object (such as a person) alone *demands* an explanation in terms of learning; the other cues are conceivably innate. Whether this cue is effective in producing perceptions of distance, rather than intellectual judgments or calculations, has therefore been an issue of some concern. For the most recent review of this issue, see Julian Hochberg, *Perception* (Englewood Cliffs, N.J.: Prentice-Hall, 1978), pp. 116–120.

14. Or at any rate it was long believed that such compositions have that effect; cf. White, *Pictorial Space*.

15. See Pirenne, *Optics*.

16. A. Guzman, "Decomposition of a Visual Scene into Three-Dimensional Bodies," in A. Graselli, ed., *Automatic Interpretation and Classification of Images* (New York: Academic Press, 1969).

17. Related to the question of shadow gradients and modeling, we have chicks' unlearned "perceptual assumption" that illumination comes from above: W. Hershberger, "Attached-Shadow Orientation Perceived as Depth by Chickens Reared in an Environment Illuminated from Below," *Journal of Comparative and Physiological Psychology* 73 (1970): 407–411. With respect to interposition: The protective coloration that serves to hide animals from each others' eyes works in large part by providing marks that will help to avoid the interruption by the animal's body of some edge or contour in the background. And a recent discussion of occlusion is given by Claes von Hofsten and Karin Lindhagen, "Perception of Visual Occlusion in 4½-month-old Infants," *Uppsala Psychological Reports* 290 (1980).

18. Max Wertheimer, "Untersuchungen zur Lehre von der Gestalt. II," *Psychologische Forschung* 4 (1923): 301–350.

19. Julian Hochberg, "Some of the Things That Pictures Are," in Calvin Nodine and Dennis Fisher, eds., *Views of Pictorial Representation: Making, Perceiving and Interpreting* (New York: Praeger, 1979); "Pictorial Functions and Perceptual Structures," in Hagen, *Perception of Pictures.*

20. The class of impossible figures of which Figure 19.4A1 is a member was described by L. S. Penrose and R. Penrose, "Impossible Objects: A Special Type of Visual Illusion," *British Journal of Psychology* 49 (1958): 31–33. This specific figure, which is particularly amenable to experimental manipulation, is from Julian Hochberg, "In the Mind's Eye," in Ralph N. Haber, ed., *Contemporary Theory and Research in Visual Perception* (New York: Holt, Rinehart & Winston, 1968).

21. Experimental research is needed here, but to my eye, it is more difficult to see that the left and right sides of 19.4A1 are inconsistently oriented than that they are oppositely oriented in 19.4A2.

22. Mary A. Peterson and Julian Hochberg, "The Opposed-Set Measurement Procedure: A Quantitative Analysis of the Effect of Local Cues and Intention in Form Perception," *Journal of Experimental Psychology: Human Perception and Performance* 9 (1983): 183–193.

23. Hochberg, "Pictorial Functions"; Dan Lloyd, *Picturing*, doctoral dissertation, Columbia University, 1982.

20

Movies in the Mind's Eye

Julian Hochberg and Virginia Brooks

Most writers on film, and most filmmakers, need no science. But any serious discussion of whether the medium was used effectively or artistically in any instance requires some understanding of how we perceive and remember moving pictures, and that must derive from research: Introspection will not serve. Scattered aspects of cognitive science have begun to appear, therefore, in recent writings on film.[1] On the other side of the aisle, students of perception and visual memory cannot afford to ignore moving pictures, but until recently they have mostly confined their attention to low-level motion phenomena, as have introductory film texts. The latter, if they write at all about perception, still proclaim that we perceive motion from successive still frames because of (heavens protect us!) "persistence of vision."[2] In any case, stroboscopic motion is only a small part of the perception of visual events, which is what film is about.

In this essay we reexamine the cognitive systems that contribute to the visually informative and artistically important characteristics of film and tape, trying to keep both the science and the art in view.

Depicting Events in Moving Pictures

There are three steps to the depiction of events in moving pictures: low-level vision, relational parsing, and action schemas. We will look at each separately.

Movement as Primitive Sensory Response

A continuous motion in the world is, of course, captured by successive displaced images on film (or their video equivalent). For most events, these displacements are small and within the range of the low-level sensory receptors of the visual system; these respond identically to the small displacements on the screen and to the differences provided from one moment to the next by smooth physical motion in the world. Recent studies of this system offer an increasingly important window on the underlying neurophysiology, and reveal some surprising phenomena (for example, reversals of direction).[3] This low-level response is preemptive and "unintelligent." Notably, it occurs between nearby successive contours regardless of what objects they belong to (see, for example, Fig. 20.3A), thereby causing many "bad cuts" (which result from this fundamental displacement-detection mechanism, rather than some violation of cinematic "grammaticality"). Many techniques aimed at achieving "seamless" editing work by avoiding such unwanted apparent motion between noncorresponding objects. In the time of Eisenstein, however, and especially in the New Wave, such visual jolts became desirable, although (or because) they slow the viewer's comprehension and make the medium itself more intrusive.

Although vision psychologists and neurophysiologists sometimes write as though these low-level mechanisms account "directly" for perceiving motion, which would, if it were true, make it easy to explain and predict what people will see, it is simply not true: We usually perceive movements very different from the displacements in the eye or on the screen. Indeed, were it not for these differences, films as we know them would not be possible, as we see next.

Framework-Relative Paths of Motion

We perceive (approximately) the framework-relative paths of motion, and not the displacements on the screen which determine low-level motion.

An object may be *perfectly stationary* on the screen and yet it will appear irresistibly to move if given a moving framework (Fig. 20.1Ai) or background (Fig. 20.1Aii), and the actual motions of the frameworks or backgrounds

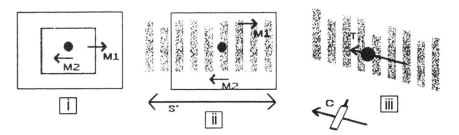

Figure 20.1A. i. Although it is perfectly stationary on the screen (indicated by the outermost rectangle), the black dot appears very strongly to move leftward (M2) if a large object, the background, or the framework actually moves rightward (Ml). ii. If the background continues to enter on the left edge of the screen and scroll off the right edge, for a total distance (s′) that is larger than the screen, the induced movement (M2) can continue as long as the filmmaker wishes it to. iii. Such scenes are usually made by moving the camera, C, in sync with the target, T, in a tracking or pan shot.

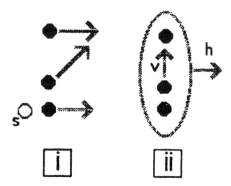

Figure 20.1B. With three dots moving on the screen, as shown by the arrows in i, a very different event is perceived, especially if only the dots are visible (that is, black dots in limbo). ii. The center dot is seen in vertical motion (arrow v) between the two end dots. If the surroundings are not completely featureless (that is, if the edges of the projection screen are dimly discernible, or there is a stationary dot, like that at s), the entire set of dots may be detected as moving horizontally (arrow h).

themselves are often not noticeable. This is part of a rich body of phenomena known as *induced motion.*[4] Something akin to Fig. 20.1Ai happens outside of the laboratory when the eye tracks a moving object in a *pursuit movement* or when a camera acts similarly in a *pan* or *track* shot (Fig. 20.1Aiii).[5] Thanks to this phenomenon, a continuous motion can be presented over a space s' that may be many times larger than the screen, in the same way that the movements of the viewer's head and eyes provide a wider prospect than the limits of gaze within any glance. The screen would be stage-bound, were it not for this resource. Similarly, the parts of an object or group of objects moving in one direction on the screen may instead be irresistibly seen as moving in another (Figs. 20.1Bi, 20.1Bii).

Neither of these demonstrations is only about dots in the laboratory. The phenomenon of Fig. 20.1A reappears in Fig. 20.1C: The rightward movement of a dancer across the screen (M2) is lost if filmed in limbo (with little or no framework), as in Fig. 20.1Ci. Indeed, the movement is perceived as *leftward* (M4) if the corps, as background, moves rightward on the screen (Fig. 20.1Cii). The phenomenon of Fig. 20.1B reappears in Fig. 20.1D: At i, we show the first and last frames in a dance movement across the stage; without a strong background, the curve that the lifted dancer's arm describes across the screen in Fig. 20.1Di is not perceived, and only the arm's movement relative to the framework provided by the moving body is perceived. Intermediate frames are shown at ii, in which the curved movement is essentially lost in any case because the dancers are kept centered by a pan shot.

In analyzing a narrative fiction film, such a microscopic approach makes it difficult to get back to the macroscopic content; in films of dance and other choreographed spectacles, and indeed in any film in which the visual content

Figure 20.1C. i. A dancer or actor actually moving rightward in space (M2) against a weak or featureless background, but tracked by the camera so as to remain stationary on the screen, will in fact appear stationary. ii. The same dancer, against a background (here, the corps) with a net rightward screen movement (that is, M3 > M4), will appear to move leftward (M4), against her true direction of movement in space.

is defined by the subject, the camera and the editing are at once relatively open to visual study and critical to an appreciation of the film. Such detailed study of the movements seems as important to an understanding of the film as it is to our understanding of cognitive process.

And that leads us to ask: If the movements we perceive may thus be very different from those we can measure on the screen, how can we say in advance what they will be? As part of a more general solution, it has been argued that the background is specified as stationary in the world because it remains otherwise invariant while moving as a whole, and that the relative motion between object and surround is attributed to the eye or camera. If that is true, then a layout of space equal to $s' = ml \times t$, where s', m are as labeled in Fig. 20.1A and t is m's duration, is also specified, as is the apparent velocity m2 of the target (although really stationary on the screen). A similar explanation has been offered for Fig. 20.1Bii, in terms of the vector that remains after subtracting the component, h, that is shared by all the moving dots.[6]

This sounds like an automatic prescription, but it cannot serve as such. For one thing, there is always a stationary visible framework—the edge of the screen—which by the preceding analysis should restrict our perceived motions to the physical displacements within that framework. But we have seen that that does not happen. Indeed, under normal viewing conditions (that is, not in limbo), both on stage and on the screen, the viewer sees the graceful curve as well as the body-relative movement (in Fig. 20.1Di), in some manner hard to describe and even harder to measure. The distinction between these two motions is analogous to the distinction between the 3D spatial layout represented in a picture and its pictorial composition: The former is viewpoint-independent, whereas the latter, which greatly affects

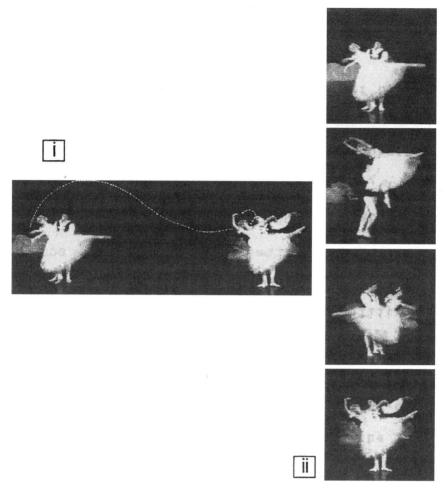

Figure 20.1D. As in Fig. 20.1B: Although the dancer's hand traces the curve across the screen as drawn in i, that curve is not seen if there is no background; the hand movements relative to the body (intermediate frames are shown in ii) are seen instead.

the feeling and aesthetics of the view, depends very much on the viewpoint of eye or camera.

Which movement actually predominates in any filmed passage seriously affects the aesthetics of the passage. The balance depends, among other things, on where the viewer attends. For example, a stationary background spot aligned as at s with the diagonal motion in Fig. 20.1Bi will, if the viewer stares at it, make the diagonal movement much more visible.[7] The filmmaker learns by trial and error—not by any principles in the production handbook—how to obtain the desired effect.

How can we know in advance what will occur and why?

A set of perceptual theories, each of which uses quite different terms (unconscious inference, perceptual logic, internalization of the laws of physics, and ecological realism), are all versions of Helmholtz's likelihood principle:[8] *We perceive that which would in our normal life most likely have produced the effective sensory stimulation we have received.*

That principle must surely be at least approximately true, or we could not survive. It is probably a good source of intuitions for filmmakers and other visual artists. But within this set of theories lie two extremely different subsets. Theories of the first class assert that some internal mental representation of the event or scene is formed within the viewer's mind, in response to the movements on screen and in the eye; such theories are frequently accused of being uneconomical and mentalistic (a term with pejorative overtones). To us, a more damaging aspect is that such theories are not predictive, because they have not addressed the nature of the representations they postulate in general; or the nature of what those representations are like in the case of moving pictures in particular.

A second kind of theory of visual perception and cognition seems much more hard-headed, specific, and based in the real world (that is, more "behaviorist"), referring only to the information offered the viewer, and to what that information specifies about the world: the extent of the surface defined in Fig. 20.1Bii, for example, or when and where we will make contact with an approaching surface or a thrown ball. In this class of theory, it may be thought that we as scientists or as moving picture craftsmen need only to know the relevant principles of physics to know what people will perceive.[9]

Don't count on it. Whether or not such nonmentalistic or physics-specific theories will ever be good or useful replacements for their mentalistic counterparts for any purposes (and we do not think they will), they fail us here for two reasons that should tell us much about visual cognition quite generally. First, they work by defining motion in a space-time coordinate system, with time as a dimension. It is easy to do this when discussing physical events that can be predicted by physical laws, such as the distance s' traversed in Figure 20.1Aii. But after some brief time, the space and movement of film gone by can exist only in a fallible viewer's limited working memory, and they do not remain unchanged somewhere simply because they were "specified" by information that has flowed past on the screen. Second, motions that follow simple physical laws that we can hope to formulate do not make up much of moving pictures in any case.

Consider the first point, that is, the role of perceptual memory as opposed to physical specification. In situations like Fig. 20.1Aii, in which a motion m1 brings some offscreen surface into view, viewers can judge when remembered objects, currently beyond the screen, will come into sight. Yet experimental measures show that such space in the mind's eye is compressed when out of sight, that is, $s' < m \times t$.[10] Studies in which an object moving at some velocity goes out of view for some brief period t, and the viewer reports whether it was early or late when it reappeared (like testing the timeliness of the return from a cutaway, or of a strolling actor's reappearance from behind an occluding object), found the ability lost within 1,200 msec.[11] In describing what the viewer gains from a moving picture, both of these kinds of study reveal mental representations (effective memories) of motion and of constructed space, rather than merely the specified physical variables. The former is thus not merely a more mystical phrasing of the latter: They have different properties. But it is even more important to us that represented movements and extents do not long outlast their presentation on the screen.

This means that, very shortly after it has occurred, the representation of an event, or of a part of an event, is different from the perception obtained during the event itself. Some specific physical information about space and time is lost with time. We assume that such losses occur as well after each change in direction or speed, or after each cutaway or change in scene. That is, unless the viewer has available some mental structure or schematic event into which the segments take their place, *and from which they can be regenerated when needed*, the continual movement in space becomes indeterminate in memory.

This, in turn, is what gives the second point—that most moving pictures are not assemblies of simple physical trajectories—its theoretical and practical importance.

Beyond Physical Trajectories: Represented Goals and Intentions

The fact is that we must parse most of the motion patterns we encounter in terms of purposeful acts, not in terms of physically specifiable trajectories. They are not the same, in that the identical act can be expressed and represented by very different physical motions. In Fritz Heider and Marianne Simmel's film (Fig. 20.2), a triad of geometric figures interacts in a rich social narrative, across more different trajectories than viewers can remember if they try to do so in terms of geometric paths, but which they can remember far better as purposive acts within a story structure.[12]

The story structure encodes the too-numerous trajectories as a smaller number of more distinctive and familiar, purposeful actions. These are the same units by which the motions of people and animals achieve recognizable organization (and which are perhaps learned by infants even before they learn simpler physical motion). All of the unrelated movements are immediately meaningful if the viewer has undertaken to construe them as purposeful and expressive actions.

The Heider and Simmel film itself was an explicit request for a new look at social psychology, at narrative, and at visual cognition. Since it appeared in 1944, social psychologists have shown that viewers agree consistently about the *breakpoints* (the bounds of staged purposive actions); they have also shown that sequences assembled from breakpoints alone are better comprehended

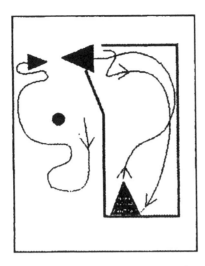

Figure 20.2. Motion paths of an animated story film by Heider and Simmel. Cast: small circle, large and small triangles (the gray triangle marks a particularly lengthy pause).

than those assembled from intermediate stills. (For this reason, films seem a natural joint venture for film theory and social psychology.)[13]

The physically defined (nonmentalistic) approaches to visual cognition say nothing about such animate events. But even if they did, we should have to abandon these approaches, designed to make mentalistic accounts unnecessary, when we consider how cuts are used in moving pictures.

Cuts, Story Structure, and the Nature of Movies in the Mind's Eye

It is not clear that any of the more mentalistic likelihood theories can be put in working order as theories about the mind. In general, although after the fact they can plausibly explain why something was seen as it was, they cannot successfully say *in advance* what movement will be perceived, or what the mental representations are like. The worst failure is that virtually all likelihood theorists (mentalistic *or* physicalistic)[14] depend on the *rigidity principle*, that is, that we perceive just that rigid 3D object which fits the changing 2D pattern of light in the eye or on the screen. This assumption can make it relatively easy to predict what surfaces or jointed structures (like people and animals) should be perceived, and why they are perceived; but the assumption is wrong. It has long been contradicted by laboratory demonstrations.[15] And it really does not apply to normally viewed moving pictures, in which changes in camera lens (close-up, longshot, and so on) and audience seating make it almost certain that *only a nonrigid and deforming object* could provide a geometrical fit to the moving image on the screen.[16] (Indeed, it seems likely to us that familiar animate bodily movements, and perhaps others as well, are perceived as opportunistic and therefore elastic fits to the motions of the extremities, rather than as rigid motions anchored at their joints, as has been claimed.)[17]

There are many other problems that current accounts of mental representation leave unaddressed.[18] That is unfortunate, because as we see next the use of cuts in moving pictures poses a clear need for a theory that is specific about the nature of mental representations of events.

We take one last stab at a nonmentalistic account, and then a first step toward a mentalistic one.

Overlapping and Nonoverlapping Cuts

In most film and video, events and layouts are conveyed by both motion-based information and by discontinuous shots. Either could be used exclusively, but that is only rarely done. The Heider-Simmel film (like the scenes in Hitchcock's *Rope*) lies at one extreme, a single continuous shot, with no change in camera viewpoint. At the other extreme, Chris Marker's *La Jetée* (1964) consists of cuts between some 424 separate shots in 27 minutes, *all but one of which contains no subject movement at all.* (There are a few camera movements within still pictures.) It is an engrossing visual narrative, despite the absence of movement. What is important to us is that *it is essentially a normal film in immediate memory, even as one watches it.* And it is hard to see how one might hope to discuss an event or a layout as communicated in this way without assuming some contribution by the viewer, some mental representation.

Overlapping cuts (Fig. 20.3A) might conceivably challenge this assumption because they potentially specify physically how the camera or eye

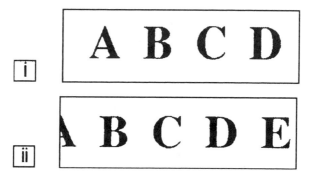

Figure 20.3A. The overlap between shots i and ii specifies that ii is leftward of i in relation to eye or camera, but strong *rightward* motion is instead seen between the noncorresponding letters, thanks to low-level motion-detection mechanisms.

Figure 20.3B. i, ii. Two successive shots, predominantly seen as a camera move from left to right.

has moved relative to the scene as a whole. This physically specified factor might in fact contribute to how we combine our successive saccadic glances at the world,[19] but it fails to predict what viewers actually perceive in overlapping cuts. Both low-level and high-level processes can subvert the technique (when indeed it has any effects at all). Depending on spacing, the low-level mechanisms mentioned earlier can provide misleading apparent motion between noncorresponding objects in successive views: For example, in Fig. 20.3A, because each letter in the second shot (ii) is just rightward of noncorresponding letters in the first shot (i), a rightward jump is seen instead of the true leftward displacement of the letters. This is a common cause of bad cuts and affects the course of looking at filmed narrative.[20] In Figs. 20.3Bi and 20.3Bii, a high-level cue as to what will come next, that is, the direction of the actors' gazes, overcomes the overlap between views (compare the longshot in Fig. 20.3C) and causes the second view (ii) to appear to lie rightward of the first (i), in the space beyond the screen.

Figure 20.3C. A more inclusive shot.

For all we know at present, therefore, even overlapping cuts may work not because their overlap automatically "specifies" anything at all, but because overlap, like an actor's gaze, *acts as a cue about what to expect.*

In any case, moving pictures also routinely use *non*overlapping cuts. Such shots, by themselves, cannot convey anything about events or layouts beyond their boundaries. Admittedly, they can be individually remembered, to a degree. After being shown a rapid sequence of unrelated stills (in laboratory research), viewers can recollect information about some of the individual shots, and they show some signs of having visual expectations about what will come next. There is also evidence of a visual buffer that stores some small number of views;[21] indeed, we know that a great many briefly viewed pictures will be recognized on a second viewing as having been seen before. But recognition memory does not of itself provide the viewer with coherent events in remembered sequence (or a remembered place larger than the separate shots). Fig. 20.4Ai represents a stationary circular aperture on the

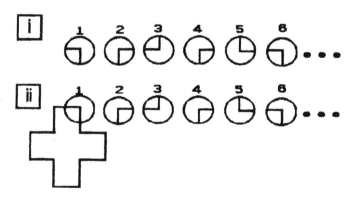

Figure 20.4A. i. The first six shots in a sequence in which the corners of a cross are successively shown through a single stationary aperture. ii. The same sequence, with the entire cross shown in the first shot.

screen (in the laboratory), through which the corners of a geometrical figure (a cross) are shown in sequence. Such sequences are not remembered. But if first shown a longshot as at Fig. 20.4Aii (1), the viewer can then test each successive view as to whether it fits the remembered cross in some regular order, and the sequence is then much better distinguished from other sequences.[22]

Without a mental structure in which to place the series of shots—their order as parts of an event, or as sample views of some spatial layout—the series is not rememberable. But it is rememberable given such a structure and the effort to apply it (that is, the attentional resources).[23] That argues that mental structure is involved in the process of event perception itself, and we must therefore try to say more about what such structure is like.

Mental Representations and Story Structures

Something like this idea is found in many traditional cognitive theories, which take the testing of mental structures as central to the perceptual process.[24] To some filmmakers, good editing poses first a visual question and then a visual answer.[25] In experimental studies of film or video cutting, using short acted or animated scenes, both the visual question posed (as in Figs. 20.4Bi–iv) and the larger story structures within which the shots are presented significantly affect how the edited shots are comprehended.[26] But we must be more explicit about such mental structures if they are to be considered seriously.

Deciding what they *cannot* be like may help us to think of what they *may* be like. The mental structures fitted to our successive glimpses at the screen and at the world cannot have the characteristics of the world itself (despite assertions that they do).[27] Movements as we remember or anticipate them do not continue to run off in time, nor do remembered or anticipated layouts continue to extend in space. As we saw earlier, we start to lose extended time and space when the supporting input ceases. In any case, it certainly does not take some 90 minutes to review in our minds the average movie's representation.

We therefore simply cannot take either the moving picture or the events and space it represents as a faithful model for the film's mental representation. It is often hard to avoid doing just that, or to avoid making the opposite error by turning to the abstract story structure instead. There are plausible theories about written story structure, in the form of hierarchical analyses which account for much of readers' memories of the story's contents.[28] Bordwell has given narrative film a related approach, which explicitly deals with cuts, distinguishing the time covered by the story from the actual screen time after editing.[29] Despite some experimental applications suggested by this approach,[30] such analyses describe the structure of the narrative film itself, as we argue next, and not the viewer's mental representation while viewing the events on the screen.

Online Perception Versus Leisurely Analysis

Even with written stories, readers probably do not normally construct de-tailed representations while reading: After they have read that Mary stirred her cup, sensitive tests reveal no trace of a spoon in the readers' minds.[31] Nor is the entire story kept in mind and used online: Subjects who were interrupted at reading regained their speed much faster after a brief review of the last few lines than they did after reviewing the preceding story structure.[32] While reading online, therefore, events that are distant in the narrative may go unconsulted, and unmentioned details are not filled in, so long as no in-consistency is encountered.[33]

When someone watches a film or tape unfold at its own pace, it seems even more likely that no filling in is done and no overall structure is con-sulted, so long as the new input is consistent with the immediately preceding or local context. And a well-made film, intended like most films in history for a single viewing, must therefore in general be *locally* comprehensible. In Fig. 20.4B, i–iv are sketches of shots 12–15 of *La Jetée*, stills of 1.27-, 2.0-, 1.0-, and 1.12-second durations, respectively. In watching the sequence, their relationship is evident without effort. Shot i poses a question; ii an-swers it (with an overlap that surely doesn't amount to physical specifica-tion); iii and iv are evidently looking at ii, following the principle in Fig. 20.3B. Using a continuous pan to connect the shots (as in Fig. 20.1) would have invited explanation in terms of relative motion detectors and invari-ants, but such explanations do not apply here (or to cutting in general). Giving the viewer appropriate acquaintance with the film prior to these shots would invite explanation in terms of story structure, but such reli-ance on overall structure would obscure the purely local comprehensibility of the shot sequence. We do not know whether the local meaning depends on the actors' gazes as a cue (perhaps by directing the viewer's attention), or whether it reveals a relatively autonomous Gricean process of construal (for example, "why else are we being shown actors looking to the left?"). The final story structure will be *essentially the same* in any case. Only the films will differ, and the perceptual and cognitive processes by which their equivalent stories are achieved will differ too. That may be important for aesthetic reasons (pacing, affective cutting tone, attentional load, looking

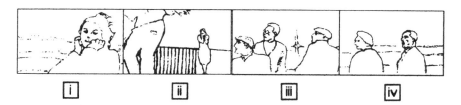

Figure 20.4B. i–iv. Sketches of shots 12–15 in *La Jetée*, all stills, by Chris Marker.

maintenance); it will be important for comprehension as well if the motions themselves are the film's subject, as in any filmed dance; and it is certainly important in any attempt to understand the perceptual processes at work in watching moving pictures. For many purposes, one might always patch such local analyses into the more conventional overall narrative analysis. But to do so one would first have to know about these local determinants, and whether they were in fact effective in the present instance.

As Thompson[34] has pointed out, there are many appropriate approaches from which to analyze film. To know what there is to comprehend in the film, to know what will arouse expectations early in the film that may later be fulfilled, to know what echoes and resonances are potentially effective, indeed to know what will be a misleading local reading of some stretch of the filmed narrative—these purposes and more require analyses in terms of overall narrative structure. Such analyses necessarily stand outside of the time flow of the film. To us, however, it is important to consider the film as it is experienced in the course of its first viewing (which for many a film will be its only viewing), thereby addressing what is most characteristic of the medium. Such an approach will distinguish one particular moving picture from another whose narrative might be summarized identically but which is very different in its moment-by-moment presentation. And such an approach scrutinizes the act of viewing itself, forcing us to attend to the rich mix of processes by which that act proceeds, and by which a mental representation of the narrated event is achieved, even though most of the steps along the way fade quickly in the course of the viewing.

In fact, considering how rapidly a filmed narrative can advance through brief and partial glimpses of previously unseen objects and events, perhaps at least three kinds of mental structure, each with different time scales and consequences, should be experimentally separated from story structure and from each other. First, there is the answer or confirmation to be obtained by the next glance. Second, there are the next expected features or landmarks, not immediately imminent, implied by the current action. Third, the viewer has a set of abstract readinesses, primed by previous events, for whatever may come afterward. Then, if a contradiction or some appeal by the film itself requires it, the viewer can consult and revise the story structure as far as it has developed. (Such appeals are very frequent. Why is that glass of milk so bright in *Suspense*? Why do we keep cutting away from the two combative adults to the rapt child in the *Third Man*? And why does the same child reappear among the crowd to stare accusingly at the camera/protagonist?) But this process will probably incur some cost in attentional resources and escape the more passive viewer. The filmmaker, knowing the story structure, can only hope that the viewer can and will make the effort and draw the right conclusions.

It seems unlikely that, aside from the endorsement of some small repertoire of local determinants (like that in Fig. 20.3B), such a detailed online analysis would be helpful to the narrative filmmaker. It seems likely that with all its limits, our storage capacities (as in speech) allow us to re-construe earlier segments in the light of later information. But such analysis will certainly be helpful in extending present perceptual psychology, which is still largely confined to the study of the individual event, into the sequence of perceptual consequences with which it must deal in real-world behavior. It will probably be helpful in the programming of interactive (and virtual-reality) media. And it will certainly be helpful where the narrative itself is of a specific visual event, as in recording some dance performance, in which different cuts and camera angles may provide totally different visual (and audiovisual) experiences.

This brings us to the last point that emerges from our argument that the motions on the screen are not simply stored intact and subject to replaying. The story structure, as it is usually laid out by a film scholar or cognitive psychologist in words and tree diagrams, also differs from what the viewer perceives and remembers, or can reconstruct, in that it is not visual. We need a notation system better fitted by visual displays than by words. Per-haps it should consist of brief high points or action features economically sampled from the flow of events; it will be relatively schematic, since details are not normally maintained unless needed; it will be mostly ego-centered, or camera-centered, with a definite viewpoint and 2D composition as dis-tinguished from an object-centered layout specified in 3D coordinates; and the amount of information that it can store depends on how redundant the viewer finds the film. Remember that striking images, regardless of their place in the story hierarchy, are sure to be recognized when next viewed, and that can itself affect the story; a shot very similar to that of Fig. 20.4Bi reappears to great effect at the end of that film.

Comic strips and their predecessors[35] are a good approximation (although some frames serve only to hold dialogue); so is the filmmaker's storyboard, especially if it follows Eisenstein's shot scripting.[36] DeWied's ingenious recent version of Bordwell's analysis, combining storyboard, breakpoints, and tree structure, seems close to what is needed.[37]

Comic strips may be popular because they approximate the ways in which we think of the visual world. La Jetée may differ little in retrospect from what it would have been with full movements. Perhaps even a visual passage that exists only for its specific flow of movements, like a nonnar-rative dance, remains with the viewer as an annotated "shot script." That representation may be hierarchical, in the limited sense that the knowl-edgeable viewer can, *if necessary*, reconstruct and insert additional boxes between the major breakpoints; it may be that specific continuous motions are noted briefly where they are important (as in Figs. 20.1C, 20.1D); and it may even be that viewers can, when needed, reenvision those movements in real time.[38] Nevertheless, we take the mental representation that is ap-proximated by this notation to be *in general* nonredundant and therefore static and discontinuous.

This is intended as a first step toward a description of the mental representation of visual events. The next step would seem to be close analysis and experimental research with moving pictures.

Notes

1. Joseph Anderson and Barbara Anderson, "The Myth of Persistence of Vision Revisited," *Journal of Film and Video* 45 (Spring 1983): 3–12, and "Motion Perception in Motion Pictures," in *The Cinematic Apparatus*, ed. Teresa DeLauretis and Stephen Heath (New York: St. Martin's Press, 1980), pp. 76–95; David Bordwell, *Narration in the Fiction Film* (Madison: University of Wisconsin Press, 1985); Virginia Brooks, "Film, Perception and Cognitive Psychology," *Millennium Film Journal* 14/15 (Fall/Winter 1984–85): 105–26.

2. There seems to be no way to put this to rest. The latest version appears in J. Cantine, S. Howard, and B. Lewis, *Shot by Shot: A Practical Guide to Filmmaking* (Pittsburgh: Pittsburgh Filmmakers, 1993). For recent criticisms, see Anderson and Anderson, "Motion Perception"; Julian Hochberg and Virginia Brooks, "The Perception of Motion Pictures," in *Handbook of Perception*, vol. 10, ed. Edward C. Carterette and Morton P. Friedman (New York: Academic Press, 1978), pp. 259–304. For a detailed history of where this incurable silliness started, see Olive Cook, *Movement in Two Dimensions* (London: Hutchinson, 1963); and Hugo Münsterberg, *The Film: A Psychological Study* (1916; reprint, New York: Dover, 1970).

3. There has been a recent explosion of work in this area. For discussion of short-range and longer-range motion mechanisms in relation to moving pictures, see Anderson and Anderson, "Myth of Persistence of Vision," and for a survey of research on the mechanisms and on the viability of the distinction, see Julian Hochberg and Virginia Brooks, "Perception of Moving Pictures Revised," in *Handbook of Perception*, ed. Edward C. Carterette and Morton Friedman, rev. ed. (in press).

4. Karl Duncker, "Über insuzerte Bewegung," *Psychologische Forschung* 12 (1929): 180–259. For a recent review, see Arien Mack, "Perceptual Aspects of Motion in the Frontal Plane," in *Handbook of Perception and Human Performance*, vol. 1, *Sensory Processes and Perception*, ed. Kenneth R. Boff, Lloyd Kaufman, and James P. Thomas (New York: John Wiley, 1986), chapter 17, pp. 1–38.

5. The question of what visuomotor information the viewer takes into account when making pursuit movements, as when tracking a target in the world, and the complexities involved when a moving or stationary viewer regards a stationary object against a moving background on a stationary motion-picture screen, are more involved than we can treat here. See Hochberg and Brooks, "Perception of Moving Pictures Revised."

6. Gunnar Johansson, *Configurations in Event Perception* (Uppsala, Sweden: Almqvist and Wiksells, 1950). For a discussion of recent work on this phenomenon, see Hochberg and Brooks, "Perception of Moving Pictures Revised." For demonstrations that the effect is not simply the result of the eye's tracking h, leaving v as the only motion on the retina, see Julian Hochberg and Peter Fallon, "Perceptual Analysis of Moving Patterns," *Science* 194 (1976): 1081–83.

7. With the stationary dot at either of the two corners which are not aligned with the diagonal, the vertical motion remains predominant, as reported by Julian Hochberg and Jeremy Beer, "Alternative Movement Organizations: Findings and Premises for Modeling (Abstract)," *Proceedings of the Psychonomic Society* (1990), p. 25; and as discussed in Hochberg and Brooks, "Perception of Moving Pictures Revised."

8. Helmholtz's rule is compressed and rephrased from his *Treatise on Physiological Optics*, vol. 3, ed. and trans. J. P. C. Southall, from the 3rd German ed. (1909–11) (Rochester, N.Y.: The Optical Society of America, 1924–25), pp. 4–13. See Julian Hochberg, "Visual Perception," in *Stevens' Handbook of Experimental Psychology*, vol. 1, ed. R. Atkinson, R. Herrnstein, G. Lindzey, and D. Luce (New York: John Wiley, 1988), pp. 295–75. For work by current advocates of that position, see Richard Gregory, *The Intelligent Eye* (London: Weidenfeld and Nicolson, 1970); Irvin Rock, "The Logic of 'The Logic of Perception,'" *Giornale italiano di psicologia* 20 (1994): 841–67; and Roger N. Shepard, "Ecological Constraints on Internal Representation: Resonant Kinematics of Perceiving, Imagining, Thinking, and Dreaming," *Psychological Review* 91 (1984): 417–47.

9. The strongest claim that perception is a direct response to stimulus information, not involving contribution from any mental representation, came from James J. Gibson, *The Ecological Approach to Visual Perception* (Boston: Houghton Mifflin, 1979). Without pursuing that claim, many visual scientists have pursued his goal of uncovering the rich, mathematically specifiable information about the world that is available to a moving observer (or one watching movies). Their recent work relevant to moving pictures is reviewed in Hochberg and Brooks, "Perception of Moving Pictures Revised." For somewhat opposing views of the information about movement into depth (a phenomenon relevant to the viewer's perception of dolly shots), see W. Warren and K. Kurtz, "The Role of Central and Peripheral Vision in Perceiving the Direction of Self-Motion," *Perception and Psychophysics* 51 (1992): 443–54; and James Cutting, *Perception with an Eye for Motion* (Cambridge: MIT Press, 1986). For a sophisticated study of how movement provides information about surface structure (for example, slopes, peaks, depressions), see J. S. Lappin and T. D. Wason, "The Perception of Geometrical Structure from Congruence," in *Pictorial Communication in Virtual and Real Environments*, ed. S. R. Ellis, M. K. Kaiser, and A. J. Grunwald (London: Taylor and Francis, 1991), pp. 425–48.

10. Jeremy M. A. Beer, "Perceiving Scene Layout through an Aperture during Visually Simulated Self-Motion," *Journal of Experimental Psychology: Human Perception and Performance* (in press).

11. Lynn A. Cooper, "Mental Models of the Structure of Three-Dimensional Objects," in *Object Perception: Structure and Process*, ed. B. Shepp and S. Ballestreros (Hillsdale, N.J.: Lawrence Erlbaum, 1989), pp. 91–119.

12. Fritz Heider and Marianne Simmel, "An Experimental Study of Apparent Behavior," *American Journal of Psychology* 57 (1944): 243–59.

13. D. Newtson and G. Engquist, "The Perceptual Organization of Ongoing Behavior," *Journal of Experimental and Social Psychology* 12 (1976): 436–50; D. Newtson, J. Hairfield, J. Bloomingdale, and S. Cutino, "The Structure of Action and Interaction," *Social Cognition* 5 (1987): 121–237.

14. See Irvin Rock, "The Logic of 'The Logic of Perception'"; and Shepard, "Ecological Constraints on Internal Representation," for mentalistic theories; and see Gibson, *Ecological Approach to Visual Perception;* G. Johansson, "Visual Space Perception through Motion," in *Tutorials on Motion Perception*, ed. A. H. Wertheim,

W. A. Wagnaar, and H. W. Leibowitz (New York: Plenum, 1982); and Shimon Ullman, *The Interpretation of Visual Motion* (Cambridge: MIT Press, 1979), for physicalistic theories.

15. Strong evidence that rigidity is not the fundamental constraint that allows us to recover three-dimensional structure from changing images, to the exclusion of static pictorial depth information, is reported by M. L. Braunstein and G. J. Andersen, "Testing the Rigidity Assumption: A Reply to Ullman," *Perception* 15 (1986): 641–44; Julian Hochberg, "Machines Should Not See as People Do, but Must Know How People See," *Computer Vision, Graphics, and Image Processing* 37 (1987): 221–37; B. J. Schwartz and G. Sperling, "Non-Rigid 3D Percepts from 2D Representations of Rigid Objects," *Investigative Ophthalmology and Visual Science*, ARVO Supplement, 24 (1983): 239 (abstract). The strategic value that the rigidity constraint offered direct theories of perception was that it made static pictorial depth cues unnecessary to any account of the perception of moving pictures, or of the perception of the world by a moving observer. Once we know that rigidity does not make the depth cues unnecessary, it becomes very hard to dispense with mental representations in one's theoretical account.

16. See Julian Hochberg and Virginia Brooks, "Perception of Still and Moving Pictures," in *International Encyclopedia of Communications*, ed. Erik Barnouw (New York: Oxford University Press, 1989); Julian Hochberg, "Representation of Motion and Space in Video and Cinematic Displays," in *Handbook of Perception and Human Performance*, vol. 1, ed. Kenneth R. Boff, James P. Thomas, and Lloyd Kaufman (New York: John Wiley, 1986), pp. 1–64.

17. For their explanation of the well-known film of actors made visible only by small lights at their joints, see G. Johansson and G. Jansson, "Perceived Rotary Motion from Changes in a Straight Line," *Perception and Psychophysics* 4 (1986): 165–70.

18. See Julian Hochberg, "Perceptual Theory and Visual Cognition," in *Cognitive Approaches to Human Perception*, ed. S. Ballesteros (Hillsdale, N.J.: Lawrence Erlbaum, 1994), pp. 269–89.

19. This was suggested by J. J. Gibson, *Perception of the Visual World* (Boston: Houghton Mifflin, 1950). It is the only explicit purely visual explanation offered for how glances combine, and it has some recent experimental support. (See D. F. Irwin, J. L. Zacks, and J. H. Brown, "Visual Memory and the Perception of a Stable Visual Environment," *Perception and Psychophysics* 47 [1990]: 35–46.) But it has also allowed Gibson and his followers to argue that the entire optic array, which remains invariant under the changing glance of eye or camera, is the effective stimulus on which perception is based—an argument that has no experimental support and much to oppose it. (See Hochberg, "Visual Perception.")

20. Julian Hochberg and Virginia Brooks, "Film Cutting and Visual Momentum," in *Eye Movements and the Higher Psychological Functions*, ed. J. W. Senders, D. F. Fisher, and R. A. Monty (Hillsdale, N.J.: Lawrence Erlbaum, 1978), pp. 293–313; G. d'Ydewalle and M. Vanderbeeken, "Perceptual and Cognitive Processing of Editing Rules in Film," in *From Eye to Mind: Information Acquisition in Perception, Search, and Reading*, ed. R. Groner, G. d'Ydewalle, and R. Parham (Amsterdam: North Holland, 1990), pp. 129–39.

21. The experimental study of montages of unrelated stills deserves more attention in film studies than it has received. For its start, see M. Potter and E. Levy, "Recognition Memory for a Rapid Sequence of Pictures," *Journal of Experimental*

Psychology 81 (1969): 10–15. For a recent review and analysis of what the data imply as to mental representations and the normal integration of our successive glances, see H. Intraub, R. Bender, and J. Mangels, "Looking at Pictures but Remembering Scenes," *Journal of Experimental Psychology: Learning, Memory, and Cognition* 18 (1992): 180–91; and H. Intraub, "Contextual Factors in Scene Perception," in *The Role of Eye Movements in Perceptual Processes*, ed. E. Chekaluk and K. R. Llewellyn (Amsterdam: North Holland, 1992), pp. 47–72, respectively.

   22. As described in Hochberg, "Representation of Motion and Space in Video and Cinematic Displays," pp. 58–60. In *Handbook of Perception and Human Performance*. K. R. Boff, L. Kaufman, and J. P. Thomas (Eds.) New York: John Wiley and Sons, 1986.

   23. Although we know of no experimental research to this point, it is clearly a demanding task, requiring both intention and concentration.

   24. Such structure testing underlies the general formulations offered by psychologists and philosophers of the past and present centuries, starting with John Stuart Mill and von Helmholtz.

   25. Karel Reisz and Gavin Millar, *The Technique of Film Editing*, 2d ed. (New York: Focal Press, 1968).

   26. R. N. Kraft, "The Influence of Camera Angle on Comprehension and Retention of Pictorial Events," *Memory and Cognition* 25 (1987): 291–307; P. S. Cowen, "Manipulating Montage: Effects on Film Comprehension, Recall, Person Perception, and Aesthetic Responses," *Empirical Studies on the Arts* 6 (1988): 97–115; R. N. Kraft, "Light and Mind: Understanding the Structure of Film," in *Cognition and the Symbolic Processes: Applied and Ecological Perspectives*, ed. R. R. Hoffman and D. S. Palermo (Hillsdale, N.J.: Lawrence Erlbaum, 1991), pp. 351–70; d'Ydewalle and Vanderbeeken, "Perceptual and Cognitive Processing."

   27. Rock, "The Logic of 'The Logic of Perception'"; Shepard, "Ecological Constraints."

   28. G. Bower, J. Black, and T. Turner, "Scripts in Memory for Text," *Cognitive Psychology* 11 (1979): 177–220; J. M. Mandler, "A Code in the Node: The Use of a Story Schema in Retrieval," *Discourse Processes* 2 (1978): 14–35; J. M. Mandler and N. S. Johnson. "Remembrance of Things Parsed: Story Structure and Recall," *Cognitive Psychology* 9 (1977): 111–51.

   29. Bordwell, D. *Narration in the Fiction Film* (Madison: Univ. of Wisconsin Press, 1987). When Bordwell's distinctions between the various scales of narrative time in moving pictures are placed against the limited resources of working memory, something like the mental shot script we discuss below seems an unavoidable attribute of online mental representation.

   30. M. A. de Wied, "The Role of Time Structures in the Experience of Film Suspense and Duration: A Study on the Effects of Anticipation Time upon Suspense and Temporal Variations on Duration Experience and Suspense" (Ph.D. diss., University of Amsterdam, 1991).

   31. B. A. Dosher and A. T. Corbett, "Instrument Inferences and Verb Schemata," *Memory and Cognition* 10 (1982): 531–39.

   32. M. Glanzer, B. Fischer, and D. Dorfman, "Short-Term Storage in Reading," *Journal of Verbal Learning and Verbal Behavior* 23 (1984): 467–86.

   33. G. McKoon and R. Ratcliff, "Inference during Reading," *Psychological Review* 99 (1992): 440–66.

34. Kristin Thompson, *Breaking the Glass Armor: Neoformalist Film Analysis* (Princeton: Princeton University Press, 1988).

35. E. H. Gombrich, *Art and Illusion: A Study in the Psychology of Pictorial Representation* (Princeton: Princeton University Press, 1961).

36. Vladimir Nizhny, *Lessons with Eisenstein*, trans. and ed. Ivor Montagu and Jay Leyda (New York: Hill and Wang, 1962), pp. 62–92.

37. de Wied, "Role of Time Structures."

38. Beer, "Perceiving Scene Layout"; Cooper, "Mental Models"; Lynn A. Cooper, "Demonstration of a Mental Analog of an External Rotation," *Perception and Psychophysics* 19 (1976): 296–302.

21

Looking Ahead (One Glance at a Time)

Julian Hochberg

Learning how to make and reproduce pictures, from the working out of the depth cues in the Renaissance through the color-mixing concerns of printing and TV, taught us most of what we knew until recently about how we perceive the world, and also did much to shape philosophy and science. Today, moving pictures raise questions that must concern cognitive psychologists and neurophysiologists, and some of the answers to those questions should help the computer scientists who work at automating movie making. We need to understand how meaningful sequential views of objects, scenes, and events are combined and remembered and how the perceptual system's anticipatory abilities help to integrate the many component processes that comprise that system.

The questions addressed here are primarily about the nature of perceived objects and scenes, which are almost all grasped through successive glimpses (or through movie cuts) of the world and its pictures, and also about some of the tools this research offers to our understanding of how the mind works. I include a brief and biased summary of the changing context in which these questions have been pursued, which has surely affected the course of the inquiry.

Pointillist Pictures for the Mind's Eye: The Old View

Beyond the point-by-point analysis of the array of light that reaches the eye, and beyond learning how to generate that array's effective pictorial surrogate by using dots or pixels of just three or four colors to match the thousands of colors that the world may present at any point, artists explored and philosophers ruminated about how a flat array of such points could represent the 3D world. The classical answer is that our perceptions of shapes, motions, depth, gestures, and above all *the integrated views of the world that span our successive glances*—all are learned associations acquired through our actions in the world. "Associations" mean clusters of memories of points or dots of light, shade, and color, plus the memories of the orders issued to move the eye or to touch some seen object, etc. In general, the mutual constraints that characterize physical objects in the world should be reflected in our perceptions of them.

Although this enormously simple approach is now clearly wrong in major and essential ways, it is also clearly right in some ways, and it survives in various guises. Scientists of various kinds map the photoreceptors' sensitivities, measure and model associative learning curves, and survey the probabilities with which the sensory inputs are likely to co-occur and thereby become associated in memory, resulting in what is termed the *likelihood principle*: We perceive what would most likely have provided the pattern of sensations received. That principle follows directly from the classical theory itself, but it would be evolutionarily bizarre if it did not fit fairly well with almost any viable theory.

In this view, to the extent that pictures provide the same *patterns* of sensations as the objects and scenes they are intended to represent, they elicit the same associations, even though they are very different both in their physical characteristics and in the light they provide the eye. Initially, moving pictures did not challenge the classical theory in any serious way: Perceived movement, whether in the real world or the movie, was in any case simply taken as a percept composed of memories of sets of sensations at successive loci in the retinal image. (There were some isolated commotions among film writers about the significance of visual persistence and of apparent motion, but those issues were ill founded; see Anderson & Anderson, 1983; Steinman et al., 2000.)

On the other hand, movie cuts (abrupt view-changes) are a different story. In normal vision, we gain an apparently coherent and continuous view of the world through a rapid series of discrete overlapping glances—ballistic saccades of about ¼ second long. How do we know where the contents of each glance fits in relation to its predecessors and successors? The generic classical answer was this: that the remembered spatial locus of each point of each glimpse's contents is corrected for the change in viewpoint, point for point, by taking into account how far the eye muscles had moved the eye. Various versions of this explanation were formulated and tested with a great deal of labor and ingenuity. Not much came of it: We do not in fact firmly transfer information about retinal position from one fixation to the next (e.g., Jonides et al., 1983).

But at least some of us had already learned from the movies that nonvisual information from the eye movement system was not *necessary* for view combination to be achieved, whether or not such information is in fact used under some circumstances. The use of cuts in films really broadcast that fact by the first decade of the 20th century and was solidly built into the seamless cutting of the Hollywood style which dominated the medium from the early to mid-1900s (see Bordwell & Thompson, 1993). Surprising some filmmakers themselves, cuts worked if properly done, showing us smart psychologists that we must find explanations that go beyond retinal-locus-corrected-by-eye-movements.

Eye movements themselves, made while looking at pictures and while reading, were themselves under heavy scrutiny by the motion picture camera in the 1930s (e.g., Buswell, 1935) and revealed something about their rate (approximately 3–4 per second), extent, and time course. We now have much less-intrusive and more-automatic instruments for tracking the gaze. But we still do not have a good account of what accrues across glances.

Movies, on the other hand, should give psychologists at least some idea of how glances are used and of their different spans in time and space, especially because the cutting room gives the film editor eyes-on feedback as to what doesn't work for integrating and anticipating successive views. Conversely, as the making of moving images aims at becoming more and more automatized, so that the cutting room no longer makes use of intimate human guidance, at least some of what psychologists and neurophysiologists discover about sequential image processing may prove useful to that industry (to the extent that the automators do not simply opt for complete virtual reality; cf. Naimark, 1991).

It's a potential incentive, anyway.

Objections and Discoveries: Perceptual Functionalism Appears

Of course, the classical approach had its opponents.

Most successful: The research from the 1940s on affirmed Hering's (1861) and Mach's (1896/1959) arguments that interactions between receptors produce new units or elements, thereby accounting directly for our perceptions of color, movement, edge, contrast, and more. Because sophisticated neuroimaging procedures now tell us that our visual infrastructure includes complexes that respond as units to those properties and even to faces, the repertoire with which any explanation of perceptual combination has to work is radically changed. Because there are surely more of such perceptual units as yet unidentified; because the relationships between such neural structures are only beginning to be charted; and because such feature-sensitive elements duplicate each other at different levels and operate at different and sometimes preemptive speeds, any likelihood theory is difficult to specify: How likely is a "rubber pencil" (Pomerantz, 1983) or the Killer Cube in Figure 21.2A?[1] Actually, once we understand them, they may become very likely, and there are now models of cortical function that apply Bayesian computation and that are supported by detailed and sophisticated brain-imaging methods (see Sajda & Kyungim, 2004), but that means that we can't use "likely" lightly.

Most dramatic: Gestaltists asserted that whole configurations, and not independent points, are the isomorphic bases of the perceptual process. The physiological mechanisms hypothesized were entropic and equilibrium seeking, like soap bubbles, or electrical force fields, or extended current flows in hypothetical brain fields, *not* like associative memories. However, by the mid-1950s, those Gestalt mechanisms already looked quite implausible, except as loose metaphors (see Hochberg, 1998). But the Gestaltists also offered organizational rules (such as proximity, good continuation, etc.) that could (in principle) be described without the global brain processes, and those rules could themselves be sidestepped by a "simplicity principle" which might, all by itself, explain most of the classical pictorial depth cues as well as the 3D appearance of Necker cube types of pattern, without *necessarily* appealing to any learned associations (cf. Attneave, 1954, for an information-based approach; and Hochberg & McAlister, 1953, for a simplicity theory).

At first, some such simplicity theory seemed plausible: that is, we perceive that arrangement/structure/interpretation that can most simply be specified or communicated, and today it still has its advocates (e.g., Leeuwenberg, 1969; van der Helm & Leeuwenberg, 2004) and those relating it to the likelihood theory (e.g., Feldman, 2004a, b; van der Helm, 2000). I, for one, believe that a much more complex simplicity principle can still work.[2] However, that entire enterprise—plus the Gestalt mystique, and much more—suffered a crippling blow from the impossible figures of Penrose and Penrose (1958) (and many earlier artists using but not seeking impossibility; see Hochberg, 1984). These are sketches of objects with parts that are opposite in 3D orientation but that are seamlessly joined by lines or edges which, through their ambiguity, veil the fact that the represented structure would be physically impossible to construct. Although one might argue that such figures don't count because they are impossible, we soon had figures that were themselves perfectly possible but that were also spontaneously perceived as structures that would be impossible (Gillam, 1979; Hochberg, 1970).

The Gestaltists were surely right in that we respond at an early level to configurations and not just to points. The proposed laws of organization and their contribution to object structure are increasingly viable (see Kubovy, 1994; Kubovy & van den Berg, 2006, for the former; and Kellman & Shipley, 1991, for the latter). *But it is wrong to consider each full configuration—each object—as reflecting a unitary infrastructure* (Hochberg, 2003). The figure-ground phenomenon itself, which Gestaltists had suggested as the indivisible basis of object assignment and shape perception, has now been convincingly shown to depend on component elements of shaped edges which face one way or the other and are subject to implicit learning (Peterson & Enns, 2005). Moreover, what structure you perceive from an assembly of such parts can depend on where you choose to attend, a point to which I return in connection with Figure 21.2.

But we have since had two related powerful discoveries that make a much more general version of the same point and make it more directly.

The first discovery shows that the human brain has top-down, forward-looking priorities. Even as visual signals from the eye and geniculate enter cortical region V1, they are modified by signals from higher cortical levels, including the prefrontal cortex, which is the topmost and most-anticipatory region (see Lennie, 1998). This must have consequences for understanding perceptual behavior and its evolution and for what perceptual phenomena are chosen to guide brain imaging. It should also affect how we model the perceptual process, and, given the discovery noted next, it almost demands research involving serial glimpses.

In the second discovery, Hoffman and Subramaniam (1995) and Kowler et al. (1995) showed that *each saccade occurs only after a shift of attention.* Because most attention shifts made in the course of normal perceptual activity are not themselves compelled by alarming stimuli, this must usually mean "only after a purposeful shift of attention." Each *purposeful* glance is aimed at some place or thing that has probably already been seen in peripheral vision during a prior glance. This vindicates older and more speculative claims that glances are normally purposeful and that they are normally directed by a perceptual question or an anticipation about what information can be found (Hochberg, 1968, 1970; Hochberg & Brooks, 1970; see also Cavanagh et al., 2001; Gottesman & Intraub, 2003; Hayhoe et al., 2003). This gives saccadic eye movements a central job—not merely do they scan the scene, like a video-camera raster, they are also carrying out their owner's *planned perceptual actions.* Learning about such plans—their size and scope and limitations—is obviously important to a more general understanding of the functions that serve perceptual inquiry.

Studying Purposeful Looking at Scenes and Objects: On the Threshold

According to this approach, purposeful saccades usually have two predecessors: (1) prior glimpses in peripheral vision (there's a blob near the barbecue; there are about six letters in the next word); and (2) the posing of a visual question (is that blob a chair or a bear? are those four letters a verb?). Only then, a skilled move brings the inquiring fovea to target.

Eye movements have usually been recorded while stationary viewers regarded text or pictures, but the eyes seem to be used in much the same way in other situations, for example, a freely moving viewer glances at the sites of planned actions well before the actions are to be performed (Hayhoe et al., 2003; Pelz & Canosa, 2001). When such glances are not actually recorded, they may be inferred, as when Gottesman and Intraub (2003) found that subjects' memories of inspected scenes show highly suggestive signs of further anticipated glances.[3] As to the saccade itself, in three to five acts per second, the high-resolution fovea jumps to some place previously seen in peripheral vision, which has extremely low acuity and is further impoverished by "crowding" (see discussion by Tripathy & Cavanagh, 2002). The fovea-periphery difference is further exacerbated to some as-yet-unknown extent in that any seen features which do not promise to help answer the visual question being asked are not responded to and are subsequently disregarded as irrelevant to the perceptual task at hand (Hochberg, 1968, 1970; Hochberg & Brooks, 1970), or perhaps are even inhibited (Lamy et al., 2004). The viewer therefore gains and retains very little raw information with each individual glance (see Intraub's 1997 review of how little raw information each glance brings).

There is now considerable research on the time course of memories of briefly exposed unrelated but meaningful pictures (see Intraub, 1981; Potter, 1976; Potter et al., 2004; Potter et al., 2002); Hollingworth (2004) finds similar time courses for the memories of individual meaningful items flagged and looked at within a meaningful scene. So far, however, little has been done on how successive views within the same object or scene are motivated, attended, and stored in the cognitive map that guides further inquiry.

It has been clear at least since Sperling (1960) that what we do not attend is likely to be not looked at, not encoded, and not remembered. This was a central feature of Neisser's (1967) comprehensive and highly influential initiation of modern cognitive psychology and in other less-comprehensive approaches (Hochberg, 1968; Treisman & Geffen, 1967) and is now the focus of a great deal of research on what has unfortunately been named "inattentional blindness" (see Mack & Rock, 1998). The consequences of inattention remain to be determined, for example, Becker and Egeth (2000) showed that even when some specific information cannot be retrieved about unattended stimuli, other information can be. I will use the term *inattentional disregard* in this essay.

Starting with Neisser and Becklen (1975), there is a growing body of movies of people in action which show that viewers cannot report clearly visible events to which they had not been prepared to attend (e.g., Levin & Simons 1997; see review by Simons, 2000). There is little research on what does get stored and how. In the next half of this essay, I describe some introductory and as yet simple research on successive attentional glimpses, gained by eye movements or by movie cuts, *within* objects (Figure 21.2) and *across* scenes (Figure 21.3), and Figure 21.4 is meant to reminds us that cuts serve as components of continuity and narrative structure.[4] First, however, I introspect and speculate briefly about what looking at representational pictures and movies might mean for the perceptual system as I have described it.

What Are *Pictures, Moving Pictures, and Our Views of the World?*

First, I suggest that our very ability to use still and moving pictures as surrogates for the world itself is an extremely consequential example of the inattentional disregard just discussed. Indeed, perceiving the world and perceiving pictures of it may not be all that different—once you grasp how to look and what to ignore.

The point of Figure 21.1A and its caption is that most depth cues offered by the real world from beyond a couple of meters can be presented

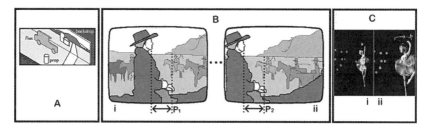

Figure 21.1. Perceptual inquiry in the world and its surrogates: The role of disregard. (A) Zones of distance (based on analysis of visual depth cues in Cutting & Vishton, 1995). The stage set symbolizes the fact that while depth information *can* be powerful in near space (from accommodation, binocular stereopsis, and parallax due to head turnings), and while parallax from limited bodily action *can* be significant for about 50 feet, after that the real world need not be that different from a flat picture screen, and whatever discrepancies and viewpoint-based distortions arise with pictures or other surrogates can simply be disregarded or dismissed. (B) A moving camera and no parallax: Grounds for dismissive disregard. Sketches of two shots taken from a sequence made as a camera sweeps (pans) over a scene of great depth (from *Red River Valley*). Because the pan is obviously revolving around a fixed point (e.g., $P_1 = P_2$), no parallax supports the pictorial depth cues, but I only temporarily perceive a discrepancy between the pictorial depth cues and the motion-revealed flatness while I am paying active attention to some occluding junction between a near and a far object. But I can simply disregard those depth-cue/flatness discrepancies, just as I disregard the distortions that abound in the movies I watch from any place other than the optical center of the particular scene being presented (cf. Cutting, 1987). And when I disregard such contraindications, the picture regains its authority as a source of visual expectations about that valley. (C) A moving camera, an optical expansion pattern, and an illusory choreography (Cutting et al., 2000, discuss the heading effect from which this demonstration derives). These shots are from a movie camera approaching point X. In the movie, the doll seems strongly to turn on the screen (arrow b in shot ii). However, when I attend to the expanding wall pattern at left and make an effort to see point X (correctly) as the center of an optical expansion pattern occasioned by the camera's heading, the doll (correctly) appears stationary in space, and its arm is correctly seen as stationary while the camera moves relative to it. But when my concentrated attention deserts mark X and its nearby expansion pattern, the filmed motion is again perceived as the doll's turning in represented space: *Even though the same expansion pattern remains in the field of view, I find it ineffectual when disregarded.*

by flat pictures, or even by suitable line drawings, which need no special learning to be grasped (see Hochberg, 1997). The objects of potential action by hand or foot (that is, the prop or the flat near the front of the pictured stage set) are in near zones, but the objects of the inquiring eye's potential action include all zones: The eye movements needed to look from one place to another on a moderately distant picture (or on a near picture viewed monocularly) are essentially the same in the 2D picture and in the 3D world it represents. And even in nearby viewing, the peripheral view that preceded the subsequent focused and attentive fixation is low resolution anyway, and the preceding foveal input is represented in working memory in an encoded form that is not likely to include any discrepant effects introduced by regarding a nearby still picture (effects which consist largely of what *doesn't* happen: the absence of parallax motion and of stereoscopic depth between what are pictured as near and far objects). Therefore, to look at a picture, keep your attention away from near-far intersections, disregard the absence of motion in what is after all a still picture, attend your dominant eye, and the picture is comprehensible. (But is itself flat, even though it represents recognizably 3D structures.)[5]

Figure 21.1B and C make much the same introspective points with moving pictures.

Looking Within Objects: The Attentional Window Offered by Glances and Cuts

Possible figures that are seen as impossible figures strongly suggest that we do not understand how we perceive objects; here we try dissecting one such stimulus. Figure 21.2A is a version of the Killer Cube as evolved from Hochberg (1970). It is nonreversing when attended at point a but periodically reverses in depth when attended at b, using opposed set procedure (Peterson & Hochberg, 1983). Moreover, when the cube is rotated (e.g., as symbolized by the upper arrow in Figure 21.2B) while it is fixated at b, it appears to move opposite to its true direction, which fits with the reports as to which wire appears nearer (Hochberg & Peterson 1987).[6] The effect obtains in Figure 21.2B even after the eye has been led to fixate the upper left region before fixating the lower right (if the latter fixation duration lasts at least 500 ms). And the procedures of Figure 21.2C show that this can happen with a cut instead of an eye movement. To help us start mapping the functions by which we perceive objects' structures through successive views, four aspects were varied: where the object is fixated after the cut (a versus b, Figure 21.2C–3) and for how long (see captions for C, D, E); the features' separations and salience (Figure 21.2C–5); and whether the diagnostic region is masked from view before the object rotates (Figure 21.2C–4a). Tentatively, disregard may be manifest 350–500 ms after attentive fixation departs past $3°$ or more of distance (thus, approximately foveal), although that depends as well on salience.

Such measures will hopefully help us to understand and eventually to model why ambiguous figures, like Necker cubes, reverse as they do; why impossible figures are not noticed as such (and why visual mazes are confusing); and these measures should also help to determine the limits of the ease and speed with which mental structures have been shown to change (Moore & Engel, 2001).

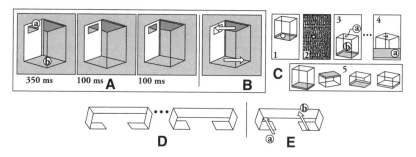

Figure 21.2. Inattentional disregard and reversal in moving objects and their pictures. (A, B) Moving one's gaze over the Killer Cube. This is a perfectly possible structure which is seen as such when attended at point a, but it periodically reverses into impossibility when attended at b. In that case, when it revolves (as shown by the top arrow in B), its motion is seen correctly when attended at a but is seen in the opposite direction (i.e., here, it is shown as counterclockwise when viewed from above) when attended at b. That accords with the reported perceived 3D structure. (C) Cutting between views of an object: An object-dissection procedure intended to preclude anticipation. This sequence keeps fixation constant (as shown in shots 1 and 3) and brings a new part of the target object into the fixated region (either a or b in 21.2C3). After a variable pause in shot 3 (350–500 ms), the animation's base is hidden (a in shot 4), the cube rotates for three or four frames, and the viewer reports the perceived direction of motion (here, counterclockwise as viewed from above). The alternative structures shown in 5 allowed the distance between features and the salience of the disambiguating feature (here, the solid bottom) to be varied, as were left-right orientations and motion directions. (D, E) Not only wires. If the shape shown at D rotates (symbolized by the string of dots) and the bottom ends are separated by approximately 3° or more, the left end appears to head away from the viewer, as shown in E, if the viewer looks at that end, and the right end appears to be heading toward the viewer, if that end is attended.

The apparent robustness of the disregard phenomenon, and the speed with which attended features provide alternative local structure, could well explain both classical reversibility (e.g., Necker cube) and the impossible objects brought forward by Penrose and Penrose (1958).

Three new candidates (not pictured here) for use with this paradigm touch on other current concerns: first, a set of more complex and realistic 3D objects, derived from displays which allow the effects of context and perspective (usually omitted from the study of pictured objects) to be embodied (Meng & Sedgwick, 2002; Sedgwick, 1990) and which can be subjected to a greater number of alternative readings; second, several sets of recognizable but reversible figure-ground stimuli that bring the vital aspects of figural *denotivity* (Peterson, 1994) and past experience into the picture; and third, sequences designed to test at what extrafoveal distances objects' substances, or "stuff" (Adelson, 2001), can serve a landmark function.

Attentive glances not only parse objects, they (and movie cuts) bring new parts of the world into view; and objects not only serve to relate their

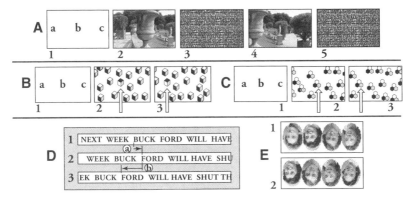

Figure 21.3. Landmarked cuts simulate (and stimulate?) saccades. The animations sampled here present two or more successive overlapping views of the same scene at exposures approximating those of saccades, and the viewer reports the perceived direction of displacement. As shown in A, a preliminary 1000-ms fixation-point display (1) is followed by two or more overlapping views (2, 4) at 200–500 ms each. (A mask, at 100 ms, follows shots 2 and 4, reducing low-level persistence and "jumps.") Performance was essentially perfect. Even at saccadic durations, therefore, visual information alone can be enough to integrate successive views, if adequate landmarks are present. But what are adequate landmarks? Using the same procedures, we found that the important difference in pop-out salience that Enns (1990) had discovered between displays like 21.3B2, 3 and 21.3C2, 3 also appeared in the ability to relate successive brief overlapping views to each other. Performance was best, not surprisingly, when the fixation point (a, b, or c) in B1 and C1 was near the landmark's locus in B3 and C3. Introspectively, it seemed that subsequent glances were biased toward where the landmark had been in C3; we are currently arranging postexposure test stimuli to assess whether that impression was correct. Sequences of similar displays built with Beck's (1967) arrays also worked. Such displacement-judgment procedures can also measure the parameters of other perceptual functions. Thus, longer sequences of overlapping shots of upright and inverted sentences, as in D, which uses no masks, and faces (E), at various rates of presentation, can serve to separate perceptual functions and their different time scales (see text).

parts to each other, they serve as landmarks in relating successive views of the world to each other. Simple attempts at exploring the second of those functions are outlined in Figure 21.3.

In perceiving the real world, our eyes execute saccadic movements prolifically, changing view by abrupt but anticipated movements. Movies, on the other hand, very often change their field of view by abrupt and unanticipated cuts. Since, as noted earlier, saccades are normally preceded by attention shifts, does that mean that the relationship between unanticipated cuts would not be comprehended even if they contained common content to act as landmarks? View sequences like Figure 21.3A, B, and C show that the displacement direction between two brief overlapping views is easily identified at rates like those of ordinary glances (approximately 200 ms) *if* the views contain a salient feature, or landmark, and that greater salience has so far yielded more reliable direction effects. Note that by very different measures, the objects here indicated by the arrows in B are more salient amid their surroundings than those in C (Enns, 1990). These correct detections occur even when masks like those shown in Figure 21.3A–3 and 5 are inserted after the second and third displays to block or reduce any avoidable low-level motion (Sperling & Lu, 1998).[7] This is only part of the task of constructing a scene from partial views, since we have not yet tested whether relationships between objects in the larger scenes can be picked up and maintained in this way or whether coordinating the cut to an antici-pated eye movement will then be needed. However, this procedure does seem to offer an alternative to reaction time or detection measures for measuring landmark salience.

The general procedure also offers measures for other perceptual func-tions. Thus, in the sequence from which three shots are shown in Figure 21.3D (in which no masks are interposed), when very brief presentations (50–100 ms) are used, displacement-direction judgments, following low-level motion (here, arrow a), show the words to be acting only as blobs of contrast, free of meaning or of salient identity whether upright or inverted. By 500 ms, when upright, the words' correct displacement direction (arrow b) can be seen *if* due attention is paid, a phenomenon of applied as well as theoretical consequence. Randomly chosen upright but unfamiliar faces will also serve as landmarks at 500 ms, but when inverted, as they are in Figure 21.3E, direction judgments are at chance even at 1000 ms, corroborating what had earlier been found through "new-old" responses (Hochberg & Galper, 1967).

To bring order and applicability to such demonstrations, we must learn more about the determinants of salience and about the range of effective window sizes and durations for various determinants of (cues to) perceived structure. But beyond anything as tractable as salience, the combination of successive views depends on the viewer's goals beyond the next fixation and on the components of narrative engagement. Researching such problems demands very different lines of inquiry, to the extent that it can be done at all.

Bringing in the World

Figure 21.4A and B reminds us that the integration of successive shots can be guided not only by configuration and landmark salience, but by narrative-based expectations, a very simple example of which are assumptions about where the actors are looking. Perhaps this taps into a relatively low-level or even hard-wired visual expectation that the next shot will reveal what the

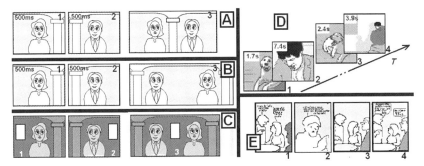

Figure 21.4. Beyond landmarks and salience: Local substories and shot tempo. (A, B) Where are we now? The almost-identical pairs of medium close-ups (1, 2) in sequences A and B are generally perceived as coming from the two different larger views in A3 and B3, respectively. (C) Increasing the salience of an opposing landmark can overcome this mutual gaze factor and thereby help us to measure its strength under varying conditions. But acquiring a more inclusive view of the object or scene is not the only reason we take successive glances or attend successive pictures. (D, E) What's going on? The shots sketched at D (from Warren Beatty's *Reds*, durations estimated from videotape) contain little motion and no auditory narrative. The prominently different durations themselves instruct us to think about the grieving man more than about the yawning dog. And this is not only a matter of how long some projected image stays in view: In the sketched comic strip at E (representative of what Garry Trudeau has done in several *Doonesbury* strips), frame 3 contains no dialogue or action except for slightly changed poses. Such emphases must pervade and shape our anticipations and interpretations of performances and communications quite generally (music, speech, dance, etc.), but the sequential visual media may provide a venue for forming and testing hypotheses about the major prosodic categories and their characteristics.

actor(s) in the first shot attended: "look where I look," as even very young children and some domestic animals know (cf. Emery, 2000; Kaminzki et al., 2005).

Alternatively, or additionally, the actors' gazes might comprise microstories, signaling what is to come or explaining what has happened; or they can be taken as instructions from the filmmaker (like arrows or pointing hands) as to the intended direction of the next shot. Note that this may overpower the landmarks and that Figure 21.4D and E have little if any overlap or shared landmarks. Filmmakers tend to avoid substantial overlap, which can produce disturbing *jump cuts* (unwanted motion between salient objects or features, which must then be cured by *cutaways*, which are brief nonoverlapping inserted views). Avoiding overlap then increases the need for other integrating factors. In cuts without landmarks, the viewer surely must require either some equivalent priming or the time to assimilate what has happened (or to deduce what the filmmaker has intended). We must turn to something that seems similar to narrative engagement as soon as we go beyond the low-level functions.

Continued motion, directed illumination, etc., can obviously provide information about the relative direction of successive views, and it would probably be easy to map the times required by such cues. Our chief concern in this section up to now has been how we combine information from successive glimpses of objects and scenes when those glimpses come through movie cuts and not self-initiated saccades, as when the shot sequence shares salient landmarks of measurable salience. In Figure 21.4C, we illustrate one method for measuring the relative effectiveness of a *non*-landmark view-combining tool, namely, actors' mutual regard. That brings us to the next question: Can we similarly devise procedures to measure other tools that are used in film (and even in comic strips) to influence and maintain looking behavior? We are now trying to measure how duration and tempo factors affect where the viewer chooses to restart an interrupted sequence, but we cannot yet assess the promise of this approach.

Looking for the Next Step

The story that unfolds over the course of a book or movie, which is usually thought of as inviting and maintaining the reader's or viewer's interest, probably has little direct and local effect on sustaining that inquiry at a glance-by-glance level (cf. Dosher & Corbett, 1982; Glanzer et al., 1984; McKoon & Ratcliff, 1992). However, much smaller *attention-based* units of social and mechanical movements, roughly comparable to what Peterson's *denotivity* and Richards and Hoffman's (1985) *codons* offer for the analysis of figural shape, have been demonstrated for the social movements (see Heider & Simmel, 1944; Scholl & Tremoulet, 2000; and see the "sprites" measured by Cavanagh et al., 2001, for a possible start at handling both types of movement). Even closer to the issue of describing perceptual anticipation and planning, Krumhansl and her colleagues have shown promising techniques that identify viewers' anticipations concerning music and dance (Camurri et al., 2004; Krumhansl & Schenck, 1997), and recent measures of how music affects attention to movies (Cohen, 2002) are clearly a start. These are particularly challenging because they take the subject's response as part of the presentation.

There are now other ways to do that. Years ago, we tried, with some very slight success (Hochberg & Brooks, 1978), to study how to maintain and manipulate visual attention and comprehension through cutting—*visual momentum* (the term derives from Spottiswoode, 1962)—using the prohibitively cumbersome eye-movement measurement methods of earlier technology. Today, there is a thriving community of video-game designers, ample software for construction and for gathering responses, and recommendations for how to cut and prime—and an inherent indifference to long-term narrative goals. Response times and accuracies are nonintrusively obtained in such contexts. Hopefully, that will help us to regain visual momentum. Modeling such behavior cannot be based only on stimulus variables: Even when the display sequence is beyond the viewer's direct control, we still face the question of how that viewer chooses where and when to look and attend and when to stop attending. Since we know that such "decisions" cannot be based on a full survey of each field of view, it must involve a creative "satisficing" (Simon, 1987) or "robust rationality" (Ben-Haim, 2004) rather than one of the optimization models, such as likelihood or simplicity, that we considered at the beginning of this chapter. This seems to be the default human condition quite generally, whether we are considering economic decisions or the structure of the Killer Cube, so it should also be evident in the way we look at movies and interactive visual displays.

Notes

1. A familiar rigid object, like a pencil, appears to bend and twist when flipped up and down at the right rate; the low-level motion is out of synchrony with the rates of other motion determinants. Surely a very careful reading of ecological contingencies and biological economies will eventually explain how we can afford such anomalies, but that makes "likelihood" esoteric and not at all a convenient rubric.

2. If we recognize that there are multiple grounds for simplicity, due in part to reaching fast "decisions" on what comes to the table at different time scales from different spare encodings (see Pizlo & Li, in press, on rapid problem solving), and that one's individual history shapes one's units of analysis (see Peterson & Enns, in press).

3. Hayhoe and her colleagues, and Intraub and hers, seem very close in their approaches to the one I am following here, which, considering their specialties, is reassuring.

4. Figures 21.1C, 21.2A, 21.3A, 21.3B, 21.4A, 21.4B, and 21.4D are drawn from demonstrations or experiments from which somewhat different versions appear in Hochberg and Brooks (2006). The demonstrations themselves and relevant data appear on http://www.inthemindseye.org.

5. That is, looking at a picture is somewhat like looking at an ambiguous figure that can be seen in one way or another, depending on how it is attended and which alternative is dominant, except that the representational alternative is by far the better encoded and remembered from glance to glance.

6. Figure 21.2A is a modified Necker cube, evolved from Hochberg (1970), strongly biased toward the *viewed-from-below* alternative at its upper left; the *viewed-from-above* alternative is normally the dominant response for cubes, which makes this arrangement (augmented by the thick wire at right) a good tool with which to demonstrate the effect.

7. Sperling and Lu present a compelling history and review of three different motion-perception functions. A mask was used in most of the present procedures to reduce or eliminate low-level motion.

References

ADELSON, E. H. (2001). On seeing stuff: The perception of materials by humans and machines. In B. E. Rogowitz & T. N. Pappas (Eds.), *Proceedings of the Human Vision and Electronic Imaging VI, SPIE Vol. 4299*, pp. 1–12.

ANDERSON, J., & ANDERSON, B. (1983). The myth of persistence of vision. *Journal of Film and Video, 45*, 3–12.

ATTNEAVE, F. (1954). Some informational aspects of visual perception. *Psychological Review, 61*, 183–193.

BECK, J. (1967). Perceptual grouping produced by line figures. *Perception and Psychophysics, 2*, 491–495.

BECKER, L., & EGETH, H. (2000). Mixed reference frames for dynamic inhibition of return. *Journal of Experimental Psychology: Human Perception and Performance, 26*, 1167–1177.

BEN-HAIM, Y. (2004). Uncertainty, probability and information-gaps. *Reliability Engineering & System Safety, 85*, 249–266.

BORDWELL, D., & THOMPSON, K. (1993). *Film art: An introduction* (4th ed.). New York: McGraw-Hill.

BUSWELL, G. T. (1935). *How people look at pictures*. Chicago: University of Chicago Press.

CAMURRI, A., KRUMHANSL, C., MAZZARINO, B., & VOLPE, G. (2004). An exploratory study of anticipating human movement in dance. In *2nd International Symposium on Measurement, Analysis and Modeling of Human Functions* (pp. 1–4). Italy: Genova.

CAVANAGH, P., LABIANCA, A., & THORNTON, I. (2001). Attention-based visual routines: Sprites. *Cognition, 80*, 47–60.

COHEN, A. J. (2002). Music cognition and the cognitive psychology of film structure. *Canadian Psychology, 43*, 215–232.

CUTTING, J. E. (1987). Rigidity in cinema seen from the front row, side aisle. *Journal of Experimental Psychology: Human Perception and Performance, 13*, 323–334.

CUTTING, J. E., ALLIPRANDINI, P. M., & WANG, R. F. (2000). Seeking one's heading through eye movements. *Psychonomic Bulletin & Review, 7(3)*, 490–498.

CUTTING, J. E., & VISHTON, P. M. (1995). Perceiving layout and knowing distances: The interaction, relative potency, and contextual use of different information about depth. In W. Epstein & S. Rogers (Eds.), *Perception of space and motion* (pp. 69–117). San Diego, CA: Academic.

DOSHER, B. A., & CORBETT, A. T. (1982). Instrument inferences and verb schemata. *Memory and Cognition, 10*, 531–539.

EMERY, N. J. (2000). The eyes have it: The neuroethology, function and evolution of social gaze. *Neuroscience and Biobehavioral Reviews, 24*, 581–604.

ENNS, J. T. (1990). Three dimensional features that pop out in visual search. In D. Brogan (Ed.), *Visual search* (pp. 37–45). London: Taylor & Francis.

FELDMAN, J. (2004a). How surprising is a simple pattern? Quantifying "Eureka!" *Cognition, 93*, 199–224.

FELDMAN, J. (2004b). *Bayes and the simplicity principle in perception*. Manuscript submitted for publication.

GILLAM, B. (1979). Even a possible figure can look impossible. *Perception, 8,* 229–232.

GLANZER, M., FISCHER, B., & DORFMAN, D. (1984). Short-term storage in reading. *Journal of Verbal Learning and Verbal Behavior, 23,* 467–486.

GOTTESMAN, C. V., & INTRAUB, H. (2003). Constraints on spatial extrapolation in the mental representation of scenes: View-boundaries vs. object-boundaries. *Visual Cognition, 10,* 875–893.

HAYHOE, M. M., SHRIVASTAVA, A., MRUCZEK, D., & PELZ, J. (2003). Visual memory and motor planning in a natural task. *Journal of Vision, 3,* 49–63.

HEIDER, F., & SIMMEL, M. (1944). An experimental study of apparent behavior. *American Journal of Psychology, 57,* 243–259.

HERING, E. (1861). *Beiträge zur Physiologie* (Vol. 1). Leipzig: Engelmann.

HOCHBERG, J. (1968). In the mind's eye. In R. N. Haber (Ed.), *Contemporary theory and research in visual perception* (pp. 309–332). New York: Holt, Rinehart & Winston.

HOCHBERG, J. (1970). Attention, organization, and consciousness. In D. I. Mostofsky (Ed.), *Attention: Contemporary theory and analysis* (pp. 99–124). New York: Appleton-Century-Crofts.

HOCHBERG, J. (1984). The perception of pictorial representations. *Social Research, 51,* 841–862.

HOCHBERG, J. (1997). The affordances of perceptual inquiry: Pictures are learned from the world, and what that fact might mean about perception quite generally. *Psychology of Learning and Motivation, 36,* 15–44.

HOCHBERG, J. (1998). Gestalt theory and its legacy: Organization in eye and brain, in attention and mental representation. In J. Hochberg (Ed.), *Perception and cognition at century's end* (pp. 253–306). San Diego, CA: Academic.

HOCHBERG, J. (2003). Acts of perceptual inquiry: Problems for any stimulus-based simplicity theory. *Acta Psychologica, 114,* 215–228.

HOCHBERG, J., & BROOKS, V. (1970). Reading as intentional behavior. In H. Singer (Ed.), *Theoretical models and processes of reading* (pp. 304–314). Newark, DE: International Reading Association.

HOCHBERG, J., & BROOKS, V. (1978). Film cutting and visual momentum. In J. W. Senders, D. F. Fisher, & R. A. Monty (Eds.), *Eye-movements and higher psychological functions* (pp. 293–313). Hillsdale, NJ: Erlbaum.

HOCHBERG, J., & BROOKS, V. (1996). Movies in the mind's eye. In D. Bordwell & N. Carroll (Eds.), *Post-theory: Reconstructing film studies* (pp. 368–387). Madison: University of Wisconsin Press.

HOCHBERG, J., & BROOKS, V. (2006). Perception and moving pictures: From Brunelleschi and Berkeley to video and video games. In P. Locher, C. Martindale, & L. Dorfman (Eds.), *New directions in aesthetics, creativity and the arts* (pp. 3–18). Amityville, NY: Baywood.

HOCHBERG, J., & GALPER, R. E. (1967). Recognition of faces: I. An exploratory study. *Psychonomic Science, 9,* 619–628.

HOCHBERG, J., & MCALISTER, E. (1953). A quantitative approach to figural "goodness." *Journal of Experimental Psychology, 45,* 361–364.

HOCHBERG, J., & PETERSON, M. A. (1987). Piecemeal organization and cognitive components in object perception: Perceptually coupled responses to moving objects. *Journal of Experimental Psychology: General, 116,* 370–380.

HOFFMAN, J. E., & SUBRAMANIAM, B. (1995). Saccadic eye movements and visual selective attention. *Perception & Psychophysics, 57,* 787–795.

HOLLINGWORTH, A. (2004). Constructing visual representations of natural scenes: The roles of short- and long-term visual memory. *Journal of Experimental Psychology: Human Perception and Performance, 30,* 519–537.

INTRAUB, H. (1981). Rapid conceptual identification of sequentially presented pictures. *Journal of Experimental Psychology: Human Perception and Performance, 7,* 604–610.

INTRAUB, H. (1997). The representation of visual scenes. *Trends in Cognitive Sciences, 1*(6), 217–222.

JONIDES, J., IRWIN, D. E., & YANTIS, S. (1983). Failure to integrate information from successive fixations. *Science, 222,* 188.

KAMINZKI, J., RIEDEL, J., CALL, J., & TOMASELLO, M. (2005). Domestic goats, *Capra hircus,* follow gaze direction and use social cues in an object choice task. *Animal Behaviour, 69,* 11–18.

KELLMAN, P., & SHIPLEY, T. F. (1991). A theory of visual interpolation in object perception. *Cognitive Psychology, 23,* 141–221.

KOWLER, E., ANDERSON, E., DOSHER, B., & BLASER, E. (1995). The role of attention in the programming of saccades. *Vision Research, 35*(13), 1897–1916.

KRUMHANSL, C., & SCHENCK, D. (1997). Can dance reflect the structural and expressive qualities of music? A perceptual experiment on Balanchine's choreography of Mozart's Divertimento No. 15. *Musicae Scientiae, 1,* 63–85.

KUBOVY, M. (1994). The perceptual organization of dot lattices. *Psychonomic Bulletin & Review, 1,* 182–190.

KUBOVY, M., & VAN DEN BERG, M. (2006). *When two Gestalt principles meet, the whole equals the sum of its parts.* Unpublished manuscript.

LAMY, D., LEBER, A., & EGETH, H. E. (2004). Effects of task relevance and stimulus-driven salience in feature-search mode. *Journal of Experimental Psychology: Human Perception and Performance, 30,* 1019–1031.

LEEUWENBERG, E. L. J. (1969). Quantitative specification of information in sequential patterns. *Psychological Review, 76,* 216–220.

LENNIE, P. (1998). Single units and visual cortical organization. *Perception, 27,* 889–935.

LEVIN, D. T., & SIMONS, D. J. (1997). Failure to detect changes to attended objects in motion pictures. *Psychonomic Bulletin and Review, 4,* 501–506.

MACH, E. (1959). *The analysis of sensations.* New York: Dover. (Original work published 1896).

MACK, A., & ROCK, I. (1998). *Inattentional blindness.* Cambridge, MA: MIT Press.

McKOON, G., & RATCLIFF, R. (1992). Inference during reading. *Psychological Review, 99,* 440–466.

MENG, J. C., & SEDGWICK, H. A. (2002). Distance perception across spatial discontinuities. *Perception & Psychophysics, 64,* 1–14.

MOORE, C., & ENGEL, S. A. (2001). Mental models change rapidly with implicitly acquired information about the local environment: A two-tone image study. *Journal of Experimental Psychology: Human Perception and Performance, 27,* 1211–1228.

NAIMARK, M. (1991). Elements of realspace imaging: A proposed taxonomy. *SPIE/SPSE Electronic Imaging Proceedings, 1457,* 169–179.

NEISSER, U. (1967). *Cognitive psychology.* New York: Appleton-Century-Crofts.

NEISSER, U., & BECKLEN, R. (1975). Selective looking: Attending to visually specified events. *Cognitive Psychology, 7,* 480–494.

PELZ, J. B., & CANOSA, R. (2001). Oculomotor behavior and perceptual strategies in complex tasks. *Vision Research, 41,* 3587–3596.

PENROSE, L., & PENROSE, R. (1958). Impossible figures: A special type of visual illusion. *British Journal of Psychology, 49,* 31–33.

PETERSON, M. A. (1994). Shape recognition can and does occur before figure-ground organization. *Current Directions in Psychological Science, 3,* 105–111.

PETERSON, M. A., & ENNS, J. T. (2005). The edge complex: Implicit memory for figure assignment in shape perception. *Perception & Psychophysics, 67,* 727–740.

PETERSON, M. A., & HOCHBERG, J. (1983). The opposed-set measurement procedure. The role of local cue and intention in form perception. *Journal of Experimental Psychology: Human Perception & Performance, 9,* 183–193.

PIZLO, Z., & LI, Z. (in press). Solving combinatorial problems: 15-puzzle. *Memory & Cognition.*

POMERANTZ, J. R. (1983). The rubber pencil illusion. *Perception & Psychophysics, 33,* 365–368.

POTTER, M. C. (1976). Short-term conceptual memory for pictures. *Journal of Experimental Psychology: Human Learning and Memory, 2, 509–522.*

POTTER, M. C., STAUB, A., & O'CONNOR, D. H. (2004). Pictorial and conceptual representation of glimpsed pictures. *Journal of Experimental Psychology: Human Perception and Performance, 30,* 478–489.

POTTER, M. C., STAUB, A., RADO, J., & O'CONNOR, D. H. (2002). Recognition memory for briefly presented pictures: The time course of rapid forgetting. *Journal of Experimental Psychology: Human Perception and Performance, 28,* 1163–1175.

RICHARDS, W., & HOFFMAN, D. D. (1985). *Codon constraints on closed 2D shapes. Computer Vision, Graphics, and Image Processing, 31,* 265–402.

SAJDA, P., & KYUNGIM, B. (2004). Integration of form and motion within a generative model of visual cortex. *Neural Networks, 17,* 809–821.

SCHOLL, B. J., & TREMOULET, P. D. (2000). Perceptual causality and animacy. *Trends in Cognitive Sciences, 4,* 299–309.

SEDGWICK, H. A. (1990). Combining multiple forms of visual information to specify contact relations in spatial layout. In P. S. Schenker (Ed.), *Sensor fusion II: Human and machine strategies, SPIE Proceedings,* 1198.

SIMON, H. (1987). Satisficing. In J. Eatwell, M. Milgate, & P. Newman (Eds.), *The new Palgrave: A dictionary of economics* (Vol. 4, pp. 243–245). New York: Macmillan.

SIMONS, D. (2000). Attentional capture and inattentional blindness. *Trends in Cognitive Sciences, 4,* 147–155.

SPERLING, G. (1960). The information available in brief visual presentations. *Psychological Monographs, 74*(498).

SPERLING, G., & LU, Z.-L. (1998). A systems analysis of motion perception. In T. Watanabe (Ed.), *High-level motion processing* (pp. 153–183). Cambridge, MA: MIT Press.

SPOTTISWOODE, R. (1962). *A grammar of the film.* Berkeley: University of California Press.

STEINMAN, R., PIZLO, Z., & PIZLO, F. (2000). Phi is not beta, and why Wertheimer's discovery launched the Gestalt revolution. *Vision Research, 40,* 2257–2264.

TREISMAN, A., & GEFFEN, G. (1967). Selective attention: Perception or response? *Quarterly Journal of Experimental Psychology, 19,* 1–17.

TRIPATHY, S. P., & CAVANAGH, P. (2002). The extent of crowding in peripheral vision does not scale with target size. *Vision Research, 42,* 2357–2369.

VAN DER HELM, P. A. (2000). Simplicity versus likelihood in visual perception: From surprisals to precisals. *Psychological Bulletin, 126,* 770–800.

VAN DER HELM, P. A., & LEEUWENBERG, E. L. J. (2004). Holographic goodness is not that bad: Reply to Olivers, Chater, and Watson (2004). *Psychological Review,* 111, 261–273.

Part II

Commentaries on Julian Hochberg's Work

Overviews

22

The Piecemeal, Constructive, and Schematic Nature of Perception

Mary A. Peterson

Julian Hochberg has long maintained that visual perception is a *piecemeal*, *schematic*, and *constructive* process, subject to influences from the viewer's perceptual intentions and expectations. Before many others were ready to admit visual perception into the cognitive domain, Hochberg adopted a cognitive view in which mental structure plays a major role in visual perception. The alternative views—that perception is wholistic and wholly stimulus-driven without influence from cognitive factors—prevailed during much of the 20th century, despite occasional arguments to the contrary. In this chapter, I will review the theoretical position that Hochberg articulated in 1968, focusing on his arguments for piecemeal perception, schematic maps, and the effects of expectation and intention on perception. I will also briefly discuss the intellectual history of, and research supporting and extending, these ideas.

Piecemeal Perception

Before 1968, prompted by Gestalt psychology, Hochberg and his colleagues were in the vanguard of the attempt to find a global simplicity metric that could account for perceived organization (e.g., Hochberg & McAllister, 1953). However, drawings of impossible objects (see Hochberg, 1968, Figure 2, reproduced as Figure 8.2, p. 76, this volume) led Hochberg to abandon this wholistic approach. Because the depth specified at one corner of a drawing of an impossible object is inconsistent with that specified at the other corners, it is not possible for the depicted object to be a connected, three-dimensional (3D) entity. Hence, a 3D perceptual solution is not globally simple. A simpler solution would be to see the drawings as patterns in two dimensions (2D). Drawings of impossible objects are nonetheless perceived to depict 3D objects. Therefore, Hochberg concluded that a global simplicity metric could not succeed as an account of human perception; instead, he proposed that the depth cues at the individual corners extend their influence locally, and that the 3D percept results from a process that combines the local cues (i.e., the pieces)

Figure 22.1. A sample cube used by Peterson and Hochberg (1983). The figure is adapted from Figure 2A in Peterson and Hochberg (1983). Copyright © by the American Psychological Association. Adapted with permission.

using limited consistency constraints. Perceived structure is not a detailed, high-fidelity image of the input. In 1982, Hochberg summarized this position in the memorable phrase "perception is not everywhere dense."

Consistent with this piecemeal view of perception, Hochberg and I (Hochberg & Peterson, 1987; Peterson & B. S. Gibson, 1991; Peterson & Hochberg, 1983) showed that cubes that were unambiguously perceived to face in one direction when observers fixated on or attended to one portion (point 1 in Figure 22.1), were nevertheless reversible and open to influence from instructed set when observers fixated on or attended to another portion of the object (point 2 in Figure 22.1). These experiments demonstrated that perceived organization was determined jointly by the fixated or attended part of the object and by the observer's perceptual set rather than by object-wide stimulus information. The cubes we used were smaller than the size of the fovea; hence piecemeal perception did not occur simply because some portions of the object were imaged in peripheral vision and registered in low resolution. We used both 2D and 3D cubes, hence these findings extended beyond pictures and into three dimensions.

Despite the evidence supporting piecemeal perception (cf. Klopfer, 1985), many investigators of vision and cognition persisted in assuming that perception was a faithful replica of the whole stimulus. Perhaps this is because under most circumstances, the piecemeal, inexact nature of the perceptual process is not available phenomenologically. It was not until recently that the compelling demonstrations of "change blindness" with pictures of natural scenes and even with real-world interactions (e.g., Rensink, O'Regan, & Clark, 1997, 2000; Simons & Levin, 1997, 1998) succeeded in dislodging the naïve view that perception is a complete record of the whole stimulus. The change-blindness research extended Hochberg's demonstrations that "perception is not everywhere dense" from a laboratory setting to a real-world setting. Along with inattentional-blindness research (Mack & Rock, 1998), the change-blindness literature is a powerful demonstration of the extent to which perception is affected by attention, intention (i.e., perceptual set), and knowledge. These factors, some of which can be traced back to Helmholtz and J. S. Mill, were also part of Hochberg's argument for perception as a constructive act (see below).

Schematic Maps

Once it is granted that perception is piecemeal in nature, the question of how different perceptual patches are pieced together must be addressed.

Hochberg (1968) proposed that the successive views obtained across glances at different scene (or object) locations were integrated via a *schematic map*. He defined a schematic map as the "program of possible samplings of an extended scene, and of *contingent expectancies* of what will be seen as a result of those samplings" (1968, p. 323). Schematic maps are perceptual-motor expectancies that serve to glue successive glimpses into a single perceptual structure (p. 324). Hochberg argued that the contents of a single glance (or a single act of attention) instantiated a schema that determined both *where* the viewer would look next and *what* he or she would expect to see at that location.

Hochberg's schematic maps are similar in spirit to Hebb's (1949) phase sequences and to Neisser's (1967) ideas regarding analysis by synthesis. They are space-time contingencies that entail finding the most likely object or scene to fit the contents of a single glance and generating an expectation regarding what will be found when the eyes are directed to another location. Hochberg claimed that coherent, organized perception occurs only when the correct schematic map is used to integrate successive views.

Hochberg investigated the role of schematic maps with a film showing, within a stationary aperture, a series of right angles that had been taken in sequence around the perimeter of an outline drawing of a solid cross (Hochberg, 1968, Figure 13, reproduced as Figures 8.12–8.14, pp. 87–88, this volume). Each frame was a surrogate for what might be seen clearly within a single glance at the cross. Observers without information regarding the object from which the frames were chosen or the implied direction of progression around the object (i.e., observers without a schematic map) perceived the right angles as the hands of a clock jumping erratically from one position to another. In contrast, observers who had seen a preview of the cross and who knew the implied direction of progression around it perceived the film as depicting a cross shifting under a stationary aperture, even to the point of detecting errors when the corner that should have been next in the progression was skipped. Here, the schematic map enabling coherent perception was given to the observers by a preview.

More recently, we (Hochberg & Peterson, 1993) tested whether observers could use past experience and the present context to arrive at the correct schematic map (the route likely used in nonexperimental settings). For each of two stimuli, three views within circular apertures (1.9° in diameter) were shown successively and cyclically in the same screen location (see Figure 22.2). Relative position information was given by shifts in the location of a white sheet on which the image seen through the circular windows appeared to have been drawn (see Figure 22.2C). There was no overlap in what was shown between views, and at least for Figure 22.2A there was little good continuation between views.

Observers viewing these displays were instructed to "try to hold" either the black or the white side of the edge as the "figure" (i.e., as the side shaped by the border between the black and white regions),[1] and to press a key

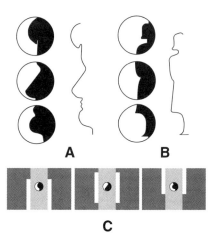

Figure 22.2. A and B. On the left of each panel are the three aperture views of the stimuli used by Hochberg and Peterson (1993). Each view was shown in isolation at the center of the field of view. C. A schematic showing that the relative location of the different views was conveyed to the subjects by movements of a white page with respect to a stationary aperture. From Hochberg and Peterson (1993).

whenever the shape that was being revealed appeared coherent. The black side of the edge portrays a known shape for which the observers presumably have a schematic map (a face profile and a woman, as shown in the outline shapes in the right panels of Figures 22.2A and 22.2B). Portions of known shapes should instantiate expectations of what would be seen if locations above or below that portion were viewed. In contrast, the complementary, white, side portrays a novel shape, for which the observers presumably do not have a schematic map; that is, no space-time expectations should be available to integrate between the aperture views of the novel shapes. If perceived coherency under aperture-viewing conditions requires schematic maps, then observers should report perceiving a more coherent shape when they try to see the black side, rather than the white side, of the edge as the figure.[2] This is what we found for upright stimuli, implying that observers do not need a preview to instantiate a preexisting schematic map (at least under circumstances where the relative locations of the different frames are implied). For inverted versions of the stimuli, observers were much less likely to report perceiving a coherent shape on the black side of the edge, suggesting that the contents of a single glance must be viewed in their canonical orientation in order for the schematic map to operate in these conditions.

How much time is required to instantiate a schematic map? We did not attempt to determine the minimum stimulus onset asynchrony needed for our effects. The answer will surely depend upon the viewer, the context, and the stimulus. In the experiments with a cross, Hochberg found that it took more than 400 ms to integrate the successively presented right angles into a schematic map. When the frames followed each other too quickly, observers perceived only the chaotically jumping hands of a clock (suggesting that apparent motion was perceived across the shortest path), even when they had knowledge regarding the object and the motion direction. Recent related research conducted by Shiffrar and Freyd (1994) showed that it takes time to fit biological motion constraints to an apparent motion display; with too short an interval between frames, observers perceived motion along the shortest path even when it was biologically impossible (e.g., even when it required perceiving a fist move through a head).

Hochberg's schematic maps are rich structures, entailing the processes involved in fitting an interpretation to the contents of the current view, motor plans regarding where to look next, and expectations regarding what will be found there. The quest to identify the processes involved in fitting an interpretation to the current view has a rich intellectual history extending back to Helmholtz and J. S. Mill, who argued that one perceives that which is *most likely* given the current input. On this view, the relationship between the stimulus and the percept is probabilistic, rather than deterministic, and past experience plays an important role in establishing what is most likely. Past experience presumably includes both the recent past (i.e., the last glance) and the more distant past (i.e., contents of schematic maps established on the basis of experience with similar stimuli).

In stressing the importance of expectations derived from past experience, the contemporary Bayesian approach to perception (Barlow, 1990; Knill & Richards, 1996) is close in spirit to the position advocated by Hochberg, by his graduate advisor, Brunswik, and by Helmholtz and J. S. Mill. It is worth noting, however, that investigators within the Bayesian tradition tend to take a wholistic view, and do not consider either the piecemeal nature of perception or the space-time expectancies into which the piecemeal views are integrated.

The space-time expectancy embodied in the schematic maps proposed by Hochberg is currently being revived in the embodied cognition framework (e.g., Barsalou, 1999) and in computational models. For instance, Briscoe (2000) summarizes a neurally plausible computational model that instantiates object recognition as learned temporal sequences in hierarchical, recurrently linked, self-organizing maps. Briscoe was inspired by the recent change-blindness experiments, by Noton and Stark's (1971) eye-movement research, and by Hebb's (1949) phase sequences. Briscoe's proposal can also be viewed as extending Hochberg's (1968) notion of schematic maps into a contemporary cognitive neuroscience framework. Much work remains to be done to investigate how space-time expectancies are established and reactivated. Many questions regarding the necessity of eye movements remain, issues that make contact with research investigating the dynamic nature of perception (e.g., Smith & Thalen, 2003).

Expectation, Attention, and Intention

Expectation, attention, and intention are critical ingredients of a cognitive approach to perception in general and of schematic maps in particular. Hochberg and Peterson (1987) attempted to investigate the expectation component of schematic maps independently of the motor component. Using a 3D wire version of the cube in Figure 22.1, we instructed observers to fixate and track a region similar to point 1 or point 2. On some trials at each fixation point, we instructed observers to try to see a local organization consistent with a cube facing downward and to the left, and on other trials, to try to see a local organization consistent with a cube facing upward and to the right (i.e., for point 2, to try to see the vertical wire in front of the horizontal wire or to try to see the horizontal wire in front of the vertical wire, respectively). These "intention instructions" carried an overt demand character, albeit an opposing demand on different trials. This is the opposed-set method introduced by Peterson and Hochberg (1983). Others had examined whether or not the viewer's expectations affected perception (e.g., Flügel, 1913; Pelton & Solley, 1968), but it was not possible to be certain that perceivers' reports in those previous experiments reflected what they perceived rather than simply what they believed they should report. The opposed-set procedure entails giving observers the same instructions while they view different portions of an object, portions that differ in their ability to support one of the two interpretations. We reasoned that if observers were reporting what they perceived, they should be differentially successful at following the instructions when they fixated the different portions of the cube. This is what we found.

We also addressed whether perception per se was affected by instructed intentions by using a procedure that Hochberg had long championed as a means to increase the likelihood that one was measuring perception rather than memory or response bias. We asked observers to report on a variable that was *perceptually coupled* to the variable to which the intention instructions referred (Hochberg & Peterson, 1987; Peterson, 1986). Perceptually coupled variables are variables that co-vary perceptually but whose relationship is typically unknown to the naïve observer (Hochberg, 1956, 1974). For instance, for oscillating 3D cubes, the perceived direction of rotation is coupled to the perceived depth orientation. Consider a cube oriented to face downward and to the left rotating in a clockwise direction. If the cube's orientation is perceived properly, its direction of rotation is perceived correctly. If the cube is perceived to be facing upward and to the right, however, its direction of rotation is perceived to be counterclockwise. Thus, reports of perceived rotation direction can be used to index perceived orientation under conditions where direct reports regarding orientation might be contaminated by the demand character of the experiment. We recorded observers' online reports of perceived direction of rotation and later used records of the cube's actual rotation direction to translate them into measures of perceived orientation. The results showed that instructed intentions *could* affect perception.

Historical Background and Contemporary Research

The question of whether or not top-down factors, such as the viewer's expectations, intentions, and motivations, affected perception has a long history (e.g., see Woodworth, 1938). The proposal that motivation and needs affected perception was taken up by the New Look psychologists whose research created a stir in the first half of the 20th century (e.g., Bruner & Goodman, 1947; Murphy, 1947). However, much of the New Look research was later shown to be a matter of response bias rather than perception (see Pastore, 1949); this was enough to reject all of the empirical findings of that school (some of it unjustifiably; see Peterson, 1999a).

At the time that Hochberg began exploring the role of the perceiver's expectations and intentions in perception, the dominant view was that perception was immune to influences from such cognitive factors (e.g., Fodor, 1984), except in those rare situations in which perceptual input was impoverished. Hochberg and his colleagues' reliance on perceptually coupled responses made a response-bias interpretation of their experiments exceedingly unlikely. Hence, their results showed the then-dominant view to be wrong. Some theorists (e.g., Pylyshyn, 1999) still attempt to maintain the traditional view by restricting perception to processes lower than those that are influenced by cognitive factors. It has always been difficult to define perception. Yet for certain questions, such as whether or not cognitive factors can influence perception, it is important to agree on a definition of what constitutes adequate reports regarding perception. Hochberg's (1956) proposed criteria—(1) online reports made while the stimulus is present, and (2) responses that could not be made if the stimulus were absent—remain useful today. Reports about perceptually coupled variables satisfy both criteria. Hence, on this definition, Hochberg and his colleagues succeeded in showing that intention affects perception (see Peterson, 1999b).

Mechanisms of Intention

An obvious next question is, how might expectations and intentions affect perception? Possibilities include allocating attention to those parts of an object or scene that support a given interpretation (e.g., Tsal & Kolbet, 1985), "priming" a representation that might be fit to a display in response to instruction (Peterson, Harvey, & Weidenbacher, 1991; Stüber & Stadler, 1999), and activating the relevant brain region (O'Craven et al., 1997). In recent years, physiological research has revealed a plethora of feedback connections from higher to lower brain regions (Van Essen & DeYoe, 1995). Hence, there exist pathways capable of mediating cognitive influences on perception. Recently, Di Lollo, Enns, and Rensink (2000) proposed a neurophysiologically informed theory of perception in which hypothesis testing is a necessary component. Their reentrant visual processing model has yet to be extended to the full space-time matrix of Hochberg's schematic maps, although it could be (see Enns & Austen, chapter 24, this volume). More work remains to be done in this domain. Cognitive neuroscience tools promise to provide some answers.

Closing Remarks

Hochberg has made his mark as a theorist who faces the hard questions in perception. Notably, he was astute enough to see that the impossible figures refuted the reigning global simplicity view that he then supported. Consequently, he abandoned that theoretical position and proposed instead a more complex, cognitive view of perception that remains contemporary today. By taking what was at that time a radical step, Hochberg earned a place as one of the major theorists of his time.

Hochberg is also an ingenious experimenter and a skilled draftsman, adept at constructing the ideal 2D or 3D display to test a hypothesis (e.g., see Figures 22.1 and 22.2). He is a true scholar of perception, with prodigious knowledge of the field, its foundations, and its historical and contemporary trends. He believes that theory should be put into practice; accordingly, he has extended his ideas into the diverse areas of art, film, and computer display design (see chapters 14 and 19–21, this volume).

I was privileged to have him as my graduate advisor.

Notes

1. This is the opposed-set instruction procedure; see the text below for further discussion.

2. Observers in Hochberg and Peterson's (1993) experiment were not informed that a known shape was portrayed on one side of the edge and not the other; they were not shown the outline versions of the face profile and the standing woman; nor did they ever view the three windows simultaneously. Therefore, the relevant schematic maps were instantiated on the basis of the information within the apertures.

References

Barlow, H. (1990). Conditions for versatile learning, Helmholtz's unconscious inference, and the task of perception. *Vision Research, 30*(11), 1561–1571.

Barsalou, L. W. (1999). Perceptual symbol systems. *Behavioral and Brain Sciences, 22,* 577–609.

Briscoe, G. (2000). Vision as temporal trace. *Spatial Vision, 13,* 215–229.

Bruner, J. S., & Goodman, C. D. (1947). Value and need as organizing factors in perception. *Journal of Abnormal and Social Psychology, 42,* 33–44.

Di Lollo, V., Enns, J. T., & Rensink, R. A. (2000). Competition for consciousness among visual events: The psychophysics of reentrant visual processes. *Journal of Experimental Psychology: General, 129,* 481–507.

Flügel, J. C. (1913). The influence of attention in illusions of reversible perspective. *British Journal of Psychology, 5,* 357–397.

Fodor, J. (1984). *The modularity of mind.* Cambridge, MA: MIT Press.

HEBB, D. O. (1949). *The organization of behavior*. New York: Wiley.

HOCHBERG, J. (1956). Perception: Toward the recovery of a definition. *Psychological Review, 6,* 400–405.

HOCHBERG, J. (1968). In the mind's eye. In R. N. Haber (Ed.), *Contemporary theory and research in visual perception* (pp. 309–331). New York: Holt, Rinehart, and Winston.

HOCHBERG, J. (1974). Higher-order stimuli and inter-response coupling in the perception of the visual world. In R. B. MacLeod and H. L. Pick, Jr. (Eds.), *Perception: Essays in honor of James J. Gibson* (pp. 17–39). Ithaca, NY: Cornell University Press.

HOCHBERG, J. (1982). How big is a stimulus? In J. Beck (Ed.), *Organization and representation in perception* (pp. 191–217). Hillsdale, NJ: Lawrence Erlbaum Associates.

HOCHBERG, J., & MCALISTER, E. (1953). A quantitative approach to figural "goodness." *Journal of Experimental Psychology, 46,* 361–364.

HOCHBERG, J., & PETERSON, M. A. (1987). Piecemeal organization and cognitive components in object perception: Perceptually coupled responses to moving objects. *Journal of Experimental Psychology: General, 116,* 370–380.

HOCHBERG, J., & PETERSON, M. A. (1993). Mental representations of occluded objects: Sequential disclosure and intentional construal. *Giornale Italiano di Psicologia, 20,* 805–820. (Monograph edition published in English in honor of Gaetano Kanizsa)

KLOPFER, D. S. (1985). Constructing mental representations of objects from successive views. *Journal of Experimental Psychology: Human Perception & Performance, 11,* 566–582.

KNILL, D. C., & RICHARDS, W. (1996). *Perception as Bayesian inference*. New York: Cambridge University Press.

MACK, A., & ROCK, I. (1998). *Inattentional blindness*. Cambridge, MA: MIT Press.

MURPHY, G. (1947). *Personality*. New York: Harper.

NEISSER, U. (1967). *Cognitive psychology*. New York: Appleton-Century-Crofts.

NOTON, D., & STARK, L. (1971). Eye movements and visual perception. *Scientific American, 224,* 34–43.

O'CRAVEN, K. M., ROSEN, B. R., KWONG, K. K., TREISMAN, A., & SAVOY, R. L. (1997). Voluntary attention modulates fMRI activation in human MT/MST. *Neuron, 18,* 591–598.

PASTORE, N. (1949). Need as a determinant of perception. *Journal of Psychology, 28,* 457–475.

PELTON, L. H., & SOLLEY, C. M. (1968). Acceleration of reversals of a Necker cube. *American Journal of Psychology, 31,* 585–589.

PETERSON, M. A. (1986). Illusory concomitant motion in ambiguous stereograms: Evidence for nonstimulus contributions to perceptual organization. *Journal of Experimental Psychology: Human Perception and Performance, 12,* 50–60.

PETERSON, M. A. (1999a). On the role of meaning in organization. *Intellectica, 28,* 37–51.

PETERSON, M. A. (1999b). Knowledge and intention can penetrate vision. *Behavioral and Brain Sciences, 22,* 389–390.

PETERSON, M. A., & GIBSON, B. S. (1991). Directing spatial attention within an object: Altering the functional equivalence of shape descriptions. *Journal of Experimental Psychology: Human Perception and Performance, 17,* 170–182.

PETERSON, M. A., HARVEY, E. H., & WEIDENBACHER, H. L. (1991). Shape recognition inputs to figure-ground organization: Which route counts? *Journal of Experimental Psychology: Human Perception and Performance, 17,* 1075–1089.

PETERSON, M. A., & HOCHBERG, J. (1983). Opposed-set measurement procedure: A quantitative analysis of the role of local cues and intention in form perception. *Journal of Experimental Psychology: Human Perception and Performance, 9,* 183–193.

PETERSON, M. A., & HOCHBERG, J. (1989). Necessary considerations for a theory of form perception: A theoretical and empirical reply to Boselie and Leeuwenberg, *Perception, 18,* 105–119.

PYLYSHYN, Z. (1999). Is vision continuous with cognition? The case of impenetrability of visual perception. *Behavioral & Brain Sciences, 22,* 341–423.

RENSINK, R. A., O'REGAN, J. K., & CLARK, J. J. (1997). To see or not to see: The need for attention to perceive changes in scenes. *Psychological Science, 8,* 368–373.

RENSINK, R. A., O'REGAN, J. K., & CLARK, J. J. (2000). On the failure to detect changes in scenes across brief interruptions. *Visual Cognition, 7,* 127–146.

SHIFFRAR, M., & FREYD, J. (1994). Apparent motion of the human body. *Psychological Science, 1,* 257–264.

SIMONS, D. J., & LEVIN, D. T. (1997). Change blindness. *Trends in Cognitive Science, 1,* 261–267.

SIMONS, D. J., & LEVIN, D. T. (1998). Failure to detect changes in people in a real world interaction. *Psychonomic Bulletin & Review, 5,* 644–649.

SMITH, L. & THELEN, E. (2003). Development as a dynamic system. *Trends in Cognitive Sciences, 7,* 343–348.

STÜBER, D., & STADLER, M. (1999). Differences in top-down influences on the reversal rate of different categories of reversible figures. *Perception, 28,* 1185–1196.

TSAL, Y., & KOLBET, L. (1985). Disambiguating ambiguous figures by selective attention. *Quarterly Journal of Experimental Psychology, 12,* 97–136.

VAN ESSEN, D. C., & DEYOE, E. A. (1995). Concurrent processing in the primate visual cortex. In M. S. Gazzaniga (Ed.), *The cognitive neurosciences* (pp. 384–400). Cambridge MA: MIT Press.

WOODWORTH, R. S. (1938). *Experimental psychology.* New York: Holt.

23

Hochberg

A Perceptual Psychologist

Barbara Gillam

Hochberg is often regarded as belonging to the cognitive end of perceptual theory. Several authors in the current volume highlight his opposition to Gibson, who denies a role for cognitive processes in perception, regarding it as a direct response to the optic array. Elsewhere, Hochberg is considered to be similar to Gregory and Rock in his emphasis on cognitive entities, which in Hochberg's case are "schema" and "expectancy." Hochberg (1974a) did indeed point to the limitations of Gibson's approach and emphasized those aspects of perception that Gibson left unexplored, such as the selection and sequencing of what to look at. This selection, according to Hochberg, is based on expectancies that are guided by schema and interrogated by eye movements to selected aspects of the scene. The issue of the selection and sequencing of views becomes especially important in considering film, where the sequence is imposed rather than selected and for which the filmmaker must control both schema and visual input. Hochberg has brilliantly explored the principles underlying the successful sequencing of views in film, which clearly often depend for success on cognitive structures set up by previous views. But is his general position a cognitive one, in the sense that he considers that what is perceived is a construction or representation rather than a response to the stimulus? I shall argue that Hochberg is strongly in the perceptual tradition in his interest in the stimulus control of perception and that the cognitive aspects of his theory complement this stimulus-bound process rather than substitute for it. I'll analyze this issue in connection with the following Hochbergian ideas: (1) the concept of schema and its role in perception; (2) the concept of local depth cues; (3) the emphasis on acquiring information for action via planned eye movements rather than from a representation; (4) the preference for strategies rather than entities in explaining perceptual selection; and (5) a strong empirical approach leading to the rejection of overriding principles for perception.

Schema

Hochberg's concept of schema is central to his thinking. From the beginning, he considered such a concept necessary to explain the selection of successive glances and the generation of expectancies guiding those glances. He had an intentional view of perception when it was novel to do so. This approach is now very strongly supported. For example, von Hofsten (2004) shows how many so-called reflexes in young infants can be shown to be intentional information-seeking behavior. However, Hochberg's schema are not similar to Gregory's "hypotheses" or Rock's "inferences." Gregory (1974) argued that perceptions are hypotheses that persist beyond the immediate stimulus input (see also Morgan, 2003). Rock (1983) believed that percepts were constructions from thoughtlike processes operating on the stimulus. Hochberg's schema do not seem to be the objects of perception in the way that these concepts are held to be, although his concept of schema is difficult to pin down, defined as it is somewhat differently at different stages of his thinking. (This is another characteristic of Hochberg's work. He is highly attuned to the implications of data and thus is constantly developing his theory in response to those data.)

Consider the definitions of schema or schematic map in Hochberg (1968), which include (1) the "program of possible samplings of an extended scene and of contingent expectancies of what will be seen as a result of those samplings" (p. 323); (2) a "matrix of space-time expectancies (or assumptions)" (p. 324); and (3) "the integrative component in visual processing, the 'glue' by which successive glimpses are joined into a single perceptual structure" (p. 324). Although the term "expectancy" implies some form of mental representation (Hochberg, 1998a), the third definition seems different from the first two and does seem to imply an ongoing representation rather like Gregory's hypotheses.

On what basis then do I conclude that, unlike Gregory and Rock, Hochberg does not generally seem to think that his schema are the objects of perceptual experience (percepts)? Hochberg (1979) likens schema to a visual image, which seems to indicate that they are at the very least impoverished relative to percepts. Hochberg (1982) states, "The attributes we perceive do not in general exist in some internal model of the object waiting to be retrieved; they are the results of our intention to perceive, and they appear in the context of the perceptual task that calls upon them" (p. 214). In 1998b (p. 281) he says, "One can argue that what is stored between glances is not visual but much more sparse and abstract—perhaps no more detailed than the representation we have when we close our eyes." In other work (Hochberg, 1995), he equates schema with "gist"[1] and considers that they are largely derived from low-resolution peripheral information. He argues that it is the invariant placement of each object fixated within the scene that integrates the glances. The scene can be interrogated at high resolution using expectancies derived from low-resolution input (see also Hochberg, 1970).

The schema thus characterized cannot be either the perception occurring within a glance nor an integration of the contents of successive glances for the latter are much richer than their encoded form (what is available in an image or when the eyes are closed). The schema guide the order in which information is input and provide an overriding plan or map which may influence and be influenced by perceptual encounters with the immediate environment occurring within a glance. In Hochberg's thinking, however, unlike Gregory's, these encounters are not just important in feeding and modifying a cognitive structure. They provide the richness of perceptual experience and interact with the sparser cognitive structures (schema) that are responsible for selection and encoding.

Hochberg regards the nature of the encoding as "mysterious," but he did have the insight, years before change blindness became famous, that "what we do not encode and store is lost to perception" (Hochberg, 1972, p. 69).

Local Depth Cues

One of Hochberg's major contributions is the observation that depth cues operate very locally. It is clear from this important work that successive glances do not modify superordinate schema that constitute the percept. For static views anyway, each glance is processed for depth, and there is no process that fits them into a coherent interpretation across glances. This is clearly shown by the Penrose "impossible" figures and also by the inability to perceive three-dimensional structure when critical features of it, such as junctions,[2] are not represented simultaneously but piecemeal (Hochberg, 1968). The Penrose figures also suggest that there is no process of vetting the perceptual response to a glance to fit a schema of coherence. Such processes are unnecessary. The world is generally coherent.

In another example of the local nature of depth processing, Hochberg points out that local diagonality can stand for vanishing-point structure (which can rarely be apprehended as a whole) in eliciting a three-dimensional percept (Hochberg, 1995). I have also argued that individual diagonals can elicit three-dimensional processing in my attempts to understand the Poggendorff illusion (Gillam, 1998).

Hochberg does not actually seem to disagree entirely with Gibson's contention that we see the world (not a representation of it) by means of responses to features or invariants in the optic array. Hochberg (1956) defines perception in terms of the immediate present. In this sense, he has more in common with Gibson than one might think. The problem he has with Gibson is not so much that perception is direct when something is looked at but that Gibson ignores the significance of the process of selecting where to look, the importance of expectancies in guiding perception, and the role of schema in determining what is encoded while looking.

The Control of Action

Befitting his education at Berkeley in the time of Tolman, Hochberg emphasizes the purposive nature of perception. In 1972 he writes, "most or all visual perception (also) involves highly skilled sequential purposive behaviors" (p. 63). His emphasis on the role of eye movements in interrogating and confirming expectancies is prescient of exciting modern research on complex action by Land and by Hayhoe, Ballard, and colleagues. These authors have found that tasks such as driving, reproducing a pattern, and making peanut butter–and-jelly sandwiches elicit remarkably similar sequences of eye movements in different individuals, who seem to use perception (frequent consultations with visual input by saccades) rather than complex encoded content to guide actions where possible (Ballard, Hayhoe, & Pelz, 1995; Land & Hayhoe, 2001). Action is guided by interrogation of the scene. Changes in the stimulus introduced at critical choice points are noticed. Others are not noticed. Hochberg has always been interested in applied perception, and it is worth noting that his position is also compatible with Brooks's robots (Brooks, 1991), which are guided by continually sampling the environment not by representing it in detail and working from memory.

Strategies and Entities in Selective Attention

The difference between Hochberg's approach and a number of traditional cognitive approaches may be found in his work on selective attention. A strong tradition in cognition is to postulate passive mental entities, such as buffers, filters, etc., to explain performance. Hochberg's (1970) attention article demonstrates his alternative to this approach in the case of selective listening. He attributes the inability to perceive material in the unattended channel to a failure of encoding rather than to the intervention of a filter. What is encoded depends on expectancies set up by prior material. This is essentially a perceptual approach in that it emphasizes active strategies of the observer in dealing with complex input rather than postulating entities to explain it. This view, as Hochberg acknowledges, has much in common with the approach of Neisser (1967).

Rejection of General Principles

On the basis of his observations, Hochberg came to reject general principles to explain what is seen in an individual case (see Hochberg, 1998b). These include the minimum principle (the idea that the perceptual resolution chosen is the simplest or the one that contains the least information), the rigidity principle (the idea that the most rigid of the geometrically possible interpretations is chosen), and the likelihood principle (the idea that what is seen is the most likely of the possible alternatives). He has emphasized that rotating figures often appear as nonrigid perceptual structures when rigid ones are possible given the stimulus (Hochberg, 1998b). He rejected the minimum principle on the basis of observers' ready perception of impossible figures as three-dimensional, despite the fact that they would be simpler with respect to information content as two-dimensional patterns (Hochberg, 1968). This example is a clever early illustration of the visual system being no better than it needs to be for the task at hand. Local information is used because it is good enough in a normally coherent world where local resolutions agree. No principle can predict such things. They must be discovered empirically. There are a number of examples in perception of the visual system not using all of the information available. For example, we (Gillam & McGrath, 1979) showed that symmetry grouping, which is much stronger for lines symmetrical about a vertical axis than for those symmetrical around a horizontal axis, does not correct for head tilt; presumably, it would rarely need to do so.

The rejection of the minimum and likelihood principles as the overarching explanatory principles of perception does not mean that simplicity may not play a role in determining particular perceptual preferences or that likelihood is not broadly important for perception to achieve (see Hochberg, chapter 21, this volume). However, perception research is largely a matter of discovering the secrets, shortcuts, approximations, and strategies of the system—something that the highly empirical Hochberg has done very well. As early as 1974(b) he speculates, "Perhaps a host of separate mechanisms and effects comprise the body of organizational phenomena and perhaps there remains no core process to explain after these are taken into account" (p. 194). This sounds similar to the "bag of tricks" idea later popularized by Ramachandran (1985) although Hochberg would probably regard perception as having more structure than that phrase implies.

Hochberg's observations of ecologically unlikely percepts in particular cases and his related warnings about assuming that perception is controlled by a few principles are especially salutary at present with the strong emergence of Bayesian approaches (Knill & Richards, 1996). These cannot account for such observations and in any case beg the question of how locally Bayesian rules are to be applied (a point made by Peterson in this book) and also to what subset of information they should be applied.

I have tried (perhaps too audaciously) in this brief account to argue that although it is tempting to put Julian Hochberg in a "cognitive" category because of his use of concepts like schema and expectancy, he nevertheless is strongly in the perceptual tradition of emphasizing the stimulus and interactions with it. He does not identify perception with stored entities and is loath to explain perception as the application of broad principles to data.

Hochberg's career shows a constant striving to understand perception as it reveals itself empirically even when that entails rejecting previously held theories or modifying major concepts. This is a rare quality that enriches his profound insights into so many areas of our field.

Notes

1. In his work on art, Hochberg also shows how painters can manipulate the "gist" and thus the expectancies and imaginative demands created in the observer of a painting by manipulating peripheral content.

2. As in so many domains, Hochberg anticipated current research in pointing out the importance of junctions in perceptual organization and object recognition. For a summary of more recent research on junctions, see Hanse and Neumann (2004).

References

BALLARD, D. H., HAYHOE, M. M.; & PELZ, J. (1995). Memory limits in sensorimotor tasks. In J. Hook, J. Davis, & D. Beiser (Eds.), *Models of information processing in the basal ganglia* (pp. 295–313). Cambridge: The MIT Press.

BROOKS, R. A. (1991). Intelligence without representation. *Artificial Intelligence Journal, 47*, 139–159.

GILLAM, B. (1998). Illusions at century's end. In J. Hochberg (Ed.), *Perception and cognition at century's end* (pp. 98–132). New York: Academic.

GILLAM, B., & McGRATH, D. (1979). Orientation relative to the retina determines perceived organization. *Perception & Psychophysics, 26*(3), 177–181.

GREGORY, R. L. (1974). Choosing a paradigm for perception. In E. Carterette & M. Friedman (Eds.), *Handbook of perception* (Vol. 1, pp. 255–283). New York: Academic.

HANSE, T., & NEUMANN, H. (2004). Neural mechanisms for the robust representation of junctions. *Neural Computation, 16*, 1013–1037.

HOCHBERG, J. (1956). Perception: Toward the recovery of a definition. *Psychological Review, 63*, 400–405.

HOCHBERG, J. (1968). In the mind's eye. In R. N. Haber (Ed.), *Contemporary theory and research in visual perception* (pp. 309–331). New York: HOLT, Rinehart, and Winston.

HOCHBERG, J. (1970). Attention, organization, and consciousness. In D. Mostofsky (Ed.), *Attention: Contemporary theory and analysis* (pp. 99–124). New York: Appleton-Century-Crofts.

HOCHBERG, J. (1972). The representation of things and people. In E. H. Gombrich, J. Hochberg, & M. Black (Eds.), *Art, perception and reality* (pp. 47–94). Baltimore: Johns Hopkins University Press.

HOCHBERG, J. (1974a). Higher-order stimuli and inter-response coupling in the perception of the visual world. In R. B. MacLeod & H. L. Pick, Jr. (Eds.), *Perception: Essays in honor of James J. Gibson* (pp. 17–39). ITHACA, NY: Cornell University Press.

HOCHBERG, J. (1974b). Organization and the Gestalt tradition. In E. Carterette & M. Friedman (Eds.), *Handbook of perception* (Vol. 1, pp. 179–210). New York: Academic.

HOCHBERG, J. (1979). Some of the things that paintings are. In C. Nodine & D. Fisher (Eds.), *Views of pictorial representation: Making, perceiving and interpreting* (pp. 17–41). New York: Praeger.

HOCHBERG, J. (1982). How big is a stimulus? In J. Beck (Ed.), *Organization and representation in perception* (pp. 191–217). HILLSDALE, NJ: Erlbaum.

HOCHBERG, J. (1995). The construction of pictorial meaning. In T. Sebeok & S. Umiker-Sebeok (Eds.), *Advances in visual semiotics: The semiotic web 1992– 1993* (pp. 108–162). Berlin: Mouton de Gruyter.

HOCHBERG, J. (1998a). A context for the second half of the century: One view. In J. Hochberg (Ed.), *Perception and cognition at century's end* (pp. 3–18). San Diego, CA: Academic.

HOCHBERG, J. (1998b). Gestalt theory and its legacy: Organization in eye and brain, in attention and mental representation. In J. Hochberg (Ed.), *Perception and cognition at century's end* (pp. 253–292). San Diego, CA: Academic.

HOFSTEN, C. VON. (2004). An action perspective on motor development. *Trends in Cognitive Science, 8*(6), 266–272.

KNILL, D. C., & RICHARDS, W. (1996). *Perception as Bayesian inference.* New York: Cambridge University Press.

LAND, M. F., & HAYHOE, M. (2001). In what ways do eye movements contribute to everyday activities? *Vision Research, 41*(25–26), 3559–3565.

MORGAN, M. (2003). *The space between our ears: How the brain represents visual space.* London: Weidenfeld & Nicolson. Ch 8.

NEISSER, U. (1967). *Cognitive psychology.* New York: Appleton-Century-Crofts.

RAMACHANDRAN, V. S. (1985). Apparent motion of subjective surfaces. *Perception, 14,* 127–134.

ROCK, I. (1983). *The logic of perception.* Cambridge: The MIT Press.

Schematic Maps and Integration Across Glances

24

Mental Schemata and the Limits of Perception

James T. Enns and Erin Austen

Julian Hochberg deserves full credit for giving serious consideration to one of the most obvious and yet overlooked limitations of the human visual system. This is the fact that vision is not uniformly detailed over the field of view. Or, as he liked to put it, "unlike objects themselves, our perception of objects is not everywhere dense" (Hochberg, 1982, p. 214). He was referring to the fact that retinal cones are concentrated near the fovea, so as to maximize spatial resolution for only the central 1–2° around the point of fixation. This limitation means that in order to view any scene in detail, a series of eye movements and fixations must be made. It also implies that our subjective experience of a wide-angled field of view that is high in detail is an illusion, as many textbook demonstrations now attest. Yet, despite this knowledge, formal theories of vision, for the most part, paid very little attention to it until rather late into the 20th century. Even David Marr's (1982) *Vision*, the book often credited with the greatest influence on vision science in the past quarter century, is remarkably silent on the consequences of this fundamental limitation.

Vision researchers have no one to blame for this oversight but themselves. Almost 40 years ago, Hochberg summarized an extensive research program in which this fundamental limitation of vision played a starring role. First presented in 1966 as an invited address at the meeting of the American Psychological Association, and later published as a book chapter titled "In the Mind's Eye" (1968), it laid out some of the consequences of this uneven density of vision.

First, Hochberg pointed out that any analysis of shape and scene perception must be conducted on the mental representation or image in the mind's eye (he called it a *schematic map* or a *mental schema*) rather than on the stimulus itself. This is for the simple reason that every shape or scene enters the mind of the observer through a series of piecemeal views. If there is a picture of an extended scene, it resides solely in the observer's mind. This insight alone rules out all Gestalt analyses of the stimulus and other coding schemes in which the analysis begins with a physical description of the extended stimulus. The proper units of analysis must be sought in the visual brain and mind.

Second, Hochberg proposed that vision be subdivided functionally into two qualitative steps: one involving perception in a momentary glance (the processes at work during a single fixation) and the other involving perception of the schematic map (the integration of multiple glances). It was this second step that he proposed influenced perception so as to make it unique in each individual and in each moment of time, through the forces of attention, learning, and development. Simply put, if the scene is formed only in the mind, then the mind can have maximum influence at the level of the scene rather than at the level of the glance.

Third, he introduced the idea that perception in the momentary glance works recursively with the perception of schemata in a mutual relationship. For example, the processes of perception in a glance might automatically evoke hypotheses (learned or innately acquired) about what lies outside the scope of spatial resolution on that glance, leading to a bias in where the next glance will be placed and what might be expected to be found there. In turn, having an expectation of a particular schema in a scene would lead to the testing of specific hypotheses in subsequent glances. This recursive aspect to Hochberg's theory made it very clear that vision in almost every circumstance is influenced as much by what lies in the mind as by what lies in the eyes of the beholder.

As has been repeated many times in history, the mere fact that these ideas were laid out in a compelling way did not in itself ensure that the larger community of vision science would embrace them. In this essay, we will summarize some recent research we have conducted that is still aimed at establishing Hochberg's points that "our perception of objects is not everywhere dense" and that expectations have a direct influence on what we see in a momentary glance.

The work was conducted in the context of what has come to be called *change blindness* (Rensink, 2002; Simons & Levin, 1997; see also contributions in this volume by Hayhoe, chapter 25, and by Simons & Levin, chapter 37). Basically, interrupting an observer's view of a scene by an eye blink, a brief flicker in the image, a brief occlusion by a passing object, or a change in viewing position can render the observer insensitive to changes in the location and identity of many objects that are not the current focus of attention. Note that these effects should not come as any surprise to those following Hochberg's work, since he pointed out that precisely this sort of "blindness" occurs when observers look at one of the Dutch artist M. C. Escher's impossible buildings. Hochberg's experiments showed that observers were slow and inaccurate in detecting inconsistencies in the details seen in separate glances at these drawings, provided that the information seen within each glance was internally consistent and structurally coherent. According to Hochberg, what it takes to detect the inconsistency in the separate glances is the formation of a very specific schema regarding the three-dimensional structure of a portion of the scene, presumably acquired from the first of the glances. This schema must then be compared with the information acquired in a second glance at another region of the scene. The problem is that such specific schemata are not the default ones we use in exploring scenes of buildings and landscapes. Rather, we simply assume that the physical objects we see will be globally coherent, even in pictures.

One of the key ingredients for effective modern demonstrations of change blindness is that the changes made to the image (by the experimenter) do not disturb the observers' general schema of the scene. Just as observers of Escher's drawings are likely to become aware of the inconsistencies once they test a perceptual schema against the details of a momentary glance, so too the successful detection of change in a scene requires observers to focus "attention" in one way or another on the location in which the change is occurring. On this, all change-blindness researchers seem to agree (Rensink, 2002; Simons & Levin, 1997). But within this broad agreement on the importance of attention, there is a considerable range of opinion on what is meant by focusing attention. The same term has been applied to *objects* that are of central interest to the observer (Rensink, 2000; Rensink et al., 1997), to scene *locations* in which a local visual transient or a unique color has recently been presented (Rensink et al., 1997; Scholl, 2000), and to increased *spatial certainty* about where changed objects will appear (Rensink, 2000; Smilek, Eastwood, & Merikle, 2000).

Our first question was whether the perception of an object is really as rich and detailed as is assumed by many modern attention researchers (Duncan, 1984; Egly, Driver, & Rafal, 1994; Wolfe, 1994; Wolfe, Klempen, & Dahlen, 2000). In this research, there is an oft-repeated claim that paying attention to an object "binds" all the features of that object, at least momentarily, thereby allowing the observer to have equal access to the entire bundle of visual features associated with an object (e.g., its relative location in the scene, its shape, color, texture, motion trajectory, etc.). The strongest evidence for this claim comes from what has been called the *two-object cost*: Reporting two visual attributes of a scene can be accomplished more rapidly and accurately when the two attributes are linked to the same attended object than when they are associated with two or more objects over which attention must be divided or rapidly switched (Baylis, 1994; Davis et al., 2000; Duncan, 1984).

In our first study (Austen & Enns, 2000), we began by differentiating the spatial distribution of attention (is attention aimed narrowly or distributed widely over space?) from the expectations of the observer (is an expected object in the fine details or in a more extended pattern?). We used the flicker method of change detection (Rensink, 2002) in which the observer's task is to view two alternating frames of a display and to indicate as soon as possible whether any item is changed in its identity from frame to frame.

The stimuli were compound letters, as shown in Figure 24.1: At the local level, they were multiple copies of the same small letter; at the global level, these smaller letters formed the shape of a larger letter. Observers were

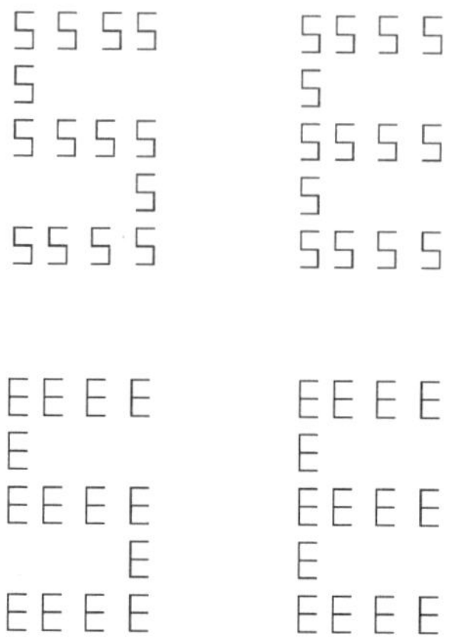

```
5 5 55      5555
5           5
5 5 55      5555
       5    5
5555        5555
```

Figure 24.1. Compound letters used in studies of change detection (Austen & Enns, 2000). Letters on the left form a global S; letters on the right form a global E. The top panel's letters are S at the local level; the bottom panel's letters are E at the local level.

```
E E E E     E E E E
E           E
E E E E     E E E E
       E    E
E E E E     E E E E
```

informed that from trial to trial the number of compound letters would vary randomly among one, three, or five. They were also told that the changed letter would be found either at the local level (the small letters that form the large letter) or at the global level (the large letter formed by the spatial configuration of the smaller letters). The cycling displays consisted of a view of one display for 200 ms, separated by a blank interval of 200 ms, and then a view of the alternate display, followed by the same blank interval. The cycling display ended when the observer pressed a key to indicate whether the two displays contained "no change" or a "change."

In Experiment 1 (Austen & Enns, 2000), the changing letter was equally often at the local and global levels. The results showed first that when attention was spatially distributed among three or five compound letters, rather than being focused on only one letter, changes were detected more readily at the global level. This is consistent with a general bias in perception favoring the global or "gist" level of structure when attention is distributed among multiple objects (Navon, 1977). Faced with the task of dividing attention among multiple objects, it appears that perception first provides access to the crude outline or gist of a scene before narrowing its scope to specific details of a single object. From Hochberg's perspective, one might say that this is consistent with perception having access to a mental schema prior to having access to the details in a momentary glance (Biederman, Rabinowitz, Glass, & Stacey, 1974; Hochstein & Ahissar, 2002).

A second finding of Experiment 1 was that when there was only a single compound letter in a display, changes in letter identity were detected equally well at the local and global levels of structure. This finding, at first blush, appears to concur with the popular modern view that a single attended object is richly represented in the mind of the observer, following only a single brief glance (Duncan, 1984).

However, the results of Experiment 2 (Austen & Enns, 2000) held a surprise for this interpretation. In this experiment, the perceptual expectations of the observer were systematically varied without influencing the response tendency. In a global bias condition, 75% of the trials involved a change to one of the global letters while the remaining 25% of those trials involved letter changes at the local level. A local bias condition involved the complementary arrangement: 25% of the changes were to global letters and 75% were to local letters. Under these conditions, observers were both faster and more accurate in detecting changes at the level that was most likely to change. Most important, this was true even when there was only a single item to attend in order to detect the change. It must be emphasized that this expectation bias on perception was not associated with any response bias: Change versus no-change trials were still equally likely, just as in Experiment 1. This finding therefore strongly suggests that the number of objects that are attended is not the only limiting factor on perception; the nature of the mental schema that observers test when they first view the attended object are also important (Archambault O'Donnell, & Schyns, 1999; Lamb, Pond, & Zahir, 2000). Even a single, visually attended compound letter is not represented in the mind such that its local and its global structure are equally accessible for report.

But how general is this conclusion? Should we draw the conclusion from these results that attended objects are generally not represented as richly and in as much detail as predicted by research on object-based attention? After all, compound letters could be criticized for having little ecological or social significance as objects. If anything, they are among the most arbitrary and artificial stimuli that could possibly be tested. Objects in the natural world are noted for their redundancy, not for their independently variable attributes at different levels of analysis. Moreover, the constituents of these stimuli— letters of the alphabet—are extremely overlearned. Perhaps attended objects are richly represented when a more natural and less familiar set of stimuli is tested.

A second study aimed at these questions (Austen & Enns, 2003) tested the perception of human faces with an experimental design very similar to the study using compound letters (Austen & Enns, 2000). Faces were chosen for several reasons. First, they are stimuli with unique social and biological significance for humans, who are experts at making the subtle visual discriminations required to identify them. Observers' expertise with faces should ensure that they are processed efficiently even when the particular faces are not well known. Second, face perception depends on "configural processing," meaning that the perception of the individual constituents and features of a face (e.g., particular nose shape, emotional expression) are highly dependent on the presence of other constituents and features (e.g., mouth shape, three-dimensional structure of the face). This strongly biases the test in favor of finding evidence of a rich representation of an attended face. If face perception turns out to be every bit as expectation-dependent as the perception of compound letters, we would be forced to conclude that their perception in a glance is also not richly detailed. Even the details of a single glance may not be

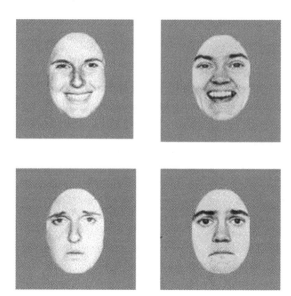

Figure 24.2. Faces used in studies of change detection (Austen & Enns, 2003). Faces on the left are both person 1; faces on the right are person 2. Upper faces show "happy" expressions while lower faces show "sad" expressions.

"everywhere dense" (Peterson & Gibson, 1991; Peterson & Hochberg, 1983).

The stimulus set we used is shown in Figure 24.2. It consisted of four faces derived from the combinations of two individuals (persons 1 and 2) posing with each of two emotional expressions (happy and sad). We again conducted two experiments, one in which change in the faces was equally likely to occur in the identity or in the emotional expression of the face (Experiment 1) and one in which the change was more likely to occur in either the identity or the emotional expression of the face (Experiment 2).

We also repeated all of our tests for both upright faces and for upside-down faces, to ensure that observers were actually processing these stimuli as faces. For example, when faces are seen in an upside-down orientation, the identity of even well-known faces is difficult to determine (Yin, 1969). In contrast, the perception of individual features is not influenced as strongly by turning the picture upside-down. It was important to include this kind of a control in our experiment, to ensure that observers were not "cheating" in our task by performing it in a way that bypasses the normal route for face perception. The results from the upside-down control conditions indicated that observers were indeed treating the images as faces.

The important result of the face study was that change detection in faces was strongly influenced by observers' expectation regarding which aspect of the face was likely to change on a given trial. Observers detected an expected change in a face, both in identity and in emotional expression, more rapidly and accurately than an unexpected change in the same face. This was true not only when attention was distributed across five faces, as would be expected by almost all theories of perception on the grounds that detection of change in an individual face would require a time-consuming narrowing of attention to an individual face. But it was equally true when observers were examining a single face, a face that was at the center of their gaze and could be attended single-mindedly because it was unaccompanied by any other stimuli. Again, it is important to emphasize that this result was not contaminated by any tendency to detect change in itself, since change and no-change trials were equally represented in all conditions of the experiment. Yet, attending to a face did not permit equally efficient change detection of expected and unexpected changes (see also Schyns & Gosselin, 2003).

We interpret these two studies as extending Julian Hochberg's original observation that "our perception of objects is not everywhere dense." That is, these results take us beyond the limitations that derive from having a fovea that registers only a small region of the visual field in much detail at any moment in time. These limitations of foveal vision are very real and must be overcome every time we view an extended scene. Yet, an even more fundamental limit on perception derives from the fact that our visual consciousness is able to focus on only one mental schema at a time. We believe that this way of framing the limitations of vision helps to clarify one of the puzzles of the change-blindness literature. The puzzle is that although focused attention is *necessary* to detect change in a scene (Rensink et al., 1997), focused spatial attention is not itself *sufficient* for reliable change detection. Its lack of sufficiency can be seen in the cases of change blindness that have been reported even when foveal viewing of an object has been ensured and attention has been drawn to the object that is about to change (Levin & Simons, 1997; Simons & Levin, 1998). Indeed, the change-detection experiments just described are another instance of this lack of immunity to change blindness when viewing attended objects.

What we believe is missing in this way of talking about attention is the important distinction between merely orienting toward *a location* or *an object* versus attending to the *match between the contents of an expected mental schema for a location (an object) and the sensory information at that location (about that object)*. Our view is that perception is fundamentally limited by the *inherently* serial nature of the schema-matching process (Di Lollo, Enns, & Rensink, 2000; Enns & Di Lollo, 2000; Kawahara, Enns, & Di Lollo, 2002), not only by the *practically* serial nature of eye movements and attention over spatial locations. Support for this view comes from many recent experiments showing the severe serial limitations on processing that remain when observers view rapid sequences of foveal images (Shapiro, Arnell, & Raymond, 1997; Visser, Bischof, & Di Lollo, 1999). The challenge for vision research in the future will be to try to understand the basis of this limit. Why is it that the massively parallel and interconnected neural system called the brain is only able to bring one mental schema to consciousness at a time? Although we do not have an answer at present, it is important to acknowledge the large contribution that Julian Hochberg has made in bringing modern researchers to the point where they are even able to pose this question.

References

ARCHAMBAULT, A., O'DONNELL, C., & SCHYNS, P. G. (1999). Blind to object changes: When learning the same object at different levels of categorization modifies its perception. *Psychological Science, 10,* 249–255.

AUSTEN, E., & ENNS, J. T. (2000). Change detection: Paying attention to detail. *Psyche, 6,* 11.

AUSTEN, E., & ENNS, J. T. (2003). Change detection in an attended face depends on the expectation of the observer. *Journal of Vision, 3,* 64–74.

BAYLIS, G. C. (1994). Visual attention and objects: Two-object cost with equal convexity. *Journal of Experimental Psychology: Human Perception and Performance, 20,* 208–212.

BIEDERMAN, I., RABINOWITZ, J. C., GLASS, A. L., & STACEY, E. W. J. (1974). On the information extracted from a glance at a scene. *Journal of Experimental Psychology, 103,* 597–600.

DAVIS, G., DRIVER, J., PAVANI, F., & SHEPHARD, A. (2000). Reappraising the apparent costs of attending to two separate visual objects. *Vision Research, 40,* 1323–1332.

DI LOLLO, V., ENNS, J. T., & RENSINK, R. A. (2000). Competition for consciousness among visual events: The psychophysics of reentrant visual processes. *Journal of Experimental Psychology: General, 129,* 481–507.

DUNCAN, J. (1984). Selective attention and the organization of visual information. *Journal of Experimental Psychology: General, 113,* 501–517.

EGLY, R., DRIVER, J., & RAFAL, R. D. (1994). Shifting visual attention between objects and locations: Evidence from normal and parietal lesion subjects. *Journal of Experimental Psychology: General, 123,* 161–177.

ENNS, J. T., & DI LOLLO, V. (2000). What's new in visual masking? *Trends in Cognitive Sciences, 4,* 345–352.

HOCHBERG, J. (1968). In the mind's eye. In R. N. Haber (Ed.), *Contemporary theory and research in visual perception* (pp. 309–331). New York: Holt, Rinehart and Winston.

HOCHBERG, J. (1982). How big is a stimulus? In J. Beck (Ed.), *Organization and representation in perception* (pp. 191–217). Hillsdale, NJ: Lawrence Erlbaum Associates.

HOCHSTEIN, S., & AHISSAR, M. (2002). View from the top: Hierarchies and reverse hierarchies in the visual system. *Neuron, 36,* 791–804.

KAWAHARA, J., ENNS, J. T., & DI LOLLO, V. (2002). Task switching mediates the attentional blink even without backward masking. *Perception & Psychophysics, 65,* 339–351.

LAMB, M. R., POND, H. M., & ZAHIR, G. (2000). Contributions of automatic and controlled processes to the analysis of hierarchical structure. *Journal of Experimental Psychology: Human Perception and Performance, 26,* 234–245.

LEVIN, D. T., & SIMONS, D. J. (1997). Failure to detect changes to attended objects in motion pictures. *Psychonomic Bulletin and Review, 4,* 501–506.

MARR, D. (1982). *Vision*. New York: Freeman.

NAVON, D. (1977). Forest before trees: The precedence of global features in visual perception. *Cognitive Psychology, 9,* 353–383.

PETERSON, M. A., & GIBSON, B.S. (1991). Directing spatial attention within an object: Altering the functional equivalence of shape descriptions. *Journal of Experimental Psychology: Human Perception and Performance, 17,* 170–182.

PETERSON, M. A., & HOCHBERG, J. (1983). Opposed-set measurement procedure: A quantitative analysis of the role of local cues and intention in form perception. *Journal of Experimental Psychology: Human Perception and Performance, 9,* 183–193.

RENSINK, R. A. (2000). Visual search for change: A probe into the nature of attentional processing. *Visual Cognition, 7,* 345–376.

RENSINK, R. A. (2002). Change detection. *Annual Review of Psychology, 53,* 245–277.

RENSINK, R. A., O'REGAN, J. K., & CLARK, J. J. (1997). To see or not to see: The need for attention to perceive changes in scenes. *Psychological Science, 8,* 368–373.

SCHOLL, B. J. (2000). Attenuated change blindness for exogenously attended items in a flicker paradigm. *Visual Cognition, 7,* 377–396.

SCHYNS, P. G., & GOSSELIN, F. (2003). Diagnostic use of scale information for componential and holistic recognition. In M. A. Peterson & G. Rhodes (Eds.), *Perception of faces, objects, and scenes* (pp. 120–145). New York: Oxford University Press.

SHAPIRO, K. L., ARNELL, K. A., & RAYMOND, J. E. (1997). The attentional blink: A view on attention and a glimpse on consciousness. *Trends in Cognitive Science, 1,* 291–296.

SIMONS, D. J., & LEVIN, D. T. (1997). Change blindness. *Trends in Cognitive Science, 1,* 261–267.

SIMONS, D. J., & LEVIN, D. T. (1998). Failure to detect changes to people during a real-world interaction. *Psychonomic Bulletin and Review, 5,* 644–649.

SMILEK, D., EASTWOOD, J. D., & MERIKLE, P. M. (2000). Does unattended information facilitate change detection? *Journal of Experimental Psychology: Human Perception and Performance, 26,* 480–487.

VISSER, T. A. W., BISCHOF, W. F., & DI LOLLO, V. (1999). Attentional switching in spatial and non-spatial domains: Evidence from the attentional blink. *Psychological Bulletin, 125,* 458–469.

WOLFE, J. M. (1994). Guided search 2.0: A revised model of visual search. *Psychonomic Bulletin & Review, 1,* 202–238.

WOLFE, J. M., KLEMPEN, N., & DAHLEN, K. (2000). Post-attentive vision. *Journal of Experimental Psychology: Human Perception and Performance, 26,* 693–716.

YIN, R. K. (1969). Looking at upside-down faces. *Journal of Experimental Psychology, 81,* 141–145.

25

Integration of Visual Information Across Saccades

Mary M. Hayhoe

One of the most important and also one of the most elusive issues in visual perception is the nature of the visual representations that span fixations. Many visual computations, such as perceiving the color or motion of a stimulus, can be accomplished within the time span of a single fixation. However, visual operations are normally embedded in the context of extended behavioral sequences. This means that many visual behaviors span several fixations. In the spatial domain, observers must maintain constancy of visual direction across different eye and head positions as a basis for coordinated actions. In the temporal domain, visual information acquired in one gaze position must be related in some way to the previous ones. Thus, some kind of internal model or representation of the environment, which persists across gaze positions, seems necessary to ensure coordinated movement. Our current understanding of the nature of this representation, however, is limited.

A large body of work in the last ten years indicates that visual representations that span fixations are very impoverished (e.g., Henderson & Hollingworth, 1999; Simons, 2000; Simons & Levin, 1997). Evidence for limited memory from prior fixations is provided by the finding that observers are extremely insensitive to changes in the visual scene during an eye movement, film cut, or similar masking stimulus (Henderson, 1992; Irwin, 1991; Irwin, Zacks, & Brown, 1990; O'Regan, 1992; Pollatsek & Rayner, 1992; Rensink, O'Regan, & Clark, 1997; Simons, 1996). Since detection of a change requires a comparison of the information in different fixations, this "change blindness" has been interpreted as evidence that only a small part of the information in the scene is retained across fixations. It is generally agreed that, following a change in gaze position, observers retain in memory only a small number of items, or "object files," consistent with the capacity limits of visual working memory, together with information about scene "gist" and other higher-level semantic information (Hollingworth & Henderson, 2002; Irwin & Gordon, 1998). For example, O'Regan and Levy-Schoen (1983) suggested that observers maintain only a "coarse semantic description" of a scene and acquire specific information as needed via directed fixations.

It is unclear, however, exactly what is meant by a "coarse semantic description" or how completely it specifies the contents of the representation that spans fixations. We are inclined to think of it as a kind of degraded photograph, perhaps with words in the place of objects. A number of recent observations suggests that this is not a very good way to think about it. Indeed, the ideas proposed by Hochberg in 1968 seem to better capture the complexity of the representations that span fixations. Long a student of film, Hochberg proposed a "space in the mind's eye" that is constructed from successive frames in a movie as the camera pans across a scene (see Hochberg, 1986, for an extensive review). The format of movies, namely, successive frames presented over time, mimics normal vision, in that successive images result from sequences of fixations. The fact that we have no trouble interpreting movie sequences suggests that the same underlying perceptual mechanisms serve both movie viewing and normal vision. Hochberg (1968) proposed that the integrated representation across fixations could be thought of as a *schematic map*. By this, he meant not an image-like representation, but a *program of possible samplings of an extended scene and of contingent expectancies of what will be seen as a result of those samplings*. As an illustration of what Hochberg meant by a schematic map, it is perhaps simplest to use his own example, that of looking at a cross like that in Figure 25.1 through an aperture that traces the contour of the cross in successive views. One can see that, given the idea of the cross and the knowledge of how the aperture is moving, the resulting sequence of images is perfectly comprehensible. Without this context, it is an uninterpretable sequence of right angles.

The schematic map is thus not merely a variety of passive visual storage, but entails the active collection of visual information via eye movements. In this sense, it is similar to the internal model of space proposed by Loomis and colleagues as a basis for guiding movements within a scene (see, e.g., Loomis & Beall, 2004). The idea of an internal model of space comes from experiments that demonstrate excellent ability to navigate and update one's position in spaces previously seen, but no longer visible. The reality of this extended schematic map, or representation of space in the mind's eye, is also revealed by the excellent accuracy of very large gaze changes to regions

Figure 25.1. A cross seen through an aperture that moves clockwise around the boundary. Alternatively, the aperture may be stationary and the cross move behind it. Individual views, shown on the right, are ambiguous. Adapted from Hochberg (1968).

outside the field of view (greater than 90°), which land within a few degrees of the target (Land, Mennie, & Rusted, 1999). The need to orient to regions outside the field of view in natural vision (for example, moving around within a room) provides a rationale for such a model of space. Interestingly, the restrictions of peripheral vision occasioned by retinal diseases are often not noticed by subjects until the field of view is drastically reduced. This demonstrates the seamless nature of the perceptual transition between locations currently in view and those out of view and is consistent with the idea of an internal model or schematic map of space in the mind's eye, where observers' *contingent expectancies* are fulfilled, following an appropriate movement.

Given that the world is rendered to our senses through the sampling process occasioned by saccadic eye movements, it is natural to suppose that knowledge of those movements and their consequences are embodied in our internal representation of the world, as Hochberg suggests. Mackay (1973) had a similar insight in his attempt to understand visual stability. He gave as an example the tactile experience occasioned by exploring a familiar object. Here, the tactile sensations occur in a sequence as a result of active exploration of the object. This is a tactile analog of the visual presentation of the cross through an aperture in Figure 25.1. It is the mental representation or schematic map of the object as a whole that provides the continuity or, by analogy, tactile "stability." Similar ideas have also been put forward by O'Regan and Noë (2001). Support for this idea comes also from a different source. It is possible to change the gain of saccadic eye movements by repeatedly shifting the target during the saccade, so that the subject lands off target. After 50 trials or so, subjects adjust the gain of their saccades so that a target in one location will generate a saccade to the location to which the target has consistently been moved. Presumably, the saccadic system interprets the repeated errors as a miscalibration. Interestingly, this change in gain does not occur if the target is blanked for the first 100 ms after landing (Bahcall & Kowler, 2000). When the target is no longer present on arrival, subjects' expectancies are violated, and the saccadic system is no longer obliged to assume responsibility for the error. This example reinforces Hochberg's suggestion that what subjects expect to see after a saccade is critically important to perception.

The spatial veridicality of the internal model of space or schematic map is probably greater than Hochberg supposed. When viewing films, observers can tolerate significant spatial inconsistencies (Hochberg, 1986). However, when we rely on the body, rather than perceptual awareness, as a device for reporting on the nature of the schematic map, there is evidence for quite astonishing spatial precision. As mentioned, above, observers can make extremely accurate movements (combined eye-head-body) up to 180°. Hayhoe (2002) also showed that memory representations integrated across saccades must include precise spatial information that is used for saccade planning.

Another important insight into the nature of the internal representation of a scene is provided by an elegant experiment by Henderson and Hollingworth (2003). They showed subjects an image of a scene viewed through narrow vertical slats that occluded 50% of the image. When the slats are shifted 180°, revealing completely new parts of the image and occluding the regions previously visible, subjects are completely unable to see the shift, unless they focus on a small detail in the scene. This makes sense if there really is a representation of a scene as a whole—something that has not been clear—and if the image is parsed as a scene plus an occluder. Just as object recognition is robust to occlusion, so too are scenes. When the occluder moves, the scene does not in fact change, and the visual system accurately reports that fact. This observation is reminiscent of Hochberg's example of the cross figure seen through an aperture. The image sequence can be parsed into a schematic representation of a cross, seen partially through the occluder.

A final observation that seems very consistent with Hochberg's schematic maps was made by Droll, Hayhoe, Triesch, and Sullivan (2004). Hochberg pointed out the importance of perceptual learning in the construction of schematic maps. Thus, seeing the cross in Figure 25.1 depends on previous experiences with seeing crosses and what happens when fixation is moved from one part of an object to another. Droll et al. (2004) asked subjects to pick up and move one of a set of virtual red or blue bricks of different sizes. They looked at subjects' sensitivity to color changes in the brick that was being moved. Figure 25.2 shows the layout of the virtual scene. In one of the conditions of the experiment, when the color of the brick changed from red to blue or vice versa, subjects reported seeing the change only about 40% of the time, despite fixating the brick for as much as a second before and after the change. If, however, the brick changed to green, a color not previously present in the scene, subjects almost invariably noticed the change. This is hard to explain if we ask the question of whether the internal representation of a scene codes low-level features or not, since a low-level feature change is detectable in one instance, but not in the other. However, both red and blue objects are always present in the scene (though not necessarily always within the field of view of the head-mounted display). Landing on either a blue or a red brick after a saccade is a frequent event, so seeing a change from red to blue requires careful monitoring of the identity of the brick in hand. A change to a new color such as green, however, violates the expectations that subjects have built up over the course of the experiment. Thus, the schema is violated. A similar observation was also made by Rich and Gillam (2000).

In summary, Hochberg's conceptualization of a schematic map seems to capture many of the observed complexities of the information integrated across saccades. A schematic map is a rather more active representation than that proposed by Irwin and others, as it entails knowledge of the movements involved in the acquisition of the information and a set of expectations of the consequences of these movements (see, e.g., Hollingworth & Henderson,

Figure 25.2. View of the virtual environment used by Droll et al. (2004). Finger position is indicated by the small dot on the face of the central brick. (The thumb is out of view behind the brick.) The subject has picked up one of the bricks and is moving it toward the front of the display to place it on one of the conveyor belts visible at the bottom of the display. The color change is made during this movement.

2002; Irwin & Gordon, 1998; O'Regan, 1992; Pollatsek & Rayner, 1992). It may also contain specific visual (rather than semantic) information, while at the same time maintain inconsistencies. Finally, it reflects the effects of perceptual experience.

References

BAHCALL, D. O., & KOWLER, E. (2000). The control of saccadic adaptation: Implications for the scanning of natural visual scenes. *Vision Research, 40,* 2779–2796.

DROLL, J., HAYHOE, M., TRIESCH, J., & SULLIVAN, B. (2004). Working memory for object features is influenced by scene context. *Journal of Vision, 4,* 152a.

HAYHOE, M. (2002). Visual short term memory and motor control. In J. Hyönä, D. Munoz, W. Heide, & R. Radach (Eds.), *The brain's eyes: Neurobiological and clinical aspects of oculomotor research* (pp. 349–363). Amsterdam: Elsevier.

HENDERSON, J. M. (1992). Visual attention and eye movement control during reading and picture viewing. In K. Rayner (Ed.), *Eye movements and visual cognition* (pp. 261–283). Berlin: Springer.

HENDERSON, J. M., & HOLLINGWORTH, A. (1999). High-level scene perception. *Annual Review of Psychology, 50,* 243–271.

HENDERSON, J. M., & HOLLINGWORTH, A. (2003). Global transsaccadic change blindness during scene perception. *Psychological Science, 14,* 493–497.

HOCHBERG, J. (1968). In the mind's eye. In R. Haber (Ed.), *Contemporary theory and research in visual perception* (pp. 309–331). New York: Appleton-Century-Crofts.

HOCHBERG, J. (1986). Representation of motion and space in video and cinematic displays. In K. Boff, L. Kauffman, & J. Thomas (Eds.), *Handbook of perception and human performance* (Vol. 1, pp. 22.21–22.64). New York: Wiley.

HOLLINGWORTH, A., & HENDERSON, J. M. (2002). Accurate visual memory for previously attended objects in natural scenes. *Journal of Experimental Psychology: Human Perception and Performance, 28,* 113–136.

IRWIN, D. (1991). Information integration across saccadic eye movements, *Cognitive Psychology, 23,* 420–456.

IRWIN, D. (1992). Memory for position and identity across eye movements. *Journal of Experimental Psychology: Learning, Memory, & Cognition, 18,* 307–317.

IRWIN, D. (1996). Integrating information across saccadic eye movements. *Curr. Dir. Psychological Science, 5,* 94–100.

IRWIN, D., & GORDON, R. (1998). Eye movements, attention, and trans-saccadic memory. *Visual Cognition, 5,* 127–155.

IRWIN, D. E., ZACKS, J. L., & BROWN, J. S. (1990). Visual memory and the perception of a stable visual environment, *Perception and Psychophysics, 47,* 35–46.

LAND, M. F., MENNIE, N., & RUSTED, J. (1999). Eye movements and the roles of vision in activities of daily living: Making a cup of tea. *Perception, 28,* 1311–1328.

LOOMIS, J., & BEALL, A. (2004). Model-based control of perception/action. In L. Vaina et al. (Eds.), *Optic flow and beyond* (pp. 421–441). Netherlands: Kluwer.

MACKAY, D. (1973). Visual stability and voluntary eye movements. In R. Jung (Ed.), *Handbook of sensory physiology* (pp. 307–331). Berlin: Springer.

O'REGAN, J. K. (1992). Solving the "real" mysteries of visual perception: The world as an outside memory. *Canadian Journal of Psychology, 46,* 461–488.

O'REGAN, J. K., & LEVY-SCHOEN, A. (1983). Integrating visual information from successive fixations: Does trans-saccadic fusion exist? *Vision Research, 23,* 765–769.

O'REGAN, J. K., & NOË, A. (2001). A sensorimotor account of vision and visual consciousness. *Behavioral & Brain Sciences, 24,* 939–1031.

POLLATSEK, A., & RAYNER, K. (1992). What is integrated across fixations? In K. Rayner (Ed.), *Eye movements and visual cognition: Scene perception and reading* (pp. 166–191). New York: Springer-Verlag.

RENSINK, R. A., O'REGAN, J. K., & CLARK, J. J. (1997). To see or not to see: The need for attention to perceive changes in scenes. *Psychological Science, 8,* 368–373.

RICH, A., & GILLAM, B. (2000). Failure to detect changes in color for lines rotating in depth: The effects of grouping and type of color change. *Vision Research, 40,* 1377–1384.

SIMONS, D. (1996). In sight, out of mind: When object representations fail. *Psychological Science, 7,* 301–305.

SIMONS, D. J. (2000). Current approaches to change blindness. *Visual Cognition, 7,* 1–15.

SIMONS, D., & LEVIN, D. (1997). Change blindness. *Trends in Cognitive Science, 1,* 261–267.

26

Scene Perception

The World Through a Window

Helene Intraub

If photoreceptors coated our bodies instead of our retinas, we'd be able to see in all directions simultaneously—thus eliminating one of the fundamental mysteries of perception. Instead, the visual field is spatially limited, preventing us from ever seeing our surroundings all at once. Retinal inhomogeneity limits the view further—with the best visual acuity restricted to the tiny foveal region (only 2° of visual angle). In a sense, it as if the world is always viewed through a "window": an imperfect window, with graded clarity. Thus, movement is critical for scene perception; ballistic saccades shift the position of the foveae up to four times per second, and head movements rapidly bring new areas into view. How we come to experience a coherent representation of our surroundings based on these discrete, inhomogeneous samples is one of the mysteries of perception.

Hochberg's (1978, 1986a) approach to the puzzle of visual coherence is multifaceted. He has addressed it through innovative analyses of both perceptual errors (visual illusions) and perceptual "successes" in the face of impoverished input (e.g., aperture viewing, perception of motion pictures). He proposes that one's current view is incorporated within a *schema*, which is a cognitive structure that includes memory for prior views as well as anticipatory projections of upcoming information as determined by the viewer's goals and actions. Successive views are understood within the context of this schema, or "mental map." He has provided numerous compelling means of exemplifying this idea. I will describe just two examples, in which he drew on situations in which sensory input is even more constrained than during normal free viewing.

In his fascinating discussion of film editing and perception, Hochberg (1986a) describes a situation in which the camera sweeps across a scene. If it sweeps to the right, layout shifts across the screen toward the left and disappears beyond the left-hand edge. Yet, he points out, "in most situations there is a compelling perception of space, in which an extent has been traversed and about which the viewer has a clear visual knowledge. That extent is larger than the screen and exists nowhere but in the mind of the viewer" (Hochberg, 1986a, p. 22.43). The viewer's representation beyond the screen is palpable—creating the sense of continuous, complex spaces that in reality do not exist (e.g., interiors of starships, old western towns) except as movie sets that are noncontinuous, truncated bits of the to-be-created world with no continuity beyond the deliberately constrained viewpoint of the camera.

Experimental support for the proposed schema has been provided by Hochberg's aperture-viewing experiments. In one study, using stop-motion photography, a pair of perpendicular lines was animated so that it rotated around the inside of a circle (Hochberg, 1978, 1986a; see Figures 8.12–8.14, pp. 87–88 of this book). Viewers reported seeing a clock face with hands at a fixed angle moving around the dial. However, the successive positions of the perpendicular lines were selected so that they were identical to what would be seen if an outline cross (⊏⊐) was moving behind a peephole. If an "establishing shot" (showing a full view of the cross) or a verbal description of the cross preceded the animation, viewers' perception was markedly different. They reported seeing an outline cross moving behind a round aperture. Perception was "concrete" enough to allow them to note when one of its four arms was skipped. This could not be based on *sensory* integration because none of the "arms" was ever actually shown in the animation (just two perpendicular lines). Nor could it be based on a "good guess" given the establishing shot, because in addition to noting a missing arm, perception of the moving cross was sensitive to the presentation rate at which successive views were shown (described in Hochberg, 1986a).

Hochberg stressed the "abstract" nature (i.e., sketchy rather than picture-like) of the mental schema that facilitates view integration (e.g., Hochberg, 1978, 1982, 1986a, 1986b). This was initially not a widely accepted view in the eye-movement literature (e.g., Davidson, Fox, & Dick, 1973), but over the years, research on eye movements and transsaccadic memory has provided widely accepted support for this position (e.g., Irwin, 1991, 1993; McConkie & Currie, 1996; Rayner & Pollatsek, 1992). Although a sketchy representation is likely to be more forgiving than a rigid sensory representation in integrating layout, there is also a cost. Lack of detail can result in the failure to detect changes from one view to the next—exemplified in cinema by film-goers' frequent failure to detect continuity errors (see Hochberg, 1986a, for an example). This important observation was subsequently supported in a series of influential papers on "change blindness" (Rensink, O'Regan, & Clark, 1997; Simons, 2000; Simons & Levin, 1997). Clearly, Hochberg's theoretical analyses and associated observations have presaged the direction of current research on scene representation. Borrowing terminology from filmmaking, I will now cut to a close-up and discuss the impact of his work on my own research in that area.

Perception Through a Window: Aperture Viewing and Boundary Extension

When I was a student, first studying Hochberg's work, it was the aperture studies that I found to be most accessible in explaining how an abstract schema could play a fundamental role in something as seemingly concrete as visual perception. Years later, these studies came to mind when I noticed a curious error in viewers' memory for photographs of scenes. They tended to remember having seen a surrounding swath of unseen but highly likely layout (see Figure 26.1) from beyond the camera's point of view. The error was not limited to their drawings but was strikingly evident in recognition tests as well. These observations were first reported by Intraub and Richardson (1989), who coined the term "boundary extension" to describe the phenomenon.

Figure 26.1. The top row shows close-up views of scenes; the middle row shows representative participants' drawings from memory; and the bottom row shows a more wide-angle view of the scenes. Note that the information added by the participant was an excellent prediction of what actually did exist just beyond the view. Column 1 is from Intraub and Richardson (1989; 15-s exposure and 2-day retention interval), and column 2 is from Intraub et al. (1996; 250-ms exposure tested minutes later).

Because it was originally inconceivable that these memory errors would occur immediately, memory was tested after relatively long retention intervals in the first experiments (e.g., 35 min or 2 days). It seemed plausible that the error reflected changes over time consistent with other known memory distortions (e.g., memory changing toward the "prototypic view" or becoming distorted due to Gestalt object completion of background objects; Intraub, Bender, & Mangels, 1992; Intraub & Richardson, 1989). Hochberg's theory, however, suggested an alternative explanation. Perhaps viewers spontaneously perceive a photograph as a "view of the world through a window" with all of the attendant expectations of continuity inherent in aperture viewing. Thus, instead of reflecting changes over time to an initially veridical representation, boundary extension might instead faithfully reflect the schematic representation that Hochberg proposed as the basis of scene perception. Anticipatory projection of layout may in fact become "visible" (in the form of boundary extension) when viewers are explicitly required to express a remembered expanse. Subsequent research ruled out long-term memory accounts (e.g., Intraub et al., 1992; for a review, see Intraub, 2002), and evidence has continued to accrue in support of the perceptual schema explanation.

Boundary extension occurs rapidly and is difficult to eliminate. For example, Intraub and Bodamer (1993) demonstrated that prior knowledge of the phenomenon can attenuate but not eliminate it—something that colleagues and experimenters in my lab have all informally experienced (see Figure 26.2). Intraub and Berkowits (1996) attempted to prevent it by encouraging more effortful encoding by inverting the to-be-remembered photographs. Not only did boundary extension persist, but the amount of extension was virtually the same in the inverted and upright conditions. Boundary extension is ubiquitous and has been reported in people ranging in age from 6 years to 84 years (Candel, Merckelbach, Houben, & Vandyck, 2004; Seamon, Schlegel, Heister, Landau, & Blumenthal, 2002). In ongoing research with Paul Quinn at the University of Delaware, using a habituation/looking procedure, we have obtained preliminary evidence that 3- to 4-month-old infants also remember having seen beyond the boundaries of a view.

Schema Theory: Caveats and Possibilities

These observations are consistent with the notion of a perceptual schema but do not prove the point. "Schema" is still a somewhat vague construct. In addressing the role of schematic construction in perception, Hochberg (1982) himself has cautioned, "All of this may be too good to be true, however, and should not be taken too seriously until we can specify better what is meant by schema (i.e., by what in Helmholtzian terms would be the premises of unconscious inference), and until we can put limits on the

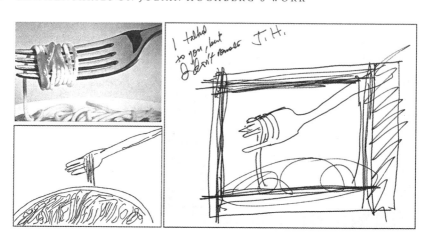

Figure 26.2. Viewers in the Intraub and Bodamer (1993) experiment studied the fork photograph (along with two other pictures that weren't tested); their drawings of the fork moments later included extended boundaries (as shown in the example in the lower left panel; pictures based on figures in Gottesman & Intraub, 1999). Although the error was pointed out to them, and they were challenged to prevent it from happening as they memorized a new set of pictures, they were unable to do so. Similarly, in 1987–1988, Julian Hochberg drew the fork picture from memory (right panel). He noted that I had mentioned the phenomenon to him, but he couldn't remember the upshot. When reminded, like most other viewers, he thought he could correct his drawing by adjusting the boundaries; however, comparison with the photo shows that he was not successful in eliminating the mentally extrapolated region (drawing reproduced with Hochberg's permission).

theory as I have been trying to put limits on the other theories of perceptual organization" (p. 214). In a later paper, he indicated disappointment at the lack of direct research addressing "the qualitative and quantitative nature of the space...behind an aperture" and then offered suggestions about how the field might begin to achieve this end (Hochberg, 1986a, p. 43).

Boundary extension may provide one means by which some of these goals can be accomplished. I will provide a brief sketch of recent and ongoing research aimed at (a) providing qualitative and quantitative assessments of anticipatory spatial representation, (b) establishing boundary conditions for the occurrence of boundary extension, and (c) developing direct tests of the potential role of boundary extension in view integration in both the visual and haptic modalities.

Perceptual Schema Theory: Not All Boundaries Are Equal

Unlike Hochberg's aperture studies, in the case of boundary extension, there is no "establishing shot." In this case, a single, isolated view elicits an anticipatory projection of layout. Thus boundary extension provides a means for focusing on the anticipatory aspects of Hochberg's proposed schema (Intraub, 1997, 2002). My colleagues and I have argued that *view boundaries* (Gottesman & Intraub, 2003) are treated by the visual system as if they were the edges of an aperture, and thus they signal the occlusion of surrounding space. Such boundaries would be expected to elicit both relatively low-level "filling-in" processes (amodal continuation of surfaces or textures; e.g., Kellman, Yin, & Shipley, 1998; Nakayama, He, & Shimojo, 1995; Yin, Kellman, & Shipley, 1997) and more high-level constructive processes based on world knowledge (e.g., knowledge about fences in Figure 26.1).

This characterization suggests a *boundary condition.* Boundary extension should not occur in memory for all types of pictures—only those in which the edges of the picture are construed as being *view boundaries* that delimit the view of an otherwise continuous environment (i.e., the edges of an aperture). To test this, Intraub, Gottesman, and Bills (1998; also see Legault & Standing, 1992) tested recognition memory for outline drawings of single objects on blank backgrounds. Such backgrounds putatively depicted "nothing"—the blank space was simply the paper on which the artist drew the object—thus the edges of the picture should not be construed as view boundaries. As predicted, boundary extension did not occur (spatial errors were bidirectional rather than unidirectional). However, boundary extension did occur for the same stimuli if viewers were instructed to *imagine* a real-world background for the object during encoding (e.g., while looking at an outline drawing of a traffic cone, the viewer was told to "imagine it is on an asphalt road that fills the background"). Boundary extension also occurred without imagination instructions, when a sketchy background was added to the outline drawings (e.g., stippling to indicate an asphalt road), which were then shown to another group of viewers.

These results show that boundary extension isn't simply the result of objects becoming compressed in memory, or a bias to remember more space between an object and a surrounding boundary. When the picture was understood to be a view of a scene, anticipatory projection of the background occurred. Gottesman and Intraub (2002) reported an analogous outcome using photographs of objects that were cut out of their natural backgrounds and presented on a blank background within a clear set of borders. When viewers construed the blank background as being a truncated view of a bland but continuous region, boundary extension occurred; but when the context was biased so that viewers interpreted the blank background as being completely unrelated to the cut-out object (i.e., not part of the picture at all but a rectangular surface on which the cut-out picture rested), boundary extension did not occur. Again, only when the display edges were construed as being *view boundaries* did boundary extension occur.

Are view boundaries "special"? All view boundaries are borders that *surround* the content of a picture. Gottesman and Intraub (2003) addressed the possibility that any surrounding boundaries in a scene will cause a spatial

Figure 26.3. In addition to the edges of the photograph itself (the *view boundaries*), each picture includes a *surrounding* boundary *within* the view: In the left panel, the surrounding boundary is an object boundary (the edge of the towel surrounding the sandal), and in the right panel the surrounding boundary is also a *view boundary* (the picture frame surrounding the photo on the desk). All view boundaries yielded boundary extension, whereas object boundaries did not (based on figures in Gottesman & Intraub, 2003).

distortion like boundary extension to occur—even if the boundaries are not view boundaries. Photographs were taken that always included a surrounding boundary *within* the view: In Figure 26.3 (left panel), a sandal rests on a towel, which is lying on a grassy field. The border of the towel surrounds the sandal; it is a surrounding boundary but not a view boundary. We expected viewers to remember seeing more grass around the objects (typical boundary extension), but would they also remember seeing a greater expanse of terrycloth around the sandal?

Drawing and reconstruction tests (in which viewers constructed the remembered view by choosing from among a set of variously sized parts) showed that boundary extension occurred beyond the edges of the picture (the view boundaries) but not beyond the edges of the towel (an object boundary). However, a surrounding boundary *within* a view did yield boundary extension when that boundary was in itself a view boundary (see the framed picture in the picture of a desktop in Figure 26.3, right panel). In the case of this "picture within a picture," boundary extension occurred not only for the picture as a whole (viewers remembered seeing more of the desk) but also for the view within the tiny picture frame on the desk.

Memory for occluded objects in scenes provides additional evidence for the special status of view boundaries. Intraub, DiCola, and Akers (2004) tested memory for the visible portion of an occluded object in a multi-object scene that was cropped either by a view boundary or by another object *within* the view. Images were presented using a multilayered graphics program so that viewers could independently adjust the boundaries of the view and the position of the objects. Using a mouse, they could move the target object behind other objects or behind the view boundary (depending on condition) and reconstruct the remembered occlusion relation. The portion of the object that remained visible in the reconstruction was measured in pixels. On average, viewers increased the visible portion of the occluded object when it had been cropped by a view boundary but *not* when it was cropped by another object *within* the to-be-remembered view (i.e., on average, object relations within the view were preserved). View boundaries are fleeting, accidental boundaries (not a part of the scene). The goal of the visual system isn't to remember the fleeting boundaries of successive fixations, but to perceive the continuous scene that is being sampled. Might anticipatory representation of the layout just beyond the given view play a role in the integration of successive views during visual scanning?

Eye Movements: Can Boundary Extension Facilitate Integration of Successive Views?

We've known for some time that a brief pictorial exposure similar to "a fixation's worth" (e.g., 250 or 333 ms) is sufficient to elicit boundary extension moments later (Intraub, Gottesman, Willey, & Zuk, 1996). Perhaps the extended region serves to prime upcoming layout during visual scanning, facilitating the integration of views into a coherent representation. However, this would only be possible if boundary extension occurred on the to-be-fixated side of a view—and there is good reason to question whether or not this would occur. Attention precedes the eyes to a to-be-fixated target, and there is evidence that it serves to enhance the detection of target details before the eyes arrive at the new location (Hoffman & Subramaniam, 1995; Kowler, Anderson, Dosher, & Blaser, 1995). Thus, if a fixation is planned near a view boundary, detail enhancement might serve to "pin down" the location of that boundary, eliminating boundary extension at that boundary.

To test the effects of a planned fixation on scene representation, Intraub, Hoffman, Wetherhold, and Stoehs (in press) monitored eye movements in the following task. Viewers centrally fixated a photograph. After 250 ms, a 50-ms cue directed the viewer to fixate an object near either the left or right boundary. A mask replaced the picture before the eyes landed. Two seconds later, the picture reappeared, and using the mouse, the viewer adjusted each of the four view boundaries independently to reconstruct the studied view. We ran four experiments, varying details of the recognition test, and boundary extension always occurred on the to-be-fixated side. In fact, the amount was similar to that obtained in a no-movement control condition in which the viewers simply maintained central fixation.

The top and bottom borders (which were never the target of the cue) also were remembered with extended boundaries. However, the *plan* to shift fixation had a striking effect on the shape of the boundary-extended region. Boundary extension was minimized or eliminated not on the to-be-fixated side, but on the side *opposite* the planned fixation. In other words, given these competing actions, following the cue, boundary extension was inhibited on the "path *not* taken." This pattern of results is consistent with the *biased competition model of attention* (Desimone & Duncan, 1995). But what is most important for the present discussion is that this change in the extrapolated region did not affect boundary extension at the leading edge of the representation—the to-be-fixated side always included an extended swath of anticipated layout. Attention may enhance the detection of specific details of a targeted object (e.g., Hoffman & Subramaniam, 1995), but layout extrapolation beyond the edge of the view occurred nonetheless. At the least, it is available to facilitate the integration of successive views during visual exploration.

Visual and Haptic Exploration: Integrating Partial Views in Different Modalities

Does boundary extension reflect the underlying mental structure of perception? Or might it be limited solely to memory for pictures (a position that would be consistent with Gibson's, 1951, acceptance of the role of mental structure in picture perception but not in perception of 3D objects and surfaces)? To determine if boundary extension occurs in memory of the 3D world, Intraub (2004) tested memory for regions of 3D space directly in front of the viewer. Small "movie sets" were constructed (e.g., kitchen counter, dining-room place setting, bureau top, carpenter's workspace) within a laboratory. Windows limited the view (see Figure 26.4). After inspecting six such scenes for 30 s each, the windows were removed, and participants reconstructed the edges of the original view. They remembered

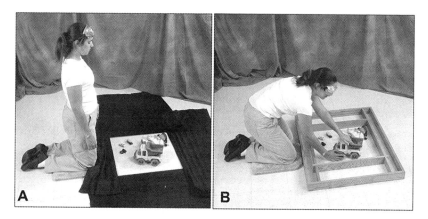

Figure 26.4. Visual exploration (panel A) and haptic exploration (panel B) of the "toys" scene. (All borders were removed prior to test.) From Intraub, 2004.

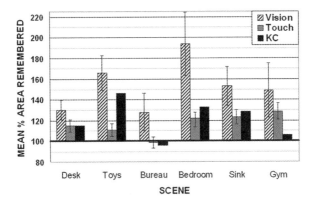

Figure 26.5. Mean percentage of the area of each region remembered by sighted participants in the visual ("vision") and haptic ("touch") conditions and the percentage of each region remembered by KC, a deaf and blind participant. Error bars show the .95 confidence interval around each mean. (Boundary extension occurs when the mean remembered area is significantly greater than 100%, that is, when 100% is *not* included in the confidence interval.) From Intraub, 2004.

having seen a sizable amount of previously unseen area, just beyond the original view. When other subjects explored the region haptically (while blindfolded), they too experienced boundary extension—remembering having *felt* beyond the edges of the window. The percentage increase in area that occurred in memory for each modality is shown in Figure 26.5.

Haptic boundary extension could not be attributed solely to sighted participants' reliance on visual representations (e.g., visualization of the felt surface) because the same results obtained when a "haptic expert," KC—a woman who has been deaf and blind since early life—explored the same scenes. The amount of extension she experienced was, in all but one case, similar to or greater than that remembered by the blindfolded-sighted participants (see "Touch," Figure 26.5). It is important to note that vision resulted in a greater amount of extension than did haptic exploration (whether the latter was performed by a haptic expert or by sighted participants who were temporarily blindfolded). This suggests that input modality may play a role in constraining extrapolation. Indeed, cross-modal conditions in an experiment similar to the one just described (Intraub, Morelli, & Turner, 2004) demonstrated that visual encoding resulted in greater boundary extension than did haptic encoding, irrespective of which modality was used during the memory test (test modality had no effect on performance).

Vision and haptics differ in many ways, but one salient characteristic is a difference in scope; the visual field is much greater than the reach of our hands (see William James's, 1890, discussion of the spatial cognition of blind and sighted individuals; and O'Regan & Noë, 2001). Put another way, a small shift of the eyes can bring considerably more new information to the observer than can a small shift of the hands. The smaller scope of the haptic modality may constrain the size of the projected region. After all, to support a coherent representation of surrounding space, spatial projection needs to be large enough to aid integration but not so large that it causes confabulatory errors and confusion.

Conclusions

Hochberg's perceptual theory has provided the groundwork for current trends in the study of scene representation and the integration of successive views. Research on transsaccadic memory and change blindness has borne out critical aspects of his claims about the schematic nature of moment-to-moment representations. Research on boundary extension shows that both immediate and long-term representations of truncated views of natural scenes typically include projections of the surrounding layout. These observations indicate that, similar to aperture viewing and cinematic communication, scene representation essentially "ignores" the spurious boundaries of a given view. Whether exploring the world through vision or touch, we sample it only a part at a time and yet experience a coherent representation of a continuous world.

A Personal Note

I had the honor, in 1987–1988, of being a National Science Foundation visiting professor in Julian Hochberg's lab. As a scientist (and as a filmmaker—a critical aspect of my life from age 9 through college), that visit meant more to me than I can say. During my stay, I wrote the first paper on boundary extension (Intraub & Richardson, 1989). I did so surrounded by students studying perception, students analyzing cinema, rotating windows, gloriously tall stacks of film canisters, and the latest in computer graphics—but, most important of all, I experienced the generous hospitality of someone who first opened the "window" for me (so to speak) on what is most exciting about perception.

Acknowledgement

Chapter preparation was supported in part by NIMH grant R01MH54688.

References

CANDEL, I., MERCKELBACH, H., HOUBEN, K., & VANDYCK, I. (2004). How children remember neutral and emotional pictures: Boundary extension in children's scene memories. *American Journal of Psychology, 117,* 249–257.

DAVIDSON, M. L., FOX, M. J., & DICK, A. O. (1973). Effect of eye movements on backward masking and perceived location. *Perception & Psychophysics, 14,* 110–116.

DESIMONE, R., & DUNCAN, J. (1995). Neural mechanisms of selective visual attention. *Annual Review Neuroscience, 18,* 193–222.

GIBSON, J. J. (1951). What is a form? *Psychological Review, 58,* 403–412.

GOTTESMAN, C. V., & INTRAUB, H. (1999). Wide-angle memory of close-up scenes: A demonstration of boundary extension. *Behavioral Research Methods, Instruments and Computers, 31,* 86–93.

GOTTESMAN, C. V., & INTRAUB, H. (2002). Surface construal and the mental representation of scenes. *Journal of Experimental Psychology: Human Perception and Performance, 28,* 1–11.

GOTTESMAN, C. V., & INTRAUB, H. (2003). Constraints on spatial extrapolation in the mental representation of scenes: View-boundaries versus object-boundaries. *Visual Cognition, 10,* 875–893.

HOCHBERG, J. (1978). *Perception* (2d ed.). Englewood Cliffs, NJ: Prentice-Hall.

HOCHBERG, J. (1982). How big is a stimulus? In J. Beck (Ed.), *Organization and representation in perception* (pp. 191–217). New York: Erlbaum.

HOCHBERG, J. (1986a). Representation of motion and space in video and cinematic displays. In K. J. Boff, L. Kaufman, & J. P. Thomas (Eds.), *Handbook of perception and human performance* (Vol. 1, pp. 22.1–22.64). New York: Wiley.

HOCHBERG, J. (1986b). Visual perception and real and represented objects and events. In N. J. Smelser & D. R. Gernstein (Eds.), *Behavioral and social science* (pp. 249–298). Washington, DC: National Academy Press.

HOCHBERG, J. (1998). Gestalt theory and its legacy: Organization in eye and brain, in attention and mental representation. In J. Hochberg (Ed.), *Perception and cognition at century's end* (pp. 373–402). San Diego, CA: Academic.

HOFFMAN, J. E., & SUBRAMANIAM, B. (1995). The role of visual attention in saccadic eye movements. *Perception and Psychophysics, 57,* 787–795.

INTRAUB, H. (1997). The representation of visual scenes. *Trends in the Cognitive Sciences, 1,* 217–221.

INTRAUB, H. (2002). Anticipatory spatial representation of natural scenes: Momentum without movement? *Visual Cognition, 9,* 93–119.

INTRAUB, H. (2004). Anticipatory spatial representation in a deaf and blind observer. *Cognition, 94,* 19–37.

INTRAUB, H., BENDER, R. S., & MANGELS, J. A. (1992). Looking at pictures but remembering scenes. *Journal of Experimental Psychology: Learning, Memory and Cognition, 18,* 180–191.

INTRAUB, H., & BERKOWITS, D. (1996). Beyond the edges of a picture. *American Journal of Psychology, 109,* 581–598.

INTRAUB, H., & BODAMER, J. L. (1993). Boundary extension: Fundamental aspect of pictorial representation or encoding artifact? *Journal of Experimental Psychology: Learning, Memory and Cognition, 19,* 1387–1397.

INTRAUB, H., DICOLA, C., & AKERS, M. (2004). *Memory for occluded objects in scenes: Are all boundaries equal?* Manuscript in preparation.

INTRAUB, H., GOTTESMAN, C. V., & BILLS, A. J. (1998). Effects of perceiving and imagining scenes on memory for pictures. *Journal of Experimental Psychology: Learning, Memory, & Cognition, 24,* 186–201.

INTRAUB, H., GOTTESMAN, C. V., WILLEY, E. V., & ZUK, I. J. (1996). Boundary extension for briefly glimpsed pictures: Do common perceptual processes result in unexpected memory distortions? *Journal of Memory and Language, 35,* 118–134.

INTRAUB, H., HOFFMAN, J. E., WETHERHOLD, C. J., & STOEHS, S. (in press). More than meets the eye: The effect of planned fixations on scene representation. *Perception & Psychophysics.*

INTRAUB, H., MORELLI, F., & TURNER, A. (2004). *Anticipatory representation of 3D scenes following visual or haptic exploration.* Manuscript in preparation.

INTRAUB, H., & RICHARDSON, M. (1989). Wide-angle memories of close-up scenes. *Journal of Experimental Psychology: Learning, Memory and Cognition, 15,* 179–187.

IRWIN, D. E. (1991). Information integration across saccadic eye movements. *Cognitive Psychology, 23,* 42–456.

IRWIN, D. E. (1993). Perceiving an integrated visual world. In D. E. Meyer and S. Kornblum (Eds.), *Attention and performance: Vol. 14. Synergies in experiment psychology, artificial intelligence, and cognitive neuroscience* (pp. 121–142). Cambridge, MA: MIT Press.

JAMES, W. (1890). *The principles of psychology* (Vol. 2). New York: Holt.

KELLMAN, P. J., YIN, C., & SHIPLEY, T. F. (1998). A common mechanism for illusory and occluded object completion. *Journal of Experimental Psychology: Human Perception and Performance, 24,* 859–869.

KOWLER, E., ANDERSON, E., DOSHER, B., & BLASER, E. (1995). The role of attention in the programming of saccades. *Vision Research, 35,* 1897–1916.

LEGAULT E., & STANDING, L. (1992). Memory for size of drawings and of photographs. *Perceptual and Motor Skills, 75,* 121.

McCONKIE, G. W., & CURRIE, C. B. (1996). Visual stability across saccades while viewing complex pictures. *Journal of Experimental Psychology: Human Perception and Performance, 22,* 563–581.

NAKAYAMA, K., HE, Z. J., & SHIMOJO, S. (1995). Visual surface representation: A critical link between lower level and higher level vision. In S. M. Kosslyn & D. N. Osherson (Eds.), *Visual cognition* (Vol. 2, pp. 1–70). Cambridge, MA: MIT Press.

O'REGAN, J. K., & NOË, A. (2001). A sensorimotor account of vision and visual consciousness. *Behavioral & Brain Sciences, 24,* 939–1031.

RAYNER, K., & POLLATSEK, A. (1992). Eye movements and scene perception. *Canadian Journal of Psychology, 46,* 342–376.

RENSINK, R. A., O'REGAN, J. K., & CLARK, J. J. (1997). To see or not to see: The need for attention to perceive changes in scenes. *Psychological Science, 8,* 368–373.

SEAMON, J. G., SCHLEGEL, S. E., HEISTER, P. M., LANDAU, A. M., & BLUMENTHAL, B. F. (2002). Misremembering pictured objects: People of all ages demonstrate the boundary extension illusion. *American Journal of Psychology, 115,* 151–167.

SIMONS, D. J. (2000). Current approaches to change blindness. *Visual Cognition, 7,* 1–15.

SIMONS, D. J., & LEVIN, D. T. (1997). Change blindness. *Trends in Cognitive Science, 1,* 261–267.

YIN, C., KELLMAN, P. J., & SHIPLEY, T. F. (1997). Surface completion complements boundary interpolation in the visual integration of partly occluded objects. *Perception, 26,* 1459–1479.

27

"How Big Is a Stimulus?"

Learning About Imagery by Studying Perception

Daniel Reisberg

In 1982, Julie Hochberg published a particularly compelling essay entitled "How Big Is a Stimulus?" (reproduced in this volume). That essay marshaled a number of arguments that Hochberg had developed in other writings and, with these arguments in view, drew the reader toward a series of important and persuasive claims: that the "effective stimulus" is sharply limited both spatially and temporally; that perception, therefore, is often determined by local cues, not global patterns; and that percepts, as a result, are "not everywhere dense" (because percepts are often "silent" or "vague" on information not contained within the local view).

What are the data that led Hochberg to these claims? In most cases, they were simple and elegant demonstrations, of the sort that are easily reproduced for the reader. The corroborating lab data were available, but almost rendered unnecessary by the "see for yourself" quality of the effects. The data included the observations that impossible figures lose their apparent three-dimensionality if they are made small (so that the contradictory vertices are all in foveal view) and the fact that Figure 27.1 is easily reversible if one fixates on point A, despite the interposition cue visible at point B.

These and other observations make it clear that information currently in foveal view has special weight in governing perceptual form and that, as a result, the percept will in many cases neglect or overrule potentially informative cues just a few degrees away from fixation, even if these other cues were themselves fixated just moments earlier. This in turn places powerful limits on what we can claim about the fullness with which successive glimpses are integrated, or about the perceiver's sensitivity to patterns that, by their nature, involve cues that are distributed in time or space.

In the 1982 essay, Hochberg offered these various arguments largely as concerns about theories of direct perception (e.g., Gibson, 1950, 1979), but the implications of the essay are broader, and, in its closing pages, Hochberg drew powerful lessons from these data about the nature of the representation that is created by perception and, in consequence, specifically warned against a reification of the percept: "One must therefore not slide into the implicit assumption that the perceptual response to an object is in any sense an

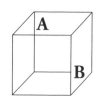

Figure 27.1. The importance of local cues. This modified Necker cube is easily reversible if one fixates on point A, despite the interposition cue visible at point B—a clear demonstration of the power of local cues in guiding perception.

object" (Hochberg, 1982, p. 214). Instead, the percept needs to be understood as inextricably tied to the perceiver's actions, intentions, and attention: "[T]he attributes that we perceive do not in general exist in some internal model of the object, waiting to be retrieved; they are the results of our intention to perceive, and they appear in the context of the perceptual task that calls upon them" (p. 214).

How do these claims about perceptual representation flow from Hochberg's data? As already mentioned, the data make it clear that local cues play a powerful role in determining how an object or scene is perceived. This strongly implies that perceptual representations must regularly be updated and revised, as new information arrives on the fovea. As a result, one's sense of the perceived object cannot be thought of as a stable and coherent model of the whole stimulus. Instead, the representation is more like an extrapolation created on the fly, guided powerfully by the small bit of information currently in view. In Hochberg's terms, this extrapolation takes the form of a "schema of expectations" that is systematically tested and adjusted as one explores the visual environment (Hochberg, 1982, p. 202). All of these claims, offered two decades ago, anticipated many current findings. For example, the fact that perceptions are not "everywhere dense" leads to the expectation that there may be large gaps in what we notice in the perceptual scene, a prediction amply confirmed (for example) by studies of change blindness (see chapter 37, this volume). Hochberg also notes the tension between our subjective sense that our perceptions are complete and coherent and the demonstrations that they are, in fact, neither ("Another good grounding," he says, for the "behaviorist's distrust of introspection or phenomenology"; 1982, p. 196). In this fashion, he anticipates the phenomenon that Levin et al. (2000) dub "change blindness blindness"—perceivers' insensitivity to the surprisingly large gaps in their perception.

Hochberg's claims also extend beyond perception. In the 1982 essay, Hochberg noted the parallels between his conclusions and some of Kolers and Smythe's (1979) claims about *mental imagery*, and, on this point, Hochberg's arguments had a profound impact on my own thinking. Although I expressed the point clumsily in my early work (e.g., Chambers & Reisberg, 1985), I was strongly influenced by the suggestions echoing through Hochberg's writings, Kolers's (e.g., Kolers & Smythe, 1979), and also Michael Kubovy's (e.g., Kubovy, 1983), suggestions that implied clearly that the debate then raging over the nature of mental imagery (e.g., Kosslyn, 1981; Pylyshyn, 1981) was cast in terms that were too coarse. Specifically, Hochberg's data led to a view that emphasized the role of *expectations, exploration,* and *activity* within perception and, by extension, within imagery. However, these factors were largely neglected by both sides of the "imagery debate," leading Hochberg (and, from slightly different perspectives, Kolers and Kubovy) to the view that our theorizing was placing too much emphasis on the *image* and not enough on the active nature of *imaging.* Indeed, Kubovy urged us all to rely less on "image" as a noun and to use it more sensibly as a verb: As he put it, we should remember, for example, that research participants don't "rotate an image"; instead, they "image a rotation" (Kubovy, 1983; for a related and more recent argument, see Kubovy & Epstein, 2001).

In my early thinking, this emphasis on imaging (the activity) served to remind me of the role of the *imager*—the source of the activity. As a result, I was led to ask what the influences are of the imager's expectations and perceptual hypotheses about the imaged form: How do these shape the image itself? How do they shape the image's function—if, for example, the imager is inspecting, and perhaps hoping to make discoveries about, the imaged form?

Moreover, Hochberg explicitly linked his position to J. S. Mill's notion of the "permanent possibility of sensation" (Hochberg, 1982, p. 205; Mill, 1865/1965). Perceptual schemata, Hochberg argued, amount to a set of expectations, and these expectations are tested against the incoming sensory data. Here, though, we meet a potential contrast between perception and imagery: In perception, there is a distal stimulus that can serve as a "permanent" source for sensations, against which perceptual hypotheses can be checked. In imagery, there is no distal stimulus and so nothing against which to check one's perceptual hypotheses. As a result, hypotheses about an imaged form cannot be confirmed *or* disconfirmed, and thus should be resistant to alteration.

It was this broad line of thought that led Deborah Chambers and me, in the 1980s, to explore the idea that visual images might be highly resistant to reinterpretation—so that, for example, one should have immense difficulty in finding the duck in a "rabbit image" or vice versa. In broad terms, our notion was that imagery, like perception, depends on the active construction of hypotheses; if so, then the imager's *intentions* in creating the image should play a huge role in shaping those hypotheses. In addition, if hypotheses in *perception* are tested against stimulus information (and thus subject to change, if inconsistent information is encountered), then hypotheses in *imagery* could not be tested, and so should not readily change. All of this was consistent with our results, and we did find that images were strongly resistant to reinterpretation (Chambers & Reisberg, 1985; for related data with auditory images, see Reisberg, Smith, Baxter, & Sonenshine, 1989).

One might worry that this result reflects some peculiar stubbornness on the part of our participants, or perhaps a failure to understand the task.

These claims can be set aside, however, in light of the further hypothesis, derived from this same theoretical base, that images *would* be subject to reinterpretation if the new organization was suggested "from above" and so not dependent on some process of testing perceptual hypotheses against sensory information. Consistent with this idea, we were able to show that images were easily reinterpreted if suitable hints were given (Reisberg & Chambers, 1991; also see Hyman, 1993). Peterson et al. (1992) extended this argument in a lovely way, showing that explicit (verbal) hints were not necessary, but that the same could be achieved by means of instructive example figures.

Our studies also examined another implication of Hochberg's position—namely, that images (like percepts) should not be "everywhere dense." Specifically, one should have a full and rich sense of *some* aspects of the imaged form (i.e., those aspects for which one has sensory expectations), but only a vague sense of the form's other aspects. Moreover, this unevenness should be tied to the imager's understanding of the image—on the notion that this understanding will shape the imager's sensory hypotheses and expectations. Chambers and Reisberg (1992) confirmed these claims for imagery, showing that a "duck image" based on Jastrow's classic figure tended to be well defined for the side of the form showing the duck's face but quite vague for the back of the head. The pattern of what was well defined and what was vague simply reversed when participants were visualizing the same form as a "rabbit image."

We were, therefore, able to make headway on important issues in the study of imagery thanks to guidance derived directly from Hochberg's work. More important, though, I am convinced that Hochberg's work—and, with that, a sharper understanding of perception—is just as useful for current studies of imagery as it was for our work on the duck/rabbit. This belief is driven in part by the increasing sophistication of cognitive neuroscience and, with that, the notion that we might be able to locate patterns that many people will regard as "the neural substrate for imagery." Some intriguing data are already available, mapping in detail the areas of the visual cortex that are activated when one is entertaining an image (e.g., Behrmann, 2000; Kosslyn et al., 1999; Kosslyn & Thompson, 2003; Mellet et al., 2000; O'Craven & Kanwisher, 2000), and one might be tempted to argue from this that we have located the neural instantiation for the image itself. In addition, let us note that the relevant areas of the visual cortex are topographically organized, with the implication that we might be able to think of imagery as involving activation patterns within these "maps"—a view just a small step removed from describing images as pixel patterns defined within a region of visual space.

These neuroscience data are certainly important, but they seem to draw us once more toward a reification of the image: On one reading of these data, the image is an internal "object" or "model," instantiated via a particular pattern of activation in the visual cortex. This is, of course, just the view that Hochberg sought to reject on the basis of plausible extrapolations from perception and just the view that Chambers and I sought to refute with our behavioral data. It is on this basis, then, that researchers in this arena would be well served by a reading of Hochberg's 1982 essay (and other writings), and this may well give them pause about endorsing a view of imagery that (once again) seems to understate the role of the imager's intentions, expectations, and activity. In my view, Hochberg's insights on these issues are now just as compelling as they were 20 years ago, and they speak to the same fundamental issues. There is, in other words, still an enormous amount to be gained from pondering Hochberg's claims about perception *and* imagery. I urge my colleagues to do so.

References

BEHRMANN, M. (2000). The mind's eye mapped onto the brain's matter. *Current Directions in Psychological Science, 9,* 50–54.

CHAMBERS, D., & REISBERG, D. (1985). Can mental images be ambiguous? *Journal of Experimental Psychology: Human Perception and Performance, 11,* 317–328.

CHAMBERS, D., & REISBERG, D. (1992). What an image depicts depends on what an image means. *Cognitive Psychology, 24,* 145–174.

GIBSON, J. J. (1950). *The perception of the visual world.* Boston: Houghton Mifflin.

GIBSON, J. J. (1979). *The ecological approach to visual perception.* Boston: Houghton Mifflin.

HOCHBERG, J. (1982). How big is a stimulus? In J. Beck (Ed.), *Organization and representation in perception* (pp. 191–217). Hillsdale, NJ: Erlbaum.

HYMAN, I. (1993). Imagery, reconstructive memory, and discovery. In B. Roskos-Ewoldsen, M. Intons-Peterson, & R. Anderson (Eds.), *Imagery, creativity and discovery: A cognitive approach* (pp. 99–122). Amsterdam: Elsevier.

KOLERS, P. A., & SMYTHE, W. E. (1979). Images, symbols, and skills. *Canadian Journal of Psychology, 33,* 158–184.

KOSSLYN, S. M. (1981). The medium and the message in mental imagery: A theory. *Psychological Review, 88,* 46–66.

KOSSLYN, S. M., PASCUAL-LEONE, A., FELICIAN, O., CAMPOSANO, S., KEENAN, J. P., THOMPSON, W. L., GANIS, G., SUKEL, K. E., & ALPERT, N. M. (1999). The role of area 17 in visual imagery: Convergent evidence from PET and rTMS. *Science, 284,* 167–170.

KOSSLYN, S. M., & THOMPSON, W. L. (2003). When is early visual cortex activated during mental imagery? *Psychological Bulletin, 129,* 723–746.

KUBOVY, M. (1983). Mental imagery majestically transforming cognitive psychology (Review of R. N. Shepard & L. Cooper, *Mental images and their transformations*). *Contemporary Psychology, 28,* 661–663.

KUBOVY, M., & EPSTEIN, W. (2001). Internalization: A metaphor we can live without. *Behavioral & Brain Sciences, 24,* 618–625.

LEVIN, D. T., MOMEN, N., DRIVDAHL, S. B., & SIMONS, D. J. (2000). Change blindness blindness: The metacognitive error of overestimating change-detection ability. *Visual Cognition, 7,* 397–412.

MELLET, E., TZOURIO-MAZOYER, N., BRICOGNE, S., MAZOYER, B., KOSSLYN, S. M., & DENIS, M. (2000). Functional anatomy of high-resolution visual mental imagery. *Journal of Cognitive Neuroscience, 12*(1), 98–109.

MILL, J. S. (1965). *An examination of Sir William Hamilton's philosophy (On the permanent possibility of sensation)*. Reprinted in R. J. Hernstein & E. G. Boring (Eds.), *A source book in the history of psychology*. Cambridge, MA: Harvard University Press. (Original work published 1865)

O'CRAVEN, K., & KANWISHER, N. (2000). Mental imagery of faces and places activates corresponding stimulus-specific brain regions. *Journal of Cognitive Neuroscience, 12*, 1013–1023.

PETERSON, M. A., KIHLSTROM, J., ROSE, P., & GLISKY, M. (1992). Mental images can be ambiguous: Reconstruals and reference-frame reversals. *Memory & Cognition, 20*, 107–123.

PYLYSHYN, Z. (1981). The imagery debate: Analogue media versus tacit knowledge. In N. Block (Ed.), *Imagery* (pp. 151–206). Cambridge, MA: MIT Press.

REISBERG, D., & CHAMBERS, D. (1991). Neither pictures nor propositions: What can we learn from a mental image? *Canadian Journal of Psychology, 45*, 336–352.

REISBERG, D., SMITH, J. D., BAXTER, D. A., & SONENSHINE, M. (1989). "Enacted" auditory images are ambiguous; "pure" auditory images are not. *Quarterly Journal of Experimental Psychology, 41A*, 619–641.

28

How Big Is an Optical Invariant?

Limits of Tau in Time-to-Contact Judgments

Patricia R. DeLucia

> Concern for molar factors is no license for ignoring the molecular.
> —Julian Hochberg, 1982

When Hochberg (1982) asked, "How big is a stimulus?" he raised issues that have critical and widespread implications for perceptual theory. The objective of this chapter is to consider these issues in the context of time-to-contact (TTC) judgments. First, I will summarize points raised by Hochberg that are most relevant to this chapter. Then I will discuss implications of these points for TTC judgments. Finally, I will discuss how heuristics may accommodate limits in the size of an effective optical invariant. I begin with a note on terminology.

Terminology

In this chapter, I will discuss optical invariants and heuristics. I will also discuss available information and effective information. An *optical invariant* refers to a higher-order variable of optical information that corresponds to, or specifies, a property of the three-dimensional (3D) environment (Gibson, 1979). A *higher-order variable* refers to a relationship between individual measures of a stimulus (Hochberg, 1978). Optical invariants remain invariantly related to properties of the environment despite transformations of the optic array (Gibson, 1979; Hochberg, 1978). It is important to distinguish between invariants and *heuristics*. The information provided by invariants predicts with 100% reliability an event that observers could perceive (Cutting & Wang, 2000). In contrast, heuristics provide information that is not necessarily veridical and varies in reliability. Heuristics increase efficiency by limiting search through the possible solutions, but do not guarantee the correct solution and can result in error (Braunstein, 1976). For example, the pictorial depth cue of relative size is a heuristic. Tau is an invariant that specifies TTC. It also is important to distinguish between *available* and *effective* information. Available information exists in the optic array independently of the visual system (Sedgwick, 1983). However, the availability of an optical invariant is inconsequential for perception if an observer cannot use it (Hochberg, 1982). Availability does not imply effectiveness.

Hochberg's Main Points

Hochberg's (1982) main premise is that the amount of information that observers can pick up or extract from a stimulus array is limited spatially and temporally; these limitations raise critical issues for direct theories of perception (Gibson, 1979).[1] One critical issue is that the effectiveness of higher-order variables depends on whether lower-order variables are above threshold. Hochberg provided a compelling example. Texture-density gradient is an optical invariant that specifies surface slant (e.g., ground plane). It is defined by the change in (optical) spacing between texture elements as a function of the distance between the elements and the observer. To extract information about surface slant, observers must extract texture-density gradient. To do so, the texture elements and their spacing and the change in density per unit distance must be above threshold. If any of these components is subthreshold, slant information is ineffective. Hochberg (1982) argued that spatial and temporal limits in the visual system determine whether higher-order variables of stimulus information are effective.

Spatial Limits

Within a single glance or fixation, limited visual acuity prevents observers from extracting detailed information throughout the visual field. Therefore, the ability to extract optical invariants depends on where the observer looks. Consider Hochberg's (1982) example of a texture-density gradient on a ground plane. Observers may not be able to detect the density of both near and far elements (and thus their difference) in a single glance; multiple glances may be necessary. In another example, Hochberg, Green, and Virostek (1978; see also Hochberg, 1981) demonstrated that the detection of the depth direction of textured surfaces varied with the distance between the observer's fixation point and the location of kinetic occlusion information. The latter was extracted less effectively when viewed with peripheral vision compared with foveal vision. These examples demonstrate that observers cannot extract higher-order information throughout the visual field with a single glance. This brings us to the importance of temporal limits.

Temporal Limits

Since observers cannot extract all information in a stimulus array with a single glance, they must scan the array with multiple fixations. However, observers cannot store all the information from one glance to another, and mental structure may be used to integrate information from successive views

(Hochberg, 1982). For example, texture-density gradient may be ineffective if the optical spacing of the near and far texture elements is not retained and integrated adequately from one glance to the next. Furthermore, it is not known how much time is necessary for observers to extract higher-order information. In short, there are strong limits on the duration and size of a stimulus pattern that is effective at any time, and therefore, it is critical to determine the size of an effective stimulus (Hochberg, 1982).

Implications

When optical invariants are not available, or are available but ineffective, how do observers perceive 3D space? One alternative is that mental structures contribute to perception (Gibson, 1966; Hochberg, 1982). According to Hochberg (1982, 1987), these include constructs of the world (mental representations or visual imagery), constructs which guide individual glances and store information (schema), and constraints by which perceived structures are fitted to a stimulus pattern (unconscious inferences). Alternatively, observers use heuristics rather than invariants. Neither alternative is consistent with a direct theory of perception. As Hochberg argued, it is critical to determine the size of the effective stimulus in order to identify the conditions under which observers can directly use higher-order variables or optical invariants.

Time-to-Contact Judgments

In this section, I consider the issues raised by Hochberg (1982) in the context of TTC judgments. The time remaining until an approaching object contacts the eye is specified directly by the inverse of the object's relative rate of optical expansion, or *tau* (Lee, 1976).[2] Simply stated, tau is the ratio of an object's optical size to its rate of optical expansion. Tau is independent of an object's size, speed, or distance from the observer (e.g., Hochberg, 1986). Theoretically, it is not necessary to perceive speed or distance to perceive TTC (Lee & Young, 1985). Therefore, tau may render pictorial depth cues and mental structures unnecessary in TTC judgments. Numerous studies are cited frequently as providing support for the use of tau, but other studies are consistent with, or provide evidence for, alternative perceptual determinants of TTC judgments (Wann, 1996).

Moreover, tau is not exempt from sensory limitations. Therefore, explanations of TTC judgments must address the issues raised by Hochberg (1982). Tau is effective only when an object's optical size and rate of optical expansion is above threshold. Consequently, tau may be ineffective for a small or far approaching object if the change in the object's optical size is subthreshold. Tau can be rendered ineffective by spatial and temporal limits.

Spatial Limits

As with texture-density gradient, limits in visual acuity constrain the effectiveness of tau. Retinal eccentricity (not scaled for cortical magnification factor) influenced various types of TTC judgments (Manser & Hancock, 1996; Meyer, 2001; Regan & Vincent, 1995). Moreover, display enhancements designed to improve TTC judgments were effective only when observers were instructed to attend to them (DeLucia, 1991). The implication is that useful information for TTC judgments may not be accessible within a single glance or attentional act (DeLucia, 1991), and effective visual information is not distributed uniformly across the optic flow field (Hochberg, 1982).

Temporal Limits

As with texture-density gradient, tau may be ineffective if optic flow information is not retained or integrated adequately from one glance to the next. Moreover, the optic array that results from moving 3D environments contains both lower-order motion and higher-order motion information (DeLucia, 1991). *Lower-order motion* refers to movements per se, or two-dimensional motions whose thresholds can be measured. Such motions do not necessarily result from the projection of 3D motion or specify properties of a 3D environment. In contrast, *higher-order motion information* refers to optical invariants that result from 3D motion. Lower-order motion is always present in higher-order motion information. Higher-order motion information is not necessarily present in two-dimensional motions. Consistent with Hochberg's (1982) argument that both lower-order and higher-order variables are important in perception, TTC judgments were influenced by lower-order motion, including optical expansion (magnitude of change in optical size), rate of expansion (change in optical size per unit time), and image velocity (change in optical position per unit time) (e.g., DeLucia, 1991; DeLucia & Novak, 1997; DeLucia & Warren, 1994; Kerzel, Hecht, & Kim, 1999; Regan & Hamstra, 1993; Smith, Flach, Dittman, & Stanard, 2001). The implication is that lower-order variables that do not specify TTC can affect TTC judgments.

Furthermore, analyses of the effects of computer aliasing on TTC information indicated that temporal limits in the visual system are relevant for TTC judgments (DeLucia, 1991, 1999). In principle, tau is available continuously at every instant in time (Tresilian, 1990). However, due to limits in the temporal resolution of the visual system, it is unlikely that optical expansion, and thus tau, is sampled continuously. The minimum time over which temporal information is integrated before being used may range from 32 ms (Morgan, 1980) to 350 ms (Smith & Gulick, 1957), depending on the task and display (DeLucia, 1991).Therefore, TTC information may not be extracted on a "frame-by-frame" basis. Rather, an averaging process may be used (DeLucia, 1991, 1999; Tresilian, 1993). In designing computer-generated images of approaching objects, it will be important to determine the effective size of the "averaging window" (De-Lucia, 1999).

Implications

When tau is not available, or is available but ineffective, how do observers judge TTC? One alternative is that mental structures contribute to such judgments. Tresilian (1995) proposed that task variables determine whether cognitive processing influences TTC judgments. Alternatively, observers use heuristics rather than invariants. Cutting and Wang (2000) proposed that when invariants are available, observers use them to guide visual performance, and when invariants are unavailable, observers use heuristics.

It is important to recognize that tau is available only when an object approaches the eye on a direct path and at a constant velocity; the law of small angles is observed; and the object is rigid and, if rotating, symmetrical (Tresilian, 1991). When such conditions are violated, tau does not provide veridical TTC information and can lead to inaccurate TTC estimation. Furthermore, even when tau is available, it may not be above threshold due to the limited spatial and temporal resolution of the visual system. Tau may not be effective when optical expansion is subthreshold or when attentional demands are high (DeLucia, Kaiser, Bush, Meyer, & Sweet, 2003). When tau is not available or is subthreshold, it is adaptive for the visual system to rely on alternative strategies. However, empirical studies suggest that mental structures and heuristics may influence TTC judgments even when tau is available or above threshold.

For example, results suggest that TTC judgments are influenced by limits in cognitive processing, such as limits in short-term memory (Novak, 1998) and limited-capacity processing (DeLucia & Novak, 1997). Furthermore, at least in some conditions, TTC judgments may be influenced by mental structures of cognitive motion extrapolation and visual imagery (DeLucia, 2004; DeLucia & Liddell, 1998; Liddell, 1998). Specifically, when observers judge the TTC of an object that is not continuously in view, they may use a cognitive model of the visible motion trajectory to extrapolate the object's motion after it is no longer visible and may also use mental images of the object to keep track of its position.

Moreover, TTC judgments were influenced by heuristics, such as pictorial depth cues (DeLucia, 1991; DeLucia & Novak, 1997). Observers reported that a large, distant, approaching object would reach them before a small, near, approaching object that was specified by tau to arrive sooner (for a review, see DeLucia, 2004). Judgments were consistent with relative size rather than with tau.[3] Similarly, judgments were influenced by other depth cues, such as height in field and occlusion (DeLucia et al., 2003). Familiar size—the only depth cue that requires past experience (and hence mental structure; Hochberg, 1978)—influenced TTC judgments even when monocular and binocular TTC information was available (DeLucia, 2004). In short, mental structures and heuristics may influence TTC judgments even when tau is above threshold.

Do Heuristics Accommodate Limits in the Size of an Effective Optical Invariant?

Why would heuristics influence TTC judgments when tau is available or above threshold? There are several reasons (DeLucia, 2004). First, the quality of some information sources varies with distance. Pictorial depth cues may be effective at relatively far distances where the effectiveness of binocular and motion information may be diminished (Cutting & Vishton, 1995). In some situations, observers may have to plan a response to an object which is too distant for tau or other relevant visual information to be effective. For example, a driver requires several seconds to begin braking to avoid collision with another vehicle and must detect the potential collision when the vehicle is relatively distant (Stewart, Cudworth, & Lishman, 1993). At the necessary distance, tau may be subthreshold. If the visual system could use only tau, perceptual-motor performance would be inflexible, if not impossible. It is adaptive for the visual system to act opportunistically (Tresilian, 1995) and to rely on a variety of sources, including heuristics.

Second, observers putatively direct their fixation and attention to various locations in space as an event unfolds and a task progresses. Fixation location determines which information sources fall in central and peripheral vision and which information sources are effective. Similarly, attention and cognitive-processing demands may enhance or attenuate the effectiveness of an information source. In short, higher-order information such as tau may be above threshold during some phases of a task but subthreshold during other phases. It is adaptive for the visual system to be prepared to rely on heuristics.[4]

Third, DeLucia et al. (2003) conjectured that the visual system does not distinguish between events in which conditions required by tau are met and those in which they are not. Therefore, it seems advantageous to use heuristics as an ongoing general strategy even when tau is above threshold.

Conclusions and Practical Implications

In 1968, Hochberg discussed the theoretical importance of the limits of the momentary glance, particularly in the context of form perception. In 1982, he discussed the importance of these limits for direct theories of perception and argued that such limitations have not been addressed adequately. In the decades since then, there have been further demonstrations that sensory limitations constrain the pick-up of optical invariants but, despite their importance, surprisingly little attention has been devoted to these issues. It is argued here that determining the size of effective visual information continues to be one of the most pressing issues for perceptual theory. If spatial and temporal limitations of the visual system render optical invariants ineffective, one must consider the contribution of heuristics and mental structures. As Hochberg (1982) argued, it is critical to determine the size of the effective stimulus in order to identify the conditions under which observers can directly use higher-order variables of information. He argued further that the nature and emphases of perceptual theory depend on the size of the effective stimulus.

Finally, Hochberg (1982) recognized that these issues have practical as well as theoretical importance. Many technologies exacerbate existing sensory limitations by reducing the observer's field of view. Therefore, the issues raised by Hochberg have important human-factors implications for design. For example, surgery is performed increasingly with the use of small cameras inserted into the body. These devices provide a reduced field of view and result in degraded depth perception and spatial orientation (similarly for night-vision goggles; DeLucia & Task, 1995). Mental models have been characterized as critical in such surgeries (Cao & Milgram, 2000). The aim of current research is to apply the issues raised by Hochberg to the design of such technologies so that surgical performance can be optimized (DeLucia, Hoskins, & Griswold, 2004; DeLucia, Mather, Griswold, & Mitra, 2006). In conclusion, it is critical to determine the size of the effective optical invariant. Such analyses will facilitate the development of perceptual theory and the design of technologies.

Acknowledgments

This chapter was written while the author was supported by the Texas Advanced Research Program under grant No. 003644-0081-2001.

Notes

1. And for Gestalt theory, which is not discussed here.
2. For brevity, discussions are limited to TTC judgments and local tau. The same arguments apply to other judgments (e.g., collision detection) and other optical TTC information (e.g., global tau).
3. This is similar to Hochberg's (1978, 1987) report that observers' judgments about the motion direction of the Ames rotating trapezoid were consistent with the depth cues of linear perspective and relative size and that the illusion occurred even when motion information was above threshold.

4. It has been proposed that the information sources that influence TTC judgments vary throughout a task or event (DeLucia, 2004; DeLucia & Warren, 1994). Therefore, it is essential to measure specific sources of visual information and judgments about spatial layout *concurrently* and *throughout* an approach event. This method contrasts with typical studies of TTC in which one judgment is measured at the end of an event. Continuous response measurement, or *online response monitoring*, is a new paradigm that is currently being pursued, and it can indicate whether (and when) the basis of performance changes from heuristics to invariants during an event (DeLucia, 2004).

References

BRAUNSTEIN, M. L. (1976). *Depth perception through motion.* New York: Academic.

CAO, C. G. L., & MILGRAM, P. (2000). Disorientation in minimal access surgery: A case study. *Proceedings of the IEA 2000/HFES 2000 Congress,* 4.169–4.172.

CUTTING, J. E., & VISHTON, P. M. (1995). Perceiving layout and knowing distances: The integration, relative potency, and contextual use of different information about depth. In W. Epstein & S. J. Rogers (Eds.), *Perception of space and motion* (pp. 69–117). San Diego, CA: Academic.

CUTTING, J. E., & WANG, R. F. (2000). Heading judgments in minimal environments: The value of a heuristic when invariants are rare. *Perception & Psychophysics, 62,* 1146–1159.

DeLUCIA, P. R. (1991). Pictorial and motion-based information for depth perception. *Journal of Experimental Psychology: Human Perception and Performance, 17,* 738–748.

DeLUCIA, P. R. (1999). Size-arrival effects: The potential role of conflicts between monocular and binocular time-to-contact information, and of computer aliasing. *Perception & Psychophysics, 61,* 1168–1177.

DeLUCIA, P. R. (2004). Multiple sources of information influence time-to-contact judgments: Do heuristics accommodate limits in sensory and cognitive processes? In H. Hecht & G. J. P. Savelsburgh (Eds.), *Advances in psychology: Vol. 135. Time-to-Contact* (pp. 243–286). Amsterdam: Elsevier-North-Holland.

DeLUCIA, P. R., HOSKINS, M. L., & GRISWOLD, J. A. (2004). Laparoscopic surgery: Are three viewing perspectives better than one? In *Proceedings of the Human Factors and Ergonomics Society 48th Annual Meeting* (pp. 1661–1665). Santa Monica, CA: Human Factors and Ergonomics Society.

DeLUCIA, P. R., KAISER, M. K., BUSH, J. M., MEYER, L. E., & SWEET, B. T. (2003). Information integration in judgments of time to contact. *Quarterly Journal of Experimental Psychology: Human Experimental Psychology, 56(A),* 1165–1189.

DeLUCIA, P. R., & LIDDELL, G. W. (1998). Cognitive motion extrapolation and cognitive clocking in prediction motion tasks. *Journal of Experimental Psychology: Human Perception and Performance, 24,* 901–914.

DeLUCIA, P. R., MATHER, R. D., GRISWOLD, J. A., & MITRA, S. (2006). Toward the improvement of image-guided interventions for minimally invasive surgery: Three factors that affect performance. *Human Factors, 48,* 23–38.

DeLUCIA, P. R., & NOVAK, J. B. (1997). Judgments of relative time-to-contact of more than two approaching objects: Toward a method. *Perception & Psychophysics, 59,* 913–928.

DeLucia, P. R., & Task, H. L. (1995). Depth and collision judgment using night vision goggles. *International Journal of Aviation Psychology, 5,* 371–386.

DeLucia, P. R., & Warren, R. (1994). Pictorial and motion-based depth information during active control of self-motion: Size-arrival effects on collision avoidance. *Journal of Experimental Psychology: Human Perception and Performance, 20,* 783–798.

Gibson, J. J. (1966). *The senses considered as perceptual systems.* Boston: Houghton Mifflin.

Gibson, J. J. (1979). *The ecological approach to visual perception.* Boston: Houghton Mifflin.

Hochberg, J. (1968). In the mind's eye. In R. N Haber (Ed.), *Contemporary theory and research in visual perception* (pp. 309–331). New York: Holt, Rinehart & Winston.

Hochberg, J. (1978). *Perception* (2d ed.). Englewood Cliffs, NJ: Prentice-Hall.

Hochberg, J. (1981). Levels of perceptual organization. In M. Kubovy & J. Pomerantz (Eds.), *Perceptual organization* (pp. 255–276). Hillsdale, NJ: Erlbaum

Hochberg, J. (1982). How big is a stimulus? In J. Beck (Ed.), *Organization and representation in perception* (pp. 191–217). Hillsdale, NJ: Erlbaum.

Hochberg, J. (1986). Representation of motion and space in video and cinematic displays. In K. R. Boff, J. P. Thomas, & L. Kaufman (Eds.), *Handbook of perception and human performance* (pp. 22.1–22.64). Toronto: Wiley.

Hochberg, J. (1987). Machines should not see as people do, but must know how people see. *Computer Vision, Graphics, and Image Processing, 37,* 221–237.

Hochberg, J., Green, J., & Virostek, S. (1978). *Texture occlusion requires central viewing: Demonstrations, data and theoretical implications.* Paper delivered at the APA Convention.

Kerzel, D., Hecht, H., & Kim, N. (1999). Image velocity, not tau, explains arrival-time judgments from global optical flow. *Journal of Experimental Psychology: Human Perception and Performance, 25,* 1540–1555.

Lee, D. N. (1976). A theory of visual control of braking based on information about time-to-collision. *Perception, 5,* 437–459.

Lee, D. N., & Young, D. S. (1985). Visual timing of interceptive action. In D. J. Ingle, M. Jeannerod, & D. N. Lee (Eds.), *Brain mechanisms and spatial vision* (pp. 1–30). Dordrecht: Martinus Nijhoff.

Liddell, G. W. (1998). Interfering and updating cognitive representations used in judgments of absolute time-to-contact in a prediction-motion task. *Dissertation Abstracts International, 58*(10), 5678B. (University Microfilms No. 9812032)

Manser, M. P., & Hancock, P. A. (1996). Influence of approach angle on estimates of time-to-contact. *Ecological Psychology, 8,* 71–99.

Meyer, L. E. (2001). The effects of retinal eccentricity on judgments about collisions. *Dissertation Abstracts International, 62*(05), 2523B. (University Microfilms No. AAT 3015713)

Morgan, M. J. (1980). Analogue models of motion perception. *Philosophical Transactions of the Royal Society of London, B290,* 117–135.

Novak, J. B. (1998). Judgments of absolute time-to-contact in multiple object displays: Evaluating the role of cognitive processes in arrival-time judgments. *Dissertation Abstracts International, 58*(10), 5679B. (University Microfilms No. 9812047)

Regan, D., & Hamstra, S. J. (1993). Dissociation of discrimination thresholds for time to contact and for rate of angular expansion. *Vision Research, 33,* 447–462.

REGAN, D., & VINCENT, A. (1995). Visual processing of looming and time to contact throughout the visual field. *Vision Research, 35,* 1845–1857.

SEDGWICK, H. A. (1983). Environment-centered representation of spatial layout: Available visual information from texture and perspective. In J. Beck, B. Hope, & A. Rosenfeld (Eds.), *Human and machine vision* (pp. 425–458). New York: Academic.

SMITH, M. R. H., FLACH, J. M., DITTMAN, S. M., & STANARD, T. (2001). Monocular optical constraints on collision control. *Journal of Experimental Psychology: Human Perception and Performance, 27,* 395–410.

SMITH, W. M., & GULICK, W. L. (1957). Dynamic contour perception. *Journal of Experimental Psychology, 53,* 145–152.

STEWART, D., CUDWORTH, C. J., & LISHMAN, J. R. (1993). Misperception of time-to-collision by drivers in pedestrian accidents. *Perception, 22,* 1227–1244.

TRESILIAN, J. R. (1990). Perceptual information for the timing of interceptive action. *Perception, 19,* 223–239.

TRESILIAN, J. R. (1991). Empirical and theoretical issues in the perception of TTC. *Journal of Experimental Psychology: Human Perception and Performance, 17,* 865–876.

TRESILIAN, J. R. (1993). Four questions of time to contact: A critical examination of research on interceptive timing. *Perception, 22,* 653–680.

TRESILIAN, J. R. (1995). Perceptual and cognitive processes in time-to-contact estimation: Analysis of prediction-motion and relative judgment tasks. *Perception & Psychophysics, 57,* 231–245.

WANN, J. P. (1996). Anticipating arrival: Is the tau margin a specious theory? *Journal of Experimental Psychology: Human Performance and Perception, 22,* 1034–1048.

29

Hochberg and Inattentional Blindness

Arien Mack

Since at least the 1980s, there has been ample, compelling evidence of the importance of attention for perceptual awareness, and over a much, much longer period, philosophers and armchair psychologists as distant from each other as Aristotle and William James have recognized the inextricable link between attention and consciousness. We now even have civil laws acknowledging the link. It is the reason that in many places in this country it has become illegal to drive while talking on a cell phone and why, if we do, we may find ourselves running into something in the road that we failed to see because we were distracted. It therefore is somewhat surprising that, despite the widely acknowledged link between attention and consciousness or attention and perception, it was not until quite recently that it has become overwhelmingly clear that we actually neither perceive nor are conscious of the many things around if us we do not attend to them. It is as if we were blind or deaf to these things even though they may be highly visible and highly audible.

There are at least three strands of research associated with this realization: research on the phenomenon of *inattentional blindness* (IB), the very name of which underscores the attention-perception connection; research on *change blindness* (CB), another inattentional blindness phenomenon specifically associated with our now well-documented incapacity to detect even large changes in scenes if we are not attending to them; and the *attentional blink* (AB), another inattention phenomenon. The term AB denotes the fact that we are frequently unable to detect a stimulus for which we are looking, if it appears fairly closely on the heels of a prior stimulus for which we also are looking and which we have detected. Most of the published research on this group of phenomena has appeared since about 1998 though some of the phenomena have a longer research history.

The Question

The question that organizes this brief essay is whether Hochberg's work, which certainly stressed the importance of attention and expectation in perception, anticipated these phenomena, and if it did not, are they nevertheless explicable within the terms of his theorizing about perception? In a quite general sense, it would seem that this group of attention-related phenomena are consistent with Hochberg's views, particularly insofar as he continually argued for the role in perception of expectation and intention, both of which are important aspects of attention. When we pay attention or search for an object, our looking is both intentional and governed by the expectation of seeing it. This is why the standard procedure for finding *preattentive* perceptual features (Triesman & Gelade, 1980) is seriously flawed, since it is based on visual search procedures which, by definition, demand attention (Mack & Rock, 1998).

Perception Without Attention

In order to determine what, if any, visual features are perceived in the complete absence of attention, it is essential that the feature or object in question is the object neither of an intention nor of an expectation. What is needed is a state of "inattentional looking." However, since this "pure" state may only occur when we are "lost in thought," it must be engineered in the laboratory. The only procedure that can dependably create inattention to a target object is one in which observers are engaged in looking intently at something else while some target of interest to the researcher is also present. This principle is the basis for the inattention procedure used in the many experiments designed to study inattentional blindness. In one frequently used version of this procedure, observers are required to report the longer arm of a briefly presented cross for several trials followed by a trial in which the cross is presented along with the target stimulus, which either can be at fixation when the cross is centered about 2° away or about 2° away from fixation when the cross is centered at fixation. Using this procedure and others like it in a large number of experiments, we found that observers very often failed to detect the target stimulus, particularly when the target appeared exactly at fixation while the cross which was the object of attention was centered 2° away (Mack & Rock, 1998).

While Hochberg's insistence on the role of attention and intention in perception is in general consistent with findings suggesting that attention is an essential component of perceiving, it is not clear whether Hochberg's theorizing anticipates these findings nor whether there are aspects of these findings which are at odds with his theory. To answer this question, it is necessary to briefly review what we know about these several kinds of inattentional blindness and then turn to Hochberg's treatment of attention, perception, and consciousness.

Inattentional Blindness

Prior to its being named inattentional blindness, a dynamic version of this phenomenon was demonstrated by Neisser (Neisser & Becklen, 1975). In one example of this work, the researchers showed observers a brief film clip in which, for example, people dressed in black or white uniforms were passing a basketball among themselves. When observers were asked to count the number of times the ball was passed between players wearing either white or black uniforms, they often failed to notice the presence of a woman who at some point during the film strolled across the court carrying an open umbrella. (Simons and Chabris, 1999, repeated a version of this, but instead of a woman with an umbrella, a man in a gorilla suit walked across the court, stopping at the center to pound his chest. The gorilla too was not seen by a significant number of observers.)

The term *inattentional blindness* is now the name given to our failure to detect even the presence of a highly visible stimulus at or near fixation when we are engaged in an attention-demanding task like the one described by Neisser or the one described above in which a target object is presented at or near fixation to observers who are asked to report the longer arm of a briefly presented cross. Under these latter conditions, particularly when the unexpected target item appears where the subject is fixating and the cross is about $2°$ away from fixation, the target is almost never detected. While most items presented under these conditions are not detected, there are, however, a few very notable exceptions. A small number of stimuli do quite reliably capture attention. The most predictable of them are one's own name and a smiley-face icon. Evidence indicates that it is the meaning of these stimuli that captures attention since if either are modified even slightly, for example, inverting the face or changing one internal vowel in the name, it is not likely to be detected. Contrary to what one might expect, none of what perceptual psychologists often think of as salient features seem to have the capacity to capture attention. Neither a brightly colored disk nor a moving or flickering one is likely to be detected under conditions of inattention. However, although unattended stimuli are, for the most part, not detected, there is evidence that they are capable of *priming*, that is, of affecting a subsequent cognitive/perceptual act. For example, if the unattended, undetected target stimulus is a word, there is a reasonable chance that it, rather than some more common word, will be given as the word completing a subsequently presented word stem composed of the initial letters of the target. So while attention is a prerequisite for conscious perception, the finding that meaning captures attention and that undetected stimuli are processed and encoded are also integral aspects of inattentional blindness and must be taken into account when the phenomenon itself is considered. As it will become clear below, nothing in Hochberg's theorizing anticipates the extent to which processing and encoding into memory occurs outside of awareness.

The Attentional Blink

The attentional blink (AB) is another instance of inattentional blindness and shares many of its characteristics, but unlike inattentional blindness, the attentional blink occurs when observers are actively searching for a target stimulus. The typical procedure for obtaining AB is one in which observers are asked to report the presence of two different targets in a rapidly presented series of visual stimuli. The second target is often missed if it occurs roughly within 500 ms of the first (Shapiro, 1994). This failure to see the second target is the AB and is the result of the fact that the second target appears during the interval in which attentional resources are absorbed in processing the first. However, like inattentional blindness, there are a few stimuli which resist the AB. Not surprisingly, these are the same few highly meaningful stimuli that also resist IB (Mack, Pappas, Silverman, & Gay, 2002; Shapiro, Caldwell, & Sorensen, 1997). In addition, there is reason here too to believe that the meaning of the undetected "blinked" target is processed and encoded although not perceived (Luck, Vogel, & Shapiro, 1996). This is significant because it lends additional weight to the view that stimuli not seen because they are unattended nevertheless are processed even to the level of meaning.

Change Blindness

The third inattention phenomenon, change blindness, occurs when observers fail to detect changes in scenes even when they are searching for them. For example, observers often fail to report a change while looking at a repeatedly shown scene cycled with a changed version of the same scene separated by a blank field. (The blank serves to mask the motion transients that, if present, would signal the occurrence of change.) It turns out, again not too surprisingly, that if the item that changes is not central to the gist of the scene, change is far more difficult to detect than if the change is one that affects gist (Rensink, O'Regan, & Clark, 1997). This, of course, is consistent with the importance of meaning for the capture of attention since what is meaningful in a scene defines its gist. In addition, this phenomenon also seems consistent with Hochberg's view that perception is not uniformly dense all over the field (Hochberg, 1968). That being the case, it makes sense that some changes might not be picked up.

Dynamic Change Blindness

Simons and his colleagues (see, for example, Simons & Levin, 1998) have demonstrated dynamic versions of change blindness in which observers frequently fail to detect a significant change following a film cut. This work in particular provides a direct link to Hochberg's work on the perception of films and particularly of nonoverlapping views in films. In two by now well-known demonstration films, Simons and his colleagues have used film cuts to produce change blindness. For example, in one film, a young man is seen sitting at a desk and then getting up. At this point, the camera cuts to the office doorway, where a young man of approximately the same height and coloring, although dressed somewhat differently, is seen talking on a hall phone. Many viewers fail to perceive that the man talking on the phone is not the young man who was sitting at the desk despite the fact that the man is the only actor in the vignette and therefore the object of attention.

Inattentional Blindness, Change Blindness, and Hochberg on Perceiving Films

While Simons and his colleagues have used film cuts to demonstrate change blindness, Hochberg (e.g., Hochberg & Brooks, 1978) is one of the only perception psychologists who has been explicitly interested in the important question of "how we combine view sequences from motion pictures in which scenes are built up by a succession of *nonoverlapping* views" (Hochberg and Brooks, 1978, p. 293). His discussion of this perceptual achievement has direct bearing on our understanding of the dynamic change-blindness film vignettes. When discussing how we perceive nonoverlapping shots, which is what the critical frames in Simons's vignettes are, Hochberg and Brooks (1978) propose that it is our knowledge of the world that "provides the glue that joins the successive views." They go on to say:

> Film editors have, in fact, said that what makes a cut good and rapid to comprehend is the successful effort of the filmmaker to provide the viewer with the visual answer to the question that he would normally have been about to obtain for himself at that time, were he able to change the scene by his own perceptuomotor acts. Once the viewer's visual question is answered, there is no further reason for him to explore the scene, and the scene goes cinematically dead. (p. 294)

If we apply Hochberg's approach to our failure to perceive the change in actors in Simons's demonstration of change blindness just described, we might understand it as a result of our normal assumptions about films in general, namely, that when we see someone getting up from a desk and next see someone talking on the phone who globally resembles that person and who remains within the same visual environment (the office), we assume it is the same person and that the filmmaker is, so to speak, answering our question about why the person got up from his desk in the earlier frame. We do not assume that the filmmaker is out to trick us. This same account would apply to another of Simons's change-blindness experiments (Simons & Levin, 1998) in which an experimenter asks a naive person for directions. While the naive person is giving the experimenter directions, a "real-life film cut" occurs in which a door carried by two unseen confederates comes between them, allowing cover for another experimenter to switch places with the first one. After the interruption, the naive person continues to give directions without noticing that she is now talking to a different person. Like the film viewer, the person giving directions assumes continuity in the world and thus fails to perceive that the person with whom she is conversing has changed. Were the person to have changed from male to female or from one kind of person to another, e.g., from a typical student on a college campus to a construction worker, we are told that the change would be picked up, making it clear that as long as the change does not seriously violate our normal assumptions, we fail to see changes that seem hard to miss.

Surely, Hochberg's recognition that our perceptions are not everywhere equally dense coupled with his view that the integration of images across successive glances or frames is heavily influenced by what we know and what we assume foreshadows the phenomenon of change blindness, even though the extent to which we fail to detect changes may not have been anticipated.

Dichotic Listening

There, however, is one aspect of inattentional blindness which appears to be completely at odds with Hochberg's theorizing about perception. It becomes evident when we examine his account of the results of dichotic-listening experiments, which can be considered auditory analogs of IB experiments. In these experiments, participants are required to shadow a message delivered to one ear while ignoring a competing message simultaneously delivered to the other ear. If, for example, the voice in the unattended ear is male and that in the attended ear is female, listeners generally are aware of this difference, but they are generally completely unaware of the content of the unattended message. However, if the subject's name is included in the unattended message, about one-third of the subjects usually report hearing it (Cherry, 1953), indicating once again that one's own name has the capacity to capture attention. The results of dichotic-listening research have generally been understood in terms of a selective filtering mechanism, which either operates early in the information-processing hierarchy to block or at least attenuate the input in the unattended channel (Treisman, 1969) or later, after the meaning of the input on both channels has been assessed

(Deutsch & Deutsch, 1963). Hochberg's alternative account (1970) completely rejects the notion of a filter. In its place, he proposes, "Suppose there is *no* filter. Suppose instead that when we have a continual flow of sounds, we rapidly forget those that are not encoded into verbal structures" (p. 107). The input from each of the two channels, in this case the phonemes, are tagged as to ear of origin and briefly stored. Those from the attended message are processed first and are encoded into morphemes and in turn into larger structures on the basis of learned transitional probabilities and expectancies, while the bits from the unattended channel fade from immediate memory and are no longer available for further processing. He accounts for the own-name phenomenon by arguing:

> If the secondary morpheme [*that is, a morpheme on the unattended channel*] were one's own name, it would have extremely high internal transitional probabilities for the listener; additionally, even the first few phonemes of one's own name probably serve as an overlearned instruction to listen actively to whatever channel carries it. (p. 109)

Therefore, according to Hochberg, what is encoded as a confirmed expectation is recalled long enough to be reproduced, and "what is not encoded is lost" (p. 110). In other words, Hochberg replaces a filtering mechanism with an immediate memory failure as the explanation for the failure to perceive the message delivered to the unattended channel, and he extends this explanation to visual inattention as well: "The loss of unencoded sensations (or of smaller units) generates the fact of selective attention" (p. 121).[1]

There, however, is a serious problem with a memory account of the failure to be aware of unattended and undetected stimuli, which is shared by the more-recent accounts of inattentional blindness that also attribute it to rapid forgetting (Moore & Egeth, 1997; Wolfe, 1999). According to these accounts, it is not that the unattended object is not detected or seen, but rather that it is quickly forgotten because it is only minimally processed and unencoded. On this view, stimuli which are not objects of attention do not receive the additional processing which, for Hochberg at least, is a function of schematic maps and expectancies that convert them from mere sensations to coherent and meaningful objects. But how do these accounts deal with the clear evidence of priming by these unreported, unseen stimuli? How are these stimuli able to prime subsequent responses and do so even semantically so that the meaning of the undetected stimuli influences subsequent responses?

So while Hochberg's emphasis on the importance of expectations, past knowledge, and intentions in the perceptual process has been abundantly supported by recent research on these various kinds of inattentional blindnesses, his effort to eliminate an attentional filter to account for the facts of selective attention and replace it with what amounts to a short-term memory failure faces what may be an insurmountable problem. It simply fails to account for the now-abundant evidence (from both priming and fMRI studies) that what is not perceived because it was not an object of attention nevertheless may be processed, and encoded, and be capable of affecting our subsequent perceptions and cognitions. What is not seen is not, as Hochberg's theorizing would have us believe, necessarily forgotten. What we see, as Hochberg so cogently argued, is heavily influenced by our intentions, expectations, and past knowledge, but what we don't see because it was not the object of attention, contra Hochberg, also may be deeply processed and stored and subject to the same top-down influences of prior knowledge which, Hochberg taught us, play so important a role in our conscious perceptions.

Note

1. It is perhaps relevant to point out that while there are clear similarities between the dichotic-listening and inattention procedures (most important, both focus attention on only one stimulus or stimulus stream and look at the fate of the unattended input), the fate of these stimuli differ. In the case of dichotic listening, the observers are aware of sounds on the unattended channel even if they are unable to say much about them, whereas in the case of inattentional blindness, the subjects are completely unaware of the unattended and unexpected stimuli.

References

CHERRY, E. (1953). Some experiments on the recognition of speech, with one and two ears. *Journal of the Acoustical Society of America, 25,* 975–979.

DEUTSCH, J., & DEUTSCH, D. (1963). Attention: Some theoretical considerations. *Psychological Review, 87,* 272–300.

HOCHBERG, J. (1968). In the mind's eye. Invited address read at September meeting of the American psychological Society, Division 3. Reprinted in R. N. Haber (Ed.), *Contemporary theory and research in visual perception* (pp. 309–331). New York: Holt, Rinehart and Winston.

HOCHBERG, J. (1970). Attention, organization, and consciousness. In D. Mostofsky (Ed.), *Attention: Contemporary theory and analysis* (pp. 99–124). New York: Appleton-Century-Crofts.

HOCHBERG, J., & BROOKS, V. (1978). Film cutting and visual momentum. In J. W. Senders, D. F. Fisher, & R. A. Monty (Eds.), *Eye movements and the higher psychological functions* (pp. 293–313). Hillsdale, NJ: Erlbaum.

LUCK, S., VOGEL, E., & SHAPIRO, K. (1996). Word meanings can be accessed, but not reported during the attentional blink. *Nature, 383,* 616–618.

MACK, A., PAPPAS, Z., SILVERMAN, M., & GAY, R. (2002). What we see: Inattention and the capture of attention by meaning. *Consciousness and Cognition, 11,* 507–527.

MACK, A., & ROCK, I. (1998). *Inattentional blindness.* Cambridge, MA: MIT Press.

MOORE, C., & EGETH, H. (1997). Perception without attention: Evidence of grouping under conditions of inattention. *Journal of Experimental Psychology: Human Perception and Performance, 112,* 339–352.

NEISSER, U., & BECKLEN, R. (1975). Selective looking: Attending to visually specified events. *Cognitive Psychology, 7,* 480–494.

RENSINK, R., O'REGAN, K., & CLARK, S. (1997). To see or not to see: The need for attention to perceive changes in scenes. *Psychological Science, 8,* 368–373.

SHAPIRO, K. (1994). The attentional blink: The brain's eye blink. *Current Directions in Psychological Science, 3,* 86–89.

SHAPIRO, K., CALDWELL, J., & SORENSEN, R. (1997). Personal names and the attentional blink: A visual cocktail party effect. *Journal of Experimental Psychology: Human Perception and Performance, 23,* 504–514.

SIMONS, D., & CHABRIS, C. (1999). Gorillas in our midst: Sustained inattentional blindness for dynamic events. *Perception, 28,* 1059–1074.

SIMONS, D., & LEVIN, D. (1998). Failure to detect changes to people during real world interactions. *Psychonomic Bulletin and Review, 5,* 644–649.

TREISMAN, A. (1969). Strategies and model of selective attention. *Psychological Review, 76,* 282–299.

TREISMAN, A., & GELADE, G. (1980). A feature integration theory of attention. *Cognitive Psychology, 112,* 97–136.

WOLFE, J. (1999). Inattentional amnesia. In V. Coltheart (Ed.), *Fleeting memories: Cognition of brief visual stimuli* (pp. 71–94). Cambridge, MA: MIT Press.

Local Processing, Organization, and Perceptual Rules

30

Framing the Rules of Perception

*Hochberg Versus Galileo, Gestalts, Garner,
and Gibson*

James E. Cutting

Julian Hochberg is our greatest synthesizer of theories and experimental
results in the field of perception, and he has been for a half century. Moreover, his only real predecessor was E. G. Boring, who in a single volume
(Boring, 1942) put together both an intellectual and rumor-filled history of
the field. Hochberg never had either aspiration. Nonetheless, in what may be
the largest collection of handbook chapters on perception that anyone will
ever write, Hochberg's corpus has covered all of the important ground many
times in the best of historical traditions—revising and reworking the past in
light of current and ongoing research and controversies.

As have many others, I have spent a good part of my intellectual life
having agreements and disagreements about perception with the several Julian
Hochbergs, the authors of those chapters and of various experimental works.
For example, occasionally I would find myself tantalized by an idea that he
had proposed several decades before, only to discover that he had disavowed
it not long before I was embracing it. But Hochberg's legacy is not continual
revolution. One thread that runs through his work is a concern with the
rules by which perception occurs. There can be no doubt that our perception of the world around us occurs in a very reliable and repeatable way.
But why? This was Koffka's query: "Why do we perceive things as we do?"
(Koffka, 1935, p. 75). Perception is rule-governed but in what form should
we express its rules? Historically, there are a number of candidates for
framing an answer. Here, I will consider four.

Galileo and Descartes: Rules as Math

We can look first to Galileo and the idea of a *mathesis universalis*. That is,
our knowledge about nature—and the mind, and hence perception—must
be written in the language of mathematics (see Klein, 1985, p. 95). No field
has embraced this idea more than physics, and few physicists more than
Wigner (1979, p. 237), who concluded: "The miracle of the appropriateness
of the language of mathematics for the formulation of the laws of physics is

a wonderful gift which we neither understand nor deserve. We should be grateful for it and hope . . . that it will extend . . . to wide branches of learning." Hochberg, although an undergraduate physics major, seems never to have been seriously tempted in this direction in his study of perception.

But, nonetheless, might perception be one of Wigner's "wide branches of learning" to which math can fruitfully be applied? Are what and how we perceive best couched in math? This is not the place to review the variety of such approaches (see, for example, Cutting, 1986, 1987, 1998), but there are many and I will return to some below. Nonetheless, there are at least two reasons to doubt that any Galilean *mathesis universalis* will solve many problems in perception. First, unconstrained, the reach of mathematics is too broad and powerful (Cutting, 1986, p. xi). For example, mathematics has proved as equally applicable to all of astrology as it has to all of astronomy, no less to perception and the mind. So, what would we have learned? Second, most of mathematics is precise, whereas most of perception is not. As noted by Hochberg (1956, p. 404) early in his career, there are always problems of ambiguity, uncertainty, and background noise: "the degree of the inter- and intra-individual variability of the relationship between stimulus and perceptual response . . . as related by the task." To be sure, ambiguity (as multistability) has been modeled with catastrophe theory (e.g., Ta'eed, Ta'eed, & Wright, 1988); uncertainty is reasonably well captured by a fuzzy logic (Massaro, 1987), and a few researchers have become interested in the fractal structure of the background noise in experimental responses (Gilden, Thornton, & Mallon, 1995; Van Orden, Holden, & Turvey, 2003). But these are not the kinds of perceptual rules that have interested Hochberg. For him, why we perceive as we do has much more to do with meaning than with math.

Descartes was also interested in a *mathesis universalis*, but his interest took a different turn than Galileo's.[1] As the methodological backbone of his *Rules for the Direction of the Natural Intelligence* (Helden, 1610/1989), Descartes's set of ideas was somewhat closer to what Hochberg endorses. Few of Descartes's rules concern psychology but Rules 14 through 16 are about representation, imagination, the senses, and memory. Hochberg has never been happy with the idea of separating these (e.g., Hochberg, 1981b), nor was Descartes. Nonetheless, following a tradition from Euclid and Arabic optics, Descartes often reduced visual perception to geometry; Hochberg never took this route.

Gestalts, Ruled by Economy

Hochberg was deeply affected by the Gestalt revolution, and he has served as its major interpreter for a long time (e.g., Hochberg, 1957, 1998). He was the first to quantify the idea of *Prägnanz*, or figural goodness, as simplicity and apply it to perception (Hochberg & McAlister, 1953). Succinctly, Hochberg later characterized this as a perceptual rule: "We perceive whatever objects or scene would most simply or economically fit the sensory pattern" (Hochberg, 1981b, p. 263). In their landmark study, Hochberg and McAlister took Kopfermann cubes (see Figure 2.2, p. 13, this volume) and counted bits and pieces of lines and their intersections, and accounted for how they were seen in two and three dimensions. Later, confronted with several of Penrose's impossible figures (e.g., Penrose & Penrose, 1958; see also Figure 8.2, p. 76, this volume), Hochberg (1962, 1968) became dissatisfied with this approach. Nonetheless, this initial work ignited several research programs in several areas.

One program was that of Leeuwenberg (1968; Leeuwenberg & Boselie, 1988), followed by various copyists (Cutting, 1981; Restle, 1979). This approach sought to account for percepts by claiming them to be the simplest among alternatives—and this idea is still very much alive (Chater & Vitányi, 2003; van der Helm, chapter 33, this volume). Indeed, it had important roots in developments from algorithmic information theory in computer science, but even these occurred well after Hochberg and McAlister. However, the problems of simplicity as applied to perception are two: First, what one perceives is not always the simplest, however "simple" be defined (e.g., Cutting, 2000; Hochberg, 1968), and second, different ad hoc sets of primitives can be rallied at any point in support of almost any calculation of simplicity (Cutting, 1987; Goodman, 1972; Hochberg, 1998). The theory is principled, but the primitives often are not. But no matter, the theory is wrong.

Shannon and Garner to Bayes: Rules as Probabilities

A third approach to rules for perception burgeoned in the 1950s after the information-theoretic work of Shannon (1948; Shannon & Weaver, 1949). Hochberg lived through and beyond this information revolution in psychology. With Attneave (1954), he was the first to apply aspects of these ideas to perception, as discussed in the previous section. Within the field of perception, the work of Garner (1962, 1970) was closest to Shannon's ideas of information as the reduction of uncertainty about a perceptual stimulus. There is something deeply attractive about this idea: There is more information in a stimulus if you know little about it, and less if you know a lot. Thus, if you are clueless about the day of the week, and I tell you it's Friday, you receive information (bits = $\log[7]$); but if you already know it is Friday, you had no uncertainty and thus received no information. The problem with this approach, however, is nontrivial—knowing in advance what the perceiver knows. But one way out of this problem for Garner was that perception was fundamentally about seeking information. Hochberg has always been sympathetic with this idea.

Garner, who was one of my graduate advisors (Cutting, 1991), was also sympathetic to Bayesian statistics, and aspects of his work can be viewed as an intellectual precursor to Bayesian approaches to perception. More recently, Knill and Richards (1996) used Bayes' rule to study scenes, and their book is the contemporary starting point for this approach. But here let me apply it to objects and information:

$$p \text{ (object | information)} = p \text{ (information | object)}$$
$$\times\, p \text{ (object)}/p \text{ (information)}, \qquad \text{Eq(1)}$$

where p is probability and p (object | information) is the probability of a particular object being present given the particular information in the visual array. Recently, there have been some stunning uses of Bayes' theorem in perception (Kersten, 1997; Weiss, Simoncelli, & Adelson, 2002), but some rather stringent constraints must be placed on the formula above. Given free rein of all possible objects and information, both the probability of any given object and of any given information source flirts with zero. Thus the latter part of the equation—p (object)/p (information)—can be wildly unstable. All of the real work in Bayesian approaches to perception is in the controlling of these "priors" (the a priori probabilities). Moreover, I claim that when the probabilities of these two are the same, we have something close to Gibson's approach, discussed below.

Four decades before the popularization of Bayesian approaches to perception, however, Brunswik (1956) was interested in these very issues. He focused centrally on what came to be known as the *cue validity* of information and the *ecological validity* of experiments. For example, Brunswik was interested in the probability that any given cue (such as relative size) specified some property of objects of the world (such as their relative depth). Quite boldly in his research program, he set out to assess such probabilities, and he worried deeply about important issues such as sampling. Hochberg's (1966) great admiration for the rigor of Brunswik, one of his own advisors at Berkeley, did not stop him from providing a withering critique. Brunswik used pictures as stimuli, and the objects in pictures have quite a different set of probabilities than do those same objects in the world. For example, faces of people have a much higher occurrence rate in photographs than they would if a camera were simply randomly pointed in any direction. Thus construed in his own terms, not only was Brunswik's search for probabilities problematic, so were his experiments. And this same critique applies generally to Bayesian approaches today. Interestingly, it is also on this ground that Gibson took on most of midcentury perceptual theory (Gibson, 1966, 1979). Although not tempted by Brunswikian or Bayesian approaches, Hochberg has nonetheless been tantalized by likelihoods, as I will return to below.

Gibson: Rules as Certainties

In 1949, Hochberg arrived at Cornell University as an instructor. Gibson arrived the same year as a full professor. The two shared my department for 15 years (Hochberg, 1990), with Hochberg rising through the ranks. Indeed, the earliest explication and defense of Gibson's emerging theoretical position in perception was in Hochberg's work (1964). The two had overlapping interests in many areas of perception, but perhaps most interestingly in film. For example, both had deep fascination about how successive shots within and across scenes were perceptually plausible—that is, why and how they worked. Not surprisingly, Gibson was most interested in what remained the same (invariant) across shots within a scene (Gibson, 1950, pp. 159–160; 1979, pp. 297–301). But Hochberg was interested in what the perceiver brought to the shot transition within and across scenes to make it interpretable, using this as a model for successive glances in the real world (Hochberg, 1978, pp. 200–211; Hochberg & Brooks, 1996, pp. 244–277). For Hochberg: As in film, so the world. For Gibson: As the world, so in film. This difference made Hochberg take the structure of film seriously, and Gibson misinterpreted it.

For Gibson, information was present in the environment and needed only to be picked up. For Hochberg, even if it were true, this was a statement that didn't answer the important questions. The observer had to find the information (necessitating eye movements) and have some strategy about where to look. Moreover, the role of the experimenter was to specify what exactly that information was. Gibson had no particular interest in the fleshing out of this idea (see Hochberg, 1981b, 1990), although an army of researchers over 30 years set out to find these invariants (see Cutting, 1993, for a review). And they found some—but not all that many.

For Gibson, the information sources to be picked up were invariants. A perceptual invariant is a concept borrowed from group theory. Any one of a group of transformations can be applied to an object, leaving it unchanged, and the six in the Galilean group—translations and rotations in orthogonal dimensions x, y, and z—were obvious candidates, but changes in lighting were also important. Early on, it looked as if invariants from projective geometry might be useful for visual perception (Gibson, 1950, p. 153n; Johansson, von Hofsten, & Jansson, 1980), and indeed some evidence was found in their support (Cutting, 1986). Later, however, their scope seemed to narrow (Niall & Macnamara, 1989; Van Gool, Moons, Pauwels, & Wagemans, 1994). Nonetheless, the attractive thing about invariants is the putative one-to-one relationship between information and the object it represents. Reworking and simplifying Bayes, Gibson believed:

$$p \,(\text{object} \mid \text{information}) = p \,(\text{information} \mid \text{object}) = 1. \qquad \text{Eq(2)}$$

That is, the information in the visual array specified the presence of the object under all normal conditions, and the object would always contain that information. Note, however, that the p here is probability, not perception. For Hochberg, and indeed even for Gibson (1979), the perceiver had to explore and find the information. The richness of the real world did not necessarily make this task easier, and it was still worth doing laboratory experiments with specially structured stimuli. About Gibson, Hochberg felt that "it was a great achievement to have framed plausible accounts of accurate perception in a normal environment, but it is not therefore pointless to study anything short of that" (Hochberg, 1990, p. 751).

Hochberg on Rules

The perceptual rule to which Hochberg has paid the most attention over the last quarter century is sometimes known as Helmholtz's rule, or the likelihood principle: "We perceive that object or event which would, under normal seeing conditions, be most likely to produce the pattern of sensations that we receive. To fit a perceived object or event to the sensory data in this way amounts to an *unconscious inference*" (Hochberg, 1981b, p. 127; see also 1981a, p. 263). Stated this way, this idea is close to a Bayesian approach to perception. But rather than being interested in the algorithm of calculating the probabilities—which drags one sideways into difficult, even arcane, frequency analyses and the shoring up of priors—Hochberg is simply interested in the fact that the mind, one's personal history, evolutionary history, and the structure of the world *all* matter.

This formulation nicely deals with a number of issues. One is the backward coupling of sensory data to objects and events without stating that the sensory data need to be shared across all peoples. Thus, issues of different sensory qualities (or qualia), as are found when comparing color-normal with color-weak individuals, are not stumbling blocks. Both groups have color sensations and, although different, those sensations correspond to objects and events in the world in a rule-like fashion within a given individual. Moreover, across individuals, we also know the reasons for differential neural patterns. In this manner, the rule takes a firm stance on the mind-body problem (e.g., Fodor, 1981)—it is a materialist point of view, avoiding the problems of central-state identity (mind-brain isomorphisms) and embracing a brand of functionalism (mind-brain correlations).

This rule also nicely sets aside discussion of any differential causes attributable to nature (biological endowment) and nurture (learning). In the phrasing of this rule, the ontogeny of perception doesn't matter. All that matters is that the senses respond in the way that they do to particular objects and events, and that they respond consistently. Similarly, perceptual differences in peoples across cultures and differences in creatures across environments can be accommodated—in both cases, the patterns of sensory data that are picked up can differ as a result of learning or endowment, and understanding both is a proper focus of perceptual research.

To be sure, there has not been universal endorsement of the likelihood principle (Leeuwenberg & Boselie, 1988). Indeed, Helmholtz's rule does put all of the onus on consistency and hedges on anything other than a "normality" of conditions—without defining normality. But the theory stands, through Hochberg, as a touchstone that every perceptual theorist must consider. Is Hochberg right? He cannot be far wrong.

Note

1. *Mathesis universalis* was a popular idea in the 17th century and may have been first promoted by the Belgian mathematician Adrianus Romanus in his *Universae mathesis idea* of 1602 (see Heffernan, 1998, p. 97n).

References

ATTNEAVE, F. (1954). Some informational aspects of visual perception. *Psychological Review, 61*, 183–198.

BORING, E. G. (1942). *Sensation and perception in the history of experimental psychology.* New York: Appleton-Century.

BRUNSWIK, E. (1956). *Perception and the representative design of psychological experiments.* Berkeley: University of California Press.

CHATER, N., & VITÁNYI, P. (2003). Simplicity: A unifying principle in cognitive science? *Trends in Cognitive Sciences, 7*, 19–22.

CUTTING, J. E. (1981). Coding theory adapted to gait perception. *Journal of Experimental Psychology: Human Perception and Performance, 7*, 71–87.

CUTTING, J. E. (1986). *Perception with an eye for motion.* Cambridge, MA: MIT Press.

CUTTING, J. E. (1987). Perception and information. *Annual Review of Psychology, 38*, 61–90.

CUTTING, J. E. (1991). Why our stimuli look like they do. In G. Lockhead & J. Pomerantz (Eds.), *Information and structure: Essays in honor of Wendell R. Garner* (pp. 41–52). Washington, DC: American Psychological Association.

CUTTING, J. E. (1993). Perceptual artifacts and phenomena: Gibson's role in the 20th century. In S. Masin (Ed.), *Foundations of perceptual theory* (pp. 231–260). Amsterdam: North Holland.

CUTTING, J. E. (1998). Information from the world around us. In J. Hochberg (Ed.), *Perception and cognition at century's end* (pp. 69–93). San Diego, CA: Academic.

CUTTING, J. E. (2000). Accuracy, scope, and flexibility of models. *Journal of Mathematical Psychology, 44*, 3–19.

FODOR, J. A. (1981). The mind-body problem. *Scientific American, 244*(1), 114–123.

GARNER, W. R. (1962). *Uncertainty and structure as psychological concepts.* New York: Wiley.

GARNER, W. R. (1970). Good patterns have few alternatives. *American Psychologist, 58*, 34–42.

GIBSON, J. J. (1950). *Perception of the visual world.* Boston: Houghton Mifflin.

GIBSON, J. J. (1966). *The senses considered as perceptual systems.* Boston: Houghton Mifflin.

GIBSON, J. J. (1979). *The ecological approach to visual perception.* Boston: Houghton Mifflin.

GILDEN, D., THORNTON, T., & MALLON, M. W. (1995). 1/f noise in human cognition. *Science, 267*, 1837–1839.

GOODMAN, N. (1972). Seven strictures on similarity. In N. Goodman, *Problems and projects* (pp. 437–446). Indianapolis, IN: Hackett.

HEFFERNAN, G. (Ed. & Trans.). (1998). *René Descartes: Regulae ad directionem ingenii: Rules for the direction of the natural intelligence.* Amsterdam: Rodopi. (Original work published 1618–1629)

HELDEN, A. V. (1989). *Sidereus nuncius; or, the sidereal messenger of Galileo Galilei.* Chicago: University of Chicago Press. (Original work published 1610)

HOCHBERG, J. (1956). Perception: Toward the recovery of a definition. *Psychological Review, 63,* 400–405.

HOCHBERG, J. (1957). Effects of the Gestalt revolution: The Cornell symposium on perception. *Psychological Review, 64,* 73–84.

HOCHBERG, J. (1962). The psychophysics of visual perception. *Audio-Visual Communication Review, 10,* 22–54.

HOCHBERG, J. (1964). *Perception* (1st ed.). Englewood Cliffs, NJ: Prentice-Hall.

HOCHBERG, J. (1966). Representative sampling and the purposes of perceptual research: Pictures of the world and the world of pictures. In K. R. Hammond (Ed.), *The psychology of Egon Brunswik* (pp. 361–381). New York: Holt, Rinehart, and Winston.

HOCHBERG, J. (1968). In the mind's eye. In R. N. Haber (Ed.), *Contemporary theory and research in visual perception* (pp. 309–331). London: Holt, Rinehart & Winston.

HOCHBERG, J. (1978). *Perception* (2d ed.). Englewood Cliffs, NJ: Prentice-Hall.

HOCHBERG, J. (1981a). Levels of perceptual organization. In M. Kubovy & J. R. Pomerantz (Eds.), *Perceptual organization* (pp. 255–278). Hillsdale, NJ: Erlbaum.

HOCHBERG, J. (1981b). On cognition in perception: Perceptual coupling and unconscious inference. *Cognition, 10,* 127–134.

HOCHBERG, J. (1990). After the revolution. *Contemporary Psychology, 35,* 750–752.

HOCHBERG, J. (1998). Gestalt theory and its legacy. In J. Hochberg (Ed.), *Perception and cognition at century's end* (pp. 253–306). San Diego, CA: Academic.

HOCHBERG, J., & BROOKS, V. (1996). The perception of motion pictures. In M. P. Friedman & E. C. Carterette (Eds.), *Cognitive ecology* (pp. 205–292). San Diego: Academic.

HOCHBERG, J., & MCALISTER, E. (1953). A quantitative approach to figural "goodness." *Journal of Experimental Psychology, 46,* 361–364.

JOHANSSON, G., VON HOFSTEN, C., & JANSSON, G. (1980). Event perception. *Annual Review of Psychology, 31,* 27–66.

KERSTEN, D. (1997). Inverse 3-D graphics: A metaphor for visual perception. *Behavior Research Methods, Instruments, & Computers, 29,* 37–46.

KLEIN, M. (1985). *Mathematics and the search for knowledge.* New York: Oxford.

KNILL, D. C., & RICHARDS, W. (1996). *Perception as Bayesian inference.* New York: Cambridge University Press.

KOFFKA, K. (1935). *The principles of Gestalt psychology.* New York: Harcourt.

LEEUWENBERG, E. (1968). *Structural information of visual patterns.* The Hague: Mouton.

LEEUWENBERG, E., & BOSELIE, F. (1988). Against the likelihood principle in visual form perception. *Psychological Review, 95,* 485–491.

MASSARO, D. W. (1987). *Speech perception by ear and by eye: A paradigm for psychological inquiry.* Hillsdale, NJ: Erlbaum.

NIALL, K., & MACNAMARA, J. (1989). Projective invariance and visual shape constancy. *Acta Psychologica, 72,* 65–79.

PENROSE, L. S., & PENROSE, R. (1958). Impossible objects: A special type of illusion. *British Journal of Psychology, 49,* 31–33.

RESTLE, F. (1979). Coding theory of the perception of motion configurations. *Psychological Review, 86,* 1–24.

SHANNON, C. E. (1948). A mathematical theory of communication. *Bell Systems Technical Journal, 27,* 379–423, 623–656.

SHANNON, C. E., & WEAVER, W. (1949). *The mathematical theory of communication.* Urbana: University of Illinois Press.

TA'EED, L. K., TA'EED, O., & WRIGHT, J. E. (1988). Determinants involved in the perception of the Necker cube: An application of catastrophe theory. *Behavioral Science, 33,* 97–115.

VAN GOOL, L. J., MOONS, T., PAUWELS, E., & WAGEMANS, J. (1994). Invariance from a Euclidean geometer's perspective. *Perception, 23,* 547–561.

VAN ORDEN, G., HOLDEN, J. G., & TURVEY, M. T. (2003). Self-organization of cognitive performance. *Journal of Experimental Psychology: General, 132,* 331–350.

WEISS, Y., SIMONCELLI, E. P., & ADELSON, E. H. (2002). Motion illusions as optimal percepts. *Nature Neuroscience, 5,* 598–604.

WIGNER, E. (1979). The unreasonable effectiveness of mathematics in the natural sciences. In E. Wigner, *Symmetries and reflections* (pp. 222–237). Woodbridge, CT: Ox Bow.

31

On the Internal Consistency of Perceptual Organization

James T. Todd

One of the central tenets of Gestalt psychology is that configurations of stimulus elements are perceptually organized to have the lowest possible structural complexity—what is often referred to as the "minimum principle." Consider, for example, the image of a Necker cube presented in the left panel of Figure 31.1. It is important to keep in mind that the actual physical structure of this figure is a 2D configuration of lines, but that is not how it is perceived. It appears instead as a 3D cube, presumably because that structure is simpler than the alternative 2D interpretation.

Although the minimum principle is frequently invoked as an "explanation" of perceptual organization, a precise definition of structural complexity is seldom provided. One of the first attempts to rectify that problem was developed by Hochberg and McAlister (1953), who proposed a formal quantitative analysis for measuring the relative complexity of possible perceptual organizations based on the number of line segments in a figure and the number of distinct angles. Empirical support for this approach was later provided by Hochberg and Brooks (1960). They asked subjects to rate the apparent three-dimensionality of wire-frame figures, like Necker cubes, that were depicted from multiple vantage points. Whereas the 3D complexity of a given object remains constant across different views, the 2D complexity of its projected image can vary dramatically. For example, the image of a cube can appear as a square or a hexagon if viewed from an appropriate vantage point. Hochberg and Brooks found that there was a strong negative correlation between the apparent three-dimensionality of an object and the 2D complexity of its optical projection. In other words, the patterns that had simple 2D interpretations were perceived as flat rather than three-dimensional, which is consistent with the minimum principle.

Despite these early attempts to make the intuitive notion of a minimum principle more scientifically rigorous, Hochberg eventually concluded that it cannot be the primary underlying mechanism for the perception of 3D shapes from line drawings. His reasons for this conversion were first laid out in 1966 in an invited address to the American Psychological Association, which was later published in Hochberg (1968). It was motivated in part by

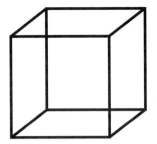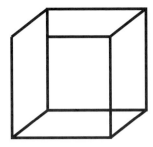

Figure 31.1. Two drawings of a wire-frame cube. The one in the left panel is mathematically and perceptually ambiguous. It can appear to face upward to the right or downward to the left. The pattern in the right panel is adapted from Peterson and Hochberg (1983). Although it is mathematically unambiguous because of the occlusion information provided by the T-junction, the other ambiguous features can still undergo a piecemeal perceptual reversal, which creates the appearance of an impossible figure.

the perceptual appearance of impossible figures (Penrose & Penrose, 1958). Because these figures have no consistent 3D interpretation, any reasonable computational instantiation of the minimum principle would predict that they should appear as 2D patterns. That is not what occurs, however. Indeed, if the incompatible features are sufficiently far apart, observers may not even notice that the depicted 3D structure is internally inconsistent. According to Hochberg (1968), this suggests that perceived 3D structure is based on a schematic map of local depth cues obtained over multiple eye fixations and that the structure of this map need not be internally consistent.

A related demonstration to support this hypothesis was first presented by Hochberg (1970) and was systematically investigated in an elegant series of experiments by Peterson and Hochberg (1983). Consider the pattern in the right panel of Figure 31.1, which is adapted from these studies. Unlike the ambiguous Necker cube in the left panel, this pattern has a unique 3D interpretation as a cube facing upward to the right. Based on the minimum principle, one would expect that the perceptual organization of this object should be quite stable, but a visual inspection of the figure reveals that it is easily reversed so that the cube appears to be facing downward to the left. When this occurs, however, the object has the appearance of an impossible figure because the inversion is incomplete. Note that the T-junction in the upper left of the pattern provides compelling information about local depth order that is not easily reversed, but this apparently does not constrain the perceived 3D structure in other regions. This can create a piecemeal inversion, in which the apparent depth order of different line segments is internally inconsistent.

Another compelling example of piecemeal inversion was discovered much later by Reichel and Todd (1990) in a study of intrinsic biases in the

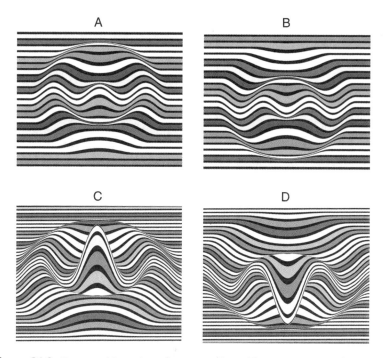

Figure 31.2. Perceptual inversion of texture surfaces. The two upper panels are identical images presented in opposite orientations. Because most observers have a perceptual bias to interpret the overall surface slant so that depth increases with height in the image plane, the apparent sign of surface relief is reversed when the image is turned upside-down. The lower panels are also identical images in opposite orientations. In this case, however, they contain occlusion information to specify the correct depth-order relations. When this is consistent with the perceptual bias, observers perceive the correct pattern of surface relief. When the image is turned upside-down so that the occlusion information is incompatible with the bias, the surface undergoes a piecemeal perceptual reversal, which creates the appearance of an impossible figure.

perception of ambiguous surfaces. The two panels labeled A and B in Figure 31.2 show images of a textured surface that are identical in all respects, except that they are presented in opposite orientations. Because these images were rendered under orthographic projection, the depicted sign of relief is mathematically ambiguous, but, for most observers, there is a strong perceptual bias to interpret the overall surface slant such that the apparent depth increases with height in the image plane. That is why the surface labeled A appears to have a small bump in its center, whereas the one labeled B appears to have a small dimple. If the figure is viewed upside down, however, the perceptual bias will cause the apparent sign of relief to become inverted, such that A will appear to have a dimple, and B will appear to have a bump.

In an effort to overcome this bias, Reichel and Todd also created stimuli with visible smooth occlusion contours to provide unambiguous information about the depicted surface depth order relations. The image labeled C in Figure 31.2 shows one example where the occlusion information is consistent with the perceptual bias. This produces a stable perception of the correct pattern of surface relief. The image labeled D shows exactly the same surface in an inverted orientation, so that the occlusion information is in conflict with the surface orientation bias. Note how this produces a piecemeal perceptual inversion with the disturbing appearance of an impossible figure. Although the occlusion information determines the perceived depth order in its immediate local neighborhood, the surface orientation bias seems to dominate the apparent structure everywhere else. What is fascinating about this figure is that it has an unambiguous 3D interpretation that is internally consistent, yet most observers have difficulty perceiving it even with conscious effort. A similar effect can also be obtained in the perception of 3D shape from shading (see Reichel & Todd, 1990).

As Hochberg first recognized in the 1970s, the phenomenon of piecemeal inversion has important theoretical implications, but it has not in my opinion received the attention it deserves, and there have been few subsequent studies to investigate its generality. It is interesting to note that in my own perception of ambiguous figures, the apparent depth order relations among different features are not completely independent of one another—even when I experience a piecemeal inversion. For example, when the patterns in Figure 31.1 switch from one perceptual organization to another, the ambiguous features almost always switch in unison. It is the unambiguous T-junctions that can appear inconsistent with the other features. All of this raises a number of important questions for future research. Are T-junctions special in this regard, or are there other local sources of information about depth order that are equally resistant to perceptual inversion? The existence of piecemeal perceptual inversion is clearly inconsistent with the idea that perceptual organization is determined exclusively by a global minimum principle, but it does not necessarily follow from this evidence that a minimum principle has no effect whatsoever. If so, how do we explain why the appearances of ambiguous features in Figure 31.1 are generally consistent with one another, or why it is impossible to perceive the myriad noncubic 3D interpretations that could also have produced the same optical projection? These are fundamental questions for the theoretical analysis of perceptual organization, but they have proven to be surprisingly elusive.

References

HOCHBERG, J. (1968). In the mind's eye. In R. Haber (Ed.), *Contemporary theory and research in visual perception* (pp. 309–331). New York: Holt, Rinehart, and Winston.

HOCHBERG, J. (1970). Attention, organization, and consciousness. In D. Mostofsky (Ed.), *Attention: Contemporary theory and analysis* (pp. 99–124). New York: Appleton-Century-Crofts.

HOCHBERG, J., & BROOKS, V. (1960). The psychophysics of form: Reversible perspective drawings of spatial objects. *American Journal of Psychology, 73,* 337–354.

HOCHBERG, J., & MCALISTER, E. (1953). A quantitative approach to figural "goodness." *Journal of Experimental Psychology, 46,* 361–364.

PENROSE, L., & PENROSE, R. (1958). Impossible objects: A special type of visual illusion. *British Journal of Psychology, 49,* 31–33.

PETERSON, M. A., & HOCHBERG, J. (1983). Opposed-set measurement procedure: A quantitative analysis of the role of local cues and intention in form perception. *Journal of Experimental Psychology: Human Perception and Performance, 9,* 183–193.

REICHEL, F. D., & TODD, J. T. (1990). Perceived depth inversion of smoothly curved surfaces due to image orientation. *Journal of Experimental Psychology: Human Perception and Performance, 16,* 653–664.

32

Piecemeal Perception and Hochberg's Window

Grouping of Stimulus Elements Over Distances

James R. Pomerantz

Julian Hochberg has always been one to take on the big questions in visual perception, and as a result, his reach of influence—including the range of people he has affected—has been long. For me, his most lasting influence is captured by one question that engaged him for years: Is there a spatial window in which perceptual organization occurs, particularly the organization governing the perception of form and of spatial layout? Hochberg argued that this window is small and that perception is principally a piecemeal affair rather than one based on global organization. Although there are cases where organization does seem to span large regions of visual space, recent evidence supports Hochberg's contention.

Global Perception

Hochberg (1981) framed his question in the context of the broadest historical theories of perception—Helmholtzian, Gibsonian, and Gestaltist—noting that they "differ in . . . the degree of *wholism* posited (i.e., the size of the structure within which constraints are strong)" (p. 255) but that "the bounds over which wholistic theories extend their analyses have not been well defined" (p. 259). Gestalt theory implied that "some overall measure of simplicity can be found and that it is to be applied to some *overall* unit (e.g., an object); otherwise there is no proposal at all" (p. 263). Going on, he observed that "the size of the unit is central. . . . I do not know of any serious and successful attempts to specify a size of unit (details, objects, scenes) within which the Gestalt principles apply, and I do not now believe that any such attempt could work" (p. 263). Pointing to impossible figures, whose existence seems strongly to imply that perceptual organization is driven by local cues with little attempt to achieve simplified, global Gestalts, Hochberg noted, "There really is very little left of the Gestalt theory, as proposed by Wertheimer, Kohler, and Koffka, that survives the facts. . . . I cannot see how . . . 'laws of organization' much larger in scope than a couple of degrees in extent can accommodate these particularistic or neoatomistic implications" (p. 266) (see also Hochberg, 1968).

Piecemeal Perception

Fast forwarding more than two decades, we began to talk of the "spotlight of attention" within which features are integrated (Treisman & Gelade, 1980). It is not much of a leap to move from Hochberg's question—the size of the window within which perceptual organization occurs—to the size of the spotlight where the binding problem is resolved, the region in which it is determined which perceptual attributes and elements go together. After all, Gestalt organization is in many respects another method of feature integration. Hochberg's inquiries foreshadowed in good measure the concept of the attentional spotlight, although it remains unclear whether Gestalt organization, concerned as it is with configuration, is part of the same process that integrates other features, such as color, depth, and motion, or instead is handled by a separate process, perhaps taking place within a different spatially bound region. In any case, I believe Hochberg's question remains alive and well today.

To illustrate the importance of Hochberg's window, reconsider his example of impossible figures: stimuli that are organized into three-dimensional interpretations that are physically impossible. They include such famous figures as the Penrose triangle and the Schuster three-pronged clevis, which appear so often in introductory psychology textbooks. Their mere existence could imply that visual organization takes place only in a piecemeal fashion, as if within a window too small to accommodate the entire figure (cf. Hochberg, 1968, for an earlier glimpse into the window metaphor). Impossible figures show that contours which are organized and interpreted correctly at the local level are not similarly organized at the global level.

Hochberg's Cube

Hochberg (1981) elevated the impossible figure to a significantly higher level when he created his seemingly innocuous variation on the Necker cube, shown in Figure 32.1. Here, one of the lines making up the drawing is truncated to yield a stimulus with a perfectly possible 3D interpretation, viz., a Necker cube whose right face is opaque. Nonetheless, it is often perceived as impossible, as a figure that twists irreconcilably in its orientation as one examines it (see also Gillam, 1978). Of course, with the traditional impossible figures too, there is always one interpretation that is possible: seeing the stimulus as lines on a flat piece of paper. Not only is this interpretation possible, it is also veridical.

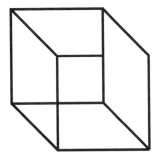

Figure 32.1. The Hochberg cube, in which one line segment of the famous Necker cube is truncated to yield a figure that, despite having a simple and wholly possible interpretation, is often seen as an impossible figure. Adapted from Hochberg (1981).

Hochberg's cube does these traditional figures one better by allowing for a perfectly possible 3D interpretation as an alternative to the impossible one(s). The fact that viewers often see—even prefer—the impossible organization suggests even more forcefully that organization stops at the local level, with little or no checking that the interpretations in one region are consistent with those in others outside a small window (at least for depth orientation in flat images). Hochberg's cube led to other similar examples, including Michael Kubovy's and my ambiguous triptych (Pomerantz & Kubovy, 1981), and these confirm that Hochberg's cube is not an isolated curiosity. Other evidence for the piecemeal-perception hypothesis comes from demonstrations that properties such as symmetry, which seem to be detected globally, are in fact detected only locally, in the regions immediately surrounding the symmetry axis (Julesz, 1975). The extreme interpretation of this outcome—that there is no global organization in perception—might at first seem at odds with everyday experience in which errors and anomalies such as those seen with impossible figures are rare. It is possible, of course, that our impression that the visual world is usually well structured globally is merely an illusion. For example, we know from work on change blindness that our impression that we are attending to and remembering the whole field of vision is often incorrect (Rensink, O'Regan, & Clark, 1997). But even so, there need be no fundamental conflict, because the world that we perceive is in fact well structured, and our regional interpretations are good ones. In true Gibsonian fashion, our percepts are so well organized because the world is typically well organized. Only when facing "trick" stimuli, usually laboratory contrivances with dubious ecological validity, will such a piecemeal system fail.

Subjective Contours

The biggest challenge to piecemeal perception comes from evidence that often our perceptions are globally structured, with the perceptual system integrating information across sizable distances. A seemingly unambiguous and powerful case is Kanizsa's (1979) subjective triangle (Figure 32.2), in

Figure 32.2. Kanizsa's subjective contour. Here, viewers perceive a whiter-than-white equilateral triangle that is not physically present, suggesting that vision is organized not only over small but over fairly large distances, as shown on the right. Adapted from Kanizsa (1979).

which the inducing elements can be separated by significant distances without disrupting our perception of the global figure.

These conflicting notions on the window for perceptual organization have surfaced in parts of my own research that have focused on the perceptual grouping of visual elements, a problem dating back to Wertheimer (1912) and the original Gestaltists. Through work with grids of dots, they showed long ago that spatial separation—proximity—was a major factor in grouping, a finding that holds up today under closer scrutiny (Kubovy & Wagemans, 1995) and is consistent with a small-sized window.

In perceiving scenes, parts of single objects are often spatially separated, as when an occluder intervenes. The finding that more widely spaced elements are less likely to group than near ones could reflect a Helmholtzian bet on the true state of the world: The farther apart they are, the less likely they are to belong to the same object. Or it could reflect the increased difficulty at greater distances of perceiving detailed relationships, such as collinearity, that would drive grouping. In any case, most of the experiments on grouping by proximity have used a competition method, i.e., one in which perceivers see dots organized either in rows or in columns. Such methods are good for demonstrating an important finding—a preference to group over shorter distances rather than longer—but they do not answer whether, in the absence of competition, grouping over longer distances fails (but see Gillam, 1981).

Grouping of Contours

Research in my lab has tested element groupings using stimuli such as those shown in Figure 32.3 and has assessed grouping through two reaction-time (RT) methods. One of them involves *Garner interference* effects (GI; Pomerantz & Schwaitzberg, 1975; see also Pomerantz et al., 2003), which measure interference from variation on a task-irrelevant element. These experiments reveal that as two curved lines (parentheses) of fixed size, as shown in Figure 32.3, are separated horizontally in panel B compared with A, grouping between them (as indexed by Garner interference) diminishes monotonically, reaching zero at about 4° of separation, even though no alternative grouping presents itself—no other contour is presented in the stimulus with which the originals can group. This result led me to conclude that visual grouping not only works better over short distances than over long ones but that it may not work over long distances at all.

It is of course possible that this conclusion applies only to this one type of grouping, of simple line segments, or this one method for measuring grouping, GI. Regarding the latter, however, similar findings have emerged from our work with a second method for measuring grouping, the *configural superiority effect* (CSE; Pomerantz, Sager, & Stoever, 1977). The CSE assesses benefits accruing from adding a noninformative context to an odd-element discrimination task whose four stimuli are arranged in an imaginary square. As shown in Figure 32.4A, in the leftmost panel, the task is to locate the target, i.e., to spot the odd quadrant, the one whose stimulus differs from that in the other three, in a speeded task in which reaction time and

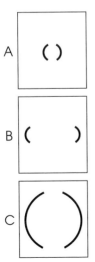

Figure 32.3. A. A pair of parentheses that groups well, both phenomenologically and by two performance measures. B. A separated pair that groups poorly, reflecting a loss of grouping by proximity. C. Restoring the proportional shape of the pair restores grouping only partially, indicating that grouping may be sensitive to absolute distances and so not be size-scale invariant.

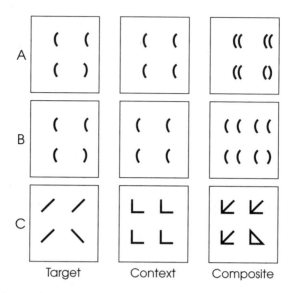

Figure 32.4. Conditions yielding configural superiority effects (CSEs), wherein it is easier to spot the odd stimulus in the rightmost composite than in the leftmost target displays, despite the fact that the added context elements are identical in all four locations. The CSE is strong in panels A and C but weak in B, reflecting a loss in grouping by proximity.

error rates are measured. Four identical context elements are added in the center panel to yield the composite shown in the right panel. Despite their noninformative nature, the context elements boost performance enormously when the elements are closely spaced, as shown in the figure. When they are moved farther apart, as in Figure 32.4B, these gains rapidly vanish. These results have been replicated many times with a range of stimulus sizes and spacings similar to those shown in Figure 32.4 (in this instance, the entire stimulus field—all four quadrants—subtends a visual angle of around 4°).

Size-Scale Invariance in Grouping?

More recently, Mary Portillo and I examined whether the decline in grouping (as measured by CSEs) when elements are separated in space might be offset by enlarging the elements, as in Figure 32.3C, so the proportions of panel A are restored while retaining the interelement distances of panel B, where little or no grouping arises. We wondered whether grouping might be size-scale invariant (and so would remain unchanged with zooming) and thus

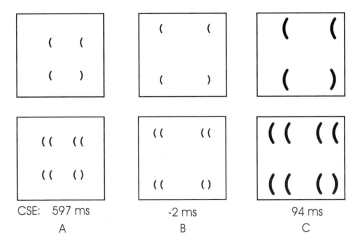

Figure 32.5. In panel A, a large configural superiority effect (CSE): Adding an identical parenthesis to each quadrant shortens RTs to locate the odd one by 597 ms. B. These identical parentheses are spaced out to allow room for subsequent zooming; the CSE drops to slightly below zero. C. Dilating the stimuli in panel A while maintaining proportions restores only a small fraction of the original CSE, only 94 ms.

that the effects observed earlier were due to configural or other changes that occur as elements are separated but kept constant in size.

Our preliminary results using the same odd-quadrant RT task clearly suggest otherwise: The CSE from elements spaced as in Figure 32.3C is barely restored at all to the levels seen with stimuli spaced as in panel A. Our specific experiment is shown in Figure 32.5. In panel A, adding a second, identical parenthesis to each quadrant speeds the localization of the odd quadrant by almost 600 ms when the two parentheses in a pair are separated by about 2° of visual angle and the quadrant centers are about 10° apart. Spacing the quadrants out as in panel B eliminates this CSE entirely, driving it slightly (albeit not significantly) below zero. In panel C, restoring the exact proportions of A while retaining the absolute physical spacing of B restores less than 20% of the original CSE (94 ms versus 597 ms). In other words, in comparing panels A and C, there appears to be no size-scale invariance for grouping, at least as measured by the CSE.

This supports Hochberg's piecemeal-perception notion even more strongly. Interestingly, this seems to contrast with impossible figures, where it may be more the proportions of the figures than their absolute dimensions that determine perceived impossibility (see Pomerantz & Kubovy's, 1981, discussion, which was motivated by Hochberg's analysis).

Grouping on a Larger Scale

From these results, one might be tempted to conclude that grouping is in fact a local operation restricted to elements within a small window. Other evidence from these same experiments, however, suggests otherwise. Returning to Figure 32.4C, we see another CSE, this one based on line orientation rather than curvature, where adding an L-shaped context makes it easier to distinguish a positive from a negative diagonal, presumably because grouping of the line segments converts them into forms, i.e., into triangles and arrows. We have noticed that in the target condition involving only the four diagonals with no context, the four diagonals seem to be grouping with each other. Specifically, perceivers sometimes are confused about which element is in fact odd, believing that it is the upper left rather than the lower right in Figure 32.4C, left panel. Their performance on the task corroborates their claim and suggests that the four diagonals group—an interquadrant grouping—to form a configuration. In doing so, three elements point toward the center (suggesting an X shape), but the fourth does not, and so it is seen to be odd (an effect we call *false pop out*; Pomerantz & Portillo, 2004). Such interquadrant grouping is occurring over larger distances than those we believed were too large to produce grouping in Figure 32.4B. Thus, it would be premature to claim that grouping never takes place over distances greater than some threshold value, because for reasons yet unknown, in some instances, persuasive counterexamples appear.

Conclusion

One conclusion to draw from this is that there may indeed be a "window" within which perceptual organization—including grouping—occurs. Perceived groupings will favor shorter distances when available, to be sure, and will often link elements separated by longer distances in the absence of closer elements. Elements outside the window do not, however, appear to group with elements inside the window. Thus, there may be an upper limit to how far two elements can be separated yet continue to group, a limit not moderated by simple changes in scale. This conclusion seems quite close to Hochberg's thinking on the matter and, following his analysis, would seem to have important implications for the major theories of perceptual organization in vision.

References

GILLAM, B. (1978). Even a possible figure can look impossible. *Perception, 8,* 229–232.

GILLAM, B. (1981). Separation relative to length determines the organization of two lines into a unit. *Journal of Experimental Psychology: Human Perception & Performance*, *7*(4), 884–889.

HOCHBERG, J. (1968). In the mind's eye. Invited address read at the September 1966 meeting of the American Psychological Association, Division 3. Reprinted in R. N. Haber (Ed.), *Contemporary theory and research in visual perception* (pp. 309–331). New York: Holt, Rinehart, and Winston.

HOCHBERG, J. (1981). Levels of perceptual organization. In M. Kubovy & J. R. Pomerantz (Eds.), *Perceptual organization* (pp. 255–278). Hillsdale, NJ: Erlbaum.

JULESZ, B. (1975). Experiments in the visual perception of texture. *Scientific American*, *232*, 34–43.

KANIZSA, G. (1979). *Organization in vision*. New York: Praeger.

KUBOVY, M., & WAGEMANS, J. (1995). Grouping by proximity and multistability in dot lattices: A quantitative gestalt theory. *Psychological Science, 6*, 225–234.

POMERANTZ, J. R., AGRAWAL, A., JEWELL, S. W., JEONG, M., KHAN, H., & LOZANO, S. C. (2003). Contour grouping inside and outside of facial contexts. *Acta Psychologica*, *114*(3), 245–271.

POMERANTZ, J. R., & KUBOVY, M. (1981). Perceptual organization: An overview. In M. Kubovy & J. R. Pomerantz (Eds.), *Perceptual organization* (pp. 423–456). Hillsdale, NJ: Erlbaum.

POMERANTZ, J. R., & PORTILLO, M. C. (2004). *False pop out*. Paper presented at the 45th Annual Meeting of the Psychonomic Society, Minneapolis, MN (November 19–21).

POMERANTZ, J. R., SAGER, L. C., & STOEVER, R. J. (1977). Perception of wholes and of their component parts: Some configural superiority effects. *Journal of Experimental Psychology: Human Perception and Performance, 3*, 422–435.

POMERANTZ, J. R., & SCHWAITZBERG, S. D. (1975). Grouping by proximity: Selective attention measures. *Perception & Psychophysics, 18*, 355–361.

RENSINK, R. A., O'REGAN, J. K., & CLARK, J. J. (1997). To see or not to see: The need for attention to perceive changes in scenes. *Psychological Science, 8*, 368–373.

TREISMAN, A., & GELADE, G. (1980). A feature integration theory of attention. *Cognition Psychology, 12*, 97–136.

WERTHEIMER, M. (1912). Experimentelle Studien uber das Sehen von Bewegung. *Zeitschrift für Psychologie, 61*, 161–265. (Translated in part in T. Shipley [Ed.], *Classics in psychology*. New York: Philosophical Library, 1961.)

33

The Resurrection of Simplicity in Vision

Peter A. van der Helm

With ups and downs since the early 20th century, simplicity has been considered a relevant factor in visual form and object perception. Since the 1990s, other sciences also have shown an interest in simplicity as a driving modeling factor. This recent interest has been triggered by intriguing findings in a mathematical research line called *algorithmic information theory* (AIT), which started in the mid-1960s. As I argue here, these AIT findings support but cannot replace the independent perceptual research line that started in the early 1950s with Hochberg and McAlister's (1953) information-theoretic simplicity idea.

In the aftermath of Shannon's (1948) ground-breaking work in classical information theory, Hochberg and McAlister (1953) proposed modeling the visual system as selecting the most simple interpretation of a proximal stimulus. More precisely, they proposed: "[T]he less the amount of information needed to define a given organization as compared to the other alternatives, the more likely that the figure will be so perceived" (p. 361). This proposal is nowadays known as the *simplicity principle*, and it marks the beginning of a paradigm shift from probabilistic to descriptive information.

Probabilistic information is the central concept in classical information theory. After Nyquist (1924) and Hartley (1928), Shannon (1948) employed the following probabilistic quantification of the information load of an object: "if an object x occurs with probability $p(x)$, then its information load is $-\log_2 p(x)$." In communication science, the term "object" would refer to a transmittable message and, in vision science, it would refer to a possible interpretation of a visual stimulus, that is, a message that the visual system could transmit to higher cognitive levels.

Hence, probabilistic information starts from known probabilities in terms of frequencies of occurrence: The more often an object is known to occur, the smaller its information load is. Tribus (1961) called the quantity $-\log_2 p(x)$ the *surprisal*: The more often an object is known to occur, the lower the surprise is when it does occur. In vision science, the idea of starting from known probabilities was put forward by Helmholtz (1909/1962). His *likelihood principle* proposes modeling the visual system as selecting the interpretation with the highest probability of specifying correctly the actual distal stimulus (cf. Hochberg, 1968, p. 89). This sounds attractive because it suggests that vision is highly veridical.

However, an individual object can be assigned a probability only by virtue of knowledge about the size of the class to which this object is taken to belong, that is, only by virtue of knowledge about the frequencies of occurrence of instantiations of this class. The likelihood principle is silent about what the classes are, but even if the classes are known, how could vision or vision science have access to the real frequencies of occurrence in this world? Ecological surveys (cf. Brunswik, 1956) might yield frequencies of occurrence, but these are frequencies of occurrence of percepts and precisely these percepts need explaining. That is, if one takes the latter frequencies of occurrence not just to fit data but also to explain data, then one falls into the circular explanation that "we see what we see" (cf. Hoffman, 1996).

Descriptive information is a concept that circumvents the foregoing problems by starting from the regularity in the internal structure of individual objects. As Hochberg and McAlister (1953) put it, the descriptive information load, or *complexity*, $c(x)$, of an individual object x is "the number of different items we must be given, in order to specify or reproduce a given pattern" (p. 361). Hence, in total, the simplicity principle proposes modeling the visual system as selecting the interpretation with the shortest descriptive code, that is, with the shortest reconstruction recipe for the stimulus. In general, the shortest codes are codes that capture the maximum regularity in objects.

The relevance of simplicity in perceptual organization had already been demonstrated by the early 20th-century Gestaltists. In fact, the simplicity principle can be seen as an information-theoretic version of Koffka's (1935) *law of Prägnanz*, which associated simplicity with energetically stable internal states of the visual system. In contrast to the early Gestaltists, who appealed to an intuitive concept of simplicity, Hochberg and McAlister's proposal paved the way for formal specifications of simplicity.

This rethinking, in the 1950s, of the role of simplicity in perceptual organization (see also Attneave, 1954) triggered, in the 1960s, the development of various coding models (e.g., Leeuwenberg, 1968; Restle, 1970; Simon & Kotovsky, 1963; Vitz & Todd, 1969). These coding models were fairly successful empirically but also created a new problem: Every coding model proposed another coding language yielding language-dependent complexities, so, which model is the right one? After having compared a half dozen of these coding models, Simon (1972) formulated this new problem as follows: "[I]f an index of complexity is to have significance for psychology, then the encoding scheme itself must have some kind of psychological basis" (p. 371). In the years that followed, no such psychological basis was proposed, and as a consequence, vision science lost much of its interest in the simplicity principle.

This loss of interest was understandable but, in a sense, also curious. Simon's (1972) conclusion was based on his empirical finding that simplicity appeared to be a stable concept: Complexities, $c(x)$, may vary in absolute value with the employed coding language but are yet highly correlated across coding languages. In the mid-1960s, in mathematics, a theoretical finding with the same thrust, namely, the *invariance theorem* (Kolmogorov, 1965; Solomonoff, 1964), did not decrease but increased the interest in simplicity and led to the rise of algorithmic information theory (see Li & Vitányi, 1997).

A central topic in AIT is the relation between probabilistic and descriptive information. A major finding in AIT is that a good alternative for the often unknown real probability, $p(x)$, of object x is provably provided by starting from the complexity $c(x)$ of x and by taking $2^{-c(x)}$ as an artificial probability of x. (See also Leeuwenberg & Boselie, 1988, who, in vision science, proposed a similar derivation of probabilities from complexities.)

Van der Helm (2000) called the quantity $2^{-c(x)}$ the *precisal*: It is higher if $c(x)$ is lower, and a lower $c(x)$ implies a more precise specification of x, that is, a specification that classifies x as belonging to a smaller subset of all possible objects. (Garner's, 1970, motto that "good patterns have few alternatives" has the same thrust.) To be clear, a precisal does not refer to a real frequency of occurrence in this world. It refers to a frequency of occurrence in a world filled by an object generator that, first, randomly selects a class of objects with the same complexity and then randomly produces an object from this class. Because class size correlates with complexity, a particular simple object thus has a higher probability of being produced than a particular complex object.

The AIT finding that precisals form a good alternative for real probabilities led, in the 1990s, to a growing interest in simplicity in various research domains. As for the relevance of AIT to vision, however, some reservations are in order. First, AIT does not provide a concrete coding language, let alone a psychological basis as called for by Simon (1972). Second, AIT does not take account of Mackay's (1950) perceptually relevant distinction between metrical and structural information. This implies, for instance, that squares and rectangles may get the same or different complexities, depending on the numerical values of the edge lengths. Third, in AIT, the precisal of an object reflects the size of the class of all different objects with the same complexity, but this form of object classification does not seem to have perceptual relevance.

Hence, without a psychologically compelling account of these issues, AIT findings cannot be translated meaningfully to vision. Fortunately, in the 1970s and 1980s, a few vision scientists kept the simplicity flame burning, most prominently within *structural information theory* (SIT). SIT arose from Leeuwenberg's (1968) coding model that employs complexities reflecting structural information only (see van der Helm, van Lier, & Leeuwenberg, 1992). In response to Simon (1972), this coding model nowadays has an adequate psychological basis which comprises a novel formalization of visual regularity that (a) underlies the choice of the complexity metric and the regularity-capturing coding rules, and (b) has proved itself by way of an empirically successful model of regularity detection (van der Helm & Leeuwenberg, 1991, 1996, 1999, 2004).

Furthermore, in line with Garner's (1962) seminal idea of inferred subsets, SIT takes an individual object to belong to a *structural class*, that is, the class of all metrically different objects with not only the same structural complexity but also the same structure (Collard & Buffart, 1983). Therefore, in SIT, an object's precisal reflects the size of the object's structural class (van der Helm, 2000). Only given such a psychologically motivated derivation of precisals can the earlier-mentioned AIT finding be translated meaningfully to vision. That is, this AIT finding suggests that vision, if guided by precisals, is fairly veridical in many worlds (i.e., rather than highly veridical in only one world).

The foregoing shows that AIT supports but cannot replace the perceptual research line that Hochberg and McAlister (1953) started. In fact, this line still moves on, for instance, within the following Bayesian framework.

First, by going from complexities $c(x)$ to precisals $2^{-c(x)}$, selecting the most simple interpretation, H, for a proximal stimulus, D, transforms into selecting the interpretation H that, in Bayesian style, maximizes the posterior precisal: $p(H|D) = p(H)^*p(D|H)$. Here, the prior precisal, $p(H)$, is derived from the (viewpoint-independent) complexity of the distal stimulus as hypothesized in H, and the conditional precisal, $p(D|H)$, is derived from the (viewpoint-dependent) complexity of the proximal stimulus D if H would be true.

Second, based on van Lier, van der Helm, and Leeuwenberg's (1994) empirically successful distinction between viewpoint-independent and viewpoint-dependent complexities in amodal completion, van der Helm (2000) argued that conditional precisals are close to real conditional probabilities. This is relevant because the conditionals are decisive in the everyday perception of a moving observer who recursively applies Bayes' rule to interpret a growing sample of proximal stimuli of the same distal scene. After each recursion step, the just-obtained posterior is taken as the prior in the next recursion step, which implies that the effect of the first priors fades away and that the conditionals become the decisive entities. Hence, if conditional precisals are indeed close to real conditional probabilities, then one may just as well use precisals instead of real probabilities, especially if the latter are unknown. Remarkably, various current Bayesian models of perception (see, e.g., those in Knill & Richards, 1996) claim to use real probabilities but actually use precisals.

Third, recent correspondence with Julian Hochberg triggered a Bayesian picture of the link between an autonomous, simplicity-guided visual system and other cognitive faculties. To answer Hochberg's (1982) question in general terms, this picture starts with a proximal stimulus with a size that, temporally, spans about 30 ms (Leeuwenberg, Mens, & Calis, 1985) and that, spatially, is determined by acuity and conspicuity (e.g., extrafoveally, a higher conspicuity may compensate for the lower acuity). Then, in Bayesian style, hypotheses about the distal stimulus are ranked on the basis of their prior precisals which, via multiplication with their conditional precisals, are weighed by the degree of consistency between the hypothesized distal stimuli and the proximal stimulus. The prior ranking reflects a form of object perception, as it is determined by object-centered representations of hypothesized distal objects. The conditional weighing reflects a form of space perception, as it is determined by relative positions of the viewer and hypothesized distal objects.

This distinction between priors and conditionals agrees with the functional distinction between the ventral ("what") and dorsal ("where") pathways in the brain (Ungerleider & Mishkin, 1982). The idea now is that the Bayesian integration of these perceptual priors and conditionals guides the hypotheses to higher cognitive levels where their ranking may be weighed by further conditional factors, such as the viewer's knowledge and intentions related to a task to be performed, yielding a final ranking in the situation at hand.

Hence, Hochberg and McAlister's (1953) simplicity idea has led to a conception of vision as a fairly reliable, autonomous source of knowledge about the external world. In this conception, vision performs an unconscious inference on the basis of knowledge-free precisals, the output of which is enriched by a gradually more and more conscious inference on the basis of internally available contextual information.

References

ATTNEAVE, F. (1954). Some informational aspects of visual perception. *Psychological Review, 61,* 183–193.

BRUNSWIK, E. (1956). *Perception and the representative design of psychological experiments.* Berkeley: University of California Press.

COLLARD, R. F. A., & BUFFART, H. F. J. M. (1983). Minimization of structural information: A set-theoretical approach. *Pattern Recognition, 16,* 231–242.

GARNER, W. R. (1962). *Uncertainty and structure as psychological concepts.* New York: Wiley.

GARNER, W. R. (1970). Good patterns have few alternatives. *American Scientist, 58,* 34–42.

HARTLEY, R. V. L. (1928). Transmission of information. *Bell Systems Technology Journal, 7,* 535–563.

HELMHOLTZ, H. L. F. (1962). *Treatise on physiological optics* (J. P. C. Southall, Trans.). New York: Dover. (Original work published 1909)

HOCHBERG, J. E. (1968). *Perception.* Englewood Cliffs, NJ: Prentice-Hall.

HOCHBERG, J. E. (1982). How big is a stimulus? In J. Beck (Ed.), *Organization and representation in perception* (pp. 191–217). Hillsdale, NJ: Erlbaum.

HOCHBERG, J. E., & McALISTER, E. (1953). A quantitative approach to figural "goodness." *Journal of Experimental Psychology, 46,* 361–364.

HOFFMAN, D. D. (1996). What do we mean by "the structure of the world"? In D. K. Knill & W. Richards (Eds.), *Perception as Bayesian inference* (pp. 219–221). Cambridge: Cambridge University Press.

KNILL, D. C., & RICHARDS, W. (Eds.). (1996). *Perception as Bayesian inference.* Cambridge: Cambridge University Press.

KOFFKA, K. (1935). *Principles of gestalt psychology.* London: Routledge & Kegan Paul.

KOLMOGOROV, A. N. (1965). Three approaches to the quantitative definition of information. *Problems in Information Transmission, 1,* 1–7.

LEEUWENBERG, E. L. J. (1968). *Structural information of visual patterns: An efficient coding system in perception.* The Hague: Mouton.

LEEUWENBERG, E. L. J., & BOSELIE, F. (1988). Against the likelihood principle in visual form perception. *Psychological Review, 95,* 485–491.

LEEUWENBERG, E. L. J., MENS, L., & CALIS, G. (1985). Knowledge within perception: Masking caused by incompatible interpretation. *Acta Psychologica, 59,* 91–102.

LI, M., & VITÁNYI, P. (1997). *An introduction to Kolmogorov complexity and its applications* (2d ed.). New York: Springer-Verlag.

MACKAY, D. (1950). Quantal aspects of scientific information. *Philosophical Magazine, 41,* 289–301.

NYQUIST, H. (1924). Certain factors affecting telegraph speed. *Bell System Technical Journal, 3,* 324–346.

RESTLE, F. (1970). Theory of serial pattern learning: Structural trees. *Psychological Review, 77,* 481–495.

SHANNON, C. E. (1948). A mathematical theory of communication. *Bell System Technical Journal, 27,* 379–423, 623–656.

SIMON, H. A. (1972). Complexity and the representation of patterned sequences of symbols. *Psychological Review, 79,* 369–382.

SIMON, H. A., & KOTOVSKY, K. (1963). Human acquisition of concepts for sequential patterns. *Psychological Review, 70,* 534–546.

SOLOMONOFF, R. J. (1964). A formal theory of inductive inference. *Information and Control, 7,* 1–22, 224–254.

TRIBUS, M. (1961). *Thermostatics and thermodynamics.* Princeton, NJ: Van Nostrand.

UNGERLEIDER, L. G., & MISHKIN, M. (1982). Two cortical visual systems. In D. J. Ingle, M. A. Goodale, & R. J. W. Mansfield (Eds.), *Analysis of visual behavior* (pp. 549–586). Cambridge, MA: MIT Press.

VAN DER HELM, P. A. (2000). Simplicity versus likelihood in visual perception: From surprisals to precisals. *Psychological Bulletin, 126,* 770–800.

VAN DER HELM, P. A., & LEEUWENBERG, E. L. J. (1991). Accessibility, a criterion for regularity and hierarchy in visual pattern codes. *Journal of Mathematical Psychology, 35,* 151–213.

VAN DER HELM, P. A., & LEEUWENBERG, E. L. J. (1996). Goodness of visual regularities: A nontransformational approach. *Psychological Review, 103,* 429–456.

VAN DER HELM, P. A., & LEEUWENBERG, E. L. J. (1999). A better approach to goodness: Reply to Wagemans (1999). *Psychological Review, 106,* 622–630.

VAN DER HELM, P. A., & LEEUWENBERG, E. L. J. (2004). Holographic goodness is not that bad: Reply to Olivers, Chater, and Watson (2004). *Psychological Review, 111,* 261–273.

VAN DER HELM, P. A., VAN LIER, R. J., & LEEUWENBERG, E. L. J. (1992). Serial pattern complexity: Irregularity and hierarchy. *Perception, 21,* 517–544.

VAN LIER, R. J., VAN DER HELM, P. A., & LEEUWENBERG, E. L. J. (1994). Integrating global and local aspects of visual occlusion. *Perception, 23,* 883–903.

VITZ, P. C., & TODD, R. C. (1969). A coded element model of the perceptual processing of sequential stimuli. *Psychological Review, 76,* 433–449.

34

Shape Constancy and Perceptual Simplicity

Hochberg's Fundamental Contributions

Zygmunt Pizlo

I first became familiar with Professor Julian Hochberg's contributions to visual perception in 1989 when Professor Robert Steinman, my doctoral advisor, suggested that I read his chapter on shape (Hochberg, 1971). I did. Reading Hochberg's chapter proved to be very inspiring. By 1971, the year the chapter appeared, most students of vision considered shape constancy to be a solved problem. They thought that shape constancy is accomplished by "taking slant into account." This explanation, which was first suggested by Alhazen (1083/1989, p. 279), was formulated explicitly by Descartes (1637/ 2001, p. 106). It was accepted by Woodworth (1938), who claimed that it was supported by Thouless (1931a, b), who had published widely cited papers, as well as by a number of similar, subsequent experiments. But, according to Hochberg (1971), there was a fundamental problem with all of this work. He pointed out that Stavrianos's (1945) paper on shape constancy (specifically, her Experiment 1) in which she showed that perceived shape and perceived slant were unrelated, makes difficulties for anyone claiming that shape constancy is accomplished by taking slant into account. Once Hochberg pointed this out, it became clear that it was important to understand the reasons for the differences between Stavrianos's and Thouless's results. I was intrigued by Hochberg's treatment of this subject, read the original papers myself, and realized that his concern was fully justified. Once I realized this, and after giving considerable thought to the geometry underlying the choice of stimuli for shape-constancy experiments, I realized that Thouless (and others) had overlooked the fact that ellipses and triangles, the only stimuli used in their experiments, have geometrical properties that make them *completely unsuitable* for studying shape constancy. Let me explain this point in some detail.

There are three geometrical facts that are critical to the argument. First, ellipses and triangles are simple shapes. That is, the shape of an ellipse is characterized by only one parameter, aspect ratio, and the shape of a triangle is characterized by only two parameters, two angles. Second, the perspective projection of an ellipse is also an ellipse, and the perspective projection of a triangle is also a triangle. Finally, a perspective projection changes the shape of a planar figure (for a given retinal position and size) with 2 degrees of freedom (Pizlo & Rosenfeld, 1992; Pizlo, Rosenfeld, & Weiss, 1997a, b). From these three geometrical facts, it follows that any ellipse can produce any other ellipse on the retina, and any triangle can produce any other triangle on the retina. Note, however, that this is not true for any other family, other than ellipses and triangles, of planar (or 3D) shapes. Consider, for example, quadrilaterals. The shape of a quadrilateral is characterized by four, not by only one or two parameters (ratio of lengths of two sides, plus three angles). This fact means that in the projection of a quadrilateral to the retina, not all parameters can be changed independently. In other words, for quadrilaterals, it is not true that *any* quadrilateral can produce any *other* quadrilateral on the observer's retina as is the case for ellipses and triangles.

Now, what is the methodological implication of using ellipses (or triangles) to study shape perception? The most striking implication becomes evident as soon as one realizes that shape constancy is probably the most important ecological problem that has to be solved by the visual system because an object with a given shape can produce a large number of different retinal images when the object is presented with different slants. The observer's task is to recognize that these different retinal images can be produced by the same shape. Success in the real world depends primarily on the veridical perception of an object on the basis of its shape. A successful solution of this shape-constancy problem is represented by the fact that a single percept corresponds to all of the retinal images produced by a given stimulus. But, because any given ellipse (or triangle) can produce, on the observer's retina, any other ellipse (or triangle), it is clear that the retinal image itself is not sufficient to tell two different objects apart, if the objects belong to the family of ellipses (or triangles). It follows logically that the only way to solve the shape-constancy problem in the case of ellipses and triangles is to take into account the slant of the shape from the observer's viewpoint. So, if one uses ellipses and triangles as stimuli, one is *forced* to employ a taking-into-account mechanism to explain the constancy. Clearly, Thouless's subjects had no choice but to take into account slant, so it is not surprising that he concluded that taking into account was necessary. Once this is understood, the question of whether his conclusion generalizes to other shapes becomes an open question. This issue was neither appreciated nor addressed by Thouless. The fact that results obtained with ellipses and triangles *do not generalize* to other shapes was demonstrated by Stavrianos, who used rectangles as stimuli in her Experiment 1. Different rectangles never produce identical images on the retina, regardless of their slants and tilts, and in general two (or more) different objects (except for ellipses and triangles) can produce identical retinal images with zero probability. As a result, in the case of rectangles (as well as in the case of all figures and objects other than ellipses and triangles), the shape-constancy problem can be solved *without* taking slant into account, as Stavrianos demonstrated. The use of rectangles by Stavrianos may have been accidental because she makes no mention of why she decided to use rectangles, instead of ellipses, in her main experiment, as Thouless had. The failure to analyze the geometry inherent in the shape-constancy problem was probably responsible for the fact that most studies of shape constancy performed after Stavrianos published used only ellipses and triangles as stimuli, producing results consistent with those of Thouless and not realizing the fundamental limitations of these results.[1]

To summarize and conclude this section, my interest in the history of shape constancy was inspired by Hochberg's (1971) chapter on shape perception. This interest, after it had been supplemented by mathematical analyses and psychophysical experiments, led me to formulate a new theory of shape constancy (Pizlo, 1994) in which shape constancy is achieved without taking slant into account.

Professor Hochberg's effect on my research interests extended well beyond my studies of shape constancy. Much of my subsequent research has been built on Professor Hochberg's elaboration of the Gestalt idea of a "simplicity principle." In the next section, I will present highlights from two of his early publications on this subject and put them into their historical context. I will also emphasize important elements in this work that are often overlooked. He anticipated several important developments well before others appreciated their importance. I will then describe some of my recent work that makes use of these elements.

Hochberg's interest in visual perception started around the time that Shannon put *information theory* on solid ground (Shannon, 1948). This watershed period is now referred to as a "cognitive revolution" (Gardner, 1987; Neisser, 1967). Representative experiments included counting *bits* of information in linguistic messages (Miller, 1951; Miller & Selfridge, 1950; Shannon, 1948), in sensory-motor channels (Fitts, 1954; Hick, 1952), in short-term memory (Miller, 1956), and in the perception of patterns (Attneave, 1954, 1959). It was reasonable to expect that messages and patterns that are simpler and have greater redundancy are easier to code, respond to, memorize, and recognize. This proved to be the case. It seemed that information theory offered the possibility of formulating a rigorous version of the Gestalt simplicity principle called the *law of Prägnanz* (Attneave, 1954).

Hochberg and McAlister's (1953) paper started a series of studies specifically aimed at doing this, that is, they set out to define the Gestalt simplicity principle as it applied to the perception of shape. According to information theory, the complexity of a stimulus is measured by the amount of information that is needed to describe the stimulus. They used stimuli like those shown in Figure 34.1. Each of the four stimuli can lead either to a 2D perceptual interpretation equivalent to the drawing itself, or to a 3D interpretation, such as a cube.[2] The complexity (or simplicity) of the 3D interpretation was the same for all four stimuli because there was only one perceived 3D interpretation (a cube). The complexity of the 2D interpretation,

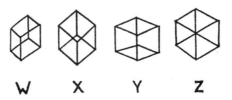

Figure 34.1. Stimuli used by Hochberg and McAlister (1953).

however, was different for each of the four stimuli. The authors conjectured that "the less the amount of information needed to define a given organization, as opposed to the other alternatives, the more likely that the figure will be so perceived" (p. 361). Hochberg and McAlister proposed three geometrical features that can be used to measure the complexity of a 2D interpretation: the number of line segments, of angles, and of points of intersection (junctions). For example, the stimulus Y has 13 line segments, 20 angles, and 8 junction points.[3] According to the authors' classification, X and W are equally complex, Y is simpler, and Z is the simplest. Therefore, Z should be perceived as a 2D pattern, whereas X and W should be perceived as cubes. This conjecture agrees with phenomenological observations, as well as with Hochberg and McAlister's experimental results.

It is important to emphasize that Hochberg and McAlister's study aimed at understanding *the role of simplicity in producing 3D percepts from 2D images*. This contrasted with the main line of research being done at the time, which concentrated on studying *the role of simplicity in producing 2D simple percepts from 2D ambiguous images* (e.g., Attneave, 1954, 1959). This distinction is fundamental, but it was overlooked by all except Hochberg and his coworkers.

Stimulated by Professor Hochberg's research on simplicity, I tried to elaborate on his ideas (Pizlo 2001; Pizlo & Stevenson, 1999). The fact that the percept can be three-dimensional when the retinal image is two-dimensional implies that the problem of visual perception is ill posed (Poggio et al., 1985). Namely, each retinal image determines an infinite number of possible 3D interpretations. In order to produce a unique and veridical percept, the visual system has to impose strong constraints on the family of possible percepts. These constraints represent regularities that are present in the physical world, such as the planarity of contours, smoothness of surfaces, and symmetry of objects (see Pizlo, 2001, for a more complete list of constraints). Because regularities can be stated in the form of simplicity constraints, this approach is related directly to the tradition that started with Gestalt psychology and was continued by Professor Hochberg. But keep in mind that the simplicity principle does not refer to distorting the 2D retinal image toward a simpler 2D percept; instead it refers to adding a priori constraints so that the combination of the 2D retinal image and the added a priori constraints results in a veridical 3D percept. It was Professor Hochberg, and only Professor Hochberg, who emphasized the importance of studying the role of the simplicity principle in producing a 3D percept from a 2D image. This is why the contemporary application of information theory to shape perception should be credited as extensions of Hochberg's studies, rather than the studies of others who concentrated on analyzing the perception of 2D patterns.[4]

A simplicity principle is not the only way to impose constraints. A *likelihood principle* is a complementary way to accomplish the same thing. The likelihood principle has usually been associated with the empiricist school of perception, according to which fundamental aspects of perception are learned in the course of one's life (Ittelson, 1960; Kilpatrick, 1961). The simplicity principle, on the other hand, has usually been associated with the nativist school of perception, according to which fundamental aspects of perception are innate. Interestingly, at the time that Professor Hochberg started his work on shape perception, there was also a third view, according to which priors are not needed (Gibson, 1950). Specifically, according to Gibson, a priori constraints, such as the simplicity principle, are important only when impoverished stimuli, such as pictures, are used. They are not needed when real 3D scenes are viewed. This was, in fact, a fundamental assumption of Gibson's entire approach, which set Gibson's theorizing apart from that of Gestalt psychologists. According to Gibson, ordinary visual stimulation provides the observer with all the information that is sufficient for accurate percepts and, as a result, a priori simplicity constraints (i.e., Gestalt rules of perceptual organization) are not needed: "Wertheimer's drawings were nonsense patterns of the extreme type, far removed from the images of a material world. His laws are applicable, therefore, to some kinds of abstract drawings and paintings . . . , but not so much to ordinary visual stimulation" (Gibson, 1950, p. 196). The early research of Attneave (among others) concentrated on studying the perception of 2D patterns and neglected the 3D world. Gibson did exactly the opposite. Only Hochberg grasped the importance of studying both in his research on shape (Hochberg, 1978).

Next, I will briefly describe another classical study, Hochberg and Brooks (1962), which is directly relevant in this context. It shows why the simplicity principle provides a more plausible way of explaining a priori constraints than does the likelihood principle when it comes to the perception of shapes in the real world. It also shows why studying the perception of 3D shapes, as represented in pictures, is important for understanding how perception works in the real world.

The subject in this experiment was a newborn boy. He was exposed to a wide variety of solid objects and taught their names as his language skills developed. His exposure to representations in the form of pictures (including movies) was prevented as completely as possible. The expectation was that at the appropriate time the boy would be able to recognize familiar objects and name them. The question remained as to whether he would also be able to name them when they were represented by pictures. The initial "training" stage of this experiment was expected to last longer than it did, because by 19 months, it was no longer possible to keep the child away from pictures without interfering significantly with the child's (and his parents') normal life. The second stage included two tests. In the first test, 21 stimuli (pictures) were used. Some were line drawings of toys and other objects. Others were actual photographs of the objects. The stimuli were presented one at a time, and the child's responses were recorded on tape. After this test, the child was given a large number of picture books to encourage "perceptual learning." After one month, a second test was administered to assess the extent of his perceptual learning. The child had free access to pictures, as well as objects, during this month. A new set of 19 stimuli was used in the second test.

In both tests, the boy had little (if any) difficulty in naming familiar objects from pictures. This means that a single 2D image of a given 3D object produced a 3D percept in the boy's mind, and the percept must have been similar (or identical) to the percept produced by viewing the 3D object itself. Furthermore, the performance in the first test was as good as in the second test. These results strongly suggest that *perceiving 3D objects from pictures is innate and that this perceptual ability involves the same mechanisms as perceiving real 3D objects.* Finally, because perceiving 3D objects from 2D images does involve a priori simplicity constraints, it is reasonable to claim that *the same set of simplicity constraints is involved in perceiving 3D scenes as in perceiving such scenes from pictures.* It follows that theories of perception derived from studying the perception of objects from pictures are relevant for the study of the perception of real objects.

In conclusion, after more than a half century of intense research that followed Professor Hochberg's early publications, it is now quite clear that his contributions have been fundamental and that his papers will figure prominently both in the history of visual perception and in the history of psychology. Professor Hochberg built a bridge between Gestalt psychology and modern contemporary cognitive psychology by clarifying Gestalt ideas, by reformulating, and by elaborating them. I, and many others, owe him a lot.

Notes

1. A few studies used trapezoids, which *are* quadrilaterals (e.g., Beck & Gibson, 1955; Kaiser, 1967). Unfortunately, the trapezoids and their slants were chosen in such a way that the retinal image itself was not sufficient to tell the various trapezoids apart. In effect, these studies, despite the fact that quadrilaterals were used, were methodologically flawed in the same way as Thouless's.

2. Obviously, there are an infinite number of 2D and 3D interpretations corresponding to each drawing. The set of these interpretations contains planar

figures with various slants and tilts and polyhedral and nonpolyhedral objects. In fact, a given 2D image can be produced by a set of unrelated points in 3D, rather than by a set of lines or quadrilaterals. It so happens that when a 2D image on the retina can be produced by a cube, the observer perceives a cube, rather than any of the other 2D or 3D possible interpretations. Hochberg and McAlister did not discuss the simplicity rule (criterion) responsible for this perceptual choice. The first formulation of such a rule was put forth by Perkins (1972, 1976), and it was subsequently elaborated by Leclerc and Fischler (1992), Marill (1991), and Sinha and Adelson (1992).

3. Hochberg and McAlister reported, in their Table 1, the number of angles minus one, rather than the number of angles itself. Also note a typo in this table. For figure Y, their table indicates, incorrectly, 17 junction points. This typo was corrected in the later reprint of this paper in Beardslee and Wertheimer (1958).

4. In his later publications, Hochberg (e.g., 1978) pointed out that the simplicity principle faces critical difficulties. The most serious one was related to the impossibility of *independently* testing two statements: (i) the visual system uses simplicity, and (ii) an explicit definition of simplicity (see also Hatfield & Epstein, 1985). By changing the definition in (ii) one can either reject or support (i). For example, one can always define simplicity in a trivial way by saying that the simplest interpretation is what the observer perceives (Hochberg, 1978, p. 141). The clue to resolving this conceptual difficulty did not begin to emerge until the late 1970s, when David Marr (1982) (and others) attempted to simulate perceptual processes on a computer. This early work showed how computationally difficult visual perception actually is. It soon became obvious that in order to produce veridical percepts from the retinal image(s), the visual system *must* use constraints, such as simplicity. In other words, computational studies showed that (i) is true and that psychophysical experiments are not needed to test this statement. How simplicity is defined in the visual system so as to make it possible for this system to produce veridical percepts quickly, as it does, remains an open question (Pizlo, 2001).

References

ALHAZEN. (1989). *The optics* (Books 1–3) (A. I. Sabra, Trans.). London: Warburg Institute. (Original work published 1083)

ATTNEAVE, F. (1954). Some informational aspects of visual perception. *Psychological Review, 61,* 183–193.

ATTNEAVE, F. (1959). *Applications of information theory to psychology.* New York: Holt.

BEARDSLEE, D. C., & WERTHEIMER, M. (1958). *Readings in perception.* New York: van Nostrand.

BECK, J., & GIBSON, J. J. (1955). The relation of apparent shape to apparent slant in the perception of objects. *Journal of Experimental Psychology, 50,* 125–133.

DESCARTES, R. (2001). *Discourse on method, optics, geometry, and meteorology* (P. J. Olscamp, Trans.). Indianapolis, IN: Hackett. (Original work published 1637)

FITTS, P. M. (1954). The information capacity of the human motor system in controlling the amplitude of movement. *Journal of Experimental Psychology, 47,* 281–391.

GARDNER, H. (1987). *The mind's new science.* New York: Basic.

GIBSON, J. J. (1950). *The perception of the visual world.* Boston: Houghton Mifflin.

Hatfield, G., & Epstein, W. (1985). The status of the minimum principle in the theoretical analysis of visual perception. *Psychological Bulletin, 97,* 155–186.

Hick, W. E. (1952). On the rate of gain of information. *Quarterly Journal of Experimental Psychology, 4,* 11–26.

Hochberg, J. (1971). Perception. In J. W. Kling & L. A. Riggs (Eds.), *Woodworth & Schlosberg's experimental psychology* (pp. 395–550). New York: Holt, Rinehart & Winston.

Hochberg, J. (1978). *Perception.* Englewood Cliffs, NJ: Prentice-Hall.

Hochberg, J., & Brooks, V. (1962). Pictorial recognition as an unlearned ability: A study of one child's performance. *American Journal of Psychology, 75,* 624–628.

Hochberg, J., & McAlister, E. (1953). A quantitative approach to figural "goodness." *Journal of Experimental Psychology, 46,* 361–364.

Ittelson, W. H. (1960). *Visual space perception.* New York: Springer.

Kaiser, P. K. (1967). Perceived shape and its dependency on perceived slant. *Journal of Experimental Psychology, 75,* 345–353.

Kilpatrick, F. P. (1961). *Explorations in transactional psychology.* New York: New York University Press.

Leclerc, Y. G., & Fischler, M. A. (1992). An optimization-based approach to the interpretation of single line drawings as 3D wire frames. *International Journal of Computer Vision, 9,* 113–136.

Marill, T. (1991). Emulating the human interpretation of line-drawings as 3D objects. *International Journal of Computer Vision, 6,* 147–161.

Marr, D. (1982). *Vision.* New York: W.H. Freeman.

Miller, G. A. (1951). *Language and communication.* New York: McGraw-Hill.

Miller, G. A. (1956). The magical number seven, plus or minus two: Some limits on our capacity for processing information. *Psychological Review, 63,* 81–97.

Miller, G. A., & Selfridge, J. A. (1950). Verbal context and the recall of meaningful material. *American Journal of Psychology, 63,* 176–185.

Neisser, U. (1967). *Cognitive psychology.* New York: Appleton.

Perkins, D. N. (1972). Visual discrimination between rectangular and nonrectangular parallelopipeds. *Perception & Psychophysics, 12,* 396–400.

Perkins, D. N. (1976). How good a bet is good form? *Perception, 5,* 393–406.

Pizlo, Z. (1994). A theory of shape constancy based on perspective invariants. *Vision Research, 34,* 1637–1658.

Pizlo, Z. (2001). Perception viewed as an inverse problem. *Vision Research, 41,* 3145–3161.

Pizlo, Z., & Rosenfeld, A. (1992). Recognition of planar shapes from perspective images using contour-based invariants. *Computer Vision, Graphics & Image Processing: Image Understanding, 56,* 330–350.

Pizlo, Z., Rosenfeld, A., & Weiss, I. (1997a). The geometry of visual space: About the incompatibility between science and mathematics: Dialogue. *Computer Vision & Image Understanding, 65,* 425–433.

Pizlo, Z., Rosenfeld, A., & Weiss, I. (1997b). Visual space: Mathematics, engineering, and science: Response. *Computer Vision & Image Understanding, 65,* 450–454.

Pizlo, Z., & Stevenson, A. K. (1999). Shape constancy from novel views. *Perception & Psychophysics, 61,* 1299–1307.

Poggio, T., Torre, V., & Koch, C. (1985). Computational vision and regularization theory. *Nature, 317,* 314–319.

Shannon, C. E. (1948). A mathematical theory of communication. *Bell System Technical Journal, 27,* 623–656, 379–423.

Sinha, P., & Adelson, E. H. (1992). Recovery of 3D shape from 2D wireframe drawings. *Investigative Ophthalmology & Visual Science, 33*(Suppl.), 825.

Stavrianos, B. K. (1945). The relation of shape perception to explicit judgments of inclination. *Archives of Psychology, 296,* 1–94.

Thouless, R. H. (1931a). Phenomenal regression to the real object. *British Journal of Psychology, 21,* 339–359.

Thouless, R. H. (1931b). Phenomenal regression to the real object. *British Journal of Psychology, 22,* 1–30.

Woodworth, R. S. (1938). *Experimental psychology.* New York: Holt.

35

Constructing and Interpreting the World in the Cerebral Hemispheres

Paul M. Corballis

My first encounter with Julian Hochberg was in the fall of 1991. I was a newly minted graduate student at Columbia University and had been assigned to be a teaching assistant for Hochberg's undergraduate perception class. I had arrived in New York a few days beforehand and wasn't at all sure what to expect from my new situation—a new city, a new course of study, and a new teaching assignment. If Hochberg's credentials and reputation as one of the giants in the field made me somewhat apprehensive, his office had me downright intimidated. It conformed exactly to my stereotype of an Ivy League professor's office (or perhaps it subsequently came to define that stereotype for me—memory can be tricky). It was a large office—two stories tall—with overstuffed bookshelves straining under their load and every flat surface piled high with yet more books and papers. Assorted pieces of equipment from long-completed experiments or demonstrations were scattered haphazardly between the piles. It was at once a perception enthusiast's gold mine and a sure sign that I would have my work cut out for me keeping on top of things in the upcoming semester.

As it turned out, my feeling of intimidation was misplaced. Hochberg was generous with his time and encouragement, and the teaching assignment quickly turned out to be a highlight of my first years at Columbia. Needless to say, the class was a tour de force. Many—or perhaps most—of the undergraduates found it somewhat cryptic, but for me it only served to underscore the reasons I had become interested in perception in the first place. I was nominally there because I knew a little about the topic, and I could help set and grade exams and explain tricky concepts to the students when required. Instead, I found myself on the receiving end of a new education in perceptual psychology. Some of the other contributors to this volume (and perhaps even a few readers) will doubtless also recall Hochberg's "big picture" approach to his class—partly a historical retrospective, partly a study of the philosophical underpinnings of the study of perception, and partly a critical review of the theoretical and empirical literature in perceptual psychology. He understood that artists always seem to be a step or two ahead of scientists when it comes to understanding the human mind, so the class was liberally illustrated with examples from the fine arts and cinema.

One of the privileges—and, perhaps, responsibilities—that came with being Hochberg's teaching assistant was to act as a sounding board for his musings about the many enduring mysteries of perception. A significant portion of the class was devoted to his long-running debates with J. J. Gibson concerning the nature of perception. The problem was to explain how the perceiver arrived at an accurate description of the distal stimulus (the arrangement of objects in the environment) from a rather impoverished proximal stimulus (the pattern of stimulation arriving at the sensory receptors). Gibson, of course, was the principal advocate of "direct perception," in which he argued that the proximal stimulus contained all of the information necessary to allow accurate perception and that perceptual systems had evolved to take advantage of the regularities in the relationships between distal and proximal stimuli (e.g., Gibson, 1950, 1979). Perception, therefore, was available directly from the proximal stimulus without requiring further interpretation. Hochberg, on the other hand, championed a "constructivist" view of perception, which emphasizes the inherent ambiguity of the proximal stimulus and the ill-posed nature of the perceptual problem. In the case of vision, for example, an infinite number of possible three-dimensional configurations of distal stimuli could, in principle, lead to a given retinal image. From this standpoint, perception must be an active process requiring construction or interpretation on the part of the viewer. This interpretation can—indeed, must—be influenced not just by the proximal stimulus, but by the experiences, expectancies, and biases of the perceiver. The idea of a cognitive component to perception was articulated by Helmholtz (1909/1962), who suggested that "unconscious inference" was necessary to translate between proximal and distal stimuli. Hochberg was always eager to discuss the underpinnings of such a process and to move beyond what amounts to a rather vague notion of "construing" the distal stimulus from the proximal. His demonstrations that direct perception could not explain some visual phenomena—even in perceptually rich situations—were compelling, but at the same time it was clear that he was unsatisfied with simply appealing to unconscious inference or its latter-day manifestations.

I served as Hochberg's teaching assistant for the fall semesters of 1991 and 1992 (I fear that the students assigned to my discussion section in that first semester got something of a raw deal, since I really only fully appreciated the intricacies of the material some way into my second tour of duty). During that time, we had many discussions that profoundly influenced my thinking about perception, but among the most influential was one that began with an off-the-cuff remark that Hochberg made at the end of class one evening. During the lecture, Hochberg had illustrated a point with an illusion. A student had raised his hand and announced that he didn't see the illusory figure the way he was supposed to. This student had become something of a class celebrity—he was vocal and interactive and almost always "got it" well in advance of the rest of the class (and sometimes in advance of the teaching assistants). Hochberg had remarked several times about his intelligence, but on this occasion as we left the classroom he said, "Perhaps that guy isn't as smart as I thought he was." I laughed, but it quickly became clear that his comment was in earnest. The idea that perception requires a kind of intelligence is one that Hochberg had a significant role in advancing, and of course it is not a foreign one to researchers in the field. It was, however, the first time I had really thought about perception as an issue of intelligent problem solving in such concrete terms.

Sometime during my first year or so of study at Columbia, my interests began to drift toward neuroscience and neuropsychology as approaches that might help to answer some of the enduring problems in psychology. I was still predominantly interested in perceptual issues but thought that a more brain-based approach might ultimately be more satisfying than the traditional psychological one. I'm sure I was caught up in the zeitgeist, too. Cognitive neuroscience was on the upswing, and perhaps some of the persistent questions would finally yield to some of the exciting new techniques that were on the horizon. Hochberg wisely cautioned against expecting too much, but I followed my instincts and joined the legions of experimental psychologists who began to self-identify as cognitive neuroscientists.

After graduating from Columbia, I moved north to Dartmouth College to spend some time in the laboratory of Michael Gazzaniga, one of the founding fathers of cognitive neuroscience. Although I was able to try my hand at a variety of techniques there, I spent the better part of the next six years studying the split-brain patients who had first made Gazzaniga famous. These are patients who have had the corpus callosum—the major forebrain commissure connecting the two cerebral hemispheres—surgically severed to relieve pharmacologically intractable epilepsy. They are interesting to cognitive neuroscientists for a number of reasons. Typically, they are outwardly normal, showing few signs of neurological impairment. However, the surgery effectively isolates each hemisphere from the other at the cortical level, so that information available to one hemisphere is, for the most part, inaccessible to the other. This allows the unique psychological attributes of each hemisphere to be studied in near-complete isolation.

More than three decades of research with these split-brain patients had led Gazzaniga to a strong conclusion: The left hemisphere is far superior to the right in performing tasks that require problem solving, reasoning, or the resolution of ambiguity. In essence, most of the attributes we associate with intelligence seem to be lateralized to the left hemisphere, perhaps because of its concomitant specialization for language production and comprehension. Gazzaniga's term the "left-hemisphere interpreter" neatly encapsulates these findings (see Gazzaniga, 2000, for a comprehensive review of the findings that led to this conclusion).

The relatively few studies of perceptual lateralization in split-brain patients had been somewhat equivocal. Most had confirmed the widely held notion of right-hemisphere superiority for visual or visuospatial functions, but a handful had failed to find any lateralization at all. On balance, it appeared that visual perception, at least, was lateralized to the right hemisphere, but that perceptual lateralization appeared to be relatively weak compared to the left hemisphere's interpretive and linguistic specializations.

The consensus on left- and right-hemisphere specializations left me somewhat unsatisfied, especially in light of the view espoused by Hochberg and others that perception is an intelligent process, requiring the active resolution of ambiguity. If intelligence and the ability to resolve ambiguity are, broadly speaking, lateralized to the left hemisphere, then shouldn't we expect to find left-hemisphere dominance for perceptual tasks too? Or does perception engage a qualitatively different intelligence, lateralized to the right hemisphere? I made it my task to find some answers to these questions.

In collaboration with Gazzaniga and Margaret Funnell, among others, I embarked on a series of studies investigating visual perception in split-brain patients. The crossed-organization human visual system allows information to be restricted to one hemisphere simply by presenting it to the contralateral side of visual fixation. Thus, stimuli presented to the left side of fixation are restricted to the right hemisphere, and vice versa. Hemispheric asymmetries can be assessed by comparing psychophysical performance for stimuli presented to either side of fixation. Tasks favoring the left hemisphere (i.e., right visual hemifield) often require elaborate control conditions to make it possible to interpret the data, since it is possible that the right hemisphere simply misunderstood the instructions but was otherwise capable of performing the task. Tasks favoring the right hemisphere (left visual hemifield) are easier to interpret, since there is essentially no chance that the left hemisphere was unable to understand instructions that the right hemisphere could implement.

We immediately began to find evidence that some perceptual abilities were indeed lateralized to the right hemisphere. In contrast to previous findings with split-brain patients, some visual functions appeared quite strongly lateralized, and some functions seemed simple enough that we characterized the performance asymmetry as a left-hemisphere deficit, rather than as a right-hemisphere superiority, although these are of course opposite sides of the same coin (Corballis, Funnell, & Gazzaniga, 2002a; Funnell, Corballis, & Gazzaniga, 1999).

Other researchers studying split-brain patients, patients with unilateral brain damage, or neuroimaging data have found similar right-hemispheric advantages for visual tasks, and several have attempted to characterize the main differences between the hemispheres in terms of their processing of visual stimuli. Most of these proposals recognize that perceptual asymmetries are not as dramatic as linguistic asymmetries and so propose that the two hemispheres divide the problem of perceiving the world between them, each focusing on a different aspect of the visual input. For example, Delis, Robertson, and Efron (1986) suggested that the principal difference between the hemispheres is the level of detail at which they process stimuli. According to this view, the left hemisphere is biased toward processing the local details of a visual stimulus, while the right hemisphere is biased toward the global organization (see Ivry & Robertson, 1998, for an updated view of this idea). A similar idea was proposed by Sargent (1982), who suggested that the left hemisphere preferentially processes the high-spatial-frequency components of a stimulus, and the right hemisphere processes the low-spatial-frequency components. A third dichotomy was proposed by Kosslyn and his colleagues (Kosslyn, Koenig, Barrett, Cave, Tang, & Gabrieli, 1989), who suggested that the difference between the cerebral hemispheres, at least in perceptual terms, lies in the way each represents spatial relationships. Because of its linguistic capabilities, the left hemisphere represents spatial information in a categorical—essentially, verbal—fashion. The right hemisphere, in contrast, uses a coordinate representation in which spatial relationships are maintained in a finer-grained fashion. As Hellige (1993) notes, these various suggestions make similar predictions for a number of perceptual situations, and it is not clear whether any of them capture the fundamental distinction between the two hemispheres' perceptual systems.

None of these division-of-labor dichotomies seemed to offer a straightforward account for some of our split-brain data. For instance, we found a right-hemisphere advantage for shape perception when amodal boundary completion was required, but no asymmetry for a similar task requiring modal completion (Corballis, Fendrich, Shapley, & Gazzaniga, 1999). We also found evidence for a right-hemisphere advantage for one instance of the line-motion illusion (in which a line that appears instantaneously appears to propagate from one end to the other) but not for another manifestation of the same illusion (Corballis, Funnell, & Gazzaniga, 2002b). Overall, the pattern of data began to suggest that the two hemispheres were roughly equivalent for low-level analysis, but that higher-level perceptual processing was lateralized to the right hemisphere. These findings suggested to me that Gazzaniga's notion of a "left-hemisphere interpreter" needed to be extended. The left hemisphere may indeed be specialized for resolving ambiguity and for problem solving in certain domains, but the right hemisphere appears to have equally sophisticated talents and to perform similar functions in the perceptual domain (see Corballis, 2003a, b).

A compelling illustration of the hemispheric differences in perceptual and logical problem solving comes from a recent split-brain study conducted at Dartmouth. In one condition, we presented the patients with a modified version of the classic Michotte studies of the perception of causality. The stimuli were a series of short movies showing one circle moving into the vicinity of a second circle, which then moved away. In some of the movies, the first circle appeared to strike the second, which immediately began to move. In other movies, there was either a small gap between the circles when the second one began to move, or there was a brief delay between the impact and the movement of the second circle. For most observers, the introduction of these spatial or temporal gaps decreases the likelihood that the movement of the second circle was caused by the collision with the first circle. Small gaps may not disrupt the perception of causality much, but larger gaps make it appear that the second circle moves of its own accord. We showed the movies to the patients lateralized to one visual hemifield so that the information would only be available to one hemisphere at a time. At the conclusion of each movie, the patients were asked to judge whether the motion of the second circle appeared to have been caused by the first circle, or whether the second circle appeared to move on its own. Somewhat surprisingly, when the movies were presented to the left hemisphere, both patients were essentially indifferent to the presence of the spatial or temporal gaps and responded more or less at random. When the movies were shown to their right hemispheres, the patients' responses mimicked the pattern produced by most neurologically intact subjects. That is, they responded that the motion of the second circle seemed to have been caused by the first circle when the gaps were small, but not when the gaps were larger. It appears that causality is, in these perceptually driven conditions, "interpreted" by the right hemisphere. In a second condition, the patients were shown a second set of movies, in which the relationship between the state of a light and a set of switches was manipulated. The patients were asked to judge whether a particular arrangement of the switches would result in the light being on or off. This condition required the patients to learn the relationships between the switches and the light and to make a determination of causality based on those learned relationships. Under these conditions, the patients' left hemispheres had no trouble performing the task, and their right hemispheres generated more or less random responses (Roser, Fugelsang, Dunbar, Corballis, & Gazzaniga, 2005).

   This dissociation between "perceptual" and "cognitive" inference hints at a neural basis for a distinction between two qualitatively different "intelligent" systems in the human brain. One is lateralized to the left hemisphere and supports the types of processes that we usually think of as intelligent—syllogistic reasoning, symbolic representation, problem solving, sequence learning, and the like. It is likely that this system is linguistically based or at least shares much of its neural and cognitive substrate with human language. The other system—which underlies perception—is probably phylogenetically much older. I have little doubt that we share much of our perceptual intelligence with the majority of other vertebrates, at least, since we share many of the same perceptual problems. I suspect that the neural substrate of this system is more widely distributed in the brain and that it is lateralized to the right hemisphere in humans essentially by default. That is, the evolution of the language-based system and its concomitants in the left hemisphere may have coopted neural territory that had previously been dedicated to perceptual processing, leaving the right hemisphere to handle perceptual problems (Corballis, Funnell, & Gazzaniga, 2000). If I am on the right track, perhaps Hochberg's student was more gifted with one variety of intelligence than the other. He definitely exhibited all of the traditional signs of intelligence, at least the left-hemisphere variety. Maybe his perceptual intelligence failed to reach the same heights.

Most, if not all, of the other contributors to this volume have a stronger claim than I to be represented in these pages. I have not spoken to Hochberg for the better part of a decade and had only a relatively brief association with him in the early days of my graduate education. Nevertheless, I consider him to be one of the strongest influences on my intellectual development. His erudition was at once stimulating and intimidating to a young graduate student, and he set the bar high for those who wished to follow him. High expectations notwithstanding, he remains one of the most intellectually generous people I have encountered. Psychology needs more like Julian Hochberg.

References

CORBALLIS, P. M. (2003a). Visual grouping and the right hemisphere interpreter. In T. Ono, G. Matsumoto, R. R. Llinas, A. Berthoz, R. Norgren, H. Nishijo, & R. Tamura (Eds.), *Cognition and emotion in the brain: Selected topics of the International Symposium on Limbic and Association Cortical Systems* (pp. 447–457). International Congress Series 1250. Amsterdam: Elsevier.

CORBALLIS, P. M. (2003b). Visuospatial processing and the right-hemisphere interpreter. *Brain and Cognition, 53,* 171–176.

CORBALLIS, P. M., FENDRICH, R., SHAPLEY, R., & GAZZANIGA, M. S. (1999). Illusory contours and amodal completion: Evidence for a functional dissociation in callosotomy patients. *Journal of Cognitive Neuroscience, 11,* 459–466.

CORBALLIS, P. M., FUNNELL, M. G., & GAZZANIGA, M. S. (2000). An evolutionary perspective on hemispheric asymmetries. *Brain and Cognition, 43,* 112–117.

CORBALLIS, P. M., FUNNELL, M. G., & GAZZANIGA, M. S. (2002a). Hemispheric asymmetries for simple visual judgments in the split brain. *Neuropsychologia, 40,* 401–410.

CORBALLIS, P. M., FUNNELL, M. G., & GAZZANIGA, M. S. (2002b). An investigation of the line motion effect in a callosotomy patient. *Brain and Cognition, 48,* 327–332.

DELIS, D. C., ROBERTSON, L. C., & EFRON, R. (1986). Hemispheric specialization for memory for visual hierarchical stimuli. *Neuropsychologia, 24,* 205–214.

FUNNELL, M. G., CORBALLIS, P. M., & GAZZANIGA, M. S. (1999). A deficit in perceptual matching in the left hemisphere of a callosotomy patient. *Neuropsychologia, 37,* 1143–1154.

GAZZANIGA, M. S. (2000). Cerebral specialization and interhemispheric communication: Does the corpus callosum enable the human condition? *Brain, 123,* 1293–1326.

GIBSON, J. J. (1950). *The perception of the visual world.* Boston: Houghton Mifflin.

GIBSON, J. J. (1979). *The ecological approach to visual perception.* Boston: Houghton Mifflin.

HELLIGE, J. (1993). *Hemispheric asymmetry: What's right and what's left.* Cambridge, MA: Harvard University Press.

HELMHOLTZ, H. L. F. (1962). *Treatise on physiological optics* (Trans. J. P. C. Southall). New York: Dover. (Original work published 1909)

IVRY, R. B., & ROBERTSON, L. C. (1998). *The two sides of perception.* Cambridge, MA: MIT Press.

KOSSLYN, S. M., KOENIG, O., BARRETT, A., CAVE, C. B., TANG, J., & GABRIELI, J. D. E. (1989). Evidence for two types of spatial representations: Hemispheric specialization for categorical and coordinate relations. *Journal of Experimental Psychology: Human Perception and Performance, 15,* 723–735.

ROSER, M., FUGELSANG, J., DUNBAR, K., CORBALLIS, P. M., & GAZZANIGA, M. S. (2005). Dissociating processes supporting causal perception and causal inference in the brain. *Neuropsychology, 19,* 591–602.

SARGENT, J. (1982). The cerebral balance of power: Confrontation or cooperation? *Journal of Experimental Psychology: Human Perception and Performance, 8,* 253–272.

36

Segmentation, Grouping, and Shape

Some Hochbergian Questions

Philip J. Kellman and Patrick Garrigan

It is a privilege to contribute a chapter to this volume honoring Julian Hochberg. Such a volume is deserved, and overdue, simply on the basis of Hochberg's contributions as one of the great perception scientists of the 20th century. What many contributors to this volume have in common, however, goes beyond that. We have benefited from Hochberg's gifts as a teacher and mentor. In the process that allows the questions, tools, and insights in a discipline to be handed off from one generation to another, he has had a special and profound influence on his students, not only from his one-on-one interactions with them but also as they have been able to observe his approach to scholarship and science.

We feel especially fortunate to be included here. Although neither author of this chapter was officially his doctoral student, Kellman was fortunate during his third year of graduate school to be part of a year-long seminar with Hochberg. Some enlightened faculty in the Psychology Department at the University of Pennsylvania at that time realized that, although their department was strong in research on basic visual mechanisms, it was not strong in perception, a topic of increasing interest among its students. Asking "Why not the best?" they arranged for Hochberg to travel to Penn every second week to teach a graduate perception seminar in 1978. This amazing seminar had an enormous impact on Kellman and on a whole group of students who had not initially come to graduate school to study perception. These included Dan Reisberg, David Smith, and Denise Varner in that seminar and others who would benefit later from the climate in the department that Hochberg's seminar helped to create, such as Tim Shipley and Felice Bedford. The idea that one seminar could actually solidify an enduring focus of interest in a department sounds inflated, but that's pretty much what happened.

With regard to key issues in perceptual science, it is striking how well Julian Hochberg's influence endures. In this chapter, we note a few of these issues and describe how they loom large in our current concerns. The chapter is brief and in parts speculative; what we are most certain will persist in the long run are not elements of our models but the basic Hochbergian questions that motivate them.

Some Hochbergian Problems

In current work, we are attempting to connect what is known about grouping and segmentation processes with issues of shape perception and representation. Three problems define much of this work, and all involve issues that Julian Hochberg worked on and in some cases helped to define. We briefly describe these three areas below.

The Problem of Shape Perception and Representation

What is shape and how do we represent it? Hochberg and his colleagues made significant contributions on these issues, such as attempts to quantify figural goodness (Hochberg, Gleitman, & MacBride, 1948; Hochberg & McAlister, 1953). He introduced these problems to a generation of investigators through his book on perception (Hochberg, 1964) and his landmark chapters, which occupy 155 pages in the 1971 edition of *Woodworth and Schlosberg's Experimental Psychology*.

Problems of Abstraction in Perception

In the classic article "In the Mind's Eye," Hochberg (1968) made the case that perception advances beyond local activations by constructing "schematic maps" from successive fixations and that these maps are abstract in that they contain selective information about shape, but not every detail of the local activations that produce them.

Connecting Early Visual Encodings With Higher Visual Representations

How do we get to schematic maps from local activations? Early cortical units respond to local areas of oriented contrast. If we think of the response to a visual pattern as an ensemble of activations like these, how do we get to the perception of contours, unity, objects, and shape?

Contemporary Issues of Shape, Schematic Maps, and the Relation of Early and Middle Vision

Although there has been progress, all of these Hochbergian questions remain important in current research.

Even within visual segmentation and grouping processes, shape issues arise. For example, interpolation processes that connect visible contours across gaps, as in occluded and illusory contour formation, appear to contribute definite contour shapes in regions that are not locally specified by stimulus

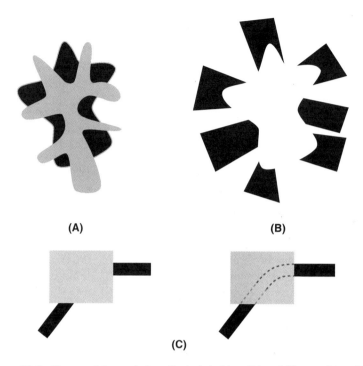

Figure 36.1. Shape and interpolation. Occluded object (A) and illusory object (B) displays with the same set of physically specified contours and gaps. Interpolation leads to similar perceived shapes in both cases. C. The display on the right indicates the perceived shape that may be produced by interpolation in the occlusion display on the left. Note that curved edges may appear in the percept despite their absence in the display presented.

information. Figure 36.1 shows illusory and occluded figures that share the same extents and locations of physically specified contours and the same gaps. Phenomenologically, they also appear to share the same completed shapes, an observation that fits with evidence and arguments that they share a common underlying interpolation process (Shipley & Kellman, 1992; Ringach & Shapley, 1996; Yin, Kellman, & Shipley, 1998; Kellman, Garrigan, & Shipley, 2005). Figure 36.1C illustrates more locally how interpolation contributes to shape of unspecified regions.

Issues of shape and abstraction must be resolved if we are to link middle vision—including contour, surface, and object perception—to known facts about early visual processing, such as the kinds of neural units located in early cortical areas (Heitger et al., 1992, 1998; Hubel & Wiesel, 1968). The typical outputs of neural-style models of these processes (e.g., Grossberg & Mingolla, 1985; Grossberg, Mingolla, & Ross, 1997; Heitger et al., 1998; Yen & Finkel, 1998). are *images*, showing the locations of activation resulting from grouping or interpolation operators (but see Yen & Finkel, 1998). It is easy to forget when viewing these outputs that the models themselves do not "know" anything about what things go together. Issues of identifying connected contours, segmenting objects, etc., remain. This point is not meant as a criticism of these models, which address a number of important issues, but only to make clear that certain crucial problems are not addressed.

The point is relevant, not only for interpolated contours, but for "real" ones as well. A viewed contour produces a large ensemble of responses in early cortical areas, but how do we arrive at a contour "token," a higher-level unit that has properties such as shape and can receive labels such as boundary assignment? One effort to assemble local activations into contour tokens is the model of Yen and Finkel (1998), which uses the synchrony of firing of active local edge detectors to combine them into a unit. Although attempting to address the next step toward object perception, the model says little about how some attribute of this token, in particular its shape, might be extracted.

This issue is crucial, because higher-level shape representations are both more and less than the early neural activations that contribute to them. They are *more* because an abstract representation of shape can be used to recognize, compare, equate, or distinguish other stimuli that differ in many particulars. They are *less* because the higher level representation necessarily omits much of the details of particular local activations.

One might say that we are concerned with some unsolved problems of schematic maps, specifically how to extract and encode contour shapes and how to get from an ensemble of local neural responses to shape tokens that allow object shape to be represented. This effort is only beginning, so we offer only sketches of the problems along with some possible elements of their solutions.

Some Guiding Principles

A few basic ideas about shape representations guide our work. Here, we describe them briefly.

Unity in Shape Representation

We assume that the outputs of perception include higher-level tokens that are larger and more abstract than the responses of orientation-sensitive units in early cortical areas. Contour tokens would appear necessary to explain ordinary observations, such as the fact that contour shapes can be discriminated and matched, and that in reversible figure-ground displays with smooth contours (as in Figure 36.2), boundary assignment (indicating which side of a contour is figure) ordinarily changes for the whole contour at once.

Figure 36.2. Contour tokens and boundary assignment. Although boundary assignment (figure-ground organization) may change as the figure is viewed, it always changes as a unit. This regularity suggests that boundary assignment operates on unitary contour tokens.

Our understanding of what these tokens are is poor. Such higher-level representations may characterize shapes of whole objects, but they also probably include descriptive units that are not so high-level, such as parts (Hoffman & Richards, 1984) and contours.

Limited Resolution in Shape Representation

Another principle guiding our work is that shape representations do not have infinitely fine grain. This is likely to be a principled difference between shape representations in biological systems and machines. In a computer vision application, if a space curve is specified by an equation, the system is able to compute the slope or any other derivative of the curve at any point on the curve. It is unlikely that human representations are equally detailed at all points, and we probably have little or no sensitivity to derivatives higher than the first (slope) (Kellman, Garrigan, Kalar, & Shipley, 2003). In short, human shape representation is far more limited, but also geared to certain tasks. An equation for a curve would not naturally indicate salient parts or their contribution to the perceived complexity of a contour. It also would not easily capture similarities of contour shapes.

More generally, we suspect that the ordinary processing of shape contours utilizes representations that usually simplify the actual contour shape. Doing so not only produces a more economical record; it also makes feasible the detection of shapes as similar or different across changes in position, orientation, scale, and the elements composing the shape. Figure 36.3 illustrates some of these points.

Recently, we have carried out experiments in which subjects make same/different judgments about successively presented smooth, curved contours. Results suggest both that complexity matters a great deal and that human shape representations are simplified relative to real shapes. Nevertheless, across a range of conditions, human judgments are quite good. After considering how a shape representation system might connect with object segmentation and interpolation processes, we suggest how economy in shape representation may be achieved, without much loss of the ability to represent and distinguish different shapes.

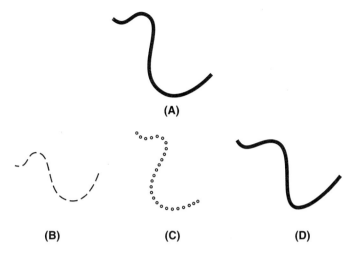

Figure 36.3. Abstract shape. The contour at the top (A) has a distinct shape, a property independent of its position, orientation, or local characteristics. Objects B and C are composed of different local elements and have different sizes and orientations, yet they are seen as having the same overall shape as in A. Object D is most similar to A in terms of overall size, orientation, and type of line, yet it is clearly the only contour in the figure with a different shape.

Constraining Interpolated Contour Shape

One specific issue that has prodded our thinking on shape representations is the shapes of interpolated contours. Evidence suggests that the visual system creates well-defined contour links across gaps in the perception of occluded and illusory objects. Data on the exact shapes of interpolated contours are sparse and conflicting. The premise above regarding the spatial grain of shape representations may provide some theoretical guidance about interpolated contours. Some models propose outputs that are unconstrained by consideration of the complexity of the interpolated contour's shape. For example, Fantoni and Gerbino (2003) suggest an interpolation scheme that progresses from two endpoints by combining two inputs (whose weights change at each point along the path), a straight-line connection between the endpoints of the visible inducing edges and their collinear extensions. This scheme produces curved interpolations that often have changing curvature at every point. Recently, Fulvio, Singh & Maloney (in press) suggested that interpolated shapes might best be described by quintic (5th order) polynomials. Even if some neural basis in terms of interactions of oriented units were able to achieve such contour connections, they would be unlikely to survive into our representations of shape. We believe that shape representations are unlikely to represent different curvatures at every point, even when the stimulus contains them. Two lines of work have suggested more constrained schemes. Analysis by J. Edward Skeath (see appendix II of Kellman & Shipley, 1991) suggested a simple shape for interpolated contours that is naturally compatible with the geometry of contour relatability, a description of the relations of real contours that support interpolation. Interpolated contours can always be composed of a constant curvature segment and a zero-curvature (straight) segment. Earlier, Ullman (1976) proposed that illusory contours can always be composed of two constant curvature segments. The Skeath/Kellman/ Shipley (1991) proposal has the virtue of providing a unique solution for the path of interpolation without an additional step in which a unique solution is chosen from a set of possible ones, as in the model proposed by Ullman. However, both proposals are compatible with economy in subsequent coding.

Aspects of a Theory Connecting Early Vision to Shape Representations

Arclets

We are developing a scheme that uses the simplicity of the circle as the link between low- and higher-level vision. We propose that neural circuits exist that combine small groups of oriented units that are linked by constant turning angles, e.g., they encode constant curvature segments (including zero curvature) of shapes. We call these *arclets* (see Figure 36.4). These are likely to include both 2D and 3D groups of oriented units, as recent work suggests that object formation is a 3D process, based on 3D positions and orientations of oriented units (Kellman, Garrigan, & Shipley, 2005).

In their application to interpolation, activation initiated by real contours spreads along restricted paths in a network of oriented units; these paths consist of arclets. This restriction, combined with one simple, additional constraint, provides a unique path of interpolation connecting any relatable edges. In their application to shape coding, the activations of arclets—units that are activated by signals in chains of several oriented units—allow a natural means of handing off the information from real and interpolated contour positions to higher-level shape representations.

A Shape Representation Scheme

We conjecture that at the level at which middle- and higher-level shape representations receive information from early visual activations (clusters of oriented units), shape representations are made up of chunks of constant curvature. The neural basis for extracting these chunks are detectors that sense patterns of activation in a layer of oriented units, such as those found in the early cortical visual areas. A given arclet is activated if a chain of oriented units forming a collinear or cocircular path is simultaneously activated. Different arclets code different curvatures. Activation of a single

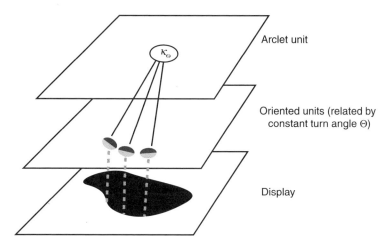

Figure 36.4. From local activations to abstract shape: proposed arclet circuits. Arclets may represent the first step toward a nonlocal description of contour shape. Oriented units simultaneously activated by a stimulus are grouped according to their relative positions and orientations. If the geometry of the contour is within the tolerance of a higher-order arclet grouping unit, a simplified, abstract representation for this part of the contour emerges from the complex array of local activations. For interpolated contours, activation spreads from the ends of visible edges only through collinear or cocircular arclet paths, leading to a unique interpolation path for relatable contours.

arclet indicates the presence of that curvature in a certain position, and activation of a series of adjacent arclets of the same curvature value signals an extended contour region having that curvature value. The encoding of a constant curvature segment extends along a contour until a transition zone, at which arclets of that curvature no longer exceed a certain threshold of accurately matching the contour (or are less well activated than some arclet having a different curvature value). A shape representation consists of a set of constant curvature values (scaled to achieve size invariance; see below) characterizing segments along a contour, along with some marking of transition zones between constant curvature segments.

One implication of this scheme, which we are currently working out and testing, is that shapes of curved contours that have continuously varying curvature must somehow be fit into the representation we are proposing. Obviously, in the limit, if a very large number of constant curvature segments can be used to represent a contour, there would be little difference between our proposal and one that invokes representations of arbitrary space curves. Therefore, one difficult task we are pursuing is to discover the representational scheme that determines how a complicated contour is parsed into segments of nearly constant curvature, as well as how these several pieces are knit together in a representation. Two early indications make us optimistic about such a scheme. First, in simple closed forms of smooth but arbitrary shape, there is an obvious complementary relationship between certain features of contours, such as the concave minima that determine the decomposition of objects into parts (e.g., Hoffman & Richards, 1984; Singh & Hoffman, 1997), and the contour segments between part boundaries. Full representations of such shapes may well be combinations of part boundaries along with constant and zero curvature segments between them. Second, although we have not devised a complete representational scheme, we have obtained preliminary data indicating that shapes with constant curvature chunks are processed more efficiently and support better discrimination performance than similar shapes with nonconstant curvatures.

Shape Invariance

Hochberg (1968) offered arguments as to why schematic maps are abstract rather than literal copies of the original input. Similar arguments not only apply to shape representation but mark its most important characteristics. As the Gestalt psychologists emphasized (and as we illustrated in Figure 36.3), two things can have the same form yet differ in the local elements comprising them. One mandate for a successful shape representation scheme is that it should make explicit what Figures 36.3A, B, and C have in common, as well as how they differ from Figure 36.3D.

This ideal has been most closely accomplished in models of high-level object recognition (e.g., Hummel & Biederman, 1992). Most models of this sort, however, focus on so-called basic-level object recognition, which refers to shape categories at the basic level of conceptual hierarchies. (For example, chairs, airplanes, and cups are basic level, whereas my favorite easy chair or the concept of vehicles are subordinate or superordinate level concepts, respectively.) In this kind of scheme, both a single-engine Cessna and a Boeing 747 will activate the final representational category "airplanes." Likewise, other research (e.g., Attneave, 1954) suggests that specific curved edges may be replaced by straight ones and still allow recognition of a shape category ("Attneave's cat").[1] Yet the invariances useful for detailed object naming are too abstract to account for human perception of the shapes of contours and objects, such as what is the same or different among the displays in Figure 36.3.

At this level of shape representation, there are important and interesting problems. One is that standard mathematical notions of curvature do not capture shape invariance. A large circle and a small circle obviously have the same shape, but they have very different curvatures (where curvature is given by the change in contour orientation per unit arc length). Use of relative curvatures or normalization by some overall size measurement (e.g., length along longest axis for a closed shape, or normalization by chord length for a curved segment of a contour) is a standard operation in computer vision (Costa & Cesar, 2000) and one that might be used to equate a shape characteristic at differing sizes in human vision (cf. Singh & Hoffman, 1997).

Arclets may offer a means of achieving scale invariance in a more natural way. Because orientation-sensitive units in early visual areas exist across a range of spatial scales, arclets would similarly span this range. There is an interesting invariant for arclets related by the same turn angle, but made of different size elements. As long as all elements within each arclet are of equal size, all arclets based on the same turn angle between oriented elements and having the same number of elements represent the same scale-invariant shape. That is, shape pieces that receive the same encoding in terms of arclet turn angle and element number differ only by a scale factor (see Figure 36.5). Thus, activating an arclet at any scale could signal two unique values (turn angle and the number of elements in the arclet) that specify scale-invariant shape for that part of the contour. Two circles of different sizes, for

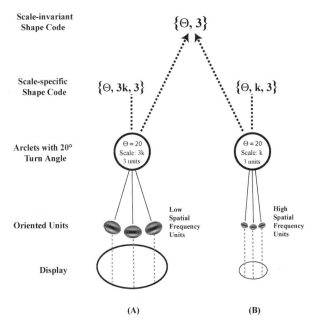

Figure 36.5. Representations consisting of sets of arclets and their relations along a contour are inherently scale-invariant. A. Large ellipse. A contour fragment is detected by an arclet made of coarse orientation-sensitive units related to each other by a 20° turn angle. B. Small version of ellipse in A. The corresponding contour fragment is detected by an arclet made of smaller orientation-sensitive units related to each other by 20° turn angles. Scale-specific representations of shape can derive from three characteristics of the best-activated arclet: turn angle, scale, and number of oriented units. Arclets made from oriented units of a given scale (spatial frequency) are scalar transforms of arclets at other scales having the same turn angle. This property makes available a scale-invariant representation of the shape of the contour fragment based on two parameters of an activated arclet: turn angle and number of oriented units activated.

example, will have contours that best match arclets at different scales, but both arclets will have the same number of elements and the same relative turn angle between them. Some constraints will be necessary in contour encoding for selecting the proper scale of arclet. For example, a slow-turning, small-scale arclet and a faster-turning, large-scale arclet could both match a large curve. It appears, however, that simple constraints, such as selecting the matching arclet of highest turn angle as the best descriptor, would resolve this ambiguity. Similarity of forms and parts across orientations may be straightforwardly given in this scheme. If curvature chunks are encoded around the border of a shape beginning at some recognizable feature, then representations will be orientation invariant. These relatively simple ingredients would allow two contours or closed shapes having the same form but differing in orientation and size to produce the invariant representations needed to support shape perception and classification.

The efforts to understand shape perception and abstraction in perceptual representations and the efforts to connect early visual activations with higher-level tokens are challenging and ongoing. We have much left to learn, but these proposals offer a sketch (a schematic map?) of how we might use certain shape tokens that begin with simple relations of oriented units to bridge the gap from low-level neural activations to higher-level representations. In pursuing these problems, we owe a great debt to Julian Hochberg, who was among the earliest researchers to grapple with the notion of representation in perception, to pinpoint key issues, and to impress his students with their importance. Although we are not yet in possession of clear answers, we are convinced, in no small part due to Hochberg's insights, that these are the crucial questions.

Note

1. Another interesting implication of Attneave's (1954) work and later research (e.g., Norman, Phillips, & Ross, 2001) for the present approach is that points of maximum curvature may be important for some aspects of shape encoding. Yet, in our scheme, such points may not be marked explicitly. One way to reconcile these ideas is to acknowledge that multiple encoding schemes exist in human shape perception. Points of maximum curvature may be extracted during early fitting of arclets (and used for various purposes) even if the final arclet representation sometimes subsumes a curvature maximum into a larger region of relatively constant curvature. These issues are under investigation.

References

ATTNEAVE, F. (1954). Some informational aspects of visual perception. *Psychological Review, 61,* 183–193.

Costa, L. da F. & Cesar, R. M. (2000). *Shape analysis and classification*. Boca Raton, FL: CRC Press.

Fantoni, C., & Gerbino, W. (2003). Contour interpolation by vector-field combination. *Journal of Vision, 3*(4), 281–303.

Fulvio, J.M., Singh, M. & Maloney, L. T. (in press). Consistency of location and gradient judgments of visually-interpolated contours. *Computer Vision and Pattern Recognition*, Proceedings, 2006.

Grossberg, S., & Mingolla, E. (1985). Neural dynamics of form perception: Boundary completion, illusory figures, and neon color spreading. *Psychological Review, 92*, 173–211.

Grossberg, S., Mingolla, E., & Ross, W. D. (1997). Visual brain and visual perception: How does the cortex do perceptual grouping? Trends in *Neurosciences, 20*(3), 106–111.

Heitger, F., Rosenthaler, L., von der Heydt, R., Peterhans, E., & Kübler, O. (1992). Simulation of neural contour mechanisms: From simple to end-stopped cells. *Vision Research, 32*, 963–981.

Heitger, F., von der Heydt, R., Peterhans, E., Rosenthaler, L., & Kübler, O. (1998). Simulation of neural contour mechanisms: Representing anomalous contours. *Image and Vision Computing, 16*, 407–421.

Hochberg, J. (1964). *Perception*. Englewood Cliffs, NJ: Prentice-Hall.

Hochberg, J. (1968). In the mind's eye. In R. N. Haber (Ed.), *Contemporary theory and research on visual perception* (pp. 309–331). New York: Holt, Rinehart, & Winston.

Hochberg, J. (1971). Perception: I. Color and shape. In J. W. Kling & L. A. Riggs (Eds.), *Woodworth and Schlosberg's experimental psychology* (pp. 395–474). New York: Holt, Rinehart & Winston.

Hochberg, J. E., Gleitman, H., & MacBride, P. D. (1948). Visual threshold as a function of simplicity of form. *American Psychologist, 3*, 341–342.

Hochberg, J. E., & McAlister, E. (1953). A quantitative approach to figural "goodness." Journal of Experimental Psychology, 46, 361–364.

Hoffman, D. D., & Richards, W. A. (1984). Parts of recognition. *Cognition, 18*, 65–96.

Hubel, D. H., & Wiesel, T. N. (1968). Receptive fields and functional architecture of monkey striate cortex. *Journal of Physiology, 195*, 215–243.

Hummel, J. E., & Biederman, I. (1992). Dynamic binding in a neural network for shape recognition. *Psychological Review, 99*, 480–517.

Kellman, P. J., Garrigan, P., Kalar, D. J., & Shipley, T. F. (2003). Good continuation and relatability: Related but distinct principles. *Journal of Vision, 3*(9), 120a.

Kellman, P. J., Garrigan, P., & Shipley, T. F. (2005). Object interpolation in three dimensions. *Psychological Review, 112* (3), 586–609.

Kellman, P. J., & Shipley, T. F. (1991). A theory of visual interpolation in object perception. *Cognitive Psychology, 23*, 141–221.

Morrone, M. C., & Burr, D. C. (1988). Feature detection in human vision: A phase-dependent energy model. *Proceedings of the Royal Society of London B, 235*, 221–245.

Norman, J. F., Phillips, F., & Ross, H. E. (2001). Information concentration along the boundary contours of naturally shaped solid objects. *Perception, 30*, 1285–1294.

RINGACH, D. L., & SHAPLEY, R. (1996). Spatial and temporal properties of illusory contours and amodal boundary completion. *Vision Research, 36,* 3037–3050.

SHIPLEY, T. F., & KELLMAN, P. J. (1992). Perception of partly occluded objects and illusory figures: Evidence for an identity hypothesis. *Journal of Experimental Psychology: Human Perception & Performance, 18*(1), 106–120.

SHIPLEY, T. F., & KELLMAN, P. J. (2001). From fragments to objects: Segmentation and grouping in vision. Amsterdam: Elsevier.

SINGH, M., & HOFFMAN, D. D. (1997). Constructing and representing visual objects. *Trends in Cognitive Sciences, 1*(3), 98–102.

ULLMAN, S. (1976). Filling in the gaps: The shape of subjective contours and a model for their generation. *Biological Cybernetics, 25,* 1–6.

WERTHEIMER, M. (1921). Untersuchungen zur Lehre von der Gestalt: I. *Psychologische Forschung, 1,* 47–58.

WERTHEIMER, M. (1958). Principles of perceptual organization. In D. C. Beardslee & M. Wertheimer (Eds.), *Readings in perception* (pp. 115–135). Princeton, NJ: D. Van Nostrand.

YEN, S. C., & FINKEL, L. H. (1998). Extraction of perceptually salient contours by striate cortical networks. *Vision Research, 38,* 719–741.

YIN, C., KELLMAN, P. J., & SHIPLEY, T. F. (1998). A common mechanism for illusory and occluded object recognition. *Journal of Experimental Psychology, 24*(3), 859–869.

Pictures, Film, and Dance

37

Ideas of Lasting Influence

*Hochberg's Anticipation of Research on Change
Blindness and Motion-Picture Perception*

Daniel J. Simons and Daniel T. Levin

Julian Hochberg has had little direct influence on our academic careers, and
we have never even met him. Our knowledge of his contributions to perception and cognition comes entirely from his writings and through discussions of the influence he has had on some of our colleagues and mentors.
Those writings have anticipated major developments in perception and cognition, often by several decades. We firmly believe that his prescient writings
will continue to influence perception research for decades to come.

The measure of Hochberg's contribution comes not from the number of
papers he published (although he has plenty), nor from extensive research on
a single topic. Rather, at least for us, Hochberg's influence comes from the
number of original ideas he has had and the number of as yet unexplored big
questions he addressed in his writing. One useful rubric for measuring the
influence of someone's writing is to examine the number of good ideas contained in each of his papers (the metric was conceived by Brian Scholl: http://
pantheon.yale.edu/~bs265/misc/musings/bjs-miscMusings.html). Most papers
in psychology have at most one or maybe two new ideas (and many have a ratio
of less than one idea/paper). In contrast, many of Hochberg's papers, particularly his book chapters, are chock full of original, creative, and important
ideas that cry out for further empirical work. Many of these ideas have yet to
receive the attention they deserve in the perception literature. A researcher who
was short of ideas could certainly mine Hochberg's writings and never run out
of important questions to address. In this essay, we describe just two examples
of Hochberg's ability to identify interesting and underexplored problems. One
involves a study he described in passing as part of a larger chapter, an experiment that anticipated the current literature on change detection by nearly
20 years. The other involves his thorough discussion of motion-picture perception, an area that still is in desperate need of empirical exploration.

The use of change detection as a tool to study visual memory has a long
history (for reviews, see Rensink, 2002; Simons & Levin, 2003), with early
research focusing primarily on changes to text or to simple arrays of dots or
letters (e.g., McConkie & Zola, 1979; Phillips, 1974). Since the 1990s,
work on change detection has focused on a surprising phenomenon now

known as *change blindness*: Observers often fail to detect large changes to photographs of real-world scenes provided that the change occurs during a brief disruption (Rensink, O'Regan, & Clark, 1997; Simons & Levin, 1997). This research has gained attention because, unlike earlier work with simple arrays, the extent of change blindness is counterintuitive to most people unfamiliar with the effects (Levin, Momen, Drivdahl, & Simons, 2000). Most people believe that they are concretely aware of the visual world and that significant changes should draw attention and be detected. When simple demonstrations illustrate the extent of change blindness, people are often surprised: These findings led researchers to the realization that our intuitions about visual attention and about the ability to notice unexpected events are inaccurate. One of the primary tools used to study change detection involves presenting an original and modified version of a scene in rapid alternation, with each scene followed by a blank screen. This "flicker" task, so-called because of the display's flickering appearance, was popularized as a tool to study change detection only in the late 1990s (Rensink et al., 1997). The 1990s also saw some of the first well-known work to use complex images in change-detection studies (Blackmore, Brelstaff, Nelson, & Troscianko, 1995; Currie, McConkie, Carlson-Radvansky, & Irwin, 2000; Rensink et al., 1997; Simons, 1996).

Although the flicker task emerged from the recent change-blindness literature as one of the best new tools for studying visual memory (e.g., Rensink, 2000), it may well be older than originally thought. In fact, it may well be original to Hochberg's work in the 1960s. In a briefly sketched study, reported in only a few sentences of a much longer chapter, Hochberg used the flicker task to study changes to facial expression in drawings (Hochberg, 1968, p. 329). His method is nearly identical to the current flicker paradigm, and even the critical findings are similar. Subjects searched for a change while an original and modified image alternated repeatedly, and change-detection performance was measured as the time (or number of presentations) taken to detect the change. Hochberg found that changes to the expression of an inverted, polarity-reversed face are detected readily if the two displays are separated by a short time, but that detection takes many cycles if the delay between displays is long enough to eliminate apparent motion. One critical finding in the change-blindness literature is that detection is easy with a short interstimulus interval (ISI) due to apparent motion but difficult with a long delay due to the need for a comparison to visual memory (Rensink, O'Regan, & Clark, 2000). Hochberg reported the same pattern. As best as we can determine, this brief mention represents the first and only use of the flicker paradigm prior to the surge of interest in change blindness in the 1990s. Moreover, unlike most studies of change detection prior to the 1990s, Hochberg used pictorial stimuli in his study. Although this finding and method appeared only as a brief mention in a densely packed chapter, it was a direct precursor for an entire subfield of research in attention and perception nearly 30 years later.

One area he studied intensively still has not reached its potential in the perception literature: the study of motion-picture perception. Since the late 1990s, research on the perception of photographs and scenes has gained renewed life in the perception literature (Henderson & Hollingworth, 1999; Intraub, 1997), largely due to increases in computer power and the availability of software that allows systematic image manipulation. Before the 1990s, research on scene perception was limited by the inability to psychophysically explore the information underlying scene perception and memory. Although it was possible to present visual scenes to an observer using a tachistoscope, altering the images in any systematic fashion was prohibitively difficult. Over the past few years, tools have become available and affordable for systematic perception research using not just static images, but also dynamic scenes and motion pictures. In the 1980s, however, despite the dearth of affordable and, more important, easy techniques for the systematic variation of motion pictures, Hochberg undertook a detailed and systematic theoretical investigation of motion-picture perception (Hochberg, 1986).

The study of motion-picture perception presents a potentially rich source of observations about human perception and a methodology that has gone largely untapped. Hochberg's work is among the few exceptions to this: He wrote the most comprehensive review of the psychological bases of motion-picture perception (Hochberg, 1986) and also conducted a wide range of experiments, many of which presaged more recent perception and attention research. For example, Hochberg explored how viewers might use gaze direction as a cue to help specify the spatial relationships among parts of a scene in a motion picture (Hochberg, 1994). More recent work has examined how observing the gaze of another person helps in tasks ranging from word learning to change detection (e.g., Flavell, 2004; O'Donnell & Langton, 2003). Hochberg also explored different types of transitions in motion-picture perception, carefully describing the perceptual nature of pans (pivots of an otherwise stationary camera), tracking (physical translations of the camera position), zooms (changes to the camera focal length), and combinations of these (Hochberg, 1986). Hochberg's exploration provided insights that filmmakers might find helpful, but also contributed to work on the perceptual bases of human way-finding and navigation, processes that use similar cues to those he carefully described (see Cutting, 1986).

Hochberg's experimental and theoretical analyses of motion-picture perception served as a beacon of rigorous analysis during a time (1960–1990) when academic work on motion pictures was dominated by a postmodern/semiotic analysis. The postmodern approach denies the cognitive and perceptual bases of motion-picture perception, adhering almost exclusively to the notion that motion-picture perception is a cultural artifact. In rejecting this approach, Hochberg adopted a thread of analysis initiated soon after the invention of motion pictures, one that explicitly compares and contrasts motion-picture perception and real-world perception. This more "classical" film theory was driven both by filmmakers' relentless experimentation (ranging from D. W. Griffith's obsessive projection-room recutting to Lev Kuleshov and V. I. Pudovkin's famous experiments on montage; see Levin & Simons, 2000) and by the theoretical analyses of experimental psychologists (e.g., Arnheim, 1974; Munsterberg, 1916). Recently, the discipline of film studies has again become more compatible with an interdisciplinary approach. The development of the "cognitive approach" to film theory (e.g., Anderson, 1996; Bordwell & Carroll, 1996; Messaris, 1994; Prince, 1993) owes much to Hochberg's persistence and creativity.

Hochberg's work will continue to anticipate developments in perception and cognition for years to come. We particularly admire not only his idea productivity, but also his ability to identify crucial new avenues of exploration and to pursue them even when they are difficult, unpopular, or neglected. Both of us can only hope to assemble the kind of broad, creative, and truly inspirational analysis of perception that has characterized Julian Hochberg's research.

References

ANDERSON, J. (1996). *The reality of illusion: An ecological approach to cognitive film theory.* Carbondale: Southern Illinois University Press.

ARNHEIM, R. (1974). *Art and visual perception: A psychology of the creative eye (the new version)* (2d ed.). Berkeley: University of California Press.

BLACKMORE, S. J., BRELSTAFF, G., NELSON, K., & TROSCIANKO, T. (1995). Is the richness of our visual world an illusion? Transsaccadic memory for complex scenes. *Perception, 24,* 1075–1081.

BORDWELL, D., & CARROLL, N. (Eds.). (1996). *Post-theory: Reconstructing film studies.* Madison: University of Wisconsin Press.

CURRIE, C. B., McCONKIE, G. W., CARLSON-RADVANSKY, L. A., & IRWIN, D. E. (2000). The role of the saccade target object in the perception of a visually stable world. *Perception and Psychophysics, 62*(4), 673–683.

CUTTING, J. E. (1986). *Perception with an eye for motion.* Cambridge, MA: MIT Press.

FLAVELL, J. H. (2004). Development of knowledge about vision. In D. T. Levin (Ed.), *Thinking and seeing: Visual metacognition in adults and children* (pp. 13–36). Cambridge, MA: MIT Press.

HENDERSON, J. M., & HOLLINGWORTH, A. (1999). High-level scene perception. *Annual Review of Psychology, 50,* 243–271.

HOCHBERG, J. (1968). In the mind's eye. In R. N. Haber (Ed.), *Contemporary theory and research in visual perception* (pp. 309–331). New York: Holt, Rinehart & Winston.

HOCHBERG, J. (1986). Representation of motion and space in video and cinematic displays. In J. P. Thomas (Ed.), *Handbook of perception and human performance: Vol. 1. Sensory processes and perception* (pp. 22.21–22.64). New York: Wiley.

HOCHBERG, J. (1994). *Binding "what" and "where" across successive views: Theories, models, tests.* Paper presented at the annual meeting of the Psychonomic Society, St. Louis, MO.

INTRAUB, H. (1997). The representation of visual scenes. *Trends in Cognitive Sciences,* *1*(6), 217–222.

LEVIN, D. T., MOMEN, N., DRIVDAHL, S. B., & SIMONS, D. J. (2000). Change blindness blindness: The metacognitive error of overestimating change-detection ability. *Visual Cognition, 7,* 397–412.

LEVIN, D. T., & SIMONS, D. J. (2000). Perceiving stability in a changing world: Combining shots and integrating views in motion pictures and the real world. *Media Psychology, 2,* 357–380.

McCONKIE, G. W., & ZOLA, D. (1979). Is visual information integrated across successive fixations in reading? *Perception and Psychophysics, 25*(3), 221–224.

MESSARIS, P. (1994). *Visual literacy: Image, mind, & reality.* Boulder, CO: Westview.

MUNSTERBERG, H. (1916). *The photoplay: A psychological study.* New York: Dover.

O'DONNELL, C., & LANGTON, S. R. H. (2003). Gaze cues attenuate change blindness in the flicker paradigm. *Journal of Vision, 3*(9), 649a.

PHILLIPS, W. A. (1974). On the distinction between sensory storage and short-term visual memory. *Perception and Psychophysics, 16,* 283–290.

PRINCE, S. (1993). The discourse of pictures: Iconicity and film studies. *Film Quarterly, 47*(1), 16–28.

RENSINK, R. A. (2000). Visual search for change: A probe into the nature of attentional processing. *Visual Cognition, 7,* 345–376.

RENSINK, R. A. (2002). Change detection. *Annual Review of Psychology, 53,* 245–277.

RENSINK, R. A., O'REGAN, J. K., & CLARK, J. J. (1997). To see or not to see: The need for attention to perceive changes in scenes. *Psychological Science, 8*(5), 368–373.

RENSINK, R. A., O'REGAN, J. K., & CLARK, J. J. (2000). On the failure to detect changes in scenes across brief interruptions. *Visual Cognition, 7,* 127–146.

SIMONS, D. J. (1996). In sight, out of mind: When object representations fail. *Psychological Science, 7*(5), 301–305.

SIMONS, D. J., & LEVIN, D. T. (1997). Change blindness. *Trends in Cognitive Sciences, 1*(7), 261–267.

SIMONS, D. J., & LEVIN, D. T. (2003). What makes change blindness interesting? *Psychology of Learning and Motivation, 42,* 295–322.

38

On the Cognitive Ecology of the Cinema

Ed S. Tan

The contribution of psychology to an understanding of the cinema has been a limited one. After Hugo Münsterberg's *The Photoplay* (1916) and Rudolf Arnheim's *Film as Art* (1933/1958), only a few scattered studies appeared in press until the late 1970s, when James Gibson devoted a chapter to motion pictures, where he observed:

> The technology of cinema and television has reached the very highest level of applied science. The psychology of the awareness provided by a motion picture, however, is non-existent, apart from an essay by J. Hochberg and V. Brooks [1978a], to whom I am indebted for much good talk about the problems of film. (Gibson, 1979, p. 292)

Gibson's chapter presented an overview of the phenomenology of film "awareness," in itself quite important but imprecise. Hochberg and Brooks posed the right questions about understanding film, which were also informed by the applied science of cinema technology. The attempts to answer these questions in their original chapter and in various more-recent papers would constitute a concise but impressive volume. The theme of the volume would be the roles of knowledge and inference going beyond what is given in the stimulus in the perception of motion pictures. On this theme, their approach differs substantially from Gibson's, which emphasizes the selective pick-up of stimulus properties and especially invariants under transformation. Although Gibson was aware of the differences between perception of the world and of film, he did not flesh out the selective process in cinematic perception, which he considered in large part a mystery, as we shall see shortly. The discrepancy between the two views of cinema will not come as a surprise if we consider Hochberg's affinity throughout his work with the classical Helmholtzian tradition, in which visual perception is explained by unconscious inference, whereas Gibson's ecological view largely rejects the same tradition.

In this essay, a review of Hochberg and Brooks's proposals on the use of knowledge in cinematic comprehension will be presented. I will first review the role of inference in the relatively simple process of perceiving motion and in the more complex understanding of the relations between shots, the

562

basic cinematic units. Then I will discuss the contribution of knowledge to grasping the potentially highly complex communicative meaning of film and the concluding proposal that cinematic knowledge is an element of the ecology of the cinema no less fundamental than its typical technical and perceptual conditions. In closing, the importance of Hochberg and Brooks's research for film theory and psychology will be discussed.

The Role of Knowledge in Film Viewing: Perceiving Motion

Two levels of complexity of the film stimulus can be distinguished that are reflected in comprehension processes. At an elementary level of comprehension, viewers have to grasp the contents of shots. A *shot* is the image that corresponds to an uninterrupted camera take. Separate shots are edited into meaningful sequences. For example, shots portraying a speaking and a listening person can be edited into a dialogue sequence. At a more advanced level, viewers have to comprehend the connections between subsequent sequences. Let us start at the elementary level.

The basic problem in the comprehension of single shots, and a classic problem in the psychology of film as well, is that of perceiving motion. A shot is a series of static frames that is experienced as a moving image. Why and how do we perceive movement? Today, the classical explanation of perception as a mental representation of movement inferred as the most likely event in the world from changes in retinal location may seem far-fetched. In continuous shots, apparent object movement is seen automatically by the same motion-detection mechanism that identifies motion in the real world. No mental representation or inference is involved, or so it seems. However, a qualification of this statement is in place on empirical grounds. Slow-acting, long-range motions can be identified that require some mental representation of objects (Hochberg & Brooks, 1996b).[1] Also, an important theoretical reservation may be made. Hochberg and Brooks point out that neurophysiological motion detectors do not *explain* motion perception, that is, they "amend but do not demolish" an account based on a mental representation of motion (Hochberg & Brooks, 1996b, p. 226).

The film medium provides motion-dependent information about the 3D spatial layouts of scenes. A relevant question to ask here is how the viewer handles complications characteristic of the cinema. For instance, camera motion often introduces ambiguity, especially in so-called following shots, where a moving camera fixates a moving object. For the viewer, the object remains in a constant position on the screen, with a background moving in the opposite direction. The fact that in such cases the viewer perceives object motion is absolutely essential for the cinema, and Hochberg and Brooks demonstrated that some construal resolving the ambiguity inherent in the stimulus is necessary. *Induced motion*, as the phenomenon is called, affects the viewers' experience of direction and speed of moving objects as a result of complex interactions of the object itself, the camera, and background motion. Especially in Hochberg and Brooks (1996a), beautiful examples are provided of the intricate aesthetics of camera movement when filming a moving human figure, examples that can only be thought of if one has studied lots of filmed dance or, even better, filmed dance oneself, as Brooks has. Movement may be seen where there is not any, reversals of direction and apparent stasis may all occur, and even in parallel. Hochberg and Brooks (1996b) demonstrated that the way that complex movements are "parsed" into components depends on factors such as fixation point and even viewer intentions. What these examples make abundantly clear is that a direct, realist explanation of film awareness, as Gibson would have had it, would soon stumble on degrees of stimulus complexity too high to capture in optical array invariants; input from other mechanisms capable of selecting candidates for pick-up would be necessary.

The Role of Knowledge in Understanding Shot Transitions in Film Sequences

The power of cinema is not only in presenting objects in motion but also in gluing separate views together into meaningful sequences. How do we understand scenes presented in pieces, and what are the limits to our understanding? Gibson's answer to the question would be that the perceptual system extracts invariants from the two shots on either side of the cut (Gibson, 1979, p. 299). The account may be correct in many cases, because changes in camera viewpoint are often only minute, resulting in overlapping views, or the same object visible in the two shots may act as a landmark. But what if the overlap is less substantial or missing? Especially in Hochberg (1986), a really superb account was given of the various issues involved in understanding discontinuous transitions in film and of relevant findings in psychological research, such as studies of aperture viewing that mimic objects seen by a moving camera. It was argued that answers based on known mechanisms of sensory integration and Gibson's extraction of invariants fail to account for frequent and simple cinematic events, such as elision of space and time. Hochberg and Brooks propose a principled answer: that films play in the mind's eye. Viewers construct an offscreen mental space from separate views, and they can link two or more successive views by the relation of each of these to this space. In constructing a mental space, overlap may even be overruled by other cues that have nothing to do with any invariance. My favorite demonstration is the one in Hochberg and Brooks (1996b, pp. 256–257), in which a scene of three human figures standing before a building, gazing forward, left, and right, is cut into four overlapping views (see Figure 38.1). Overlap between successive views, the simplest source of invariance, is constituted by parts of a line of text and by "landmarks" in the

Figure 38.1. Gaze direction as a cue for the construction of the spatial layout of successive views. Reprinted from Hochberg and Brooks (1996b). Copyright © 1996. Used with permission from Elsevier. The original caption stated: "Layout in the mind's eye: not 'stimulus information,' but effective and less effective cues. Successive views (A and D, ca. 1 s; B and C, ca. 0.5 s) presented in continuous cycle (A–D, D–A, . . .). In this sequence, depicted gaze direction is opposed to the information provided by landmarks, and by the line of text; gaze direction prevails, in that A is predominantly reported to appear at the right and D at the left of the overall space."

background building: a column and a window. It turned out that the direction of the gazes of the figures in consecutive shots is the effective cue in the construction of the scene, overriding landmarks and text, just as experienced filmmakers would probably have predicted and as readers can verify. Gaze direction is a factor that goes far beyond the (mathematical) invariants to be picked up from the optical array offered by the screen and is in fact far removed from anything immediately given in the film stimulus.

The explanation based on the construction of a mental space allowed Hochberg and Brooks to address more specific and interesting questions about the role of the stimulus in relation to the use of knowledge, such as what parts of objects or events can be elided without affecting the experience of spatial or temporal continuity. Figure 38.2 illustrates the effective elision of events, making the point that some parts of an object or event are good building blocks for perceiving a three-dimensional object or a comprehensible scene, whereas others are not.

Comprehension of entirely discontinuous transitions, such as in alternating views of two characters simultaneously in different places ("parallel editing"), demands inference and knowledge use. It is here that Gibson admits that he is defied by the riddle of cinematic perception: "There is no overlap of structure between such alternating shots, but there must be some common invariants. What are they?" (Gibson, 1979, p. 300). If rhetorical questions can have an answer, Hochberg and Brooks's would be this: Expectations that guide the comprehension of cuts to new scenes and ones that are remote from the

Figure 38.2. What makes ellipses comprehensible? Reproduction of Figure 22.36 from Hochberg (1986). Copyright © 1986, John Wiley and Sons, Inc. This material is used with permission of John Wiley and Sons, Inc. The original caption stated: "Effective elision of events. (a) Two views through judiciously placed apertures of the same house, selected to be (i) informative and (ii) less informative. (b) A short event. (c) and (d) Sequences of four views chosen from (b), so as to be informative and uninformative, respectively. (e)(i) Sequence of man hopping across room, repetitively; (ii) subset of (i) chosen so that a man is perceived to float across room ('pixillation [*sic*],' a specialized form of strobing)."

566

previous one in terms of narrative time derive from knowledge of narrative in general and narrative films in particular. Thus, understanding nonoverlapping transitions requires recognizing larger story units, like complex events and episodes and rules for which of these can and cannot be left out of stories, to be explored by literary-analysis types of study (Hochberg, 1986, p. 22.50). However, a translation is required of such narrative structures into mental representations that are realistic in the sense that they include visual features, such as a definite viewpoint and a 2D composition layout. Theoretical or empirical proposals as to the nature of these representations are lacking at present (Hochberg & Brooks, 1996a, p. 382).

High-Complexity Knowledge Use: Film Viewing as a Communicative Act

Hochberg (1986) pointed out that perhaps the most complex cognitive process in cinematic understanding is watching film as a communicative act, "in which the viewer expects that the filmmaker has undertaken to present something in an intelligible fashion and will not provide indecipherable strings of shots" (p. 22.53). This *pragmatic* rather than *syntactic* or *morphological* understanding may act as a basis for instant problem solving, required when a viewer meets new stylistic options that cannot be dealt with using knowledge from previous examples, as is often the case in artistic cinema, but also in innovative commercial films. I would add to this that pragmatic understanding involves an awareness of cooperation with the filmmaker, in which viewers expect that their efforts will be sufficiently rewarded. In this respect, Hochberg and Brooks's research into *visual momentum*, or viewer interest (Brooks & Hochberg, 1976; Hochberg & Brooks, 1978b) has to be mentioned. They investigated the influence of cutting-rate and specific shot-content factors on variations of glance rate and looking preference, thus uniquely contributing to an understanding of the typical arresting effect of cinema viewing. There is no other research in perception psychology that helps us in understanding why, for example, a static shot "goes dead," as filmmakers say, if it is not refreshed in time by a slightly different view, or how the contents of the shot interact with "refresh rate." In a series of inventive experiments, Hochberg and Brooks gathered evidence for an impetus to gather visual information. Looking preference increased with cutting rate and with the complexity of shot contents. One of the findings implied that a delay of comprehension, caused by removing peripheral stimulus information signaling a change of contents, sustained visual momentum. Comparing the results of this research with film practice, it may be hypothesized that current cutting strategies meet the viewers' typical motivation for cognitive inquiry. The reward of comprehension is carefully dosed by varying the time allowed to the viewer to inspect objects and scenes, dependent on their novelty and complexity. It may also be expected that cutting strategies and corresponding expectations vary from one genre to another and that, in the less-current case, viewers still rely on the communicative intentions that they ascribe to the filmmaker.

The Cognitive Ecology of the Cinema

In explaining what film really is, Hochberg and Brooks focused on characteristic perceptual conditions set by cameras, cinematic displays, and editing practices, thus defining the ecology of cinematic perception, which differs from the ecology of the real world. They described the "canonical arrangement" of camera, projector, screen, and viewer, in which the viewer's eye receives the same sheaf of light rays from the scene's layout as did the camera when registering the scene. In this arrangement, there are already numerous ways in which identical arrays for the camera and for the viewer's eye are provided. However, viewers can deal with substantial deviations from the canonical arrangements, as everybody who has ever watched a movie from the front row side aisle may confirm.[2] Some violations of the canonical arrangement are even expressly *built into* most motion pictures (Hochberg, 1986, p. 22.18). An important example is the abundant use made by filmmakers of quasi movements, such as zooms and pans that replace real camera movements of dolly and tracking shots, respectively. In these cases, the viewer ignores departures from rigidity of shape and non-uniformities of movement in virtual space (Hochberg & Brooks, 1986, p. 22.20). Furthermore, the ecology of the cinema does not neatly fit with the paradigmatic conditions of research into the visual system in general. Hochberg and Brooks (1996b, p. 217) warned that current explanations of apparent motion are geared toward forming and testing theories about the structure of neurophysiology, rather than at explaining the perception of movement in moving pictures. More important, they have made it clear how far removed cinematic comprehension is from a solely bottom-up data-driven process and that it needs an intelligent mind's eye. The minimum achievement of the mind's eye is perceptual inference, enabling or even forcing us to see what is most likely to fit the sensory pattern. The likelihood of the candidates depends on knowledge, specified or instantiated in perceptual maps through which the mind's eye can more or less freely roam. The ecology of the cinema, then, is not determined by technical or perceptual conditions. It is a profoundly cognitive ecology: It includes the availability of knowledge obtained in the world and even more specifically in the cinema itself, which is shared by film viewers and filmmakers. It also contains the goals and intentions of viewers and filmmakers in a collaborative effort to make film viewing not only a coherent but also an involving experience. I believe that it is implied in this view that the viewer's competence may surpass canonical knowledge and involve a form of discovery. When knowledge of the world and knowledge obtained from known film examples are insufficient for comprehension, the viewer may engage in active problem solving and in large part constructing a most-likely inference. Which films do incite such constructive problem solving in which viewers is a matter to be decided upon by film theory and the sociology of the cinema.

Bridging the Gap Between Film Disciplines

If the study of perception and of film are neighboring houses, then Hochberg and Brooks provided one with a roof and the other with a foundation, the joint result being that they could be recognized *as* neighboring houses, not in the least by their inhabitants. Hochberg and Brooks provided perceptual psychologists with an outlook on higher mental processes sheltering perception from a flood of uninterpretable visual data. At the same time, they donated to film theorists a view on the basics of perception, pinpointing where and how "blind" sensory mechanisms and fast cognitive processes give way to slower, more-complex ones that interface with knowledge of the world and of narrative and film structures. In this way, they have opened up a scientific investigation of individual differences in film viewing—due to knowledge and "set" and the role of cultural conventions in understanding film—associated with narrative and film structures, including style.

Hochberg and Brooks's contribution to psychology at large, as the science of the mind, may be that, in studying cinematic perception, they created an outstanding case for the *poverty-of-the-stimulus* argument (Fodor, 1983), which states that if the output is richer than the input, then some work must have been performed by a "smart" cognitive module. They showed that film perception involves input from modules that add enrichment with knowledge from the social and cultural world. In this way, they helped to reintroduce content into psychological explanation, without getting stuck in gratuitous "flirtations with mentalism," as they call it, by neglecting sensory components of motion-picture perception (Hochberg & Brooks, 1996, p. 206).

A firsthand knowledge of the theory of film practice, generally absent in both psychologists and film theorists, enabled Hochberg and Brooks to explain why choices that are made in professional film production are considered good and bad, or at least why they matter. (And, by the way, I believe that it also helped them to develop an extraordinary talent for displaying the content of moving images in marvelous graphics that merit a place in one of Edward Tufte's volumes, 1990, 1997, on the most ingenious visualizations ever.) They have repeatedly observed that the marriage of filmmaking and explaining film is more than ever necessary, because now that the cinematic experience can be invoked by completely digitally produced images, we need a full understanding of the regularities that underlie perception and comprehension of the moving image. The flipside of the coin of digital production is that understanding film by making film (or versions of it) is becoming affordable to every psychologist interested in cinema and to every film scholar interested in the psychology of film viewing. Hochberg and Brooks, as film-viewing and film-creating psychologists, inspired a theoretical and experimental approach to the study of cinema aimed at understanding how it works.

I would like to close this chapter with a quote from Hochberg (1986, p. 22.60) that perfectly answers Gibson's complaint: "[The] need, the scientists, and the tools are now all in place, and we may expect rapid progress in this field of inquiry."

Notes

1. This is just one example of Hochberg's argument running throughout his work that fundamental processes need at least some control by higher-order influences. The most convincing one to me is his discussion of the role of Gestalt-like organization in figure-ground segregation in picture perception, which is of course fundamental to film perception as well (e.g., Hochberg, 1992–1993, 1998).

2. The phenomenon has been investigated by Cutting (1987).

References

ARNHEIM, R. (1958). *Film as art.* London: Faber & Faber. (Original work published in German, 1933)

BROOKS, V., & HOCHBERG, J. (1976). Control of active looking by motion picture cutting rate [Abstract]. *Proceedings of the Eastern Psychological Association, 49.*

CUTTING, J. E. (1987). Rigidity in cinema seen from the front row, side aisle. *Journal of Experimental Psychology: Human Perception and Performance, 13,* 323–334.

FODOR, J. A. (1983). *The modularity of mind.* Cambridge, MA: MIT Press.

GIBSON, J. J. (1979). *The ecological approach to perception.* Boston: Houghton-Mifflin.

HOCHBERG, J. (1986). Representation of motion and space in video and cinematic displays. In K. R. Boff, L. Kaufman, & J. P. Thomas (Eds.), *Handbook of perception and human performance: Vol. 1. Sensory processes and perception* (pp. 22.1–22.64). New York: Wiley.

HOCHBERG, J. (1992–1993). The construction of pictorial meaning. In T. A. Sebeok & J. Umiker-Sebeok (Eds.), *Advances in visual semiotics* (pp. 109–162). Berlin: Mouton-de Gruyter.

HOCHBERG, J. (1998). Gestalt theory and its legacy. In J. Hochberg (Ed.), *Perception and cognition at century's end* (pp. 253–306). San Diego, CA: Academic.

HOCHBERG, J., & BROOKS, V. (1978a). The perception of motion pictures. In E. C. Carterette & M. P. Friedman (Eds.), *Handbook of perception* (Vol. 10, pp. 259–304). New York: Academic.

HOCHBERG, J., & BROOKS, V. (1978b). Film cutting and visual momentum. In J. W. Senders, D. F. Fisher, & R. A. Monty (Eds.), *Eye movements and the higher psychological functions* (pp. 293–313). Hillsdale, NJ: Erlbaum.

HOCHBERG, J., & BROOKS, V. (1996a). Movies in the mind's eye. In D. Bordwell & N. Carroll (Eds.), *Post-theory* (pp. 368–387). Madison: University of Wisconsin Press.

HOCHBERG, J., & BROOKS, V. (1996b). The perception of motion pictures. In M. P. Friedman & E. C. Carterette (Eds.), *Cognitive ecology* (pp. 205–292). New York: Academic.

MÜNSTERBERG, H. (1916). *The photoplay: A psychological study*. New York: Appleton & Co.

TUFTE, E. R. (1990). *Envisioning information*. Cheshire, CT: Graphics Press.

TUFTE, E. R. (1997). *Visual explanations*. Cheshire, CT: Graphics Press.

39

Hochberg on the Perception of Pictures and of the World

H. A. Sedgwick

The Concept of Functional Fidelity

Pictures seem to pose a critical problem for perceptual theory because when looking at pictures we reliably report seeing things that are not there. A picture is a flat surface that, as Hochberg says, "acts not as a dappled surface, but as a substitute or surrogate for spatial arrangements of other entirely different objects" (1962, p. 23).

Two tempting and diametrically opposed resolutions of this problem readily present themselves. One is that picture perception is based on learned conventions associating certain pictorial forms with certain real objects; there is no intrinsic visual connection between a picture and what it represents, and so the problem is removed from the realm of perceptual theory. The other resolution is that a successful picture works by presenting to the eye the same array of light as would come from the object that the picture represents; picture perception is thus the same as ordinary perception, and so poses no special problem for perceptual theory.

In what is certainly one of the most dramatic and resonant studies in the history of experimental psychology, Hochberg and Brooks (1962) demolished both of these theories with one blow. They raised their own child to the age of almost 2 years with no (or minimal) exposure to pictures. The child, then being able to speak, was shown line drawings of various familiar objects (a car, a shoe, a doll, etc.) and identified them effortlessly. Picture perception is thus not a convention, like language, because the child had no opportunity to learn such conventions. Neither does picture perception depend on the light from the picture being the same as the light from the object, because a physical description of the wavelengths, intensities, and distribution of the light from a car would have almost nothing in common with the physical description of the light coming from a line drawing of the same car. Noting that line drawings can sometimes communicate even more effectively than relatively high-fidelity photographs, Hochberg (1962, p. 30) wrote: "Perfect physical fidelity is impossible and would not be of psychological interest if it were achieved, but perfect *functional* fidelity . . . is completely achievable and is of considerable psychological interest."[1]

Since the 1960s, Hochberg has engaged in a sustained investigation of what constitutes the "functional fidelity" linking a picture to what it represents (Hochberg, 1962, 1972, 1978a, 1978b, 1979, 1980, 1983, 1984, 1986a, 1994, 1996). The result is a uniquely rich and detailed body of ideas and findings that draws on perceptual theory to help explain how pictures work and that examines pictorial perception to enrich perceptual theory. It follows from this intertwining of concerns that much of Hochberg's work on pictures is, and is intended to be, directly applicable to all of perception. On the other hand, this work also displays a deep interest in pictures per se and the distinctive problems they pose for perceptual theory. This interest extends not only to pictures created specifically for laboratory study but also to historical paintings and drawings created by artists for diverse cultural purposes.[2]

The Role of the Optic Array in Producing Functional Fidelity

Hochberg (1962) examines the functional fidelity of line drawings, which in reality are just ribbons of pigment deposited on a surface. He gives a detailed analysis of the ways in which physical surfaces at different depths "will produce optic arrays similar to that produced by an outline drawing" (p. 33). His analysis centers on the importance of edges in perceiving the shape of an object, for which he offers evidence from retinal rivalry, metacontrast, and camouflage. He argues that "[a]s far as shape is concerned, what isn't edged is not perceived, and what is perceived is edged" (p. 34). Either through early experience or evolution, he suggests, "we enter early childhood with the tendency to see an *edge of a surface* each time a sufficiently large luminous discontinuity (or other stimulus for 'contour') confronts our eyes" (p. 34).

The Role of Peripheral Vision in Producing Functional Fidelity

Not all of the elements of functional fidelity can be found in the relations between the optic arrays produced by pictures and by physical surfaces. Instead, most aspects of functional fidelity depend on the characteristics of the human visual system. To take one example, a key feature of human vision, well known but often neglected in perceptual theory, is the inhomogeneity of the retina, which provides detailed vision only at the center of gaze and increasingly coarse vision in the periphery. Hochberg has made this distinction central to his understanding of perception both of pictures and of the world. Eye movements are essential to scan the optic array, and peripheral vision takes on a dual role with respect to them. As he writes (1996, p. 172), "The eye has the wide field of peripheral vision as a form of online storage, a very impoverished reminder of where the fovea had been directed and a preview of what it might find at other loci in the field of view." In Hochberg's view, the functional fidelity of pictures depends in part on the limitations of peripheral vision: "With their low resolution (no detail, no texture, etc.) peripheral views of the real world and of its pictures must differ little from each other, and the contours at objects' edges, corners, and occlusions must be most important."

The low resolution of peripheral vision also suggests to Hochberg an ingenious, if partial, solution to the problem of how the observer deals with the cues that identify the picture as an object in itself, a flat, pigmented, physical surface. As Gibson (1951) had noted, one salient difference between pictures and real scenes is that a picture is delimited by its edges, which specify that the picture is actually a flat surface. Hochberg (1962, p. 40), while acknowledging this, suggests:

> [P]erhaps one sees a picture as a tridimensional scene merely by keeping his gaze away from the edges of a picture. This specialized restriction of gaze—and perhaps a decreased attention to the binocular localization [of the picture surface] through suppression of the contribution of one edge—may well comprise all or most of the "learning" to use pictures of objects or scenes.

The Role of Schematic Maps in Producing Functional Fidelity

Complementing peripheral vision, in Hochberg's view, are the use of mental structures—schematic maps—that "motivate successive glances of perceptual inquiry, guide the acts by which the questions are answered, serve as the criteria that terminate the inquiry, and provide for storing the results of the inquiry" (1996, p. 171). He approximates the situation arising from a series of fixations by displaying pictures, such as a line drawing of a house, through small circular apertures that show only fragments of the picture, and he argues that in seeing the house through holes in a near surface, "the viewer must fit some imaginary object to the fragmentary stimulus display" (1980, p. 56). The point of this demonstration, which Hochberg notes is not quite the same situation as in normal perception, is that such an ability "exists in our perceptual repertory" (1980, p. 58). In a crucial statement, he explains the existence of such mental structures by saying:

> [P]ictures are not unique in being ambiguous and incomplete: The objects of the world, as they are glimpsed within each momentary glance, are usually partially hidden from sight, and are ambiguous and incomplete as far as usable stimulus information is concerned. I believe that the *usable*

stimulus information in each momentary glance is inadequate to determine a truthful perception of the world in terms of that stimulation alone; I believe that mental structures of sensory expectation are developed to bridge the successive glances at the world; that the differences between realistic pictures and many of the scenes they represent may be negligible to the momentary glance; and that pictures therefore draw on mental structures normally developed in the service of seeing the real world. (1980, p. 59)

Hochberg thus believes there to be multiple, complexly related determinants of perception, both of pictures and of the world; these appear to include the usable focal information in the momentary glance, the much sparser but usable peripheral information in the momentary glance, sensory expectations concerning successive glances, and perhaps other mental structures, such as those that "imagine" complete objects when only partially occluded objects are visible.

The Role of the Creator in Producing Functional Fidelity

An important insight of Hochberg's is that the functional fidelity of pictures is not mechanically guaranteed by the process of their creation but instead depends upon the person who creates the picture: "The artist and photographer must still 'compose' their pictures if scenes and objects are to be recognizable (and also to lead the eye where it should go . . .)" (1962, p. 43). He offers detailed analyses of several compositional devices whereby artists increase the functional fidelity of their pictures. For example, he describes a technique, which he calls *focal chiaroscuro*, used by Rembrandt:

A few areas of the picture are provided with relatively sharp detail and with reflectances in the middle range, whereas the remainder of the painting is either very dark or very light, and is executed in a blurred and sketchy way that *looks natural only to peripheral vision*. This procedure, and the composition of the painting, constrains the viewer's gaze predominantly to the focal regions. (1980, p. 82)

A related example is the technique of *sfumato*, introduced by Leonardo da Vinci, in which the edges of represented objects are blurred. In Hochberg's words:

I believe that such blurring serves at once to make the discrepancy between picture and real edge less determinate; to simulate the blurring that must normally prevail in the retinal image of a horizon . . . when the eye is focused on the near bulge of a convex object; and most important, by tending to keep the viewer from looking directly at the blurred edge, to obtain the advantage of reducing the conflict between real and represented edge depth. (1980, p. 66)

Linear perspective can produce compelling depth in a picture but is also a source of problems for the artist. A realistic-perspective picture has only one correct viewpoint. From any other viewpoint, the virtual space that is geometrically specified by the picture's perspective is distorted in various ways (Pirenne, 1970; Sedgwick, 1980, 1991). Moreover, with a picture that subtends a wide visual angle, objects in the periphery of the picture may appear distorted even when viewed from the correct viewpoint. Hochberg discusses a variety of ways that artists deal with these problems. Leonardo da Vinci's solution, called *synthetic perspective* (Hochberg, 1996, p. 164), is to draw the perspective from multiple viewpoints, each local to a portion of the picture. Alternatively, Hochberg points out (1996, p. 166), the picture's creator may choose to avoid the use of obvious perspective (by not introducing extended receding edges) and may instead use more robust information for depth, such as is provided by interposition (and, one might add, by the ground plane; see Sedgwick, 2003).

The Artistic Subversion of Functional Fidelity

Hochberg couples the recognition of the creator's role in enhancing the functional fidelity of a picture with the recognition that conversely the picture's creator may deliberately lessen its functional fidelity. In a fascinating analysis of techniques used in some of Matisse's paintings, Hochberg shows how Matisse uses the Gestalt principle of good continuation to deliberately flatten the perceived depth: The T-junctions normally created by interposition are avoided by rounding the interrupted line so that it continues into the interrupting line; and lines and edges that are at different distances in the depicted scene are made to coincide on the picture surface so that they appear to be in the same depth plane (1980, p. 73). Hochberg also discusses how Cézanne flattened his pictures in foveal vision by "repeat[ing] the color of the background for a short distance within the object's outline" (1980, p. 88). Hochberg argues that, with techniques such as those that deliberately flatten its depth, "the picture proclaims to the viewer that it is the purposive creation of an individual painter, and that it cannot be considered mainly in terms of the scene that it presents" (Hochberg, 1980, p. 88).

The Limits of Prediction

Finally, although a picture may have good functional fidelity, and we may have a good understanding of how this fidelity is achieved, Hochberg points out that this does not mean that we can predict what a given viewer will perceive when looking at a picture. As he says, because of the very limited extent of detailed vision, "[w]hen one looks at a picture, one does not (and cannot) direct the eyes everywhere" (1996, p. 170). Although studies of viewers' eye movements when looking at pictures have been able to make broad statistical generalizations to the effect that more-informative areas of a picture are looked at more than less-informative areas (Buswell, 1935), and although Hochberg in his earlier work expressed a guarded optimism about eventually "knowing where people will look in a pictorial display" (1962, pp. 51–52), his later work seems to reject this possibility, both for pictures and for the real world. He concludes:

> One therefore looks at pictures (and at the world) piecemeal. Perceptions must fit that set of limited glances . . . that are free to continue at length or to terminate after only a very small proportion of the visual field has been brought to detailed foveal vision. *Because glances are purposeful, elective actions, one cannot in advance say what parts of the information in the light offered to the eye by picture or world will in fact be sampled.* (1996, p. 171)

The Role of Pictures in the General Study of Perception

One very important consequence of the concept of the functional fidelity of pictures is that it provides a theoretical justification for the use of pictures in the more general study of perception. Much of the perceptual research preceding Hochberg, including most of the work of the Gestalt psychologists, as well as a significant portion of Hochberg's own perceptual research, uses pictures in the investigation of perception. As an example of this, we may follow one theoretically central thread of research. One of the earliest demonstrations in perceptual psychology, and still one of the most famous, was Necker's 1832 line drawing of a transparent rhomboid, more commonly drawn as a cube, which demonstrated that the same physical display could be seen in two distinct organizations and that which organization was seen could be influenced by where one fixated (cited in Boring, 1942, pp. 268–269). Kopfermann (1930, cited in Koffka, 1935, p. 159) demonstrated that the two-dimensional patterns produced by different views of a transparent cube differed from each other in the degree to which they were seen as two- or three-dimensional. Koffka (1935, p. 159) used line drawings of these Kopfermann cubes to argue that the perception of tridimensionality depended on Gestalt principles of organization such as "good shape" and "good continuation." Hochberg and McAlister (1953), asserting that "empirical study of the Gestalt principles of perceptual organization is . . . frequently made difficult by their subjective and qualitative formulation," used similar line drawings of the Kopfermann cubes in an attempt to validate a quantitative measure of simplicity that could predict whether a figure would be perceived as two- or three-dimensional. This approach, by Hochberg's own account (2003), was later shown to be untenable by using the Penrose and Penrose (1958) line drawing of an "impossible" triangle. By modifying the Penrose drawing into a rectangular form that could then be stretched or compressed, Hochberg (1962) created his influential demonstration (discussed by many of the commentators in this volume) that the depth cues in a figure are only effective locally, so any global measure of simplicity must be unable to predict the perceived organization of the figure. Gillam (1979) closed this circle of demonstrations by showing that an elongated Necker cube constituted a "possible, impossible figure," both of whose ends were perceived to face forward without any obvious appearance of impossibility, thus showing that globally inconsistent local organizations could be preferred in perception even when a simpler globally consistent organization was possible. That this whole sequence of research, in which Hochberg's contributions are central, has anything to tell us about perception in general, rather than just about line drawings, depends on the functional fidelity of pictures.

Conclusion

This brief commentary has been able to give only some of the gist of Hochberg's extensive work on pictures and the concept of functional fidelity, but it is perhaps enough to suggest the complexity and importance of this work and the degree to which Hochberg's more-general theories of the visual perception of the world draw on his work on pictures.

Notes

1. Here, as elsewhere in this essay, the use of italics in the quotation is Hochberg's.
2. Several of Hochberg's papers on pictures are included in the present volume (chapters 5, 12, 15, and 19 are Hochberg 1962, 1972, 1980, and 1984, respectively, and chapter 6 is Hochberg & Brooks, 1962). Complementary to Hochberg's work on pictures, and extending it through the inclusion of motion and events, is his work, in collaboration with Virginia Brooks, on film (Hochberg, 1986b, 1989; Hochberg & Brooks, 1973, 1978a, 1978b, 1989, 1996a, 1996b; Hochberg, Brooks, & Fallon, 1977). Two of these papers are also included here (chapters 14 and 20 are Hochberg & Brooks, 1978a and 1996a, respectively). This work on film is discussed by several of the other commentaries in this volume.

References

BORING, E. G. (1942). *Sensation and perception in the history of experimental psychology.* New York: Appleton-Century-Crofts.
BUSWELL, G. T. (1935). *How people look at pictures.* Chicago: University of Chicago Press.

GIBSON, J. J. (1951). What is a form? *Psychological Review, 58,* 403–412.

GILLAM, B. (1979). Even a possible figure can look impossible! *Perception, 8,* 229–232.

HOCHBERG, J. (1962). The psychophysics of pictorial perception. *Audio-Visual Communications Review, 10,* 22–54.

HOCHBERG, J. (1972). The representation of things and people. In E. H. Gombrich, J. Hochberg, & M. Black (Eds.), *Art, perception and reality* (pp. 47–94). Baltimore: Johns Hopkins University Press.

HOCHBERG, J. (1978a). Visual art and the structures of the mind. In S. S. Madeja (Ed.), *The arts, cognition and basic skills* (pp. 151–172). St. Louis, MO: CEMREL.

HOCHBERG, J. (1978b). Art and perception. In E. C. Carterette & M. P. Friedman (Eds.), *Handbook of perception* (Vol. 10, pp. 225–258). New York: Academic.

HOCHBERG, J. (1979). Some of the things that paintings are. In C. F. Nodine & D. F. Fisher (Eds.), *Perception and pictorial representation* (pp. 17–41). New York: Praeger.

HOCHBERG, J. (1980). Pictorial function and perceptual structures. In M. A. Hagen (Ed.), *The perception of pictures* (Vol. 2, pp. 47–93). New York: Academic.

HOCHBERG, J. (1983). Problems of picture perception. *Visual Arts Research, 9,* 24.

HOCHBERG, J. (1984). The perception of pictorial representations. *Social Research, 51,* 841–862.

HOCHBERG, J. (1986a). Visual perception of real and represented objects and events. In N. J. Smelser & D. R. Gerstein (Eds.), *Behavioral and social science: Fifty years of discovery* (pp. 249–298). Washington, DC: National Academy Press.

HOCHBERG, J. (1986b). Representation of motion and space in video and cinematic displays. In K. Boff, J. Thomas, & L. Kaufman (Eds.), *Handbook of perception and human performance* (Vol. 1, pp. 1–64). New York: Wiley.

HOCHBERG, J. (1989). The perception of moving images. *Iris, 5,* 41–68.

HOCHBERG, J. (1994). Construction of pictorial meaning. In T. A. Sebeok & J. Umiker-Sebeok (Eds.), *Advances in visual semiotics: The semiotic web 1992–93* (pp. 110–162). Berlin: Mouton de Gruyter.

HOCHBERG, J. (1996). The perception of pictures and pictorial art. In M. P. Friedman & E. C. Carterette (Eds.), *Cognitive ecology* (pp. 151–203). New York: Academic.

HOCHBERG, J. (2003). Acts of perceptual inquiry: Problems for any stimulus-based simplicity theory. *Acta Psychologica, 114,* 215–228.

HOCHBERG, J., & BROOKS, V. (1962). Pictorial recognition as an unlearned ability: A study of one child's performance. *American Journal of Psychology, 75,* 624–628.

HOCHBERG, J., & BROOKS, V. (1973). *The perception of television displays.* New York: Experimental Television Laboratory of the Education Broadcasting System.

HOCHBERG, J., & BROOKS, V. (1978a). Film cutting and visual momentum. In J. W. Senders, D. F. Fisher, & R. A. Monty (Eds.), *Eye movements and the higher psychological functions* (pp. 293–313). Hillsdale, NJ: Erlbaum.

HOCHBERG, J., & BROOKS, V. (1978b). The perception of motion pictures. In E. C. Carterette & M. P. Friedman, *Handbook of perception* (Vol. 10, pp. 259–304). New York: Academic.

HOCHBERG, J., & BROOKS, V. (1989). Perception of still and moving pictures. In E. Barnouw (Ed.), *International encyclopedia of communications* (Vol. 3, pp. 255–262). New York: Oxford University Press.

HOCHBERG, J., & BROOKS, V. (1996a). Movies in the mind's eye. In D. Bordwell & N. Carroll (Eds.), *Post-theory: Reconstructing film studies* (pp. 368–387). Madison: University of Wisconsin Press.

HOCHBERG, J., & BROOKS, V. (1996b). The perception of motion pictures. In M. P. Friedman & E. C. Carterette (Eds.), *Cognitive ecology* (pp. 205–292). San Diego, CA: Academic.

HOCHBERG, J., BROOKS, V., & FALLON, P. (1977). Motion organization effects with successive static displays ("stop action"). *Scandinavian Journal of Psychology, 18,* 187–191.

HOCHBERG, J., & McALISTER, E. (1953). A quantitative approach to figural "goodness." *Journal of Experimental Psychology, 46,* 361–364.

KOFFKA, K. (1935). *Principles of Gestalt psychology.* New York: Harcourt, Brace & World.

KOPFERMANN, H. (1930). Psychologische Untersuchungen uber die Wirkung zweidimensionaler Darstellungen koperiicher Gebilde. *Psychologische Forschung, 13,* 293–364.

PENROSE, L., & PENROSE, R. (1958). Impossible figures: A special type of visual illusion. *British Journal of Psychology, 49,* 31–33.

PIRENNE, M. H. (1970). *Optics, painting and photography.* Cambridge, UK: Cambridge University Press.

SEDGWICK, H. A. (1980). The geometry of spatial layout in pictorial representation. In M. Hagen (Ed.), *The perception of pictures* (Vol. 1, pp. 33–90). New York: Academic.

SEDGWICK, H. A. (1991). Effects of viewpoint on the virtual space of pictures. In S. R. Ellis (Ed.), *Pictorial communication in virtual and real environments* (pp. 460–479). London: Taylor & Francis.

SEDGWICK, H. A. (2003). Relating direct and indirect perception of spatial layout. In H. Hecht, R. Schwartz, & M. Atherton (Eds.), *Looking into pictures* (pp. 61–75). Cambridge, MA: MIT Press.

40

Celebrating the Usefulness of Pictorial Information in Visual Perception

Jeremy Beer

I encountered Julian Hochberg's constructivist approach to perception as his doctoral student at Columbia University. In the years since, this approach has continued to influence the design of my experiments, especially those examining the moving viewer's perception of scenes and events, and to guide my thinking about perception in general. One of its particular strengths is that it has transcended polemic, not because it lacked unifying principles and strong opinions (indeed, some of these principles and opinions have provoked heated debate), but rather because the approach was so purely empirical. In my recollection, whenever Hochberg encountered a conflict between two theories of perception, he would work swiftly to articulate an unambiguous prediction from each and then craft an experimental test to determine which would prevail. In devising this empirical test, he would always pose a specific question regarding the perceptual component of interest; importantly, this question was usually not "Can the viewer use this class of information?" but rather the more probing "*Does* the viewer use this class of information even when other sources are available?" Observing this rigorous empirical approach in Hochberg's laboratory taught me to be careful about wielding a rigid and universal theoretical hammer to attack questions in perception.[1] The experiments I performed with him taught me that the factors underlying a perceptual competence can change in the presence of stimulus transformations, and also that tolerance of such transformations is engineered into some of these underlying perceptual components.

Hochberg's view of perception has remained particularly influential to me in three areas: the respective roles of motion versus pictorial information in the perception of three-dimensional configurations and events; the similar conflict between dynamic and pictorial information in the judgment of time-to-contact; and the effects of display boundaries on the dimensions of space perceived by the viewer.

Ames Phenomena: Pictorial Cues Versus Motion in Depth and Event Perception

Throughout my time at Columbia, a squadron of Ames windows and Ames-derived objects stood prominently in the Hochberg lab, defying bystanders to ignore their persistent rubberiness. These devices hold a personal significance for me because I remember everyone in the lab discussing them, playing with them, and feeling taunted by them over the years, in spite of the fact that we were all continually and variously engaged in any number of other projects.

The Ames object is a trapezoidal contour with converging edges and shading cues painted on both faces, which induces the illusion of a rectangular window slanting into depth. Because of the pictorial depth cues of linear perspective and relative size (whereby objects that subtend lesser visual angles are perceived as farther away than objects that subtend greater visual angles), Ames windows are almost always perceived as if the shorter edge is more distant, even when it actually juts forward. This leads to the classic Ames effect in which the trapezoid is rotated about a vertical axis, and the viewer instead perceives a window yawing back and forth in oscillation.

We employed the Ames objects in a sequence of experiments and demonstrations, all of which were constructed to pit the pictorial depth cues against motion information. The pictorial cues are misleading much of the time (viz., whenever the short edge is not farther away). In contrast, the motion information should specify the object's actual layout and slant, if viewers are capable of extracting a rigid configuration from the dynamic image transformations that occur during the object's, or their own, actively initiated movement.

In spite of this, none of our experiments was successful in reliably banishing the Ames objects' tendency to induce motion and depth illusions when viewed from any vantage point other than directly above, or within a short distance. Not content with the classic Ames demonstration in which the continuously rotating trapezoid appears to swing back and forth, we tried using an entertaining variety of devices to defeat the painter's cues. We replaced the painted shading with texture patterns, such as uniformly spaced dots, which increased the information specifying the trapezoid's flatness and introduced an optical motion gradient that was unbiased by false illumination cues; nevertheless, the perspective of the converging edges and the relative size of the vertical edges prevailed, and the rotating object still appeared to swing like a screen door. We pierced the window with a solidly mounted metal rod, and it still appeared to swing, now as an impossible figure with an apparently flexible bar repeatedly violating the continuity of its solid parts. We constructed a new figure comprising two Ames trapezoids back to back, and placed this rigid, planar, hexagonal figure in a yawing oscillation (an actual movement that resembled the illusion of yawing oscillation described above), and it appeared to crease along its central spine like a butterfly. Finally, we froze the original trapezoid in a fixed orientation with the short edge in front and had viewers generate motion by swaying their own vantage point from side to side. These movements made the stationary object appear to swing, because the perception of the trapezoid's optical deformation was coupled with the illusory, reversed perception of its slant: Assuming the depth cues' accuracy, the opening and closing of the object's image could be explained only if the window were yawing in synchrony with the viewer's movements. The fact that the cues were inaccurate does not alter their strength, nor their coupling with the viewer's interpretation of optical deformation. Throughout these situations, it became increasingly difficult to dismiss the pictorial cues as artifacts of a painted world, because they worked so effectively against motion information specifying the actual, rigid distal configuration. (See Hochberg, 1986, for a more detailed description of the conditions under which the Ames effects are observed.)

Augmenting visual displays with depth information has remained a fertile topic of inquiry. Van den Berg and Brenner (1994) and Vishton, Nijhawan, and Cutting (1994) claimed that adding veridical depth information enhances heading perception during self-motion (though Ehrlich et al., 1998, reported subsequently that this addition is not useful without an appropriate extraretinal eye-movement signal), and adding depth information to optic flow patterns reportedly increases MST neurons' heading selectivity and sensitivity during ocular pursuit (Upadhyay, Page, & Duffy, 2000).[2] In addition, the enhancement or addition of pictorial depth cues has been shown to influence the effectiveness of vehicle displays. Some years ago, I built up some virtual clouds to introduce illusory depth cues in a synthetic flight environment and found that these objects were capable of distorting a pilot's judgment of the aircraft sink rate in a landing approach task (Beer et al., 1998). And new-generation "pathway in the sky" aviation displays are designed specifically to add veridical perspective and relative size cues to the pilot's visual environment (Snow et al., 1999). My interest in these pictorial cues continues unabated, and some of my most vivid recollections about titrating visual depth information empirically remain those of our playful efforts to make the Ames window stand up for itself and look like an unyielding object in the Hochberg lab.

Relative Size Versus Motion in Time-to-Contact Judgment

The second area in which Hochberg's emphasis on pictorial depth information has proven influential in perception is that of time-to-contact judgments. Patricia DeLucia has produced a notable body of work in this area, which includes findings relevant to self-motion control, collision avoidance, and interceptive action (see chapter 28, this volume). Like the

Ames investigations, these studies juxtaposed optical motion information (which could, in theory, specify irrefutably the time remaining until a viewer will contact an approaching or approached object) and pictorial depth cues (which might be configured to alter or contradict the optically specified solution). In these experiments, DeLucia constructed environments in which the raw expansion information specified one perceived configuration while the pictorial cue of relative size could specify a contradictory solution. This line of research continued Hochberg's tradition of articulating conflicting predictions from competing theories clearly and then testing the predictions unambiguously.

An object's optical expansion can specify the time remaining until the object reaches the observer or vice versa (Lee, 1976); if the expansion remains above threshold, this information source is largely independent of the object's size. But, according to the relative-size cue, larger images typically belong to nearer objects (see above); for this reason, an observer approaching two objects that subtend different visual angles will expect to reach the larger object first, because it looks nearer. DeLucia first effected the competitive comparison between optical expansion and relative size in a paradigm that required the viewer to judge which of two approaching objects would arrive first (DeLucia, 1991). Large, distant objects were generally judged to arrive at the viewer's position before small, near objects that would actually have arrived sooner. In a subsequent study, DeLucia (1994) instructed subjects (who were controlling their movement in a visual self-motion simulation) to approach a fixed object as closely as possible and then jump over it without colliding. As was the case with the approaching objects, the landmarks' projected size influenced control movements consistently, with subjects jumping earlier to clear large objects than to clear small objects that they were approaching at equal speeds. These two sets of findings indicate that predictive models of distance perception and self-motion control must include the effects of pictorial information, particularly relative size.

It is worth noting that the interaction between visual-motion and pictorial-depth information, explored in these first two research areas, can cause unexpected perceptual consequences, particularly in observers viewing unfamiliar scenes. Once, while flying in a plane at high altitude, I looked down through a fine-grained layer of high clouds to a coarser layer of lower, larger clouds and experienced the shocking and persistent perception that the large clouds (which looked nearer, but weren't) were blasting forward at twice the speed of the aircraft. After some head scratching, I managed to reconcile this perception with my disbelief in 1000-knot jetstreams, by considering that relative size can alter the perception of distance in optic flow environments: I must have been fixating the small, near clouds, seeing them as more distant, and then misinterpreting the motion parallax caused by the large, far clouds streaming in my retinal field in the same direction as my own travel (Figure 40.1). When an observer moves through the world and fixates a stationary object located apart from the direction of

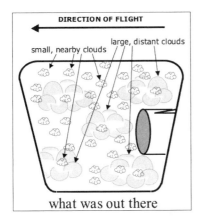
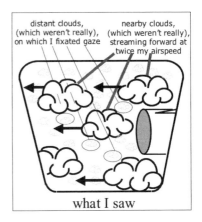

Figure 40.1.

locomotion, nearer stationary objects typically stream away from the aim point in the retinal field, while more-distant stationary objects stream toward it in the same direction as the viewer's movement (Cutting, 1986; Cutting et al., 1992). If the respective objects' relative nearness is perceived correctly, this retinal streaming is interpreted as an unsurprising manifestation of their fixedness in the world, whereas if the perceived order of nearness is altered by a misleading depth cue, the streaming can be perceived as an indicator of object motion (in this case, disconcertingly rapid motion).

Effects of Display Boundaries on the Perception of Extended Scenes

The third way in which Hochberg has been profoundly influential is through his emphasis on how a scene is typically perceived across a succession of views, and on how this perception can be affected by the geometric boundaries governing the successive views. Shortly before I completed my doctorate in 1992, he expressed this emphasis forcefully and eloquently in a conversation regarding the proposed dichotomy between "what" and "where" processing streams in the brain (Ungerleider & Mishkin, 1982). Hochberg was clearly uncomfortable with the possibility that this dichotomy could be overinterpreted and adopted as dogma, in the face of evidence indicating that the divergence between the two classes of information is not absolute. I remember particularly his pointing out that sometimes a perception of the "what" kind is ambiguous or impossible unless and until the viewer manages to integrate information across a succession of "where" perceptions. In one demonstration of this principle, he displayed successive close-up views through a round aperture of the individual corners of a cross-shaped figure, which was much larger than the aperture (Hochberg, 1986). The sequence of partial still views was unintelligible, looking like a disjointed set of pictures of a clock face, unless some integrating structure was provided. One way to convey this structure was to present a prior "longshot" view of the entire object as seen from afar. Alternatively, the partial views could be tied together by moving the object behind the aperture to reveal its features over time. In the latter case, the perception of global shape depended on viewers' ability to integrate visual motion across time and thereby build up a defining group of "where" relationships among the object's components.

This building up of a spatial percept over time and across views comprised the foundation for my dissertation research, which examined the metric of the extended space that viewers can perceive when a viewing aperture (or a movie camera, or the viewer's limited instantaneous field of view) moves relative to the figures or landmarks in a scene. Examples of this perceptual competence include a driver's ability to maintain spatial awareness of other cars on the road as they move into and out of view (e.g., from the windshield to the rear-view mirror) and also the moviegoer's ability to understand the layout of a room depicted by a moving camera even when the room is never shown in its entirety.[3]

In a series of experiments, we used chronometric modeling to map the extended spaces that viewers perceived while observing simulated self-motion displays in which the camera tracked laterally (Beer, 1993). The viewer's task was to press a button during the camera movement to predict the emergence onscreen of a widely displaced peripheral target landmark, whose position in the scene had been shown in a prior longshot, or panoramic view (Figure 40.2). The experiments identified two characteristics of viewers' ability to perceive the dimensions of an extended scene configuration as revealed by a moving camera. First, viewers were able to integrate optic flow over time; specifically, they perceived their depicted self-motion fairly accurately as the integral of camera speed over time (including changes in speed and pauses in the movement), up to a limiting boundary. Within this boundary, it was determined that when the camera moved, viewers could predict the emergence of the target landmark at close to the ideal response time. This ideal time corresponded with the span of a camera movement that should be required to reveal the target, as specified in the prior view: The wider the lateral spacing of the target, the later the response, *up to the limiting boundary.*

The second characteristic identified in these experiments comprised this limiting boundary, beyond which the geometry of the perceived space defined by the button presses changed. When the prior panoramic view displayed a scene configuration so large that viewers had to integrate the lateral optic flow across an imagined span that was wider than the close-up view could display at one time, systematic distortions emerged in the space perceived beyond the edges of the screen. In particular, while the timing of

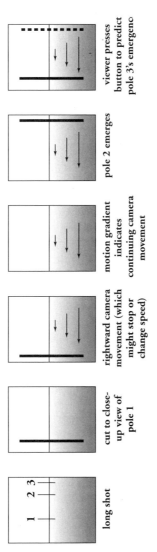

long shot

cut to close-up view of pole 1

rightward camera movement (which might stop or change speed)

motion gradient indicates continuing camera movement

pole 2 emerges

viewer presses button to predict pole 3's emergenc

Figure 40.2.

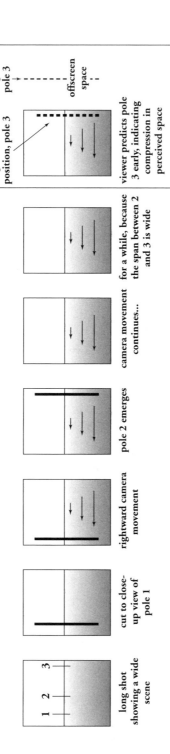

Figure 40.3.

long shot showing a wide scene

cut to close-up view of pole 1

rightward camera movement

pole 2 emerges

camera movement continues...

for a while, because the span between 2 and 3 is wide

viewer predicts pole 3 early, indicating compression in perceived space

predicted position, pole 3

correct position pole 3

offscreen space

the prediction responses continued to lengthen linearly with target distance when these very wide scenes were displayed (as it should if viewers were retaining information accurately from the prior view and using it to integrate the subsequent camera-motion information), the slope of the response-time curve flattened. Viewers were compressing these scenes perceptually and predicting the target landmark's emergence early, and the more the imagined span exceeded the width of the close-up view, the greater the scene compression became (Figure 40.3). This compression effect indicated that while viewers are capable of using remembered information in conjunction with optic flow to perceive and generate expectations about scenes extending beyond the edges of the display, there are boundaries beyond which this perception departs from a Euclidean metric. Nevertheless, it remains true that to the extent a remembered geographic configuration comprises a "what" representation, generating it by integrating motion information across a succession of partial views constitutes a perceptual building up among "where" representations, just as Hochberg suggested.

Conclusion

In these and in other areas of inquiry, Hochberg's approach to perception has influenced me meaningfully, as it has influenced the fields of vision science, human engineering, and film theory. Had I not stumbled into a teaching assignment with him many years ago, I would not have been drawn in by his enthusiasm for projective geometry, by his rigorous emphasis on the importance (and the limitations) of optic flow, and by his unflagging celebration of pictorial information in perception. This celebration has enriched my understanding and experience, because thinking about perception is its own reward, a reward that is particularly satisfying when one is exploring among the landmarks, textures, monuments, shadows, vehicles, and figures of a novel environment.

Notes

1. Minimum principles, assertions of direct perception, and computational reverse-projection algorithms are examples of theoretical tools that turn brittle when it is demonstrated that viewers tolerate certain inconsistencies in a visual display. These inconsistencies include the coexistence of mutually contradictory spatial information, impossible geometric transformations, and the depiction of nonrigidity in the structure of distal objects.

2. In this last study, the depth information comprised the addition of speed planes (texture planes whose disparate distances are coded by their relative optical-expansion rates). In this context, the "depth cue" to which the neurons responded was the ordered motion parallax that emerges among multiple objects as the viewer

moves through the three-dimensional world, or among multiple vertices as they move in a structured configuration. Like many information sources, this one is not bulletproof: If it were, there would be no Ames phenomenon.

3. This ability to perceive extended spaces behind and beyond the edges of the screen is demonstrated clearly when one is given the opportunity to explore an actual scene that has been viewed previously in a cinematic sequence or a computer-generated graphic rendering. With the advent of virtual architectural tours and simulated mission rehearsals, the commercial and operational application of this perceptual competence is becoming commonplace. Its power remains striking, however, as I discovered a few months ago at a diner near Barstow, California, which I had seen previously in the strange and atmospheric film *Bagdad Café*. As I entered the store, I was familiar with its configuration; I knew in a relative sense where the tables and counter and adjoining rooms would be (though according to the research described above, I might not have known exactly how many steps would be required to move from one of these features to another).

References

BEER, J. M. A. (1993). Perceiving scene layout through an aperture during visually simulated self-motion. *Journal of Experimental Psychology: Human Perception and Performance, 19,* 1066–1081.

BEER, J. M. A., GHANI, N., PREVIC, F. H., & CAMPBELL, J. M. (1998). Speed can influence aim-point judgments even before illusory depth cues enter the picture. *Perception, 27* (Suppl.: *Proceedings of the European Conference on Visual Perception*), 58.

CUTTING, J. E. (1986). *Perception with an eye for motion.* Cambridge, MA: MIT Press.

CUTTING, J. E., SPRINGER, K., BRAREN, P. A., & JOHNSON, S. H. (1992). Wayfinding on foot from information in retinal, not optical, flow. *Journal of Experimental Psychology: General, 121,* 41–72.

DELUCIA, P. R. (1991). Pictorial and motion-based information for depth perception. *Journal of Experimental Psychology: Human Perception and Performance, 17,* 738–748.

DELUCIA, P. R. (1994). Pictorial and motion-based depth information during active control of self-motion: Size-arrival effects on collision avoidance. *Journal of Experimental Psychology: Human Perception and Performance, 20,* 783–798.

EHRLICH, S. M., BECK, D. M., CROWELL, J. A., FREEMAN, T. C., & BANKS, M. S. (1998). Depth information and perceived self-motion during simulated gaze rotations. *Vision Research, 38,* 3129–3145.

HOCHBERG, J. (1986). Visual perception of real and represented objects and events. In N. J. Smelser & D. R. Gerstein (Eds.), *Behavioral and social science: Fifty years of discovery* (pp. 249–298). Washington, DC: National Academy Press.

LEE, D. N. (1976). A theory of visual control of braking based on information about time-to-collision. *Perception, 5,* 437–459.

SNOW, M. P., REISING, J. M., LIGGETT, K. K., & BARRY, T. P. (1999). Flying complex approaches using a head-up display. In R. S. Jensen (Ed.) *Proceedings of the 10th International Symposium on Aviation Psychology* (pp. 1–7). Columbus: Ohio State University.

UNGERLEIDER, L. G., & MISHKIN, M. (1982). Two cortical visual systems. In D. Ingle, M. Goodale, & R. Mansfield (Eds.), *Analysis of visual behavior* (pp. 549–586). Cambridge, MA: MIT Press.

UPADHYAY, U. D., PAGE, W. K., & DUFFY, C. J. (2000). MST responses to pursuit across optic flow with motion parallax. *Journal of Neurophysiology, 84,* 818–826.

VAN DEN BERG, A. V., & BRENNER, E. (1994). Humans combine the optic flow with static depth cues for robust perception of heading. *Vision Research, 34,* 2153–2167.

VISHTON, P. M., NIJHAWAN, R., & CUTTING, J. E. (1994). Moving observers utilize static depth cues in determining their direction of motion. *Investigative Ophthalmology & Visual Science, 35*(Suppl.), 2000 (Paper #3444).

41

Mental Structure in Experts' Perception of Human Movement

Dale S. Klopfer

My favorite figure in Hochberg's (1964) *Perception* text shows a row of seven "scribbles," each paired with a name (p. 100). The reader is invited to learn the name paired with each scribble and then to test him- or herself on a second row showing the scribbles in a different order. The scribbles, it turns out, are caricatures in profile, drawn so that their facial features match the names—the scribble paired with the label *Baby* looks like a baby, the one paired with *Ape* looks like an ape, and so on—but the resemblance is typically not seen unless the scribbles are rotated 90° clockwise. In their original orientation, the scribbles resemble Arabic script, and it is harder to learn the correct labels for the scribbles when they are rotated. One reason that I admire this figure is that it demonstrates elegantly how we fit sensory input to mental structures and how that process depends upon experience. Another is that I suspect that Julie drew those scribbles, and I like to visualize him beaming as he showed them to friends and colleagues.

The work described here, done in collaboration with Jackie Nelson-Paunil, extends the line of the scribbles by exploring the role of experience in the perception of human movement. Following from Chase and Simon's (1973) work with expert chess players, we expected that viewers with extensive experience studying dance and human movement would see dance sequences differently from their less-experienced counterparts.

Few psychologists have concerned themselves with the study of how dance is perceived. Virginia Brooks offered a detailed analysis of why the experience of watching a live dance performance can be so different from watching the same performance on film (Brooks, 1984). When making a film of a live performance, the director can inadvertently alter the sense of composition and rhythm that the choreographer intended by choosing poor shooting angles, changing the focal length of the lens inauspiciously, or editing sequences together without regard to maintaining continuity in how space and time are perceived. Brooks outlined principles for how dance ought to be filmed and called for empirical work to be done that would establish them.

An example of the sort of empirical work that Brooks described is Margot Lasher's studies of the cognitive representation of a short sequence of dance steps. She proposed that ballet sequences are made up of event units; their cognitive representations include a preparatory phase and a completing phase (Lasher, 1981). Preparatory phases include positions or steps in which a dancer is relatively stable and has a low center of gravity, as when both feet are on the ground. In completing phases, the dancer is unstable and typically has a higher center of gravity, as when balancing on one leg with arms raised. Lasher asked subjects to watch a sequence of ballet steps and then judge whether a two-step memory probe seen subsequently was contained in the original sequence. The probes were either preparatory-then-completing steps or completing-then-preparatory steps, and they either appeared in the original sequence as shown or were in the reverse order from how they appeared in the original sequence. Subjects falsely identified reversed (incorrect) unseen preparatory-then-completing probes as being in the original sequence, and correctly rejected reversed completing-then-preparatory probes. In addition, subjects readily identified seen (correct) preparatory-then-completing probes but had difficulty with the seen completing-then-preparatory probes. This pattern of results suggests that it is not necessarily the steps themselves that are encoded but whether they are relatively stable or unstable and whether they appear in a particular order. Lasher speculated that when watching dance, viewers use preparatory-then-completing event units to anticipate upcoming movements, looking, for example, for periods of relative stability that are punctuated by moments of instability.

The participants in Lasher's studies were not experts in dance but still demonstrated that they used cognitive representations while perceiving simple ballet sequences. It seems reasonable to expect that extensive experience with dance would result in the development of more-elaborate mental representations of movement at both finer and coarser levels of detail, consistent with current thinking on perceptual learning (see Goldstone, 1998). For example, an expert could see when the precise positioning of a dancer's foot was incorrect, and she would also be able to encode a longer sequence of choreographed steps than would a novice, corresponding, perhaps, to what is referred to as a *dance phrase* (Maletic, 1987).

Not surprisingly, experienced dancers have better memory for dance sequences than do less-experienced dancers. When asked to reproduce sequences that were eight steps long, skilled dancers exhibited better recall than did unskilled dancers (Starkes, Caicco, Boutilier, & Sevsek, 1990; Starkes, Deakin, Lindley, & Crisp, 1987). These findings are consistent with the idea that experience fosters an improved ability to encode and remember choreographed movements, perhaps by accessing cognitive representations of the sort that Lasher described.

It is interesting to compare different dance styles, such as ballet and modern dance (see McDonagh, 1976). Ballet is highly structured, consisting of well-established body positions, postures, facings, and movements, nearly all of which have verbal labels. Modern dance, on the other hand, is far less constrained; one could argue that movement in modern dance is constrained only by gravity and the laws of physics. Unlike in ballet, there are no "correct" positions or body alignments in modern dance (except in the mind of the choreographer). It is only a slight exaggeration to say that ballet epitomizes structure in dance whereas modern dance can be nearly without structure and less predictable.

Starkes et al. (1987) found that skilled ballet dancers' recall of a short choreographed ballet sequence was better than that of less-skilled ballet dancers. When the same elements or steps of the choreographed sequences were assembled randomly into unstructured sequences, however, memory was the same for both groups. This skill-by-structure interaction parallels Chase and Simon's (1973) findings that expert chess players recalled where pieces were on a chessboard far better than did novices, but only when the pieces were in positions taken from actual games; when pieces were randomly placed on the board, experts and novices performed similarly. The explanation of this finding is that chess experts have learned thousands of patterns of chess pieces that can occur in game situations, and they access these higher-order representations when encoding the chessboards. As a result, experts recall more pieces correctly than do novices, but only if the chessboards reflect the structure and constraints of the game. Analogous claims can be made for experienced and less-experienced ballet dancers.

Starkes et al. (1990) reported a different pattern of results in a subsequent study of experienced and less-experienced modern dancers. College-aged dancers with experience in a variety of dance styles were asked to recall short structured and unstructured modern dance sequences; a group of students with limited instruction in modern dance was asked to do likewise. The experienced dancers remembered the structured and unstructured sequences equally well; the novices remembered them equally poorly. That is, there was a main effect of skill level on recall but no skill-by-structure interaction.

It is tempting to believe that the presence and absence of the skill-by-structure interaction in ballet and modern dance, respectively, is due to the difference in the two dance styles. In a structured domain, the difference between random and structured stimuli is larger than in a less-structured domain. It is possible that the skilled modern dancers were unable to learn the limited structure of their dance style whereas the skilled ballet dancers were able to learn the rich structure of theirs. Yet, it might also be the case that the skilled ballet dancers were more highly skilled in ballet than the skilled modern dancers were in modern dance. Consequently, it is difficult to know whether the absence of a skill-by-structure interaction with modern dance is due to the minimal structure of modern dance or to differences in skill between the experienced ballet and modern dancers.

We sought to demonstrate a skill-by-structure interaction in the perception of dance using a within-groups design and an adaptation of

Newtson's (1973) technique for studying event perception. Newtson's participants watched a filmed event (e.g., someone repairing a radio) and pressed a button whenever an action unit occurred. There is substantial agreement across observers on the location of these action units, indicating that there is general consensus on how the behavior stream is parsed into smaller units (Newtson, 1973; Newtson, Engquist, & Bois, 1977; Newtson, Hairfield, Bloomingdale, & Cutino, 1987; Zacks, Tversky, & Iyer, 2001). We asked participants watching a filmed dance sequence to press a button whenever a movement unit occurred with the hope that there would be consensus, particularly among experts, on how dance sequences are parsed.

Because modern dance has minimal structure yet still consists of identifiable rhythmic movements, we expected that both experts and novices would be able to identify movement units when segmenting a modern dance performance. (Similarly, if people were asked to parse the scribbles seen horizontally into easily reproducible elements, there would likely be general agreement on where those points would be.) The ballet sequence, however, possessing the rich structure and vocabulary that only the experts would appreciate, would be difficult for the novices to segment.

Our experts were 16 certified movement analysts (CMAs) who were attending the national conference of the American Alliance for Health, Physical Education, Recreation, and Dance in 1998. All of the CMAs had received formal training in dance notation from the Laban Institute of Movement Studies and had an average of 15 years of professional dance experience, primarily in ballet and modern dance. Our novices were introductory psychology students, most of whom had no dance experience beyond the age of 10. CMAs were tested in a hotel room at the conference; novices were tested in a laboratory setting.

Our choice of filmed dance sequences was necessarily idiosyncratic. We used sequences containing a single dancer under the further conditions that the sequence contain no cuts and the performer must be visible in full view at all times (i.e., no close-ups). The ballet video (97 seconds long) showed a light, up-tempo piece with a ballerina performing a series of turns, leaps, and traveling steps. The modern piece (344 s) was slow and consisted of many rhythmic, circular movements and a great deal of work on the floor. For practice, we showed a movie clip of Fred Astaire tap dancing (73 s). We also showed a videotape of a mime (Marcel Marceau) at a party to explore how its narrative structure influenced the parsing of stylized movements. The results we obtained with the mime sequence are not germane to the current hypothesis and will not be reported here.

All sequences were presented in black-and-white and without sound. The tap sequence was always shown first, with the presentation of the remaining sequences counterbalanced across participants. Participants watched the sequences and pressed a button whenever a movement unit had occurred; no definition of movement unit was provided. The time stamp of each button press was recorded. We divided each sequence into 1-second bins and coded a button press that occurred during an interval as a "1" and the absence of a button press as a "0." The ballet sequence, then, yielded an array of 97 possible ones and zeros for each viewer.

As we did not know a priori how the movement units would be defined, we inferred them from points in the sequences where viewers agreed that a movement unit had just occurred. We recognized that there would necessarily be some agreement on the locations of the movement units by chance alone. For example, if two viewers pressed the button 50 times during a 100-s sequence (i.e., had press rates of 50%), by chance alone there would be 25 intervals during which they both pressed the button. To discriminate random from meaningful agreement, we used the viewers' press rates to compute the levels of chance agreement, which we then compared to the levels of agreement that were actually obtained. Accordingly, we could test whether the viewers agreed with each other more than would be expected by chance.

We found that we could reject the random model as a way of characterizing the responses from both CMAs and novices who segmented the modern sequence. Given the free-form nature of modern dance, viewers may have responded to sensory characteristics of motion, or *movement features* (Zacks, 2004), and perhaps to aspects of *temporal texture*, rhythmic motions that have statistical regularity, such as swaying or rocking (Polana, 1994, cited in Rao, Yilmaz, & Shah, 2002). Without analyzing the movements themselves, however, we cannot say to what the viewers responded, or whether the novices and CMAs responded to the same movements.

As for the ballet sequence, we rejected the random model as a way of characterizing the responses of the CMAs but retained it for describing the novices' responses. These findings were expected because the novices lacked the vocabulary of ballet movements that presumably enabled the CMAs to segment the ballet sequence into commonly agreed-upon units.

Because the modern piece was longer than the ballet, we wondered if novices' ability to agree upon the locations of movement units in the former but not in the latter were due to a practice effect. When we analyzed the responses to the first 100 s of the modern piece, however, novices still showed significant agreement. We also wondered if the novices couldn't agree upon the locations of movement units in the ballet piece because the tempo was too fast for them to detect movement units. Consequently, we showed the ballet sequence at half-speed to a second group of novices, but they still responded randomly.

It may be that both the novices and CMAs used "lower-order" aspects of stimulation (e.g., movement features) or general knowledge of human movement to segment the modern piece. Alternatively, the novices may have segmented the piece based upon lower-order stimulus information whereas the CMAs, who had experience with modern dance, may have responded to higher-order aspects of movement at a coarser level of analysis (see Zacks, 2004). The average press rates of the novices and CMAs did not differ, however, suggesting that the grain size of the movement units for both groups was the same.

The CMAs' experience with ballet appeared to confer an advantage in identifying movement units over the group with no dance experience. The CMAs agreed upon the locations of movement-unit boundaries in the ballet sequence whereas the novices did not. Because of their ballet experience, the CMAs knew, for example, that an *arabesque* is a pose that is often used to mark the end of a sequence of steps and that a *rond de jambe* is a circular movement of the leg that has well-defined beginning and ending points. This knowledge surely played a role in how they segmented the ballet sequence.

The dramatic difference between the segmenting of the ballet sequence by the CMAs and novices was presaged by what Julie wrote in "In the Mind's Eye": "Something like the way in which schematic maps seemed to bring . . . otherwise meaningless sequences . . . into manageable chunks . . . must surely be found in the perception of social movements and events" (Hochberg, 1968, p. 329). He called these mental structures *schematic sequences*, and he asserted that it is in these structures "that the effects of learning can be found." As it is with the scribbles, so it is with dance.

Acknowledgments

This research was supported by an interdisciplinary research grant from the College of Education and Human Development at Bowling Green State University awarded to J. Nelson-Paunil. We thank Donald Paunil for software support and Deanna Chase Elliot for help in testing the CMAs. I thank Mary Peterson and Barbara Gillam for the opportunity to contribute to this volume and for their helpful comments. Thanks are due as well to Patricia C. Smith for her critical reading of this chapter.

References

BROOKS, V. L. (1984). Why dance films do not look right: A study in the nature of the documentary of movement as visual communication. *Studies in Visual Communication, 10,* 44–67.

CHASE, W. G., & SIMON, H. A. (1973). Perception in chess. *Cognitive Psychology, 4,* 55–81.

GOLDSTONE, R. L. (1998). Perceptual learning. *Annual Review of Psychology, 49,* 585–612.

HOCHBERG, J. E. (1964). *Perception.* Englewood Cliffs, NJ: Prentice-Hall.

HOCHBERG, J. (1968). In the mind's eye. In R. N. Haber (Ed.), *Contemporary theory and research in visual perception* (pp. 309–331). New York: Holt, Rinehart, and Winston.

LASHER, M. D. (1981). The cognitive representation of an event involving human motion. *Cognitive Psychology, 13,* 391–406.

MALETIC, V. (1987). *Body, space, expression: The development of Rudolf Laban's movement and dance concepts.* New York: Mouton de Gruyter.

McDonagh, D. (1976). *The complete guide to modern dance.* Garden City, NY: Doubleday.

Newtson, D. (1973). Attribution and the unit of perception of ongoing behavior. *Journal of Personality and Social Psychology, 28,* 28–38.

Newtson, D. Engquist, G., & Bois, J. (1977). The objective basis of behavior units. *Journal of Personality and Social Psychology, 35,* 847–862.

Newtson, D., Hairfield, J., Bloomingdale, J., & Cutino, S. (1987). The structure of action and interaction. *Social Cognition, 5,* 191–237.

Rao, C., Yilmaz, A., & Shah, M. (2002). View-invariant representation and recognition of actions. *International Journal of Computer Vision, 50,* 203–226.

Starkes, J. L., Caicco, M., Boutilier, C., & Sevsek, B. (1990). Motor recall of experts for structured and unstructured sequences in creative modern dance. *Journal of Sport & Exercise Psychology, 12,* 317–321.

Starkes, J. L., Deakin, J. M., Lindley, S., & Crisp, F. (1987). Motor versus verbal recall of ballet sequences by young expert dancers. *Journal of Sport Psychology, 9,* 222–230.

Zacks, J. M. (2004). Using movement and intentions to understand simple events. *Cognitive Science, 28,* 979–1008.

Zacks, J. M., Tversky, B., & Iyer, G. (2001). Perceiving, remembering, and communicating structure in events. *Journal of Experimental Psychology: General, 130,* 29–58.

Part III

*Julian Hochberg: Biography
and Bibliography*

Julian Hochberg

Biography

Julian Hochberg was born on July 10, 1923, in New York City. Like so many highly distinguished scientists, he attended the College of the City of New York (City College), majoring in physics. He was a graduate student at Berkeley in the latter days of Tolman and the time of Brunswik. On completion of his Ph.D., he took up his first academic appointment in 1949 as an instructor at Cornell, where he became a professor in 1960. He moved back to New York City in 1965 as a professor at New York University. In 1969, he became a professor at Columbia University, where he remained until his retirement.

Julian Hochberg

Hochberg has received many honors, among them election to the National Academy of Sciences, the American Academy of Arts and Sciences, and the Society of Experimental Psychologists; his awards include a Guggenheim fellowship, the Warren Medal of the Society of Experimental Psychologists, and an honorary degree from Columbia University. He has also assumed many responsibilities, including the presidencies of the Eastern Psychological Association and of two divisions of the American Psychological Association (Division 3: Experimental Psychology and Division 10: Psychology and the Arts); the chair of Section J (Experimental Psychology) of the American Association for the Advancement of Science, appointments to National Academy of Sciences and National Research Council committees in sensory processes and human factors, and two terms as chair of the Psychology Department at Columbia University. In addition, he has also served on the boards of major journals, including *Psychological Review*, *American Journal of Psychology*, *Journal of Experimental Psychology: General*, and *Journal of Experimental Psychology: Human Perception and Performance*. A list of his publications in chronological order follows.

Bibliography

HOCHBERG, J. E., GLEITMAN, H., & MacBRIDE, P. D. (1948). Visual threshold as a function of simplicity of form. *American Psychologist, 3,* 341–342.

HOCHBERG, J., & GLEITMAN, H. (1949). Toward a reformulation of the perception-motivation dichotomy. *Journal of Personality, 18,* 180–191.

HOCHBERG, C. B., & HOCHBERG, J. E. (1950). Familiar size as a "cue" in the perception of "depth" in figures with reversible perspective. *American Psychologist, 5,* 263–264.

HOCHBERG, J. (1950). Figure-ground reversal as a function of visual satiation. *Journal of Experimental Psychology, 40,* 682–686.

HOCHBERG, J., & BITTERMAN, M. E. (1950). The use of painted grids and circuits in the construction of psychological apparatus. *American Journal of Psychology, 63,* 90–91.

HOCHBERG, J., TRIEBEL, W., & SEAMAN, G. (1951). Color adaptation under conditions of homogeneous visual stimulation (Ganzfeld). *Journal of Experimental Psychology, 41,* 153–159.

HOCHBERG, J., & BITTERMAN, M. E. (1951). Figural after-effects as a function of the retinal size of the inspection figure. *American Journal of Psychology, 64,* 99–102.

MURPHY, G., & HOCHBERG, J. (1951). Perceptual development: Some tentative hypotheses. *Psychological Review, 58,* 332–349.

HOCHBERG, C. B., & HOCHBERG, J. (1952). Familiar size and the perception of depth. *Journal of Psychology, 34,* 107–114.

HOCHBERG, C. B., & HOCHBERG, J. (1953). Familiar size and subception in perceived depth. *Journal of Psychology: Interdisciplinary & Applied, 36,* 341–345.

HOCHBERG, J., & McALISTER, E. (1953). A quantitative approach to figural "goodness." *Journal of Experimental Psychology, 46,* 361–364.

HOCHBERG, J., & BECK, J. (1954). Apparent spatial arrangement and perceived brightness. *Journal of Experimental Psychology, 47,* 263–266.

HOCHBERG, J., & SMITH, D. (1954). The effect of "punishment" (electric shock) on figure-ground perception. *Journal of Psychology: Interdisciplinary & Applied, 38,* 83–87.

HOCHBERG, J. (1954). *Methods in psychology.* Ithaca, NY: Office of Naval Research.

HOCHBERG, J., & TRIEBEL, W. (1955). Figural after-effects with colored stimuli. *American Journal of Psychology, 68,* 133–135.

HOCHBERG, J., & SMITH, O. W. (1955). Landing strip markings and the "expansion pattern": I. Program, preliminary analysis and apparatus. *Perceptual & Motor Skills, 5,* 81–92.

HOCHBERG, J., RYAN, T. A., & HABER, S. (1955). "Perceptual defense" as an interference phenomenon. *Perceptual & Motor Skills, 5,* 15–17.

HOCHBERG, J., & HAY, J. (1956). Figural after-effects, after-image, and physiological nystagmus. *American Journal of Psychology, 69,* 480–482.

HOCHBERG, J. (1956). Perception: Toward the recovery of a definition. *Psychological Review, 6,* 400–405.

HOCHBERG, J., & SILVERSTEIN, A. (1956). A quantitative index of stimulus-similarity: Proximity vs. differences in brightness. *American Journal of Psychology, 69,* 456–459.

HOCHBERG, J., & McALISTER, E. (1955). Relative size vs. familiar size in the perception of represented depth. *American Journal of Psychology, 68,* 294–296.

HOCHBERG, J. (1957). Effects of the Gestalt revolution: The Cornell symposium on perception. *Psychological Review, 64,* 78–84.

HOCHBERG, J. (1957). Form and visual detection. In J. W. Wulfeck & J. H. Taylor (Eds.), *Form discrimination as related to military problems. NAS/NRC, 561,* 129–133.

HOCHBERG, J. (1957). Psychophysics and stereotype in social perception. In M. Sherif & M. O. Wilson (Eds.), *Emerging problems in social psychology* (pp. 117–141). Oklahoma City: University of Oklahoma Press.

HOCHBERG, J. (1957). Spatial representation: Theme 10 [Abstract]. *Proceedings of the International Congress of Psychology.* Brussels.

HOCHBERG, J., LAMBERT, W. W., & RYAN, T. A. (1957). *Vocabulary for psychology.* New York: Data-Guide.

HOCHBERG, J., & HARDY, D. (1958). Brightness and proximity factors in grouping. *Perceptual & Motor Skills, 10,* 22.

HOCHBERG, J., & BROOKS, V. (1958). Effects of previously associated annoying stimuli (auditory) on visual recognition thresholds. *Journal of Experimental Psychology, 55,* 490–491.

HOCHBERG, J., & HARDY, D. (1960). Brightness and proximity factors in grouping. *Perceptual & Motor Skills, 10,* 22.

HOCHBERG, J., DAY, R., & HARDY, D. (1960). Hue and brightness differences, contours and figural after-effects. *American Journal of Psychology, 73,* 638–639.

HOCHBERG, J., & BROOKS, V. (1960). A psychophysical study of "cuteness." *Perceptual & Motor Skills, 11,* 205.

HOCHBERG, J., & BROOKS, V. (1960). The psychophysics of form: Reversible-perspective drawings of spatial objects. *American Journal of Psychology, 73,* 337–354.

HOCHBERG, J. (1960). Social perception: Substance and strategy. In J. G. Peatman & E. L. Hartley (Eds.), *Festschrift for Gardner Murphy* (pp. 145–156). New York: Harper.

Hochberg, J., & V. Brooks. (1962). Compression of pictorial space through perspective-reversal. *Perceptual & Motor Skills, 16,* 262.

Hochberg, J. (1962). Nativism and empiricism in perception. In L. Postman (Ed.), *Psychology in the making* (pp. 255–330). New York: Knopf.

Hochberg, J., & Brooks, V. (1962). Pictorial recognition as an unlearned ability: A study of one child's performance. *American Journal of Psychology, 75,* 624–628.

Hochberg, J. (1962). The psychophysics of pictorial perception. *Audio-Visual Communication Review, 10,* 22–54.

Hochberg, J., & V. Brooks. (1963). Graphic symbols: Things or holes? *American Journal of Psychology, 76,* 326–329.

Hochberg, J. (1963). On the importance of movement-produced stimulation in prism-induced after-effects. *Perceptual & Motor Skills, 16,* 544.

Hochberg, J. (1964). Contralateral suppressive fields of binocular combination. *Psychonomic Science, 1,* 157–158

Hochberg, J. (1964). Depth perception loss with monocular suppression: A problem in the explanation of stereopsis. *Science, 145,* 1334–1336.

Hochberg, J. (1964). *Perception.* Englewood Cliffs, NJ: Prentice-Hall.

Hochberg, J., & Brooks, V. (1964). Recognition by preliterate children of reversible-perspective figures. *Perceptual & Motor Skills, 19,* 802.

Bower, T., Goldsmith, W. M., & Hochberg, J. (1964). Stereodepth from after-images. *Perceptual & Motor Skills, 19*(2), 510.

Hochberg, J. (1964). Stimulus factors in literacy: Graphic communication, verbal and non-verbal. *Project Literacy Reports,* No. 1, July, Cornell University, Ithaca, NY.

Hochberg, J. (1964). A theory of the binocular cyclopean field: On the possibility of simulated stereopsis. *Perceptual & Motor Skills, 19,* 685.

Hochberg, J., & Berko, M. (1965). Phenomenal displacement in delayed auditory feedback: I. Disparate inter-aural intensities. II. High intensity effects. *Psychonomic Science, 2,* 389–390.

Hochberg, J. (1966). Reading pictures and text: What is learned in perceptual development? *Proceedings of the 18th International Congress of Psychology, 30,* 18–26.

Hochberg, J. (1966). Representative sampling and the purposes of perceptual research: Pictures of the world and the world of pictures. In K. Hammond (Ed.), *The psychology of Egon Brunswik* (pp. 361–381). New York: Holt, Rinehart and Winston.

Hochberg, J., & Galper, R. E. (1967). Recognition of faces: I. An exploratory study. *Psychonomic Science, 9*(12), 619–620.

Hochberg, J. (1968). In the mind's eye. Invited address read at the September 1966 meeting of the American Psychological Association, Division 3. In R. N. Haber (Ed.), *Contemporary theory and research in visual perception* (pp. 309–331). New York: Holt, Rinehart, and Winston.

Girgus, J., & Hochberg, J. (1970). Age differences in sequential form recognition. *Psychonomic Science, 21,* 211–212.

Hochberg, J. (1970). Attention, organization, and consciousness. In D. Mostofsky (Ed.), *Attention: Contemporary theory and analysis* (pp. 99–124). New York: Appleton-Century-Crofts.

Hochberg, J. (1970). Components of literacy: Speculations and exploratory research. In H. Levin and J. Williams (Eds.), *Basic studies on reading* (pp. 74–89). New York: Basic.

Hochberg, J., & Brooks, V. (1970). Reading as intentional behavior. In H. Singer (Ed.), *Theoretical models and processes of reading* (pp. 242–251). Newark, DE: International Reading Association.

Zimmerman, R. R., & Hochberg, J. (1970). Responses of infant monkeys to pictorial representations of a learned visual discrimination. *Psychonomic Science, 18*(5), 307–308.

Zimmerman, R. R., & Hochberg, J. (1971). The facilitation of picture discrimination after object discrimination learning in the neonatal monkey and probably vice versa. *Psychonomic Science, 24*(5), 239–241.

Hochberg, J. (1971). Perception: Color and shape. In J. Kling & L. Riggs (Eds.), *Woodworth and Schlosberg's experimental psychology* (pp. 395–474). New York: Holt, Rinehart and Winston.

Hochberg, J. (1971). Perception: Space and movement. In J. Kling & d L. Riggs (Eds.), *Woodworth and Schlosberg's experimental psychology* (pp. 475–550). New York: Holt, Rinehart and Winston.

Galper, R. E., & Hochberg, J. (1971). Recognition memory for photographs of faces. *American Journal of Psychology, 84,* 351–354.

Hochberg, J., & Girgus, J. (1972). Age differences in shape recognition through an aperture in free-viewing situation. *Psychonomic Science, 28,* 237–238.

Hochberg, J., Gombrich, E., & Black, M. (1972). *Art, perception and reality.* Baltimore: Johns Hopkins University Press.

Hochberg, J., & Brooks, V. (1972). *The perception of television displays.* New York: Educational Television Laboratory of the Educational Broadcasting Corporation.

Hochberg, J. (1972). The representation of things and people. In E. H. Gombrich, J. Hochberg, & M. Black (Eds.), *Art, perception and reality* (pp. 47–94). Baltimore: Johns Hopkins University Press.

Hochberg, J., & Galper, R. E. (1974). Attribution of intention as a function of physiognomy. *Memory & Cognition, 2,* 39–42.

Hochberg, J. (1974). Higher-order stimuli and inter-response coupling in the perception of the visual world. In R. B. MacLeod & H. L. Pick, Jr. (Eds.), *Perception: Essays in honor of James J. Gibson* (pp. 17–39). Ithaca, NY: Cornell University Press.

Hochberg, J., & Brooks, V. (1974). The integration of successive cinematic views of simple scenes. *Bulletin of the Psychonomic Society, 4,* 263.

Hochberg, J. (1974). On the control of saccades in reading. *Vision Research, 15,* 620.

Hochberg, J. (1974). Organization and the Gestalt tradition. In E. C. Carterette & M. P. Friedman (Eds.), *Handbook of perception* (Vol. 1) (pp. 179–210). New York: Academic.

Hochberg, J. (1974). Toward a speech-plan/eye-movement model of reading. In R. A. Monty & J. W. Senders (Eds.), *Eye movements and psychological processes* (pp. 397–416). Hillsdale, NJ: Erlbaum.

Hochberg, J., & Fallon, P. (1976). Perceptual analysis of moving patterns. *Science, 194,* 1081–1083.

Hochberg, J. (1977). Contemporary theories of perception in historical perspective. In B. Wolman (Ed.), *International encyclopedia of neurology, psychiatry, psychoanalysis and psychology.* New York: Van Nostrand Reinhold for Aesculapius.

Hochberg, J., & Gellman, L. (1977). The effect of landmark features on "mental rotation" times. *Memory & Cognition, 5*(1), 23–26.

HOCHBERG, J., FALLON, P., & BROOKS, V. (1977). Motion organization effects with successive static displays ("stop action"). *Scandinavian Journal of Psychology, 18,* 187–191.

HOCHBERG, J. (1978). *Art and visual perception.* In E. Carterette & M. Friedman (Eds.), *Handbook of perception* (Vol. X, pp. 225–258). New York: Academic.

HOCHBERG, J., & BROOKS, V. (1978). Film cutting and visual momentum. In J. W. Senders, D. F. Fisher, & R. A. Monty (Eds.), *Eye movements and the higher psychological functions* (pp. 293–313). Hillsdale, NJ: Erlbaum.

HOCHBERG, J. (1978). *Motion pictures of mental structures.* Presidential address of the Eastern Psychological Association.

HOCHBERG, J. (1978). *Perception* (2d ed.). Englewood Cliffs, NJ: Prentice-Hall.

HOCHBERG, J., & V. BROOKS. (1978). The perception of motion pictures. In E. Carterette & M. Friedman (Eds.), *Handbook of perception* (Vol. X, pp. 259–304). New York: Academic.

HOCHBERG, J. (1978). Perceptual constancy. *Science, 201,* 1218–1219 (Review).

HOCHBERG, J. (1978). Visual arts and the structures of the mind. In S. S. Madeja (Ed.), *The arts, cognition and basic skills* (pp. 151–172). St. Louis, MO: CEMREL.

HOCHBERG, J. (1979). Sensation and perception. In E. Hearst (Ed.), *Experimental psychology at 100* (pp. 89–142). Hillsdale, NJ: Erlbaum.

HOCHBERG, J. (1979). Some of the things that paintings are. In C. Nodine & D. Fisher (Eds.), *Views of pictorial representation: Making, perceiving and interpreting* (pp. 17–41). New York: Praeger.

HOCHBERG, J., GIRGUS, J., & GELLMAN, L. H. (1980). The effect of spatial order on piecemeal shape recognition: A developmental study. *Perception and Psychophysics, 28*(2), 133–138.

HOCHBERG, J. (1980). Pictorial functions and perceptual structures. In M. A. Hagen (Ed.), *The psychology of representational pictures* (pp. 47–93). New York: Academic.

HOCHBERG, J. (1981). Levels of perceptual organization. In M. Kubovy & J. Pomerantz (Eds.), *Perceptual organization* (pp. 255–278). Hillsdale, NJ: Erlbaum.

HOCHBERG, J. (1981). On cognition in perception: Perceptual coupling and unconscious inference. *Cognition, 10,* 127–134.

HOCHBERG, J. (1982). How big is a stimulus? In J. Beck (Ed.), *Organization and representation in perception* (pp. 191–217). Hillsdale, NJ: Erlbaum.

HOCHBERG, J. (1983). Constancy. In E. Craighead & C. B. Nemeroff (Eds.), *Encyclopedia of psychology* (Vol. 3, pp. 278–281). New York: Wiley.

HOCHBERG, J. (1983). Form perception: Experience and explanations. In P. C. Dodwell & T. Caelli (Eds.), *Figural synthesis* (pp. 1–30). Hillsdale, NJ: Erlbaum.

PETERSON, M. A., & HOCHBERG, J. (1983). The opposed-set measurement procedure: The role of local cue and intention in form perception. *Journal of Experimental Psychology: Human Perception & Performance, 9,* 183–193.

HOCHBERG, J. (1983). Perception. In I. Darien-Smith (Ed.), *Handbook of physiology: Section 1. The nervous system. Vol. III. Sensory processes* (pp. 75–102).

HOCHBERG, J. (1983). Perception. In E. Craighead & C. B. Nemeroff (Eds.), *Encyclopedia of psychology* (Vol. 2., pp. 497–500). New York: Wiley.

HOCHBERG, J. (1983). Problems of picture perception. *Visual Arts Research, 9,* 7–24.

HOCHBERG, J. (1983). Unconscious inference. In E. Craighead & C. B. Nemeroff (Eds.), *Encyclopedia of psychology* (Vol. 3, pp. 449f.). New York: Wiley.

HOCHBERG, J. (1983). Visual perception in architecture. *Via, 6,* 26–45.

HOCHBERG, J. (1984). The perception of pictorial representations. *Social Research, 51,* 841–862.

HOCHBERG, J. (1986). Parts and wholes: A response to Arnheim. *New Ideas in Psychology, 4,* 285–293.

HOCHBERG, J. (1986). Representation of motion and space in video and cinematic displays. In K. R. Boff, L. Kaufman, & J. P. Thomas (Eds.), *Handbook of perception and human performance: Vol. I. Sensory processes and perception* (pp. 22:1–64). New York: Wiley.

HOCHBERG, J. (1986). Visual perception of real and represented objects and events. In N. J. Smelser & D. R. Gerstein (Eds.), *Behavioral and social science: Fifty years of discovery* (pp. 249–298). Washington, DC: National Academy Press.

HOCHBERG, J. (1987). Machines should not see as people do, but must know how people see. *Computer Vision, Graphics, and Image Processing, 37,* 221–237.

HOCHBERG, J., & PETERSON, M. A. (1987). Piecemeal organization and cognitive components in object perception: Perceptually coupled responses to moving objects. *Journal of Experimental Psychology: General, 116,* 370–380.

HOCHBERG, J. (1988). Visual perception. In R. Atkinson, R. J. Herrnstein, G. Lindsey, & D. Luce (Eds.), *Stevens' handbook of experimental psychology* (Vol. I, pp. 295–375). New York: Wiley.

HOCHBERG, J. (1989). Combining views. In J. I. Elkind, S. K. Card, & J. Hochberg (Eds.), *Human performance models for computer-aided engineering* (pp. 159–165). Washington, DC: National Academy Press.

ELKIND, J. I., CARD, S. K., & HOCHBERG, J. (1989). *Human performance models for computer-aided engineering.* Washington, DC: National Academy Press.

PETERSON, M. A., & HOCHBERG, J. (1989). Necessary considerations for a theory of form perception: A theoretical and empirical reply to Boselie and Leeuwenberg (1986). *Perception, 18*(1), 105–111.

HOCHBERG, J. (1989). The perception of moving images. *Iris, 5,* 41–68.

HOCHBERG, J., & BROOKS, V. (1989). Perception of still and moving pictures. In E. Barnouw (Ed.), *International encyclopedia of communications* (Vol. 3, pp. 255–262). New York: Oxford University Press.

DeLUCIA, P. R., & HOCHBERG, J. (1991). Geometrical illusions in solid objects under ordinary viewing conditions. *Perception & Psychophysics, 50*(6), 547–554.

HOCHBERG, J., & PETERSON, M. A. (1993). Mental representations of occluded objects: Sequential disclosure and intentional construal. *Giornale Italiano di Psicologia, 20,* 805–820.

COOPER, L., & HOCHBERG, J. (1994). Objects of the mind: Mental representations in visual perception and cognition. In S. Ballesteros (Ed.), *Cognitive approaches to human perception* (pp. 223–239). Hillsdale, NJ: Erlbaum.

HOCHBERG, J. (1994). Perceptual theory and visual cognition. In S. Ballesteros (Ed.), *Cognitive approaches to human perception* (pp. 269–289). Hillsdale, NJ: Erlbaum.

HOCHBERG, J. (1994). Vector analysis, perceptual intention, and the hidden rules of visual perception (or mental structure). In G. Jansson & S. S. Bergström (Eds.), *Perceiving events and objects* (pp. 417–435). Hillsdale, NJ: Erlbaum.

HOCHBERG, J. (1995). The construction of pictorial meaning. In T. Sebeok & S. Uniber-Sebiok (Eds.), *Advances in visual semiotics: The semiotic web 1992–1993* (pp. 108–162). Berlin: Mouton de Gruyter.

HOCHBERG, J., & BROOKS, V. (1996). Movies in the mind's eye. In D. Bordwell & N. Carroll (Eds.), *Post-theory: Reconstructing film studies* (pp. 368–387). Madison: University of Wisconsin Press.

HOCHBERG, J., & BROOKS, V. (1996). The perception of motion pictures. In M. C. Friedman & E. C. Carterette (Eds.), *Cognitive ecology* (pp. 205–292). San Diego, CA: Academic.

HOCHBERG, J. (1996). The perception of pictures and pictorial art. In M. P. Friedman & E. C. Carterette (Eds.), *Cognitive ecology* (pp. 151–203). San Diego, CA: Academic.

HOCHBERG, J. (1997). The affordances of perceptual inquiry: Pictures are learned from the world, and what that fact might mean about perception quite generally. In R. Goldstone, D. Medin, & P. G. Schyns (Eds.), *Perceptual learning: Handbook of learning and motivation* (Vol. 36, pp. 15–44). San Diego, CA: Academic

HOCHBERG, J. (1998). A context for the second half of the century: One view. In J. Hochberg (Ed.), *Perception and cognition at century's end* (pp. 3–21). San Diego, CA: Academic.

HOCHBERG, J. (1998). Gestalt theory and its legacy: Organization in eye and brain, in attention and mental representation. In J. Hochberg (Ed.), *Perception and cognition at century's end* (pp. 253–306). San Diego, CA: Academic.

HOCHBERG, J. (Ed.). (1998). *Perception and cognition at century's end.* San Diego, CA: Academic.

HOCHBERG, J. (2003). Acts of perceptual inquiry: Problems for any stimulus-based simplicity theory. *Acta Psychologica, 114*(3), 215–228.

HOCHBERG, J. E., & KRANTZ, D. (2004). Brunswik and Bayes. *Contemporary Psychology: APA Review of Books, 49*(6), 785–787.

HOCHBERG, J. (2005). Jacob Beck: Reminiscence and appreciation. *Spatial Vision, 18*(2), 143–145.

Name Index

Note: Page numbers followed by n refer to endnotes.

Wartofsky, M., 258, 274, 361, 364, 373, 374n4, 374n9
Washburn, M. F., 114, 124
Wason, T. D., 392n9
Weaver, W., 497, 503
Webb, I. B., 216, 227
Weber, C., 58
Weidenbacher, H. L., 425, 428
Weinstein, M., 57
Weinstein, S., 59
Weiss, I., 526, 532
Weiss, Y., 498, 503
Weld, H. P., 9
Werner, H., 29
Werner, J., 59
Wertheim, A. H., 392n14
Wertheimer, M., 29, 286, 313, 314, 375n18, 509, 512, 517, 554
Wetherhold, C. J., 461, 466
White, J., 373n1, 374n2, 374n5, 374n6, 374n14
Whittle, P. A., 101, 124
Wieland, B. A., 195, 205
Wiesel, T., 91, 98, 544, 553

Wigner, E., 495–496, 503
Wilcocks, R. W., 105, 124
Willey, E. V., 461, 466
Wohlgemuth, A., 349, 359
Wolfe, J. M., 441, 447, 489, 491
Woodworth, R. S., 22, 72, 84, 124, 230, 237, 274, 316, 328, 425, 428, 525, 533
Wright, J. E., 496, 503
Wundt, W., 59, 73, 97, 345, 349, 359

Yantis, S., 412
Yen, S. C., 545, 554
Yilmaz, A., 596, 598
Yin, C., 459, 466, 544, 548, 554
Yin, R. K., 444, 447
Young, D. S., 211, 475, 481

Zacks, J. L., 393n19, 448, 453
Zacks, J. M., 595, 596, 598
Zahir, G., 443, 446
Zinchenko, V., 113, 121, 124
Zola, D., 557, 561
Zollner, P., 342, 355n7, 359
Zuk, I. J., 461, 466

Subject Index

Note: Page numbers followed by *f, t,* or n indicate figures, tables, or notes; those in boldface refer to whole papers by Hochberg.

accommodation, 35, 45
action units in dance, 595–597
active listening, 108–110, 141
active looking, 114–121, 116*f,* 118*f,* 162
active reading, 117–118
active vs. passive stimulation, 314–315
acuity, 241*f,* 246–247, 247*f. See also* peripheral and foveal vision
aesthetic preference and visual momentum, 218, 218*t*
affective cutting tone, 208
Africans, 203n11
aftereffects, 202n2, 344–345
age identification in portraits, 176–177
algorithmic information theory (AIT), 518–522
ambiguity
 concept of, 27–28
 figural goodness and ambiguous stimuli, 11
 of outline drawings, 167, 245, 248–249
 pictorial, 44–47
 pictorial representation, mental structures and, 240
 Rorschach ink blots and, 56n9
 usefulness of concept, 55n3
Ames trapezoid
 direct theory and, 309, 325n1
 mental structure theories and, 282, 296–297
 motion parallax and, 234*f,* 236
 optical flow pattern and, 286–287
 pictorial depth cues vs. motion information, 582–583
 size-distance coupling and, 196, 199, 201
analogs, 109
analytic introspection, 33–34, 34*f*

anorthoscopic perception, 342–343
aperture viewing. *See* successive aperture viewing
arclets, 548–549, 549*f,* 551–552, 551*f*
art. *See* pictorial representation; picture perception
articulatory intentions, 95
associationism, 192, 396
atomism, 188–191
attensity, 53–55, 54*f*
attention
 boundary extension and, 461–462
 change blindness and, 441–443, 445
 consciousness and, 483
 pre-attentive perception, 484
 spotlight of, 510
attention, selective
 active-looking model, 114–121, 116*f,* 118*f*
 active reading and, 117–118
 attention, organization, and consciousness, **100–124**
 auditory, 106–111, 106*f,* 140–141
 cognitive vs. perceptual approach and, 432
 eye movements and, 111–114, 112*f,* 115, 121
 overview, 100–102
 pictorial features, fit to, 259–260, 259*f*
 picture perception and psychophysics of attensity, 53–55, 54*f*
 purposive behaviors and, 161
 schematic maps and, 116–117
 in tachistoscopic presentations, 102–106, 104*f,* 105*f*
 See also inattentional blindness (inattentional disregard)

620